GOD LIVED WITH THEM

GOD LIVED

WITH THEM

SWAMI CHETANANANDA

Advaita Ashrama
(Publication Department)
5 Dehi Entally Road
Kolkata 700 014

Published by
Swami Mumukshananda
President, Advaita Ashrama
Mayavati, Champawat, Himalayas
from its Publication Department, Kolkata
Email : advaita@vsnl.com
Website : www.advaitaonline.com

ISBN 81-7505-198-1

Printed in India at
Trio Process
Kolkata 700 014

CONTENTS

Sri Ramakrishna: Dakshineswar, 1884

PREFACE

The melting glaciers of the high Himalayas form the river Ganges, which flows thousands of miles over the plains and supplies life-saving water to millions of people. Similarly, Sri Ramakrishna, who for most of his life remained absorbed in samadhi — the acme of spiritual experience — out of compassion descended to the relative plane of human existence to alleviate human suffering. His condensed spirituality, as it were, melted and flowed through his disciples who later carried his life-giving message to the world.

The present book *God Lived with Them* contains the life stories of sixteen monastic disciples of Sri Ramakrishna, whereas *They Lived with God* (published by Shepherd and Walwyn of London and the Vedanta Society of St. Louis in 1989 and Advaita Ashrama of Calcutta in 1991) contains the life stories of twenty-eight prominent householder devotees. Taken together, these forty-four biographies depict how Sri Ramakrishna's teachings manifested and came to fruition in his disciples' lives. To me, Sri Ramakrishna is like a chandelier and his disciples and devotees are like bulbs of different wattages radiating the light, or wisdom, of their Master. I feel blessed that for the last five years I have been able to travel, mentally of course, with these sixteen disciples from each one's birth to his death. I observed their unique love and faith in their guru, their purity and renunciation, their training and austerity, their struggle and longing for God, their spiritual unfoldment and unselfish service to humanity.

Among the sixteen monastic disciples, five went to college (two graduated), ten did not finish their formal education, and one was completely unlettered — but all of them learned from their guru true spirituality, which no educational institution could provide. Sri Ramakrishna was an extraordinary teacher and his methods were unique. Through his subtle spiritual influence, he enflamed his disciples' hearts, thereby creating hunger and passion for God. As a result, they became so inebriated with divine bliss that they almost forgot the world. Recognizing each disciple's uniqueness, Sri Ramakrishna made each one a role model and an ideal spiritual teacher in his own right. After Sri Ramakrishna's death, five of them came to the West for varying periods.

Swami Vivekananda stated about the uniqueness of his guru: "The man at whose feet I sat all my life — and it was only a few ideas of his that I try to teach — could [hardly] write his name at all. All my life I have not seen another man like that, and I have travelled all over the world. When I think of that man, I feel like a fool, because I wanted to read books and he never did.... He was his own book."

The disciples learned the greatest truths from their Master in simple language: "The goal of human life is to realize God." "Lust and gold is maya. As long as the cloud of maya exists, you do not see the effect of the Sun of Knowledge. A *sannyasi* [monk] must renounce both 'lust and gold.'" "Unite the mind and the speech." "Let there be no theft [hypocrisy] in the chamber of your heart." "Know truth for yourself, and there will be many to whom you can teach it afterwards; they will all come."

Some of Sri Ramakrishna's westernized disciples were amazed when they saw how their Master faced agnostics, atheists, sceptics, and materialists, and silenced them through his infallible logic, apt and convincing illustrations, magnanimous personality, and spiritual power. Yet at the same time, he always encouraged his disciples to question him and not to follow him blindly. "Test me as the money-changers test coins," he said. "Before you decide to accept a guru watch him by day and by night."

Those who read this book will gain some insight into how the disciples were trained and perfected by their wonderful teacher Sri Ramakrishna, and how they themselves later became conduits of his spiritual power. Sometimes the Master was strong like a thunderbolt and other times tender like a flower; sometimes he crushed their egos by scolding them and again overwhelmed them with his unselfish love. He checked their physiognomies, read their minds, guided their eating and sleeping habits, and demonstrated to them how to practise karma, jnana, bhakti, and raja yogas. When he initiated them, he empowered them and removed the obstacles to their spiritual journey. He taught them the technique of reading one's life like a book rather than depending solely on the scriptures, or swallowing others' ideas. Most importantly, he always kept before them the shining ideal of renunciation, never allowing the slightest compromise with the basic principles of truth and purity. He sang, danced, played, had fun and cracked jokes with them, and also taught them how to pray, meditate, and be immersed in God-consciousness.

The disciples learned from their Master a constructive, positive, and scientific religion that never says "believe," but "see" — "I see, and you too can see." Touching different parts of an elephant, blind men describe the elephant in various ways and then quarrel about their experience. But a man with normal sight sees the whole elephant and does not argue with others. Similarly if a person sees God, he will not form any sect or quarrel with others. Sri Ramakrishna showed his disciples the whole elephant, so what they preached was a nonsectarian, universal religion: the divinity of the soul, the unity of existence, the oneness of the Godhead, and the harmony of religions.

We know very little about the disciples of Buddha, Christ, or Chaitanya, who spread the message of their masters. We are fortunate that so much information is available about Sri Ramakrishna's great disciples. In fact, one could write a large volume on each disciple, but the aim of this book is to present the highlights of their lives. *God Lived with Them* contains some new details that have been collected from many Bengali books, magazines, and diaries; it also includes information gathered from other sources published in English. In addition to details concerning the disciples themselves, the readers will get glimpses of the ancient Vedantic mystical tradition as illustrated in these biographies.

As these lives shine in their own glory, I have avoided interpreting them. The facts of their lives have been presented chronologically in simple language with exhaustive references given in the endnotes. I have mainly cited three sources to give authenticity to this book: what Sri Ramakrishna said to or about the disciples; what the disciples said about themselves; what brother disciples, and other monks and devotees who were close to the disciples, reminisced or wrote about them. To maintain continuity of thought, I could not omit the repetition of some episodes that were connected with more than one of the lives. For brevity and readability, I have edited, paraphrased, or condensed some quotations or writings from the existing published materials in English as well as from my translations of the Bengali source materials. Throughout this book I have initially used respectful words, such as, "Sri" or "Swami," and subsequently used them sparingly, since in the West it is considered more intimate when formal titles are not used.

In conclusion, I would like to point out that these disciples of Sri Ramakrishna were not ordinary human beings: some were *ishwarakotis* (godlike souls, born with a special spiritual message for humanity), some were *nityamuktas* (ever-free souls who have never been caught by maya), and according to Sri Ramakrishna, some had been born as disciples of previous divine incarnations, such as Rama, Krishna, and Christ. They were eternal companions of God, reborn in order to fulfill a divine mission.

These disciples were actors in the divine drama of Sri Ramakrishna and played their respective roles according to his wishes. Towards the end of his life, Sri Ramakrishna remarked: "God becomes man, an Avatar, and comes to earth with His devotees. And the devotees leave the world with Him.... A band of minstrels suddenly appears, dances, and sings, and it departs in the same sudden manner. They come and they return, but none recognizes them."

I am grateful to the Vedanta students who helped edit and type the manuscript of this book. I am thankful to the devotees who provided financial help to publish this book. May Sri Ramakrishna bless us so that by recognizing him and his disciples we can attain perfection.

St. Louis   Chetanananda
1 May 1997
Centenary of the Ramakrishna Mission (1897-1997)

SRI RAMAKRISHNA
(A BIOGRAPHICAL INTRODUCTION)

Religion declines when people talk about religion but do not practise it, or when people use it for their own selfish motives. Religion becomes polluted when hypocrisy and dishonesty, lust and greed, jealousy and hatred, ego and fanaticism are rampant in people's minds. Krishna declared in the Bhagavad Gita: "When religion declines and irreligion prevails, I incarnate myself in every age to establish religion." As the same moon rises in the sky again and again, so the same God descends to the earth as a human being in different places and in different times to fulfill the need of the age and to point out the goal of human life. This is not a myth: the lives of Rama, Krishna, Buddha, Moses, Christ, Muhammad, Chaitanya, and Ramakrishna attest to the Gita's statement.

Sri Ramakrishna was born on Wednesday, 18 February 1836, in Kamarpukur, a small village sixty miles northwest of Calcutta. In the spring of 1835 his father, Khudiram Chattopadhyay, had gone to visit the holy city of Gaya to perform a rite for his ancestors in the Vishnu Temple. One night in his sleep, Khudiram had a vision. A luminous being gazed at him affectionately and then said in a sweet voice: "Khudiram, your great devotion has made me very happy. The time has come for me to be born once again on earth. I shall be born as your son."[1]

Khudiram was filled with joy until he realized that he did not have the means to carry out such a great responsibility. So he said: "No, my Lord, I am not fit for this favour. I am too poor to serve you properly."[2] "Do not be afraid, Khudiram," said the Lord. "Whatever you give me to eat, I shall enjoy."[3] Khudiram awoke, convinced that the Lord of the universe was going to be born into his household. He then left Gaya and returned to Kamarpukur before the end of April.

On Khudiram's return, his wife, Chandra, told him of an experience she had had in front of the Yogi Shiva Temple next to their house. Chandra said: "I saw that the holy image of Lord Shiva inside the shrine was alive! It began to send forth waves of the most beautiful light — slowly at first, then quicker and quicker. They filled the inside of the temple, then they came pouring out — it was like one of those huge flood waves in the river — right towards me! I was going to tell Dhani [a neighbour woman], but then the waves washed over me and swallowed me up, and I felt that marvellous light enter into my body. I fell down on the ground, unconscious. When I came to myself, I told Dhani what had happened, but she did not believe me. She said that I'd had an epileptic fit. That cannot be so, because since then I have been full of joy and my health is better than ever. Only — I feel that light is still inside me, and I believe that I am with child."[4]

Khudiram then told Chandra about his vision, and they rejoiced together. The pious couple waited patiently for the divine child's birth the following spring. Because of Khudiram's experience at Gaya, Sri Ramakrishna was named "Gadadhar," meaning "Bearer-of-the-Mace," an epithet of Vishnu. Ramakrishna grew up in Kamarpukur. He was sent to school where he learned to read and write, but he soon lost interest in this "bread-earning education" and quit school altogether. However, he continued to constantly learn by watching people in his rural village. He was *shrutidhar*, which means that whatever he heard once, he never forgot.

When he was six or seven years old, he had his first experience of cosmic consciousness. "One morning," he recalled in later life, "I took some parched rice in a small basket and was eating it while walking along the narrow ridges of the rice fields. In one part of the sky, a beautiful black cloud appeared, heavy with rain. I was watching it and eating the rice. Very soon the cloud covered almost the entire sky. And then a flock of cranes came flying by. They were as white as milk against that black cloud. It was so beautiful that I became absorbed in the sight. Then I lost consciousness of everything outward. I fell down and the rice was scattered over the earth. Some people saw this and came and carried me home."[5]

Khudiram died in 1843. Ramakrishna keenly felt the loss of his father and became more indrawn and meditative. He began to visit the small village inn where pilgrims and especially monks would stop on their way to Puri. While serving these holy people he learned their songs and prayers. Following the brahminical tradition, Ramakrishna was invested with the sacred thread when he was nine years old; this allowed him to perform the ritualistic worship for the family deities. He had some friends with whom he would play, sing, and act out religious dramas. Once during *Shivaratri* (a spring festival of Lord Shiva) he lost outer consciousness while enacting the role of Shiva. On another occasion, while going to worship the Divine Mother in a neighbouring village, he again went into samadhi.

In 1850 Ramkumar, Khudiram's eldest son, opened a school in Calcutta. As a secondary profession, he performed religious rituals in private homes. It soon became difficult for him to manage both responsibilities, so in 1852 he brought Ramakrishna to assist him in performing the rituals. On 31 May 1855 Ramkumar accepted the responsibility of officiating at the dedication ceremony of the Kali Temple of Dakshineswar that had been founded by Rani Rasmani, a wealthy woman of Calcutta. Ramakrishna was present on that occasion. Soon afterwards he moved to Dakshineswar and in time became a priest in the temple. Ramkumar died in 1856.

Ramakrishna now began his spiritual journey in earnest. While worshipping the Divine Mother, he questioned: "Are you true, Mother, or is it all a fiction of the mind — mere poetry without any reality? If you do exist, why can't I see you? Is religion, then, a fantasy, a mere castle in the air?"[6] His yearning for God-realization became more and more intense day by day. He prayed and meditated almost twenty-four hours a day. Then he had a remarkable experience:

> There was an unbearable pain in my heart because I could not see the Mother. Just as a man wrings a towel with all his strength to get the water out of it, so I felt as if my heart and mind were being wrung out. I began to think I should never see Mother. I was dying of despair. In my agony, I said to myself: "What's the use of living this life?" Suddenly my eyes fell on the sword that hangs in the temple. I decided to end my life with it, then and there. Like a madman, I ran to it and seized it. And then — I had a marvellous vision of the Mother, and fell down unconscious. . . . It was as if houses, doors, temples, and everything else vanished altogether; as if there was nothing anywhere! And what I saw was an infinite, shoreless sea of light; a sea that was consciousness. However far and in whatever direction I looked, I saw shining waves, one after another, coming towards me. They were raging and storming upon me with great speed. Very soon they were upon me; they made me sink down into unknown depths. I panted and struggled and lost consciousness.[7]

After this vision it was not possible for Ramakrishna to continue performing the worship in the temple. He entrusted this responsibility to his nephew Hriday, and spent more than two years in a God-intoxicated state. In 1859 he returned to Kamarpukur and lived with his mother for a year and seven months. During this time, Ramakrishna's mother arranged his marriage to Sarada Mukhopadhyay, a very young girl from Jayrambati, a few miles west of Kamarpukur. After the marriage Ramakrishna returned alone to Dakshineswar in 1860.

Once at Dakshineswar Ramakrishna was caught up again in a spiritual tempest. He forgot his home, wife, family, body, and surroundings. He described his experiences during that period:

No sooner had I passed through one spiritual crisis than another took its place. It was like being in the midst of a whirlwind — even my sacred thread was blown away, and I could seldom keep hold of my *dhoti* [cloth]. Sometimes I'd open my mouth, and it would be as if my jaws reached from heaven to the underworld. "Mother!" I'd cry desperately. I felt I had to pull her in, as a fisherman pulls in fish with his dragnet. A prostitute walking the street would appear to me to be Sita going to meet her victorious husband. An English boy standing cross-legged against a tree reminded me of the boy Krishna, and I lost consciousness. Sometimes I would share my food with a dog. My hair became matted. Birds would perch on my head and peck at the grains of rice that had lodged there during the worship. Snakes would crawl over my motionless body.

An ordinary man couldn't have borne a quarter of that tremendous fervour; it would have burnt him up. I had no sleep at all for six long years. My eyes lost the power of winking. I stood in front of a mirror and tried to close my eyelids with my finger — but then, suddenly, I'd be filled with ecstasy. I saw that my body didn't matter — it was of no importance, a mere trifle. Mother appeared to me and comforted me and freed me from my fear.[8]

In 1861 a nun called Bhairavi Brahmani came to Dakshineswar to initiate Ramakrishna into tantric disciplines. The Master practised sixty-four methods of Tantra and attained perfection through all of them. He then practised other methods of the Vaishnava tradition, such as *vatsalya bhava* (the affectionate attitude towards God) and *madhura bhava* (the lover's attitude towards the beloved). In 1864 Ramakrishna was initiated into sannyasa by Tota Puri, a Vedanta monk, and attained *nirvikalpa samadhi*, the highest nondualistic experience, in only three days.

In 1866 Ramakrishna practised Islam under the guidance of a Sufi named Govinda Roy. The Master later mentioned to his disciples: "I devoutly repeated the name of Allah, and I said their prayers five times daily. I spent three days in that mood, and I had the full realization of the sadhana of their faith."[9]

In 1873 Ramakrishna met Shambhu Charan Mallik, who read the Bible to him and spoke to him of Jesus. One day Ramakrishna visited Jadu Mallik's garden house, which was adjacent to the Dakshineswar temple. In his living room there was a picture of the Madonna with the child Jesus sitting on her lap. While Ramakrishna was gazing at this picture, he saw that the figures of the mother and child were shining and rays of light were coming forth from them and entering his heart.

For the next three days he was absorbed in the thought of Jesus, and at the end of the third day, while walking in the Panchavati, he had a vision of a foreign-looking person with a beautiful face and large eyes of uncommon brilliance. As he pondered who this stranger could be, a voice from within said: "This is Jesus Christ, the great yogi, the loving Son of God, who was one with his Father and who shed his heart's blood and suffered tortures for the salvation of mankind!" Jesus then embraced Ramakrishna and merged into his body.[10]

After realizing God in different religions as well as in different sects of Hinduism, Ramakrishna proclaimed: "As many faiths, so many paths." In this present age, Ramakrishna's teachings are the antidote to narrowness, bigotry, fanaticism, and intolerance towards different religions. He said: "It is not good to feel that one's own religion alone is true and all others are false. God is one only, and not two. Different people call on him by different names: some as Allah, some as God, and others as Krishna, Shiva, and Brahman. It is like the water in a lake. The Hindus call it 'jal,' the Christians 'water,' and the Muslims 'pani.'"

The precious jewels of spirituality that he had gathered through hard struggle during the first three-quarters of his life were now ready to be given to humanity. In 1875 Ramakrishna met Keshab Chandra Sen, a popular Brahmo leader who was considered a spiritual luminary. Keshab and his followers began publishing the life and teachings of Ramakrishna in their journals, and as a result many people, especially young Bengalis, came to know about the saint of Dakshineswar.

Through direct experience Ramakrishna realized that the form of the Divine Mother was one with the formless Supreme Brahman, like fire and its burning power, like milk and its whiteness. The Divine Mother once said to the Master: "You and I are one. Let your life in this world be deep in devotion to me, and pass your days for the good of mankind. The devotees will come."[11]

As a loving father is anxious to leave his accumulated wealth to his children, so a true guru wants to give his spiritual treasures to his disciples. After his first vision Ramakrishna had to wait nearly twenty-five years for his disciples and devotees. We can read in the scriptures or in the lives of the mystics about the aspirants' longing for God but never about God's longing for the aspirants. Here is a testimony in Ramakrishna's own words:

> There was no limit to the longing I felt at that time. During the day-time I somehow managed to control it. The secular talk of the worldly-minded was galling to me, and I would look wistfully to the day when my own beloved companions would come. I hoped to find solace in conversing with them and relating to them my own realizations. Every little incident would remind me of them, and thoughts of them wholly engrossed me. I was already arranging in my mind what I should say to one and give to another, and so on. But when the day would come to a close I would not be able to curb my feelings. The thought that another day had gone by, and they had not come, oppressed me. When during the evening service the temples rang with the sound of bells and conch-shells, I would climb to the roof of the *kuthi* [bungalow] in the garden and, writhing in anguish of heart, cry at the top of my voice: "Come, my children! Oh, where are you? I cannot bear to live without you." A mother never longed so intensely for the sight of her child, nor a friend for his companions, nor a lover for his sweetheart, as I longed for them. Oh, it was indescribable! Shortly after this period of yearning the devotees began to come.[12]

Ramakrishna's disciples and devotees arrived between 1879 and 1885, and he became busy training them to carry out his mission. He was an extraordinary teacher. He stirred his disciples' hearts more by his subtle influence than by actions or words. Ramakrishna trained each disciple according to his own natural aptitude, as he knew everyone's past, present, and future. He never thrust his ideas upon anyone. To those young men who were destined to be monks he pointed out the steep path of both external and internal renunciation. When teaching the would-be monastic disciples the path of renunciation and discrimination, he would not allow householder devotees to be near them.

When the flower blooms, bees come of their own accord. People from all over flocked to Ramakrishna and he would sometimes talk about God as much as twenty hours a day. This continued for years. His intense love for humanity would not allow him to refuse help to anyone. In the middle of 1885, this physical strain resulted in throat cancer. When his disciples tried to stop him from teaching, he said: "I do not care. I will give up twenty thousand such bodies to help one man."[13] Ramakrishna was moved from Dakshineswar to Calcutta and later to Cossipore for medical treatment.

Towards the end of his life, Ramakrishna distributed ochre cloths (the symbol of monasticism) to some of his young disciples, thus forming his own Order. He made Narendra (later, Swami Vivekananda) their leader, who later came to America to represent Hinduism, or Vedanta, at the 1893 Parliament of Religions in Chicago. He summarized Ramakrishna's message to the modern world in his lecture "My Master":

> Do not care for doctrines, do not care for dogmas or sects or churches or temples. They count for little compared with the essence of existence in each man, which is spirituality; and the more a man develops it, the more power he has for good. Earn that first, acquire that, and criticize no one; for all the doctrines and creeds have some good in them. Show by your lives that religion does not mean words or names or sects, but that it means spiritual realization.[14]

Sri Ramakrishna passed away on 16 August 1886 at the Cossipore garden house; his body was cremated on the bank of the Ganges. Sri Ramakrishna revealed his divine nature many times to his disciples. A couple of days before the Master's passing, while he was suffering from excruciating pain from cancer, Vivekananda was seated near his bed. Seeing Ramakrishna's emaciated body Vivekananda thought to himself: "Well, now if you can declare that you are God, then only will I believe you are really God Himself." Immediately Sri Ramakrishna looked up towards Vivekananda and said: "He who was Rama and he who was Krishna is now Ramakrishna in this body."[15]

SWAMI VIVEKANANDA: LONDON, 1896

1

ॐ

SWAMI VIVEKANANDA

"D o you see a light when you are falling asleep?" "Yes, I do. Doesn't everyone?" The boy's voice was filled with wonder.

Soon after they first met, Sri Ramakrishna asked Narendra this question; his reply provided the Master with a deep insight into the past, the nature, and the destiny of this remarkable youngster who would later become Swami Vivekananda. In Vivekananda's adult years he himself described this supernormal faculty: "From the earliest time that I can remember, I used to see a marvellous point of light between my eyebrows as soon as I shut my eyes to go to sleep, and I used to watch its various changes with great attention. That marvellous point of light would change colours and get bigger until it took the form of a ball; finally it would burst and cover my body from head to foot with white liquid light.

"As soon as that happened, I would lose outer consciousness and fall asleep. I used to believe that was the way everybody went to sleep. Then, when I grew older and began to practise meditation, that point of light would appear to me as soon as I closed my eyes, and I would concentrate upon that."[1]

Sri Ramakrishna had a vision before Narendra was born:

One day I found that my mind was soaring high in samadhi along a luminous path. As it ascended higher and higher, I found on both sides of the way ideal forms of gods and goddesses. The mind then reached the outer limits of that region, where a luminous barrier separated the sphere of relative existence from that of the Absolute. Crossing that barrier, the mind entered the transcendental realm, where no corporeal being was visible. But the next moment I saw seven venerable sages seated there in samadhi. It occurred to me that these sages must have surpassed not only men but even the gods in knowledge and holiness, in renunciation and love. Lost in admiration, I was reflecting on their greatness, when I saw a portion of that undifferentiated luminous region condense into the form of a divine child. The child came to one of the sages, tenderly clasped his neck with his lovely arms, and, addressing him in a sweet voice, tried to drag his mind down from the state of samadhi. That magic touch roused the sage from his superconscious state, and he fixed his half-open eyes upon the wonderful child. In great joy the strange child spoke to him: "I am going down. You too must go with me." The sage remained mute, but his tender look expressed his assent. No sooner had I seen Narendra than I recognized him to be that sage.[2]

Later Sri Ramakrishna disclosed the fact that the divine child was none other than himself.

Swami Vivekananda was born in Calcutta at 6:49 a.m. on Monday, 12 January 1863, and was given the name Narendranath Datta. Bhuvaneshwari Devi, Narendra's mother, had practised austerities and prayed to Vireshwar Shiva of Varanasi to give her a son. She was delighted that the Lord had answered her prayer. Bhuvaneshwari Devi was deeply religious and raised her children according to the ancient spiritual traditions of India. She taught Narendra: "Remain pure all your life; guard your own honour and never transgress the honour of others. Be very tranquil, but when necessary, harden your heart." His father, Vishwanath Datta, was an attorney of the Calcutta High Court. He was extremely generous, and had a progressive outlook in social and religious matters, owing perhaps to the influence of the Western education he had received.

Brought up and educated in nineteenth-century Calcutta, Narendra was introduced at an early age to the principles of Western thinking, which taught that one should not accept anything without evidence. Although he was a brilliant student and well-versed in history, philosophy, literature, and contemporary Western thought, he firmly held his conviction: Do not believe a thing because you read it in a book. Do not believe a thing because another has said it is so. Find out the truth for yourself. That is realization.

Sri Ramakrishna said about him: "Narendra is a great soul — perfect in meditation. He cuts the veils of maya to pieces with the sword of knowledge. Inscrutable maya can never bring him under her control."

Once a cobra appeared when Narendra was meditating with his friends. The other boys were frightened; they shouted a warning to him, and ran away. But Narendra remained motionless. The cobra, after lingering for a while, crawled away. Later he told his parents: "I knew nothing of the snake or anything else. I was feeling inexpressible joy."

At the age of fifteen he experienced spiritual ecstasy. He was journeying with his family to Raipur in Central India, and part of the trip had to be made in a bullock cart. On that particular day the air was crisp and clear, the trees and creepers were covered with blossoms, and birds of beautiful plumage sang in the forest. The cart was moving through a narrow pass where the lofty peaks rising on both sides almost touched each other. Narendra caught sight of a large beehive in the cleft of a giant cliff. The hive must have been there a very long time. Suddenly his mind was filled with awe and reverence for the Divine Providence, and he lost outer consciousness. Perhaps this was the first time that his powerful imagination helped him to ascend to the realm of the superconscious.

Once during his days as a student, Narendra had a vision:

> While at school one night I was meditating behind closed doors and had a fairly deep concentration of mind. How long I meditated in that way I cannot say. After the meditation was over I remained seated. Then from the southern wall of that room a luminous figure stepped out and stood in front of me. It was the figure of a *sannyasin* [monk], absolutely calm, with shaven head, and staff and *kamandalu* [water pot] in either hand. He gazed at me for some time, and seemed as if he would address me. I, too, gazed at him in speechless wonder. Suddenly a kind of fright seized me. I opened the door and hurried out of the room. Then it struck me that it was foolish of me to run away like that; perhaps he might say something to me. But I have never seen that figure since. I think it was the Lord Buddha whom I saw.[3]

Principal William Hastie of General Assembly's Institution (now Scottish Church College) remarked: "Narendranath is really a genius. I have travelled far and wide but I have never yet come across a lad of his talents and possibilities, even in German universities, amongst philosophical students."[4] Dr. Brajendra Nath Seal, Narendra's fellow student, who later became a leading Indian philosopher, wrote: "Undeniably a gifted youth, sociable, free and unconventional in manners, a sweet singer, the soul of social circles, a brilliant conversationalist, somewhat bitter and caustic, piercing with the shafts of a keen wit the shows and mummeries of the world, sitting in the scorner's chair but hiding the tenderest of hearts under that garb of cynicism; altogether an inspired bohemian but possessing what bohemians lack, an iron will; somewhat peremptory and absolute, speaking with accents of authority and withal possessing a strange power of the eye which could hold his listeners in thrall."[5]

Narendra was a well-rounded person: he was a musician, debater, gymnast, philanthropist, an ideal yogi, mystic, ascetic, worker, and philosopher. He was energy personified. Some years later he told one of his English disciples: "In my childhood I used to observe an inexhaustible force arising in me, overflowing in my body, as it were. I used to become restless and could not keep quiet. This was why I used to fidget all the time.... My insides would vibrate, as it were, and make me restless to do something."

Romain Rolland, the famed French writer and Swami Vivekananda's biographer, wrote: "He was tall (five feet, eight and a half inches), 170 pounds, square-shouldered, broad-chested, stout, rather heavily built; his arms were muscular and trained to all kinds of sports. He had an olive complexion, a full face, vast forehead, strong jaw, a pair of magnificent eyes, large, dark and rather prominent, with heavy lids, whose shape recalled the classic comparison to a lotus petal. Nothing escaped the magic of his glance, capable equally of embracing in its irresistible charm, or of sparkling with wit, irony, or kindness, of losing itself in ecstasy, of plunging imperiously to the very depths of consciousness and of withering with its fury. But his preeminent characteristic was kingliness. He was a born king and nobody ever came near him either in India or America without paying homage to his majesty."[6]

In his intense desire to realize the truth, young Narendra practised meditation; he studied different religious and philosophical systems of the East and the West; he met different religious leaders, but nothing was of any avail. He even joined the Brahmo Samaj, a socio-religious organization, and asked its leader, Devendranath Tagore, "Sir, have you seen God?" Devendranath was embarrassed and replied: "My boy, you have the eyes of a yogi. You should practise meditation."

Narendra's spiritual struggle continued. His first introduction to Ramakrishna occurred one day in a literature class, when he heard Principal Hastie lecturing on Wordsworth's *The Excursion* and the poet's nature-mysticism. Hastie told his students that with purity and concentration such transcendental experience was possible, but in modern times had become extremely rare. "I have known only one person," he added, "who has realized that blessed state, and he is Ramakrishna of Dakshineswar. You will understand it better if you visit this saint."

First Meetings with Sri Ramakrishna

Ramchandra Datta, Narendra's cousin and a devotee of Ramakrishna, was aware of Narendra's genuine hunger for God. Ramchandra told him, "If you really want to cultivate spirituality, then visit Ramakrishna at Dakshineswar." However, Narendra first met Ramakrishna in Calcutta in November 1881 at the house of the Master's devotee Surendra Nath Mittra. Surendra had arranged a religious gathering and had invited Narendra to entertain the Master and the devotees with his devotional singing. The Master was extremely impressed with Narendra and after a few inquiries asked him to visit him at Dakshineswar.

Narendra first visited Dakshineswar sometime in the early part of 1882. He entered the Master's room by the western door that faces the Ganges. Indifferent to his external appearance, Narendra's clothes were disheveled; his impressive eyes were partly indrawn. Ramakrishna marvelled: "How is it possible that such a great spiritual aspirant can live in Calcutta, the home of the worldly-minded?" There was a mat spread out on the floor. The Master asked him and his friends to sit on it, and then asked Narendra to sing a song. Narendra sang a song of the Brahmo Samaj:

Let us go back once more, O mind, to our proper home!
Here in this foreign land of earth
Why should we wander aimlessly in stranger's guise? ...

This song put the Master into ecstasy. When the singing was over, he took Narendra to the northern veranda and closed the door. With tearful eyes the Master said to Narendra: "You've come so late! Was that proper? Couldn't you have guessed how I've been waiting for you? My ears are nearly burned off, listening to the talk of these worldly people. I thought I should burst, not having anyone to tell how I really felt." Then with folded hands he said: "I know who you are, my Lord. You are Nara, the ancient sage, the incarnation of Narayana. You have come to earth to take away the sufferings and sorrows of mankind."[7] The rational Narendra was dumbfounded, regarding this as the babble of an insane person.

When they returned to the Master's room, Narendra's mind was agitated by the strange words and conduct of Ramakrishna. However, he asked the Master: "Sir, have you seen God?" Without a moment's hesitation Ramakrishna replied: "Yes, I have seen God. I see Him as I see you here, only more clearly. God can be seen. One can talk to Him. But who cares for God? People shed torrents of tears for their wives, children, wealth, and property, but who weeps for the vision of God? If one cries sincerely for God, one can surely see Him." "That impressed me at once," said Narendra later. "For the first time I found a man who dared to say that he had seen God, that religion was a reality to be felt, to be sensed in an infinitely more intense way than we can sense the world." Narendra felt that Ramakrishna's words were uttered from the depths of his inner experience. Still, he could not comprehend the Master's words and conduct. Bewildered, he bowed down to the Master and returned to Calcutta.

A month later Narendra returned to Dakshineswar and found the Master alone in his room. Ramakrishna was glad to see Narendra and asked him to sit on the corner of his bed. After a few minutes the Master drew near him in an ecstatic mood, muttered some words, fixed his eyes on him, and placed his right foot on Narendra's body. At his touch Narendra saw, with open eyes, the whole world vanishing — the walls, the room, the temple garden, and even himself were disappearing into the void. He felt sure that he was facing death. He cried out loudly: "Ah, what are you doing to me? Don't you know that I have parents at home?" Listening to this, the Master laughed and then touching Narendra's chest, said: "All right, let it stop now. It will happen in its own good time." With this Narendra became normal again.

Narendra was proud of his strong body, sound mind, and rational intellect; but he felt helpless in front of Ramakrishna: he could not control himself. During his third visit to Dakshineswar he tried his utmost to be on guard. The Master went for a walk with Narendra to Jadu Mallik's garden house where they both sat down in the parlour. Then the Master went into an ecstatic mood and touched Narendra, who lost outer consciousness. In that state the Master asked Narendra questions about his past, his mission in the world, the duration of his present life, and so on. The answers only confirmed what he had seen about Narendra in the vision he had experienced many years before. Later the Master told his other disciples: "Narendra is a great soul, perfect in meditation. The day he recognizes his true self he will give up his body by an act of will, through yoga."

Master and Disciple

According to Hindu tradition, the disciple must obey the guru without question. However, the influence of Western thinking did not allow Narendra to accept this; he was determined to test for himself everything that Ramakrishna taught him. He felt it was wrong for someone to surrender freedom of judgement to another. After their third meeting, Narendra felt the Master's superhuman spiritual power, but he was still somewhat sceptical. His scepticism made him one of the most reliable of all the witnesses to Ramakrishna's greatness. Later he said to a Western disciple: "Let none regret that they were difficult to convince. I fought my Master for six long years, with the result that I know every inch of the way."[8]

The meeting of Narendra and Ramakrishna was an important event in the lives of both. It was like a meeting between the Occident and the Orient, the modern and the ancient. Ramakrishna tamed the rebellious Narendra with his infinite patience, love, and vigilance. The Master was fully convinced of Narendra's divine nature and mission to the world. He could not bear the slightest criticism of Narendra and told devotees: "Let no one judge him hastily. People will never understand him fully."[9]

Ramakrishna did not hesitate to praise Narendra's greatness in the presence of one and all, which sometimes embarrassed Narendra. One day Keshab Sen and Vijaykrishna Goswami, who were leaders of the Brahmo Samaj, visited Dakshineswar with a number of Brahmo devotees. Narendra was also present. The Master remarked: "If Keshab possesses one virtue which has made him world-famous, Naren is endowed with eighteen such virtues. I have seen in Keshab and Vijay the divine light burning like a candle flame, but in Naren it shines with the radiance of the sun." Narendra later vehemently protested to the Master: "Sir, people will think you're mad if you talk like that. Keshab is famous all over the world. Vijay is a saint. And I am an insignificant student. How can you speak of us in the same breath? Please, I beg you, never say such things again."

"I cannot help it," replied the Master. "Do you think these are my words? The Divine Mother showed me certain things about you, which I repeated. And She reveals to me nothing but the truth."[10]

"How do you know it was Mother who told you?" Narendra objected. "All this may be a fiction of your own brain. Science and philosophy prove that our senses often deceive us, especially when there's a desire in our minds to believe something. You are fond of me and you wish to see me great — that may be why you have these visions."[11]

The Master was perplexed. He appealed to the Divine Mother for guidance, and was told: "Why do you care what he says? In a short time he will accept every word of yours as true."

Ramakrishna's affection for Narendra astonished everyone. If Narendra could not come to Dakshineswar for a long time, the Master cried for him or he went to see him in Calcutta. Ramakrishna knew that he would not live long in this world, so he was eager to train his foremost disciple as early as possible. One Sunday the Master went to visit him at the Brahmo Samaj Temple, where Narendra sang devotional songs during the evening service. When he arrived in the middle of the service, there was a commotion among the congregation to see the saint of Dakshineswar. The preacher was annoyed and abruptly ended his sermon, and the ushers turned out all the gaslights in order to make people leave the building — a move which resulted in a chaotic stampede to the doors in the darkness.

Narendra was greatly pained by the Master's humiliation. He managed to elbow his way to Ramakrishna's side, then he led him out through a back door, got him into a carriage and rode with him to Dakshineswar. Narendra reprimanded the Master, but Ramakrishna didn't care a bit about the scolding or his humiliating experience with the Brahmos. Then Narendra told him severely: "It is written in the Puranas that King Bharata thought so much about his favourite deer that he himself became a deer after his death. If that's true, you should beware of thinking about me!" The Master was simple, much like a little boy. He took these words very seriously, because Narendra was a man of truth. Ramakrishna went to the temple and returned shortly, beaming with delight and exclaimed: "You rascal, I won't listen to you anymore. Mother says that I love you because I see the Lord in you. The day I shall not see Him in you, I shall not be able to bear even the sight of you."

As a member of the Brahmo Samaj, Narendra was committed to the belief in a formless God with attributes, and he despised all image worship. His friend Rakhal (later, Swami Brahmananda) also became a member of the Brahmo Samaj, even though he was devotional by nature. Later, under Ramakrishna's influence, Rakhal returned to the worship of God with form. When Narendra saw Rakhal bowing down before the images, he scolded his friend for breaking the Brahmo pledge. Rakhal was too soft-natured to argue, but he was hurt and began to avoid Narendra. The Master intervened, saying to Narendra: "Please do not intimidate Rakhal. He is afraid of you. He now believes in God with form. How are you going to change him? Everyone cannot realize the formless aspect of God at the very beginning."[12] That was enough: Narendra never interfered with Rakhal's practice again.

Ramakrishna knew that Narendra's mind was naturally inclined to the path of knowledge, so he initiated him into the teachings of nondualistic Vedanta. Sometimes he asked Narendra to read aloud passages from the *Ashtavakra Samhita* and other Vedanta treatises so that he could grasp the essence of the Vedanta philosophy, which teaches that Brahman is the ultimate Reality, existence-consciousness-bliss absolute. The individual soul is Brahman and nothing else. The world is shown to be nothing but name and form, all of which is apparent, not real, having only a relative existence.

In the beginning it was hard for Narendra to accept the nondualistic view that "everything is really Brahman," because he was then a staunch follower of the Brahmo Samaj, which taught a theistic philosophy. He said to the Master: "It is blasphemous, for there is no difference between such philosophy and atheism. There is no greater sin in the world than to think of oneself as identical with the Creator. I am God, you are God, these created things are God — what can be more absurd! The sages who wrote such things must have been insane." The Master didn't mind Narendra's outspokenness at all. He smiled and said: "You may not accept the views of these seers. But how can you abuse them or limit God's infinitude? Go on praying to the God of Truth and believe in any aspect of His that He reveals to you."[13]

One day while chatting with Hazra at Dakshineswar, Narendra ridiculed the Vedantic experience of oneness: "How can this be? This jug is God, this cup is God, and we too are God! Nothing can be more preposterous!" When the Master heard Narendra's comment from his room, he came out and inquired: "Hello! What are you talking about?" Ramakrishna touched Narendra and went into samadhi. Later Narendra graphically described the effect of that touch:

The magic touch of the Master that day immediately brought a wonderful change over my mind. I was stupefied to find that there was really nothing in the universe but God! I saw it quite clearly but kept silent, to see if the idea would last. But the impression did not abate in the course of the day. I returned home, but there too, everything I saw appeared to be Brahman. I sat down to take my meal, but found that everything — the food, the plate, the person who served, and even myself — was nothing but That. I ate a morsel or two and sat still. I was startled by my mother's words: "Why do you sit still? Finish your meal," and began to eat again. But all the while, whether eating or lying down, or going to college, I had the same experience and felt myself always in a sort of comatose state. While walking in the streets, I noticed cabs plying, but I did not feel inclined to move out of the way. I felt that the cabs and myself were of one stuff. There was no sensation in my limbs, which, I thought, were getting paralyzed. I did not relish eating, and felt as if somebody else were eating. Sometimes I lay down during a meal, after a few minutes, got up and again began to eat. The result would be that on some days I would take too much, but it did no harm. My mother became alarmed and said that there must be something wrong with me. She was afraid that I might not live long. When the above state altered a little, the world began to appear to me as a dream. While walking in Cornwallis Square [now Azadhind Bag], I would strike my head against the iron railings to see if they were real or only a dream. This state of things continued for some days. When I became normal again, I realized that I must have had a glimpse of the Advaita [nondual] state. Then it struck me that the words of the scriptures were not false. Thenceforth I could not deny the conclusions of the Advaita philosophy.[14]

One day Ramakrishna's whole attitude to Narendra suddenly seemed to change. The Master looked at him without the least sign of pleasure and remained silent. Narendra thought that the Master was in a spiritual mood. He waited for a while, and then went to the veranda and began talking to Hazra. In the evening Narendra bowed down to the Master and left for Calcutta. On his next several visits, the Master's mood towards Narendra did not change. He received him with the same apparent indifference. Ignored by the Master, he spent the days with Hazra and other disciples and returned home as usual. Finally, after more than a month, the Master asked Narendra, "Why do you come here, when I don't speak a single word to you?" "Do you think I come here just to have you speak to me?" Narendra answered. "I love you. I want to see you. That's why I come." The Master was delighted. "I was testing you," he told Narendra, "to see if you'd stop coming when you didn't get love and attention. Only a spiritual aspirant of your quality could put up with so much neglect and indifference. Anyone else would have left me long ago."[15]

Narendra was very bold and frank. He did not speak about people behind their backs. He took delight in criticizing the Master's spiritual experiences as evidence of a lack of self-control. He would even make fun of his worship of Kali. "Why do you come here," the Master once asked him, "if you do not accept Kali, my Mother?" "Bah! Must I accept her," Narendra retorted, "simply because I come to see you? I come to you because I love you." "All right," said the Master, "before long you will not only accept my blessed Mother, but weep while repeating her name."[16]

As Ramakrishna tested Narendra in various ways before accepting him as a disciple, so did Narendra test Ramakrishna before he accepted him as the guru. Narendra heard that the Master's renunciation was so absolute that he could not bear the touch of money. One day Narendra arrived at Dakshineswar and found that the Master had gone to Calcutta. Suddenly he felt a desire to test the Master. He hid a rupee under the Master's mattress and waited for him. The Master returned, but no sooner had he touched the bed than he drew back in pain, as if stung by a scorpion. The Master called a temple attendant to examine the bed, and the rupee was discovered. Narendra admitted that he had put the money there. The Master was not displeased at all. He said to Narendra: "You must test me as the money-changers test their coins. You mustn't accept me until you've tested me thoroughly."[17]

On another occasion, the Master put Narendra to a difficult test. He said to him: "As a result of the austerities I've practised, I have possessed all the supernatural powers for a long time. I am thinking of asking the Mother to transfer them all to you. She's told me that you'll be able to use them when necessary. What do you say?"

"Will they help me to realize God?" Narendra asked. "No," said the Master, "they won't help you to do that. But they might be very useful after you have realized God and when you start doing His work." "Then let me realize God first," said Narendra. "After that, it will be time enough to decide if I need them or not. If I accept them now, I may forget God, make selfish use of them, and thus come to grief." The Master was greatly pleased to see Narendra's single-minded devotion.

Ramakrishna emphasized the practice of chastity to his young disciples, whom he considered to be future monks. He told Narendra that if a man maintains absolute chastity for twelve years, his mind becomes purified and open to the knowledge of God. When the Master heard that Narendra's parents were arranging his marriage, he wept, holding the feet of the image of Kali. With tears in his eyes he prayed to the Divine Mother, "O Mother, please upset the whole thing! Don't let Narendra be drowned." However, Narendra's unwillingness forced his parents to cancel the marriage.

The Training of Narendra

Only a good student can be a good teacher. The Katha Upanishad says, "Wonderful is the expounder [of the Atman] and rare the hearer; rare indeed is the experiencer of Atman taught by an able preceptor" (1.2.7). Ramakrishna was an avatar, an incarnation of God who came to the world to establish the eternal religion; he made Narendra a vehicle to carry out his mission. In the parable of the four blind men and the elephant, Ramakrishna recounted how each man touched a different part of the elephant, declared his partial understanding, and then they began to quarrel among themselves. But one with clear vision sees the whole elephant and does not quarrel. People with only partial realization form sects, but those who have full realization cannot form sects. Ramakrishna therefore trained Narendra to have full realization and carry his message of the harmony of religions to the modern world.

On 5 March 1882, the Master asked Narendra: "How do you feel about it? Worldly people say all kinds of things about the spiritually minded. But look here! When an elephant moves along the street any number of curs and other small animals may bark and cry after it; but the elephant doesn't even look back at them. If people speak ill of you, what will you think of them?"

Narendra replied, "I shall think that dogs are barking at me."

The Master smiled and said: "Oh, no! You mustn't go that far, my child! God dwells in all beings. But you may be intimate only with good people; you must keep away from the evil-minded. God is even in the tiger; but you cannot embrace the tiger on that account. You may say, 'Why run away from a tiger, which is also a manifestation of God?' The answer to that is: Those who tell you to run away are also manifestations of God — and why shouldn't you listen to them?"

On 19 August 1883, Ramakrishna went to the veranda and saw Narendra talking to Hazra, who often indulged in dry philosophical discussions. Hazra would say that the world is unreal, like a dream: worship, food offerings to the Deity, and so forth, are only hallucinations of the mind. He would repeat, "I am He." When the Master asked Narendra what they were talking about, Narendra replied with a smile: "Oh, we are discussing a great many things. They are rather too deep for others."

Ramakrishna replied: "But pure love and pure knowledge are one and the same thing. Both lead the aspirants to the same goal. The path of love is much easier."

On 25 June 1884, Ramakrishna advised his disciples to dive deep in God-consciousness, and then sang a song: "Dive deep, O mind, dive deep in the Ocean of God's beauty. If you descend to the uttermost depths, there you will find the gem of love." Then he continued: "One does not die if one sinks in this Ocean. This is the Ocean of Immortality." Once he said to Narendra: "God is the Ocean of Bliss. Tell me if you want to plunge into It. Just imagine there is some syrup in a cup and that you have become a fly. Now tell me where you will sit to sip the syrup." Narendra answered: "I will sit on the edge of the cup and stretch out my neck to drink, because I am sure to die if I go far into the cup." Then Ramakrishna said to him: "But my child, this is the Ocean of Satchidananda. There is no fear of death in It. This is the Ocean of Immortality."

On 11 March 1885, M. recorded in *The Gospel of Sri Ramakrishna*:

Many of his devotees were in [Ramakrishna's] room. Narendra did not believe that God could incarnate Himself in a human body. But Girish [a devotee] differed with him; he had the burning faith that from time to time the Almighty Lord, through His inscrutable Power, assumes a human body and descends to earth to serve a divine purpose. The Master said to Girish: "I should like to hear you and Narendra argue in English." The discussion began; but they talked in Bengali.

Narendra: "God is Infinity. How is it possible for us to comprehend Him? He dwells in every human being. It is not the case that he manifests Himself through one person only."

Master (*tenderly*): "I quite agree with Narendra. God is everywhere. But then you must remember that there are different manifestations of His Power in different beings. At some places there is a manifestation of His *avidyashakti* [God's power manifesting as ignorance], at others manifestation of His *vidyashakti* [God's power manifesting as knowledge]. Through different instruments God's Power is manifest in different degrees, greater or smaller. Therefore all men are not equal."

Ram: "What is the use of these futile arguments?"

Master (*sharply*): "No! No! There is a meaning in all this."

Girish (*to Narendra*): "How do you know that God does not assume a human body?"

Narendra: "God is 'beyond words or thought.'"

Master: "No, that is not true. He can be known by pure *buddhi* [intellect], which is the same as the Pure Self. The seers of old directly perceived the Pure Self through their pure buddhi."

Girish (*to Narendra*): "Unless God Himself teaches men through His human Incarnation, who else will teach them spiritual mysteries?"

Narendra: "Why, God dwells in our own heart; He will certainly teach us from within the heart."

Master (*tenderly*): "Yes, yes. He will teach us as our Inner Guide. . . . I clearly see that God is everything; He Himself has become all. . . . I cannot utter a word unless I come down at least two steps from the plane of samadhi. Shankara's nondualistic explanation of Vedanta is true, and so is the qualified nondualistic interpretation of Ramanuja."

Narendra: "What is qualified nondualism?"

Master: "It is the theory of Ramanuja. According to this theory, Brahman, or the Absolute, is qualified by the universe and its living beings. These three — Brahman, the world, and living beings — together constitute One."

Narendra was sitting beside the Master. He touched Narendra's body and said: "As long as a man argues about God, he has not realized Him. The nearer you approach to God, the less you reason and argue. When you attain Him, then all sounds — all reasoning and disputing — come to an end. Then you go into samadhi — into communion with God in silence."

Narendra's Struggle

In the early part of 1884, Narendra's father died unexpectedly of a heart attack. Unfortunately he left behind many unsettled debts, and the once well-to-do family was suddenly thrust into acute poverty. To add to their troubles, some relatives filed a lawsuit with the intent of depriving them of their home. Since Narendra was the eldest son, the responsibility for the family's welfare fell upon his shoulders. He had just passed his B.A. examination and had been admitted to law school. Many times he attended classes without having eaten and was often faint with hunger and weakness. He had no job and, moreover, no previous work experience. Forced by circumstances, Narendra began visiting business and government offices, barefooted and shabbily dressed, looking for a job. Occasionally, one of his friends, who knew the gravity of his situation, anonymously sent modest amounts of money to Narendra's mother. His friends invited him now and then to their homes and offered him food, but the thought of his hungry mother, sisters, and brothers at home prevented him from eating. At home he would eat as little as possible in order that the others might have enough. This first contact with the harshness of life convinced Narendra that unselfish sympathy is rare in this world. There is no place here for the weak, the poor, and the destitute.

Misfortune does not come alone. Narendra related: "Various temptations came my way. A rich woman sent me an ugly proposal to end my days of penury, which I sternly rejected with scorn. Another woman also made similar overtures to me. I said to her: 'You have wasted your life seeking the pleasures of the flesh. The dark shadows of death are before you. Have you done anything to face that? Give up all these filthy desires and remember God.'"[18]

One day, after a futile search for a job, he sat down in the shade of the Ochterloney Monument in the *maidan* (a large park). A friend who happened to be with him wanted to console him with a song: "Here blows the wind, the breath of Brahman; it is His grace we feel." Narendra furiously blurted out: "Be quiet! That fanciful nonsense is all right for people living in the lap of luxury — people who have no idea what hunger is — people whose nearest and dearest aren't going in rags and starving. No doubt it sounds true and beautiful to them —as it did to me, in the old days. But now I've seen what life is really like. That song is just a pack of lies."[19]

Despite what he had said to his friend in the maidan, Narendra did not lose his inborn faith in God and His mercy. He used to repeat the Lord's name as he got out of bed in the morning. One day his mother overheard him and said bitterly: "Hush, you fool! You have been crying yourself hoarse for God since your childhood. Tell me what has God done for you?" These words stung Narendra to the quick. A doubt crept into his mind about God's existence and His providence.

It was not in Narendra's nature to hide his feelings. He began to tell people aggressively that God did not exist and that praying to him was also futile. The rumour soon spread that Narendra had become an atheist, and furthermore that he was mixing with people of bad character. Gossip spreads faster than the gospel. The Master heard it, but he paid no attention. One day a friend of Narendra tearfully said to the Master, "Sir, we never dreamed Narendra would sink so low!" Immediately the Master said sharply: "Silence, you scoundrels! The Mother has told me that it is simply not true. I shan't look at your face if you speak to me again that way."

Narendra remembered his past spiritual experiences when he came in contact with the Master, and he was firmly convinced that he had not been born to earn money, support a family, or seek worldly enjoyments. He secretly prepared to renounce the world as his grandfather had done and even fixed a date. When he heard that the Master was visiting a devotee in Calcutta, he decided to see him before he left home forever. When they met, the Master persuaded Narendra to accompany him to Dakshineswar. When they arrived in his room, the Master went into ecstasy and sang a song, which clearly indicated that he knew Narendra's secret plan. That night he sent the others away and said to Narendra with tears: "I know you have come to the world to do Mother's work; you can never lead a worldly life. But, for my sake, stay with your family as long as I'm alive."[20]

Narendra agreed. The next day he returned home and very quickly found a temporary job in an attorney's office, which was sufficient to cover the bare existence of his family. Unable to find a permanent solution to the financial problems of his family, however, Narendra went to the Master one day and asked him to pray to the Divine Mother on his behalf, as Narendra had faith that She listened to the Master's prayers. The Master told him to go to the temple and pray to Her himself for help, assuring him that his request would be granted. Narendra went to the temple with great anticipation. But as soon as he came before the image of the Divine Mother, he saw Her as living and conscious; he forgot the world and the pitiable condition of his mother, sisters, and brothers. In ecstatic joy he prostrated before Her and prayed: "Mother, give me discrimination! Give me renunciation! Give me knowledge and devotion! Grant that I may have an uninterrupted vision of Thee!" He went back to the Master and told him what had happened. The Master sent Narendra to the temple to pray again, but the same thing happened. The third time he remembered his intention, but he felt ashamed to ask for something so small from the Mother of the Universe. At last, at Narendra's request, the Master blessed him, saying, "All right, your people at home will never be in want of plain food and clothing."[21]

Narendra was relieved that his family would no longer suffer from starvation, and the Master was relieved that Narendra had accepted the worship of God with form. He knew that the concept of God as Mother would make Narendra's spiritual life fuller and richer. Later Narendra said to one of his Western disciples: "I used to hate Kali and all Her ways. That was my six years' fight, because I would not accept Kali." "But now you have accepted Her," interjected the disciple. "I had to," said Narendra. "I had great misfortunes at that time. My father died, and so on.... Ramakrishna dedicated me to Her. And you know I believe that She guides me in every little thing I do, and just does what She likes with me."[22]

Ramakrishna gave love and freedom to his disciples so that they could grow in their own way. Throughout the rest of his life, Narendra would frequently say: "Ever since our first meeting, it was the Master alone who always had faith in me — no one else, not even my own mother and brothers. That faith and that love of his have bound me to him forever. The Master was the only one who knew how to love and who really loved. Worldly people only feign love to gratify their own self-interest."

Last Days with Sri Ramakrishna

Ramakrishna was a wonderful teacher, and he taught more by the silent influence of his inner life than by words or even by personal example. To live with him demanded of the disciple purity of thought, humility, truthfulness, and renunciation. He acted as a father, mother, and friend to his young disciples. He would joke and have fun with them and at the same time remind them that the goal of human life is God-realization. They learned from their Master how to synthesize the four yogas (jnana, karma, bhakti, and raja), the harmony of religions, the true meaning of the scriptures, and the worship of God in human beings.

One day at Dakshineswar when the Master was seated in his room, he talked about three salient disciplines of the Vaishnava religion: love of God's name, compassion for all living beings, and service to the devotees. Repeating the word *compassion* he went into samadhi. After a while he returned to normal consciousness and said to the devotees: "How foolish to speak of compassion! Man is an insignificant worm crawling on the earth — and he is to show compassion to others! This is absurd. It must not be compassion, but service to all. Recognize them as God's manifestations and serve them." Only Narendra understood the implication of the Master's words. Leaving the room, he said to the others:

What a wonderful light I have discovered in those words of the Master! How beautifully he has reconciled the ideal of bhakti with the knowledge of Vedanta, generally interpreted as dry, austere, and incompatible with human sentiments! What a grand, natural, and sweet synthesis! . . . Those following the paths of karma [action] and yoga [contemplation] are similarly benefitted by these words of the Master. The embodied being cannot remain even for a minute without activity. All his activities should be directed to the service of man, the manifestation of God upon earth, and this will accelerate his progress towards the goal. If it be the will of God, I shall one day proclaim this noble truth before the world at large. I shall make it the common property of all — the wise and the foolish, the rich and the poor, the brahmin and the pariah.[23]

Only a jeweller knows the value of a diamond. Ramakrishna knew the worth of his beloved disciple Narendra, so he made him the leader of his group of disciples. He told his disciples:

Narendra belongs to a very high place — the realm of the Absolute. He has a manly nature. So many devotees come here, but there is no one like him.

Every now and then I take stock of the devotees. I find that some are like lotuses with ten petals, some like lotuses with a hundred petals. But among lotuses Narendra is a thousand-petalled one. Other devotees may be like pots or pitchers; but Narendra is a huge water-barrel. Others may be like pools or tanks; but Narendra is a huge reservoir like the Haldarpukur. Among fish, Narendra is a huge red-eyed carp; others are like minnows, or smelts, or sardines. Narendra is a very big receptacle, one that can hold many things. He is like a bamboo with a big hollow space inside. Narendra is not under the control of anything. He is not under the control of attachment or sense pleasures. He is like a male pigeon. If you hold a male pigeon by its beak, it breaks away from you; but the female pigeon keeps still. I feel great strength when Narendra is with me in a gathering.[24]

In the middle of 1885 Ramakrishna contracted throat cancer. For the convenience of his treatment he was first taken to Calcutta and then to Cossipore, a suburb of Calcutta. Without concern for his body, he continued to train his disciples. When they begged him not to strain himself, he replied: "I do not care. I will give up twenty thousand such bodies to help one person." Sarada Devi, the Master's wife, cooked for him, and Narendra and other young disciples took charge of nursing him. One day the Master distributed ochre monastic robes to Narendra and some of his young disciples and thus formed his own monastic order. He later told Narendra: "I leave them all to your care. See that they practise spiritual disciplines even after my passing away and that they do not return home."

Another day he wrote on a piece of paper, "Naren will teach people." When Narendra expressed opposition the Master said: "But you must. Your very bones will do it."

Ten years later Narendra described his Master's message to humanity: "First make character — that is the highest duty you can perform. Know Truth for yourself, and there will be many to whom you can teach it afterwards; they will all come. This was the attitude of my Master. He criticized no one. For years I lived with that man, but never did I hear those lips utter one word of condemnation for any sect. I learned from my Master that the religions of the world are not contradictory or antagonistic. They are but various phases of one eternal religion."[25]

Ramakrishna's illness showed no signs of abating in spite of the best available care and treatment. When Narendra realized that the Master would not live long, he intensified his own spiritual practices. One day he entreated Ramakrishna for the experience of nirvikalpa samadhi, the highest realization of Advaita Vedanta. But the Master reprimanded him: "Shame on you! You are asking for such an insignificant thing. I thought that you would be like a big banyan tree, and that thousands of people would rest in your shade. But now I see that you are seeking your own liberation." He said further: "There is a state higher than that. It is you who sing, 'O Lord, Thou art all that exists.'" The Master wanted his disciple to see God in all beings and to serve them in a spirit of worship.

One evening, however, when Narendra was meditating with one of his brother disciples at Cossipore, he suddenly became aware of a light at the back of his head, as if a lamp had been placed there. It gradually became more brilliant until finally it seemed to burst. He was engulfed by that light and lost body consciousness. After some time, he began to regain normal consciousness and cried out, "Where is my body?" His amazed brother disciple assured him: "It is here. Don't you feel it?" He then rushed to the Master's room upstairs and told him of Narendra's condition. "Let him stay in that state for a while," remarked the Master, "he pestered me long enough for it." For a long time Narendra remained immersed in samadhi, forgetting space, time, and causation. After regaining normal consciousness, he entered the Master's room, and Ramakrishna told him: "Now the Mother has shown you everything. But this realization, like the jewel locked in a box, will be hidden away from you and kept in my custody. I will keep the key with me. Only after you have fulfilled your mission on this earth will the box be unlocked, and you will know everything as you have known now."[26]

Narendra once narrated how the Master had transmitted his power into him: "Two or three days before Sri Ramakrishna's passing away, he called me to his side and looked steadily at me and went into samadhi. Then I felt that a subtle force like an electric shock was entering my body! In a little while I also lost outward consciousness and sat motionless. How long I stayed in that condition I do not remember. When consciousness returned I found Sri Ramakrishna shedding tears. On questioning him, he answered me affectionately: 'Today, giving you my all, I have become a beggar. With this power you are to do much work for the good of the world before you return.' I feel that that power is constantly directing me to this or that work. This body has not been made for remaining idle."[27]

A couple of days before Ramakrishna's passing away, when the Master was in excruciating pain, a thought flashed across Narendra's mind: "Well, now if you can declare that you are God, then only will I believe you are really God Himself." Immediately the Master looked up towards Narendra and said distinctly: "O my Naren, are you still not convinced? He who in the past was born as Rama and Krishna is now living in this very body as Ramakrishna — but not from the standpoint of your Vedanta [which posits that each soul is potentially divine], but actually so."[28]

After Sri Ramakrishna's Passing Away

Ramakrishna passed away on Sunday, 16 August 1886, plunging his devotees and disciples into an ocean of grief. The young disciples wanted to continue worshiping Ramakrishna's relics at the Cossipore garden house, but they had no means to support themselves. The householder devotees, who had supported the Master, asked them to return home. However, three disciples had already left home forever, and they had no place to go. Narendra was helpless.

One evening early in September, while Surendra Nath Mittra was meditating in his household shrine, Ramakrishna appeared to him and said: "What are you doing here? My boys are roaming about, without a place to live. Attend to that, before anything else." Hearing the Master's command, Surendra hurried to Narendra and told him everything that had happened. He promised to provide the same amount of money every month as he had given for the Cossipore house prior to Ramakrishna's passing. Immediately Narendra and the disciples began to search for a house, and found one at Baranagore, midway between Dakshineswar and Calcutta. Dreary, dilapidated, and deserted, it was a building that had a reputation of being haunted by evil spirits. It had two storeys; the lower one was infested with lizards and snakes. This house was chosen because of its low rent and proximity to the Cossipore burning-ghat, where the Master's body had been cremated.

M. wrote about the first Ramakrishna monastery at Baranagore in *The Gospel of Sri Ramakrishna*: "The members of the Math [monastery] called themselves the 'danas' and the 'daityas,' which means the 'ghosts' and the 'demons,' the companions of Shiva. They took these names because of their utter indifference to worldly pleasures and relationships.... Narendra and the other members of the Math often spent their evenings on the roof. There they devoted a great deal of time to discussion of the teachings of Sri Ramakrishna, Shankaracharya, Ramanuja, and Jesus Christ, and of Hindu philosophy, European philosophy, the Vedas, the Puranas, and the Tantras."

In later years, Narendra reminisced about the early days in the monastery:

> After the passing away of Sri Ramakrishna we underwent a lot of religious practice at the Baranagore Math [monastery]. We used to get up at 3:00 a.m. and after washing our faces, etc. — we would sit in the shrine and become absorbed in japam and meditation. What a strong spirit of dispassion we had in those days! We had no thought even as to whether the world existed or not.... There were days when the japam and meditation continued from morning till four or five in the afternoon. Ramakrishnananda waited and waited with our meals ready, till at last he would come and snatch us from our meditation by sheer force.... There were days when the monastery was without a grain of food. If some rice was collected by begging, there was no salt

to take it with! On some days there would be only rice and salt, but nobody cared for it in the least. We were then being carried away by a tidal wave of spiritual practice. Oh, those wonderful days![29]

In the middle of December 1886, Narendra and eight other disciples went to Antpur, the birthplace of Baburam (later, Swami Premananda) for a retreat. One night they made a fire in the courtyard and sat around it for meditation. Suddenly Narendra was inspired to talk about Christ's love and renunciation and his self-sacrifice for the good of humanity. In front of that sacred fire, the disciples vowed to embrace the monastic life. In a joyous mood they returned to their rooms and someone discovered that it was Christmas Eve — all felt doubly blest. After a week of retreat, they returned to Baranagore, and in the early part of 1887, took formal monastic vows. Narendra took the name of Swami Vividishananda. Later, prior to his journey to America, he changed his name to Swami Vivekananda at the request of Raja Ajit Singh of Khetri.

Many years later, Narendra said to one of his disciples: "One eye shed tears of grief when I left home, because I hated to leave my mother, grandmother, brothers, and sisters; and the other eye shed tears of joy for my ideal."[30] Luxury and too many material possessions take the mind away from God. That is why most mystics remove themselves from family ties and worldly possessions. This is one of the initial tests of a spiritual journey. God embraces those souls and makes everything favourable for them who are endowed with purity and renunciation, poverty and humility, devotion and longing.

As a Wandering Monk

There is a saying, "The monk is pure who goes, and the river is pure that flows." In 1888 Vivekananda left the monastery to live as a penniless wandering monk. He carried a staff, a water pot, and his two favourite books — Bhagavad Gita and *The Imitation of Christ*.

He first went to Varanasi, known as the city of light and a capital of ancient Indian culture. During his journey he met many holy people and scholars. One day while visiting the Durga Temple, he was attacked by a troop of monkeys. While he was running away, a monk shouted to him, "Face the brutes." Swamiji stopped and looked defiantly at the ugly beasts. They quickly disappeared. Later, as a preacher in America, he shared this experience with people and told them to face the dangers and vicissitudes of life and not run away from them. Vivekananda knew his life's mission and felt a tremendous power within himself. He left the city of Varanasi with these prophetic words: "When I return here the next time, I shall burst upon society like a bombshell, and it will follow me like a dog."[31]

On his way to Hardwar, he stopped at the Hathras Railroad Station. There he met Sharat Chandra Gupta, the assistant station master, whom he accepted as his disciple. When Sharat asked the swami to stay with him longer, he replied: "My son, I have a great mission to fulfill. My guru asked me to dedicate my life to the regeneration of my motherland. Spirituality has fallen to a low ebb and starvation stalks the land. India must become dynamic again and earn the respect of the world through her spiritual power."[32]

One day during his travels in the Himalayas, Vivekananda sat for meditation under a pipal tree by the side of a stream. There he experienced the oneness of the universe and man — that man is a universe in miniature. He realized that all that exists in the universe also exists in the body, and further, that the entire universe can be found contained in a single atom. He jotted down this experience in a notebook: "In the beginning was the Word, etc. The microcosm and the macrocosm are built on the same plan. Just as the individual soul is encased in the living body, so is the Universal Soul in the living Prakriti [Nature] — the objective universe. . . . The dual aspect of the Universal Soul is eternal. So what we perceive or feel is this combination of the Eternally Formed and the Eternally Formless."[33]

During Vivekananda's itinerant days, he had various kinds of spiritual experiences. Once in a vision he saw an old man standing on the bank of the Indus chanting Vedic hymns: he distinctly heard the invocation of the Gayatri mantram from the Rig Veda. The swami believed that through this vision he had recovered the musical cadences of the early Aryans. He also experienced the presence of the Cosmic God in all beings.

Vivekananda visited Pavhari Baba, the famous yogi of Gazipur, and learned from him the secret of work: "Pay as much attention to the means of work as to its end." The yogi told him, "Live in the house of your guru like a cow," which means that one should cultivate the spirit of service and humility. There are many wonderful stories about Pavhari Baba. Once a cobra entered his cave; later, the yogi said to his frightened disciple, "It was a messenger who came from my beloved." Another day, a dog ran off with the yogi's bread and he followed, praying humbly, "Please wait, my Lord; let me butter the bread for you."

While at Gazipur Vivekananda suffered from stomach trouble and lumbago. He decided to take hatha yoga initiation from Pavhari Baba in order to cure his ailment. However, that night Ramakrishna appeared before him, looking at him intently as if very grieved. This vision was repeated for twenty-one nights. He gave up the idea of initiation, reproaching himself for lacking complete faith in the Master.

Vivekananda travelled over almost all of India, mostly on foot, visiting places of history and pilgrimage. He was thus able to gain firsthand experience of the Indian people. Seeing the poor and deplorable conditions of the masses, he was at times moved to tears. He had suffered great poverty himself and had deep compassion for the suffering of others. Once he remarked, with his usual vigour, that a God who could not in this life give a crust of bread was not to be trusted in the next for the kingdom of heaven. He observed that religion was not the crying need of India, and recalled Sri Ramakrishna's pithy saying, "Religion is not for an empty stomach."

In his travels, Vivekananda met the maharajas of Khetri, Alwar, Mysore, Ramnad, and many other dignitaries. He boldly told them that the prosperity of India depended upon uplifting the masses by introducing good education, modern science, and industry. However, they did not show sufficient interest. Later, he expressed his feelings: "May I be born again and again, and suffer thousands of miseries so that I may worship the only God that exists, the only God I believe in, the sum total of all souls — and above all, my God the wicked, my God the miserable, my God the poor of all races, of all species, is the special object of my worship."[34]

In February 1891, Vivekananda arrived at Alwar, Rajputana (western India) and met Maharaja Mangal Singh. He was very Westernized, and, although a Hindu, had no faith in worshipping images that to him were nothing but clay or stone figurines. Swamiji tried in vain to explain to him that Hindus worshipped God alone, using the images as symbols. The maharaja was not convinced. Then Vivekananda asked the prime minister to take down a picture of the maharaja that was hanging on the wall; at Vivekananda's request it was handed to him. He then commanded the prime minister and others to spit on it. Everyone was horrified. He said to the audience: "Maharaja is not bodily present in the photograph. This is only a piece of paper. It does not contain his bones, flesh, and blood. It does not speak or behave or move in any way as the maharaja does, yet all of you refuse to spit on it, because you see in this photo the shadow of the maharaja. Indeed, in spitting on the photo, you feel that you insult your master, the Prince himself." Turning to the maharaja, he continued: "See, Your Highness, though this is not you in one sense, in another sense it *is* you. That was why your devoted servants were so perplexed when I asked them to spit on it."[35] The maharaja realized his mistake and begged Swamiji's blessings.

While travelling in western and southern India, Vivekananda heard about the Parliament of Religions that was to be held in Chicago in 1893. A group of Indian rulers and influential people requested that he attend in order to represent Hinduism, the religion of Vedanta, but he refused. He was waiting for the Master's call. In December 1892, at Kanyakumari, sitting on the last bit of Indian rock in the Indian Ocean, he received his call to go to the West.

One day, while in Madras, Swamiji had a symbolic dream: He saw Sri Ramakrishna walking into the water of the ocean and beckoning him to follow. He also heard the command: "Go!" Although Swamiji was now certain of his journey, he still felt it necessary to have Holy Mother Sarada Devi's permission and blessing. He wrote to Swami Saradananda: "I have had a vision in which the Master told me to go to the West. My mind is quite disturbed. Please tell Holy Mother everything and let me know her opinion." Saradananda went to Holy Mother and read Swamiji's letter to her. Holy Mother did not give her opinion immediately, but asked Saradananda to wait. After a couple of days, Holy Mother had a dream. She saw Ramakrishna walking over the ocean waves and asking Narendra to follow him. Then Holy Mother told Saradananda: "Please write to Naren that he should go to the West." Swamiji was overjoyed when he received Holy Mother's approval and blessing.

In Madras, Vivekananda's followers began to raise money and make the necessary arrangements for his departure. In the meantime, Raja Ajit Singh of Khetri, who was a disciple of Swamiji, asked him to come to Khetri and bless his newborn son. He also offered to provide the ticket for his passage to America. Swamiji consented and went to Khetri for the birthday function. One evening while he was there, the maharaja invited him to attend a musical performance by a dancing girl. However, Vivekananda sent word that, as a monk, he was not permitted to enjoy secular pleasures. The girl was hurt when she heard the message and sang this plaintive song, which reached the swami's ears:

> Look not, O Lord, upon my sins!
> Is not same-sightedness Thy name?
> One piece of iron is in the image in the temple,
> And another, the knife in the hand of the butcher;
> Yet both of these are turned to gold
> When touched by the philosophers' stone.
> So, Lord, look not upon my evil qualities. . . .

Swamiji was deeply moved. This dancing girl, whom society condemned as impure, had taught him a great lesson: Brahman, the ever-pure, ever-free, ever-illumined, is the essence of all beings. He immediately realized his mistake and joined the party. He later said: "That incident removed the scales from my eyes. Seeing that all are indeed the manifestation of the One, I could no longer condemn anybody."[36]

On his way to Bombay Swamiji stopped at the Abu Road Station and met Swamis Brahmananda and Turiyananda. When he told them that he was going to America they were greatly excited. He explained to them: "I have now travelled all over India. . . . But alas, it was agony to me, my brothers, to see with my own eyes the terrible poverty and misery of the masses, and I could not restrain my tears! It is now my firm conviction that it is futile to preach religion amongst them without first trying to remove their poverty and sufferings. It is for this reason — to find more means for the salvation of the poor of India — that I am now going to America."[37]

The Columbian Exposition at Chicago in 1893

Vivekananda left Bombay on 31 May 1893 and reached Chicago on 30 July via Colombo, Penang, Singapore, Hong Kong, Canton, Nagasaki, Kobe, Osaka, Kyoto, Tokyo, Yokohama, Vancouver, and Winnipeg. Soon after his arrival in Chicago, he went to the information bureau of the Exposition and heard some heartrending news: The forthcoming Parliament of Religions would not open before the second week of September; no one without credentials from a bona fide organization would be accepted as a delegate; and the date to be registered as a delegate had passed. Moreover, he knew no one in Chicago and did not have sufficient money to pay the exorbitant hotel charges.

He managed to stay in Chicago for nearly two weeks and observed the World's Fair, which had been arranged in connection with the four-hundredth anniversary of Columbus's discovery of America. Marie Louise Burke states: "The primary purpose of the World's Columbian Exposition of 1893 was to bring together the fruits of man's material progress. Everything imaginable was on exhibit — not only the achievements of Western civilization, but the better to show these off, life-size models of the more backward cultures of the world."[38]

God plays in mysterious ways. Someone suggested that Vivekananda go to Boston, where living expenses would be much lower. Earlier, on the train from Vancouver to Chicago, he had met Katherine Sanborn of

Boston. She had invited him to be her guest, so he now left for Boston to stay with her. She introduced the swami to John Wright, a professor of Greek at Harvard University. He wrote some introductory letters for Vivekananda to some of his friends who were connected with the Parliament: "Here is a man more learned than all our learned professors put together." In addition, Professor Wright bought the swami's railroad ticket back to Chicago.

It was late evening when Vivekananda arrived in Chicago. Unfortunately, he had lost the address of the committee in charge of Parliament delegates. He did not know where to turn for help, and no one came forward to assist this strange-looking foreigner. Swamiji spent his first night without food, in an empty wagon that he found in the railroad station. The next morning, by divine providence, he met Mrs. George W. Hale. She took him into her home and later introduced him to her personal friend, Dr. J. H. Barrows, the president of the Parliament. Through him, the swami was accepted as a representative of Hinduism and was lodged with the other delegates.

The World's Parliament of Religions was one of the most significant events in the history of the world, because this was the first time all great religions of the world assembled on the same platform. On 11 September 1893, in the opening session of the Parliament, Vivekananda reiterated the eternal message of Vedanta: "As the different streams having their sources in different places all mingle their water in the sea, so, O Lord, the different paths which men take, through different tendencies, various though they may appear, crooked or straight, all lead to Thee." Mrs. S. K. Blodgett, an American lady who first saw Vivekananda at the Parliament, said later: "I was at the Parliament of Religions at Chicago in 1893, and when that young man [Vivekananda] got up and said, 'Sisters and Brothers of America,' seven thousand people rose to their feet as a tribute to something, they knew not what. When it was over, I saw scores of women walking over the benches to get near him, and I said to myself, 'Well, my lad, if you can resist that onslaught, you are indeed a god.'"[39]

On 27 September 1893, in the final session of the Parliament, Vivekananda concluded his speech: "If the Parliament of Religions has shown anything to the world, it is this: It has proved to the world that holiness, purity, and charity are not the exclusive possessions of any church in the world, and that every system has produced men and women of the most exalted character. In the face of this evidence, if anybody dreams of the exclusive survival of his own religion and the destruction of the others, I pity him from the bottom of my heart and point out to him that upon the banner of every religion will soon be written, in spite of resistance: 'Help and not Fight,' 'Assimilation and not Destruction,' 'Harmony and Peace and not Dissension.'"

"I Have a Message to the West"

The American news media gave Vivekananda a great deal of publicity, and he became widely known. The homes of some of the wealthiest people of American society were opened to him, and he was received as an honoured guest. But Swamiji never swayed from his monastic ideals or from the service he had set out to perform. He began lecturing all over the Midwest as well as on the East Coast and in some southern states of the U.S.A. Vivekananda founded the Vedanta Society of New York in November 1894. On 30 December 1894, at the Brooklyn Ethical Society, Swamiji declared: "I have a message to the West, as Buddha had a message to the East."[40]

Vivekananda taught Vedanta to the West, the universal philosophy and religion of the Upanishads, which originated thousands of years ago in India. Western audiences heard something new in his powerful words: Sectarianism, bigotry, superstition, intolerance were swept aside to make room for the harmony of all religions. It was an overwhelming message of goodwill and brotherly love. "The swami had little patience with the constant harping on original sin in the West," wrote Swami Atulananda, a Western monk. "Why do you dwell on sin so much?" he exclaimed. "You are heirs of immortal bliss. We Hindus refuse to call you sinners! Ye are the children of God, holy and perfect beings. It is a sin to call man a sinner, it is a libel on human nature." Atulananda continued: "Thus the swami cleared the theological atmosphere of the West. He sounded the trumpet call of glad tidings, of hope, of cheer, of salvation for all. And a new thought wave swept over America. The swami brought the gospel of the divinity of human beings.

"Swami Vivekananda had come to speak the truth, not to flatter the American nation to win their applause and sympathy. He had great reverence for Christ and his teachings, but he saw flaws in current Christianity.... In Detroit, before a large audience he exclaimed: 'I have come to make you better Christians. Remember Christ's saying, "Blessed are the peace-makers, for they shall be called the children of God." Everything that has selfishness for its basis must perish. If you want to live, go back to Christ. Go back to him who had nowhere to lay his head. Go back to him. . . . Better be ready to live in rags with Christ than to live in palaces without him.'"[41]

Vivekananda redefined religion for his Western audience, saying: "You must bear in mind that religion does not consist in talk, or doctrines, or books, but in realization. It is not learning but *being*." "The old religions said that he was an atheist who did not believe in God. The new religion says that he is an atheist who does not believe in himself." "Religion is the idea which is raising the brute unto man, and man unto God. . . .Take religion from human society and what will remain? Nothing but a forest of brutes. Sense-happiness is not the goal of humanity. Wisdom is the goal of all life."

The supreme goal of human life, according to Vivekananda, is to manifest the divinity that is within all beings. How is this done? Vivekananda described the methods in detail in his talks on the four yogas: karma yoga, the path of unselfish action; bhakti yoga, the path of devotion; jnana yoga, the path of knowledge; and raja yoga, the path of meditation. These yogas, or spiritual paths, help people to unite themselves with God, or Brahman, so they can overcome all the weaknesses and problems in their lives and attain supreme bliss and freedom.

Truth is always simple, as the teachings of all great teachers of the world demonstrate. Since Vivekananda had himself experienced the Ultimate Reality, he could make the truths of Vedanta understandable to all. He wrote to one of his disciples: "To put the Hindu ideas into English and then make out of dry philosophy and intricate mythology and queer, startling psychology, a religion which shall be easy, simple, popular, and at the same time meet the requirements of the highest minds — is a task only those can understand who have attempted it. The dry, abstract Advaita must become living — poetic — in everyday life; out of hopelessly intricate mythology must come concrete moral forms; and out of bewildering yogi-ism must come the most scientific and practical psychology — and all this must be put in a form so that a child may grasp it. That is my life's work."[42]

Establishing the Vedanta Movement in the West

During his lecture tour, Vivekananda came in contact with many well-known Western personalities. Robert Ingersoll, the famous orator and agnostic, cautioned Swamiji not to be too bold because people were intolerant of alien religious ideas. "Fifty years ago," he said, "you would have been hanged if you had come to preach in this country, or you would have been burnt alive. You would have been stoned out of the villages if you had come even much later."[43]

The great electrical inventor Nikola Tesla was impressed hearing Swamiji talk about the Vedantic *prana* (energy), *akasha* (space), and the *kalpas* (cycles) — which according to Tesla were the only theories modern science could entertain. Vivekananda also met John D. Rockefeller; and the swami tried to help him understand that God had given him wealth so that he might have an opportunity to do good to others. Rockefeller was annoyed that anyone would dare talk to him that way; he left the room without even saying goodbye. A week later he visited Swamiji and brought a paper that set forth his plans to donate an enormous sum of money to a public institution. "Well, there you are," he said. "You must be satisfied now, and you can thank me for it." Swamiji quietly read it and said: "It is for you to thank me."[44]

Harriet Monroe and Ella Wheeler Wilcox, two famous American poets, heard Vivekananda's lectures and became his great admirers. Swamiji also left a lasting impression on Professor William James of Harvard University; Dr. Lewis G. Janes, president of the Brooklyn Ethical Association; Mrs. J. J. Bagley, the wife of the Governor of Michigan; Sarah Farmer, the founder of Green Acre Conference; Mrs. Sara C. Bull, the wife of Ole Bull, the celebrated Norwegian violinist; Sarah Bernhardt, the famous French actress; and Madame Emma Calvé, the well-known French opera singer. Calvé wrote in her autobiography: "It has been my good fortune and my joy to know a man who truly 'walked with God,' a noble being, a saint, a philosopher, and a true friend. His influence upon my spiritual life was profound. He opened up new horizons before me, enlarging and vivifying my religious ideas and ideals, teaching me a broader understanding of truth. My soul will bear him eternal gratitude. The extraordinary man was a Hindu monk of the Order of the Vedanta. He was called the Swami Vivekananda, and was widely known in America for his religious teachings."[45]

After lecturing extensively, Swamiji realized that mere talk was not enough; he needed to train some sincere souls who would continue spreading the message of Vedanta in his absence. In the summer of 1894 Swamiji was invited to speak at a "Humane Conference" held at Green Acre, Maine. Christian Scientists, spiritualists, faith healers, and groups representing similar views participated in the conference. On 31 July 1894 Vivekananda wrote to his devotees, the Hale sisters, who lived in Chicago:

> The other night the camp people all went to sleep under a pine tree under which I sit every morning à la India and talk to them. Of course I went with them and we had a nice night under the stars, sleeping on

the lap of Mother Earth, and I enjoyed every bit of it. I cannot describe to you that night's glories — after the year of brutal life that I have led, to sleep on the ground, to meditate under the tree in the forest! The inn people are more or less well-to-do, and the camp people are healthy, young, sincere, and holy men and women. I teach them all *Shivoham, Shivoham* — "I am Shiva, I am Shiva" — and they all repeat it, innocent and pure as they are, and brave beyond all bounds, and I am so happy and glorified.

In the same letter, Swamiji inspired his American sisters, who sincerely helped his Western work: "Wealth goes, beauty vanishes, life flies, powers fly — but the Lord abideth forever, love abideth forever.... Stick to God. Who cares what comes, in the body or anywhere? Through the terrors of evil, say, 'My God, my Love!' Through the pangs of death, say, 'My God, my Love!' ... Do not go for glass beads, leaving the mine of diamonds. This life is a great chance. What! Seekest thou the pleasures of this world? He is the fountain of all bliss. Seek the highest, aim for the highest, and you shall reach the highest."[46]

While in New York in the early part of 1895, Swamiji met Miss Josephine MacLeod and her sister Betty (who later married Francis Leggett). They not only worked for Vedanta, but also took care of Swamiji's personal needs. In the middle of 1895, when Swamiji was exhausted from lecturing in New York, Mr. Leggett invited him to his retreat cottage at Camp Percy, New Hampshire. On 7 June 1895, Vivekananda wrote to a friend about his visit to the camp: "It gives me a new lease on life to be here. I go into the forest alone and read my Gita and am quite happy."

After a short visit to Camp Percy, Swamiji went to Thousand Island Park on the Saint Lawrence River in New York State. Miss Elizabeth Dutcher, a Vedanta student, gave her cottage to Swamiji so that he could rest there as well as give classes for sincere students. Swamiji stayed there nearly seven weeks and taught his American students the uplifting philosophy of Vedanta along with the lives and teachings of other great teachers of the world; these teachings were later published as *Inspired Talks*. In Thousand Island Park Swamiji initiated some of his male and female students into sannyasa and brahmacharya, reminding them again and again: "Find God. Nothing else matters." He emphasized morality as the basis of spiritual life. Without truth, nonviolence, continence, noncovetousness, cleanliness, and austerity, he repeated, there could be no spirituality.

On the morning of 7 August 1895, he went for a walk with Sister Christine and Mrs. Mary Funke. They strolled about half a mile up a hill covered with trees, and sat under a low-branched tree. Vivekananda suddenly said to them: "Now we will meditate. We shall be like Buddha under the Bo-tree." Vivekananda became so still that he seemed to turn to bronze. Then a thunderstorm came, and it poured rain. The swami was absorbed in meditation, oblivious to everything around him. Mrs. Funke raised her umbrella and protected him as much as possible. After a while Vivekananda regained his outer consciousness, and looking around, said, "Once more am I in Calcutta in the rains." That evening he left for New York.

In mid-August, Swamiji left for Paris, where Mr. Francis Leggett had invited him to be his guest. Before he left, however, both Miss Henrietta Müller and E.T. Sturdy invited him to London to teach Vedanta. Swamiji was also eager to do some constructive Vedanta work in England, and decided to establish a society there. For that purpose, he brought from India Swami Saradananda, and later Swami Abhedananda. During his first visit to the West, Vivekananda travelled to England three times: From September to November 1895, from April to July 1896, and from October to December 1896. Miss Margaret Noble (later, Sister Nivedita) wrote in her book *The Master as I Saw Him*:

It is strange to remember, and yet it was surely my good fortune, that though I heard the teachings of my Master, the Swami Vivekananda, on both the occasions of his visits to England in 1895 and 1896, I yet knew little or nothing of him in private life, until I came to India in the early days of 1898.

"What the world wants today, is twenty men and women who can dare to stand in the street yonder and say that they possess nothing but God. Who will go?" He [Swami Vivekananda] had risen to his feet by this time, and stood looking round his audience as if begging some of them to join him. "Why should one fear?" And then, in tones of which, even now, I can hear again the thunderous conviction, "If this is true, what else could matter? *If it is not true, what do our lives matter?*"[47]

During his second visit, the swami electrified English audiences with his jnana yoga lectures. In addition he gave a series of lectures at the Royal Society of Painters in Watercolours in Piccadilly, in clubs, educational societies, and in private circles. The British press expressed great admiration for him. Vivekananda wrote to a disciple in Madras, "In England my work is really splendid." Vivekananda attracted some sincere British followers who dedicated their lives for his mission. Two of them were J. J. Goodwin, who became his stenographer and recorded many of his lectures, and Margaret Noble, who later went to India and established a school for women.

Professor Max Müller, the well-known orientalist, wrote an article entitled "A Real Mahatman," about Sri Ramakrishna (*Nineteenth Century*, August 1896). He invited Vivekananda to his Oxford residence, and they became close friends. Later, in Germany, the swami met Professor Paul Deussen, another famous Indologist, who believed the system of Vedanta to be one of the "most majestic structures and valuable products of the genius of man in his search for Truth."

Vivekananda left England on 16 December 1896 and travelled overland to Naples, the port of departure to India. Mr. and Mrs. Sevier, who later helped to establish the Advaita Ashrama in Mayavati, accompanied him. On their way to India, the group visited Milan, Florence, and finally Rome, where they spent Christmas week. Swamiji was impressed with the magnificent art collections of Italy, as well as the grandeur of the cathedrals. At Naples, Goodwin joined the party and they left for India on 30 December 1896.

The Return to India

On the eve of his departure from London, an English friend had asked him, "Swami, how will you like your motherland after three years' experience in the luxurious and powerful West?" His significant reply was: "India I loved before I came away. Now the very dust of India has become holy to me, the very air is now holy to me; it is the holy land, the place of pilgrimage."[48]

Vivekananda and his devotees arrived in Colombo, Sri Lanka, in the afternoon of 15 January 1897. On that same day, the people of Colombo gave Vivekananda a royal reception. The swami gave his first public lecture in the East, entitled "India, the Holy Land," on the following day. Pointing to Indian spiritual tradition, the swami said: "Slow and silent, as the gentle dew that falls in the morning, unseen and unheard, yet producing a most tremendous result, has been the work of the calm, patient, all-suffering spiritual race upon the world of thought."[49]

Vivekananda's journey from Colombo to Madras was eventful. As soon as the swami touched Indian soil, Bhaskar Setupati, the Raja of Ramnad, received his beloved guru cordially and arranged everything for him and his Western followers. Swamiji received overwhelming receptions at Kandy, Anuradhapuram, Jaffna, Pamban, Rameswaram, Ramnad, Paramakudi, Madura, Trichonopoly, and Kumbhakonam.

It is amazing that an unknown monk became a national hero. The enthusiasm of the people reached its peak in Madras, where extensive preparations had been made for Vivekananda's reception. It was the people of Madras who had first recognized the swami's greatness, and had equipped him for his journey to America. The city streets were profusely decorated and seventeen triumphal arches had been erected. As soon as he got off the train, thousands of people received him with thundering shouts and applause. An elaborate procession was formed and he was taken to Castle Kernan, where arrangements had been made for his stay in the city. Vivekananda gave four lectures in Madras. All of his lectures from Colombo to Almora were recorded by his English disciple, J. J. Goodwin, and later published.

Swami Vivekananda began to awaken the sleeping, subjugated nation with the clarion call of Vedanta: "Arise! Awake! And stop not till the goal is reached!" "Strength, strength is what the Upanishads speak to me from every page. Be not weak. Will sin cure sin, weakness cure weakness? Stand up and be strong." "The first step in getting strength is to uphold the Upanishads, and believe: 'I am the Soul. I am the Omnipotent, I am the Omniscient.' Repeat these blessed saving words.... These conceptions of Vedanta must come out, must not remain only in the forest, not only in the cave, but they must come out at the bar and the bench, in the pulpit, and in the cottage of the poor man."

Vivekananda's bold message reverberated all over India and awakened the national consciousness:

My India, arise! Where is your vital force? In your Immortal Soul. Each nation, like each individual, has one theme in this life, which is its centre, the principal note round which every other note comes to form the harmony. If any one nation attempts to throw off its national vitality, the direction which has become its own through the transmission of centuries, that nation dies.... In one nation political power is its vitality, as in England. Artistic life, in another, and so on. In India religious life forms the centre, the keynote of the whole music of the national life.

Vivekananda reminded his countrymen to be unselfish and to cultivate love for the masses: "Feel, therefore, my would-be reformers, my would-be patriots! Do you feel? Do you feel that millions and millions of the descendants of gods and of sages have become next-door neighbours to brutes? Do you feel that millions are starving today and millions have been starving for ages? Do you feel that ignorance has come over the land as a dark cloud? Does it make you restless? Does it make you sleepless?

Has it made you almost mad? Are you seized with that one idea of the misery of ruin, and have you forgotten all about your name, your fame, your wives, your children, your property, even your own bodies? If so, that is the first step to becoming a patriot."

Swamiji wrote:

For the next fifty years let all other vain Gods disappear from our minds. This is the only God that is awake: our own race — everywhere His hands, everywhere His feet, everywhere His ears, He covers everything. All other Gods are sleeping. Why should we vainly go after them, when we can worship the God that we see all around us, the *Virat* [the Cosmic God]? The first of all worships is the worship of the Virat, of those all around us. These are all our Gods — men and animals; and the first Gods we have to worship are our own countrymen.

Swamiji wanted to uplift the masses through his "man-making religion" and "man-making education." He said: "Men, men — these are wanted: everything else will be ready; but strong, vigorous, believing young men, sincere to the backbone, are wanted. A hundred such and the world will be revolutionized." At the same time he cautioned his followers: "Let no political significance ever be attached falsely to my writings or sayings. . . . I will have nothing to do with political nonsense. I do not believe in politics. God and Truth are the only policy in the world. Everything else is trash."

Vivekananda had a tremendous impact all over South India. After visiting the South, he and his party took a boat from Madras to Calcutta. The steamer reached Budge Budge on 19 February, and he boarded a special train for Sealdah, Calcutta. Some of his brother disciples and thousands of people gave the swami a wonderful reception: triumphal arches decorated the streets, and his unharnessed carriage was drawn by students in a huge procession with music and religious songs. Gopallal Seal Villa, a garden house on the bank of the Ganges, was arranged for the swami and his party.

On 28 February 1897 the people of Calcutta honoured him with a public reception. Raja Benoy Krishna Deb presided and thousands of people attended. In response to the welcome address, Vivekananda spoke briefly about his work in the West, and how Vedantic teachings could improve the lives of the masses. He also paid a touching tribute to Sri Ramakrishna, "my teacher, my master, my hero, my ideal, my God in life." "If there has been anything achieved by me," he said with deep feeling, "by thoughts or words or deeds, if from my lips has ever fallen one word that has ever helped anyone in the world, I lay no claim to it; it was his. But if there have been curses falling from my lips, if there has been hatred coming out of me, it is all mine, and not his. All that has been weak has been mine; all that has been life-giving, strengthening, pure and holy has been his inspiration, his words, and he himself. Yes, my friends, the world has yet to know that man."

In 1897 the birth anniversary of Sri Ramakrishna was celebrated at the Dakshineswar temple garden. Vivekananda joined the festival along with his brother disciples and devotees. He walked barefoot on the holy ground, and was emotionally overwhelmed remembering his days with the Master. Vivekananda tried to speak a few words, but could not be heard over the noise of the large crowd around him. While Vivekananda was in Calcutta people flocked to him incessantly to pay their respects, or to hear his exposition of Vedanta. As a result, his health broke down and he left for Darjeeling, a Himalayan resort, for a much-needed rest. Swamiji regained his health to some extent, and then returned to Calcutta at the end of April 1897.

Vedanta was never an organized religion; it has been practised by mendicants all through the ages. However, Vivekananda felt the need of a monastic order that would carry the message of Vedanta all over the world, although he knew the pros and cons of organized religion. While he was in America this thought came to his mind: "To organize or not to organize? If I organize, the spirit will diminish. If I do not organize, the message will not spread."[50] On 1 May 1897 Vivekananda called a meeting of the monastic and lay devotees of Ramakrishna at the Calcutta residence of Balaram Basu and discussed the establishment of his Vedanta work on an organized basis. Swamiji proposed to the members present that the association should "bear the name of him in whose name we have become sannyasins, taking whom as your ideal you are leading the life of householders, and whose holy name, influence, and teachings have within twelve years of his passing away, spread in such unthought-of ways both in the East and in the West." All the members enthusiastically accepted the swami's proposal, and the Ramakrishna Mission Association came into existence. Swamiji then delineated the aims and ideals of the Ramakrishna Order, which are purely spiritual and humanitarian in nature and completely dissociated from politics.

Swamiji was overjoyed to see the auspicious beginning of his work in India. Inspired by Vivekananda, Mr. and Mrs. Sevier became involved in building the Advaita Ashrama at Mayavati in the Himalayas, where Westerners could practise nondualistic Vedanta. Swamiji sent Swami

Ramakrishnananda to start a centre in Madras, and Swamis Akhanda-nanda and Trigunatitananda started extensive famine relief work in Murshidabad and Dinajpur. Swamiji encouraged his brother disciples to spread out all over India. On 9 July 1897 Swamiji wrote to Mary Hale in Chicago: "Only one idea was burning in my brain — to start the machine for elevating the Indian masses, and that I have succeeded in doing to a certain extent. It would have made your heart glad to see how my boys are working in the midst of famine and disease and misery — nursing by the mat-bed of the cholera-stricken pariah and feeding the starving chandala, and the Lord sends help to me, to them, to all."

From May 1897 to the end of that year, Swamiji travelled and lectured extensively in northern India. He was overextending himself, sacrificing his health and comfort for the regeneration of India. Finally, his doctors advised him to go to a cool place in the Himalayas; he therefore went to Almora, a Himalayan resort. On 29 May he wrote to his doctor: "I began to take a lot of exercise on horseback, both morning and evening. Since then I have been very much better indeed. . . . You ought to see me, Doctor, when I sit meditating in front of the beautiful snow-peaks and repeat from the Upanishads, 'He has neither disease, nor decay, nor death; for verily, he has obtained a body full of the fire of yoga.'" On 3 June 1897 he wrote to Christine Greenstidel: "As for myself, I am quite content. I have roused a good many of our people, and that was all I wanted. Let things have their course and karma its sway. I have no bonds here below."

From Almora Vivekananda went to Punjab and Kashmir. Wherever he travelled, he inspired people to organize in order to carry on the work of practical Vedanta. In Jammu he had a pleasant meeting with the maharaja of Kashmir, and he discussed with him the possibility of founding a monastery in Kashmir for training young people. In Lahore the swami gave a number of lectures, and brought harmony between the Arya Samajists and the orthodox Hindus, two antagonistic sects. Swamiji was very much against religious dogmatism, fanaticism, and personality cults; he knew that a personality cult grows speedily and dies quickly. Vivekananda preached the eternal, universal principles of Vedanta. One day at Lahore when Lala Hansaraj, the leader of the Arya Samaj, was defending his orthodox view about the Vedas, Swamiji said to him: "Sir, you emphasize that there can be only one interpretation of the Vedas, which I consider a kind of fanaticism. I know it helps to spread a sect rapidly. Again a personality cult spreads faster than scrip-tural dogma. I have the power to bring one-third of the population of the world under the banner of Sri Ramakrishna, but I have no intention of doing that, because that will counteract my guru's great message of harmony, 'As many faiths so many paths,' and a new sect will originate in India."[51]

Before returning to Calcutta, he visited Dehra Dun, Delhi, Alwar, Khetri, Ajmere, Jodhpur, Indore, and other places in northern and western India.

Training the Disciples

Vivekananda spent most of 1898 training his Indian and Western disciples and working to consolidate what had already been started. During this period he also travelled to Darjeeling, Almora, and Kashmir.

In 1892 the Ramakrishna Monastery had been moved from Baranagore to Alambazar, and then in February 1898 it was moved to Nilambar Mukherjee's garden house in Belur village. A plot of land was purchased there on the bank of the Ganges. Under Swamiji's direction, the brother monks supervised the levelling of the grounds, and the construction of the living quarters and the shrine. Several young men joined the monastery, inspired by Vivekananda's message. Besides conducting classes on Vedanta scriptures, the swami spent hours with them in meditation and devotional singing. Vivekananda also engaged Swami Swarupananda and the Seviers to start an English monthly magazine, *Prabuddha Bharata*, in Mayavati, Himalayas, and asked Swami Trigunatitananda to start the Bengali magazine *Udbodhan* in Calcutta. During that time, he also initiated Miss Margaret Noble into brahmacharya and gave her the name "Nivedita," the Dedicated One.

In March 1898 there was an outbreak of plague in Calcutta. Vivekananda immediately made plans for relief work, but there was no money. He told his brother disciples: "We shall sell, if necessary, the land which has just been purchased for the monastery. We are sannyasins; we must be ready to sleep under the trees and live on alms as we did before. Must we care for the monastery and possessions, when by disposing of them we could relieve thousands of helpless people suffering before our own eyes?"[52] Fortunately, monetary help came from the public, and the Ramakrishna monks and Nivedita did extensive relief work in the city.

When the plague was under control, Swamiji left Calcutta with his Western disciples and went to Almora to rest as well as to train them for work in India. They learned from Vivekananda the Indian way of life, its history, religion, philosophy, and tradition. Sister Nivedita recorded these talks in her book *Notes of Some Wanderings with the Swami Vivekananda*. Mrs. Ole Bull and Miss Josephine MacLeod were with Swamiji during this Himalayan journey. "How can I best help you?" asked Miss MacLeod. The swami replied, "Love India." This remarkable American woman followed Vivekananda till her death. What a great service she gave to India! Mrs. Ole Bull was also a great devotee; she contributed financially to build the Belur Monastery. In Almora the swami heard that Pavhari Baba and J. J. Goodwin had died. He exclaimed in grief when on 2 June 1898 he received the cable announcing Goodwin's death, "My right hand is gone!" He wrote a beautiful condolence letter to Goodwin's mother in England, and he also wrote a poem in his honour entitled "Requiescat in Pace."

On 11 June 1898 Swamiji and his party left Almora for Kashmir. While in Kashmir, the maharaja received Vivekananda with the utmost respect and offered him a plot of land to build a monastery and a Sanskrit college. Unfortunately this plan was later cancelled, because the British government did not approve it. While in Kashmir Swamiji decided to make a pilgrimage to Amarnath, the ice lingam of Lord Shiva in the glacial valley of the western Himalayas. Even today, it is a very difficult journey. He asked Nivedita to accompany him, so that she might have firsthand experience of the Hindu pilgrim's life. On 2 August 1898 the swami and Nivedita entered the cave and worshipped the Lord. There Vivekananda had an overwhelming spiritual experience. He never disclosed it fully, except to say that he had been granted a boon by Amarnath, the Lord of Immortality, not to die until he himself willed it.

On 8 August the party arrived at Srinagar, where they remained until 30 September. During this period the swami's mood was directed to Kali, the Divine Mother. He composed a poem about her, and later went to visit Kshir Bhavani, a temple dedicated to the Mother that had long ago been destroyed by Muslim invaders. Here he had a vision of the Goddess. Observing the ruins of the temple, Vivekananda felt sad and said to himself: "How could the people have permitted such sacrilege without offering strenuous resistance? If I had been here then, I would never have allowed such a thing. I would have laid down my life to protect the Mother." Thereupon he heard the voice of the Goddess saying: "What if unbelievers should enter my temple and defile my image? What is that to you? Do you protect me, or do I protect you? My child, if I wish I can have innumerable temples and magnificent monastic centres. I can even this moment raise a seven-storeyed golden temple on this very spot." After his return, referring to this experience, he said to his disciples: "All my patriotism is gone. Everything is gone. Now it is only 'Mother! Mother!' I have been very wrong.... I am only a little child."[53]

The party left Kashmir on 11 October and went to Lahore. The Western disciples left for Agra and Delhi to sightsee, and the swami returned to Belur Math on 18 October. After this pilgrimage his health again deteriorated. He suffered terribly from asthma.

On 12 November 1898, the day of the Kali worship, Holy Mother inaugurated the Nivedita Girls' School in Calcutta. At the end she "prayed that the blessings of the Great Mother of the universe might be upon the school and that the girls it should train might be ideal girls." Thus the swami encouraged Nivedita to educate Indian women, and gave her complete freedom to run the school.

On 9 December 1898 Belur Math was formally consecrated when Vivekananda installed the Master's relics in its shrine. Swamiji carried the urn of relics on his own shoulder, and on his way he said to a disciple: "The Master once told me, 'I will go and live wherever you take me, carrying me on your shoulder, be it under a tree or in the humblest cottage.' With faith in that gracious promise I myself am now carrying him to the site of our future Math. Know for certain, my boy, that so long as his name inspires his followers with the ideal of purity, holiness, and charity for all men, even so long shall he, the Master, sanctify this place with his presence."[54]

Vivekananda was in an ecstatic mood after the consecration: He was relieved to find a permanent place for the Master. Belur Math became the headquarters of the Ramakrishna Order. He told the monks and devotees: "It will be a centre in which will be recognized and practised a grand harmony of all creeds and faiths as exemplified in the life of Sri Ramakrishna, and religion in its universal aspect, alone, will be preached. And from this centre of universal toleration will go forth the shining message of goodwill, peace, and harmony to deluge the whole world."[55]

Vivekananda was an embodiment of renunciation and purity, and he reminded the monks that all power comes from those virtues. In the Belur Math rule book, he stated the monks' primary goal: "This monastery is established to work out one's own liberation, and to train oneself to do good to the world in every way, along the lines laid down by Sri Ramakrishna." One day one of his disciples expressed a desire to go into seclusion in order to practise austerities. The swami reprimanded him: "You will go to hell if you seek your own salvation! Seek the salvation of others if you want to reach the Highest. Kill out the desire for personal liberation. This is the greatest spiritual discipline."[56] This statement shows what an unselfish, gigantic heart Vivekananda had!

Second Visit to the West

On 16 December 1898 Vivekananda announced that he would return to the West to meet his old friends and to see the progress of the Vedanta work that he had started. The monks and devotees welcomed the idea, thinking the sea voyage would restore his failing health. Vivekananda left from Calcutta on 20 June 1899, accompanied by Swami Turiyananda and Sister Nivedita. This journey turned into a wonderful education for both of them: Swamiji taught Turiyananda how to work in the West and Nivedita how to work in the East. Nivedita wrote: "It was while we sat chatting in the river [Ganges] on the first afternoon, he suddenly exclaimed: 'Yes, the older I grow, the more everything seems to me to lie in manliness.'"[57] Another day, the swami said to Nivedita: "Social life in the West is like a peal of laughter, but underneath, it is a wail. It ends in a sob. The fun and frivolity are all on the surface: really, it is full of tragic intensity. Now here [India], it is sad and gloomy on the outside, but underneath are carelessness and merriment."[58]

Vivekananda's belief in the effectiveness of Vedanta grew through his travels and observations, experiences and insights He saw it not as a mere religion or philosophy, but rather as a means by which science and religion could become reconciled, and material prosperity and spirituality blended. He noticed that the East was strong in noble religious and spiritual traditions even though it suffered from grinding poverty; the West, however, for all its technological advancements and affluence, suffered from spiritual poverty. There was no reason, he thought, why East and West could not profit from each other's strengths by removing each other's weaknesses.

Vivekananda arrived in London on 31 July 1899 and stayed there a few weeks. He met with some old friends, but his fragile health did not allow him to give lectures. He then left for New York with Turiyananda and two American devotees, and arrived there on 28 August. It was arranged that the swamis would live temporarily at Ridgely Manor, Francis Leggett's beautiful country home. The entire fall Vivekananda rested and recuperated. He was happy to see the activities of the Vedanta Society of New York (which he had founded in November 1894) under the leadership of Swami Abhedananda, and he engaged Turiyananda to give classes in Montclair, New Jersey.

Vivekananda was in a relaxed mood at Ridgely. "There are many memories," writes Maud Stumm, an American devotee, "connected with those days at Ridgely. Nearly every day Swami was wonderful in a new way —

and now it would be music that he dwelt upon, now art, and once he burst into the morning-room, declaring for 'Liberty.' 'What do I care if Mohammed was a good man, or Buddha! Does that alter *my* own goodness or evil? Let us be good for our own sake on our own responsibility!'"[59]

Miss MacLeod wrote in her reminiscences: "In the evening, sitting around the great fire in the hall of Ridgely Manor, he would talk, and once after he came out with some of his thoughts a lady said, 'Swami, I don't agree with you there.' 'No? Then it is not for you,' he answered. Someone else said, 'O, but that is where I find you true.' 'Ah, then it was for you,' he said showing that utter respect for the other man's views. One evening he was so eloquent, about a dozen people listening, his voice becoming so soft and seemingly far away; when the evening was over, we all separated without even saying goodnight to each other. Such a holy quality pervaded. My sister, Mrs. Leggett, had occasion to go to one of the rooms afterward. There she found one of the guests, an agnostic, weeping. 'What do you mean?' my sister asked, and the lady said, 'That man has given me eternal life. I never wish to hear him again.'"[60]

On 22 November Vivekananda left for Los Angeles via Chicago and stayed in southern California from 3 December 1899 to 22 February 1900. While in southern California he gave several lectures in Los Angeles and Pasadena. During his last six weeks there he stayed with the Mead sisters (Mrs. Carrie Mead Wyckoff, Mrs. Alice Mead Hansbrough, and Miss Helen Mead) at their house at 309 Monterey Road in South Pasadena. (The house, now owned by the Vedanta Society of Southern California and carefully restored to its original state, is surprisingly small.) Mrs. Hansbrough became the swami's private secretary during his California trip. During his stay in Pasadena he often played with the Mead sisters' children, and sometimes would join them for picnics or sightseeing. After lunch Swamiji would generally recline on the couch in the living room, and there he would read or talk while Mrs. Wyckoff busily pursued her various household tasks. "Madam," he said one day to her, "you work so hard that it makes me tired. Well, there have to be some Marthas, and you are a Martha."[61] Another day the swami asked Ralph, Mrs. Wyckoff's son, "Can you see your own eyes?" Ralph answered that he could not, except in a mirror. "God is like that," the swami told him. "He is as close as your own eyes. He is your own, even though you can't see Him."[62]

Vivekananda then travelled to northern California, where in April 1900 he founded the Vedanta Society in San Francisco. Swamiji's oratory and magnetic personality overwhelmed the people. "He once told us,"

Mr. Thomas Allan recounted, "that he had such faith in the Divine Mother that if he had to speak on a subject that he knew absolutely nothing about, he would get on his feet, for he knew that Mother would put the words into his mouth."[63] Mrs. Edith Allan wrote in her reminiscences: "Although I attended all Swamiji's public lectures both in San Francisco and Alameda, it was ... close contact with Swamiji that I most deeply cherish. Once after being quiet for some time Swamiji said: 'Madame, be broad-minded, always see two ways. When I am on the Heights, I say "I am He," and when I have a stomachache, I say "Mother, have mercy on me." Always see two ways.' On another occasion he said: 'Learn to be the witness. If there are two dogs fighting on the street and I go out there, I get mixed up in the fight; but if I stay quietly in my room, I witness the fight from the window. So learn to be the witness.'"[64]

Swamiji was bold and fearless. He never tried to please or flatter others: he told people what was good for them. Ida Ansell, Swamiji's stenographer, wrote in her memoirs: "What becomes of one's individuality when one realizes his oneness with God? 'You people in this country are so afraid of losing your in-di-vid-u-al-i-ty!' he would exclaim. 'Why, you are not individuals yet. When you realize your whole nature, you will attain your true individuality, not before. In knowing God you cannot lose anything. There is another thing I am constantly hearing in this country, and that is that we should live in harmony with nature. Don't you know that all the progress ever made in the world was made by conquering nature? We are to resist nature at every point if we are to make any progress.'"[65]

During his second visit to America Swamiji worked mainly in California. While there, he had a premonition of his approaching end; in April 1900 he wrote to Miss MacLeod, "My boat is nearing the calm harbour from which it is never more to be driven out." Before finishing his mission to the world, Swamiji sang his swan song; he poured out the quintessence of Vedanta:

> In this country [America] the king has entered every one of you. You are all kings in this country. So with the religion of Vedanta. You are all Gods. One God is not sufficient.... You want to be democratic in this country. It is the democratic God that Vedanta teaches. There is a chance of Vedanta becoming the religion of your country because of democracy.[66]
>
> Don't repent! Don't repent!... Spit, if you must, but go on! Don't hold yourselves down by repenting! Throw off the load of sin, if there is such a thing, by knowing your true selves — The Pure! The Ever Free!... That

man alone is blasphemous who tells you that you are sinners.... This world is a superstition. We are hypnotized into believing it real. The process of salvation is the process of de-hypnotization.... This universe is just the play of the Lord — that is all. It is all just for fun.[67]

Stand up and fight! Not one step back, that is the idea. Fight it out, whatever comes. Let the stars move from the spheres! Let the whole world stand against us! Death means only a change of garment. What of it? Thus fight! You gain nothing by becoming cowards. Taking a step backward, you do not avoid any misfortune. You have cried to all the gods in the world. Has misery ceased? ... This bending the knee to superstitions, this selling yourself to your own mind does not befit you, my soul. You are infinite, deathless, birthless. Arise! Awake! Stand up and fight!

Enter not the door of any organized religion. Religion is only between you and your God, and no third person must come between you. Think what these organized religions have done! What Napoleon was more terrible than these religious persecutions? If you and I organize, we begin to hate every person. It is better not to love, if loving only means hating others. That is no love. That is hell![68]

Swamiji left for New York from California on 30 May 1900; on his way he stopped in Chicago to meet his old friends and devotees. He was the guest of the Hale family and exchanged many old reminiscences. Swami Nikhilananda recorded a touching incident from this visit: "On the morning of his departure, Mary came to the swami's room and found him sad. His bed appeared to have been untouched, and on being asked the reason, he confessed that he had spent the whole night without sleep. 'Oh,' he said, almost in a whisper, 'it is so difficult to break human bonds!' He knew that this was the last time he was to visit these devoted friends."[69]

After arriving in New York on 7 June 1900, he sent Turiyananda to northern California to start a retreat, which later became Shanti Ashrama. Swamiji gave a few more lectures and classes in New York and then left for Paris on 26 July 1900 to attend the Congress of the History of Religions, where he spoke twice. On 24 October 1900 he left Paris for the East with Monsieur and Madame Loyson, Jules Bois, Madame Calvé, and Miss MacLeod. He visited Vienna, Constantinople, Athens, and Cairo. "What a pilgrimage it was!" recalled Madame Calvé. "Science, philosophy, and history had no secrets from the swami. I listened with all my ears to the wise and learned discourse that went on around me.... One day we lost our way in Cairo. I suppose, we had been talking too intently. At any rate, we found ourselves in a squalid, ill-smelling street, where half-clad women lolled from windows and sprawled on doorsteps. The swami noticed nothing until a particularly noisy group of women on a bench began laughing and calling to him.

"'Poor children!' he said. 'Poor creatures! They have put their divinity in their beauty. Look at them now!' He began to weep. The women were silenced and abashed. One of them leaned forward and kissed the hem of his robe, murmuring brokenly in Spanish, 'Hombre de Dios, hombre de Dios! [Man of God].'"[70]

In Cairo, the swami felt intuitively that something was wrong in India, not knowing that Mr. Sevier was on his deathbed at Mayavati. He became restless to return to India and left alone on the first available boat to Bombay.

Towards the End

Vivekananda disembarked in Bombay and immediately took a train to Calcutta, arriving at Belur Math unannounced late on the evening of 9 December 1900. His brother monks and disciples were jubilant to have their leader return. Later Swamiji was given the sad news of Mr. Sevier's passing away. On 11 December he wrote to Miss MacLeod: "Alas, my hurrying was of no use. Poor Captain Sevier passed away, a few days ago — thus two Englishmen [the other was Mr. Goodwin] gave up their lives for us — us the Hindus. This is martyrdom, if anything is."

On 27 December 1900 Vivekananda left for Mayavati to console Mrs. Sevier. He arrived there on 3 January 1901. Swamiji's love and concern assuaged Mrs. Sevier's grief; she loved him as her own son. He stayed there for a couple of weeks and then returned to Belur Math on 24 January. During this time the swami received invitations for a lecture tour to East Bengal (now Bangladesh), and also his mother expressed a desire to visit the holy places in that part of the country. On 26 January 1901 he wrote to Mrs. Bull: "I am going to take my mother on a pilgrimage.... This is the one great wish of a Hindu widow. I have only brought misery to my people [family] all my life. I am trying to fulfill this one wish of hers."

On 28 March 1901 Swamiji, in spite of his poor health, left for Dhaka with a large party. He gave two public lectures in Dhaka and exhorted the people there to cultivate manliness and the faculty of reasoning. To a sentimental young man he said: "My boy, take my advice: develop your muscles and brain by eating good food and by healthy exercise, and then you will be able to think for yourself." On another occasion, addressing the youths of Bengal who had very little physical stamina, he said, "You will be nearer to God through football than through the Bhagavad Gita."[71]

On 5 April Vivekananda and his party left Dhaka and visited Chandranath in Chittagong, Kamakhya in Guwahati, and Shillong. Swamiji's health was failing rapidly. In addition to the diabetes from which he had been suffering, he had another severe attack of asthma at Shillong. While the swami was in pain, someone overheard him murmuring to himself: "What does it matter! I have given them enough for fifteen hundred years!"[72] On another occasion he said to a Western devotee: "The spiritual impact that has come here to Belur will last fifteen hundred years — and this will be a great university. Do not think I imagine it, I see it."[73]

Returning from East Bengal, Vivekananda led a relaxed life in Belur Math, surrounded by his pets: his dog, Bagha; the she-goat, Hansi; an antelope; a stork; several cows, sheep, ducks, and geese; and a kid called Matru who was adorned with a collar of little bells, with whom the swami ran and played like a child. The animals adored him. Matru used to sleep in his room. When Matru died he grieved like a child and said to a disciple: "How strange! Whomsoever I love dies early."

Vivekananda had completed the mission that Ramakrishna had entrusted to him. Keeping his mind on his beloved guru, Vivekananda waited for his own great departure. Sometimes he would talk to his disciples about the Master. Swami Shuddhananda recorded:

> Swami Vivekananda was then Narendranath; he was visiting Ramakrishna regularly at Dakshineswar. Pointing to Narendra's well-combed curly hair, the Master teased him about his foppishness. Narendra was also unsparing; he pointed out to the Master his varnished shoes, hubble bubble, mattress, bolster, and so on. Then the Master told him, "Look here, the amount of austerity I practised for God-realization, if you can do one-sixteenth of that, I shall arrange for you to sleep on a costly bedstead putting mattress upon mattress." Swamiji practised severe austerity in his life; and then when he returned from the West, his Western disciples presented him with a spring bed and mattress [which are still preserved in his room]. While lying on that Western mattress and remembering those words of the Master, Swamiji would tell that incident to his disciples with tears.[74]

In spite of his illness Vivekananda kept a watchful eye on the monks and the activities of the monastery. He gave regular classes on Vedanta scriptures, conducted meditation in the shrine, inspired the workers with a spirit of virile confidence in themselves, and paid strict attention to discipline and cleanliness. One day he found that Swami Shivananda had missed the morning meditation in the shrine. He said to him: "Brother, I know you do not need meditation. You have already realized the highest goal through the grace of Sri Ramakrishna. But you should meditate daily with the youngsters in order to set an example for them."[75] Shivananda obeyed that command till his old age.

Ramakrishna had always been very particular about cleanliness and Swamiji followed his example. He would check the beds and rooms of the monks, and asked that they be kept clean. Once the sweeper was sick and the privy was not cleaned for three or four days. Swamiji noticed this and decided to clean it himself. One morning at four o'clock, without informing anybody, he began scrubbing the privy. Some young monks saw him in the dark and rushed to him, asking that he return to his room so that they could clean it. But he did not stop until he had finished the task.[76] An ideal teacher is the person who practises what he teaches. Swamiji thus demonstrated the role of an ideal teacher.

Sometimes he talked to the poor labourers who were levelling the ground; he also supervised cooking arrangements, and would sing devotional songs with the monks. At other times he imparted spiritual instructions to visitors. His fragile body did not dampen his desire to work. When urged to rest, he said to a disciple: "My son, there is no rest for me. That which Sri Ramakrishna called 'Kali' took possession of my body and soul three or four days before his passing away. That makes me work and work and never lets me keep still or look to my personal comfort."[77] Vivekananda continued to train his disciples: "In every country, nations have their good and bad sides. Ours is to do good works in our lives and hold an example before others. No work succeeds by condemnation. It only repels people. Let anybody say what he likes, don't contradict him. In this world of maya, whatever work you take up will be attended with some defect. 'All undertakings are beset with imperfections, as fire with smoke' (Gita, 18.48). But will you, on that account, sit inactive? As far as you can, you must go on doing good work." Later, he disclosed his life's experience: "After so much tapasya, austerity, I have known that the highest truth is this: He is present in all beings. These are all the manifested forms of Him. There is no other God to seek for! He alone is worshipping God, who serves all beings."[78]

Towards the end of 1901, Kakuzo Okakura, a famous artist, and Mr. Hori came to Belur Math from Japan. Later, Reverend Takuno Oda, a Buddhist abbot, came to invite Vivekananda to attend the Congress of Religions in Japan. Because of his ill health, the swami could not go; but he agreed to go with them to Bodh Gaya, where Buddha had attained illumination. Swamiji, Miss MacLeod, Okakura, and others left for Gaya on 27 January 1902. Sister Nivedita wrote about this visit:

When the winter again set in, he [Vivekananda] was so ill as to be confined to bed. Yet he made one more journey, lasting through January and February 1902, when he went first to Bodh Gaya and next to Varanasi. It was a fit ending to all his wanderings. He arrived at Bodh Gaya on the morning of his last birthday [January 29], and nothing could have exceeded the courtesy and hospitality of the Mahanta [head of the monastery]. Here, as afterwards at Varanasi, the confidence and affection of the orthodox world were brought to him in such measure and freedom that he himself stood amazed at the extent of his empire in men's hearts. Bodh Gaya, as it was now the last, had also been the first of the holy places he had set out to visit. And it had been in Varanasi, some few years back (when he was an unknown monk), that he had said farewell to one, with the words, "Till that day when I fall on society like a thunderbolt I shall visit this place no more!"[79]

The maharaja of Varanasi offered Swamiji a sum of money to establish a monastery there. He accepted the offer and later sent Shivananda to organize the work. Vivekananda also inspired a group of young men who had started a small organization for the purpose of providing destitute pilgrims with food, shelter, and medical help. He said to them: "You have the true spirit, my boys, and you will always have my love and blessings! Go on bravely; never mind your poverty. Money will come. A great thing will grow out of it, surpassing your fondest hopes." Swamiji wrote an appeal for their support and named the institution "Ramakrishna Home of Service."

"I Shall Never See Forty"

Vivekananda returned to Belur Math on 7 March 1902. He had accomplished his mission, and knew his end was near. Swamiji began to withdraw himself, delegating the responsibility of the monastery to his brother disciples. "How often," he said, "does a man ruin his disciples by remaining always with them! When men are once trained, it is essential that their leader leave them, for without his absence they cannot develop themselves."[80] He was a true sannyasin, free from all attachments.

Miss MacLeod wrote in her memoirs: "One day in April [1902] he said, 'I have nothing in the world. I haven't a penny to myself. I have given away everything that has ever been given to me.' I said, 'Swami, I will give you fifty dollars a month as long as you live.' He thought a minute and then he said, 'Can I live on that?' 'Yes, O yes,' I said, 'but perhaps you cannot have cream.' I gave him then two hundred dollars, but before the four months were passed he had gone.

"At Belur Math one day, while Sister Nivedita was distributing prizes for some athletics, I was standing in Swamiji's bedroom at the Math, at the window, watching, and he said to me, 'I shall never see forty.' I, knowing he was thirty-nine, said to him, 'But Swami, Buddha did not do his great work until between forty and eighty.' But he said, 'I delivered my message and I must go.' I asked, 'Why go?' and he said, 'The shadow of a big tree will not let the smaller trees grow up. I must go to make room.'"[81]

Sometimes Swamiji was in an exalted mood. Bodhananda, a disciple of Vivekananda, recalled:

> Once Swamiji said that he would do the worship of Sri Ramarkrishna that day. So all of us went to watch Swamiji do it. We were curious to see how he would perform the ritual. First, in the usual way he took his seat as worshipper and meditated. We meditated too. After a pretty long time we sensed that someone was moving around us. I opened my eyes to see who it was. It was Swamiji. Taking the tray of flowers meant to be offered to Sri Ramakrishna, he got up. But instead of placing them before the Lord, he came to us, and touching the flowers with sandal paste, placed one on the head of each disciple.
>
> Considered from the ordinary traditional standpoint, this was an antitraditional act. Imagine flowers meant for the Lord, offered by Swamiji to his disciples! Generally after the worship service, the leftover flowers are set aside to be thrown away. But instead of doing this, Swamiji approached the altar and offered what remained in the tray before the picture of Sri Ramakrishna. He also carried out the usual rites. Then he indicated that the time had come for food offering; so we all got up to leave the room. It is a custom in India that during the food offering no one should be in the shrine except the worshipper. We heard from outside Swamiji saying, addressing Sri Ramakrishna, "Friend, please eat!" Then he came out of the shrine and closed the door. His eyes were bloodshot with emotion.

Bodhananda later explained the significance of Swamiji's worship:

> Actually Swamiji did not worship the disciples. In placing a flower on the head of each one of us, he really offered the flower at the feet of Sri Ramakrishna in each disciple. Thereby he awakened His presence in us. That presence took different aspects in everyone. Some were devotional; others had the jnana [knowledge] aspect predominant. By his act of worship, Swamiji awakened the Divine in us. The remaining flowers were not in any way defiled. The same divine presence, which

Swamiji saw in the photograph of Sri Ramakrishna on the altar, he also saw in his disciples; and at the altar he offered the remaining flowers. Lastly, Swamiji's relation to his Chosen Deity was that of a friend. That is why, in offering the food, he addressed Sri Ramakrishna by that term.[82]

Another day, touching the casket of Sri Ramakrishna's relics, Vivekananda asked himself: "Does the Master really reside here? I must test it." Then he prayed, "Master, if you are truly present here, bring here the maharaja of Gwalior [who was then visiting Calcutta] within three days." The next day Vivekananda left for Calcutta on some business. However, when he returned later that afternoon, he was told that the maharaja of Gwalior had stopped there earlier. He had been passing by the Grand Trunk Road near the monastery in his car and had sent his younger brother to see if the swami was in. Since Vivekananda was not there, the maharaja had gone away disappointed.

When Swamiji heard this news, he remembered his test. He immediately rushed to the shrine, and holding the urn of relics on his head, repeatedly said: "Master, you are true! You are true! You are true!" At that time Swami Premananda entered the shrine for meditation, and he was bewildered. Later Swamiji told Premananda and the monks about his test, and all marvelled at this proof of the Master's presence in the shrine.[83]

One day Swamiji came downstairs and sat on the canvas cot under the mango tree in the courtyard, facing west, as he often did. The monks around him were busy with their activities. One was sweeping the courtyard with a broom. Swami Premananda was climbing the steps to the shrine after his bath. Suddenly Vivekananda's eyes became radiant. Surcharged with spiritual fervour, he said to a disciple: "Where will you go to seek Brahman? He is immanent in all beings. Here, here is the visible Brahman! Shame on those who, neglecting the visible Brahman, set their minds on other things! Here is the visible Brahman before you as tangible as a fruit in one's hand! Can't you see? Here — here — here is Brahman!"[84] These words struck the people around him like an electric shock. For about fifteen minutes no one could move or function. Premananda went into ecstasy; others experienced an indescribable peace and joy. At last Vivekananda said to Premananda, "Now go to worship," and all were released. The disciples were amazed to witness the spiritual power of Vivekananda.

Swamiji explained this phenomenon on another occasion: "He who has realized the Atman becomes a house of great power. From him as the centre, and within a certain radius, emanates a spiritual force, and all those who come within this circle become animated with his ideas and are overwhelmed by them. Thus without much religious striving they inherit the results of his wonderful spirituality. This is grace."[85]

On 15 May 1902, Swamiji wrote to Miss MacLeod: "I am somewhat better, but of course far from what I expected. A great idea of quiet has come upon me. I am going to retire for good — no more work for me." His brother disciples were worried by his contemplative mood. They remembered the Master's forecast that Naren would merge forever into samadhi as soon as his mission was over, and that he would refuse to live in his physical body once he realized who he was. A brother monk one day quite casually asked him, "Do you know yet who you are?" The unexpected reply, "Yes, I now know!" awed everyone present into silence. Nobody dared to probe further. Another day he said to Saradananda: "I don't see that girl [Mother Kali] anymore. She has withdrawn her hand from me."[86]

A few days before his passing away, one of his boyhood friends came to Vivekananda and asked for some financial help. Swamiji asked Bodhananda to give his friend two rupees from his wallet. Bodhananda checked the wallet and said that if the friend was given two rupees there would not be much left. Immediately Swamiji said: "Do you think I care for that? Give him two rupees plus a little more." Then he continued: "In a room, if one window is open and the corresponding window is closed, there is no ventilation; so let it go by one window and it will come by the other."[87]

A week before the end, Vivekananda asked Shuddhananda to bring him the Bengali almanac. Swamiji turned several pages and then kept it in his room. He was seen several times on subsequent days studying the almanac intently, as if looking for something auspicious. It did not strike anyone what his intention might be; only after his death did they realize that he was selecting an auspicious day for his departure as Sri Ramakrishna had done.

Three days before his passing away, while walking on the spacious lawn of the monastery with Premananda, Swamiji said to him, pointing to a particular spot on the bank of the Ganges, "When I give up the body, cremate it there." Today on that very spot stands a temple in his honour.

Sister Nivedita left a vivid account that includes many significant facts in connection with Vivekananda's passing away and his foreknowledge of it:

When June closed ... he knew well enough that the end was near. "I am making ready for death!" he said to one who was with him, on the Wednesday before he died. "A great tapasya [austerity] and meditation has come upon me, I am making ready for death."

Once in Kashmir, after an attack of illness, I had seen him lift a couple of pebbles, saying, "Whenever death approaches me, all weakness vanishes. I have neither fear, nor doubt, nor thought of the external. I simply busy myself making ready to die. I am as hard as *that*" — and the stones struck one another in his hand — "for I *have* touched the feet of God!"

Did we not remember, moreover, the story of the great nirvikalpa samadhi of his youth, and know, when it was over, his Master had said: "This is your mango. Look! I lock it in my box. You shall taste it once more, when your work is finished!"

It was on the last Sunday before the end that he said to one of his disciples, "You know, the *work* is always my weak point! When I think that might have come to an end, I am all undone!"

On Wednesday [2 July] of the same week, the day being *Ekadashi* [the eleventh day of the moon, which orthodox Hindus observe by fasting], and himself keeping the fast in all strictness, he insisted on serving the morning [noon] meal to the same disciple [Nivedita]. Each dish as it was offered — boiled seeds of the jackfruit, boiled potatoes, plain rice, and ice-cold milk — formed the subject of playful chat; and finally, to end the meal, he himself poured the water over the hands, and dried them with a towel.

"It is I who should do these things for you, Swamiji! Not you for me!" was the protest naturally offered. But his answer was startling in its solemnity — "Jesus washed the feet of his disciples." Something checked the answer — "But that was the last time!" — as it rose to the lips, and the words remained unuttered.[88]

On his last day, Friday, 4 July 1902, Vivekananda got up very early in the morning as usual and went to the shrine for meditation. He was not sick at all. During breakfast he was in a jovial mood, teasing Premananda and recalling many events of olden times. He had fruit, milk, and tea. A fresh shad [*ilish*] fish from the Ganges was bought from a fisherman, and it was shown to him. Shad fish is a delicacy for Bengalis. Seeing the fish, Swamiji in fun said to a novice from East Bengal: "Don't you worship the first shad of the season in your part of the country? Let me see how you do that."

At 8:00 a.m. he again entered the shrine for meditation. When at 9:30 a.m. Premananda entered the shrine to perform the daily worship, Swamiji asked him to carry his *asana* (carpet) to the Master's bedroom, which was adjacent to the shrine, and shut all doors and windows. Swamiji dusted the Master's bed with his own hand, and again sat for meditation. Never before had he performed such meditation in the monastery. What transpired there, no one knows. He finished his meditation at 11:00 a.m., and then began to sing a song about Kali in his sweet voice which the monks heard from downstairs. The words to the song are:

Is Kali, my Mother, really black?
The Naked One, though black She seems,
Lights the Lotus of the heart.
Men call Her black, but yet my mind
Does not believe that She is so:
Now She is white, now red, now blue;
Now She appears as yellow, too.
I hardly know who Mother is,
Though I have pondered all my life:
Now Purusha, now Prakriti,
And now the Void, She seems to be.
To meditate on all these things
Confounds poor Kamalakanta's wits.

Descending the stairs of the shrine, he walked back and forth in the courtyard of the monastery. He appeared indrawn, as if travelling to a distant land. Suddenly Swamiji said to himself: "If there were another Vivekananda, then he would have understood what this Vivekananda has done! And yet — how many Vivekanandas shall be born in time!"[89] His statement was overheard by Premananda, who was standing on the veranda of the chapel. Never before had Swamiji spoken like this.

Then he expressed a desire to worship Mother Kali at the monastery the following day: It was Saturday, and there was a new moon, a very auspicious time for Mother's worship. Soon after, Ishwar Chandra Chakrabarty, Ramakrishnananda's father and a devout worshipper of Mother, came to visit Vivekananda. Swamiji was delighted to see him and expressed his intention of worshipping Mother Kali. He asked Shuddha-nanda and Bodhananda to procure all the necessary articles for the ceremony.

After instructing the disciples to make preparations for the Kali worship, Swamiji asked Shuddhananda to bring the Shukla-Yajur Veda from the library. When it was brought, Swamiji asked him to read the mantram beginning with the words *sushumnah suryarashmi*, with Mahidhara's commentary on it (Vajasaneyi Samhita, 18.40). Listening to part of it, Swamiji remarked: "This interpretation of the passage does not appeal to my mind. Whatever may be the commentator's interpretation of the word 'sushumna,' the seed or the basis of what the Tantras, in later ages, speak of as the sushumna nerve channel in the body, is contained here in this Vedic mantram. You, my disciples, should try to discover the true import of these mantras and make original reflections and commentaries on the scriptures."

The purport of Mahidhara's commentary may be put thus: "That Moon, who is of the form of *gandharva* (a demi-god), who is sushumna, that is, giver of supreme happiness to those who perform sacrifices, and whose rays are like the rays of the Sun — may that Moon protect us brahmins and kshatriyas! We offer our oblations to Him! His (Moon's) *apsaras* (nymphs) are the stars who illuminate all things — we offer our oblations to them."[90] Swamiji's desire to perform the Kali worship and his discussion of the sushumna suggest what he was thinking about at the time: He was planning to give up his body like a true yogi, passing through the six centres of the sushumna and merging the Paramatman in the *sahasrara* (crown of the head).

At noon he heartily enjoyed his lunch with the monks in the dining room. Because of his illness, he had generally taken his meals in his room. That day Swamiji relished various kinds of fish preparations, and humourously told Premananda: "I was very hungry because of fasting on the Ekadashi day. With great difficulty I skipped eating the cups and plates." Again, humourously, he said to his brother disciple in English, "Fish need water to swim"; and then with a chuckle, "Please give me a glass of water." He talked awhile and then went to his room to rest. After fifteen minutes he came out of his room and told Premananda: "Let us go and study. Day sleep is not good for a monk. Today I did not get any sleep. I got a little headache, because of a long meditation. I see, my brain is getting weak nowadays!"

He went to the library and called the brahmacharins to attend the class on Sanskrit grammar (*Laghu Kaumudi* by Varardaraja). One who attended the class wrote: "The class lasted for nearly three hours [1:00 to 4:00 p.m.]. But no monotony was felt. For he [Swamiji] would tell a witty story or make *bons mots* now and then to lighten his teaching, as he was wont to do. Sometimes the joke would be with reference to the wording of a certain aphorism, or he would make an amusing play upon its words knowing that the fun would make it easier for recollection. On this particular day he spoke of how he had coached his college friend, Dasharathi Sanyal, in English history in one night by following a similar process. He, however, appeared a little tired after grammar class."[91] Swamiji wanted each disciple to be original and not to follow him blindly. Warning against false prophets who might come in the future, he said to the boys: "If any man ever imitates me, kick him out. Do not imitate me."

At 4:30 p.m. Vivekananda drank some water and a cup of hot milk. Then he went for a walk with Premananda to Belur bazar, one mile away. He felt good and talked to his brother disciple on many interesting subjects. Seeing a garden on the way, he began to describe Mr. Leggett's big and beautiful garden at Ridgely Manor, and how in America a few people are able to manage large gardens by using machinery. By the by, he said to Premananda: "Why should you imitate me? The Master would forbid one to imitate others. Don't be extravagant like me." He also mentioned his plan for establishing a Vedic college in the monastery. In order to have a clearer understanding of what Swamiji felt on the matter, Premananda asked, "What will be the good of studying the Vedas?" Swamiji replied, "It will kill superstitions."

At 5:30 p.m. he returned to the monastery from his walk. He sat on a bench under the mango tree and said, "My health is so good today, which I have not felt for a long time." Swamiji talked to Premananda and other monks about the history of European civilization and also colonial history. "India is immortal," he said, "if she persists in her search for God. But if she goes in for politics and social conflict, she will die."[92] He also talked to Ramakrishnananda's father for some time.

At 6:30 p.m. when he found that some monks were taking tea, he went to them and said, "Will you give me a cup of tea?" He enjoyed the tea with them. When the vesper bell was rung at 7:00 p.m., he got up and went to his room upstairs. Bodhananda, who was Swamiji's secretary and kept his little bit of cash, reminisced: "I was standing by the stairway down on the ground floor. It was the month of July. In India the mosquitoes are so numerous and so dangerous that you get malaria from them, and no one can sleep in bed without the curtains. He had discovered that the curtains of some monks were torn, and his last command to me was, 'See that they all get new mosquito curtains.'"[93] Even in his last moments Vivekananda showed his great love and concern for the monks!

Entering his room, Swamiji said to his attendant Brahmachari Brajendra: "My body is very light today. I feel fine. Please give me my rosary." He sat facing the Ganges. Before he began his meditation, he asked Brajendra to go to the other room, and instructed him, "Wait and meditate till I call you." After an hour, at 8:00 p.m., the swami called Brajendra and asked him to fan his head. Swamiji told him to open all the windows of his room, because he was feeling hot. Then, he laid himself down on his bed on the floor. He still had the rosary in his hand. After a while Swamiji said to him: "All right, no more need for fanning! It would be better if you give a little massage to my feet." Soon, he seemed to fall asleep, and one hour passed in this manner. Vivekananda was lying on his left side and the brahmacharin was massaging his feet. He then moved and lay down on his back; shortly after that, he cried out like a baby cries for its mother. Towards the end, Brajendra noticed that Swamiji's right hand trembled a little, there was perspiration on his forehead, he breathed a deep breath, and his head rolled down by the pillow. There was silence for a minute or two, and again he breathed in the same manner; his body became still. It was 9:10 p.m.

Brajendra thought that Swamiji was in samadhi, but he was scared and puzzled. He rushed downstairs and told Swami Advaitananda about Swamiji. Immediately the old swami went to Swamiji's room, placed his hand on his heart, and checked the pulse. There was no breathing. Then Advaitananda asked Bodhananda, who had just arrived and was cooking Swamiji's meal, to check the pulse. After doing this for a while, he stood up and cried aloud. Advaitananda then told Nirbhayananda: "Alas! What are you looking at? Hurry to Dr. Mahendra Nath Majumdar of Baranagore, and bring him here as soon as you can." Within a couple of minutes Premananda arrived and found Swamiji motionless. He, Nishchayananda, and Ramakrishnananda's father began to chant "Ramakrishna" loudly into Swamiji's ears, hoping that he would return from samadhi. Swamiji's eyes were fixed in the centre of his eyebrows, and his face had assumed a divine expression with a sweet smile.

Nirbhayananda and another monk crossed the Ganges at night — the former went to the doctor at Baranagore and the latter went to Calcutta to inform Swamis Brahmananda and Saradananda. Both arrived at Belur Math at 10:30 p.m. After a thorough examination, Dr. Majumdar found no sign of life; he still tried artificial respiration, but failed. "There was," said a brother disciple, "a little blood in his nostrils, about his mouth, and in his eyes." According to the Yoga scriptures, the life breath of an illumined yogi passes out through the opening on the top of the head, causing the blood to flow in the nostrils and the mouth. Vivekananda passed away at the age of thirty-nine years, five months, and twenty-four days, thus fulfilling his own prophecy, "I shall never see forty."

In the beginning of his mission Vivekananda had said, "I am a voice without a form." Towards the end, he said: "It may be that I shall find it good to get outside of my body — to cast it off like a disused garment. But I shall not cease to work! I shall inspire men everywhere, until the world shall know that it is one with God."[94]

SWAMI BRAHMANANDA: VARANASI, 1903

2

ॐ

SWAMI BRAHMANANDA

It is extremely painful for a spiritual person who thinks constantly of God to talk or hear about mundane things. Once a novelist said to Sri Ramakrishna that the duties of a man were "eating, sleeping, and having sex." Sri Ramakrishna scolded him, telling him that he was impudent: "What you do day and night comes out through your mouth. A man belches what he eats. If he eats radish, he belches radish."[1] Ramakrishna would feel a burning sensation on his lips whenever he had to talk with worldly people. He desperately searched for companions with whom he could talk about God.

One day Ramakrishna fervently prayed to the Divine Mother: "Mother, it is my desire that a boy with sincere love for God should always remain with me. Give me such a boy."[2] A few days later, sitting under the banyan tree at Dakshineswar, he had a vision of a boy. He told this to his nephew Hriday, who immediately explained its significance with joy: "Uncle, you will have a child." "What do you mean?" said Ramakrishna with surprise. "I look upon all women as my mother. How can I have a son?"

Sri Ramakrishna had a second vision: "Just a few days before Rakhal's coming I saw Mother putting a child into my lap and saying, 'This is your son.' I shuddered at the thought and asked her in surprise, 'What do you mean? I too have a son?' Then She explained with a smile that it would be a spiritual child, and I was comforted. Shortly after this vision Rakhal came, and I at once recognized him as the boy presented by the Divine Mother."[3]

Sometime in the middle of 1881, Sri Ramakrishna had another vision. He saw two boys dancing on a full-blown lotus floating on the Ganges. One of the boys was Krishna and the other was the same boy whom the Mother had previously placed on his lap. That very day Rakhal, crossing the Ganges, came to Dakshineswar from Konnagar; the Master immediately recognized him as his spiritual son.

Rakhal Chandra Ghosh was born on Tuesday, 21 January 1863, at Sikra Kulingram, a village thirty-six miles northeast of Calcutta; he was brought up in rural Bengal. His father, Anandamohan Ghosh, was a wealthy landlord, who also made a good deal of money trading salt and mustard seed. His mother, Kailashkamini, was devoted to Krishna, so she named her son Rakhal (literally "cowherd boy," a playmate of Krishna). When Rakhal was five years old, his mother died while giving birth to quadruplets. To maintain the household and to raise Rakhal, Anandamohan married Hemangini Sen, a daughter of Shyamlal Sen of Calcutta. She was a loving young woman and cared for Rakhal as if he were her own son.

Rakhal was a handsome, energetic young boy. He was good at sports, gardening, and fishing. His early academic career was excellent. He was fond of devotional singing. When the village minstrel would sing kirtan, he would listen with rapt attention and try to learn the songs. As a young boy, he would practise meditation in the Kali Temple, and during Durga Puja he would sit behind the priest and meditate like a yogi. From his childhood Rakhal was quiet by nature and deeply religious.

In 1875 when Rakhal was twelve, Anandamohan took him to Calcutta for his higher education. He was admitted to the Training Academy and later the Metropolitan School, and stayed with his stepmother's family. Rakhal met Narendranath Datta in a nearby gymnasium. They became close friends as they were the same age and had a similar religious inclination. As a member of the Brahmo Samaj, Narendra was committed to belief in a formless God with attributes, and thus did not believe in Hindu gods. In his enthusiasm he persuaded Rakhal to embrace the Brahmo creed. Rakhal was by nature devotional and contemplative. He began to neglect his schoolwork and gradually lost all other worldly interests. Anandamohan was disturbed when he heard of Rakhal's spiritual inclination. To divert his son's mind from God to the world, he arranged Rakhal's marriage. Without any enthusiasm, Rakhal obediently accepted his father's decision.

In the middle of 1881 Rakhal married Vishweshwari Mittra, an eleven-year-old sister of Manomohan Mittra, who was a devotee of Ramakrishna. Ironically, it was his bride's brother who took Rakhal to Ramakrishna in

June or July 1881, and later made it possible for him to renounce the world. As soon as the Master saw Rakhal, he told Manomohan with a smile, "A wonderful receptacle!" Then the Master asked him, "What is your name?" "Rakhal Chandra Ghosh." Hearing the word "Rakhal," the Master went into ecstasy and softly uttered: "That name! Rakhal — the cowherd boy of Vrindaban!" After regaining normal consciousness, the Master treated him as his own and at last said, "Come again."

During one of his visits to Dakshineswar in 1881, Rakhal had a spiritual experience. Ramakrishna later recalled: "Rakhal had his first religious ecstasy while sitting here [in his room] massaging my feet. A Bhagavata scholar had been expounding the sacred book in the room. As Rakhal listened to his words, he shuddered every now and then. Then he became altogether still. His second ecstasy was at Balaram Basu's house. In that state he could not keep himself sitting upright; he lay flat on the floor. Rakhal belongs to the realm of the Personal God. He leaves the place if one talks about the Impersonal."[4]

Because Rakhal believed in the personal aspect of God, when he went to the Kali or Krishna temples with the Master, he would bow down to the deities; this was against the Brahmo creed. One day Narendra observed this and took him to task because Rakhal's action was in violation of his pledge. Rakhal had a gentle nature, so rather than argue with Narendra he began to avoid him. Knowing Rakhal's predicament, the Master said to Narendra: "Please do not intimidate Rakhal. He is afraid of you. He now believes in God with form. How are you going to change him? Everyone cannot realize the formless aspect of God at the very beginning."[5] From then on, Narendra, a true lover of freedom, never interfered with the new direction of Rakhal's religious attitude. They remained close friends until the end of their lives.

In the beginning Rakhal visited the Master now and then; later he began staying at Dakshineswar. His father objected to this, telling him to concentrate on his studies. When he found that Rakhal did not listen, he became angry and put his son under lock and key. There is a saying: "The more love is obstructed, the more intense it becomes"; lonely, homebound Rakhal longed for the Master. On his part Ramakrishna worried about Rakhal, and he went to the temple and prayed: "Mother, my heart is breaking for Rakhal. Please bring him back to Dakshineswar."

The Divine Mother answered his prayer. One day while Anandamohan was absorbed in looking over some legal documents, Rakhal quietly left the room and then ran to Dakshineswar. Anandamohan knew where Rakhal had gone, but could not do anything for a few days since he was busy with a lawsuit. Although there was little chance of winning that case, Anandamohan did win. He felt that his victory was due to his son's virtue and the blessings of Ramakrishna. He went to Dakshineswar to see his son, as well as to see the saint there. Rakhal was scared when he saw his father in the distance, but the Master reassured him: "Why are you frightened? Parents are living gods. As soon as your father arrives, bow down to him respectfully. If the Divine Mother wishes, everything will be favourable."[6]

When Anandamohan arrived, Ramakrishna gave him a hearty welcome and Rakhal humbly bowed down to him, which melted his father's heart. The Master praised Rakhal: "Ah, what a nice character Rakhal has developed! Look at his face and every now and then you will notice his lips moving. Inwardly he repeats the name of God, and so his lips move. Youngsters like him belong to the class of the ever-perfect. They are born with God-consciousness.... Ah, what a sweet nature Rakhal has nowadays! And why shouldn't it be so? If the yam is a good one, its shoots also become good. Like father, like son."[7] Anandamohan was overjoyed listening to Ramakrishna's spiritual talk and the praise of his son. Moreover, he noticed that some lawyers and deputy magistrates were among Ramakrishna's visitors; he was eager to get acquainted with them to advance his personal interests. Anandamohan returned home without raising much objection to his son's living with the Master, but asked him to send Rakhal home now and then.

"As for the family of Rakhal's wife," the Master said later, "they raised no objection — because the ladies used to come here very often. Soon after Rakhal first came here, his mother-in-law brought Vishweshwari, his wife. I wanted to see if she would stand in the way of Rakhal's devotion to God. I examined her physical features minutely and saw that there was no cause for fear. She represented an auspicious aspect of the Divine Shakti. I sent word to the *nahabat* [i.e., to Sarada Devi] to give her a rupee and unveil Vishweshwari's face."[8] (This is the traditional ceremony by which a mother-in-law welcomes her daughter-in-law. Since Rakhal was the spiritual son of Ramakrishna and Sarada Devi, Vishweshwari became their daughter-in-law.)

Living with Sri Ramakrishna

Ramakrishna behaved towards Rakhal as a mother to her child; Rakhal acted like a little child rather than a boy of eighteen. It was a mystical relationship beyond human comprehension. M. recorded on 29 March 1883 in *The Gospel of Sri Ramakrishna*:

Rakhal was not feeling well. The Master was greatly worried about him and said to the devotees: "You see, Rakhal is not well. Will soda-water help him? What am I to do now? Rakhal, please take the prasad from the Jagannath Temple."

Even as he spoke these words the Master underwent a strange transformation. He looked at Rakhal with the infinite tenderness of a mother and affectionately uttered the name of Govinda [a name of Krishna]. Did he see in Rakhal the manifestation of God Himself? The disciple was a young boy of pure heart who had renounced all attrac-tion to lust and greed. And Sri Ramakrishna was intoxicated day and night with love of God. At the sight of Rakhal his eyes expressed the tender feelings of a mother, a love like that which had filled the heart of Mother Yasoda at the sight of the Baby Krishna. The devotees gazed at the Master in wonder as he went into deep samadhi.[9]

Later Ramakrishna recalled: "In those days, Rakhal had the nature of a child of three or four. He treated me just like a mother. He would keep running to me and sitting on my lap. He wouldn't move a step from this place. He never thought of going home. I forced him to, from time to time, lest his father should forbid his coming here altogether.... Sometimes I fed him and played with him to keep him happy. Often I'd carry him around on my shoulders."[10] On one occasion the Master was so struck with his simplicity that he burst into tears as he said: "You are so simple! Ah, who will look after you after I am gone."[11]

A real guru acts in two roles — loving mother as well as chastising father — to train his disciple. The Master did not spoil his spiritual son. "When he did anything wrong," said Ramakrishna, "I scolded him. One day he took butter from the temple prasad and ate it without waiting for me. 'How greedy you are,' I said. 'You ought to have learnt, from being here, to control yourself!' He shrank into himself with fear and never did that again."[12]

One day Rakhal was very hungry and mentioned it to the Master. There was no food in his room, so the Master went to the Ganges and called loudly: "Hello, Gaurdasi! Please come. My Rakhal is hungry." After a short while Gauri-ma and Balaram arrived at Dakshineswar by boat with *rasagollas* (cheese balls soaked in sweet syrup). Immediately the Master called: "Come, Rakhal! They have brought rasagollas. Come and eat. Didn't you say you were hungry?" Embarrassed, Rakhal blurted out: "Sir, why are you talking about my hunger in front of others?" "What does it matter?" said the Master. "Since you are hungry, you should eat. What is the harm in saying so?"[13]

Once Rakhal found a coin on the street. Out of kindness he picked it up and gave it to a beggar. As a child finds joy in telling his mother everything, so it was Rakhal's nature to inform the Master of everything. When the Master heard what Rakhal had done, he reprimanded him: "Why would a person who does not eat fish go to the fish market? If you did not need money, why did you touch it?"[14] What wonderful logic! The Master wanted his spiritual son to be free from lust and gold, the two great obstacles in spiritual life.

One early afternoon Rakhal arrived from Calcutta and found the Master alone, resting on his bed. He asked Rakhal to sit on the bed and massage his feet. At first Rakhal was reluctant, but the Master insisted, saying: "Look, there is a tangible result from serving a holy man." Soon after he began massaging the Master's feet, he saw the Divine Mother, in the form of a girl of seven or eight, circle the Master's bed a few times and then enter into his body. This vision overwhelmed Rakhal. The Master then said to Rakhal with a smile: "Did you see the result of serving a holy man?"[15]

On 22 July 1883, while rubbing oil on the Master's body on the semi-circular veranda, Rakhal requested the highest spiritual experience from him. But the Master ignored his demand. When Rakhal persisted, the Master scolded him harshly. In a temper tantrum, Rakhal threw away the oil cup and stalked off with the intention of never returning. Before he got past Jadu Mallick's garden house, his feet suddenly became numb and he was forced to sit helplessly on the ground. The Master sent his nephew Ramlal to bring him back. The all-forgiving Master said to Rakhal: "Look, could you go? I drew a boundary line there."[16]

That afternoon, Rakhal and M. were in the Master's room. They heard Ramakrishna talking with the Divine Mother: "O Mother, why hast Thou given him only a particle?" After a brief pause, he added: "I understand it, Mother. That little bit will be enough for him and will serve Thy purpose. That little bit will enable him to teach people." M. felt that the Master was transmitting spiritual powers to his disciple, and he recorded: "Sri Ramakrishna was still in a state of partial consciousness when he said to Rakhal: 'You were angry with me, weren't you? Do you know why I made you angry? There was a reason. Only then would the medicine work. The surgeon first brings an abscess to a head. Only then does he apply an herb so that it may burst and dry up.'"[17]

A couple of evenings later, Rakhal saw the Master walking towards the Kali Temple, and he followed him. Ramakrishna entered the temple, but Rakhal sat for meditation in the *natmandir* (the hall in front of the Mother's temple). After a while he suddenly saw a brilliant light, like that of a million suns, rushing towards him from the shrine of the Divine Mother. He was frightened and ran to the Master's room.

A little later Ramakrishna returned from the shrine and saw Rakhal. "Hello," asked the Master, "did you sit for meditation this evening?" "Yes, I did," answered Rakhal. He then related what had happened. The Master told him: "You complain that you don't experience anything. You ask, 'What is the use of practising meditation?' So why did you run away when you had an experience?"[18]

Spiritual life is not always easy. It has many ups and downs. Rakhal had to pass through various ordeals and difficulties. He later recalled:

One morning I was meditating in the Kali Temple. I could not concentrate my mind. This made me very sad. I said to myself: "I have been living here so long, yet I have not achieved anything. What is the use of staying here then? Forget it! I am not going to say anything about it to the Master. If this depressed condition continues another two or three days, I shall return home. There my mind will be occupied with different things." Having decided this in the shrine, I returned to the Master's room. The Master was then walking on the veranda. Seeing me, he also entered the room. It was customary after returning from the shrine to salute the Master and then eat a light breakfast. As soon as I saluted the Master, he said: "Look, when you returned from the shrine, I saw that your mind seemed to be covered with a thick net." I realized that he knew everything, so I said, "Sir, you know the bad condition of my mind." He then wrote something on my tongue. Immediately I forgot my painful depression and was overwhelmed with an inexpressible joy.[19]

Another day Rakhal was meditating in the natmandir, and the Master arrived in an ecstatic mood. Addressing Rakhal, Sri Ramakrishna said: "Look, this is your mantram and there is your Chosen Deity."[20] Immediately Rakhal saw the luminous form of God in front of him and was overwhelmed. He was convinced that his guru had the power to show God to anyone. Filled with ecstatic devotion Rakhal fell at the feet of the Master and again became absorbed in meditation.

Under Ramakrishna's guidance Rakhal began to practise intense spiritual disciplines. He forgot day and night as well as food and family. The Master taught his spiritual son various kinds of spiritual disciplines, such as *asanas* (postures), *mudras* (gestures), japam, meditation, yoga, and other practices. One day, the Master initiated Rakhal into the path of Shakti before the Divine Mother and taught him how to practise meditation on the different centres of the kundalini. Rakhal used to secretly practise these disciplines. Rakhal recalled: "Once I was meditating in the Panchavati at noon while the Master was talking about the manifestation of Brahman as sound [*Shabda-Brahman*]. Listening to that discussion, even the birds in the Panchavati began to sing the Vedic songs and I heard them."[21]

While practising sadhana, Rakhal developed some occult powers. Once a worker in the temple garden became sick, and there was no one to look after him. Rakhal served him day and night. One night the patient was in deep pain. Since he had no medicine, Rakhal sat near his head and began to repeat a mantram. After a while he became drowsy; a beautiful, luminous girl of twelve then appeared before him. Recognizing her to be a goddess, Rakhal asked, "Mother, will this patient be cured?" "Yes," replied the girl and disappeared. The next day the patient was miraculously cured.[22]

Ramakrishna was a hard taskmaster. He always insisted that his disciples unite their mind and speech. One day when Rakhal returned from Calcutta, the Master asked: "Why can't I look at you? Have you done anything wrong?" "No," Rakhal replied; because he understood "wrong action" to mean stealing, robbery, or adultery. The Master again asked, "Did you tell any lies?" Then Rakhal remembered that the day before, while chatting and joking with two friends, he had told a fib. The Master told him: "Never do it again. Truthfulness alone is the spiritual discipline in the *kaliyuga* [the dark age]."[23]

Ramakrishna demonstrated his teachings through his life and actions. Rakhal later recalled:

> Oh, how deep was the Master's devotion to truth! If he happened to say that he would not eat any more food, he could not eat more, even if he was hungry. Once he said that he would go to visit Jadu Mallik [whose garden house was adjacent to the Dakshineswar temple garden] but later forgot all about it. I also did not remind him. After supper he suddenly remembered the appointment. It was quite late at night, but he had to go. I accompanied him with a lantern in my hand. When we reached the house we found it closed and all apparently asleep. The Master pushed back the door of the living room a little, placed his foot inside the room, and then left.[24]

Ramakrishna seldom travelled alone. Someone always went with him to protect his body in case he went into samadhi. On 2 May 1883 the Master attended the Brahmo festival at Nandanbagan, Calcutta, accompanied by M., Rakhal, and a few devotees. At 9:00 p.m. when the worship service was over, the host was busy serving dinner to his important visitors, forgetting the Master and his devotees. M. recorded:

> Master (*to Rakhal*): "What's the matter? Nobody is paying any attention to us!"
> Rakhal (*angrily*): "Sir, let us leave here and go to Dakshineswar."
> Master (*with a smile*): "Keep quiet! The carriage hire is three rupees and two annas. Who will pay that? Stubbornness won't get us anywhere. You haven't a penny, and you are making these empty threats! Besides, where shall we find food at this late hour of the night?"[25]

After a long time, dinner was served to the Master and he returned to Dakshineswar late at night. Rakhal learned from the Master that it would have been inauspicious for the household if a holy man had left the place without eating.

Sometimes people who go to yogis or holy men have worldly motives, such as to win a lottery or to be cured of a terminal disease. One day, while the Master was talking with Rakhal in the northeastern veranda of his room, he saw a phaeton enter the temple compound. Immediately he rushed to his room and told Rakhal to tell the people in the carriage that he was not available. "Does a holy man live here?" asked one visitor. "Yes," answered Rakhal. Through inquiry he learned that they had come for medicine from the holy man for their sick relative. Rakhal told them: "Sri Ramakrishna does not give any medicine, but Durgananda Brahmachari, who lives near the Panchavati, does." When they left, Rakhal came to the Master, who told him: "I saw a gloom of tamas in them, so I couldn't look at them. That is why I ran away to my room." He then asked Rakhal: "When you see a person, can you recognize his character?" "No, sir," answered Rakhal. That day the Master taught him various signs by which one can recognize the character of a person. This later helped him to manage the Ramakrishna Order.[26]

In the early part of 1884, while walking towards the pine grove, Sri Ramakrishna fell near the garden railing and dislocated a bone in his left arm. He had been in an ecstatic mood at the time and no one was with him. Rakhal felt guilty about this accident. The Master consoled him: "You aren't to blame for it, though you are living here to look after me; for even if you had accompanied me, you certainly wouldn't have gone up to the railing."

Gradually Rakhal became so absorbed in japam and meditation that it became difficult for him to serve the Master. On 20 June 1884 Sri Ramakrishna said to M.: "Rakhal is getting into such a spiritual mood that he can't do anything even for himself. I have to get water for him. He isn't of much service to me.... Rakhal now lives here as one of the family. I know that he will never again be attached to the world. He says that worldly enjoyments have become tasteless to him. His wife came here on her way to Konnagar. She is fourteen. He too was asked to go to Konnagar, but he didn't go. He said, 'I don't like merriment and gaiety.'"

When an avatar is born as a human being, he behaves like a human being. A great soul like Rakhal — who was an *ishwarakoti* (a godlike soul), *nityasiddha* (an ever-perfect soul), and a companion of Krishna — had a little boyish jealousy. "It was quite unbearable for him," said Sri Ramakrishna, "if I loved anyone but him. He would feel wounded at heart. At that I felt greatly concerned lest he should harm himself by being jealous of those whom Mother would bring here."[27]

In August 1884 Rakhal became sick and was sent to Calcutta for treatment. Later he went to Vrindaban with Balaram for a change. Just prior to that the Master saw in a vision that the Mother was removing Rakhal from Dakshineswar. He eagerly prayed for his spiritual son: "Mother, he [Rakhal] is a mere boy, quite ignorant; that is why he sometimes feels piqued. If, for the sake of your work, you remove him from here for some time, keep him in a good place and in a blissful mood."[28]

In Vrindaban Rakhal again became sick, which greatly concerned the Master. He knew that Rakhal's past life was connected with Krishna in Vrindaban; if he were to remember that, he might give up the body. The Master prayed to the Mother and She comforted him. Gradually Rakhal got well and stayed there nearly four months.

After returning from Vrindaban, Rakhal went to his home in Calcutta. He visited the Master at Dakshineswar and met the new young disciples. He realized then that his guru belonged to all as the moon shines equally upon all; and his jealousy left him forever by the grace of his guru.

The Master noticed that various entanglements were hovering over Rakhal. His relatives and friends were insisting that he take a job and lead a regular householder's life. On 1 March 1885 the Master said to Manomohan, Rakhal's brother-in-law: "You may take offence at my words, but I said to Rakhal, 'I would rather hear that you had drowned yourself in the Ganges than learn that you had accepted a job under another person and become his servant.'"[29]

On 7 March 1885 Ramakrishna said: "Rakhal is now enjoying his 'pension.' Since his return from Vrindaban he has been staying at home. His wife is there. But he said to me that he would not accept any work even if he were offered a salary of a thousand rupees."[30] On 16 April

Ramakrishna said to Girish: "Rakhal has now understood what is good and what is bad, what is real and what is unreal. He lives with his family, no doubt, but he knows what it means. He has a wife. And a son has been born to him. But he has realized that all these are illusory and impermanent. Rakhal will never be attached to the world. He is like a mudfish. The fish lives in the mud, but there is not the slightest trace of mud on its body."[31]

If a devotee sincerely loves God, He makes everything favourable for him. Shyama Sundari, Rakhal's mother-in-law, was a devotee of the Master and she understood Rakhal's spiritual inclination. One day Manomohan's aunt said to her: "It seems that your son-in-law is turning into a monk. Why don't you try to bring his mind back to the world, for your daughter's sake?" "What can I do?" answered Shyama Sundari. "Everything depends on the will of the Lord. If my son-in-law becomes a monk, I shall regard it as a great blessing."[32]

The divine play of an avatar and his disciples is beyond the reach of human understanding. Although most of the time they are established in God-consciousness, they sometimes act like human beings. Ramakrishna told some devotees that Rakhal had a little desire for enjoyment and by the grace of the Mother it was now over. Through the grace of the Master Rakhal demonstrated true renunciation: He was from a well-to-do home and had a young wife and a child, but he left everything for God.

"Oh, what superhuman power the Master had!" recalled Rakhal. "At that time we thought it was merely a peculiar power with him, but we could not understand the nature of it. Now we realize what a wonderful power it was! One day I said to him: 'Sir, I cannot get rid of lust. What shall I do?' He touched me in the region of the heart, muttering some indistinct words. All lust vanished from me forever! I have never felt its existence since then."[33]

In the middle of 1885 Ramakrishna developed throat cancer, and Rakhal began to stay with him at Dakshineswar. On 9 August 1885 M. recorded in the *Gospel*:

It was nine o'clock in the evening. Sri Ramakrishna was sitting on the small couch. It was Mahimacharan's desire to form a *brahmachakra* [a mystic circle prescribed in Tantra] in the presence of the Master. Mahima formed a circle, on the floor, with Rakhal, M., Kishori, and one or two other devotees. He asked them all to meditate. Rakhal went into an ecstatic state. The Master came down from the couch and placed his hand on Rakhal's chest, repeating the name of the Divine Mother. Rakhal regained consciousness of the outer world.[34]

In September 1885 Ramakrishna was taken to Calcutta for treatment; he lived there for three months. Then on 11 December 1885 he was moved to the Cossipore garden house. Rakhal served the Master along with other disciples. Sometime in the middle of January 1886, the elder Gopal wanted to distribute twelve pieces of ochre cloth and twelve rosaries among some monks. Pointing to his young disciples, the Master said to him: "You won't find better monks than these. Give your cloths and rosaries to them." Instead, Gopal offered them to the Master and he himself distributed them to Rakhal and other young disciples.

Ramakrishna's health was gradually deteriorating. On 15 March 1886 M. writes:

> Like a mother showing her tenderness to her children, he [Sri Ramakrishna] touches the faces and chins of Rakhal and Narendra. A few minutes later he says to M.: "If the body were to be preserved a few days more, many people would have their spirituality awakened.... Such is not the will of God."
>
> Rakhal (*tenderly*): "Please speak to God that He may preserve your body some time more."
>
> Master: "That depends on God's will." ...
>
> Rakhal: "We pray that you may not go away and leave us behind."
>
> Sri Ramakrishna smiles and says: "A band of minstrels suddenly appears, dances, and sings, and it departs in the same sudden manner. They come and they return, but none recognizes them."[35]

Once at the Cossipore garden house Ramakrishna remarked: "Rakhal has the keen intelligence of a king. If he chose, he could rule a kingdom." Narendra understood that the Master wanted Rakhal to be the future leader of his disciples, so he told his brother disciples, "Henceforth, we shall call Rakhal our *Raja*, king." The Master was pleased when he heard this. Later Rakhal became known in the Ramakrishna Order as *Maharaj*, or Great King.

Days of Austerity and Pilgrimage

After Sri Ramakrishna's passing away on 16 August 1886, his disciples were drowned in sorrow. Rakhal and the others felt helpless, and moreover, some had no place to live. But with the financial help of Surendra Mittra and the guidance of Narendra, they established the Ramakrishna Monastery at Baranagore. In the third week of January 1887 they took their final monastic vows by performing the traditional *viraja homa* (fire ceremony) in front of the Master's picture. Rakhal became Swami

Brahmananda. Shortly after this, his father went to the monastery to persuade him to return home. But he calmly and firmly said to his father: "Why do you take so much trouble to come to me? I am quite happy here. Now bless me that I may forget you and you may forget me."

Cutting off all family ties and attachments, Brahmananda became so absorbed in japam and meditation that he almost forgot the world. In *The Gospel of Sri Ramakrishna*, M. recorded a conversation he had had with Brahmananda in the Baranagore Monastery:

Rakhal (*earnestly*): "M., let us practise śadhana [spiritual disciplines]! We have renounced home for good. When someone says, 'You have not realized God by renouncing home; then why all this fuss?', Narendra gives a good retort. He says, 'Because we could not attain Ram, must we live with Shyam and beget children?' Ah! Every now and then Narendra says nice things."

M.: "What you say is right. I see that you too have become restless for God."

Rakhal: "M., how can I describe the state of my mind? Today at noontime I felt great yearning for the Narmada [a holy river in Central India, favoured by ascetics].... Many people think that it is enough not to look at the face of a woman. But what will you gain merely by turning your eyes to the ground at the sight of a woman? Narendra put it very well last night, when he said: 'Woman exists for a man as long as he has lust. Free from lust, one sees no difference between man and woman.'"

M.: "How true it is! Children do not see the difference between man and woman."

Rakhal: "Therefore I say that we must practise spiritual discipline. How can one attain Knowledge without going beyond maya?"[36]

In November 1888 Brahmananda went to Puri for a short time, and then in the early part of 1889 he visited Kamarpukur and Jayrambati, the birthplaces of Ramakrishna and Holy Mother. In December 1889 Brahmananda decided to practise intense austerities alone in the holy places of India. He received permission from Holy Mother and Swami Vivekananda, but they insisted that Swami Subodhananda go along and look after him.

Brahmananda and Subodhananda first went to Varanasi via Deoghar and stayed a month. From Varanasi they went to Omkarnath, situated on the bank of the holy river Narmada. Here Brahmananda lived continuously in samadhi for six days, completely oblivious of the outside world. After Omkarnath they visited Panchavati, on the bank of the river Godavari, a holy place connected with the life of Ramachandra. They then

went to Bombay, and from there by steamer to Dwaraka, a place associated with Krishna. They also visited Bet-Dwaraka, Porbandar, Junagad,
Girnar, Ahmedabad, and Pushkar. Brahmananda was not an ordinary
pilgrim. He saw the living presence of gods and goddesses in these holy
places. Later he said: "Spiritual life begins after *nirvikalpa samadhi* [the
highest transcendental experience]."[37]

In February 1890 Brahmananda and Subodhananda arrived at Vrindaban, the place where Krishna sported as a child. Here they lived on alms
and passed their time in intense spiritual practices. On 29 March 1890 Brahmananda wrote a letter to Balaram Basu, describing his spiritual struggle:

> Who can understand the divine play of God? Man experiences hap-
> piness and misery according to his own karma. This is true of every
> man — whether he is learned or ignorant, good or wicked. Rare indeed
> is a person in this world who enjoys uninterrupted peace and bliss!
> Blessed is he who is free from desires, for he lives in the kingdom of
> peace. There is more misery than happiness in this world, and most
> people live in misery. If God is all-merciful then why do his children
> suffer so much? Only God knows the answer to this mystery, and not
> ordinary human beings.
>
> Man suffers because of his ignorance, which manifests as "I" and
> "mine." The really happy and fortunate man is he who has given up
> his ego and has surrendered his life, mind, and intellect to God, and
> has nothing to call his own.
>
> The nature of the mind is to dwell on worldly objects, because it is
> created out of the three *gunas* (sattva, rajas, and tamas) which also con-
> stitute the outer world. It is only through divine grace that a man can
> withdraw his mind completely from the external objects and put it on
> God....
>
> Presently my mental condition is not good at all.... I am praying to
> God that I may remain absorbed in the thought of the Master. That is
> the one desire of my heart.[38]

A great receptacle like Brahmananda was not satisfied with a few
visions or momentary experiences. He was feeling the agony of separation from the Master. He plunged into deep meditation and remained
most of the time in an indrawn mood. Subodhananda would beg food for
him; sometimes Brahmananda would eat it and sometimes not. Although
the two brother disciples lived together, they hardly spoke to one another.

Also living in Vrindaban at this time was Vijaykrishna Goswami, a
Vaishnava saint who had known Brahmananda when he was living with
Ramakrishna at Dakshineswar. One day Vijay asked him: "The Master

gave you all that is covetable in spiritual life: visions and samadhi. Why then do you still practise so much austerity?" Brahmananda humbly answered: "The experiences and visions I got by his grace, I am now trying to attain as my permanent possession."[39]

Observing Brahmananda's hardship, rigorous disciplines, and long meditation and prayer, Subodhananda said to him: "The Master looked upon you as his son. You are the veritable son of the Lord. It does not befit you to sit like a beggar seeking his grace." Brahmananda replied: "What you say, brother, is true. The Master loved us so dearly that he gave us everything he had to give. Still we have not attained peace. This shows that it now lies with us to do the rest for the fulfillment of life's objective. Uddhava was Krishna's dear friend, yet Krishna said to him: 'If you want to properly realize any spiritual truth, you must go to some solitary place in the Himalayas and practise austerity. I can grant you some miraculous visions, if you like. But that won't be enough. It is much greater to contemplate and meditate on Him.' Indeed, without meditation and contemplation none can know anything about God."[40]

In April 1890 Subodhananda left for a pilgrimage to Hardwar, and Brahmananda remained alone in Vrindaban. The spiritual journey is truly "a flight of the alone to the Alone." Forgetting the world and his body, Brahmananda again plunged into the inner realm. In May Brahmananda heard that two important disciples of the Master had died: Balaram and Surendra. He grieved for them. In September he left Vrindaban and went to Kankhal (Hardwar) in the foothills of the Himalayas — an important place for ascetics. Here he met Vivekananda, Turiyananda, Saradananda, and other brother disciples. In November they all went to Meerut to see Swami Akhandananda, who was recuperating from a severe illness. In Meerut these disciples lived together for nearly six weeks and spent their days in meditation, study, discussion, and devotional singing as they had done in the Baranagore Monastery.

In January 1891 Vivekananda left to travel alone in other parts of India. Brahmananda and Turiyananda went to Jwalamukhi, a holy place in Punjab. During the next two years they visited many holy places in Punjab, Sind, Rajputana, and Maharashtra. In April 1893 in Bombay they unexpectedly met Vivekananda, who was then making preparations to attend the Parliament of Religions in Chicago. The swamis then went to Mount Abu and from there proceeded to Vrindaban in July 1893.

As God tests the faith of mystics, so mystics also verify God's grace. One day Turiyananda said to Brahmananda: "Today I shall not go out to beg for food. Let us see if Radha [the spiritual consort of Krishna and the goddess of Vrindaban] will feed us."[41] Both swamis passed the whole day and night in meditation, and the next morning a man brought various kinds of food for them. On another occasion, when they were practising austerities near Lake Kusum (a suburb of Vrindaban), Turiyananda received only a little dry bread from begging. Offering that to Brahmananda, he said: "Maharaj, the Master used to take such wonderful care of you. He would feed you with delicacies, and I am feeding you this dry, tasteless bread." So saying, he burst into tears.[42]

Monks depend solely on God. They sometimes follow the example of a python that attracts its prey without moving. In Vrindaban, Brahmananda took a vow of self-surrender, accepting only what God provided for him without asking; that day a devotee provided his food and other necessities, unasked. Another day while he was meditating a man put a new blanket in front of him and left. After a short while a thief came and took away the blanket. Brahmananda silently observed the play of maya and smiled.

Temptation is one of the tests of spirituality. The Queen of Bharatpur heard about Brahmananda and Turiyananda, and came to visit them at Lake Kusum. She was very much impressed by Brahmananda's serene face and offered some sweets to him. When the swami opened one of the sweets, he found a gold coin inside. Immediately he put the sweet down, informed Turiyananda about the queen's rich offering, and both secretly left the place.

The swamis then went to Ayodhya, the birthplace of Ramachandra. They could not remain there long because of a famine. One day Turiyananda went to beg for food and was given some boiled *kachu* (an edible root). As soon as they had eaten their throats began to sting and burn, and gradually their mouths and tongues swelled. Seeing Brahmananda suffering, Turiyananda went out to find a lime, an antidote for the allergy. He found a lime grove, but he could not see any fruit on the trees. He sought out the owner of the grove but was told that the fruit was out of season. Passing the grove again, he keenly searched the trees, and he unexpectedly saw a lime. With the permission of the owner, he plucked the lime and ran back to Brahmananda with it. It immediately relieved his painful throat. That night Brahmananda lamented, addressing Ramakrishna: "Master, why did you take me from home if you could not provide a morsel of food? Tomorrow morning if I get hot *khichuri* [rice and lentils cooked together] and pickles, I shall understand that you are with me."

The next morning the swamis went to bathe in the Saraju River. A monk arrived and said to Brahmananda: "Swami, I understand that both of you fasted yesterday. Please come to my cottage and have some prasad, which I offered to Lord Rama." The monk served hot khichuri and pickles to the swamis. They greatly enjoyed the meal. The monk then said: "Blessed am I! For the last twenty-four years I have been practising sadhana here in order to have a vision or to hear the voice of Lord Rama. Today the Lord has blessed me." Tears trickled from the monk's eyes. At Brahmananda's request, he elaborated: "While I was sleeping last night I saw that Lord Rama touched my body with his soft hand and said: 'Get up! I am hungry. Cook khichuri and offer it to me. Tomorrow morning you will see two devotees bathing at the ghat of the Saraju River. They are fasting. Offer my prasad to them.' It is by your grace that I had the vision of Lord Rama." While returning to their cottage Brahmananda related to Turiyananda the mystery behind the incident.[43]

When Brahmananda left Calcutta to practise austerity, his wife Vishweshwari raised their little child, Satyananda, and lived like a nun. She practised severe austerities and died in the fall of 1891. The boy was then raised by his uncle, and occasionally lived with his grandfather. The disciples of the Master were very fond of the boy and wanted him to become a monk. Unfortunately, in 1895 Satyananda was severly injured in an accidental fall: His chest was badly injured. When he returned to Calcutta, Brahmananda visited his son several times. His wealthy father, Anandamohan, tried everything to save Satyananda, but he died on 20 April 1896 at the age of ten.[44] Shortly after, Anandamohan passed away. Brahmananda absorbed all these tragedies and remained as unperturbed as a mountain.

During this period of sadhana, Brahmananda heard about Vivekananda's success at the Parliament of Religions in America in September 1893. Vivekananda was now urging his brother disciples to band together and carry on the mission of the Master. In 1892 the Ramakrishna Math had been moved from Baranagore to Alambazar. In January 1895 Brahmananda created a great stir of enthusiasm among his brother disciples when he returned to them at the Alambazar Monastery.

With Swami Vivekananda

Vivekananda returned to Calcutta from the West on 19 February 1897, and received a wonderful reception from his brother disciples and the public. When Vivekananda's carriage reached Pasupati Basu's house in Baghbazar, Brahmananda came forward and garlanded their leader. Swamiji bowed down to Brahmananda and remarked with respect: "The son of the guru should be treated as the guru himself." Brahmananda also immediately bowed down to Vivekananda, saying: "The elder brother is like one's father."[45] Swamiji then handed over to Brahmananda all the money he had collected from the West for the Indian work, and said: "Now I am relieved. I have handed over the sacred trust to the right person."

Because there was not enough room in the Alambazar Monastery, it was arranged that Swamiji and his Western disciples should stay in Gopallal Villa in Baranagore. After the civic reception in Calcutta on 28 February, Swamiji accompanied Brahmananda and others to Darjeeling to rest as well as to discuss the future of the Ramakrishna Order. On 1 May 1897, Vivekananda, Brahmananda, and other disciples and devotees of Ramakrishna gathered in Balaram Basu's house, Calcutta, and formed the Ramakrishna Mission. Vivekananda became the general president and Brahmananda became the president of the Calcutta centre.

Vivekananda was the leader of the Order, and Brahmananda was his friend, philosopher, and guide. He implemented Swamiji's plans concerning the management of the Alambazar Monastery as well as the Ramakrishna Mission's philanthropic activities. Brahmananda was extremely practical and endowed with strong common sense. Sweet and loving by nature, he had above all other qualities, a tremendous spiritual power that enabled him to evaluate people's abilities.

In February 1898 the monastery was moved from Alambazar to Nilambar Mukherjee's garden house in the Belur village; a plot of land was purchased there on the bank of the Ganges. Under Swamiji's direction, the brother monks took the responsibility of levelling the ground and building the living quarters and shrine. On 9 December 1898 Swamiji consecrated the relics of Sri Ramakrishna in the shrine of Belur Monastery.

Brahmananda used to handle the accounts, keep the monastery's diary, supervise the monastery, and give spiritual instructions to the novices. "Whenever you give lectures," Maharaj said to the monks, "please use Sri Ramakrishna's teachings as much as possible, because it is easy to understand the true import of the scriptures through his teachings. The Master used to say that there should not be any theft [i.e., hypocrisy] in the inner chamber of the heart. He had great affection for the simple-hearted. He used to say: 'I don't care for flattery. I love the person who calls on God sincerely.' The Master also said that all impurities of the mind disappear when one calls on God with a sincere heart."[46] Once a Western gentleman came to Swamiji with some spiritual questions. He sent the gentleman to Brahmananda, saying, "There is a dynamo working and we are all under him."[47] Another time Swamiji said to his disciple Sharat Chakrabarty: "Even I have not the spirituality that Rakhal has. He is the jewel of our monastery, our king."[48]

Brahmananda was always concerned about Swamiji's health, as he suffered from asthma and other ailments. One day Girish Ghosh came to visit Swamiji at Belur Math and heard that he was sick in bed. After a while, Girish saw Swamiji downstairs and said, "I heard that you had become seriously ill." Swamiji said jokingly: "You see, when I close my eyes to sleep, I see Raja's [Brahmananda's] face full of anxiety for me. I am walking now, so that he will be happy. He wants to make me a patient. As a matter of fact I am all right." Afterwards Swamiji praised Brahmananda's administrative capacity: "I have been stunned to see Raja's work. How nicely he is running the monastery. Sri Ramakrishna used to say about him, 'He could run a kingdom.'"[49]

On 20 June 1899, at the request of his Western devotees and brother disciples, Vivekananda left for the West to recover his health. He returned to Belur Math in December 1900; still his health was poor. He knew that he would not live long, so he resigned from the presidency of the Ramakrishna Math and Mission and made Brahmananda president. The swami held this paramount position until he died more than two decades later.

The relationship between Vivekananda and Brahmananda was wonderful. Both were *nityasiddhas* and *ishwarakotis*, born to fulfill the mission of Sri Ramakrishna. They had known each other from their school days and had perfect mutual trust and understanding. Whenever Vivekananda's pets disrupted Brahmananda's flower and vegetable gardens in the monastery, they would have a childish war of words that was very amusing to anyone who witnessed it. Vivekananda introduced a rule that every monk must go to the shrine very early in the morning and practise meditation; absentees would have to beg for their food that day outside the monastery. One morning Swamiji found that Brahmananda and some other monks were not in the shrine. He reminded them of the rule and left for Calcutta, because it would have been unbearable for him to see the sad plight of his brother disciples. After his return the next day, he was overjoyed when he heard that Brahmananda had had a sumptuous meal at a rich merchant's house in an adjacent village.

Sharat Chakrabarty recorded the following incident that took place in 1902:

> The disciple [Sharat] passed the preceding night in Swamiji's room. At 4:00 a.m. Swamiji roused him and said, "Go ring the bell to wake up the monks and brahmacharins from sleep." Following this order, the

disciple rang the bell near the monks who hurriedly got up, and after washing they went to the shrine for meditation.

According to Swamiji's instruction, the disciple rang the bell vigorously near Brahmananda's room, which made him remark: "Good heavens! This *Bangal* [Sharat, originally from Bangladesh] has made it too hot for us to stay in the Math." When the disciple reported this to Swamiji, he laughed heartily and said, "Well done!"[50]

Swamiji wanted a ghat and an embankment built on the bank of the Ganges at Belur Math; Swami Vijnanananda, an ex-engineer, was entrusted with completing the project. He underestimated the cost, but Brahmananda took the risk of finishing it. When Swamiji learned that the budget had been exceeded, he scolded Brahmananda harshly. The swami went to his room, closed the door, and cried profusely. Afterwards Swamiji tearfully apologized: "Brother, please forgive me. I know how much the Master loved you and never said a harsh word to you. And I, on the other hand, for the sake of this petty work, have verbally abused you and given you pain. I am not fit to live with you. I shall go away to the Himalayas and live in solitude." Brahmananda, also upset, said: "Don't say that, Swamiji. Your scolding is a blessing. How can you leave us? You are our leader. How shall we function without you?"[51] Gradually both of them calmed down.

One day after lunch while Swamiji was resting at Belur Math, he asked his disciple Sharat Chakrabarty to give him a little massage. Sharat was happy for the opportunity to serve his guru; but Swamiji didn't like his massage because, out of respect, Sharat massaged him gently. Swamiji asked him to call Brahmananda, who had just then gone to rest. When Brahmananda arrived, Swamiji said: "Raja, I don't feel good today. I asked this Bangal to give me a massage, but he did not do it well. So I have called you." Immediately Maharaj began to massage Swamiji vigorously, like an expert, and continued for a couple of hours. When the exhausted Brahmananda returned to his room, Sharat went to him and said: "Maharaj, I have come to you to resolve my confusion. I have heard that you are the spiritual son of the Master, and I have seen how much Swamiji respects you. I don't understand why Swamiji asked you to give him a massage." At this Brahmananda said: "What do you say? Don't you know he is the Lord Shiva Himself!"[52]

After fulfilling his mission, Vivekananda prepared to depart from this world by relinquishing his responsibilities, mainly to Brahmananda and Saradananda. When Sister Nivedita asked for some advice about her school, Vivekananda wrote her back on 12 February 1902: "In a previous letter, I have written you what little I had to suggest. . . . I recommend you none — not one — except Brahmananda. That 'Old Man's' [Sri Ramakrishna's] judgements never failed — mine always do. If you have to ask my advice or to get anybody to do your business, Brahmananda is the only one I recommend, none else, none else; with this my conscience is clear."[53]

Vivekananda had tremendous faith in Brahmananda's loyalty. He would say: "Others may desert me, but Raja will stand by me till the last." Vivekananda passed away on 4 July 1902. Brahmananda cried like a child over his body. When Saradananda lifted him up, Brahmananda said: "It is as if the whole Himalayan Mountains have disappeared from before my eyes!"

As President of the Ramakrishna Order

Undoubtedly, the passing away of Vivekananda was a great blow to the monks; but Brahmananda came forward to hold the helm of the Ramakrishna Mission with his vast experience and strong common sense, with unselfish love and unbounded compassion, and above all with the personality of a spiritual giant. He could read a person's character at a glance, and he guided the monks accordingly. He told them: "Give the whole of your mind to God. If there is no waste of mental energy, with a fraction of your mind you can do so much work that the world will be dazed."[54]

As head of the organization, Brahmananda boldly and calmly faced problem after problem. On 14 July 1902 Turiyananda arrived in Belur Math from America, and the news of Swamiji's passing broke his heart. Brahmananda and Saradananda received him warmly. Swami Trigunatitananda was sent to San Francisco in place of Turiyananda. Trigunatitananda had been editing and managing the *Udbodhan* magazine, which had been started by Swamiji. The magazine was passing through a financial crisis. Brahmananda made Swami Shuddhananda editor, and came forward to rescue it by raising money and collecting articles from devotees. He himself wrote an article in Bengali entitled "Guru" and began to contribute Sri Ramakrishna's teachings serially.

After Swamiji's passing away Sister Nivedita became involved in India's freedom movement. Brahmananda and Saradananda explained to her that the Ramakrishna Order had no connection with politics, so she had to choose either to be a member of the freedom movement or of the Ramakrishna Order. She chose the former. But Brahmananda was always affectionate towards her and helpful in her educational work. He asked her to write a biography of Swamiji, which was later published as *The Master as I Saw Him*.

Brahmananda was more interested in building the character of the members of the Order than in framing rules and regulations that would restrict the monks' freedom. He knew from his experience that religion finds its fulfillment in love and freedom. On the other hand, no organization can function without some guidelines. While framing some rules for the Ramakrishna Math at Alambazar, Vivekananda had said: "Look here, we are going to make rules, no doubt; but we must remember the main object thereof. Our main object is to transcend all rules and regulations. We naturally have some bad tendencies which are to be changed by observing good rules and regulations, and finally we have to go beyond even all these, just as we remove one thorn by another and throw both of them away."[55]

Kumud Bandhu Sen, a lay devotee, told the following incident, which took place in his presence:

> A meeting of the disciples of Ramakrishna had been called at Balaram Basu's house. Probably the year was 1897. The purpose was to consider organizational matters concerned with the new association. Swamiji had brought a proposed table of detailed regulations of conduct. He passed it out for all to study. All considered it carefully, and each except Maharaj made comments, suggested changes, and gave approval. But Maharaj remained silent.
>
> Then Swamiji asked: "Raja, what is the matter? Why don't you say something? Don't you like it?" Maharaj replied: "No, Naren. I don't like so many rules and regulations." Then Swamiji took the draft of that section and without a word just tore it up and threw the pieces away.[56]

At Alambazar Monastery Swamiji had dictated twenty-four rules to Swami Shuddhananda for the guidance of the newly-admitted brahmacharins; and he had framed the general rules at Nilambar Babu's garden house at Belur, which were recorded by Swami Shivananda.

"One morning at Belur Math," wrote Swami Basudevananda, "these rules of the Ramakrishna Order were read aloud in Swami Brahmananda's room. The revered swami was seated on his small cot absorbed in deep meditation. Swami Shuddhananda was the reader. When the reading was over, Brahmananda said: 'Swamiji did not utter these rules from the physical plane; he raised his mind to a higher realm and then gave dictation and Tarak-da [Swami Shivananda] wrote them down. He delineated them with a view to spreading the ideas and ideals of Sri

Ramakrishna and for the good of humanity. Everyone, whether man or woman, rich or poor, high or low, has an equal right to the spiritual heritage and service of Sri Ramakrishna. Blessed is he who serves the Master and follows his teachings! Accept those instructions of Swamiji with candid faith; practise them in your lives and then spread them in all directions. As a result you will see that the evil influence of the Dark Age will diminish and the Golden Age will come in sight.'"[57]

On another occasion, Swami Dhirananda asked Brahmananda to make some rules for the young monks. He replied: "Swamiji has already made the rules for us. We do not need to add any new ones. Add more love, attain more devotion, and help others to move towards the ideal of God." Swami Abhedananda remarked about Brahmananda: "Love was the dominant theme of his character. As the first president of the Ramakrishna Order he enforced no other law but love; and by that sheer force of love he could dominate over one and all."[58]

Brahmananda seldom attended the trustee meetings of the Order, as most of the time he was away from the monastery. Saradananda, the general secretary, managed the day-to-day administration with Brahmananda's approval and consultation. Even when Brahmananda was in Belur Math, he was reluctant to attend the meetings. One day a trustee, a disciple of Swamiji, asked him: "Maharaj, why do you make such difficulty about attending the meetings?" The swami answered: "Look, the whole world appears shadowlike to me. It is very difficult for me to come and attend to all these details."[59]

"Nevertheless," wrote Swami Ashokananda, "he was very alert about what was going on in the Order. How he knew all the things that were taking place nobody could find out; but he knew. And sometimes he could be very embarrassing. Say you had just come to him from another centre; he would ask you, 'Well, how is the cow doing? How is the calf? Was there a good harvest in the vegetable garden? How is the orchard? How many mangoes were there this season?' I remember he once asked me about a cow and a calf. I felt so embarrassed because I could not give him a right answer at all. He knew everything, kept watch over everything — not only the details of the external work, but the spiritual condition of the monks as well. He could guide them, and he would give those who were earnest as much help as they wanted."[60]

Once Saradananda said to a young monk: "When I say something, you should judge and discriminate whether I am right or wrong, but when Maharaj says something you may safely accept it as true without the slightest doubt."[61]

7

In Northern India

During his presidency, Brahmananda travelled extensively in various parts of India to organize the activities of the Order. In the middle of 1903 he went to Varanasi and stayed there for a month. He collected some funds to help the Ramakrishna Advaita Ashrama, which was struggling financially. A few young devotees of Swamiji had started the "Poor Men's Relief Association," which later became the "Ramakrishna Mission Home of Service." Brahmananda officially affiliated the group with the Order and arranged to buy some land adjacent to the Home of Service and to construct some buildings on it. He then went to Kankhal (Hardwar), where Swami Kalyanananda, a disciple of Swamiji, had started to serve sick monks in three thatched huts. With the help of a Calcutta devotee, Brahmananda arranged to buy fifteen acres of land, and he sent Vijnanananda to supervise the construction of some buildings.

Although he was the head of a large organization, karma could not bind him. Whenever he had time and opportunity he would practise sadhana in one of his four favourite holy places: Varanasi, Kankhal, Vrindaban, and Puri. As a true mystic, he could monitor the time when the spiritual current flows in those places. He said: "Each place has its own time, when it is favourable for spiritual disciplines. The auspicious time in Vrindaban is midnight; in Varanasi, from 3:00 a.m. to dawn; in Puri, afternoon; in Bhubaneswar and Belur Math at 4:00 a.m."

About Kankhal he remarked: "It is a holy place. Here it does not take much effort to be absorbed in japam and meditation. The very atmosphere is wonderful. The presence of the Mother Ganges and the majestic Himalayas make the mind calm spontaneously. The unobstructed sound of Om is always vibrating in the air." He said about Varanasi: "Kashi [Varanasi] is beyond the universe — a great place saturated with consciousness. A person gets ten times the results if he practises spiritual disciplines here, and the mantram becomes living very quickly."[62]

After staying one month at Kankhal, Maharaj went to Vrindaban and practised sadhana with Turiyananda. During this time, Brahmananda recalled how a spirit helped his steadfast devotions:

At that time Turiyananda and I were living together and practising japam and meditation punctually. We did not talk to each other unless we needed to. At 8:00 p.m. we would eat some bread that we got from begging, and then go to bed. Just at midnight we would get up, and after washing we would sit for meditation. One night while I was asleep, I was pushed by someone and heard a voice: "It is twelve. Will you not sit for meditation?" I immediately got up and was a little groggy. I thought that Turiyananda had broken my sleep, but he informed me that he had not. Quickly I finished washing and sat for meditation. I saw a Babaji (a Vaishnava saint) repeating his mantram silently in front of me. Seeing him I was a little scared. I was repeating my mantram and from time to time I would look at him. As long as I was seated on my carpet, I saw him standing, repeating his mantram. Later I used to see him daily in the same way repeating his mantram.[63]

"One day in Vrindaban," Swami Ambikananda recalled, "I accompanied Maharaj to the temple of Radharaman. Expert musicians gather there every day in the prayer hall and worship the deity with devotional songs. Maharaj introduced me to the musicians and said, 'This boy likes to sing the praises of the Lord.' This pleased them. They let me sing and accompanied me with drums and cymbals. Everyone liked my singing, and one of the priests brought a basket of sweets for Maharaj and said to him, 'I shall send this basket to your cottage.' Maharaj looked at me, pleased, and remarked, 'See what a nice present I get for your singing!'"[64]

It is a great education to live with a God-intoxicated person. From Vrindaban Brahmananda went to Vindhyachal via Allahabad. Ambikananda later reminisced:

The first night Maharaj, my father, our host, and I slept in the same room. It was nearing midnight when I felt a gentle touch. I woke up. I saw Maharaj dressed and covered with a heavy blanket. He said to me: "Get up and dress yourself in warm clothing. I want you to come with me." Without any hesitation I did as I was told, though it did not occur to me at the time to inquire where we were going. Maharaj took a lantern in one hand and a stick in the other, and asked me to follow him. We went outside. It was the night of the new moon and pitch-dark. The path was uneven. Realizing that I was stumbling, Maharaj gave me the lantern to carry and held me by the hand. I asked him then, "Where are we going?" He replied, "To see the Divine Mother."

When we entered the temple compound we found the place crowded with worshippers. Some were counting beads and others were chanting the praises of the Divine Mother. There was an intense spiritual atmosphere. The door of the temple was still closed. The priests were decorating Mother's image for the special occasion. When the doors opened, the pilgrims stood up and moved forward slowly to have the *darshan* [sight] of Mother. In the meantime the priests caught sight of Maharaj. Seeing his benign face and impressed by his personality, they stopped the pilgrims from proceeding and let Maharaj enter first. He was still holding my hand, and I was following him. When Maharaj stood before the image of the Divine Mother, he exclaimed: "Ah! How beautiful, how beautiful!" The next moment he was in ecstasy. There was perfect silence in the temple. The priests and pilgrims watched Maharaj's God-intoxicated state in amazement. After a while, still in an ecstatic mood, Maharaj asked me to sing a song to the Divine Mother. While I was singing, tears of joy fell from the outer corners of his eyes. It was a divine sight to behold. Maharaj asked me to sing another song, after which we prostrated before Mother and came out in the courtyard. Maharaj sat down in one corner to perform japam and asked me to sit also. I said, "What shall I do?" Maharaj replied: "Think of the presence of Divine Mother. Later I shall instruct you." We stayed for a while and returned to the house before daybreak.[65]

Brahmananda visited Varanasi several times. In April 1908 he laid the foundation stone of the hospital building of the Home of Service. Again he went to Varanasi in 1912, and then in March he went to Kankhal and stayed until fall. He arranged to have Durga Puja (the annual worship of the Divine Mother) in the ashrama. He told a monk who was dispensing homeopathic medicine in the hospital: "Look, my child, your work pertains to life and death. Don't be overconfident about your capability. When you give medicine, pray to Sri Ramakrishna, 'Master, help me to select that medicine which will cure this patient.' Then you will feel that the Master is working through you."[66] This was his last visit to Kankhal.

In November 1912 Holy Mother went to Varanasi with her retinue and stayed at a devotee's house near the two Ramakrishna centres. Brahmananda and other monks accompanied her to show the activities of the Ramakrishna Mission Home of Service. Greatly pleased with the visit, she remarked: "Sri Ramakrishna is ever present in the place, and Mother Lakshmi always casts her benign glance upon it." As a token of appreciation she gave a ten rupee note as a donation, which is still preserved in the centre.

Coincidentally, M. was then in Varanasi. He had often expressed the view that the Master did not approve of anyone's performing social service before realizing God, which caused ideological conflict among some monks. At Brahmananda's request, a monk said to M.: "Mother has just told us that the activities of the Home of Service were service to the Master himself and that he was tangibly present here. Now what do you say?" M. replied with a laugh: "How can I deny it anymore?"[67]

Brahmananda had unbounded devotion to Holy Mother. He used to go every morning to pay his respects to her. Fearful of being overwhelmed with emotion, he would bow down to her from the courtyard instead of going upstairs where she was. One day Golap-ma said: "Rakhal, the Mother asks why a devotee propitiates Shakti, the Divine Mother, at the beginning of worship?" Brahmananda replied: "It is because the key to the knowledge of Brahman is in the Divine Mother's keeping. There is no way of communing with Brahman unless the Mother graciously unlocks the door."[68]

One day Holy Mother visited Sarnath, about seven miles from Varanasi, where Buddha had preached his first sermon after attaining nirvana. Swami Nikhilananda wrote:

Swami Brahmananda and three other devotees followed her in another carriage. The Mother went around the place looking at the various ruins associated with Buddha and his followers and noticed that several European visitors, too, were doing so. Referring to the visitors, she said: "They built all this in a previous birth, and now they have come back again to see what they did centuries ago. They are speechless with wonder, admiring these amazing relics." While returning to Varanasi, Holy Mother, at the earnest request of Brahmananda, exchanged carriages with him. On the road, the swami's carriage had an accident, though nobody was seriously hurt. When the Mother heard about it she said: "I was fated for this mishap, but Rakhal, by force as it were, took it on his own shoulders. I had several children with me; who knows what would have happened to them?"[69]

As a tree bends when it bears too much fruit, so a real spiritual person bends with humility. Brahmananda taught the monks through his life and actions. Swami Kamaleswarananda recorded the following incident that Maharaj told him:

Once it arose in the Master's mind that if he could clean the privy, he would believe that his ego had gone. One night he translated his idea into action.

The other day I went to visit Lord Vishwanath with a few monks; I was dressed in nice clothing and looked like a dignified "Swami." I saw a sweeper sweeping the courtyard of Vishwanath. I found an opportunity to test my humility. I approached the sweeper and asked him to give me his broomstick. I offered him a coin, because seeing that I was a monk he was reluctant to give it to me. I took the broomstick from his hand, and cleaned the Lord's place. For a couple of hours I got so much joy that I can't describe it. My heart was full. There is an inexpressible joy in humility. I felt more joy cleaning the temple than visiting the deity.[70]

Brahmananda had collected some teachings of Sri Ramakrishna in Bengali, which were first serially published in the *Udbodhan* and later translated into English under the title *Words of the Master*. During this visit to Varanasi he completed the book. When he was working on the manuscript of those teachings he would not allow anybody to stay in his room. Sometimes Maharaj would get up at midnight and ask his attendant to bring the manuscript to him. Once, after correcting it, he said, "The Master came and told me: 'I didn't say that. I said this.'"[71] Saradananda wrote in his introduction to that book: "The present brochure is from the pen of one who was regarded by the Master as next to Swami Vivekananda in his capacity for realizing religious ideals. It is indeed the work of grateful love of the beloved disciple — one who, more than anyone else, lived constantly with the Master — to set the Master correctly before the public, seeing how his invaluable words are being roughly handled, deformed, and distorted nowadays at the hands of many."

Karma yoga is inscrutable. It is a wonderful path for purifying the mind; but if it is not performed in the right spirit, it breeds ego, power struggles, bickering, and dissension. In Varanasi the Ramakrishna Advaita Ashrama and the Home of Service are located side by side; some untrained monks of both centres formed rival groups and started to quarrel among themselves. Turiyananda and Saradananda tried to reconcile their differences but failed. Brahmananda was then at Bhubaneswar. When he was informed of the situation, he replied: "Don't do anything. I am coming to see for myself."

On 20 January 1921 Brahmananda arrived at Varanasi. The novices were scared to death, thinking that the swami would punish them, or at least call some meetings. He did not call any meeting or raise any question regarding work or quarrels. He simply announced that all the monks from both centres would have to meditate with him in the morning and evening, and that there would be devotional singing and questions and answers after meditation. Thus a few days passed. Then, on Swamiji's birthday he initiated forty members of the ashramas into sannyasa and brahmacharya. He lifted their minds to such a high level that they forgot all their friction. One of the ringleaders was so inspired that he left for the Himalayas to perform austerities. Peace returned to both centres.

Seeing that Brahmananda had won the battle without a fight, Saradananda complimented him: "It would be proper for you to be a king rather than a monk. Where both Turiyananda and I could not figure out the solution, how easily you solved this crucial problem!"[72] A disciple of Brahmananda wrote in his reminiscences:

Maharaj had the power to change the atmosphere of a place and to make it vibrate with his spirituality. In his company he could make everybody roll with laughter, and then suddenly, when he became silent, the place would be surcharged with a divine presence. Swami Turiyananda once remarked that Maharaj used to create such an atmosphere around himself that everyone present would be filled with some of his spiritual mood. Many people used to come to Maharaj for the purpose of seeking advice about their problems. But once they were near him they felt no necessity to ask for any solution. Problems solved themselves in his presence, and people would forget themselves, their egoism, temporal pleasure and pain, and be filled with intense divine bliss.[73]

During this last visit to Varanasi Brahmananda gave nine spiritual discourses to the monks, which are invaluable for seekers of God. The spiritual teachings of Brahmananda from 1897 to 1922 were first published in Bengali as *Dharma-prasange Swami Brahmananda*, and have been fully translated into English as *A Guide to Spiritual Life*. This book is a classic in practical Vedanta literature.

In South India

In 1897 Vivekananda had sent Ramakrishnananda to Madras to spread the message of the Master in South India. In 1908 Ramakrishnananda invited Brahmananda to visit, and went to Puri himself to escort him to Madras. Before leaving Madras, Ramakrishnananda told Sister Devamata (Laura Glenn, an American devotee) and Brahmachari Rudra to make everything ready to receive Maharaj. "Remember," he reiterated, "Swami Brahmananda was like his own son and when you see him, you have a glimpse of what Sri Ramakrishna was. The self in Brahmananda is entirely annihilated. Whatever he says or does comes directly from the Divine Source."[74]

Ramakrishnananda accommodated Brahmananda in his room, which had been renovated especially for that purpose. He said: "The Master and his son will stay inside. I will stay out in the entrance hall and serve them. What more do I want?"[75] He told the South Indian devotees: "You have not seen the Master; be content to see Maharaj." One day a devotee brought some fruits for Ramakrishna, but Ramakrishnananda offered half to Maharaj, saying: "To offer these fruits to Maharaj is as good as offering them to Sri Ramakrishna, for the Master eats through his mouth."[76] V. Krishnaswami Iyer asked Ramakrishnananda whether the new swami would give any lecture in Madras. Smiling, Ramakrishnananda replied: "What is there in lectures? He never gives lectures. Men such as he can impart religion by a mere look or touch."[77]

Sister Devamata recorded some touching incidents about Brahmananda in her *Days in an Indian Monastery*:

> Sometimes Swami Brahmananda's approval was wholly dumb and unspoken. One day he laid in my hands a folded pongee shawl with the words: "Sister, can you mend this for me? Some insect has eaten little holes all through it. I prize it because it was given me by Ram Babu [a devotee of Ramakrishna]." I took it home, tinted some sewing silk the exact shade and darned each little hole with meticulous care. It consumed the whole day and in the evening I sent the shawl back. Swami Brahmananda was delighted with it and showed it to everyone explaining that I had done it, but he never mentioned it to me. He did not wish to cheapen a loving service by an ordinary expression of thanks.
>
> One evening while he was at Madras, he went into samadhi during *arati* [vesper service]. He sat on the rug at the far end of the hall, his body motionless, his eyes closed, a smile of ecstasy playing about his lips. Swami Ramakrishnananda was the first to observe that he did not move when the service was over. Realizing what had occurred, he motioned to one of the young swamis to fan his head.... For half an hour no one stirred — a boy who was crossing the hall did not even draw back his foot. Perfect stillness pervaded the monastery — a radiant, pulsing stillness.[78]

During Christmastime Brahmananda asked Sister Devamata to arrange a Christmas party in Western fashion. She could not get a Christmas tree, but she bought a plum cake, glacé fruits, and other items from an English shop. The boys brought green branches from the jungle and bound them to the pillars in the hall and decorated the entrance with mango leaves and garlands. A Christmas altar was set up, and bread and wine were offered as a symbol of the Christian Eucharist. Sister Devamata narrated the event:

> Swami Brahmananda asked me to read the story of Christ's birth and I chose the account of Saint Luke. When I finished reading, the intense stillness in the air led me to look toward Swami Brahmananda. His eyes were open and fixed on the altar, there was a smile on his lips, but it was evident that his consciousness had gone to a higher plane. No one moved or spoke. At the end of twenty minutes or more the

look of immediate seeing returned to his eyes and he motioned to us to continue the service. Lights, incense and burning camphor were waved before the altar, the evening chant and hymn were sung, all those present bowed in silent prayer and the Christmas Service was ended

As he was eating he remarked to me: "I have been very much blessed in coming to your house today, Sister." I answered quickly, "Swami, it is I who have been blessed in having you come." "You do not understand," he replied. "I have had a great blessing here this afternoon. As you were reading the Bible, Christ suddenly stood before the altar dressed in a long blue cloak. He talked to me for some time. It was a very blessed moment."[79]

After staying some days in Madras, Brahmananda was accompanied by Ramakrishnananda on a pilgrimage in South India. First the swamis went to Rameswaram, on the coast of the Indian Ocean, and stayed three days as the guests of the Raja of Ramnad. After their arrival, both swamis went to visit the Lord Shiva and then returned to the palace. Brahmananda scolded his attendants who were busy unpacking the luggage: "Can t these things wait? You have come here to worship the Lord and that is what you should attend to first." On the second day Brahmananda and Ramakrishnananda ceremoniously worshipped the Lord with Ganges water that Maharaj had brought from Varanasi.

From Rameswaram on the way to Madras they stopped at Madurai to visit the famous Meenakshi Temple, and stayed three days in the city. Ramakrishnananda wanted to escort Maharaj to the inner sanctuary so that he could see the Mother closely. Customarily, only brahmins are allowed to enter there, and Brahmananda was born as a *kshatriya* (royal or warrior caste). At the entrance Ramakrishnananda shouted, "*Alwar, Alwar*" (i.e., an illumined Vaishnava saint), and as a result the priests did not stop them.[80] In the temple Brahmananda had a wonderful vision, which he later described: "When I stood in front of the deity, I saw the living image of Mother Meenakshi coming towards me, and I lost outer consciousness."[81] Realizing that Maharaj was in ecstasy, Ramakrishnananda held him up for nearly an hour in the midst of a large crowd; and he himself chanted the glory of the Divine Mother with tearful eyes. Afterwards the swamis came out of the shrine. Then they returned to Madras. Ramakrishnananda took Brahmananda to Kanchipuram where he visited Mother Kamakshi, Shiva and Vishnu, the famous deities.

On 20 January 1909 Brahmananda inaugurated the Ramakrishna Ashrama in Bangalore. It was a grand celebration. The high officials of the

Mysore State attended the function. Brahmananda read his address, which made an excellent impression on the audience. This was the only time that Brahmananda ever spoke in public. In Bangalore Maharaj was so impressed with *Ramnam Sankirtan* (choral singing in praise of Lord Ramachandra), that he introduced it to the Order, and he himself would join in the singing.

Swami Umananda, a disciple of Brahmananda, was working in Madras. He became ill with smallpox and was admitted to the hospital, where Ramakrishnananda visited him every day. A couple of days before he passed away, Umananda expressed a desire to see Maharaj. When Ramakrishnananda communicated this to Brahmananda, he showed concern but did not go to the hospital, thinking that the disease might be contagious. After Umananda's death, Ramakrishnananda said with tearful eyes: "Maharaj, you are so cruel! Umananda wanted to see you once in his final hours, and you did not go!" Immediately Maharaj became grave and then slowly said: "Shashi, is it enough to see a person through the eyes? Have I not been there?" Ramakrishnananda bowed down and said: "Maharaj, please forgive me; I did not understand you."[82]

Ramakrishnananda died in 1911. In July 1916 Brahmananda revisited South India. He laid the foundation stone of the new monastery building in Madras, and then went to Bangalore on 12 August. This time he extensively visited the important holy places of the South: Chamunda Devi in Mysore, Lord Padmanava in Trivandrum, Kanyakumari (the Virgin Goddess) at Cape Comorin, Perambudur (the birthplace of Ramanuja), Lord Ranganath at Trichi, and Lord Balaji Venkateshwara in Tirupati. When Brahmananda visited those holy places, the deities would manifest themselves to him. From time to time he would talk about his visions: "In Kanyakumari, I was about to burst into laughter out of joy. I saw the goddess as an eight- or ten-year-old girl, giggling. It was a beautiful, awesome, living form."[83] In Tirupati Maharaj saw the Divine Mother in the image of Lord Venkateshwara. His body shivered in ecstasy. Later he said to Swami Sharvananda: "I have distinctly seen the form of the Divine Mother. Please inquire about it."[84] After inquiry and close examination of the image and sanctuary, it was found to have been originally a Shakti temple, later converted into a Vishnu temple, probably under the influence of Ramanuja.

In April 1921 Brahmananda went to Madras with Shivananda and inaugurated the Madras Students' Home. Then he spent the summer in Bangalore and returned to Madras in October. Following his suggestion, Durga Puja was performed with the image in the monastery. Swami

Ashokananda recalled: "Once I managed to ask him a certain question very early in the morning.... He told me plainly: 'You know I cannot do anything without the command of God.' Yes, he was so close to God that we believed, and with good reason, that he was always in contact with Him. I have heard that he often saw God in the form of Sri Ramakrishna and in other forms as well."[85]

In Madras a dozen nuns from Maharashtra lived in a convent, and Gopala (Baby Krishna) was their Chosen Deity. They heard about Brahmananda and invited him to visit their shrine. Maharaj went there with some monks. When Maharaj sat in a chair, the chief nun placed a silver tray below his feet. Then each nun washed Maharaj's feet with scented water and wiped them with her hair. His feet were then placed on a velvet cushion and the nuns worshipped him with a garland, flowers, and sandalpaste. When the worship was over, each nun carried a small pitcher of milk on her hip and a glass in her hand. Then, encircling Maharaj, they began to dance and sing this famous song of their Saint Namadeva:

> Drink this milk, my Lord, Gopala,
> Drink this milk, O Son of Nanda,
> This I, Namadeva, bring you
> Milked with my own hands....

Considering Maharaj to be the living Gopala, the nuns poured milk into his mouth, but it ran down his chin because he was in samadhi, and they wiped his chin with a handkerchief. When he regained outer consciousness, he asked his attendant to sing a song. Later, hearing about this incident, Saradananda remarked, "Here the memory of Maharaj's real nature began to awaken."[86]

In East Bengal

In January 1916 Brahmananda went to Dhaka with Premananda and a few other monks to lay the foundation stone of the Ramakrishna Math. On the way, they visited the holy temple of Kamakhya at Guwahati. He stayed there for three days and performed a special worship to the Divine Mother. Then the party stopped at Mymensing for five days. One day while walking on the bank of the Brahmaputra River, Maharaj exclaimed, "My mind is merging into the Infinite." On 13 February, after arriving at Dhaka, Maharaj laid the foundation stone of the centre. One morning Maharaj said: "Last night I saw the Master dancing here. The Master himself is preaching; we are only instruments."[87]

On their arrival at Dhaka, great enthusiasm was generated in that historic city. Many distinguished people and young students flocked to visit the disciples of Ramakrishna. Maharaj inspired and initiated many of them. He visited the ashrama of Vijaykrishna Goswami, and also Deobhog (Narayangunj), the birthplace of Saint Durga Charan Nag. Brahmananda was impressed with the rural beauty of the place and the devotion of the people.

When Brahmananda was at the railway station, waiting for the train to Calcutta, a young girl who was a devotee's sister bowed down to him and asked for some advice. Maharaj told her: "Daughter, the train is coming. I don't have much time, but I will give you knowledge in one sentence: Read *The Gospel of Sri Ramakrishna* regularly every day. That is enough. You will find in this book the truth of all religions."[88]

In Puri and Bhubaneswar

Many times Brahmananda visited Puri, a lovely city on the coast of the Bay of Bengal. Once Sri Ramakrishna had advised Rakhal to go on a pilgrimage to Puri rather than to Gaya, because in Gaya he might merge into the divine and not return to the relative world. In Puri Brahmananda used to stay at Shashi Niketan, a retreat home of Balaram Basu. The holy shrine of Lord Jagannath (Krishna), the wholesome climate, and the panoramic view of the seacoast kept him in a highly spiritual mood. Quite often Brahmananda would experience ecstasy while visiting the deities — Jagannath, Balaram, and Subhadra (Krishna, his brother, and his sister) — in the inner sanctuary of the temple. One day he saw a cowherd boy in place of the deities; perhaps he saw his own real nature as the eternal companion of Krishna. During the Chariot Festival of Jagannath, according to custom, he would help pull the chariot containing Lord Jagannath's image. He experienced all-pervading consciousness in Puri and established a monastery at Chakratirtha, near the coast.

One day Atal Bihari Maitra, the deputy magistrate of Puri, said to Swami Sharvananda (a disciple of Maharaj): "What kind of monks are you! You have no occult powers." Hearing this Maharaj said: "It is easy to get occult powers, but difficult to acquire purity of mind. It is this purity of mind that really matters."[89]

In 1917 while returning from Puri, Brahmananda stopped at Bhubaneswar to visit the famous Lingaraj Shiva Temple. He stayed there three days and felt a wonderful spiritual atmosphere. He arranged to purchase a plot of land for a monastery. The monastery was dedicated on 31 October

1919. He commented: "This place is very conducive to practising yoga. It is a place of Lord Shiva — a hidden Varanasi. Practising a little spiritual discipline here, one can accrue immense results. It is a healthy place. After getting tired from working in other places, the monks may come here to rest as well as practise meditation."[90] He also advised the householder devotees to build homes around the centre and to lead a quiet life in solitude.

Maharaj visited Bhubaneswar many times for health reasons, and also trained some monks in that isolated retreat. One day he reminisced about Sri Ramakrishna: "The Master's body was so tender that once while breaking a *luchi* [crispy fried bread] his finger was cut." At this a gentleman remarked: "How is it possible for a person to cut his finger by breaking a luchi?" Brahmananda immediately became silent. If anyone interrupted him, his mood would break and he could not talk further.[91]

In 1920 Pandit Kshirod Prasad Vidyavinod went to see Brahmananda at Bhubaneswar. Kshirod lamented: "There was a possibility of my seeing Sri Ramakrishna, but it was my bad luck that I did not. I was then a student. After hearing about the Master, one day I left for Dakshineswar. After arriving at Alambazar I thought: The Master knows what is in everybody's mind. If he exposes my secret thoughts in front of everybody, I will be embarrassed. This fear sent me back home." Maharaj said, "Since you went to Alambazar to see the Master, take it for granted that you did see him." "No, Maharaj, I did not see him." Remembering his bad luck, Kshirod bent his head and began to sob. As soon as he lifted his face, he saw Sri Ramakrishna seated in Brahmananda's place.[92]

In Belur Math and Calcutta

Although Belur Math is the headquarters of the Ramakrishna Order, Brahmananda was not there most of the time. He was busy founding new centres and inspiring monks and devotees. He handed over the management of the daily activities to Premananda and Shivananda. When he stayed at Belur Math in between his travels, a festive mood would prevail among the monks. Many devotees and distinguished people would come to see him and receive spiritual instructions.

Brahmananda lived a God-intoxicated life, yet at the same time he knew what went on around him. He would supervise the care of the trees, flowering plants, vegetable garden, and dairy; he would check the cleanliness of the shrine as well as the rooms of the monks; he would inquire about the health and spiritual progress of the monks and brahmacharins.

He was a loving father, compassionate guru, and at the same time a stern taskmaster. He could not bear any lack of discipline among the monks. He reminded them: "This is Swamiji's Math. If you cannot live according to his wishes, leave the monastery! Swamiji gave his very life to build this organization and to give you everything to facilitate your spiritual practice and growth. Try to realize the infinite love he bore for you."[93]

A monk recorded in his diary:

It is winter, December 1915. Nowadays Maharaj has made a rule that all monks and brahmacharins should rise at 4:00 a.m., and should sit for japam and meditation by 4:30 a.m. Some practise meditation in the shrine, some in Maharaj's room, and others on the veranda facing the Ganges. An attendant of Maharaj has been entrusted with the duty of ringing a bell at ten minutes to four. Maharaj gets up about 3:00 a.m. His sleep is very short. After practising meditation for two to two and a half hours, all assemble in his room by 7:00 a.m. and sing devotional songs for about an hour. Then Maharaj gives spiritual instructions to all. He elevates the mind of each six or seven steps.[94]

Brahmananda also taught the monks the secret of work:

Simply carrying out some undertaking is not sufficient. It must be done in the right spirit, knowing that one is serving the Lord without any personal motive. Keep three-fourths of your mind fixed on God, and with the remaining one-fourth do whatever you have to do. If you follow this method, you will be an ideal karmayogi and you will attain peace and joy. On the other hand, if you only get involved in activities without practising meditation, ego and pride will crop up and quarrels and dissensions will ensue, thus disturbing the equanimity of your mind. Therefore I tell you, stick to your sadhana by all means whether you work or not. . . . Each and every work is equally important — whether it is meditation or household duties. Do it with the right spirit. Work is worship.[95]

One day Maharaj wanted to test the depth of the monks' morning meditation. He ordered each monk to peel a potato and bring it to him. He checked those potatoes, and then held one up and declared that the peeler of that one had had deep meditation. That person was Swami Shuddhananda, a disciple of Vivekananda. Maharaj noticed that he had removed the skin of the potato so neatly that no flesh was wasted.

One time a rich merchant lost his young wife. To assuage his grief, he came to Belur Math to live with the monks. After some time he felt uplifted by the influence of the holy company and decided to donate all of his money and his business to the Ramakrishna Mission. At that time the financial condition of the Order was poor. Premananda was moved by the donor's good intention, and he informed Maharaj of the offer. The farsighted Brahmananda realized that the merchant's renunciation was temporary, and that the Order would be in trouble if it accepted this donation. Without disclosing this insight, he told Premananda, with folded hands: "Brother, having the company of the holy that man got renunciation, and having his company shall we be involved in the world?"[96] Needless to say, the offer was not accepted.

There was a young monk in the monastery who was very obstinate and quarrelsome. One day Premananda forcefully took him to Brahmananda and said: "Maharaj, this fellow is short-tempered, he quarrels with other monks and even with me. Please touch his head with your palm so that he can be freed from anger." Maharaj jokingly said: "Brother Baburam, today my palm is not good; you better put your palm on his head." But Premananda insisted and pushed the monk's head near Maharaj's feet. His joking mood immediately disappeared. He became calm and serious. He began to rub the monk's head with his palm. Premananda then pushed the monk aside and placed his own head near Maharaj and requested him to touch it, which he did. Then Premananda loudly called to the other monks: "Hello! Please come and take the blessings of Maharaj. He has become *kalpataru* [the wish-fulfilling tree] today." All the monks, and even the servants, rushed to Brahmananda. A doctor devotee was in the bathroom; before he arrived Maharaj had gotten up from his seat. When Premananda asked Maharaj to bless the doctor, he replied, "The power that came has gone."[97]

One day Brahmananda told the monks about the supernatural power of a mantram. Swami Nikhilananda recalled:

Sri Ramakrishna taught Maharaj a mantram by repeating which one could bring a particular person to one's place. Many years later, Maharaj was at Belur Math when he heard of the arrival of a prominent maharaja in Calcutta; there was no chance of the maharaja's visiting Belur Math. Swami Brahmananda wanted to test the efficacy of the mantram taught him by the Master. He used it and within a short time the ruler of the native state sent his private secretary to the Math to find a convenient time for his visit there. Maharaj was pleased with the power of the mantram. But suddenly he remembered that the Master had asked him never to use it.[98]

One day a devotee came to Belur Math and complained: "Maharaj, I have visited this place for such a long time, still I feel that I am an outsider." Maharaj indignantly told him to go whimper to Premananda.

Later, in front of all the monks, he repeated what that devotee had said. Then Brahmananda said to the devotee: "Do you know the purport of what you said? Go home and try to reflect on it. Go to the Ghosh Sect [an esoteric tantric school], and you will get the result in three days. Be a devotee. Be a devotee." Again, addressing Shivananda, Maharaj said: "Sir, some people come here and complain that they have been coming to Belur Math for a long time and still they are not achieving anything. What does it mean?" Shivananda replied: "They want more. Their stomachs are not yet full." Maharaj said: "It may be that the food has been supplied but has not reached their stomachs." "Yes, it may be possible," replied Shivananda.[99] Maharaj indicated that that devotee would not have visited Belur Math the second time if he had not gotten anything.

One day Brahmananda said to M.: "The Master came this time to make a bridge between Jiva and Shiva [human beings and God]. See how easy it has now become to realize the Lord!"[100]

Brahmananda was a man of few words. His life was his teaching. Rather than preaching religion he demonstrated it. Swami Basudevananda recalled:

It was 2:00 or 3:00 p.m. on a hot summer day. Swami Brahmananda was seated in his room at the Belur Monastery. His attendant was fanning him. As soon as I entered his room he said: "Welcome. It is very hot today. Let us meditate on the snow-clad Himalayas; then the whole atmosphere will be cool. Do you know this mystery? First empty the mind completely. There should not be any *samskaras* [impressions]. Then the mind will automatically fill itself with God-consciousness. When water is poured out of a pitcher, does the pitcher remain empty? At once it is filled with space. Didn't space exist in the pitcher before? Yes, it did. It existed mixed with water. We see only the gross water [and not the subtle space], so we think only the water exists. Similarly, although the impressions of external objects and Pure Consciousness are both in the mind, we perceive only the mind's gross impressions because they are within the reach of our senses. We do not see the Pure Consciousness, which is also in the mind.

"If one can make the mind free from impressions, Pure Consciousness, which is Satchidananda, will be immediately revealed. Otherwise, through discrimination one can get a little inkling of Satchidananda. One should discriminate, combining devotion and meditation, and then one will understand the real import of the scriptures, the teachings of the holy men, and Sri Ramakrishna.

"Again, when a particular *sattvic* [good] impression is established in the mind, replacing other worldly impressions, then that established impression becomes luminous by the light of Brahman. At that time the snow-clad mountain turns into an effulgent form like the living Shiva, and that radiance of Shiva makes the body-mind organism of the meditator cool and calm.

"Thus, after cleansing the mind-lake, whatever ideal, or *Ishtam* [chosen form of God], you place there will be radiant and living. Brahman, the Pure Consciousness, cannot be reflected on a polluted, muddy mind-lake where many worldly waves are agitating.

"Now go ahead. I have given you a very secret teaching. Keep it secret and practise it wholeheartedly. Have you not read Sri Ramakrishna's parable of the wonderful tub of dye? Whenever the dyer was requested to dye a cloth a particular colour, he would dip it into that miraculous tub and it would immediately be dyed that colour. This mind-lake is like that wonderful tub of dye."[101]

During that time Belur Math was infested with mosquitoes. Maharaj suffered from malaria and typhoid fever. Once he remarked: "I move around because of this horrible malaria! Otherwise who would want to stay away from this glorious monastery? . . . This Belur Math is like Kailash [the abode of Shiva]. Here the guru and the Ganges are present. Swamiji also left his body here. This is Vaikuntha [the abode of Vishnu]."[102] Another time he said to Shivananda: "Tarak-da, I shall never be able to cut my attachment for Belur Math. Even after my death I shall watch Belur Math from above."[103] The damp climate and water of Belur Math did not suit Brahmananda, so from time to time he would stay at Balaram's house in Calcutta. Ramakrishna Basu, Balaram's son, was very devoted to Maharaj and served him wholeheartedly.

Many young people and devotees would come to Maharaj to have his holy company and listen to his inspiring teachings. He was an awakener of souls. Sometimes he would remind the devotees of Ramakrishna's message:

The Master often said, "God can be attained if one loves him with the combined force of these three attractions: the chaste wife's love for her husband, the mother's love for her child, and the worldly man's love for worldly possessions. . . ."

Sri Ramakrishna's message in this age is renunciation of lust and gold. [*Pointing to the monks*] You have joined the monastery in order to become holy men. Renunciation of lust and gold is the ornament of a holy man, and it is the only means of attaining God. As one progresses on the path of spirituality, one is confronted by many kinds of temptations. Cravings — such as for woman and gold, for name and fame — arise again and may lead one farther away from God. Unless you beware of this thief in the form of cravings he will steal all the goodness in you, and you will drown in the bottomless ocean of worldliness. But, on the other hand, there is the ocean of divine grace — if anyone will sincerely call on Him but once. The Master used to say: "If you move one step towards Him, He comes down ten steps towards you."[104]

Swami Nirvanananda related a touching incident that took place in 1918 at Balaram's house. One day after lunch, when Brahmananda was about to rest, a teenage girl came with her brother to see him. When Nirvanananda told this to Maharaj, he said that he could see her at 4:00 p.m. But when the girl insisted, Maharaj allowed her to see him in his room. As soon as she saw him, she began to weep. Then pointing to a picture of Sri Ramakrishna, she said, "He has asked me to come to you." Maharaj said to her affectionately, "Tell me what has happened, my child."

Then she told her story. She had been married at the age of fourteen, and her husband died only two weeks after their marriage. (In India at that time this was a disastrous situation. A Hindu widow could not remarry and had to depend on her husband's family for the rest of her life.) Faced with this gloomy future, she wholeheartedly prayed: "O Lord, what will become of me? I am so lonely and helpless. What shall I do? Please show me the way." After a year or so, one night Sri Ramakrishna appeared to her in a dream and said: "Don't weep. My son Rakhal is living in Baghbazar. Go to him. He will help you." She had never heard of Ramakrishna or Rakhal.

Without telling her in-laws about the dream, she came to visit her mother in Tollygunj, South Calcutta. Her mother knew about Sri Ramakrishna. Directed by her mother, she went to Saradananda at Udbodhan, and he sent her to Maharaj. The girl was with Maharaj for two hours and during that time he initiated her. He then asked Nirvanananda to feed the girl and her brother. The girl later became a nun and established a convent.[105]

As a Guru

The *Guru Gita* explains the word *guru*: *gu* means "darkness or ignorance"; *ru* means "destroyer." He or she who destroys or removes the ignorance of the disciple is a guru. Brahmananda was a real guru. He had the power to impart samadhi, or illumination, to anybody. Once Boshi Sen, a young devotee, said to Brahmananda, "Maharaj, you are miserly." "Why do you say so?" asked the swami. "Because you have the power to give the experience of God to others, but you are withholding it." Maharaj gravely said, "Who wants God?"

After becoming president of the Ramakrishna Order, Brahmananda began to initiate people, but was very selective. He strongly believed that the disciple and the guru must know and evaluate each other before initiation. Sometimes people had to wait many years before receiving initiation from him. There were three known reasons that prevented him from initiating indiscriminately. First, he followed the injunction of the scriptures, "Don't make too many disciples." Second, he remembered what the Master had said to Keshab Sen: "Why don't you study their nature? Is there any good in making anybody and everybody a disciple?" Third, many times after giving initiation he would become ill, as he had absorbed the disciples' sins.

However, Holy Mother asked Brahmananda to give initiation to more people, since she alone could not handle all the aspiring devotees. In 1916 Maharaj went to the Minerva Theatre to see a drama about Ramanuja, the exponent of qualified nondualistic Vedanta. The play portrayed how after Ramanuja's initiation, his guru told him that whoever repeated the mantram would be liberated, but were he to divulge it to anyone, he himself would go to hell. The largehearted Ramanuja immediately went to a crowded place and shouted: "I have just received a mantram from my teacher, and whoever repeats this will attain liberation. Here it is, take it!" This particular scene moved Maharaj and he shed tears. From then on he became more liberal in giving initiation.

Brahmananda's spiritual instructions are simple, direct, and practical. He taught mostly from his own experience rather than by quoting from the scriptures. Swami Vishuddhananda recalled: "On one occasion, in the house of Balaram Basu, Maharaj said: 'You practise meditation and japam; you progress a little, then comes a period of dryness. It seems that the doors are entirely closed. At that time it is necessary that you stick to your spiritual practices with infinite patience; by so doing you will find one day that all of a sudden the doors are opened. What a great joy it is then! In spiritual life many such thresholds have to be crossed.'

"Once Maharaj said to a devotee: 'When you meditate, you should imagine that God is standing before you like the mythical wish-fulfilling tree.' Another day he said to the same devotee: 'At the time of meditation you should imagine that you are in mid-ocean; on all sides there are mountain-high waves, and God is standing before you ready to help you.' In Madras, while I accompanied him on a walk, Maharaj said to me, 'Just do one thing: always try to remember God. I also do that.'"[106]

Girish Chandra Ghosh, a devotee of Sri Ramakrishna, told the following story about Brahmananda's extraordinary spiritual power:

Compared to myself, Rakhal is only a young boy. I know that the Master regarded him as his spiritual son, but that is not the only reason I respect him. Once I was suffering from asthma and various kinds of ailments. As a result, my body became very weak and I lost faith in Sri Ramakrishna. With a view to getting rid of that dry spell, I engaged pandits to read the Gita and the Chandi to me. But still I had no peace of mind. Some brother disciples came to see me, and I told them about the unhappy state of my mind, but they only kept silent. Then one day Rakhal came and asked me, "How are you?" I replied: "Brother, I am in hell. Can you tell me the way out?" Rakhal listened to me and then burst into laughter. "Why worry about it?" said he. "As the waves of the ocean rise high, then go down again, and again rise, so does the mind. Don't be upset. Your present mood is due to the fact that it will lead you to a higher realm of spirituality. The wave of the mind is gathering strength." As soon as Rakhal left my house, my doubt and dryness disappeared and I got back my faith and devotion.[107]

There is not much glory in making a good man better. Once Brahmananda said to a monk, "If you can't make a bad man good, why did you become a monk?" Maharaj was a friend and saviour of the fallen, the dejected, and the lowly. When Ramakrishna was alive, Girish had taken many actors and actresses from his theatre to the Master for blessings. Later they would visit Holy Mother and Brahmananda. (At that time actresses were not accepted by society because, for the most part, they were prostitutes.) Tara, one of Girish's actresses, described in her memoirs how Brahmananda's love and blessings changed her life:

Ever since I was a little girl I worked on the stage with Girish Chandra Ghosh and heard from him about Sri Ramakrishna. There was a photograph of Sri Ramakrishna in every theatre with which Girish Babu was connected, and the actors and actresses used to bow down to the Master's photograph before they appeared on the stage....

My first visit to Belur Math took place about six years ago [1916]. I was then depressed and restless. Life seemed unbearable to me. I began to seek out places of pilgrimage. In this unhappy state of mind I finally went to Belur Math. Binodini, the finest actress of Bengal at the time, was with me. When I was seven years old she introduced me to the theatre, and again it was she who introduced me to the monastery.

It was past noon when we came to the Math. Maharaj had finished his lunch and was about to go to his room to rest. At that moment we arrived and prostrated before him.

Maharaj said: "Hello, Binode! Hello, Tara! So you have come! You are too late. We have already finished our lunch. You should have let us know that you were coming."

We could see how worried he was about us. He immediately ordered fruit prasad, and arrangements were made to fry luchis for us. We went first to the shrine, then had our prasad, and afterwards were shown around the Math by a swami. Maharaj did not have his rest that day.

We were brought up to revere holy men. But along with respect and faith I felt much fear of them. I was impure — a fallen woman. And so when I touched the holy feet of Maharaj, I did it with great hesitancy, afraid to offend him. But his sweet words, his solicitude and love dispelled all my fear.

Maharaj asked me, "Why don't you come here often?" I replied, "I was afraid to come to the Math." Maharaj said with great earnestness: "Fear? You are coming to Sri Ramakrishna. What fear can there be? All of us are his children. Don't be afraid! Whenever you wish, come here. Daughter, the Lord does not care about externals. He sees our inmost heart. There should be no fear in approaching Him."

I could not hold back my tears. My lifelong sorrow melted as the tears fell from my eyes, and I realized: Here is my refuge. Here is someone to whom I am not a sinner, I am not an outcast.[108]

Once in Dhaka, Premananda said to Brahmananda, "Swamiji was a saviour of the lowly and redeemer of the sinners." Brahmananda immediately replied: "I am also a saviour of the lowly and a redeemer of the sinners." Tabu (Matiswar Sen), a young devotee, used to visit Maharaj every day at Balaram's house and would give personal service to him. Unfortunately, one day he committed an immoral act (probably adultery), and Maharaj heard about it. Tabu was ashamed to show his face. One day he secretly came to meet some of his friends, but he accidentally encountered Maharaj. Affectionately Maharaj asked Tabu, "Have you seen the big horns of a buffalo?" "Yes, Maharaj," replied Tabu. Then Maharaj remarked: "Look, if a mosquito sits on its horn, does the buffalo feel it or register any pain? Know us to be like that."[109]

Another time Brahmananda said: "Remove all fear and weakness from your mind. Never debase yourself by thinking about sin. Sin, however great it may seem in the eyes of man, is nothing in the eyes of God. One glance of His can uproot the sins of millions of births in a moment. In order to divert human beings from the path of sin, the scriptures mention heavy punishments for the sinner. Of course every action bears a result, and evil actions disturb one's peace of mind."[110]

In 1921 at Varanasi a young monk asked: "Maharaj, I am practising japam and meditation mechanically and am not acquiring any taste for them. What should I do?"

Maharaj replied: "Is it possible to get that taste in the beginning? You will have to struggle hard to attain it. Direct all your energy to that one pursuit. . . . Every night before you go to bed think for a while about how much time you have spent in doing good deeds, how much you have frittered away doing useless things, how much you have utilized in meditating, and how much you have wasted doing nothing at all.

"In the beginning it is good to make a routine and then follow it strictly. It does not matter whether your mind likes it or dislikes it. You must practise your japam and meditation as a daily routine. . . . You have received the precious mantram from your guru. Now dive deep into the ocean of Satchidananda. You have no self-reliance. Self-effort is indispensable in spiritual life. Do something for a period of at least four years. Then if you have not made any tangible progress come back and slap my face!"[111]

The effect of holy company is infallible; it may come immediately or after a period of time. Those who came in contact with Brahmananda experienced a definite change in their lives. Brahmananda reminded the devotees: "The holy company you keep, the spiritual talk you hear, all make an impression on your mind. In the course of time you will realize the effects of these things and the momentous changes that they will bring about in your life. A bumble-bee hiding in a fragrant flower offered in the worship touches the feet of the Lord. Similarly, by the grace and association of a holy man, one surpasses even the gods and attains liberation."[112]

A real guru sometimes teaches through silence. Once Swami Satprakashananda came from Dhaka to see Brahmananda at Udbodhan. He bowed down to Maharaj and sat at his feet. Dhirananda (Maharaj's attendant) introduced him to Maharaj, saying, "He has some questions." Maharaj looked at him graciously and said, "You have seen a holy man, have bowed down to him and touched his feet, what more questions can there be?" Satprakashananda wrote, "Evidently he meant that this was enough to solve my problems and remove all doubts and difficulties from within."[113]

Maharaj once told Swami Prabhavananda: "There are times when it becomes impossible for me to teach anyone. No matter where I look, I see only God wearing many masks. Who am I, the teacher? Who is to be taught? How can God teach God? But when my mind comes down again to a lower level, I see the ignorance in man and I try to remove it."[114]

Some Glimpses of Swami Brahmananda

Sri Ramakrishna once remarked about Brahmananda: "Rakhal is like the kind of mango that looks green even when ripe." He meant that within Rakhal was a great spiritual power that he kept hidden from the outside world. Behind Brahmananda's grave exterior, he was like a frolicsome boy. He would joke and have fun with the monks and devotees. M. once told Vishwananda, a disciple of Maharaj: "Observe how Maharaj acts and you will have some idea of what Sri Ramakrishna was like. When his mind came down to the finite plane, his sense of humour was very keen." "This was also true of Maharaj," wrote Prabhavananda. "One of his favourite jokes was to have some fruits or sweets placed beside a disciple who was meditating. When the disciple had finished his meditation he would find his favourite dishes laid out before him. Later Maharaj would ask, 'Well, did you get the fruits of your austerities?'"[115]

Ashokananda recalled:

Everything he [Maharaj] did used to touch people's hearts at the deepest level. Once a gentleman who came to visit him was asked to wait a few minutes, the swami would come. The few minutes ran into half an hour, and when Maharaj finally came, he said to the man in a rather embarrassed way: "You see, I was playing cards; I couldn't break away. Please don't mind." He said it with such simplicity that he stole the heart of that man.

His childlike moods were delightful. I remember seeing him once at a distance with a young brahmacharin attendant. He was dancing playfully about like a little boy and making gestures in imitation of a striking cobra. You would think a stalwart, middle-aged man would look very odd playing like that. But I can tell you, it was the most beautiful thing to see. Why? Because this childlikeness was natural with him.

He was always fond of children; he liked to play with them, and they responded to his affection. One day when he was visiting Balaram Basu's family he dressed himself in a bearskin that covered him from head to foot and, thus disguised, appeared before Balaram's grandchildren to scare them. They screamed with genuine alarm, but after the first cry one little boy said through his tears: "I know it's you, Maharaj. You can't frighten me! But why did you do it?" Then Swami Brahmananda laid aside the bearskin and took the little boy on his lap.[116]

Kiran (later, Swami Aseshananda), who was staying at Udbodhan, was sent to Brahmananda by Saradananda for his brahmacharya vows. When he approached Maharaj for his blessings, the swami was quiet for a while. Finally he said: "Yes I will, but there is one condition. You must pay me 108 rupees in advance as *guru-dakshina* [honorarium for the guru]. Otherwise I can't initiate you." Stunned, Kiran replied: "Maharaj, I have no money. It is impossible for me to pay such a large amount. If you don't bless me, I am lost." Then Maharaj gravely said: "I have a suggestion that will solve your problem. Swami Saradananda is very rich! He has all the money from the Udbodhan. You are his attendant. Go to Swami Saradananda and get him to pay that amount for you."

"While I was standing there, speechless," Aseshananda later wrote, "Maharaj called another candidate over to him and said: 'Govinda, you come from Midnapore. You will have to dance after the fashion that Orissa people are fond of, for me. If you do it well, I will give you brahmacharya.' Without hesitation, Govinda performed the dance with suitable gestures of hand to our great delight. Maharaj was pleased with his performance and laughed heartily.

"Not knowing what else to do, I returned to Udbodhan and narrated the whole story to Swami Saradananda with great seriousness. He nodded gravely: 'Very well, you may return to Belur Math and tell Maharaj that I am his and everything in Udbodhan belongs to him as well. What he asks for will be given.'

"Relieved, I returned immediately to Belur Math, prostrated before Maharaj, and repeated Swami Saradananda's message. But to my surprise and dismay, Maharaj shook his head. 'Empty words!' he shouted. 'How am I to know if he will do as he promises with nothing in writing? You are his secretary. Prepare something for him to sign. When I have his signature, then I will believe it.'

"Again I returned to Udbodhan, my mind in a turmoil. . . . Sadly I told Swami Saradananda this latest development. . . . The next day we both went to Belur Math and approached Maharaj. After a few moments in his presence, Swami Saradananda suggested it would be better if I waited outside. At length, Swami Saradananda came out of Maharaj's room and spoke to me, 'It has been arranged that you will have your brahmacharya vows with the others.'"[117]

Swami Satprakashananda wrote in his memoirs:

One day at the beginning of the winter season in 1917, in the drawing room of Balaram Mandir, Maharaj asked me to bring him pen, ink, and a piece of writing paper. When he began to dictate in English, I took down what he said. . . . The letter was addressed "To the Abbot, Belur Monastery." At the time, Swami Shivananda was in charge at the Belur Math, as respected Swami Premananda was lying ill in a small room of the Balaram Mandir.

The gist of the letter was: "The Christmas celebration will surely be observed at your Math. On that occasion we — a party of monks — are coming to the Math. Your hospitality is well known. Certainly at the conclusion of the ceremony, according to the usual custom in Christmas celebrations, there will be an arrangement for the taking of drinks. We are nonvegetarians and are fond of varied courses of meat dishes. In anticipation of a sumptuous feast, we extend to you our heartfelt thanks. May your function be crowned with success in all possible ways — that is our earnest wish."

When I had written the letter, I handed it to him for his signature. But instead of putting his own name, he signed "Premananda" and told me, "Go and read the letter to Swami Premananda." Hearing the contents of the letter and finding his signature forged, Swami Premananda simply smiled and said, "Maharaj has a childlike nature." One thing has to be especially noted here — both Swamis Premananda and Shivananda were vegetarians.

Later Maharaj asked me to go to Belur Math and deliver the letter to Swami Shivananda, but cautioned me not to mention that he had sent it. After reading through the letter, Swami Shivananda looked at me and said, laughing: "Maharaj has sent this. Is it not?" I kept silent. Swami Shivananda understood, "Silence is acquiescence."[118]

One morning when Maharaj was walking on the lawn of Belur Math, a young man humbly addressed him: "I want to meet Swami Brahmananda. I would like to be a monk." Pointing to Swami Shivananda, who was then taking tea, Maharaj said: "You see that heavy-set person at the table, he is Brahmananda." The young man bowed down to Shivananda and said: "I have come to you." Seeing that unknown person, Shivananda asked, "Could you tell me the name of the person whom you want?"

"Swami Brahmananda."

"He is walking there on the lawn," said Shivananda.

"Sir, he has told me that you are Swami Brahmananda."

"No, I am not. Swami Brahmananda is walking there."

When the young man returned to Maharaj and reported everything, Maharaj said: "No, I am not Brahmananda. You see, great souls sometimes delude people and do not like to be caught. Go again and hold his feet firmly."

The young man again went to Shivananda, got a nice scolding from him, and returned to Brahmananda again. Maharaj said to him: "I have already told you that great souls delude people, and even beat people. But you should not leave him. Hold his two feet firmly." The young man became confused, and tears came from his eyes. Then Maharaj compassionately said: "All right, you can stay in the monastery."[119]

"It has been said," wrote Christopher Isherwood, "that Brahmananda was so entirely fearless that others could not feel fear in his presence. Once, when he was walking with two devotees in the woods of Bhubaneswar, a leopard appeared and came straight towards them. He stood still and confronted it calmly until it turned tail. Again, while he was going along a narrow lane in Madras, attended by two monks, a maddened bull came charging to meet them. The young men tried to protect their guru, who was already an elderly man, by standing in front of him; but he pushed them behind him with extraordinary strength and fixed his eyes upon the bull. It stopped, shook its head from side to side, and then trotted quietly away."[120]

Like other mystics, Brahmananda loved to be in solitude; at times he had no inclination to receive visitors. In 1916 when Maharaj was staying in Bangalore, Josephine MacLeod (an American devotee of Swamiji) tried to have an interview with him. Whenever Maharaj would see her coming from a distance, he quickly disappeared into his room. He then sent Swami Nirmalananda to tell her, "Maharaj is not well today."

"After three days of trying, Miss MacLeod struck upon a plan. She put on a green dress which blended with the lush green scenery, and thus camouflaged, crept slowly along behind the trees and bushes towards the swami's veranda. Suddenly she lept in front of him and exclaimed, 'Naughty boy, now how will you escape?' The swami, embarrassed, stammered, 'Today I am quite all right.' Laughing, Joe said: 'What else can you say? You have to admit it. I caught you, didn't I?'"[121]

It is amazing and amusing to observe how a knower of God lives in this world and behaves with people. Sri Ramakrishna said about such an illumined soul: "He acts like a child or a madman or an inert thing or a ghoul. While in the mood of a child, he sometimes shows childlike guilelessness, sometimes the frivolity of adolescence, and sometimes, while instructing others, the strength of a young man."[122]

Swami Sambhavananda recalled some of Maharaj's practical jokes:

There was a "strong man" who advertised in the paper. The advertisement showed a picture of this man, fearfully muscular, with the caption: "If you want to become like me..." Maharaj would ask his cook or brahmachari attendant to take a stance like that of the muscleman and call out: "If you want to become like me..."

Maharaj liked to play word games with Swami Baradananda. In one kind of game the first person tries to think of a word for which the opponent cannot find a rhyming word. For example, Maharaj might call out "cricket." If Swami Baradananda could think of no rhyming word he would lose that round. But if he replied, for example, "wicket," then Maharaj lost, unless he in turn would think of a third rhyming word. One evening Maharaj kept Swami Baradananda playing the game for an hour and a half. Swami Baradananda was in the kitchen and Maharaj was on the veranda. I was the go-between, carrying the words back and forth. Swami Baradananda finally got bored with the game and sent me to Maharaj with the message, "It is late at night." Quickly Maharaj sent back his response, keeping intact his record for rarely being defeated, "Tell him 'good night.'"[123]

There are hundreds of stories about Brahmananda's playful jokes. Once a devotee complained: "Maharaj, people come to hear your spiritual talk, and you entertain them with funny jokes." Maharaj answered seriously: "Look, householders are burning with miseries almost all the time, so I give them some momentary joy. There are very few persons in this world who want spirituality. Those who are sincere, I talk to them about God; and I know they will listen to my spiritual instructions and follow them. That is why I don't talk about spiritual matters to all. It is not so easy to practise spiritual disciplines — it needs good *samskaras* [tendencies] from a previous life."[124]

Unconditional love and compassion are the two main traits in the mind of an illumined soul. Brahmananda's love was completely natural and he would shower it on each and all — even the animals, trees, and plants were not deprived of it. He fed the dog of the monastery; he regularly visited the cowshed and supervised the cows. He kept his eyes on the flower and vegetable gardens of each monastery. Under his supervision South Indian flower and fruit trees were planted in North Indian centres and vice versa. He had a wide range of knowledge in gardening matters. He taught the monks how to water and fertilize the trees and how to control pests. Maharaj had a keen interest in plant life. Boshi Sen reminisced:

Once he expressed a desire to see some of J. C. Bose's famous experiments showing the sensitivity of plants to external stimuli. When he visited the [Bose Research] Institute, he watched the experiments we demonstrated for him with great interest. That evening he was still preoccupied with what he had seen in the laboratory. "There was a time," he told me, "when Thakur [Sri Ramakrishna] could not step on the grass but would jump from one bare spot to another to avoid hurting the grass. At that time we simply didn't believe that grass could be sensitive. From what I saw today, I realized how infallibly true his perceptions were."[125]

Later in Bhubaneswar he said: "Trees have life. If you serve them you will feel it. Trees never become ungrateful. He who serves them will receive flowers and fruits in return." In Bangalore, when he saw the rose garden of Lalbagh, Maharaj remarked, "Look, the celestial maidens are laughing." And pointing at the green lawn, he said, "As if the Divine Mother has spread green velvet." With his mystical eyes he would see the worship of the Cosmic God all around him. One day a brahmacharin at Belur Math was picking flowers from the garden for worship of the Master. Observing him plucking the big ones in front, Maharaj told him sharply: "What are you doing? Do you want to make that tree devoid of flowers? You think Sri Ramakrishna is seated only in the shrine and does not come to the garden. Pick those flowers for worship that are hidden under the leaves and always leave some flowers in each tree."[126] Maharaj saw that those trees were also worshipping the Cosmic God with their blossoms.

Towards the End

Sri Ramakrishna had made a prediction about Brahmananda to his close disciples: "When Rakhal knows his real nature, his body will not last anymore." The Master never told Rakhal about this vision, and he forbade his disciples to reveal it as well. About 1910, when Saradananda was publishing *Sri Sri Ramakrishna Lilaprasanga* (*Sri Ramakrishna, The Great Master*) in Bengali, Premananda went to visit him in Udbodhan. Saradananda read to Premananda from his manuscript about the Master's vision concerning Maharaj. Startled, Premananda said: "Sharat, what have you done? Maharaj is still living. Don't you remember what the Master said: 'When Rakhal knows his real nature, his body will not last anymore.'"[127] Immediately Saradananda removed that part from his manuscript and also called back the proof from the press and destroyed it.

One night, while Maharaj was living at Balaram's, he suddenly had a vision of Sri Ramakrishna. The Master appeared before Maharaj and disappeared without saying anything. Brahmananda sat on his bed and tried to understand the meaning of that vision. He then said to his attendant:

"Suddenly my sleep broke, and I saw the Master standing near my bed. He didn't say a single word. I couldn't figure out the cause of his sudden appearance and disappearance." Pausing a little he gravely said: "I have no desire in my mind. I don't even have the desire to chant his name — only to surrender and surrender."[128]

On 1 January 1921, while Maharaj was in Balaram's house, Ramlal, Sri Ramakrishna's nephew, came from Dakshineswar to see him. Immediately Maharaj became jubilant. Ramlal was very dear to him and reminded him of his days in Dakshineswar. Maharaj would tease Ramlal since he was very simple and guileless. Maharaj said to him: "Brother, you will have to dress this evening as a gypsy woman and sing the songs that the Master used to sing." Ramlal shyly replied: "Maharaj, it is not the monastery. It is a devotee's house; moreover, people may misunderstand me, especially women." But when Maharaj insisted, Ramlal agreed.

In the evening Maharaj's attendants borrowed ladies' garments and jewelry from Balaram's family and decorated Ramlal. Maharaj sat on his chair in the big hall; the disciples and devotees sat around him, and the ladies watched from the veranda. As soon as Ramlal entered the hall the audience smiled. He began to sing and dance, twisting his waist and gesturing with his hands before Maharaj. This is part of that song:

> *Ekbar broje chalo brojeswar dinek duyer mato*
> O Lord of Vraja [Krishna is the Lord of Vraja; Vraja refers to his childhood haunt, Vrindaban], let us go to Vraja for a few days.
> *(O tor) mon mane to thakbi setha noile asbi druta*
> If you like that place, stay there or return quickly.
> *Age Rakhal chile akhan raja hoyecho*
> Previously you were a cowherd, and now you have become a king, etc.

When Ramlal repeated the last line, Maharaj's smiling face turned grave. That first line had reminded him of his real nature, and immediately the whole atmosphere changed.[129] He realized what Sri Ramakrishna had seen in a vision long ago about his true nature. He also understood why the Master had silently appeared before him. Maharaj began to prepare himself for his final journey, fulfilling his unfinished mission.

On 19 January 1921 Maharaj left for Varanasi with Saradananda to settle an organizational problem, and then returned to Belur Math on 16 March. Then he left for Bhubaneswar with Shivananda on 1 April and afterwards went to Madras on 25 April. This was his last visit to South India. He initiated many people, inspired the monks, and solidified the activities of the Order there. Then in November he returned to

Bhubaneswar and went to Belur Math on 12 January 1922. He attended
Sri Ramakrishna's birthday celebration at Belur Math on 28 February, and
initiated three monks into sannyasa. Then one day he said to a monk:
"Today I shall initiate. Call all who want initiation." His attendant
Baradananda remarked: "He never speaks that way. Is he going to give
up his body?" Another day he said to one of his brother disciples: "I am
now relinquishing my responsibilities. Please take care of everything."[130]

On 22 March Brahmananda left Belur Math for Balaram's house.
Before departing he carefully studied the plan for the Master's temple
that had been made under Swamiji's direction and reminded the monks
that it was their duty to complete the project. On 24 March Maharaj contracted cholera at Balaram's and all the best physicians of Calcutta
attended him. He recovered from cholera within a week, but his diabetes
(which started in 1918) now took a serious turn. All kinds of treatment
— allopathic, homeopathic, and ayurvedic — were administered to him,
but to no avail.

He told his attendants: "Take me to Bhubaneswar. If I drink that well-
water, I shall be all right. I don't care for this polluted air of Calcutta. The
air of Bhubaneswar is clean — take me there." One attendant said to him,
"Maharaj, you are too weak at present."

When Kaviraj Shyamadas Vachaspati, a noted ayurvedic physician,
came to see Brahmananda, he wore a religious mark, *vibhuti* (ashes) on
his forehead. Observing it Maharaj remarked, "Sir, the mark of Shiva,
which is on your forehead, signifies that Shiva alone is real, everything
else is unreal." M. visited Maharaj and asked him if he had any pain.
Maharaj calmly replied, "Pain takes to its wings when I think how joyfully I passed each day with the Master."[131]

On Saturday, 8 April, the burning sensation in his body and his thirst
for water increased. At noon, seeing the ladies of Balaram's family crying,
Maharaj said to them: "Why are you so afraid? I bless you all." In the
evening Dr. Durgapada Ghosh came and inquired about his discomfort.
Maharaj answered with a line from *Vivekachudamani*: "'To endure all kinds
of afflictions without caring to redress them' — this is my present condition" (verse 24). All of a sudden his face glowed and he became absorbed
in deep meditation.

At 9:00 p.m. he touched the hand of his attendant, who was seated
nearby, and blessed him saying: "Don't be afraid, my son. You have
served me well. Be absorbed in God. I bless you — you will attain the
knowledge of Brahman. I say you will attain the knowledge of Brahman."
After a while he blessed other monastic attendants: "Never forget God,

and you will realize the highest good. Do not grieve. I shall be with you always." Then he inquired about Saradananda, who would stay the whole day with Maharaj and at night would return to Udbodhan. A monk immediately ran to Udbodhan to bring Saradananda.

A deep silence pervaded the room. The monks and devotees encircling Maharaj were anxious. He opened his eyes again and began to speak: "I am floating on the banyan leaf of faith in the ocean of Brahman. Vivek — my Vivek — Vivekananda-dada [brother]! Baburam-da, Baburam-da [Premananda]! Jogen — Jogen [Yogananda]! I see the feet of Sri Rama-krishna!" Thus he was seeing and addressing the deceased disciples of the Master.

In the meantime Saradananda arrived. Seeing him Maharaj said: "Brother Sharat, you have come. My knowledge of Brahman and Vedanta are getting mixed up. You are a knower of Brahman, please tell me about it."

"My goodness!" replied Saradananda, "You are full of that knowledge. The Master gave you everything."

Then Maharaj said: "The Master is real and so is his *lila* [divine play]. I have almost reached Brahman — only a little veil is left."[132] He wanted to drink a little lemonade and then said with a smile: "Look, what is this? I am saying Brahman, Brahman, and again lemonade, lemonade!" He continued: "Father in Heaven — look, this is a wonderful idea. It is also a path of God."

When Saradananda suggested that he sleep after drinking a little lemonade, Maharaj said: "My mind is in the realm of Brahman. It does not come down. All right, pour lemonade into Brahman!" After sipping a little he said: "Aha-ha, Brahman — the Reality — the vast ocean! *Om Parabrahmane namah* [salutations to the supreme Brahman]; *Om Paramat-mane namah* [salutations to the supreme Atman]!" When Maharaj described his experience of Brahman, all felt peace and serenity in their hearts.

He slowly calmed down. His face was glowing with joy and he gazed without blinking as if he were meditating, or seeing something. After a while he exclaimed in his sweet voice:

Ah, here is the full moon — Ramakrishna! I want the Krishna of Rama-krishna. I am the cowherd boy of Vrindaban. Put anklets on my feet. I want to dance holding the hand of my Krishna. *Jhum — Jhum — Jhum!* [It refers to the sound of the anklets.] Krishna, Krishna, Krishna has come. Can't you see him? You don't have the eyes. Aha-ha, how beau-tiful! My Krishna — on the lotus — of Vrindaban! It is not sad-Krishna.

My play is over now. Look, the child Krishna is caressing me. He is calling me to come away with him. I am coming. . . . Om Vishnu, Om Vishnu, Om Vishnu![133]

Maharaj greeted Shivananda and Abhedananda who came to see him. Saradananda later said: "This time we shall not be able to keep Maharaj anymore. His vision of Krishna on the lotus, which the Master forbade us to disclose to him, has come out from his own lips."

The doctors expected him to fall into a coma, but he was fully conscious until the end. Boshi Sen wrote in his memoirs: "An hour before he gave up his body, he ceased speaking and seemed to have withdrawn to some distant realm beyond the reach of any of us. I was very gently stroking his palm and wondering whether he still remembered that old playful pressure of his thumb. At the same instant I felt it, light but unmistakable, Maharaj's last bequest to me."[134]

Ramakrishna's prophecy about his spiritual son Rakhal proved to be true. At 8:45 p.m. on Monday, 10 April 1922, Swami Brahmananda passed away. The next day his body was carried from Calcutta to Belur Math and cremated on the bank of the Ganges. Later a temple was built on that spot.

The monks and devotees lost their spiritual teacher, but they preserved some of his precious verbal testimonies in their records. Once in Belur Math a young monk asked Brahmananda: "Maharaj, does Sri Ramakrishna exist even now?" Maharaj answered: "I see you have lost your mind. Having renounced hearth and home, why are we leading such a life? He exists always. Pray to him day and night for his vision. He will dispel all your doubts and will make you understand his true nature."

"Do you see the Master nowadays?"

"Yes," replied Maharaj, "I see him whenever he shows himself out of his mercy. Anyone who has his grace can see him. But how many people have that love and longing to see him?"[135]

3

ॐ

Swami Shivananda

Some people think marriage is a form of bondage, and once married there is little chance of making any progress in spiritual life. But in the Hindu tradition, marriage is regarded as sacred. Most of the gods are married, and so are the *avatars*, or divine incarnations. If married life were unwholesome and unholy, the ancient sages would have said this. On the contrary, these saintly lawgivers sanctified all four stages of life and called them *ashramas*: *brahmacharya-ashrama*, or student life; *garhastha-ashrama*, or householder's life; *vanaprastha-ashrama*, or forest-dweller's life; and *sannyasa-ashrama*, or monastic life. They gave plenty of freedom for individuals to switch from one stage to another; for example, if a student feels intense renunciation he or she may embrace the monastic life without going through the intermediary stages.

Sri Ramakrishna married in order to demonstrate how to transcend ordinary marriage. He had no physical relationship with his wife, as he saw the Divine Mother in all women. Four of his monastic disciples were married, and Swami Shivananda was among them. Tarak (Shivananda's premonastic name) had to marry against his wishes. His father did not have enough money to pay the dowry for his youngest daughter Niroda's marriage, so he arranged for an exchange marriage. This meant that Tarak would have to marry his brother-in-law's sister, so that neither party would have to pay any dowry. Tarak's wife, Nityakali, was a highly evolved soul; unfortunately she died within a year of the marriage. As

9

Courtesy: Vedanta Society of Southern California

SWAMI SHIVANANDA

it is said: Birth, marriage, and death are not in the hands of human beings.

Though he was married Shivananda maintained unbroken chastity, and became known as *Mahapurush* (great soul) in the Ramakrishna Order. It is said that the Master touched a part of Tarak's body and said, "Dive deep in the ocean of Satchidananda," and this extinguished his lust forever.[1] Shivananda later related:

In those days when we used to visit the Master I frequently had to go home, because I was married. It was distasteful to me. Somehow or other I would spend the night at home repeating the name of the Lord. . . . I spoke about it to the Master and prayed that my worldly bondage be destroyed. After hearing my story, the Master asked me to perform a certain ritual and said in a tone of assurance: "Have no fear. I am here to protect you. Think of me and perform this ritual. Nothing adverse will happen to you. I am telling you that even if you sleep in the same room with your wife, you will be free from danger. You will see it will rather intensify your spirit of renunciation."

The Master prescribed the same ritual for Swami Brahmananda. I went through the ritual as instructed and didn't have any trouble. In the course of conversation I once mentioned this incident to Swamiji [Vivekananda]. He was very much surprised and remarked: "What do you say! It is the characteristic of a Mahapurush. You are certainly one." Since then he started calling me by this name, and others did the same.[2]

Taraknath Ghosal was born on Thursday, 16 November 1854, at Barasat, a small town east of Calcutta. His father, Ramkanai Ghosal, was a devout brahmin and a worshipper of the Divine Mother. In his house he established a Panchamundi (a tantric place of worship in which five skulls are placed under the ground), where he would practise tantric sadhana. His wife, Vamasundari, was a loving, spiritual woman. Ramkanai, a successful lawyer, was very generous to the poor and to holy people. He was the secretary of the local school and provided room and board to nearly thirty poor students in his house. His and Vamasundari's first child was a daughter named Chandi. The holy couple prayed to Lord Tarakeshwar Shiva for a son and performed austerities for a year. One night Vamasundari had a dream in which Lord Shiva appeared before her and said: "I am pleased with your devotion. I bless you. You will be the mother of a spiritual son."[3]

Because the child was born by the grace of Tarakeshwar Shiva, his parents named him Taraknath. An astrologer made a horoscope, which indicated that the child either would be a monk or a king. Later, when Tarak became a monk, he threw the horoscope into the Ganges, and thus renounced the memory of his past life. Tarak had two other younger sisters, Kshiroda and Niroda. Vamasundari died within three months of Niroda's birth. Tarak was then nine years old, and his young heart cried for his loving mother. However, his father married again. About the same time, his elder sister Chandi died, leaving two children. In addition, his second sister Kshiroda became a widow. These family misfortunes placed the seeds of renunciation in Tarak's young mind.

He began his education at the Barasat Missionary School and later went to high school. He was a good student, but did not care much for academic education. He was serious and deeply indrawn by nature, and he found delight in prayer and meditation. His headmaster remarked about him, "Tarak's character had such depth and purity that we were all charmed and impressed by it."[4]

When he was in the tenth grade, Tarak learned that his father's income had been reduced. In order to help the family financially, he left school and looked for a job. He worked for some years for the railways, first in Ghaziabad and then in Mughalsarai, in northern India. He later expressed the feelings he had during that time: "Since my boyhood I didn't care for family life, and I had a spiritual inclination in my heart. I shall never be bound to this world by getting married — this idea was deep in my mind. I had an innate desire to travel to various holy places. I used to work for the railways and call on God."[5]

While he was working in Mughalsarai, Tarak spent long hours practising meditation. He later recalled: "Then the idea of samadhi would agitate my mind. How to be absorbed in the bliss of samadhi forgetting the world — this keen desire occupied me most of the time. I was very fond of the meditation pose of Shiva and Buddha. I tried to attain samadhi month after month — I rarely slept at night. I had that one thought — how to attain samadhi."[6] One day while they were talking about samadhi, his roommate Prasanna mentioned the name of a person who had experienced genuine samadhi: Sri Ramakrishna of Dakshineswar.

At this time, as mentioned earlier, Tarak had to marry against his wishes. He took full responsibility for his young wife, Nityakali, and explained to her his hunger for God. Tarak also gave her spiritual advice and guided her in leading a spiritual life.

At the request of his friends, Tarak moved to Calcutta, where he was offered a position with the mercantile firm of Machinnon, Mackenzie, and Company. He stayed at a relative's house in Calcutta and during the weekends would visit his wife at Barasat. At that time the Brahmo Samaj Movement under the leadership of Keshab Chandra Sen was very popular in Calcutta. Keshab's soul-stirring sermons and rational approach to religion appealed to Tarak and he became a member of the Brahmo Samaj. But this movement did not quench his insatiable hunger for God; at night, he would cry and pray to God for samadhi.

First Meetings with Sri Ramakrishna

One Saturday in May or June of 1880 Tarak met Sri Ramakrishna at the Calcutta home of Ramchandra Datta. One of Ram's relatives, who was a devotee of the Master, worked with Tarak in the same office. He had shared with Tarak all he knew about the Master, and had told him that the Master would be at Ram's that night. Tarak had also read much about Ramakrishna in Keshab's paper, *Dharmatattwa*, so he wanted very much to see him. When Tarak arrived at Ram's house, he found Sri Ramakrishna in ecstasy. Oblivious of his surroundings, the Master asked, "Where am I?" Someone answered, "At Ram's house." "Which Ram?" "Doctor Ram." "O, yes!" Then he remained silent for a while.

Tarak later recalled this first meeting: "That evening I went to Ram Babu's house. I found the Master sitting in a room crowded with people. The Master was in an ecstatic mood. I saluted him and sat nearby. One can well imagine my surprise when I heard him talking eloquently on a subject which I had been so eager to know about — samadhi! I remember that he elaborated on nirvikalpa samadhi. He said that very few can attain it and that if one attained it, one's body dropped off in twenty-one days."[7]

Tarak did not get a chance to talk to the Master on this occasion, but a month later he went to see him. One Saturday evening after work he and a friend took a boat to Dakshineswar. In the dim light of an oil lamp he saw the Master seated cross-legged in his room, with three or four others on the floor in front of him. Ramakrishna asked affectionately, "Have you seen me before?" Tarak answered that he had recently seen him at Ram's house. Tarak bowed down to the Master, putting his head on the Master's lap, and the latter gently caressed his head. Tarak reminisced: "At once I felt a deep attachment for the Master. I felt as if I had known him a long time. My heart became filled with joy. I saw in him my tender, loving mother waiting for me. So with the confidence, faith, and certitude of a child, I surrendered myself to him, placing myself entirely under his care. I was certain that at last I had found him for whom I had been searching all these days. From then on I looked upon the Master as my mother."[8]

The vesper service in the different temples began and the sound of bells, drums, and symbols reverberated in the temple garden. Ramakrishna was in a divine mood. Shortly he asked Tarak, "Do you believe in God with form or without form?" "In God without form," replied Tarak. "You can't but admit the Divine Shakti [who manifests Herself in many forms] also," said the Master. He then accompanied Tarak to the Kali Temple, where the evening service was taking place. The Master prostrated before the image of the Mother. Tarak at first hesitated to follow his example, as he was a member of the Brahmo Samaj (which did not approve of image worship). But suddenly the thought flashed across his mind: "Why should I have such prejudices? Even if this image is only an image, God must still be present in it, since He is everywhere."[9] Tarak then prostrated before the image of the Mother.

After returning from the temple, the Master asked Tarak to stay overnight with him, but Tarak declined because he had already promised to stay with his friend who lived in Dakshineswar. The Master was pleased and remarked: "One should keep one's word. Speaking the truth is the austerity in this kaliyuga." After a pause the Master said, "All right, come tomorrow."

When Tarak returned the next afternoon, the Master received him cordially. He talked to him about spiritual life, served prasad that had come from the temple as supper, and arranged his bed in the southern veranda, which was adjacent to his room. That night there were no other visitors. Tarak recalled:

> Out of joy I did not sleep that night. At midnight I saw that the Master was in ecstasy and pacing naked in his room. He was also muttering something. Shortly he came to the veranda and asked me, "Hello, are you sleeping?" "No, sir," I replied. "Could you chant a little of Lord Rama's name?" After I chanted Rama's name for some time, he calmed down. Thus I passed that night with joyful intoxication. In the morning while I was taking leave bowing down to the Master, he said, "Come again — alone."[10]
>
> During my second or third visit I was serving him when he suddenly touched my chest while in an ecstatic mood. That touch made me lose outer consciousness and sent me into a deep meditative state. I do not know how long I remained in that state. As a result, everything became revealed to me. I realized that I was the Atman, eternal and free. I realized that the Master was the Lord born as man for the good of humanity, and that I was on earth to serve him. He gave me a similar blessing another day under the banyan tree in the Panchavati.[11]

Ramakrishna recognized Tarak as one of his inner circle. Later Tarak reminisced:

One day Sri Ramakrishna said: "Well, so many people come here. I seldom ask anyone about his home and family, or desire to know anything about these things. But when I first met you I felt that you belonged here, that I would like to know the particulars of your home, parents, and the like. Can you tell me why? Where is your home and what is your father's name?" In reply I told him I came from Barasat and my father's name was Ramkanai Ghosal.

Hearing this, the Master said: "Indeed! You are Ramkanai Ghosal's son! Now I understand why the Mother aroused this desire in me for information about your home. I know your father very well. He is the attorney for Rani Rasmani's estate. The Rani and her family always thought highly of your father, and whenever he would visit the garden at Dakshineswar, they would do everything to make him comfortable, carefully arranging his accommodation, meals, servants, and the like. He is certainly a highly developed *sadhaka* [spiritual aspirant].

"[In the early days — 1850s] whenever he came here, he would take his bath in the Ganges, put on a red silk garment, and enter the Mother's temple. He looked like a veritable Bhairava [celestial attendant of Shiva]. He was tall, stout, and fair-complexioned, and his chest was always red. He meditated for long periods in the Mother's temple. And he used to bring with him a musician who would sit behind him singing songs symbolically describing the nerve centres in the human body, as well as songs about Mother Kali. Your father would be absorbed in meditation, with tears streaming down his cheeks. When he left the temple after meditation his face would be flushed with spiritual emotion and nobody would dare approach him.

"At that time I was suffering from an unbearable burning sensation all over my body. When I met your father, I said: 'Well, you are a devotee of the Mother and so am I. I also practise meditation, but can you tell me why I feel a burning sensation all over my body? Look, the burning sensation is so intense that the hairs of my body have been singed. It is sometimes excruciating!' Your father recommended that I wear an amulet bearing the name of my Chosen Deity. Strange as it may seem, with the wearing of this amulet, the burning sensation at once diminished. Would you ask your father to visit me sometime?"

In those days I was living in Calcutta, going home only occasionally. My father was very pleased when I told him about Sri Ramakrishna, and he came one day to see the Master. On another occasion the Master said: "Your father's spiritual practices were attended with some desire for worldly objects. As a result of his spiritual practices, he amassed much wealth and also spent it nobly."[12]

On one occasion Tarak requested the Master to give him the experience of samadhi. The Master told him: "You will get it. Don't be impatient. The Divine Mother will bless you at the right time." Another day the Master took Tarak to the Panchavati and wrote a mantram on his tongue, which put him into deep meditation, and he lost consciousness of his body. Later the Master brought him back to normal consciousness by rubbing his chest with his fingers. This is a kind of tantric initiation in which a guru imparts spiritual power to his disciple. Swami Saradananda wrote in *Sri Ramakrishna, The Great Master* that the Master's touch roused an upsurge of longing for God in Tarak's mind — suddenly all the knots of his heart were loosened.

Tarak recalled his wonderful experiences during his early encounters with the Master:

> When I first started visiting the Master, I often felt inclined to cry. One night I was crying uncontrollably by the riverside near the bakul tree. The Master was in his room, and he inquired where I had gone. When I returned he asked me to sit down and said: "The Lord is greatly pleased if one cries to him. Tears of love wash away the mental impurities accumulated through the ages. It is very good to cry to God."
>
> Another day when I was meditating in the Panchavati grove, my concentration became very deep. The Master came towards me from the pine grove, and as soon as he looked at me, I burst into tears. The Master stood still. I felt something creeping up inside my chest, and I was overcome by a fit of shaking. The Master said that my crying was not insignificant. It was a type of ecstasy. I then followed him to his room where he gave me something to eat. The awakening of the kundalini [the spiritual energy] was an easy matter for him. He could do this even without a touch, but by a mere look.[13]

Days with Sri Ramakrishna

Sri Ramakrishna did not teach his disciples through books or sermons but through the example of his own life. At every moment, with every movement he demonstrated how to practise religion. Tarak was fortunate to live with and serve the Master at Dakshineswar and Cossipore. Like the other disciples, Tarak recalled his experiences and his observations of the Master. These reminiscences are important testimonies about the life of an avatar. That is why it is better to reproduce them rather than to paraphrase. Tarak recalled:

His hands were very tender. But why speak just of his hands! His entire body was so. For instance, a type of *luchi* [fried bread] with a hard crust once cut his finger.

At night the Master would eat perhaps one or at the most two small luchis with a little porridge. Because he could not digest whole milk, Holy Mother would add water and cook it with farina, making a pudding. He would take a little of that. In the cupboard there would be sweets made of fresh cheese. Whenever he was hungry he would eat one or two pieces or perhaps half of one piece, giving the rest to others who were there. His ways were like those of a child. It was as if he himself were a child.

Once the Master said, "In the future many white-complexioned devotees will come here." God is all-merciful. He is not limited by time, place, or person. Blessed we are! We had the opportunity to serve the Master, making betel-rolls and preparing tobacco for him. How fortunate we are! We served the Master and we received so much love and affection from him! His compassion and love for us were infinite.

In those days we used to sleep on the floor of his room. At bedtime the Master would tell us how to lie down. He would say that if we were to lie flat on our backs and visualize the Mother in our hearts while falling asleep, then we would have spiritual dreams. He asked us to think of spiritual things while going to sleep. During the summer we used to sleep on the veranda and were bothered by mosquitos.

The Master looked upon Swami Brahmananda as Gopala [the boy Krishna]. Occasionally he would send him to visit his relatives at home, but when Swami Brahmananda was not with him the Master had great difficulty taking care of himself. One night at 1:00 a.m. the Master came out to the veranda where I was sleeping and asked, "Could you chant the name of Gopala for me?" I chanted for an hour. Some nights when he did not have anybody around him, he would call the night guard to chant the name of Rama for him. What love the Master had for the name of God!

We saw how little the Master slept. Now and then he might get an hour or half an hour of sleep at the most. Most of the time he was absorbed in samadhi, and the remaining time he spent in spiritual moods. These moods became very pronounced at night. He would spend the whole night repeating the name of Mother or Hari. When we stayed with the Master at Dakshineswar we were filled with awe. He had no sleep at all. Whenever we awoke we would hear him talking with the Divine Mother in a state of spiritual inebriation. He would pace back and forth in the room, all the while muttering something inaudibly. Sometimes he would wake us in the middle of the night and say: "Hello, my dear boys! Have you come here to sleep? If you spend the whole night in sleep, when will you call on God?" As soon as we heard his voice, we would quickly sit up and start to meditate.

While coming down from nirvikalpa samadhi and still under its influence, Sri Ramakrishna would try to describe that state, but he was never successful. Eventually he would say: "I wish very much to tell you about it, but I cannot. Somebody shuts my mouth." Really, that state cannot be described. "Only he who has had the experience can understand it."

The Master would not readily allow me to render personal service to him. This often pained me very much. Then, from an incident that happened one day, I learned why he was so unwilling. Who, indeed, can understand his motives? On that day I stayed at Dakshineswar. Other devotees were there also. After spending a long time in his room talking about religious matters, he got up and proceeded towards the pine grove to answer the call of nature. Usually one of the devotees would follow him on such occasions with his water pot to pour water on his hands, as he could not touch anything metal. When he went to the pine grove that day, I carried the water pot and waited at the proper place for his return. On his way back, when he found me standing there with the water pot, he said: "Now, look here. Why did you do such a thing? Why did you come with the water pot? How can I accept water from your hand? Can I accept service from you? I honour your father as a guru." I was struck with wonder. Only then did I realize why he would not allow me to render service to him. The Master had infinite moods. How could we fathom them? We can understand only that which he allows us to understand.

The Master's words were so impressive and instructive that I felt tempted to take notes. One day at Dakshineswar I was listening to him and looking intently at his face. He was explaining many beautiful things. Noticing my keen interest, the Master suddenly said: "Look here! Why are you listening so attentively?" I was taken by surprise. He then added: "You don't have to do that. Your life is different." I felt as if the Master had divined my intention to keep notes and did not approve of it, and that was why he had spoken in that way. From that time on I gave up the idea of taking notes of his conversations, and whatever notes I already had I threw into the Ganges.[14]

Sometime in the middle of 1883, Tarak's wife, Nityakali, fell ill and died. Tarak performed the customary ritual for his departed wife, then resigned from his job and decided to lead the life of a monk. When Tarak told his father of his determination, tears began to trickle down his father's cheeks. Ramkanai asked Tarak to salute their family deity in the shrine and then blessed him, placing his hand on his son's head: "May you realize God! I myself tried to renounce the world and realize Him, but I failed. Therefore I bless you that you may attain God!" When Tarak told the Master about this, he was quite pleased to hear it and said, "It is good that this has happened!"

Tarak was first amongst the disciples to renounce worldly attachments. He lived mostly with Ramakrishna during the last three years of the Master's life. Sometimes he would live at Dakshineswar, and sometimes the Master would arrange for him to stay at Ram's house in Calcutta. Tarak cooked his own food and practised meditation in some solitary parks (Beadon Square and Hedua in Central Calcutta) or in the cremation ground (Keoratala ghat at South Calcutta). He also lived for some time at Kankurgachi Yogodyana (Ram's retreat in East Calcutta).

"I was so happy there all by myself," recalled Tarak. "For lunch I used to procure from the neighbourhood a little rice and one or two simple dishes. For supper I prepared over the open *dhuni* fire [a fire used by wandering monks] a few pieces of unleavened bread and roasted an eggplant or a couple of green bananas. And I ate only these, washing them down with drinks of water. Day and night I used to be absorbed in my spiritual practice beside the dhuni fire, and right there snatched my sleep and rest. The fire would sometimes attract snakes, but for some reason or other they avoided me."[15]

From time to time Tarak would visit the Master at Dakshineswar. On 8 June 1883 when Tarak arrived, Ramakrishna was in the Mother's temple. He was pleased to see Tarak and showed his affection by touching his chin. In addition to guiding the disciple, the real guru also protects him from evil influence. The Master knew that Tarak was very close to Nityagopal, who often experienced ecstasy during *kirtan* (devotional singing) and at the same time mixed freely with women. One day the Master privately told Tarak: "Look, don't be too close to Nityagopal. His path is different; he does not belong to this place." Tarak immediately stopped associating with him. Another time a Vaishnava monk, whose order accepted Krishna but not Radha, came to Dakshineswar. He was a good sadhu but very dry. Seeing that Tarak was visiting him often, the Master cautioned him: "His philosophy may be good, but it does not appeal to me. I love God as well as His *lila* [divine play]."[16] Tarak at once withdrew himself from that monk.

In February 1884 Sri Ramakrishna had an accident. One day Tarak came and inquired about the Master's health. In reply he smilingly said: "One night in the garden as I was looking at the moon, my feet became entangled in the wire fence, and I fell down fracturing my left wrist. The after-effect is still there, and they have bandaged me tightly. They refuse to take the bandage off. I can hardly call on my Divine Mother with comfort. Tell me, does one enjoy calling on the Mother in such a predicament? Sometimes I feel, what nonsense is this! Let me out of this body, snapping all ties! Then again I think, no, let the pleasant play of the Mother continue. There is fun in this too."[17]

After hearing this Tarak said, "Sir, you can certainly heal yourself if you so wish." The Master replied, "What! I can cure myself by a mere wish?" The Master paused awhile, then continued: "No, aches and pains of sickness are preferable. Sickness scares away worldly people who visit here with ulterior motives, and I am left alone." The next moment he talked to the Divine Mother, "Mother, you have made a wonderful device." He then began to sing a devotional song and went into samadhi. After a while the Master regained his normal consciousness and talked to the Mother again like a petulant child: "Mother, you were never born. So how can you understand the pain of embodiment?"[18]

In 1884 Tarak went on a short pilgrimage to Vrindaban, the childhood playground of Krishna. On 7 September 1884 he visited the Master, carrying with him some sacred dust and prasad that he had brought from the holy city.

By the middle of 1885 Sri Ramakrishna had developed throat cancer. On 20 September 1885 he was in his room at Dakshineswar when a physician from Calcutta came to examine him. The Master asked the devotees, "Well, people ask why, if I am such a holy person, I should be ill?" Tarak replied, "Bhagavan Das Babaji, too, was ill and bedridden a long time." The Master objected: "But look at Dr. Madhu. At the age of sixty he carries food to the house of his mistress; and he has no illness." A devotee said: "Sir, your illness is for the sake of others. You take upon yourself the sins of those who come to you." When a devotee asked the Master to tell the Mother to cure his disease, the Master replied, "I cannot ask God to cure my disease."[19]

On 26 September 1885 Sri Ramakrishna was taken to Calcutta for treatment. He stayed at a house in Shyampukur till 11 December and then was moved to the Cossipore garden house. Tarak joined the other brother disciples there to serve the Master. He later reminisced:

Sri Ramakrishna was seriously ill and was staying at the Cossipore garden house while under treatment. Most of us were living there with him to nurse him. Taking turns, we waited on him day and night. Surendra, a well-to-do householder devotee, arranged for all the necessities.

A cook had been engaged, but when he fell ill, we had to take turns cooking. Our meals were very plain, usually consisting of rice or unleavened bread, lentils, vegetables, soup, or similar dishes. We were in such a mental state that we didn't pay any attention to food at all. We ate whatever we could get. In the first place, the Master was terribly sick, and secondly we were all deeply absorbed in severe spiritual disciplines.

One night it was my turn to cook for the household. As I was adding the final spices to the vegetables, the smell spread through the house and reached the Master upstairs. He asked the nearby attendant: "What is cooking? Excellent! The aroma of the spices is everywhere! Who is the cook?" When he learned that I was the cook, he said, "Go and bring me a little of it," and he tasted a tiny bit of the preparation. Because of the cancer in his throat he could hardly swallow anything. With great difficulty he would eat a little farina cooked in milk, but most of the time he was not able to swallow even that.[20]

Sometime in the middle of January 1886, the elder Gopal wanted to distribute twelve pieces of ochre cloth and rosaries to some monks. The Master pointed to his young disciples and said: "You won't find better monks than these. Give your cloths and rosaries to them." Instead, Gopal offered them to the Master and he himself distributed them among his young disciples. Tarak received an ochre cloth, the garb of a monk, directly from the Master.

Apart from serving the Master, the disciples began to practise various kinds of sadhanas (spiritual disciplines) under his guidance. Sometimes Tarak would spend the whole night in meditation in the Panchavati grove at Dakshineswar and then would return to Cossipore in the morning. In the early part of 1886, Narendra, Tarak, and some other disciples began to study the life and teachings of Buddha and were captivated by his renunciation, forbearance, love, and compassion. One night in the early part of April, without informing anyone, Narendra, Tarak, and Kali left for Bodh Gaya, where Buddha attained nirvana.

After arriving at Bodh Gaya, they spent days in meditation under the famous bodhi tree where Buddha attained enlightenment. On the third night Narendra felt an intense longing for Buddha. He was overwhelmed by emotion and burst into tears, tenderly embracing Tarak, who was meditating next to him. It is said that Narendra saw Buddha enter into Tarak's body.

While they were in Gaya, the other disciples were worried about them, but the Master kept quiet. When the three returned to Cossipore, the Master, moving his index finger in a circle and waving his thumb, said, "No spirituality anywhere!" Then pointing to himself he said: "This time all is here. You may roam about wherever you please, but you will not find anything [spirituality] anywhere. Here all the doors are open."[21]

Days of Austerity and Pilgrimages

Sri Ramakrishna passed away on 16 August 1886, and his young disciples were grief stricken. At first, they thought that the Master was in samadhi, so they chanted the Lord's name for the whole night. The next day Dr. Mahendralal Sarkar came to examine Sri Ramakrishna, and declared that he was dead. In the afternoon the disciples carried the body to the Cossipore cremation ground, and after the cremation brought the Master's relics back to the Cossipore garden house. They decided to place the relics on the altar and continue worshipping Sri Ramakrishna. Holy Mother gave her approval of the plan. Tarak, Latu, and the elder Gopal stayed at the Cossipore garden house as they had no other place to go; the other disciples came during the day to talk about the Master.

Because the young disciples had to vacate the garden house by the end of August and had no means to rent a place for worship, Ramchandra Datta suggested that they install the Master's relics at his retreat in Kankurgachi. The helpless disciples had to yield to this, but they secretly took away the major portion of the relics in an urn, which they kept at the house of Balaram Basu. One day about this time Sri Ramakrishna appeared before Surendra Nath Mittra, a rich and generous devotee, and asked him to provide a place for the disciples to live and worship. Surendra joyfully told Narendra about his vision, suggested that he create a centre, and agreed to pay all necessary expenses. Very soon the disciples established the Ramakrishna monastery at Baranagore, which was between Dakshineswar and Calcutta. Tarak and the elder Gopal were the first to live full time in the monastery.

During December 1886, Tarak and some other disciples went to Antpur, the country home of Baburam. Inspired by Narendra, they took informal vows of monasticism during a night-long vigil around a sacred fire. Later they discovered that their vigil had taken place on Christmas Eve. A month later they took formal monastic vows, performing the traditional *viraja homa* (fire) ceremony in Baranagore. Narendra gave the name "Swami Shivananda" to Tarak, knowing his Shiva-like nature.

Sri Ramakrishna bound his disciples with a cord of love. Shivananda later remarked: "We had so much deep love for each other that we were ready to sacrifice our lives for each other." From the very inception of the Ramakrishna Math, the disciples tried to create a spiritual atmosphere through their austerities, japam, meditation, devotional singing, and scriptural study. Shivananda lived at Baranagore for about two and a half years, developing his own spiritual life and helping to consolidate the new monastery. He nursed monks who fell ill, and did household work, such as cutting vegetables for cooking, carrying water from the Ganges, sweeping and dusting the rooms, and even cleaning the toilets.

In the beginning of 1889 Shivananda felt an urge to lead the free, detached life of an itinerant monk. He left for Kedarnath and Badrinarayan, two famous Himalayan holy places. It was a long and arduous journey. During those days pilgrims had to walk hundreds of miles on foot. On the way he visited several holy places in northern India. He was overjoyed to see the perpetual snow range of the Kedar peak (23,000 feet); the shrine itself was at 12,000 feet above sea level. After staying there a few days, he left for Badrinarayan. Shivananda wrote to Brahmananda: "It has been four days since I arrived at Badrinarayan — a beautiful place situated right on the bank of the river Alakananda, surrounded by snow peaks. Here the Alakananda flows through snow. In certain spots the river is so wholly covered with snow that the water is not visible at all. While coming to Badrinarayan I had to walk over snow part of the way, sometimes as long a distance as half a mile. And yet this place does not seem to be so dreadfully cold as Kedarnath."[22] Shivananda stayed there for a few days and attended the worship service of Lord Vishnu.

"Of the mountains I am the Himalayas," said Krishna in the Gita. On the top of this vast, panoramic mountain range, in the depth of its caves, and on the banks of its rivers, the rishis of ancient India lived and discovered the truths of Vedanta. Monks therefore find great joy in visiting the holy places of the Himalayas. After visiting Badrinath, Shivananda went to Almora, in another part of the Himalayas. On the way to Srinagar, he met Gangadhar, (later, Swami Akhandananda) who had come down from Tibet. On seeing each other after such a long time, the brother disciples embraced and wept for joy. Shivananda asked Gangadhar to return to Baranagore Math, but he declined and returned to Tibet.

During his stay in Almora, Shivananda met some sincere seekers of truth and talked to them about spiritual life. Lala Badrishah Thulghoria, a rich local merchant, became an ardent devotee and welcomed Shivananda to his home. He was very happy to serve Shivananda, but he was unhappy that he did not have a son to maintain his family line. One day Lalaji humbly asked Shivananda to bless him so that he would have a son. Pleased with his devotion and service, the swami prayed to the Lord. By God's grace, in due course a male child was born. Badrishah named him "Siddhadas" — a servant of the saint. Later, Badrishah's Almora home became the residence for visiting Ramakrishna monks, including Swami Vivekananda.

Towards the end of 1889 Shivananda returned to the Baranagore Monastery and stayed there two years. In October 1891 he again left on a pilgrimage and visited Prayag, at the confluence of the Ganges and Jamuna rivers; Omkarnath Shiva, on the bank of the river Narmada; Panchavati, on the bank of the river Godavari in Central India; Bombay, and Poona. He practised austerities in all these places. In the early part of 1892 the Baranagore Monastery was moved to Alambazar. During the time of Sri Ramakrishna's birth anniversary, Shivananda returned to Alambazar and received the sad news that his father had passed away. Towards the end of March 1892, Shivananada and Ramakrishnananda went to visit Kamarpukur, the birthplace of Sri Ramakrishna, and Jayrambati, the birthplace of Holy Mother. The swamis met some people who had personally known Ramakrishna, and they heard many stories about him. Hearing the sweet reminiscences of Sri Ramakrishna's boyhood days and seeing the places associated with him made him alive in their minds. Out of devotion they rolled on the dusty courtyard of Ramakrishna's parental home. Both swamis also stayed with Holy Mother at Jayrambati and cooked for her one day. Unfortunately, Shivananda contracted malarial fever; as soon as he partially recovered both the swamis returned to Alambazar.

At the end of 1892 Shivananda again left the monastery and visited Kurukshetra, near Delhi, where Krishna delivered the message of the Gita to Arjuna. He then visited Jwalamukhi, Saroe, and other holy places in the northwestern part of India. He later recalled: "In those days I felt great restlessness and longing to realize God. While walking I would practise the recollectedness of God and pray to Him earnestly. I disliked the company of people and avoided roads ordinarily frequented by travellers. Towards evening I found shelter somewhere and spent the night absorbed in my own thoughts. If a person lives this way, having no possessions, he develops full resignation to God. He becomes established in the idea that God alone is his protector in prosperity as well as in adversity."[23] The Himalayas had a special attraction for Shivananda. In the middle of 1893 he returned to Almora and stayed several months. While there he met E. T. Sturdy, a young English theosophist, who was leading the life of a Hindu monk and practising raja yoga. He was greatly attracted to Shivananda's personality and later heard about Vivekananda's success in America. Upon his return to England he invited Vivekananda there and made all the arrangements for him to preach Vedanta.

On 2 October 1893 Shivananda left Almora for Rameswaram, which is in South India on the shore of the Indian Ocean. On his way he visited Agra, Vrindaban, Jaipur, Abu, and Bombay, finally arriving in Madras. In the meantime the news of Vivekananda's success at the Parliament of Religions in Chicago had reached India. Swamiji's followers were delighted to have Shivananda in Madras and showed him Swamiji's inspiring letters written to them from America. From Madras Shivananda visited the most important holy places in South India: Kanchi, Chidambaram, Bangalore, Madurai, Rameswaram, and Sri Rangam. After attending the Ramakrishna birth anniversary festival with the Madras devotees, Shivananda returned to the Alambazar Monastery. Swamiji wrote from America praising Shivananda's work in Madras.

Sometimes traditional monks observe a vow called *chaturmasya*: during the rainy season, they stay in one place for four months and practise intense sadhana. Shivananda decided to go to Uttar Kashi, a remote part of the Himalayas, to observe *chaturmasya*. Uttar Kashi is a lovely place on the bank of the Ganges where many hermits live, but in those days few people went to Uttar Kashi because of its inaccessibility. Shivananda found a small cottage on the Ganges and begged for food once a day. Most of the time he remained absorbed in japam and meditation.

It is always good to hear directly from a seeker of God about the struggle and hardship of his spiritual journey. Later Shivananda recalled:

This body did a lot of mountain climbing, visited many places, and practised much austerity. There were times when I did not have more than one piece of cloth with me. Many nights I slept under a tree. I had a feeling of great dispassion and never thought about physical comfort, finding joy in austerity alone. I wandered a great deal, carrying no possessions, but was never in any trouble. The Master stayed by me and protected me from all dangers and difficulties, and I never went hungry.[24]

In the early part of 1895 he went to visit Khanderao Baba at Brahmavarta (or Vithur), near Kanpur. That monk had practised austerity for thirty-eight years at one spot on the bank of the Ganges. Speaking with him, Shivananda realized that he was a knower of Brahman. The swami also met great souls like Trailanga Swami, Swami Bhaskarananda, Chameli Puri, and Magniram Brahmachari in Varanasi. "I was on my way to Vithur to see a holy man," recalled Shivananda later. "At noon I was resting under a tree. Till then I had no food, and there was no village nearby either. In the meantime a big ripe bel fruit fell from a bel tree and cracked open near me. I looked around and found no one. Then I picked up that bel fruit and ate it, which was my meal for the day."[25]

Swami Vividishananda wrote in *A Man of God*:

> For over a decade the swami travelled in different parts of India, some-times in the Himalayas, sometimes on the plains, and sometimes in deserts or forests, and always he lived a life worthy of a man of God.... Mahapurush had experienced samadhi three times as a young man during the lifetime of the Master. The austerities and meditations of his itinerant period established him in that blessed state, enriching his life and giving him the necessary depth and strength to shoulder the responsibilities of the great task ahead of him. On the anvil of those years and the ones in which he began doing works of service were forged the character and personality later adored as Mahapurush, the head of the Order, who constantly lived in God and overflowed with love and blessings to all.[26]

With Swami Vivekananda

In February 1896 Shivananda returned to Alambazar Monastery. In the meantime Vivekananda had written from America, exhorting his brother disciples to stay together, inspiring them to spread the message of Ramakrishna all over India and to perform philanthropic activities among the impoverished masses in India. Shivananda responded accordingly. Once he explained the philosophy behind his work: "The Master does his own work. You and I are only instruments. Fix your mind on him — he will make you do what is to be done. Work done out of ego accomplishes nothing. What good does it do to the world? He who has performed much austerity, God makes him an instrument and works through him. He only works in the right spirit. Work that lacks the spirit is a waste of energy."[27]

In January 1897 Vivekananda arrived in South India; Shivananda went to Madurai to receive him. Shivananda later wrote about this trip:

To receive Swamiji some monks of our Order, including myself, were at the Madurai station. Alighting from the royal carriage lent by the Raja of Ramnad, Swamiji greeted us by embracing us warmly.... All of us were lodged at the state guest house. In the afternoon the leading citizens of the city gathered at the Madurai College and presented Swamiji with an address of welcome, to which he gave a reply. That was the first time I heard him speak publicly and I was certainly struck by his gift of speech. Hitherto we had lived and travelled together, but never had I seen him manifest such dynamic eloquence. He had a wonderful command of the English language, and when he spoke he gave one the impression that he was speaking in his own mother tongue.... In Madras Swamiji stayed for about five or six [actually nine] days and gave as many public lectures. Then, accompanied by a few disciples from Madras, Swamiji boarded a steamer bound for Calcutta. His Western disciples and we his brothers were also in the party. On board the steamer Swamiji had animated religious discussions with some Christian missionary passengers, who learned a great deal from him. The deck of the steamer became, as it were, an auditorium, attracting the entire passenger community.... Finally, Swamiji arrived in Calcutta, where he was given a tremendous public ovation. In Calcutta he gave two or three public lectures. After a long time we were again together at the Math with Swamiji. Words fail to describe the joy we had in his company in those days.[28]

After arriving in Calcutta, Vivekananda was exhausted and became ill from overwork. He left for Darjeeling, a Himalayan resort, for a rest. Shivananda again went to Almora for sadhana, and he was advised by Swamiji to start a centre there (which came into existence in 1916). From Darjeeling, Vivekananda returned to Calcutta and established the Ramakrishna Mission on 1 May 1897, and on 6 May he left for Almora to rest, accompanied by Shivananda. One day in Almora, Swamiji taught Shivananda how to read other people's minds. Then at the request of Swamiji, Shivananda went to Sri Lanka to preach Vedanta, and stayed there for about seven to eight months. He conducted classes on the Bhagavad Gita and raja yoga, which were attended by many educated Hindus and Europeans. Shivananda trained Mrs. Picket, a capable and serious Western student, and then sent her to teach Vedanta in Australia and New Zealand. During his stay in Sri Lanka, the swami visited various famous temples, including the Tooth Temple, where Buddha's teeth are enshrined. In February 1898 Shivananda returned to Calcutta. Later, a monk asked Shivananda whether he liked Sri Lanka or not. Shivananda replied: "I am happy everywhere. I never feel discontented in any place. If one can live in God, one can be happy anywhere."[29]

On 13 February 1898 the Ramakrishna Math was moved from Alambazar to Nilambar Babu's garden house in Belur. The disciples purchased a piece of land at Belur on the bank of the Ganges on which to build the future headquarters of the Ramakrishna Order. On 27 February Swamiji carried the relics of Sri Ramakrishna to the new site and worshipped the Master. Shivananda and other disciples and devotees of the Master were present on that auspicious occasion. Finally, on 2 January 1899, the monastery was moved from the rented house to Belur Math. Swamiji announced that all monks should join in daily scripture class in the monastery. Shivananda took an active part in these classes and would answer the questions of the monks. The following are some questions and answers from these sessions.

14 March 1898

Question: Why does truth suffer from persecution so often at the hands of opponents?

Shivananda: Truth can never suffer, for it is transcendental, not physical. We see the body suffer, not the real person. Persecution, instead of hurting the truth, always brings out its pristine glory all the more.

15 April 1898

Question: How can it be proved that this world is unreal and Brahman alone is real?

Shivananda: If we observe closely the changeableness of things outside as well as within, we can be convinced of the unreality of the entire world. Every change perceived by the senses as happening outside has its counterpart within us. In proportion as the outer world is changeable, so is the inner world. By the reality of a thing is meant truly its existence at all times, eternally. Unfortunately, in this world of phenomena there is nothing that remains unchanged even for a second. Now with the idea of finding the ultimate truth, if we push our analysis further, we shall see that at the back of all changeable phenomena is the immutable Brahman. First, gross objects, then subtle and subtler objects — whatever we analyze in the outer world — we fail to find any permanence in them. Baffled, we finally turn within ourselves. This self-withdrawal or abstraction is the only way to the knowledge of Brahman or the Supreme Reality.[30]

Vivekananda made a rule in the monastery that all monks would have to get up at 4:00 a.m., and then after washing, meditate in the shrine; otherwise they would have to beg for alms that day. One day Shivananda did not hear the bell and, as a result, missed the morning meditation. Swamiji noticed this, and later said to him: "Tarak-da, we made the rule that those who did not come to the shrine would have to live on alms that day." Shivananda replied, "Of course, I am leaving the monastery right now for alms, and whatever I shall get that I will eat." After Shivananda left to beg for alms, the food was offered to the Master in the shrine as usual and the lunch bell was rung, but Swamiji did not go to the dining hall. Instead, he waited on the western veranda. When Shivananda returned, Swamiji joyfully asked: "Tarak-da, what did you bring? I have not eaten any food obtained by begging for a long time. [It is customary in India for monks to live on food obtained by begging from door to door as bees collect honey from flower to flower.] Let us share the food and eat together." The two brother disciples happily enjoyed that pure food.[31]

Sri Ramakrishna trained his disciples to be organized in their actions, and he insisted that they keep each thing in its proper place. Accordingly, Swami Vivekananda made a rule in Belur Math that anyone who smoked a hubble-bubble should put it back in a particular place after smoking and not just leave it here or there. One day a hubble-bubble was found on the front veranda of the monastery. Swamiji became angry when he saw it. When he inquired who had left it there, someone told him that it was Swami Shivananda. Immediately Swamiji called him in a loud voice, "Tarak-da!" Hearing Swamiji's thundering voice, all were scared — even Swami Shivananda. No sooner had the swami arrived than Swamiji threw the hubble-bubble on the floor and broke it into pieces. Then he said to Swami Shivananda, "Now you collect money, buy a new hubble-bubble, and keep it in its proper place."[32]

Vivekananda went to the West again in June 1899 and returned to India in December 1900. After arriving at Belur Math, Swamiji heard the sad news of Mr. Sevier's death in Mayavati, Himalayas. Accompanied by Shivananda and Sadananda, Swamiji left for Mayavati to console Mrs. Sevier. It was a bad winter with a great deal of snow and rain, and Mayavati was sixty-five miles away from the Kathgodam Railroad Station. They reached Mayavati on 3 January. After staying there for a couple of weeks, they returned to the plains. At Pilibhit, Swamiji asked Shivananda to spread the Master's message in that area and to raise some money for the monastery. During this time Shivananda travelled to various places in Uttar Pradesh and towards the end of 1901, he went to Kankhal to help Swami Kalyanananda. In February 1902 when Swamiji went to Varanasi to improve his health, Shivananda stayed with him, and then returned to Belur Math.

Later Shivananda reminisced with the monks: "A couple of weeks before Swamiji's passing away, we were standing beneath the mango tree in the courtyard. Swamiji came down from the shrine. Having a prophetic vision, he said, 'Look, the spiritual current of this place will continue for seven to eight hundred years.' We are witnessing a little, you will see more in the future. Believe in my words. The Master and the Divine Mother are guiding this Order."[33]

While Swamiji was in Varanasi, the Maharaja of Bhinga invited Swamiji to his palace and offered him 500 rupees to start a centre in Varanasi. Swamiji didn't accept the money at that time, but he later asked Shivananda to go to Varanasi and start a centre there. Shivananda left Belur Math in the fourth week of June; Swamiji died on 4 July 1902.

At Varanasi

From 1902 to 1909 Shivananda concentrated on establishing a permanent centre in Varanasi, with the maharaja's help. He named the centre *Sri Ramakrishna Advaita Ashrama*, with the idea that one can be established in Advaita (nonduality) by moulding oneself on the life and teachings of Sri Ramakrishna. He decided to preach Vedanta by practising it in daily life rather than by lecturing about it from the pulpit. He practised severe austerities in Varanasi and set an example for others. When he experienced no communion with God he would lament. One day he said to Swami Nirbharananda: "Chandra, this day is gone in vain. Neither have I seen the Master today nor have I shed tears for him."[34]

A monk wrote in his diary about Shivananda's daily life:

His bed was a blanket and a tiger skin. Even in cold winter he would sleep on the floor of the hall, first spreading straw and the tiger skin over it, and then covering himself with a blanket. Sometimes at 2:00 a.m. he would sit for meditation near the fireplace. In the morning he would open the shrine, and then he would chant for a long time from the Gita, Chandi, and Upanishads. Afterwards, supervising the household work, he would take his bath and perform ritualistic worship. Whatever food was available, he would offer to the Master, and he lived on that prasad with others. There was no arrangement for special food. He seldom would go out of the ashrama. He was absorbed in his own mood, and sometimes he would sing in a low voice. He would meditate in the afternoon also. After vespers he would remain absorbed in meditation till the food was offered to the Master. He was so grave that we were afraid to talk to him.[35]

When the maharaja's donation (500 rupees) was exhausted, the ashrama faced a terrible financial crisis. Unfortunately, when Shivananda collected one hundred rupees to pay the house rent, that money was stolen by an employee. Shivananda was then reproached by the landlord for not paying the rent. Later, it was arranged for the rent to be paid in installments. Gradually, when the people came to know about the swami and his financial difficulties, they began to help him. Shivananda opened a free nursery school in the ashrama for poor children, and he also distributed Vivekananda's lectures printed in Hindi. Many scholars of Varanasi visited the swami and learned from his personal spiritual experience.

In spite of his stern exterior, he would serve the monks like a loving mother. Once he said to a senior monk: "You know, the boys living here are like young cobras [which means they possess the same deadly poison as a mature cobra]. You should not belittle them. Those who have taken refuge in the Master are great."[36]

In Belur Math and Other Places

In 1909 Shivananda handed over the management of the Varanasi Advaita Ashrama to his assistant monk and returned to Belur Math. Although Swami Brahmananda was the president, Swami Premananda managed the monastery. When Premananda visited Calcutta or other places, Shivananda would perform ritualistic worship and manage the monastery in his place. Regarding his worship at Belur he once said: "Our worship in the shrine was more an act of love and devotion, having none of the external grandeur of ritualistic observances as is prevalent now. While doing the worship we would think of the Master as visibly present, just as we had seen him at Dakshineswar in his room seated on his cot; we would worship him, following the simplest procedure. Although we observed some of the orthodox rules and forms, we never stressed them. Sri Ramakrishna is the lord of our hearts, and what he wants from us is genuine devotion and self-dedication."[37]

Swami Atulananda, a Western swami then known as Gurudas, recalled:

I met the swami [Shivananda] at the western tea-veranda of the main monastery building at Belur on the very day when I arrived from America. He was seated on a bench smoking his hubble-bubble. There were several other monks besides a number of devotees present at the place. After introduction and exchange of greetings, the swami was kind enough to make me sit beside him on the bench — a signal honour. Referring to the peculiar sound produced by the hubble-bubble, he joked and wanted me to believe that there was a live frog inside that made the noise. Then showing me how to smoke the hubble-bubble, he was gracious enough to let me use his own pipe. At the time I took the incident rather casually, because in our society smoking is an everyday affair, involving no etiquette or ceremony. Besides, I thought of the incident as a plain joke, never realizing that it could have any other meaning. But later as I became better acquainted with Hindu society and its customs, it dawned upon me that by letting me use his own pipe Mahapurush paved the way for my easy acceptance as a member, in addition to making a gesture of endearment.[38]

Shortly before Sri Ramakrishna's birth anniversary in 1910, Lady Minto, the wife of the then viceroy and governor-general of India, paid a visit to Belur Math. Shivananda received her cordially and showed her around the monastery. Lady Minto was under the impression that it was Swami Vivekananda who had founded the Ramakrishna Order. But Shivananda told her: "Neither Vivekananda nor the disciples founded the Order. It was Sri Ramakrishna himself who initiated the Order during his last illness at Cossipore. At that time the Master took Swamiji aside and taught him how to organize and conduct the work, telling him the secrets of the monastic organization to be."[39] Lady Minto was surprised to hear this.

In the same year Shivananda, Turiyananda, Premananda, and Brahmachari Gurudas went to Amarnath, the famous ice cave in Kashmir. It was a difficult pilgrimage. After spending three months in Kashmir and visiting various places, Shivananda returned to Varanasi, where he contracted blood dysentery. When he returned to Belur Math he was again attacked by dysentery. He was then sent to Calcutta for treatment, where he recuperated after a prolonged illness. Later he adopted a very strict diet, which he followed all through his life. Day after day he ate plain rice with bland soup without complaint. He truly followed that famous saying of the Bhagavata, "He who has controlled the tongue has controlled everything." Saradananda humourously named that tasteless, odorless soup, "Mahapurush's soup."

After Sri Ramakrishna's birth anniversary in 1912, Shivananda, Brahmananda, and Turiyananda went to Kankhal (Hardwar) and stayed seven months. The monastic community was inspired by the disciples who told them stories of their guru, Sri Ramakrishna. This oral tradition of spirituality is vital to the growth of the younger generation in the Order, and is generally lacking in organized religion. Moreover, religious festivals, devotional singing, and spiritual discourses remove the monotony of life.

Brahmananda arranged for the celebration of Durga Puja in the ashrama and invited many monks from outside the Ramakrishna Order.

When not travelling, Shivananda would answer letters from the devotees. On 15 July 1912 he wrote:

Continue your japam and meditation as usual. It will not do any harm to you. First place a picture of Sri Ramakrishna in front of you, then close your eyes and imagine that form in your heart. Pray to him with earnest love and meditate on his divine qualities in the following way: He is Satchidananda (Existence-Knowledge-Bliss Absolute). Now he has been born as a human being to clear the path of liberation for humankind, as he did in previous ages. In this age he himself has taken the form of Ramakrishna and awakened faith and devotion in many — he is doing the same at present and will do so in the future. He is our father, mother, friend, guru — our all in all. Thus surrender yourself to him.[40]

On 16 June 1913 Shivananda went to Almora at the invitation of Paltu Kar, a householder devotee of the Master. He lived there for a year and a half, talking to the devotees about spiritual life and practising sadhana. During this time he wrote some wonderful letters that indicated his mental condition. Here are some excerpts:

17 September 1913: You have asked me: "What do I desire — the Lord or liberation?" My answer: "The Lord." You also desire the Lord; if you find Him, liberation will be assured like the fruit in the palm.[41]

30 October 1914: There is not any particular special method to call on God — only try to love Him. If you ask, "How shall I love Him?" The answer is this: "When you cannot stay without calling on Him, without thinking of Him, then only you know that He is loving you." If He does not love, none can love Him. He is our all-in-all — in life as well as in death.[42]

On 6 November 1914 Shivananda returned to Varanasi and met Brahmananda, Premananda, and Turiyananda. When the disciples came together, they talked about the Master and their experiences. This would uplift the spirits of the young monks and devotees. One day a devotee lamented to Shivananda about his sinful life. The swami replied: "Haven't you heard Sri Ramakrishna's words on this subject? He used to say: 'Sins are like a mountain of cotton. Even as a tiny spark of fire reduces to ashes mountain-high cotton, so does a little of divine grace [reduce to nothing] heaps of sins.' Don't be afraid. Call upon the Lord and repeat his sacred and potent name; nothing else will be needed."[43]

In November 1914 Shivananda returned to Belur Math. After Ramakrishna's birth anniversary in the spring of 1915, the swami went to Ranchi to attend the Ramakrishna festival. A devotee reminisced:

The swami was here only for three or four days, and yet during that short time he gave us such heavenly joy!... As he was recounting some intimate incidents from the lives of Sri Ramakrishna and Holy Mother, a devotee said in a note of sadness: "Maharaj, we merely hear about the Master; we do not have the good fortune of seeing him with our eyes." Quickly the swami rejoined: "Why! He who hath seen the son, hath seen the Father. I and my Father are one." Startled by his statement we stood there looking at him with admiration. His solemn words are still echoing in our ears.[44]

After returning to Belur Math from Ranchi, Shivananda again left for Almora on 8 April 1915. Shivananda accompanied Turiyananda who was then suffering from diabetes. It was thought that the Himalayan climate would be beneficial for his health. Shivananda's loving care and arrangement of proper diet considerably improved Turiyananda's health. This time Shivananda concentrated on building a permanent ashrama in Almora as he had been asked to do by Swamiji. A piece of land was purchased and construction was started with the help of local devotees. To collect more funds and building materials he came down to Varanasi on 5 November 1915 and finally returned to Belur Math on 5 March 1916 via Prayag.

In 1916 and 1917 Premananda was busy travelling and preaching in East Bengal, and from time to time he became ill. During his absence Shivananda managed the Belur Monastery. When the ailing Premananda died in 1918, Shivananda lamented: "I felt in my heart an emptiness that cannot be described in words. Many times I was tempted to go back to the Himalayas and remain there absorbed in a transcendental spiritual state — in samadhi beyond all relative categories — having nothing to do with the world anymore."[45] But this wish of Shivananda's was never fulfilled because he had to take complete responsibility for the management of the monastery.

The disciples of Sri Ramakrishna were genuine role models. They trained monks by setting the routine for meditation, scriptural study, and karma yoga. As soon as the shrine door was open in the morning, Shivananda would go in to meditate and would remain there till 7:00 a.m. After returning to his room, he would greet the monks and inspire them with spiritual conversation. He would also inquire about their health and welfare. Shivananda kept a vigilant eye on the Master's worship service and food offering, the flower and vegetable gardens, the dairy, and the welfare of the neighbours. Sometimes he would visit the Belur Math headquarters and give advice to the trustees.

Since the earliest days, Belur Math has conducted a free clinic and dispensary for the benefit of poor neighbours as well as monastics. The monk in charge of the clinic recalled:

It was the rainy season. All around there was sickness, especially malarial fever. The number of outside patients visiting the clinic was growing fast. To make the situation worse the compounder [pharmacist] assisting me fell ill. I found it very difficult to manage the work alone. One day Mahapurush dropped in at the clinic and after hearing the report of the work said: "I see that you are having a hard time doing the work by yourself. Shall I help you a little?" In reply I said: "Why, Maharaj? No. That is not necessary. Please bless me that I may manage it myself." There was no end to his worries when anyone happened to be sick at the Math. He would insist on having reports twice or thrice a day, eager to know how the patients were doing. Ah! How concerned he was for us! How deep was his love for us![46]

Shivananda's lifestyle was very simple. He regularly wrote letters to the monks and devotees himself. In the afternoons he would meet with devotees and answer their spiritual questions or talk about his days with the Master and Swamiji. He would attend the vesper service and afterwards meditate in the shrine. He would partake of the Master's prasad and plain food along with other monks. His clothing was also very simple. Until 1922 he had two pieces of cloth, a short-sleeved shirt, a chadar, and one pair of slippers. He had another set of clothing and shoes that he used while visiting Calcutta and other places.

In July 1920 Holy Mother passed away in Calcutta, and her body was cremated in Belur Math. Shivananda suppressed his own grief, and consoled the devotees. On 12 August 1920 he wrote in a letter:

He who feels more keenly the loss of the Mother will certainly see her more within, thereby enjoying genuine peace. She was not an ordinary woman or a seeker on the path — not even one of those who attained the Goal. She was verily a manifestation of the Divine Mother — the Primal Energy, ever perfect. She is indeed the Mother of the universe, the same as the dormant spiritual power, the indwelling spirit in every living being. Blessed is the devotee who received initiation from her and had a taste of her utterly selfless love. The devotee who even once felt the touch of her loving hands in blessing is bound to be spiritually awakened, if he is not already awakened. This is my sincere conviction.[47]

On 6 February 1921 Mahatma Gandhi and his wife, Motilal Nehru, Mohammed Ali, and other national leaders visited Belur Math during the birthday celebration of Swami Vivekananda. Shivananda received them cordially and took them to the shrine and the room where Vivekananda had lived and passed away. Shivananda thought very highly of Gandhi because of his sincerity of purpose, sacrifice, and love for the masses of India. Gandhi showed keen interest in the activities of the monastery and touched some of the relics of Sri Ramakrishna with devotion. Seeing a huge crowd in the monastery courtyard, Gandhi gave a short talk:

> Please do not think for a moment that I have come here with the idea of preaching my doctrine of noncooperation and the spinning wheel. I am here to offer my humble homage and salutations to the sacred memory of Swami Vivekananda on his birthday. I have studied Swamiji's writings well. As a result, my love for India has grown. To the youth of the country I have this appeal: Please do not leave empty-handed the monastery where Swamiji lived, moved, and died without accepting some of his great ideas.[48]

On 1 April 1921 Shivananda left for South India with Brahmananda, who had been invited to open the Students' Home in Madras. On the way they stopped at Bhubaneswar and Waltair and arrived in Madras on 25 April. On 14 June they went to Bangalore, where they stayed nearly four months. On 11 September Shivananda wrote to a monk: "I went to Mysore for a few days. There I visited the vast shrine of Mother Chamundi on the top of a hill, and recited the Chandi [the glory of the Divine Mother]. From there I visited the temple of Narayana in Melkot [thirty-two miles from Mysore], where Ramanuja began to preach his philosophy of qualified nondualism. It is one of the main holy places of the Vaishnavas."[49] About the Goddess Chamundi he said later: "Ah! The Mother is vibrantly living there. Through her grace I had a wonderful *darshan* [vision]!"[50]

From Bangalore, Shivananda and Brahmananda returned to Madras. They attended Durga Puja and Kali Puja in Madras, then left for Bhubaneswar on 19 November, and finally returned to Belur Math on 12 January 1922. On 10 November 1921 Swami Abhedananda had returned permanently to Belur Math from America. Shivananda and Brahmananda were happy to see Abhedananda after fifteen years. In the meantime, the devotees of East Bengal invited Shivananda to visit Dhaka. On 13 February 1922 Shivananda left for Dhaka with Abhedananda and some other monks.

Although Shivananda was not a public speaker, his inspiring heart-to-heart talks roused spiritual hunger in the devotees' minds. Some wanted initiation from him, but he declined. Shivananda was not interested in becoming a guru. One morning he said to a monk: "Last night I saw Holy Mother in a dream. She told me, 'My son, if you do not give initiation who else will?' You see, I have now received the order from the Mother."[51] However, Shivananda wrote to Brahmananda for advice. Brahmananda joyfully replied: "Do initiate people by all means, without any hesitation. Whoever will receive initiation from you will certainly be blessed."[52] One day in Dhaka, Shivananda said in the course of conversation: "Once in Dakshineswar the Master said to Swamiji, Maharaj, and myself, 'You will have to initiate many people in the future.' Can the Master's words be otherwise? He said that so many years ago, and now it has come true."[53] In both Dhaka and Mymensingh Shivananda initiated many devotees.

One day in Dhaka a devotee approached Shivananda: "We are poor. Will you be kind enough to visit our home in spite of that?" "You are right," said the swami, "we don't go to the house of a poor person." The devotee left depressed. The next day Shivananda and his attendant walked two miles to that devotee's home. Overwhelmed with joy the man exclaimed: "What great fortune! Maharaj, welcome to our poor home." Shivananda said with a smile: "We do not go to the house of a poor person. We visit the devotee's house that is God's dwelling place — and that is the house of the richest person."[54]

Towards the end of March 1922 Brahmananda contracted cholera. Then his diabetes, which had started in 1918, took a serious turn. As soon as Shivananda heard this news, he rushed to Calcutta. Brahmananda was very happy to see him. Shivananda told him: "Maharaj, without you how will we live? Please use your willpower so that you can be cured." The best doctors in Calcutta attended him, but Brahmananda's condition steadily deteriorated. Shivananda began to pray to the Master for Brahmananda's recovery. Three days before Brahmananda passed away, Sri Ramakrishna appeared before Shivananda while he was praying. But as soon as Shivananda asked the Master to cure Brahmananda, he turned his face and disappeared. This happened three times that night. At last Shivananda understood that the Master would no longer keep his spiritual son in this world. Brahmananda died on 10 April 1922.

As President of the Ramakrishna Order

In 1901 Vivekananda had made Shivananda one of the trustees of Ramakrishna Math and Mission, and in 1910 he had become the vice-president. After Brahmananda passed away in 1922, Shivananda was elected president of the Ramakrishna Order. As president he acted as an instrument in the Master's hands. One day he remarked: "The Master is an expert player. He can win the game with a valueless cowrie [shell coin in ancient India]. What do I have? Neither have I learning nor intellect, neither am I a speaker nor am I good-looking; still the Master is using me as an instrument for doing his work."[55] Shivananda's humility was phenomenal. Moreover, his allegiance, love for, and faith in the Master were exceptional.

Most of the time Shivananda lived in Belur Math, but from time to time he visited other centres of the Order and inspired the monks and devotees. In January 1923 he went to Varanasi to dedicate a building in the Ramakrishna Advaita Ashrama, which was constructed in the memory of Swami Adbhutananda, who had died in 1920. Shivananda then visited Allahabad and stayed a few days with Swami Vijnanananda, a brother disciple. The two brother disciples exchanged notes and indulged in reminiscences of their early days with the Master in Dakshineswar. One day both swamis went by boat to visit the confluence of the Ganges and the Jamuna.

Shivananda then went to the Ramakrishna Mission centre at Kankhal at the invitation of Swami Kalyanananda. A couple of days after his arrival it snowed on the peaks of the Himalayan range. Shivananda was very happy to see the panoramic view of the snow-clad mountains. He remarked: "For years I haven't seen snow. So Shiva, the Lord of the mountains, has been gracious to reveal himself in his white form today! Ah, how magnificent it is! Without snow the Himalayas do not look right."[56] One day he took his bath in the holy water of the Brahmakunda and chanted, glorifying God. Later he recalled: "At the time when we were in this region practising austerity — that was long ago — the whole area was like a forest and very solitary. One could scarcely see a human being anywhere in those days. Now the place has grown into something like a town. It doesn't have the seclusion of the olden times."

Shivananda returned to Belur Math on Sri Ramakrishna's birthday. On that auspicious day he initiated some monastics into sannyasa and brahmacharya. The public festival of the Master, which was usually attended by thousands, was held on the following Sunday. The previous night there was torrential rain, and water had even entered the kitchen. The senior monks were very apprehensive about the weather, and they asked Shivananda's advice. Without saying a word, Shivananda left for the shrine with his rosary. After a while he came out with a radiant face, reciting the following verse from the Bhagavata: "Thou hast saved us ever from poisonous water, wild animals and demons, from rain, storm, lightning and fire, from our enemies and fears, O Lord!" Then, with great assurance, he said: "Go on making preparations for the celebration as usual. Through His grace everything will be all right."[57] Strangely enough, the clouds cleared and the sun shone forth; the festival went off well.

During Shivananda's presidency, the activities of the Ramakrishna Math and Mission expanded considerably. Several new centres were opened in India, Singapore, Europe, North America, and South America. He inspired the monks to carry out philanthropic activities and at the same time advised them to harmonize the four yogas in their lives so that they could realize the Atman. One day he said to a monk: "Please practise japam and meditation regularly, because that is the source of power. Do not curtail time from meditation." Another day a monk suggested that the monks should place more emphasis on meditation than activity. Shivananda gravely answered: "The importance of meditation was in the past, is in the present, and will be in the future also. You are talking about work? Without practising japam and meditation, one cannot work according to the ideal of Sri Ramakrishna and Vivekananda. One should work and worship simultaneously."[58]

After dedicating the Vivekananda Temple on 28 January 1924 and the Brahmananda Temple on 7 February 1924 in Belur Math, Shivananda left for South India on 7 April with Swamis Sharvananda and Bodhananda. On their way to Madras they stopped in Bhubaneswar and Waltair. One day Shivananda and his party were invited for lunch by a devotee. While leaving the swami noticed some poor people in the alley fighting for the leftover food. Unable to bear it, he asked his host to feed them. Shivananda reminded him of Swamiji's message: "Make the poor of humanity your God. The service of these living gods is the religion of this age."

In Madras Shivananda contracted malaria and suffered for more than a week. When his fever subsided, the doctors advised him to go to a cool resort in the hills. Arrangements were made for Shivananda and his attendants to go to Springfield near Kunoor in the Nilgiri Hills, 6,000 feet above sea level. Many maharajas, wealthy people, and Europeans had bungalows there. Although he went to Springfield to recover his health, he attracted and initiated many people of Ootacamund, Malabar, and Madras. He wanted to open a centre in the Nilgiri Hills, where the monks could practise sadhana.

The scripture says the wishes of the knower of Brahman are always fulfilled. Shivananda wrote in a letter: "Mysterious is the power of the Master! A low caste washerman has donated two acres of land. He had a dream: His chosen deity, Mother Sitala, said to him, 'Very soon some people will come to you for a piece of land to establish a monastery. Be sure to give them what they want.' Having this dream for three consecutive nights, he thought, 'Nobody is coming to me for land.' One day while searching for the land, the local devotees met the washerman and told him what they were looking for. Immediately he said, 'For all these days I have been searching for you. Please come along and take two acres of land from my twenty-two acres.' Forthwith, he executed a registered deed of transfer for it."[59] Detailed plans were then made so that an ashrama could be established quickly.

On 23 July 1924 Shivananda left Kunoor for Bangalore. On the way he visited the Nattarampalli Ashrama for six days. He stayed in Bangalore for four and a half months and initiated many people. On 11 December he returned to Madras; the next day, he opened Ramakrishna Mission's newly constructed high school building. On 7 January 1925 Shivananda left Madras for Bombay. On the way he stopped for a few days at Cuddapah, a small town where some Hindu and Muslim devotees had established the "Ramakrishna Samaj." The devotees gave a reception for Shivananda and afterwards Sharvananda gave a lecture. Shivananda opened the new library hall and the community hall of the Samaj.

About this visit Shivananda said later:

A Muslim whom I met in Cuddapah is so highly esteemed that he received the title of Khan Bahadur from the British Government. He belongs to the Sufi sect of Islam, but is very devoted to the Master. In Cuddapah there is a little ashrama dedicated to Sri Ramakrishna. The Khan Bahadur, the local collector who is also a Muslim, and several others were responsible for founding the ashrama. We stayed there for a few days. Almost every morning and evening I found the Khan Bahadur seated in a corner of the shrine room in deep humility, intently looking at the portrait of the Master on the altar. He is convinced that the Prophet Muhammad was born as Sri Ramakrishna for the good of the world.[60]

On 12 January Shivananda and his party arrived in Bombay. The Ramakrishna Ashrama was then in a rented house at Khar, in the western part of Bombay. Inspired by Shivananda, the local devotees purchased two plots of land in Khar, and on 6 February the swami laid the foundation stone of the new ashrama. He remarked: "In times to come, the Lord's work here will have splendid success. He is managing his work; we are simply instruments." While in Bombay Shivananda met many people every day and also initiated some devotees. After attending the celebration of Vivekananda's birth, the swami left Bombay for Belur Math. On the way he stopped at Nagpur and stayed for a week. There was no ashrama at Nagpur, but some devotees who were interested in the teachings of Ramakrishna and Vivekananda had bought a piece of land on which to build a centre. Shivananda laid the foundation stone on the newly purchased land, and also initiated some devotees.

After nearly a year's travel in South India and Bombay, Shivananda returned to Belur Math on 19 February 1925. During this period he tried to consolidate the activities of the Order and establish new centres. His deeply spiritual life and captivating personality created enthusiasm in the minds of the people wherever he went. His visits and talks were also responsible for many new monastic recruits to the Order.

All four yogas — karma, jnana, bhakti, and raja — are harmoniously practised in the Ramakrishna Order. Shivananda always encouraged the monks to devote more time to meditation, but at the same time to serve suffering humanity. He reminded the monks: "It is true that work brings attachment; but this Order of the Master, Holy Mother, and Swamiji is different. This Order does not stand exclusively for spiritual practices — the practice of renunciation and austerity only. This Order has a mission that will reestablish the religion of the age. Here one must perform action along with contemplation. Those who will work at our [the disciples of the Master] direction will never get attached. The Master himself will be responsible for them."[61]

According to Vedanta philosophy the real nature of human beings is the Atman, which is actionless; It cannot be attained through action. Some people think that if we do not perform actions we will be established in the Atman, but this notion is wrong. The Vedantic tradition states that unselfish action purifies the mind, then spiritual practices make the mind one-pointed, which eventually leads to the experience of the Atman. Shivananda wrote to a monk:

> May the Lord give you indomitable enthusiasm and courage! Know for certain that the ashrama is bound to flourish. Don't worry on that score. Never forget what Swamiji said regarding work. Whatever you do in connection with the monastery or in the way of service to the country is not inferior to spiritual practice. All that you do is His work — even japam and meditation. Never doubt this. Even as repeating His name and thinking about Him is spiritual practice, so is the service of humanity when done selflessly. You are wholly mistaken, in fact, irrational, if you think that you have wasted your life in doing service. Spiritual practice is not of one kind only; it is various. It is renunciation of the ego or the self.[62]

In January 1926 Shivananda visited the Ramakrishna Mission Vidya-pith, at Deoghar, which is in the state of Bihar. Deoghar is a holy place, famed for its temple dedicated to Lord Shiva (Baidyanath). On 28 January Shivananda opened the new school building at Vidyapith and installed the picture of Sri Ramakrishna. He remarked: "Eventually this school will grow immensely. I see clearly that many wonderful things will happen here." One day he went to visit Lord Shiva in the temple, where he had a spiritual experience.

During his brief stay in Deoghar, Shivananda caught a chill that developed into a bad cold accompanied by asthmatic spells. One night the swami could not sleep. The next morning, in spite of his sickness, he cheerfully greeted everyone as usual. He told them his experience:

> I suffered a great deal last night. I felt almost suffocated. The passages of my nose became stopped up because of my cold, and the asthma was very much worse. I did not feel at ease whether sitting, reclining, or lying down.... Gradually I felt as if all my senses would stop and life would leave the body. Being at a loss what to do, I started meditating. It being the meditation of an old man [which came from his lifelong practice], my mind soon became absorbed within. I noticed then that there was no pain or suffering and the mind became quiet and placid. The storm and stress of the outer world could not reach there. After remaining in that state awhile my mind came down to the external world.[63]

Curious, a monk asked: "What is that, Maharaj?" The swami replied: "That is the Atman." Shivananda's experience substantiates this verse of the Katha Upanishad: "The Purusha, not larger than a thumb, the inner Self, always dwells in the hearts of men. Let a man separate him from his body with steadiness, as one separates the tender stalk from a blade of grass. Let him know that Self as the Bright, as the Immortal" (2.3.17).

On his way back to Belur from Deoghar, Shivananda stopped at Jam-tara in Bihar, where there is a retreat centre of the Ramakrishna Order. He installed a picture of the Master in a newly built shrine, and stayed for a few days. One evening while he was meditating in his room, he suddenly exclaimed three times: "Great good has happened in this wilderness." Another day Shivananda arranged a feast for the poor tribal people and was delighted as he saw them enjoying their meal. He remarked: "Ah! They are the veritable manifestations of the Lord." In the middle of February 1926 the swami and his party returned to Belur Math.

The first convention of the Ramakrishna Math and Mission, a momentous event for the Ramakrishna Order, took place on 1 April 1926 in Belur

Math. Monks and devotees arrived from various centres in India as well as abroad. Four direct disciples of Sri Ramakrishna attended the convention. Swami Saradananda was the committee chairman and Swami Shivananda was its president. Here are excerpts from Shivananda's speech:

Children of Sri Ramakrishna, please allow me to express my sincere felicitations at your congregating together in this convention of the Ramakrishna Math and Mission held for the first time in the annals of the Ramakrishna Order. This convention, I am confident, will afford you a unique opportunity of comparing notes with one another regarding the various works carried on by the different centres that you have met here to represent and also of hearing from the few surviving disciples of Bhagavan Sri Ramakrishna about the ideas and ideals of religion as expressed in and through the life of our Master, which will undoubtedly go a great way towards increasing the necessary solidarity of this organization....

From my little experience I tell you, children of Sri Ramakrishna, that our organization lasts as long as the spirit of God pervades its atmosphere. Love, catholicity, purity, and selflessness are the cornerstones of our organization. No man-made laws can save it from ruin when selfishness eats into its vitals. If you all try to become perfect — keeping intact your allegiance to this Math, which gives you every kind of facility for reaching that perfection — you will add a leaf to the life of the organization. Swamiji shed his blood for the Math. His spirit is still hovering over us. This Math is the visible body of Sri Ramakrishna. All those that have gone before us are still with us in spirit to help us in all possible ways. We must unfurl all sails so that we may take advantage of the divine wind that is ever blowing to take us to the destined goal....

I have fullest confidence in you all who have been earnestly endeavouring to realize this lofty ideal in life. You do not hesitate to brush aside any personal considerations however strong, for the realization of this ideal — and I clearly find Sri Ramakrishna, our Light and Guide, working from behind you and through you. His benign hands are at the back of all of your activities. It is his grace alone that has enabled your works to be crowned with success within such a short period of time. Putting your faith in our Lord every one of you can say, "Let me stand where I am and I shall move the world." I exhort you with all the earnestness at my command not to be disturbed or discouraged by momentary failures. Failures are but the stepping-stones to success. Viewing success and failure alike, work on with unwavering faith in him and victory will be yours at the end. I only pray that your surrender may be complete. Be like the arrow that darts from the bow. Be like the hammer that falls on the anvil. Be like the sword that pierces its object. The arrow does not murmur if it misses the target. The hammer does not fret if it falls on a wrong place. And the sword does not lament if it is broken in the hands of its wielder. Yet there is a joy in being made, used, and broken; and an equal joy in being finally set aside.

I invoke the blessings of Sri Ramakrishna on you all so that he may give you strength and courage to realize Truth in this very life.[64]

The convention continued for a week, and it was a great success. Many papers were read by the monks and by other prominent people. A working committee was formed that consisted of some young swamis who would stay in the headquarters and manage the detailed activities of the Order under the supervision of the president, general secretary, and the trustees, thus lightening the burden of Shivananda and Saradananda. It was also extremely important for the young generation to learn the traditions from the direct disciples and to pass them on to the next generation.

The majority of human problems are caused by misunderstandings or lack of communication. There is bound to be a certain amount of friction or difference of opinion in any group where many people live and work together. This is true in a family setting, as well as in a monastery or convent. Once Shivananda reminded the monks:

Look here, the Master used to say that one should see the ocean in a drop of water. It was not just a superficial opinion of his; it was a con-viction — the outcome of his actual experience. Otherwise, we could not have stayed with him. Instead of seeing our faults, he graciously attracted us to his side and let us live with him as we were. Who is there that is absolutely stainless? All those who have come here have one aim, and that is to be free from imperfection. Nobody came here perfect. These minor weaknesses will eventually disappear through his grace. If one can be resigned at his feet, he will set everything right.[65]

On 2 May 1926 Shivananda again left for South India. On the way he stopped at Bhubaneswar, Puri, and Waltair, reaching Madras on 11 May. The monks and devotees were happy to have Shivananda in their midst, and he initiated many people and talked to them about the Master, Holy Mother, and Swamiji. On 4 June he went to Ootacumund and stayed in the bungalow of the abbot of the Tirupati Temple. He mentioned: "The spiritual atmosphere of this place is very elevating; the mind naturally runs after the Infinite." Most of the time while he was there he remained indrawn, as if living in a different world. One can guess where his mind was from this conversation:

> The other day as I sat here silently watching the blue mountain ranges I experienced something. I saw a luminous figure coming out of this body [*meaning his own*], and it grew and grew, till at last it enveloped the whole world. [*Heaving a deep sigh he then remarked*]: The Master is my Paramatman, the supreme Self. It is He who pervades the whole universe. "A quarter of His is this whole universe; His other three immortal quarters are in the bright region" (Purusha Sukta).[66]

One morning Shivananda and his attendant went for a walk. On the way Shivananda saw a Western woman who was a Christian missionary. He cordially said "good morning" to her. But that woman cast him a scornful look and then turned her face and walked away without returning the greeting. She was angry because the Ramakrishna Mission was working among the poor in the Nilgiri Hills. The attendant monk was hurt and spoke out: "Maharaj, why did you greet her? She left, humiliating you!" "It does not matter," Shivananda answered. "One should respect women of all countries. 'The Divine Mother manifests in all women of the world'" (Chandi).[67]

On 24 September 1926 Shivananda inaugurated the building of the new ashrama in Ootacamund. During his stay there he came in contact with various sincere devotees. Later he told this incident:

> One year I visited the Nilgiri Hills. Learning that I was there, a Muslim doctor and his family came all the way from Bombay to see me. After inquiry I found that he was a famous physician in Bombay who had been educated in England and had a very good practice. He was accompanied by his wife and two sons, who were very handsome in appearance.
>
> In the course of conversation the doctor said to me, "We have come to see you, but my wife is particularly eager to speak to you." Saying this, he moved to the adjoining room. His wife saluted me with great devotion, and disclosed many intimate things relating to her spiritual life. Since childhood she has been a devotee of Krishna. She worships the child Krishna and occasionally has visions of him. After reading the Master's life and teachings she has become very much devoted to him. It is her conviction that her chosen deity, Krishna, has been born again as Ramakrishna.
>
> I noticed that she has profound love and devotion for the Master. She is quite intense in her spiritual practices, and the Master has

blessed her in many ways. When taking leave of me, she knelt down and bowed to me, saying, "Please bless me by touching my head with your hand. You had the blessed privilege of associating with Sri Ramakrishna, and you were blessed by him. Please touch my head with the hand that once touched Sri Ramakrishna." And how she wept! I said to myself again and again: "Glory be unto the Lord! Blessed is Thy power."[68]

After staying five months in Ootacamund, Shivananda visited Bangalore, Madras, and Nattrampally, at last reaching Bombay on 22 December. Two years previously he had stayed in a rented place, but now the centre had its own building and shrine. Shivananda installed Sri Ramakrishna's picture in the shrine, and was happy to see the activities of the ashrama. Then on his way to Belur Math he stopped at Nagpur again and his holy presence inspired the local devotees to expedite the construction of the new ashrama. He returned to Belur Math on 22 February 1927.

Shivananda's health began to break down. In addition to asthma, he had high blood pressure. But he had no time to rest: he used to initiate devotees regularly, give counsel to the monks, and handle the problems of the Order that others could not handle. In August 1927 Saradananda, the general secretary of the Ramakrishna Order, had a stroke and died. Shivananda was overwhelmed with grief, and his health deteriorated even further. The doctors advised him to go to a resort, and a wealthy devotee invited Shivananda to live in his Seth Villa at Madhupur in Bihar, which is known for its excellent water and climate. The swami stayed in that quiet villa for two months and his health improved considerably.

On 27 November 1927 Shivananda went to Varanasi; it was his last visit. He stayed in the Ramakrishna Advaita Ashrama for nearly two months and initiated quite a number of people. Shivananda was in an exalted mood in Varanasi. One morning when the monks of both ashramas came to greet him, the swami said: "Look, I had a very delightful experience last night. In the dead of night I suddenly saw before me a divine figure of white complexion with matted hair and three eyes. His luminous form lighted up the whole place. Ah, what a beautiful, lovely, compassionate face! The vision roused my spiritual energy upward, and my whole being was gradually absorbed in divine bliss. In the meantime I saw that the form gradually vanished, and in its place stood Sri Ramakrishna with a smiling face. Pointing to me, the Master said, 'You will have to live a little longer, for you still have something more to do.' As the Master said this, my mind came down to the normal plane and the body began functioning as usual. It is all his will. I was in a blissful state. The

Master is none other than Vishwanath himself." A curious monk asked: "Did you have the vision in a dream?" "No, no," replied the swami, "I was wide awake."[69]

Shivananda managed the Ramakrishna Order through his magnanimous personality as well as his spiritual power. One evening in Varanasi a young brahmacharin expressed his unwillingness to work according to Shivananda's instructions. The brahmacharin later became repentant and apologized: "Maharaj, you alone know what is best for me. I am ready to do whatever you want me to do." With great tenderness Shivananda said: "That's right. You have rightly understood. It will certainly be good for you if you listen to us and follow our instructions implicitly. Whatever we say comes directly from Sri Ramakrishna. These days I live wholly united with the Master."[70]

Shivananda began to initiate people in 1922, but he never claimed that he was a guru. One day in Varanasi he said to a monk: "The Master has effaced from my mind the idea that I am the guru. Shiva alone is the true guru, and in this age it is Sri Ramakrishna. It is the Master who inspires the devotees to come here, and I tell them as he prompts me from within. He is the Soul of my soul."[71]

On 15 January 1928 Jawharlal Nehru came to visit the Ramakrishna Mission Home of Service in Varanasi, and he was delighted to meet Shivananda. A few days later, his wife, Kamala Nehru, came to Shivananda for a blessing and spiritual instruction. She became a devotee and visited the swami in Belur Math many times. The entire Nehru family maintained a good relationship with the swamis of the Ramakrishna Order.

Shivananda left Varanasi on 15 February 1928 and arrived at Patna on the same day. He stayed there for a few days, initiated some people, and then returned to Belur Math on 19 February. This was his last outing as president of the Order.

Once a senior monk asked Shivananda to take disciplinary action against a monk and expel him from the Order. Shivananda listened to the accusations attentively and then asked the senior monk, "Does he not have one or two good qualities?" When the senior monk mentioned a couple of the monk's good qualities, Shivananda's face radiated with joy and he exclaimed, "That is enough!" That monk stayed in the Order.[72]

Another time Shivananda told the monks: "You cannot reform people by simply talking and reprimanding. If you have the spiritual power, redirect and change the inner tendencies of people. Talk to the Lord and pray to Him so that He may do the work of reforming. If He is gracious, then in a trice bad tendencies will undergo wholesale transformation."[73]

In March 1928 Swami Paramananda, head of the Vedanta Centre in Cohasset, Massachusetts, visited Belur Math. On 3 March he requested Shivananda: "Maharaj, I am making a movie of Belur Math, and our American devotees want to see the swamis also. If it is not inconvenient for you, please come downstairs."[74] Shortly Shivananda came down and walked in the monastery compound with Subodhananda and some monks and devotees. This film taken by Paramananda is the only motion picture we have of any direct disciples of Sri Ramakrishna. [The original film is in the archives of Ananda Ashrama, Cohasset. However, it was included in the video *Ramakrishna: A Documentary*, produced by the Vedanta Society of St. Louis.]

In the late 1920s the renowned French writer Romain Rolland began to write the biographies of Sri Ramakrishna and Swami Vivekananda. Shivananda assigned Swami Ashokananda to help provide Romain Rolland with all the available information, and Shivananda himself answered many of the writer's questions. Rolland acknowledged in the preface of *The Life of Ramakrishna*: "I owe a great deal to the present venerable head of the Belur Math and Superior of the Order, Swami Shivananda, who has been good enough to give me his precious personal memories of the Master."

After returning from the West, Vivekananda had the idea to build a temple for Sri Ramakrishna in Belur Math. At that time he directed Vijnanananda in designing the temple. When he saw the plans, Swamiji said: "The temple will be constructed later, and I shall see it from above." In the beginning of 1929 the trustees of the Order finally decided to have the foundation stone laid by Shivananda. Arrangements were made and Shivananda laid the stone on Sri Ramakrishna's birthday (13 March 1929) in the presence of Abhedananda, Vijnanananda, M., and many monks and devotees. (On 14 January 1938 the Ramakrishna Temple of Belur Math was at last dedicated by Vijnanananda, a direct disciple of the Master.)

Some Glimpses of Swami Shivananda

Swami Shivananda was an extraordinary teacher and a guru by divine right. His own life was a commentary on what he preached. He never stood upon a public platform or addressed large audiences. But he kept his spiritual treasures open for seekers of God. He solved their spiritual problems, and answered their questions on religion and philosophy from his own personal experience. As to his own realization, Shivananda once exclaimed: "I am happy. I have realized the *purnam* (the Infinite) by the grace of the Master." He then joyously chanted the peace mantram of the Brihadaranyaka Upanishad: "All that is invisible is verily the Infinite. All that is visible is also the Infinite. The whole universe has come out of the Infinite, which is still the Infinite."[75]

One day Swami Kamaleshwarananda told Shivananda, "I want to study the Upanishads with you." Shivananda replied: "Can you study our lives? Our lives are verily Upanishads. Here you will find the quintessence of the scriptures.... The light that I received from the Master I am sharing with you. The flame of one lamp lights another — thus we are all connected."[76]

Swami Satprakashananda recalled: "Once during a walk at Belur Math I asked Mahapurushji. 'Maharaj, some take initiation from the Holy Mother and others from Swami Brahmananda. Is there any difference between the two?' He said in reply: 'No, I do not see any difference whatsoever — the same Ganges water is coming out of two taps. The same grace of the Master is flowing out through the Holy Mother and Maharaj; the One Substance is in two receptacles. But look here, what do you mean by "*taking* initiation?" They receive it, they receive it. It is *given*, it is *given*.' No sooner did I hear this than my inner eyes were opened with regard to initiation, and a great problem was solved for me. Dependence on the Divine coupled with self-reliance ruled my heart."[77]

It is amazing how Shivananda, through his realization, solved both scriptural questions and the monks' spiritual problems. Swami Nikhilananda wrote:

I do not remember having asked him any spiritual or philosophical question. I do not believe he ever claimed to be a scholar or philosopher. Whatever instructions he gave to the devotees came from his direct experience, couched in simple language, and his profound faith that he acted as an instrument of Sri Ramakrishna, who guided him in his words, thoughts, and action. The ego was completely absent in him. Once I asked him a much-debated question about the present birth being the last one in the case of those who have taken shelter at Sri Ramakrishna's feet. In reply he said that it was his belief also. I argued that according to the scriptures, only those who are completely free from desires are not reincarnated and such desirelessness is not possible unless one directly experiences Brahman in the nirvikalpa samadhi. Mahapurush Maharaj said: "I am not a scholar. I do not know the scriptures. Can you tell me what is the cause of rebirth? Is it not unfulfilled desires?" I agreed. "Tell me," he said, "suppose you are at the point of death and Sri Ramakrishna appears before you. Suppose he asks you if you have any unfulfilled desire for which you want to assume another human body. What will you say?" I said: "I do not believe I have any desire to fulfill for which I would like to come back to this world again." "Then this is your last birth. This desirelessness one feels through the Master's grace," said Mahapurush Maharaj.

On another occasion, when I had just returned from Comilla [in Bangladesh] after a long absence, I saluted Mahapurush Maharaj and told him in the course of conversation that I was not making any spiritual progress. "None whatsoever?" he asked. I said that I did not feel any. "Listen, my child, perhaps you mean to say that you have not made as much spiritual progress as you would desire. Let me tell you something. You must be happy to see me after a long time. Are you not?" "Certainly, Maharaj," I replied. He said: "I am also very happy to see you. What is the cause of this mutual attraction? Neither you nor I have any blood relationship. You are happy to see me because you love God. I too am happy because I love God. This love of God binds us both together. On account of this love of God we feel happy when we see each other. When you were away I missed you. You too must have missed me. This love of God is the sure sign of spiritual progress."[78]

There is a saying, "Every saint has a past, every sinner has a future." If a child's body is filthy, does the mother throw it away? She washes the child and takes it on her lap again. Similarly, an illumined guru purifies the minds of impure souls. Swami Apurvananda recorded:

One morning Swami Shivananda, after lying down for a while, was seated on his cot. He seemed solemn and indrawn, but suddenly said to the attendant standing near: "Will you go and see if there is someone who wants initiation?" The attendant looked here and there and then went downstairs, where he found a woman who wanted initiation. After inquiry he was startled by the information she gave about herself. She was young and had come from a village.... She told the story of her sinful life and said that, although born in a brahmin family, she had kept bad company and gone astray.... In a remorseful tone she said, "May I not see him [Mahapurushji] once?"

When the attendant, looking disturbed, returned to the swami, the latter inquired very earnestly, "Tell me, is someone there?" The attendant reluctantly replied, "Maharaj, it is a lady who wants initiation, but ... " Before the attendant could finish what he felt he must say, Mahapurush remarked: "What of that? Ask her to bathe in the Ganges and come to me after visiting the shrine. Sri Ramakrishna is the redeemer of the fallen. He came especially to uplift them. What will happen to them if he does not come to their rescue? One could not then call him the saviour of the fallen."

The swami was ready to shower his blessings upon her. Later, when after her bath, she came for initiation he said, as if he knew everything about her: "What is there to fear, my daughter? You will certainly be blessed, since you have taken refuge in Sri Ramakrishna, our Master and saviour. Say this: 'Whatever sins I have committed in this life and in lives past, I offer them here [i.e., to the Master] and I will sin no more.'" After initiation the woman appeared to be an altogether new person.

Later that day the swami remarked: "Do you know why there is so much sickness in this body — so much suffering? The sins of others are being worked out in this body; if not, why should it suffer so much?"[79]

In the last part of his life, Shivananda could not travel because of his illness and old age. However, people came from all over the country to receive his blessings. It was not possible for him to remember the names of all his disciples. Once, seeing his prolonged meditation, an attendant asked, "Why do you need to meditate so much?" The swami answered: "Not for myself, my child. I initiate many people into spiritual life, but not all can keep up the necessary practices. Others find it possible to do so, yet make little headway. When I concentrate, their faces flash before me and I pray for them, removing the obstructions to their progress."[80]

One night he told his attendant: "Today the queen of Balangir came. She made a great statement. While leaving she bowed down and told me in tears: 'Maharaj, you have many devotees like me, but I have none like you.' This great statement was made by Radha to Krishna. The attitude of the gopis was to surrender completely to Krishna."[81]

Purna Haldar, an old fisherman from Bally, would catch fish in the Ganges, not far from the monastery. As he was feeble and bent with age, most of the time his catch was poor and not sufficient to provide a meagre living. Shivananda used to watch this old man from the upper veranda, and his heart would go out to him. In order to help him, Shivananda instructed the monk in charge of the kitchen to buy whatever he caught and to pay him handsomely. In addition, the swami now and then would give him cloth and other things. For a few days the swami did not see Purna, and then after inquiring learned that he had died. Immediately he sent a monk with sufficient money and clothes to his widow, so that she could perform rites for her departed husband. Afterwards he sent money to Purna's widow regularly.[82]

One noon after dinner, Shivananda saw a cobbler mending shoes while seated under the mango tree in the monastery courtyard. He told his attendant: "Ah, we all have had our meals, whereas this man is drudging there with an empty stomach. Go and give him a good quantity of offered fruits and sweets." The attendant obeyed and on his return found Shivananda standing by the window of his room with a half rupee in his hand, looking intently at the cobbler. Seeing the man eating, Shivananda remarked: "Ah, did you notice this? The man must have been awfully hungry. That is why he began to eat right away. Stand here and watch. I am having a little fun." Saying this, he dropped the coin in front of the man, who looked up and understood the situation. Overwhelmed with gratitude and joy, the man saluted him with folded hands and put the coin in his pocket. Later, finding a monk bargaining with the cobbler regarding the price for the work done, Shivananda reproached him: "Ah! The man is poor. Why bargain with him?"[83]

One night a thief entered the room of Josephine MacLeod [Joe], an American devotee of Swamiji, who was staying in the guest house of Belur Math. When the thief grabbed her locket reliquary, which contained Vivekananda's hair, Joe woke up and shouted. Swami Punyananda and some others were staying downstairs. They hurriedly ran and caught the thief at the head of the stairs. Punyananda gave him a good beating, tied him with a rope, and took him to the veranda of the Math building.

In those days every morning Shivananda would walk through the Math compound inspecting everything, especially the dairy. On his way that morning, Shivananda saw the thief and said to him jokingly: "Look, is this a place where one should come to steal? If these boys take turns beating you, you will die." The swami left after saying this.

After a while Shivananda returned from his rounds and began eating his breakfast. Then Joe entered his room and informed the swami: "Mahapurush Maharaj, you have heard that a thief entered my room; I think he is a devotee. Otherwise why would he take my locket leaving so many things in the room? You know, that locket is a reliquary containing Swamiji's hair. I believe his devotion for Swamiji was the motive for stealing it." Childlike, Shivananda at once believed the words of Joe. He asked Punyananda to release the thief, take him to the Ganges, and make sure that he had a bath and changed into the new cloth that he had sent for him. When Shivananda's orders were carried out, the thief went to bow down before Shivananda. The swami affectionately asked him: "Hello, would you like to become a monk?"[84] Although the thief's answer was unrecorded, his mind undoubtedly carried this memory throughout his life.

The scriptures say that a knower of Brahman wanders in this world sometimes like a child, sometimes like a madman, sometimes like a wise man and sometimes like a fool. He is ever happy with supreme bliss. One day Shivananda wished to eat from a gold plate. His attendants were in a dilemma, as it was not possible for the poor monastery to buy a gold plate. A monk with presence of mind remarked: "The tender banana leaf is also called goldleaf." (The inner stalk of the tender banana leaf is golden in colour, and it can remind one of a gold plate.) Immediately Shivananda said: "You are right. Henceforth I shall eat on a banana leaf." His attendants were relieved. They spread the banana leaf on his regular plate and then served food to the swami.[85]

One night Shivananda asked his attendant, "Could you buy a big catfish tomorrow?" "Yes, Maharaj," answered the monk. The next day he went to the market and bought a big live catfish for the swami, who was pleased to see it. First he said, "Make a nice fish curry out of it." The next moment he said: "Well, this fish was in a small tank. How nice it would be if we let it go in the Ganges! This fish will be happy. Now please release it into the Ganges." Immediately the swami's order was carried out. The fish disappeared, wiggling its tail. Shivananda's face reflected the fish's joy of freedom, and he exclaimed: "How wonderful! What joy!"[86]

Shivananda had tremendous love and respect for Swamiji and Brahmananda. Sometimes he would enter Swamiji's room and carefully check every little article in it. Once while looking at a group picture his eyes fell on his own figure, and he began to laugh. "Eh, who is this rogue, here?" he said. "This one became a saint, having been with saints!" Referring to six disciples of the Master who were earmarked as ishwarakotis [godlike souls], Shivananda remarked: "Swamiji, Maharaj, and a few others belonged to that category. I was not so high, but now I also have become an ishwarakoti through his grace."[87]

Swami Apurvananda recorded: "One afternoon after his rest the swami was seated on his bed facing the west. Sometimes he meditated closing the eyes and sometimes looking at a picture of the Master on the wall. The door and the window of the western veranda were open. Suddenly Mahapurushji raised his head upright and pointing to the mango tree in the courtyard, said: 'Look, such a great amount of power has accumulated within me that if I tell that tree, "Be liberated," it will be liberated. I can make people free just by looking in a particular direction.' Saying so he again bent his head and became absorbed in meditation."[88]

In spite of his old age and illness, he kept track of the monastery activities, especially the Master's service. He reminded the monks and the devotees: "The Master himself is present in Belur Math, for Swamiji installed him here. Know this as the truth."[89] He guided the worshipper in serving Sri Ramakrishna: "After daily worship recite some hymns to the Master. In the afternoon instead of making several garlands, make one jasmine garland for the Master, and spend the remaining time in japam, meditation, and studying the scriptures. In the summer after putting the Master to bed, you must fan him for some time." The swami himself demonstrated how to prepare a betel roll and tobacco for the Master.[90]

Swami Jnanadananda recalled: "One day I was sweeping the courtyard of the Math near the mango tree. After I finished sweeping, Mahapurush Maharaj said, looking at the courtyard: 'Hello, what are you doing? The Master walks here. I still see dust and used match sticks on the courtyard. Clean this place with special care, so that the Master can walk with joy and his feet won't get dirty.' After this I realized that the Master dwells everywhere in the monastery. Although we do not see him, the swami does."[91]

Swami Nikhilatmananda reminisced: "I used to mop the floor of the shrine every day. Sometimes the rainwater would flood the southern veranda of the shrine. One day after it rained I did not mop the veranda. Mahapurush Maharaj observed it from his room. Calling me to his room he said: 'Look, is it the way to serve the Master? The Master can't walk on the veranda because of the rainwater. His feet will get wet. What are you doing here? I see the Master walking on that veranda every afternoon. My child, always be careful so that the Master may not feel discomfort. He is the Soul of our souls, the Lord of the universe. "If he is pleased, the whole world will be pleased."'"[92]

Seeing God in everything and everywhere is the culmination of the Vedantic experience. Shivananda's mind was full of Ramakrishna. He once told Brahmananda in Belur Math: "Raja, I see the Master even these days. Were it not so, it would be unbearable for me to live."[93] Pointing to the picture of Sri Ramakrishna, Shivananda said to the devotees: "Don't think of this picture of the Master as an ordinary picture. He himself dwells in it and listens to the prayers of the devotees."[94]

On another occasion Shivananda said: "In this age the name of Sri Ramakrishna is the mantram for liberation. Rama and Krishna — the combination of these two incarnations is simultaneously manifested in Ramakrishna. If you chant the name of Ramakrishna, you will get the result of japam of the Rama mantram as well as the Krishna mantram. He was born to liberate sinners and sufferers, and showed a simple and beautiful path for God-realization."[95]

Towards the End

Swami Shivananda began to complete his role in Ramakrishna's drama. He carried the Master's message wholeheartedly and distributed it among the masses. Pointing to his own body he told a monk: "This is not just an ordinary body; it has its own distinction. God-realization has been attained in and through this body. This body has touched Bhagavan Sri Ramakrishna, lived with him, served him. The Master has made this body a vehicle for the propagation of his message for this age. Otherwise this body is nothing but a cage of flesh and blood.... Should he feel it necessary to maintain this body longer, he will do so. Else, I am ready to depart at his first call. I am waiting for his call."[96]

After illumination only compassion motivates the mind of a *jivanmukta*, one who is free while living. Shivananda struggled to keep his mind on the relative plane so that he could help others. Swami Ashokananda wrote: "During the day he would have many things scattered over his bed. Though his assortment varied, it would contain something like the following: a stick, a musical instrument, *The Gospel of Sri Ramakrishna*, the Gita, the Chandi, Sanskrit texts and Bengali folk tales, as well as books that were plentifully illustrated. At times he might playfully shake the stick at the attendants, or finger the musical instrument, and very often he read. The monks did not at first understand why he wanted his bed cluttered with so many things, but one day he said: 'My mind wants to rush towards the Absolute all the time. That is why I am trying with all these trifling diversions to hold my mind down. Just as a mother gives her child toys to keep it engaged, so I am also trying by various means to make my mind forget the Absolute.'"[97]

As a Vedanta monk Shivananda was strong and uncompromising; he always reminded the monks of the ideal: "Renunciation of lust and gold! If you can renounce lust of the flesh and the greed for wealth, everything will be all right.... Above everything, a monk should observe the vow of chastity and poverty.... Purity and guilelessness should be your watchwords. The Master forgives all failings except hypocrisy and self-deception. Those who play false and take to hypocritical ways do not belong here. The Master does not allow them to remain in the Order; he removes them. Only those who are genuine can stay."[98]

However, Shivananda was soft and tenderhearted, and he acted like a loving mother in the monastery. During the malaria season he would go to the kitchen and guide the cook in preparing a special diet for the sick monks. A monk recalled: "A Western woman was staying in the Belur guest house and she was sick. I was seated in the Mother's Temple. I saw Mahapurushji walking from the Math building to the guest house carrying an orange in his hand for that woman. His face was serene and he was absorbed within himself. It was an unforgettable scene."[99]

His love seemed perennial and inexhaustible. Even animals and birds shared in his affection and care. He would regularly go to the dairy and feed the cows bananas, molasses, and barley powder. Quite often people would see the old swami stroking the cows in the monastery compound. He would ask his attendant to spread grain on the roof adjacent to his room so he could watch the birds enjoying their food. His pet dog, Kelo, would get baths and special dinners. Pointing to Kelo, Shivananda would say, "Kelo is my dog and I am the dog of the Master."[100] One night the swami was meditating in his room when a cat entered, crying "mew mew." Shivananda bowed to the cat with folded hands, and then said to his attendant: "The Master has kept me in such a state that I see everything as conscious. I see the play of consciousness in the wall, door, bed, and even in this cat."[101]

Swami Shivananda was keen to spread the message of the Master throughout the world. During his presidency the following swamis of the Ramakrishna Order were sent to North America, South America, and Europe: Swami Prabhavananda in 1923; Swamis Dayananda and Akhilananda in 1926; Swamis Madhavananda and Jnaneswarananda in 1927; Swami Vividishananda in 1928; Swami Devatmananda in 1930; Swamis Ashokananda and Nikhilananda in 1931; Swami Vijayananda in 1932; Swami Yatiswarananda in 1933. These swamis and others worked hard to carry out the mission of Vedanta inaugurated by Vivekananda. It was a golden era for the Order.

The disciples of the Master departed one after another: M., the recorder of the *Gospel*, and Swami Subodhananda died in 1932. The death of these dear ones caused grief to Shivananda's heart. Sometimes he would say: "Almost all are now gone. With whom shall I talk? There is no longer any joy in conversation." Dhan Gopal Mukherji, one of Shivananda's disciples who had been abroad for many years, came to Belur to see him; but seeing the swami's fragile health, he burst into tears. Shivananda consoled him: "When Buddha was about to attain *pari-nirvana*, final release from the body, Ananda was overwhelmed with grief. At this Buddha said: 'Why are you weeping, Ananda? This life lasts for fifty, sixty, or at the most a hundred years. But I am about to attain eternal life.'"[102]

As the days passed, Shivananda's health failed rapidly because of high blood pressure and asthma, and finally he became bedridden. Sometimes he would apologize to his attendants, "I am putting all of you to so much trouble." In spite of his ill health, he continued to have various visions and spiritual experiences. One evening he said to an attendant: "Put the holy ashes of the Lord Shiva on my forehead, and spread a silk chadar on the bed. Look, the Master has come." Another afternoon he said to his attendants: "Just now Swamiji and Maharaj came and said to me, 'Tarak-da, let us go!' Did you not see them?"[103]

On 24 April 1933 Shivananda expressed a desire to see the monastery. His monastic disciples carried him in a chair. He bowed down to all the temples, visited the dairy, the flower and vegetable gardens, the stores and offices. At last he bowed down to the Mother Ganges. His face was beaming with joy. This was his final tour around the monastery, and his last words were: "Whatever is true will happen. Truth alone triumphs in the end. Truth alone persists. That which is false does not last. Therefore one should not regret it."[104] Although Shivananda did not write any books, his inspired conversations were recorded and published in *For Seekers of God*. Many monks and devotees also left their valuable reminiscences of the swami, which were printed in Bengali in three volumes as *Shivananda Smriti Samgraha*.

On 25 April Shivananda initiated three devotees. Compared to other days, he was feeling better. At 11:00 a.m. he had his lunch. While drinking a little buttermilk after his meal his right hand suddenly began to tremble and he put his cup down. A stroke of apoplexy paralyzed his right side and his speech became impaired. He tried to say something to his attendant but failed. Immediately the attendant called other swamis and helped Shivananda lie down on the bed. At once word was sent to Calcutta for expert medical help, and several doctors hurried to the monastery. All effort was made to provide the best medical care, and several doctors attended Shivananda daily.

The news of Shivananda's critical condition spread rapidly, and for months monks and devotees came from far and near just to see his face. Akhandananda came from Sargachi and Vijnanananda came from Allahabad to see their beloved brother disciple. Abhedananda, another disciple of the Master, also came to visit Shivananda. Although Shivananda could not talk, he could understand and express his feelings. He would receive his visitors with a smile and sometimes greet them by lifting his left hand. Seeing him one knew that the swami was in bliss and had no body consciousness.

Looking at Shivananda's serene and joyful face, Pandit Pramathanath Tarkabhushan, an authority on the Hindu scriptures, remarked: "I have read in books about *jivanmuktas*, or illumined souls; today I have seen one face to face in the flesh. The swami seemed to be in deep samadhi all the time, once in a while coming down to the normal plane. I am indeed very much blessed in meeting this supreme yogi. I have studied about samadhi in the scriptures, thought about it and discussed it a great deal. But never before have I had the good fortune to see a man established in samadhi."[105]

On 3 February 1934, nine months after the stroke, Shivananda developed pneumonia. His condition slowly deteriorated. Several eminent doctors struggled to keep this great soul alive. Swami Shivananda lived to see Sri Ramakrishna's birth anniversary on 15 February and the public festival on Sunday, 18 February. He passed away at 5:36 p.m. on Tuesday, 20 February 1934. At the final moment Shivananda's face beamed with joy and the hair of his head stood on end, both considered to be auspicious signs.

The monks chanted Shankara's *Six Stanzas on Nirvana*, Pushpadanta's *Shiva Mahimnah Stotram*, the Upanishads, and the Gita. Abhedananda came and offered flowers at the feet of Shivananda and recited a line from the Bhagavata, "O great soul, my salutations at your lotus feet." According to the traditional custom, Shivananda's body was bathed with Ganges water, decorated with flowers and sandalpaste, and then consigned to the flames of the funeral pyre on the bank of the Ganges. Hundreds of monks and devotees solemnly repeated: "Glory be unto Sri Ramakrishna!"

If anyone ever asked where he would go after leaving the body, Swami Shivananda replied that his rightful place would be in Ramakrishnaloka (abode of Ramakrishna) with the Master. His life is a glowing example of a person who continuously lived in God-consciousness. One day he humbly said to a monk: "Look, I am my Master's dog. As a dog protects the precious wealth of its master from robbers, so I am protecting the valuable spiritual treasures [discrimination, renunciation, knowledge, devotion] of the Master in this monastery. He who stays here like a faithful dog will attain the greatest good."[106]

4

ॐ

SWAMI PREMANANDA

As a little child needs constant care and protection, so does a *paramahamsa*, an illumined soul, who frequently goes in and out of samadhi. In this God-intoxicated state, the paramahamsa is completely oblivious of his body and surroundings; as a result, he is subject to the risk of accidental injury. The paramahamsa's body is extremely precious because it is God's instrument to benefit humanity. That is why it is the disciples' duty to protect their guru's body.

On 20 June 1884 Sri Ramakrishna said to M. (the recorder of *The Gospel of Sri Ramakrishna*): "You see, I am having some difficulty about my physical needs. It will be nice if Baburam lives with me. The nature of these attendants of mine is undergoing a change. Latu is always tense with spiritual emotion. He is about to merge himself in God. Rakhal is getting into such a spiritual mood that he can't do anything even for himself. I have to get water for him. He isn't of much service to me."[1] Moreover, Rakhal had to visit home occasionally. Although several devotees lived with the Master, he could only bear the touch of certain people during his ecstasy. On 30 June he told Baburam: "Do stay with me. It will be very nice. In this mood I cannot allow others to touch me."[2]

Matangini, Baburam's mother, was a devotee of the Master. When she visited Dakshineswar during this time, the Master asked her, "Will you give me something?" "Yes, sir, whatever you ask." "Will you give me your son? I want a pure-hearted boy to live here. I am greatly pleased even when he gives me a glass of water." Matangini at once agreed: "It is my good fortune, sir, that you will accept him and that he will live with you.

SWAMI PREMANANDA

But, does anybody give away her son for nothing?" Ramakrishna smiled and asked, "What shall I give you?" Matangini humbly said, "I have just two requests: one is that I may have unflinching devotion for God; the other is that none of my children dies before I do." Sri Ramakrishna granted her those boons.[3]

Baburam Ghosh was born at 11:55 p.m. on Tuesday, 10 December 1861, at Antpur, a village thirty miles from Calcutta. His father, Taraprasanna Ghosh, and mother, Matangini Devi, came from two well-to-do and aristocratic families of the same village. Both were pious and devoted to their family deity, Lakshmi-narayan. They had one daughter, Krishnabhavini, who was married to Balaram Basu (a devotee of Sri Ramakrishna) and three sons: Tulsiram, Baburam, and Shantiram. Through Balaram, his family and his wife's family became devotees of the Master.

Very little is known about Baburam's early life. He was an extremely handsome child with a fair complexion. It is said that even as a little boy of four or five he could not bear the idea of marriage. If he were teased about it, he would vehemently protest, waving his hands, "Don't say that! Oh, don't make me marry! I would die."[4] When he was eight, Baburam would imagine a beautiful wooded place on the bank of the Ganges where he would live in a hut with another monk and meditate on God. These holy wishes were fulfilled when Baburam came in contact with Sri Ramakrishna in Dakshineswar.

Baburam studied for a few years in his village school, then his mother sent him to his uncle in North Calcutta to continue his education. He was first admitted to Banga Vidyalaya, then to Aryan School, and finally to Metropolitan School, Shyambazar, where M. was the headmaster, and Rakhal was his classmate. Later, Baburam reminisced about his early life: "My mother now and then would shut herself up in a room and meditate all day. If we happened to return home from Calcutta on those days, we had to live in a neighbouring house and meet her the next day. She was very strict in her discipline. She would never allow us to stay with her in the village home, lest that spoil our education. But she would never utter a harsh word to her daughters-in-law or even to servants. . . . I was very naughty as a young boy. So I have got some scars on my forehead. Swamiji used to say, 'He is no boy who has no scars on his head.'"[5]

First Meetings with Sri Ramakrishna

In Pascal's immortal words: "You would not have looked for Me, if you had not found Me." From his very childhood Baburam knew his goal; he was looking for a guru who could help him to reach it. One day he went to Hari Sabha at Jorasanko to listen to discourses on the Bhagavata, and there he saw Sri Ramakrishna, without knowing who he was. However, sometime before, Matangini and Tulsiram had visited the Master at Dakshineswar. Observing Baburam's religious inclination, Tulsiram told him to visit the Master, who, like Sri Gauranga, lost all consciousness of the world while uttering the name of God.

Baburam had learned that Rakhal often visited the Master. The next day in school he asked Rakhal more about the saint of Dakshineswar. They planned to visit him the next Saturday after school hours, probably on 8 April 1882. Baburam reminisced about that memorable visit:

> Swami Brahmananda and I went to Hathkhola ghat [in West Calcutta] to take a boat for Dakshineswar, and there we met Ramdayal Babu. Learning that he was also going to see Sri Ramakrishna, we got in a boat together. It was almost dusk when we reached Rani Rasmani's Kali Temple. We went to the Master's room and were told that he had gone to the temple to pay obeisance to the Mother of the Universe. Asking us to stay there, Swami Brahmananda went towards the Mother's temple to find the Master. Soon I saw him holding onto the Master very carefully and guiding him, saying: "Steps. Go up here, down here." I had already heard that the Master would often become overwhelmed with ecstasy and lose outer consciousness. Therefore I knew that he was in an ecstatic mood when I saw him coming, reeling like a drunken man. He entered the room in that state and sat on a small bedstead. Shortly afterwards he came back to normal consciousness.[6]

When Ramakrishna inquired about the newcomer, Ramdayal introduced him. Ramakrishna said: "Ah, you are a relative of Balaram. Then you are related to us also. Well, what is your native place?" "Antpur, sir." "Ah, then I must have visited it. Kalu and Bhulu of Jhamapukur also belong to that place, don't they?" "Yes, sir. But how do you know them?" "Why, they are sons of Ramprasad Mittra. When I was at Jhamapukur, I used to go frequently to their house as well as to that of Digambar Mittra."[7]

Saying this, the Master caught hold of Baburam's hand and said: "Come closer to the light. Let me see your face." In the dim light of an earthen lamp he thoroughly examined Baburam's face, hands, and feet, and he expressed great satisfaction. Then he weighed Baburam's forearm by placing it on his palm. It was one of his ways of judging a person's spirituality; if it was lighter than ordinary he would say that this showed a "beneficent intelligence." Observing the auspicious signs, the Master expressed with joy, "Very good, very good."

Baburam recalled his first night at Dakshineswar:

A few hours were spent delightfully in religious talk. We took our supper at 10:00 p.m. and lay down on the southeast veranda of the Master's room. Beds were arranged for the Master and Swami Brahmananda in the room. But scarcely had an hour passed when the Master came out of his room with his cloth under one arm and came to our bedside. Addressing Ramdayal Babu, he asked affectionately, "Are you sleeping?" Both of us quickly sat up in our beds and replied, "No, sir." The Master said: "Look, I have not seen Narendra for a long time, and I feel as if my whole soul were being forcibly wrung like a wet towel. Please ask him to come once and see me. He is a person of pure sattva qualities. He is Narayana himself. I cannot have peace of mind if I don't see him now and then."

Ramdayal Babu had been visiting Dakshineswar for some time, so the childlike nature of the Master was not unknown to him. Seeing that childlike behaviour, he knew that the Master was in ecstasy. He tried to console the Master by promising that he would see Narendra first thing in the morning and ask him to come, and similar other things. But the Master's mood was not at all alleviated that night. Knowing that we were getting no rest, he would return to his room now and then for some time. But after a while he would forget and again come back to us and begin speaking of Narendra's good qualities, expressing pathetically the terrible anguish of his mind on account of Narendra's long absence.[8]

In the morning Baburam found the Master quite normal, and there was no trace of anxiety on his face. He was overwhelmed observing the Master's love for Narendra and he thought Narendra must be a very hardhearted person. The Master asked Baburam to walk around the Panchavati grove, where he had practised sadhana. Baburam was astonished to find that it was exactly like the wooded place on the Ganges that he had envisioned in his boyhood. Then the Master sent Baburam to visit the deities in the temples, which he did. When he took leave of the Master, the latter affectionately said, "Come again."

Three days after the first visit, Ramdayal met Baburam at Baghbazar and informed him that the Master had asked for him. Baburam was moved by the Master's kindness. On the following Sunday he arrived at Dakshineswar at 8:00 a.m. When he saw Baburam, the Master said: "It is nice that you have come. Go to the Panchavati, where they are having a picnic. Carry this firewood there. Narendra has come. Have a talk with him."[9] At the Panchavati Baburam found Rakhal, who introduced him to Narendra and some other young devotees of the Master. They were having great fun. Baburam had heard about Narendra's greatness beforehand, and now he was impressed by Narendra's large, expressive eyes and handsome, vigorous form. His friendly jokes and humour, fiery conversation, and heavenly singing captivated Baburam's mind. He quickly realized that Narendra was a brilliant man who excelled in everything.

One afternoon Baburam came to visit the Master at Dakshineswar. As soon as he arrived the Master said to him: "Baburam, it is good that you have come. This gentleman [*pointing to Deven Majumdar*] has come from Calcutta and now is suffering from a high fever. He can't return by himself, so take him immediately to his home by boat. I have so many things to tell you. Please come another day." Baburam took the dust of the Master's feet, and left for Calcutta with Deven.[10]

Love is reciprocal. As the disciples loved the Master, he also loved them dearly. Later, Baburam reminisced: "The Master used to cry whenever I left Dakshineswar to return to Calcutta. Oh, how can I explain to you how much he loved us! He would go to Calcutta in a carriage just so he could feed Purna [a young devotee]. He would wait near the school where Purna went, send someone to bring the boy, and then feed him delicacies.... One day he was found waiting outside Balaram Babu's house where I was staying. Balaram Babu was not at home, and the Master was hesitant to go inside, thinking he might not be welcomed. He had come to see me. Someone finally called him in. His love knew no bounds, and one drop of it completely filled us. Each one thus thought himself to be the most beloved of the Master."[11]

Baburam was twenty when he first met the Master, though he appeared to be much younger. He was very handsome, about five feet eight inches tall, and rather slim. He had black hair and a complexion like pure gold. In the beginning he visited the Master only on holidays, so that his family would not think that he was neglecting his studies. On 20 June 1884 the Master asked M.: "Tell me, does Baburam intend to continue with his studies? I said to him, 'Continue your studies to set an example to others.'... I don't want Baburam to tear himself away from his family. It may make trouble at home."[12]

During these first visits, Ramakrishna recognized through his yogic vision that Baburam had been born as a part of Radha, the spiritual consort of Krishna. On 20 June 1884 the Master said to M.: "I noticed the other day that Baburam ... has a feminine nature. In a vision I saw Baburam as a goddess with a necklace around her neck and with women companions about her. He has received something in a dream. His body is pure. Only a very little effort will awaken his spiritual consciousness."[13] On other occasions he described Baburam as a *nityasiddha* (ever-perfect soul) and an *ishwarakoti* (godlike soul). The Master earmarked six of his disciples as *ishwarakotis*: Narendra, Rakhal, Baburam, Yogin, Niranjan, and Purna.

On 30 June 1884 the Master again said to M.: "Yesterday I came to know Baburam's inner nature. That is why I have been trying so hard to persuade him to live with me. The mother bird hatches the egg in proper time. Boys like Baburam are pure in heart. They have not yet fallen into the clutches of 'woman and gold.' They are like a new pot. Milk kept in it will not turn sour....I need Baburam here. I pass through certain spiritual states when I need someone like him."[14] About Baburam's purity, the Master used to say, "He is pure, pure to the very marrow of his bones."[15]

In the Company of the Master

Baburam was deemed a proper attendant for Sri Ramakrishna because of his absolute purity. He was one of those fortunate souls whose touch the Master could bear during samadhi, and many were the occasions when he was found supporting the Master in that state lest he should fall and be injured. Later, Baburam reminisced: "Sri Ramakrishna was the embodiment of purity. A man earned a lot of money by taking bribes. One day this person touched the Master's feet while he was in samadhi and he cried out in pain. During the Master's samadhi we had to hold him so he would not fall, but we were afraid. We thought that if we were not pure enough, then, when we touched him during samadhi, he would publicly cry out in pain. So we prayed for purity. It was the Master's grace that I was allowed to live with him."[16]

On 21 September 1884 Ramakrishna went to the Star Theatre to see the play *Chaitanya Lila* (The Divine Play of Sri Chaitanya). Baburam recalled: "Before we left Dakshineswar, he said to me: 'Look, if I go into samadhi there, people will turn towards me and there will be a commotion. If you see me on the verge of samadhi, talk to me about various other things.' But when he went to the theatre he could not stop going into samadhi, even though he tried. I began to repeat the name of God, and slowly he came round. Such experiences of *bhava* [ecstasy], *mahabhava* [great ecstasy], and samadhi were natural with him. He had to struggle hard in order to hold his mind down to the normal plane."[17]

Sometime in 1884 Baburam begged the Master for samadhi. Ramakrishna consoled him, saying: "All right, I shall ask the Divine Mother about it. Does anything happen by my will, my child?" But Baburam insisted on samadhi; he then had to return to Antpur on business. In the meantime, the Master expressed his concern to others: "You see, Baburam wept much and asked for samadhi before he left. What will happen? If he does not have it, he will have no regard for the words of this place [*meaning himself*]." He then prayed to the Mother: "Please grant, Mother, that Baburam may have a little ecstasy or other spiritual experience." The Mother replied, "He will not have ecstasy; he will have knowledge." This relieved the Master to some extent.

In 1885 Baburam was preparing for his Entrance examination, but after meeting the Master he cared very little for study. On 7 March 1885 Ramakrishna said to Baburam: "Where are your books? Aren't you attending to your studies? (*To M.*) He wants to stick to both [God and the world]. That is very difficult. What will you gain by knowing God partially? ... One procures the thorn of knowledge to remove the thorn of ignorance; then one goes beyond both knowledge and ignorance." "That's what I want," said Baburam. "But, my child," said the Master, "can you attain it by holding to both? If you want that, then come away." Baburam said joyfully, "Take me away from the world."[18]

Baburam failed his Entrance examination. A few days later he came to Dakshineswar with Vaikunthanath Sanyal. Baburam was very much afraid of what the Master would say. When Vaikuntha told Baburam's bad news to the Master, he made light of it. "Well," he said, "that is very good. You have failed to pass; now you are free from all passes." (In Bengali, "pass" is the same word as "fetter.")

With Baburam's formal education at an end, his spiritual education began under the Master's guidance. He received his mother's approval and began living at Dakshineswar permanently. On 7 March 1885 the Master said to M. in front of Baburam: "I have been seeking one who has totally renounced 'woman and gold.' When I find a young man, I think that perhaps he will live with me; but everyone raises some objection or other."[19] Baburam had no objection, so the Master called him *daradi*, the companion of his soul.

Living with Ramakrishna was a great education. He taught his disciples through his life, not merely with words. Baburam watched the Master day and night and imbibed the spirit of renunciation and purity, which are the two main pillars of spiritual life. Later, Baburam recalled:

> One night I was sleeping in the Master's room. In the dead of night I woke up and found him pacing from one end of his room to the other,

saying: "Mother, I do not want this. Do not bring me honour from men. Don't, Mother, don't. I spit on it." Saying this, he paced back and forth like a madman. I was filled with wonder. I thought: "How strange! People are so eager for name and fame, and he is pleading with the Mother not to give it to him! Why is this happening before me? Is it to instruct me?"

The Master could not bear any kind of bondage. If the edge of his mosquito curtain was tucked under the mattress, he would feel suffocated. It was instead dropped around the edge of his bed. He could not even button his shirt. We had to do that for him. And neither could he bolt his door. He saw God in everything. One day someone tore a piece of new cloth in front of him and he cried out, "Oh, pain!"

Once I saw a person secretly put money under the Master's mattress when he was not in his room. Later when the Master came back, he could not go near the bed. His renunciation was phenomenal. Can an ordinary person conceive of such things? We have seen his ideal life, so we speak with conviction.

Sometimes the Master would entertain us by imitating a dancing girl, placing one hand on his waist and moving his other hand about. Again, through humour, tales, and parables, he would explain to us the most intricate philosophies, which were confusing even to scholars. His wonderful skill in teaching left a deep impression on our hearts forever. The Master was adept in explaining the supreme spiritual truths in simple, sweet language.

"Never see faults in others. Rather see your own faults," said the Master. Once, in front of the Master, some visitors were criticizing the character of Satish Giri, the abbot of the Tarakeshwar Monastery. Immediately Sri Ramakrishna diverted their attention to the abbot's good qualities. The Master did not like his devotees to gossip.

We saw how lovingly the Master used to receive the devotees at Dakshineswar! He would ask, "Do you want to chew a betel roll?" If the devotee said, "No," he would then ask, "Would you like to smoke tobacco?" Thus, in so many ways he would take care of the devotees.

The Master showered his grace on Girish Chandra Ghosh and even on many prostitutes. One day the ladies of Balaram Babu's family were sitting before the Master in his room when a prostitute named Ramani passed along the road nearby. The Master called to her and asked, "Why don't you come nowadays?" The ladies were scandalized to hear the Master talking with a prostitute.

Shortly afterwards the Master took them to visit the shrines. When they reached the Kali Temple the Master said to the Mother: "Mother, Thou indeed hast become the prostitute and the chaste woman!" The ladies understood that they were wrong in hating Ramani, that the Master spoke with her, knowing her to be the Mother Herself, and that they should not be so proud of their chastity, for it was all due to the Mother's will.

Once the Master assured a devotee: "Have you committed a sin? Don't be afraid. Take a vow, 'I will not sin anymore.' I shall swallow all of your sins."[20]

One day Sri Ramakrishna was resting in his room at Dakshineswar. Baburam and some other young boys were with Hazra on the eastern porch of the Master's room. Hazra said to Baburam and others: "You are all mere boys! You are visiting Sri Ramakrishna off and on, and he just keeps you satisfied with fruits and sweets. Hold him — press him — and get something [power, wealth, and so on] from him." As soon as the Master heard this from his room he jumped up from his bed, rushed to the veranda, and shouted: "Baburam, come to my room right now. Don't listen to his calculating advice. The beggar pesters the rich man, saying, 'Sir, give me a pice! Give me a pice!' Being disgusted with the beggar, the rich man throws a small coin to him, saying, 'Take this and get out of here.' You are my very own. You will not have to ask for anything from me. Whatever I have, it is all yours."[21]

As the mother bird protects her fledglings, so the Master guarded his young disciples from various evil influences. One day at Dakshineswar the Master said to Baburam: "I can't touch you today. Did you do anything wrong?" "No, sir." "Then why can't I touch you?" After a while Baburam remembered that in the morning while chatting with his friend he had said something which was not true. He confessed it to the Master. Baburam realized that Sri Ramakrishna's life was established in truth, and that truthfulness is the key to God-realization.[22]

Baburam used to give personal service to the Master, such as sweeping the floor, making his bed, and preparing tobacco and betel-rolls. He used to rub the Master's body with oil before his bath, and would fan him when necessary. Baburam would accompany Ramakrishna whenever he visited the devotees' houses or theatres in Calcutta. One day at Balaram's house in Calcutta, Baburam was pouring water for the Master to wash his hands. Downstairs a few schoolgirls were playing. The Master watched a girl swirling a bunch of keys tied in the corner of her sari (cloth). Pointing to that girl, the Master said to Baburam: "Look, girls tie boys like that bunch of keys and spin them around. Likewise do you want to move around in their hands?"[23] Baburam realized that the Master was instructing him to be free from the temptation of women.

Bhartrihari said in his *Vairagyashatakam* (One Hundred Verses on Renunciation): "Everything is fraught with fear in this world, renunciation alone makes one fearless." Sri Ramakrishna advised his young monastic disciples to renounce both externally and internally; he advised his householder disciples to renounce internally. Many years later Baburam related how the Master taught the monastic disciples: "Very little of the Master's teachings is recorded in the *Gospel*. M. used to visit the Master occasionally and would note down his teachings as he heard them. . . . His teachings to the monastic disciples were given in private. As soon as the householder devotees would leave the room, he would get up and lock the door and then speak to us living words of renunciation. He would try to impress upon our young minds the emptiness and vanity of worldly enjoyments."[24].

The Master kept a watchful eye over his would-be monastic disciples. He gave them spiritual instructions and would send them at night to different areas in the temple garden to practise meditation. He generally kept Baburam and Rakhal near him. He even told the Holy Mother how many pieces of *chapati* (unleavened bread) should be given to each disciple. Baburam was supposed to have four, but Holy Mother gave him six. When the Master came to know about it, he immediately went to the nahabat and complained that her indiscreet affection might ruin Baburam's future life. The Holy Mother firmly replied: "Why are you so much worried because he had a couple more chapatis? I shall look after his future. Please don't make an issue about his food." The Master understood that Holy Mother's action was justified as she exercised her motherly prerogative towards her children.

Every action and word of Sri Ramakrishna's was meaningful. He was a very light eater but would eat his meal consisting of various dishes. One day he said to Baburam and others: "Do you know why I eat my meal with all these items? If I ate all the items mixed together [which would lead him to the experience of oneness], my mind would merge into the Infinite and never return. For you people I keep my mind on a lower plane by creating desires, such as, I shall eat my rice with five kinds of curries, and so on." The Master kept some small, harmless desires, so that he could function in the world and help his devotees.

Baburam later recalled about his spiritual training: "The Master encouraged us to read the scriptures and holy books. He kept some books such as *Mukti O Tahar Sadhan* [Liberation and Its Practice] in his room and sometimes asked us to read them to him. When a person reads about God, his mind is absorbed in Him. . . . We saw him working in the garden, and also sweeping his room. He could not tolerate work done in a slip-shod manner. He himself did everything precisely and gracefully, and he taught us to do the same. He would scold us if we did not put tools and other things back in their proper places."[25]

In the middle of 1885 Ramakrishna developed throat cancer, moved to Calcutta for treatment, and finally settled in Cossipore. Baburam stayed with the Master and served him along with other disciples. Ramakrishna continued to train his disciples, and one day distributed twelve pieces of ochre cloth and twelve rosaries among them. Baburam was blessed by the Master with an ochre cloth and a rosary.

The Master tied his disciples with a cord of love. Sometimes they would share their sweet memories with each other. Many years later (15 August 1915) Baburam wrote to Swami Abhedananda who was then preaching Vedanta in America: "Do you remember when you and I were together at the Cossipore garden house, and the Master remarked, 'Your relation-ship is between Self and Self.' Do you remember what else he said? He said: 'You are like monkeys; and I am the monkey-trainer holding in my hand the ropes tied around your waists. The monkey-trainer pulls the rope if the monkeys become too troublesome.' Please bear in your mind, brother, that we are monkeys in his hand."[26]

In spite of his fatal illness, the Master would make fun and tell jokes with his disciples. Holy Mother recalled:

> While living in the Cossipore garden, I was once climbing the steps, carrying a bowl with five pounds of milk. I felt giddy and the milk spilt on the ground. My ankles were badly sprained. Naren and Baburam ran there and took care of me. There was a great inflammation of the feet. The Master heard of the accident and said to Baburam: "Well, Baburam, it is a nice mess I am in now. Who will cook my food? Who will feed me now?" He was then ill with cancer of the throat and lived only on farina pudding. I used to make it and feed him in his room in the upper storey of the house. I had then a ring in my nose. The Master touched his nose and made a sign of the ring by making a circle with his finger, in order to indicate me. He then said, "Baburam, can you put her (*making the sign*) in a basket and carry her on your shoulder to this room?" Naren and Baburam were convulsed with side-splitting laughter. Thus he used to cut jokes with them. After three days the swelling subsided. Then they helped me to go upstairs with his meals.[27]

Baburam learned how his compassionate guru served mankind, and he later followed Ramakrishna's example in his own life. Years later he recalled: "When he was suffering from the excruciating pain of cancer, every day he would wait for seekers of God to come. Sometimes he would look out at the street and say: 'What has happened? Nobody has come today.' . . . He could not talk but only whisper. He was hungry but could not eat. He found no relief either in sitting or in lying down. Day and night he felt a burning sensation all over his body. In spite of all this terrible suffering, he never stopped showering his grace on people and helping them realize God. This went on for a year and a half. If this is not crucifixion, I don't know what it is."[28]

The disciples were desperate to save their Master's life. They knew that Sri Ramakrishna had the power to heal himself, but he was reluctant to bring his mind from God to his body. One day the Master had a hard time swallowing anything; then he said, "I shall eat later on in my subtle body through a million mouths." Baburam responded: "I do not care for your million mouths or your subtle body. What I want is that you should eat through this mouth and that I should see this gross body."[29]

Ramakrishna could not ordinarily eat any food if it was touched by an impure person or cooked by a nonbrahmin. He observed his brahminical caste rules, as he came to fulfill and not to destroy. Baburam recalled: "One day the Master asked me [Baburam was a nonbrahmin] to cook food for him and he ate from my hand. He was so gracious to me! A day or two before his passing away he asked all of us to feed him pudding, and thus he withdrew all his restrictions."[30]

Days of Wandering and Austerity

Sri Ramakrishna passed away on 16 August 1886. Baburam temporarily moved to his mother's Calcutta residence. Shortly thereafter, the disciples established the first Ramakrishna Monastery at Baranagore with the help of Surendra Mittra, a lay disciple of the Master. Baburam joined the group. In the middle of December 1886, Baburam's mother invited the Master's disciples to her country home in Antpur. Narendra, Baburam, Sharat, Shashi, Tarak, Kali, Niranjan, Gangadhar, and Sarada travelled to Antpur by train, singing devotional songs along the way.

One cold night, a bonfire was lit in the courtyard. The disciples gathered around it and meditated for a long while. Then Naren began to tell them the story of Jesus, placing emphasis on his great renunciation. Greatly inspired, the disciples took the vow of renunciation in front of the *dhuni* fire. Later, they discovered that this evening had been Christmas Eve, and they felt that a more propitious time for their vow could not have been chosen. After returning to Baranagore, the disciples took formal sannyasa, performing *viraja homa* (a special fire ceremony) in late January 1887. Narendra gave Baburam the name "Premananda," meaning "bliss of divine love," remembering the Master's remark that Sri Radha herself, the goddess of love, was partially incarnated in him.

At Baranagore the disciples lived a very austere life. They had difficulty meeting their bare necessities: if they had rice to cook, they had no money to buy salt. However, it was of no concern to them whether they ate or slept. They spent hours in meditation and other spiritual practices — they were seized by a desire to merge themselves in God. Ramakrishnananda was the caretaker of the monastery, and he took it upon himself to look after the monks and see that they ate at least one meal a day. Premananda would help with the household work as well as the Master's worship. One day he fell from a tree while picking flowers and fractured his right wrist. He forgot his pain by thinking of the Master. Later, Premananda told a touching episode about Swamiji: "After the Master's passing away Swamiji used to cry for him so much secretly at night that his pillow would get wet and I would put it in the sun in the morning to dry."[31]

We know very little of Premananda's life at the Baranagore Monastery, nor do we find a detailed account of his wanderings during this time. In the last part of February 1887, after Sri Ramakrishna's birth anniversary, Premananda left for Puri with Saradananda and Abhedananda. They stayed six months at Emar Monastery and attended the Chariot Festival of Jagannath. They lived on prasad from the temple and would pass their days in meditation and japam. During his stay in Puri, Premananda had typhoid fever, but he soon recovered through the loving care of his brother disciples. Towards the end of August they left Puri, and after visiting Bhubaneswar, Konarak, Udaygiri and Khandagiri, they returned to Baranagore.

Sometime in 1889 Premananda went to Varanasi, where he met the great illumined soul Trailanga Swami and the learned ascetic Swami Bhaskarananda. In 1890 he went to Gazipur to see Vivekananda, who was then staying with the great yogi Pavhari Baba. Premananda became ill there, and was sent back to Varanasi to live with Abhedananda. On 13 April 1890 Premananda's brother-in-law, Balaram Basu, died. Upon hearing this sad news, the swami returned to Calcutta to console his sister.

The Ramakrishna Monastery was in Baranagore from 1886 to 1892, and in Alambazar (near Dakshineswar) from 1892 to 1897. While living in Alambazar, Premananda went to Dakshineswar quite often. He would practise japam and meditation for long hours either in the Panchavati or in the Master's room. Forgetting food and rest, he lived on the memory of the Master. He was extremely simple, humble, and self-effacing. Although the monastery was their permanent home, from time to time the disciples would travel to various holy places in India for pilgrimage and to practise spiritual disciplines.

Recalling the olden days in Alambazar Monastery, Turiyananda wrote to Premananda on 20 November 1915: "The memory of all past associations with you gives me great joy. And why shouldn't it be so? You are so full of the Master that there is no room within you for anything else. This reminds me of an incident that took place at the Alambazar Monastery. As you spoke that day, you invoked the memory of the Master in all visible things. At that time I observed in you the truth of this saying, 'Wherever the eyes fall, there the Lord manifests.' You did not see anything that did not remind you of the Master. I don't know whether you remember it or not, but it is indelibly imprinted on my mind. That day I realized what it is to be merged in God."[32]

In 1895 Premananda visited various holy places in northern India, and at last settled at Kalababu's Kunja, Balaram Basu's retreat in Vrindaban. He would spend the entire day absorbed in the contemplation of God, and in the evening he would visit the deities in the temples. In December 1895 Ramakrishnananda wrote two letters to Premananda describing vividly the Master's visit to Vrindaban, which he had heard from Hriday, the Master's nephew, who had accompanied him. These letters (see *Ramakrishna as We Saw Him*, 159-60) helped Premananda to visualize the Master's pilgrimage to Vrindaban.

After some time, Brahmachari Kalikrishna (later, Swami Virajananda) joined him. During the Swing Festival of Krishna, they and Bhaktamal, a Vaishnava monk, decided to circumambulate Vrindaban (a long tedious journey that takes many days). Bhaktamal asked Premananda to put on a pair of shoes, but the latter refused as it would be disrespectful to the holy place. Living on alms, they stayed in Barsana, the birthplace of Radha, for a month and a half. At last they returned to Vrindaban. Shortly thereafter Kalikrishna became ill; Premananda took him to Etawah for treatment. They stayed with Hariprasanna (later, Swami Vijnanananda) who was working there as an engineer.

In Etawah they heard the news that Vivekananda was returning to India from the West. Towards the end of 1896 they left for Calcutta; but on the way they stopped at Burdwan to visit Holy Mother at Jayrambati. They stayed there for a couple of weeks. One day during his walk, Premananda saw beautiful lotuses in a pond and his devotion for the Mother

13

swelled in his heart. Kalikrishna did not know how to swim, so Premananda got into the water and picked some lotuses to offer to Holy Mother. When he came out of the water, Kalikrishna noticed that nearly twenty leeches were stuck on his body. As soon as they were removed, Premananda began to bleed. Holy Mother was very worried and cautioned him not to do such a thing again. From Jayrambati they went to Antpur via Tarakeshwar. At last they arrived at Alambazar Monastery, where they learned that Swamiji had reached Calcutta four or five days earlier.

After returning from the West, Vivekananda introduced a daily routine in Alambazar Monastery: in the morning — meditation, chanting, exercise, karma yoga; in the afternoon — scripture class, question and answer sessions, vespers, meditation. If a monk did not get up early in the morning, he had to beg for his food that day. Once Premananda woke up late. He went to Swamiji and said: "I am sorry I did not get up early today; brother, you made the rule that one should be punished for that reason. Please punish me." Immediately Swamiji gravely said, "Baburam, could you imagine that I would punish you?" Tears rolled from Swamiji's eyes. Brahmananda mediated the situation, saying: "It is not a question of punishment. According to the rule, one is supposed to beg food that day, that's all."[33] Premananda left to beg for his food.

In March 1897 Ramakrishnananda left for Madras to start a centre, and Premananda assumed the responsibility of the worship service. The Ramakrishna Monastery was moved from Alambazar to Nilambar Babu's garden house in Belur on 13 February 1898; and finally Swamiji consecrated the Belur Math on 9 December 1898. In the meantime Premananda had left for a pilgrimage to northern India on 4 April 1898 and returned in December during the consecration ceremony. Premananda then resumed his worship service, and Swamiji made him one of the trustees of Belur Math.

One morning at 9:00 o'clock Premananda was about to start worship in Belur Math's old shrine. Swamiji came to the shrine to bow down to the Master. Seeing Premananda, Swamiji said: "Brother, all these days you have been worshipping the Lord with flowers and sandal paste; now start worshipping the living gods. Go to Belur village and serve the poor and the afflicted." Then Swamiji asked his disciple Brahmachari Nandalal to perform the worship and Premananda left the shrine to obey his leader's order. In the village he found an old, sick widow and offered her treatment from the monastery's charitable dispensary; but the woman refused his help. Then he came across a few unwashed children in another area; he brought them to the monastery, cleaned them with soap and water, fed them, and sent them back to their homes. When Premananda was asked, he told Swamiji about his experience, "When I was serving them, I felt I was actually serving the Master through living gods."[34]

Sri Ramakrishna made Vivekananda the leader of his disciples. It is really astounding how they obeyed and respected him. One day in Belur, Sharat Chandra Chakrabarty had a dream that he was worshipping his guru, Vivekananda. He told Swamiji about his dream and begged for permission to worship him. Swamiji had to acquiesce. When the ceremony was over, Swamiji said to the disciple: "Well, your worship is finished. Now Premananda will be in a rage at your sacrilegious act of worshipping my feet in the flower tray meant for Sri Ramakrishna's worship." Before his words were finished, Premananda entered the room. Swamiji said to him: "Look, what a sacrilege he has committed! With the articles of the Master's worship, he has worshipped me." Premananda said with a smile: "Well done! Are you and the Master different?"[35]

In the beginning, in order to train the novices, Swamiji made a rule that nobody should nap in the afternoon. One day Swamiji learned that Premananda was sleeping; perhaps he had not slept the previous night. But Swamiji ordered his disciple: "Go drag him from the bed. Pull him out by the feet." The disciple obeyed his guru. Premananda cried: "What are you doing? Stop! Stop!" He did not stop. Premananda understood that Swamiji was behind it, so he did not say anything. After vespers, Swamiji was pacing in the northern veranda of his room. As soon as he saw Premananda, he embraced him and said: "Brother, our Master used to treasure you in his heart, and I am such a person that I asked that you be dragged from your bed! I am not fit to live here."[36] Then he began to sob uninterruptedly. Premananda had a hard time consoling Swamiji that day.

There is a saying, "Only he who loves, can rule." The brother disciples recognized the greatness of Swamiji, who was completely free from selfishness or any personal motivation. He was a real leader. He did not compromise the ideal or dilute the truth. One afternoon Swamiji was holding a class for the junior monks, which continued till evening. Seeing nobody in the shrine for vespers, Premananda went to the classroom and said to the young monks: "What are you doing? Aren't you coming to vespers? Finish the class and come." Swamiji immediately became angry with Premananda and said harshly: "Is it your idea that what I am doing here is not worship? When you ring the bell in the shrine, is only that worship?" He continued to berate Premananda.

Premananda was crestfallen. He went away and finished the vesper service by himself, and then disappeared. All of the monks searched for him everywhere, but could not find him. Swamiji lamented his harshness towards Premananda. He went to the shrine of Sri Ramakrishna and struck his forehead again and again on the threshold, begging forgiveness for having spoken so rudely. It is said that he struck his forehead so many times and with such intensity that the skin broke and his forehead began to bleed. At last Premananda was discovered seated alone on the roof, very morose and melancholy. The monks brought him down to Swamiji and the latter embraced him and begged his forgiveness.

Swami Vivekananda passed away on 4 July 1902. Three days earlier, while walking on the spacious lawn of the monastery with Premananda, Swamiji had pointed to a spot on the bank of the Ganges and said, "When I give up the body, cremate it there." On the day that he died Swamiji had breakfast and lunch with Premananda. He was in a jovial mood, and gave classes to the monks. After 4:00 p.m. Swamiji walked with Premananda to Belur bazar and back, a mile each way. Swamiji felt good and talked to his brother disciple on many interesting subjects. He also mentioned his plan for establishing a Vedic college in the monastery. In order to have a clearer understanding of what Swamiji felt on the matter, Premananda asked, "What will be the good of studying the Vedas?" Vivekananda replied, "It will kill superstitions."[37]

Manager of Belur Math

Before his passing away, Vivekananda gave two instructions to Premananda: first, to manage Belur Math, the headquarters of the Ramakrishna Order; second, not to initiate anyone. "If you make disciples," he said, "then your disciples will quarrel and compete with Brahmananda's." Premananda obeyed Swamiji. Swami Brahmananda was the president of the Ramakrishna Order, so he had to travel all over India to give initiation and to promote the cause of the organization. As a result, Premananda was practically in charge of Belur Math. Apart from his regular worship service, he trained the monks, entertained the devotees and visitors, supervised the kitchen, dairy, and garden, took care of the sick monks, collected money for the maintenance of the monastery, and sometimes went on lecture tours. His body was fragile, but his magnetic personality attracted many people to him. Sri Ramakrishna was living to him, and he had an ability to imprint that feeling in others.

Premananda taught more through the example of his life than through his words. A monk recorded his daily routine: He would go to bed at 11:00 p.m. and get up at 3:00 or 3:30 a.m. After washing, he would go to the shrine and perform the morning service to the Master, and then he would meditate with the monks for a couple of hours. Then, if Swami Brahmananda was at Belur, all would go to his room and bow down to him, and there would be devotional singing. At 8:00 a.m. Premananda would instruct the monks to do their respective duties. He himself would sit with some monks, cutting and cleaning vegetables for lunch. It was quite a job because a large meal, with various dishes, was prepared for many monks and devotees.

Premananda taught the monks practical Vedanta: how to blend work and worship in daily life. Even while chopping vegetables he would talk about the Master and relate many stories. His watchful eyes were everywhere. If someone peeled a potato a little too deeply, the swami would remind him that the vegetables had been bought with the devotees' hard-earned money and great sacrifice of their comfort; it was not proper for the monks to misuse those things. Premananda could not tolerate any waste, and he imprinted this idea in the minds of newcomers.

He also joined the monks in pulling out weeds from the courtyard, cutting fodder for the cows, and making cow dung balls for fuel by mixing cow dung with coal dust. He did not just give orders. "All work here is sacred," he would say, "whether you cut vegetables, whether you prepare cow dung balls, whether you go out to give lectures or worship in the chapel — everything is service unto the Lord. You have to learn to do everything with an equal sense of reverence and sanctity in your heart."[38]

True religion means the manifestation of perfection within. Premananda insisted on this perfection in every action. Swami Ashokananda recalled: "He continually impressed upon the minds of the monks that they had to be completely devoid of ego, completely devoid of any kind of carelessness, completely devoid of any kind of worldly desire. Everything had to be done perfectly from beginning to end. Once he explained the reason for it: 'My boys, one day you will have to do very responsible things. If you don't learn the habit of responsibility in small things, you will not learn the habit of responsibility in big things. You will cheat.'"[39]

After cutting vegetables, he would bathe in the Ganges, and then he would go to the shrine to perform the ritualistic worship of Sri Ramakrishna. It was a simple but very intense worship, with at least half an hour of meditation. It would end about 10:30 a.m; then he would carry the flower tray and offer flowers to the Mother Ganges. Afterwards he would take some prasad; if there were any devotees or guests he would talk about the teachings of the Master, or he would go to supervise the vegetable garden and dairy. At 11:30 a.m. he would offer cooked food to the Master and then eat his lunch. After a little rest he would answer letters, and then give a class to the monks. In the afternoon he would go for a walk, and in the evening he would perform the vesper service and sit for meditation. Afterwards Premananda would join the monks and devotees in the visitors' room, where there was either devotional singing or reading and discussion from Vivekananda's works, or he would reminisce about the Master. When the bell for food offering was rung, Premananda would go to the shrine to offer food to the Master and then close the shrine for the day. He would then eat supper. Before retiring he would attend to the needs of visiting devotees, making sure that they had beds to sleep in, and that they were all comfortable and properly cared for. This was his daily life.

Swami Rameswarananda recalled:

From early morning till he went to bed, Swami Premananda spent his whole time serving the Master, the monks, and the devotees. He was an embodiment of service.

His service to the Master was living, as if he could see the Master rising from bed, washing his mouth, eating his meals, resting in his bed, and walking in the garden. He would instruct the monks: cut the overgrowth of the thorny rose plants, otherwise they will stick to the cloth of the Master. Watch so that he may not find difficulty walking in the monastery compound. Don't put too much lime in the betel-roll; it will burn the tongue of the Master. He preferred to eat warm food; don't serve cold food to him. When you make sandalpaste for worship, there should not be any rough particles in it. In Dakshineswar the Master loved flowers and the sweet fragrance of incense; therefore, decorate the Master's shrine with flowers and burn incense. Putting the Master to bed, drop the mosquito curtain, and mentally massage his feet. Keep a glass of water on a stool next to the Master's bed, if by chance he gets up he may drink it. Change the cloth on the Master's picture on the altar every day.

In 1916-17 I used to perform worship in the shrine. One day Swami Premananda asked me: "Is the clothing of the Master okay? My boy, look carefully. After offering a new cloth to the Master, I was about to put it on; then the Master told me through a vision, 'Baburam, you are going to have a new cloth, and my shirt is torn. Don't you love me anymore?' Then both of us went to the shrine and found that the Master's shirt had been chewed by a mouse."[40]

Service to the Devotees

Premananda's life depicts how a person acts, behaves, and lives in this world after God-realization. His heart swells with love and compassion for people's suffering, and he acts without any ulterior motive or selfishness. Work turns into worship for him. The Hindu scriptures say: "Those who are devoted to God are not true devotees, but those who are devoted to the devotees of God are true devotees." Premananda taught the monks that service to the Master and service to the devotees are not different. He quoted the saying of Sri Ramakrishna, "*Bhagavata-Bhakta-Bhagavan* — the scripture, the devotee, and God — all three are the same." Another time he said: "The Master called from the roof of the *kuthi* [bungalow] in Dakshineswar, 'O devotees, wherever you are, please come.' Is that call only for a few of us? He called you and many more. All the devotees of the Master have not yet arrived."[41]

When flowers bloom, bees come of their own accord. Premananda's love and magnetic personality attracted many people to Belur Math, and sometimes they even came at odd times. College boys from Calcutta used to gather there; he always received them as a loving mother. He considered it a great privilege for the monks to serve devotees with food and hospitality, love and spirituality. Sometimes he gave his own food to the devotees and went without. Devotees would sometimes come after dinner was over, and he himself would go to the kitchen and start cooking. The monks, of course, did not want him to do that. But he would say, "You have worked so hard, let me cook." Sometimes people would come late at night, and if they wanted to eat, the monks would get up and prepare a meal. If there were no extra beds, they would give their own beds to these visitors. A monk recalled: "I didn't have any time to sleep in those days. I would just lie down on a bench for two to three hours." If there was any grumbling among the young monks, Premananda would say: "Look, people suffer so much in the world. They come to Sri Ramakrishna's place to get some peace. It is your duty to make them feel welcome. It will be of great benefit to you; it will be of great benefit to them."[42]

Some devotees once came with a baby who was crying for food. Premananda immediately set aside some milk for the Master's offering, and gave the rest to the baby. A rich family from Calcutta came to Belur Math by car, and was about to leave without having prasad. Premananda asked a monk to run and give some prasad to them. The next day they sent a good quantity of sweets and others things for offering to the Master.

Premananda commented: "Look, if the monks serve the devotees, the Master makes them serve himself as well as the monks. But you serve them without any motive."[43]

Once a devotee from Madras fell asleep on the upstairs veranda. Premananda noticed this at midnight. He immediately set a mosquito curtain over his bed and began to fan him. The devotee woke up and was overwhelmed when he saw Premananda fanning him. On another occasion many devotees came to the monastery and they left their shoes in the courtyard and went to the shrine. In the meantime, it started raining. A brahmacharin rushed to bring those shoes to the veranda, and he began to lift them with his foot. Observing the brahmacharin's feeling of superiority, Premananda said, "Carry the devotees' shoes on your head."[44] In Varanasi he said to a monk, "Look, a monk's bag should have two openings [which means things will come in from one side and will go out through the other]. You serve a person who donates money and neglect another who cannot afford to; that is not proper conduct for a monk."[45]

Swami Brahmananda was the president of the board of trustees and Premananda was a trustee. Once in the trustee meeting Swami Shuddhananda read the financial report and told Brahmananda that there was a four hundred rupee deficit in connection with the service to the devotees. Brahmananda asked, "Brother Baburam, how shall we tackle this deficit?" Premananda replied, "Maharaj, I have spent this money for serving the devotees, so I shall collect it by begging."[46] Another time Shuddhananda proposed to Brahmananda that there should be some rules and regulations about the devotees' staying in Belur Math. Premananda said: "Look, Shuddhananda, as long as we are alive, let it continue this way; when we die, you can open a hotel for the devotees. . . . It is the Master who brings the devotees and they bring everything for him. Likewise, it is the Master who is eating and also who is feeding the devotees. What can we say about it?"[47]

During India's struggle for independence, some young men severed themselves from the freedom movement and joined the Ramakrishna Order. Sometimes plainclothes police officers would come to Belur Math to keep track of these ex-revolutionaries. A police spy reminisced about Premananda's greatness: "Under the instruction of higher authority, I went to Belur Math for an inspection. It was a hot summer noon. I walked all the way. When I arrived, I was exhausted, and sat on a bench. It was quiet; it seemed all were resting. All of a sudden, a person came and began to fan me with a palm leaf fan. Afterwards he gave me some prasad and a glass of cold water. I ate and felt greatly relieved. He knew who I was, still he served me."[48]

Love sees no faults. A young man from a noble family of Calcutta had fallen in with undesirable companions and through their influence had taken drugs. This was very painful for his relatives, who tried their best to correct his behaviour, but all their efforts failed. In desperation, his brother, who was a monk, sought the help of Premananda. Premananda quietly listened to his story, and then went to visit the boy. After a long talk, he convinced him to come to the monastery for a visit the following day, which he did. He continued to come to Belur many times afterwards. Gradually, the spiritual presence of Premananda began to change his character. "How much tenderness and affection he bestowed on me," he recalled later. "My relatives and friends abandoned me, but his love sustained me. He knew all my misdeeds, and still he loved me!" Eventually he renounced the world and joined the Order as a monk.[49]

Training the Young Monks

It is extremely difficult to train monks. They first observe the teacher's life and then secondly his scholarship. Only a man of purity, renunciation, love, and learning can train monks. Premananda was endowed with the first three qualities from his very birth. Although he did not have much formal education, day and night he read the living Upanishad, that is, the life and teachings of Sri Ramakrishna.

Once a young man came to Premananda and expressed his desire to become a monk. The swami told him: "Now you are a student. Finish your bachelor's degree and then join the monastery. Swamiji had a B.A. degree." The young man said, "Swami, is it not possible to become a monk without a B.A. degree? You have no B.A. degree." Premananda, addressing a monk, said, "Look, what this boy says! My boy, whatever learning we needed, the Master gave us. We don't need any degrees."[50]

Premananda was an inspirer of souls. He reminded the monks: "Never forget that the goal of human life is to realize God, to have His vision. That is why you have renounced hearth and home. Struggle hard to have love and devotion for Him. Yearn for Him with a longing heart. You are men. Be gods! Teach others by the example of your own life." After a few minutes of silence he continued, "I see very clearly that after we are gone, multitudes will come to learn from you young men."

"Who will listen to us?" said a young monk.

Premananda: "Don't think that you are inferior to us. You have received the grace of the Holy Mother. Do you think we have become great just because people take the dust of our feet? No! We first saw Sri Ramakrishna and then renounced the world; you are great indeed because you have renounced the world without seeing him!"

The young monk: "The Master made you great."

Premananda: "No! The Master did not make us great, he made us 'nobodies.' You also have to become 'nobodies.' Wipe out all vanity from the mind. The Master used to say, 'When the ego dies, all troubles cease.' 'Not I, not I, but Thou, O Lord.'"[51]

Premananda was an embodiment of humility, patience, forbearance, and forgiveness. One day he revealed his mind to a senior monk: "After finishing my morning meditation and japam when I come down the stairs of the shrine, I repeat again and again this mantram of the Master, 'sha, sha, sa — forbear, forbear, forbear. He who forbears, survives; and he who does not, perishes.'"[52] Devoid of any trace of pride and egotism, he felt himself to be an instrument in the hands of the Master. In Belur Math Premananda had to act as a loving mother as well as a chastising father. He scolded the monks to correct their shortcomings, but his tender heart cried afterwards. Sometimes while walking alone in the courtyard of the monastery, he would admonish himself: "O Baburam, be careful! O Baburam, be careful!" Some of his letters indicate his inner feelings:

> I do not harbour the idea that I am good. I have come to learn. There is no end to learning. May the Master give us right understanding — this is my prayer. By observing the faults of others we gradually become infected by them. We have not come to look at their faults and to correct them. It is only to learn that we are here. Lord, Thou art everything. Whom should I scold? Everything is He; there is only a difference in the quantity of dust that covers the gold.[53]

Despite his humility, Premananda could be stern if necessary. He laid great stress on gentleness of behaviour. "Be gentle first," he would often repeat, "if you want to be a monk." He said regretfully: "Nowadays no one pays any attention to social and common good manners and gentle behaviour. The Master used to take extreme care to teach us these things."

A monk wrote: "By his eloquent and impassioned appeals he would firmly impress upon the novitiates the high ideals of Sri Ramakrishna and

Swami Vivekananda. As he held out vividly before their imagination the wonderful renunciation of the Master, his keen thirst for God-realization, his unheard-of devotion to truth, his strenuous religious practices and austerities, his wonderful realizations, and his profound love and kindness for his disciples — he would appear to be lifted out of the mundane plane and his words would electrify the audience. Thus he moulded the young minds in the cast of a new ideal."[54]

Premananda did not care for one-sidedness; he encouraged the monks to practise all four yogas — karma, jnana, bhakti, and raja — according to the ideals of Vivekananda. "You should learn," he said, "how to work in every walk of life — be it a worshipper in the shrine, a cook in the kitchen, a cowherd in the cowshed, or a sweeper in the toilet. Be they great or small, all works should receive your equal attention. Always take as much care of the means as of the ends."[55] He could not bear the monks to be even slightly indifferent or careless towards their work. He scolded them vehemently, yet he was quick to forgive and forget the faults of all. Premananda's scoldings are now legendary in the Ramakrishna Order.

Swami Gnaneswarananda recalled:

Because Swami Premananda was so loving to all, he was often referred to as the "Mother of the Math." He could also be quite stern at times, but it was always for our good. I was once severely reprimanded by him. There had been talk about the Bhagavad Gita, and I had said, "Yes, I have read it." Immediately Swami Premananda said, "My boy, say I *am reading* it. Never say I have read the Gita. One can never finish reading the Gita."

Another time we were weeding the Math garden. Swami Premananda was watching us and he noticed that one of the boys was not pulling the weeds out by the roots. He called out to him: "My boy, you must pull the weeds out by the roots, otherwise, you are simply fooling yourself and wasting time. If you do not realize the necessity of rooting out weeds in the garden, how can you weed out your old faults and tendencies? How can you understand the real meaning of spiritual life?" And he added, significantly, "Weed them out, boys! Weed them out, roots and all."

On another occasion, Swami Premananda chastised us for talking too much: "You talkative fools! You talk nothing but nonsense. Let not your tongue talk; let your character speak!" And again, "Why do you buzz so much? You bees evidently haven't yet found the honey."[56]

One day Premananda asked a brahmacharin to cut fodder for the cows and sent him to the cowshed. The brahmacharin began his duty with overconfidence, and shortly cut his finger. Premananda stopped by the cowshed on his usual rounds to see how different work was going on. The boy tried to conceal his bleeding finger, but could not evade Premananda's vigilant eyes. He said sharply: "You are careless! I asked you to cut the fodder, not your finger. Didn't I? You can see your finger bleed. But do you know how it makes another's heart bleed? I thought you were a very clever boy, but you have proved yourself a fool and me a greater one. Shame on you! You considered the work very trivial!"[57] Then he took the boy to the dispensary and had his finger bandaged.

Knowing that Premananda was a strict disciplinarian, Brahmananda sometimes would tease his brother disciple. One morning the monks were in Brahmananda's room upstairs and were engaged in spiritual talk. It began to grow late. Premananda found that the boys had not come downstairs to start their respective duties. So he shouted from downstairs: "Hello, up there! You boys come down now. The Master's lunch has not yet been arranged." Out of fun Brahmananda asked the boys to go to Premananda and to say: "Sir, please give us liberation. Then we will have no more difficulty with our meditation, prayer, and other disciplines. Surely you can do this for us." Overhearing Brahmananda's joke, Premananda shouted: "All right, you practise your samadhi. To that I have no objection. I will handle everything by myself. But just once let me find the noise of the marketplace arising in your minds, and I'll pull you by the ears and soon put you back to work!"[58]

A monk was in charge of the kitchen store. One day while pouring oil, a few drops fell on the floor. Premananda saw it. He called to the monk: "Why are you wasting the Master's oil? The devotees donate their hard-earned money for the Master's service. You will not have to work here anymore. I bow down to you." Premananda bent his head and left the place. The monk felt terrible. He continued his work, but did not eat any food for a few days except for drinking Ganges water. When Premananda heard about it, he embraced the monk and said: "Are you mad at me? Who else do I have other than you? If you do not do right, shall I not scold you? Know for certain, a monk's scolding purifies the mind."[59] Premananda then gave him prasad and removed his mental agony.

Once he approached a brahmacharin who had been spending much of his time working in the garden: "Are you studying the scriptures or doing only the work of a coolie?" The brahmacharin sheepishly replied: "One of our brothers reads and we listen. Moreover, I don't know Sanskrit well." Swami Dhirananda jokingly remarked, "Out of fear of study he left home, and now here you are asking him to study?" Ignoring the joke, Premananda named a new English book and then sternly said to the brahmacharin: "Read that book from beginning to end within three months. Otherwise, you take just enough fare from the office for a ferry across the Ganges [which meant he would have to leave the monastery]."[60]

During those days scripture classes were held every evening in the visitors' room of the monastery. One evening after meditation, Premananda came there and found no one. The room was dark. He was greatly annoyed at this. When the news spread that Premananda was waiting in the classroom, other monks came. All were silent when Premananda asked why the class was not being held. At last a brahmacharin said: "We find it difficult to hold the class in this room. The devotees who come to the Math are often found lying down or sleeping here." The compassionate swami replied: "Do you know how many worries and troubles they have in their lives? They are tormented in the world, so they come here for peace and rest. This place vibrates with a holy atmosphere and the gentle breeze of the Ganges. Where will you find such a peaceful place? Let them sleep. What are you here for? You have renounced everything to awaken people. The Master and Swamiji came to awaken the whole world. You have come to work for them. Can you not awaken these few people? Seeing you awakened, their sleep will break."[61]

When Brahmananda, Turiyananda, or any other direct disciples of the Master were at Belur Math, Premananda would ask the young monks to serve them and associate with them. He told the monks: "Having the company of God, they have become gods. They are not ordinary people. Your life will be blessed if you associate with them and serve them." If Brahmananda was displeased with any monk, Premananda would take that monk to him and humbly plead: "Maharaj, this boy is good. Please don't be mad at him. If you bless him by placing your palm on his head, all of his shortcomings will go away." Saying this, Premananda grasped Maharaj's hand and touched the head of the monk.[62]

Once, after the evening service, Premananda sat for meditation in a corner of the southern veranda of the old shrine. The usual time passed but he did not get up. When he came to offer the food, the attendant of the shrine found Premananda sitting motionless. He presumed that sleep had overtaken the swami's tired body, and he called him repeatedly, but in vain. He returned after the shrine service and called him again — still there was no response. He then held a light before him. Slowly Premananda opened his eyes. When he was asked if he had fallen asleep, Premananda answered through a mystical song: "I am awakened and will sleep no more. I am awake in the state of yoga. O Mother, I have given back Thy mystic sleep to Thee and have put sleep to sleep." Turning to the attendant he said: "When you find me in that state, don't call me or cry aloud, but repeat the Master's name in my ears. That will bring me back."[63]

On Pilgrimage and with Brother Disciples

Premananda did not travel as much as some of his brother disciples did. In the early part of his monastic life, he accompanied his mother to Rameswaram, an important holy place in South India. Later, in 1906 he went to Puri, the holy place of Jagannath. One day he happened to notice a Christian missionary standing before the Jagannath Temple, strongly upbraiding Hinduism. He could not bear to hear Hinduism denounced in that sacred place. He loudly began to chant the name of the Lord: "Hari bol! Hari bol!" The crowd quickly picked it up, and the missionary's voice was drowned out. The priests immediately expressed their gratitude to Premananda and said, "We had been fearful of taking any action to stop the missionary." Premananda quickly left the place, abashed and sad at heart over his impulsive action. That night Sri Ramakrishna appeared to him in a dream and asked him: "Why did you break up that gathering? That man was also spreading my name and teachings. Tomorrow you must find the missionary and apologize." The next morning, after a considerable search, Premananda located the house of the missionary and humbly asked his forgiveness.[64]

In 1910 Premananda went with Shivananda and Turiyananda to see Amarnath, the ice lingam of Shiva in Kashmir. Later Premananda wrote to Sister Devamata: "Just imagine what a glorious experience it was for all of us — both the vision of that great white cave of Amarnath at an altitude of about eighteen thousand feet and the toilsome journey through the most enchanting and soul-stirring scenery in the world."[65] They also visited Kshirbhavani, and they stayed in a houseboat for a month in Srinagar. After visiting Kankhal, Hardwar, and Varanasi, Premananda returned to Belur Math in December 1910.

In 1914 Premananda went to Varanasi to bring Brahmananda back to Belur Math. Brahmananda was reluctant to leave the city of Lord Shiva. "But, Maharaj," said Premananda, "Swamiji is our Lord Shiva, and he resides in Belur." Brahmananda remained silent. Then Brahmananda went to visit Prayag (Allahabad) and Premananda followed him. One afternoon Premananda suddenly prostrated himself flat before his brother disciple. Brahmananda immediately became excited and said: "Brother, what are you doing? Get up! Get up!" But Premananda remained firm. "I will not. Not until you agree to return to Belur Math." Premananda's love and humility won. Brahmananda smiled: "Rise, brother, rise. I will come back."[66]

A remarkable incident took place during this trip that was later narrated by Swami Prabhavananda:

> It was in Varanasi in October 1914. Swami Premananda used to visit the temples of Lord Vishwanath and Mother Annapurna after taking his bath in the Ganges. I would accompany him. One day after we finished worship in the temple of Annapurna, the head priest placed a garland of marigolds around Swami Premananda's neck. When the swami was about to take the garland off to give it to me, I saluted him: "No, Maharaj, keep it yourself. You look so beautiful." The word "beautiful" reminded the swami of God's beauty, and he went into ecstasy. His face flushed, and then a light began to emanate from his whole body. Walking slowly, he left the temple, and I followed him. The temple lane was crowded as usual, but on either side of us people stared at the swami and made way. It was quite evident that everyone present saw him illumined. He was completely absorbed in the thought of God and oblivious of his surroundings. As we approached the outer gate of the monastery, Swami Nirbharananda, the abbot, saw us from the veranda. He immediately ordered the monks to prepare a special welcome for Swami Premananda. We entered the monastery grounds to the sound of bells and conch shells. As the swami got to the veranda, he took off the garland and placed it around the neck of the abbot. For a brief moment he danced in ecstatic joy. Gradually the ecstasy abated, and the divine light disappeared.[67]

Although Premananda was essentially gentle-natured, he was neither emotional nor sentimental. But sometimes he would become God-intoxicated, and his blissful mood would unfailingly draw others into an elevated state. Once during Durga Puja in Belur Math, the monks were singing devotional songs. Premananda suddenly became filled with divine joy and urged Saradananda: "Brother, you will have to sing a song. Don't you see how much joy is flowing here? But unless you sing, this flow of joy will not be complete." Saradananda protested that he had not sung for a long time. However, unable to avoid the loving request of Premananda, Saradananda sang and later joined in dancing with other brother disciples. He was quite bulky. The next day he remarked, "Alas, Brother Baburam made me dance in my old age."[68]

The disciples of Sri Ramakrishna had great love and respect for each other. Premananda and Shivananda were together once in Belur Math during the Shivaratri festival. Addressing Shivananda, Premananda said, "This is our Lord Shiva! Brother Tarak is our Shiva!" Another day Brahmananda told the monks about Premananda: "Listen, if you can follow sincerely one or two things that Premananda says, your lives will be blessed. Is he an ordinary man? He is so pure that in whatever direction he looks, everything in that direction becomes pure."[69]

Once during the Master's birth anniversary, M. came to Belur Math to pay his homage to the Master. He was not well. After saluting the Master in the shrine, M. sat under the mango tree in the courtyard. He carried some puffed rice for refreshment and inquired if there was any curd (yogurt) in the storeroom. A young monk went to check and found a pot of curd that had not yet been offered to the Master; for that reason, it could not be given to M. While the monk was returning from the storeroom, Premananda learned from him that M. needed curd. Premananda immediately took the pot and, standing in front of the Master's picture, offered it to him with closed eyes. He then gave it to the monk to serve M. Afterwards Premananda told a monk, with emotion: "Today the Master saved me from a grave error. Do you know M. was an intimate companion of the Master? The Master eats food through the mouths of these devotees. Have you not read in the *Gospel*, where the Master says that if you feed one of them, you will attain virtue equivalent to feeding one thousand monks? In the Ramakrishna incarnation, M. is the Sage Vyasa [the recorder] and again the Sage Narada [the singer]. Day and night the gospel of the Master comes from his lips like a fountain. The Master saved me today from a serious mistake."[70]

Ego separates human beings from God; that is why Sri Ramakrishna always taught his disciples to be humble. Even after his passing away, the Master kept watch on his Baburam. Premananda was a strict vegetarian and had a little hidden repugnance for people who ate fish; this attitude occasionally would surface in his words and dealings. One night the Master told him in a vision: "Look, Baburam, my children eat a little fish. Why do you make so much fuss about it? Do you think that you have achieved everything because you don't eat fish?" The next morning Premananda got up and first went to the kitchen and touched his tongue to the fish-cutting knife. He said to himself: "I am Baburam; why should I hurt others' feelings?" Afterwards he sent someone to the market to buy good fish; he then cut them, cooked them, and served them to the monks himself. After lunch he apologized to the monks: "The Master used to say, 'The poison of the big cobra and the little cobra is the same.' [The same divinity abides in an illumined soul as well as in a young monk.] I beg forgiveness from all of you. I must not say anything that could hurt others' feelings."[71]

Premananda's whole life was one of complete self-surrender. Behind every action was the subtle but commanding presence of Sri Ramakrishna. Sometimes this presence became visible and Premananda would be blessed with a vision of his beloved guru. However, this did not always occur under the most pleasant of circumstances. Once Premananda gave a pumpkin from the monastery garden to a poor brahmin. Seeing the brahmin taking away the pumpkin, Brahmananda said to Premananda, "If you freely distribute the vegetables in this way, how shall we manage the Master's service here?" Premananda was hurt. He put his towel on his shoulder and marched out of the Belur compound, prepared to leave for good. But the moment he reached the gate, his towel was suddenly snatched from him, and in an instant tightened around his neck. He turned, only to find the figure of Sri Ramakrishna standing in front of him. "Where are you going, my child?" the Master said. "How can you go away, leaving me here?" Overwhelmed by the experience, Premananda rushed to Brahmananda and prostrated himself at his feet.[72]

Premananda was one of the few disciples of the Master who had free access to Holy Mother. She was very fond of him, and Premananda was also very devoted to her. Whenever any monk would go to visit Mother at Udbodhan, Premananda would send flowers, vegetables, and milk for her, asking the monk to convey his salutations to her. Because he never initiated anyone, he would send the devotees to Holy Mother or Brahmananda for initiation. Premananda's face actually glowed when he spoke about Holy Mother. He once said that those who differentiated between her and the Master would never make any spiritual progress; she and the Master were like the two sides of one and the same coin. In the course of a talk at Belur Math he said to the devotees: "We have seen that she had a much greater capacity than the Master. She was the embodiment of Power, and how well she controlled it! Sri Ramakrishna could not do so, though he tried. His power became manifest through his frequent ecstasies, which were seen by all. The Mother repeatedly experienced samadhi, but others did not know of it. What wonderful self-control she exercised! She cov-

14

ered herself with a veil, like a young bride in her husband's home. The people of Jayrambati thought she was busy day and night looking after her nephews and nieces."[73]

As a Preacher

Life inspires life. Sometimes a great scholar with wonderful oratory cannot impress the audience; on the other hand, a person with a few words — not well arranged and perhaps ungrammatical — can make an immense impression. Vivekananda commented: "Words, even thoughts, contribute only one-third of the influence in making an impression, the man, two-thirds. What you call the personal magnetism of the man — that is what goes out and impresses you."[74] Premananda was a magnetic and powerful speaker, and he talked based on his experience. He spoke from his heart — and the voice of the heart is understood by all. He pointed out again and again that religion lies in practice and not in theory. Purity and dispassion are two indispensable conditions for God-realization. During his stay at Dakshineswar, Premananda started to record some of Sri Ramakrishna's teachings. But the Master told him: "That is not your task. Many beautiful words of wisdom will burst forth from your lips."[75]

If Holy Mother was in Calcutta, Premananda would always ask her permission to go anywhere to lecture. In 1914 Premananda was invited to speak during the Ramakrishna festival at Malda, North Bengal. He came with the devotees to Udbodhan to receive the Mother's permission, but she refused it because Premananda had been sick only a fortnight before. When the devotees again importuned Holy Mother about the trip, she asked Premananda if he wanted to go. He replied with great emotion: "What do I know, Mother? I shall carry out your order. If you ask me to jump into fire, I will jump; if you ask me to plunge into water, I will plunge; if you ask me to enter into hell, I will enter. What do I know? Your word is final." At last Holy Mother gave him permission, but she asked him to return soon. To the devotees she said: "You see, they are all great souls. Their bodies are channels for doing good to the world. Look after their physical comfort and ease."[76]

In Malda Swami Premananda gave a lecture entitled "Serve Human Beings as God." He emphasized Vivekananda's karma yoga, practical Vedanta, and concluded that the religion of this age is to serve mankind. While he was lecturing, a gentleman asked him to speak about love and devotion; but Premananda ignored him. But when the man repeated himself, Premananda said: "Who will listen to love and devotion? I don't find anybody here who is fit to listen to it." Then the swami continued: "Sir, listen to a story. Once a street hawker was calling out, 'Who wants to buy love? Who wants to buy love?' People opened their front doors and inquired about the price. The hawker said: 'Price? It is priceless! But I can sell this invaluable love in exchange for a head. Are you ready to give up your heads?' People immediately shut their doors." Then pointing to the audience, Premananda said, "Is there anybody here ready to give up his head [the ego]?" Everyone kept quiet.[77]

In 1901, after returning from East Bengal (now Bangladesh), Vivekananda had said to Premananda, "I have left East Bengal for you." It was a prophetic statement. Every year from 1913 to 1917, Premananda visited East Bengal, sometimes alone and once with Brahmananda. Swami Ashokananda recorded: "His visits were all epic events. Wherever he went, thousands of people — old and young, Hindus and Muslims — were attracted to him. And when he would leave a place, even after a visit of only a few days, people would run after him, crying. He probably would be going off in a horse carriage, and they would run to keep up with him. For miles people would follow him like that, shedding tears as if someone very near to them were dying. These are the real miracles of the spirit. He would just pull their hearts out; he bought them up, as it were, with his love — Hindus and Muslims alike."[78] As a result of Premananda's extensive preaching in East Bengal, many young men joined the Ramakrishna Order.

Premananda was an illumined soul, and he was beyond caste, creed, and religious sect. Knowing his universal attitude, the Muslim Nawab Salimulla of Dhaka invited Premananda to his palace. Premananda carried the Master's prasad to the Muslim devotees. He met the Begums (Muslim women of royal families) in the palace of Nawab Gani, told them the life story of Sri Ramakrishna, and shared his message of the harmony of religions. Salimulla had read Swami Vivekananda's works and was attracted to the activities of the Ramakrishna Mission. He invited Premananda to consult with him about opening a centre in Dhaka for Muslim youths. Salimulla's sister, Begum Akhtara Banu, donated some money for the construction of the Ramakrishna Math in Dhaka, in her father's memory. Later some Muslim women became very drawn to Premananda and visited Belur Math.

Knowing Premananda's successful mission in Dhaka, Turiyananda wrote to him: "You are the precious jewel-casket of Sri Ramakrishna. As an embodiment of love, you are distributing love like the gopis of Vrindaban.

Brother, save some love for us."[79] Observing Premananda's great enthusiasm for preaching, Brahmananda cautioned him not to overdo it, as his body was very fragile. To this Premananda said: "I am perfect, eternally free. I am a follower of Swamiji, and it is he who asked me to carry the message of Sri Ramakrishna to every village."[80] On another occasion, Premananda asked Holy Mother: "Mother, I don't have any learning, but people from various places invite me to speak. What shall I do?" Mother replied: "My son, don't worry. The Master will speak sitting on your tongue. He is with you."[81]

On one occasion Premananda was ready to go to East Bengal, and the devotees were waiting for him in the boat at Belur ghat. They were supposed to take the train from Calcutta, and then take a steamer. Premananda went to the shrine to get the Master's permission. A monk who happened to be there heard Premananda talking to the Master, but he didn't hear the Master's response. At last Premananda said, "All right, Master, I shall not go." He then came downstairs and told the devotees that he would not go that day. The devotees were disappointed; but the newspaper later reported that the steamer he was supposed to take from Goalanda to Dhaka had been sunk by a cyclone.[82]

In 1915 Premananda visited Rarikhal in Dhaka and stayed at the house of the famous scientist Jagadish Chandra Bose. The caretaker of the house gave him a nice room, but the bed was infested with bedbugs. As soon as he went to bed, he was attacked by them. He asked his attendant to light the lantern. The bedbugs temporarily disappeared when they saw the light, but they returned when it was turned off. Premananda sat on his bed and passed the whole night in meditation. The next day he continued his busy schedule, lecturing and talking to the people, and so on. When he was reminded to take rest, he said, "My body does not get tired talking about the Master."[83]

The devotees of Rarikhal invited Premananda to their Ramakrishna festival. They collected donations from Hindu villagers, but not from the Muslims, believing that they would not help a Hindu cause. But the Muslims had seen Premananda; some of them had talked with him; and the Muslim community was aware of his holiness. "Does he belong to the Hindus only?" they said. "He is also our *pir* [Muslim saint]." A Muslim delegation came to Premananda and said: "What have we done that we were not asked for contributions for this festival? Why have we been left out?"[84] They felt aggrieved. So Premananda sent volunteers to the Muslim community to collect funds, which they gladly gave for the Master's festival. He said in a public meeting: "We Hindus and

Muslims are like two brothers. If we sincerely worship our respective gods without keeping any hatred for each other, our divine sight will open. Only then shall we realize all are one."[85] It is amazing how Premananda's unselfish love and feeling brought harmony between the Hindus and Muslims!

After returning to Belur Math, Premananda was stricken by cholera. Two reputable doctors treated him. One day he lost outer consciousness and the monks almost lost hope. Gradually he opened his eyes and said feebly: "Don't fear. I shall not die, because my mother is still alive." (Sri Ramakrishna had given his mother the boon that her children would not die before she did.) Premananda recovered from his illness and left for Puri, where he stayed for three months. In September 1915 he returned to Belur Math.

In January 1916 Premananda again left for East Bengal with Brahmananda and a group of monks. They visited Kamakhya (a famous place for Mother worship), Mymensingh, and Dhaka. On this occasion Brahmananda laid the foundation stone of Ramakrishna Mission in Dhaka. While there the swamis stayed at Agnes Villa and met some revolutionaries who were fighting for India's freedom. Swami Nikhilananda was then a college student and connected with a revolutionary society. He wrote in his memoirs:

One morning I went to the Villa with two members of our revolutionary society. Swami Premananda took us to a small room in which there were two beds. Swami Brahmananda was seated on one of them. Swami Premananda took his seat on the other. After saluting Swami Brahmananda we sat on the floor.

Swami Premananda introduced us to Swami Brahmananda and said to him: "Maharaj, look at these young men. They are all fine boys, but completely misguided. They have become revolutionaries in order to serve India. Please give them right advice." Usually very reserved, Swami Brahmananda asked us in an earnest voice to give up the method of violence and follow in the footsteps of Swami Vivekananda. He said that we must first build our character and only then take up the service of the country. By way of illustration he said: "If gunpowder is damp it will not explode. However you may try to ignite it, you will only be wasting match sticks. But if the powder is dry, one match will be enough to produce the explosion." He emphasized that Swami Vivekananda was a real patriot and that we should follow his instructions.

"But, sir," I said, "you have not understood Swami Vivekananda.

We read in his books that he wants us to shed our blood for India's freedom. That is what the revolutionaries are doing. You have not understood Swami Vivekananda's teachings."

That was too much for Swami Premananda. "You idiot!" he exclaimed. "You do not know with whom you are talking. We knew Swamiji for over twenty years. We ate together, played together, talked together, and discussed our plans of work together — and we have not understood him! And you fools have read a few pages of his books and understand him completely!" Then, addressing Swami Brahmananda, he said: "Maharaj, did you hear that? He said that you did not understand Swamiji. Do you think he has the intelligence of a horse? Let me see if he can carry me on his back!"

Suddenly he left his bed and asked me to go down on all fours. Sitting on my back, with his feet hanging down on both sides, he asked me to take him round the room, as if I were a real horse. I did as I was asked. After a minute or two he dismounted and said to me that everything would be all right. Swami Brahmananda looked at the whole affair benignly and again advised us first to mould our character. We left the room — and that was the end of my connection with the revolutionary society.[86]

One day Premananda and Brahmananda went to visit Deobhog, the home of Nag Mahashay (Saint Durga Charan Nag) who was an ideal householder disciple of Sri Ramakrishna. Premananda bowed down in front of his cottage and lamented, "Oh, if Nag Mahashay were alive today!" Brahmananda also said: "What a holy place! Nag Mahashay was a great soul, so this place is vibrating with consciousness!" Then the swamis and devotees sang and danced in ecstasy in the courtyard. They chanted: *"Hari haraye namah, Krishna yadavaya namah; Yadavaya namah Krishna Madhavaya namah."* (Salutation to Hari; Salutation to Krishna; Salutation to Yadava and Madhava).[87]

Premananda returned to Belur Math on 26 February 1916. On 5 March he told the monks: "During my last visit to Dhaka I used to talk day and night with the devotees. This would often cause insomnia. Of course I would repeat and explain only the words of the Master — myself I know nothing — yet I could not sleep at night. That was because I am but a small 'vessel.' But we have seen the Master going again and again into ecstasy and samadhi — it was so natural with him."[88] On another occasion he said: "Who will preach? Nobody is needed to preach Sri Ramakrishna. He is preached by himself. Wherever I go, I see the glory of the Master. Out of mercy he took me to all those places to see how he was spreading his ideas among the people."[89]

On Sunday, 5 March 1916, the annual general meeting of the Ramakrishna Mission was held at Belur Math. When the agenda of the meeting
was completed, Brahmananda asked Premananda to give a talk. Premananda spoke to the audience:

Elephants have two sets of teeth: one outside — the tusks, and another
inside to chew food. The activities of our Mission are like the elephant's
tusks. Whatever work you may do — managing hospitals or conducting relief work — unless you have character, all will be in vain. What
is wanted is character, purity, steadfast devotion to God. If you have
them, you will prosper, otherwise you will totally fail.

(To the lay members) It is no good being only members of the Mission. You must build up your own character, you must make the whole
world your own through love, so that people may find inspiration
from your selflessness, renunciation, and purity. You must drive away
all egotism and pride from your heart and consider yourselves as servants of the Lord and thus serve humanity.

Our Master never sought name and fame, and so they have come
to him in profusion. Swamiji often said in his later life that he was disgusted with name and fame. Be you all men of character. Grow into
gods. Only then will the work of the Mission prosper. This is my
earnest prayer to you all.[90]

In 1917 Premananda made his last visit to East Bengal. In Mymensingh,
a Muslim teacher heard Premananda say that all religions are true and
the same God exists in all beings. To test Premananda, the Muslim teacher
asked: "Sir, you are preaching a wonderful catholic attitude, but can you
partake of food from my plate?" [An orthodox Hindu will never eat food
touched by a Muslim.] "Yes, I can," replied Premananda. Immediately
some food was brought on a plate, and without the slightest hesitation
he partook of it from the hands of the Muslim teacher.

One day at Dhaka, Premananda and other monks and devotees were
invited to dinner at a devotee's home. Premananda was speaking to the
group with his usual fervour. In the audience was the curator of a
museum, who was a sceptic. In the course of the talk, Premananda said,
"Pray to God for spiritual treasures, such as devotion, knowledge, power
of discrimination, dispassion, and so forth." The curator interrupted:
"Why should we pray to God? Does he not know what we need?" Premananda answered: "Yes, if you feel that way — if you are convinced that
God knows all your needs and will fulfill them, then you don't have to
pray. But many pray to God for the fulfillment of their worldly desires,
for material things. Is it not wise to pray to him for the eternal instead of

the evanescent? Who but a fool will approach the King of kings for a trifle? If you pray to God, pray to him for the highest."[91]

A real teacher must be ready to sacrifice himself and to set an example for others. Premananda's favourite saying was: If you want to be a *sardar* (leader), be *sirdar* (ready to sacrifice one's head). One day Premananda was visiting Hasara, a village close to Dhaka. On the way he saw a pond full of water hyacinth, a terrible pest in East Bengal that pollutes water and fosters the breeding of mosquitos, which carry malarial fever. Many people suffer and die from malarial epidemics. He asked the young men who accompanied him to clear the pond. To set an example he himself got into the water to remove some of them. This seriously affected his health.

Towards the End

Either because of physical exhaustion in Dhaka or from eating tainted food, Premananda contracted a high fever. He returned to Belur Math in the middle of June 1917. Doctors diagnosed it as *kala-azar*, a malignant fever that was then difficult to cure and frequently fatal. During the rainy season the climate of Belur Math was not good, so he was taken to Udbodhan first and then to Balaram's house for treatment.

Premananda followed his guru's teaching "renounce lust and gold" till death. Once in Calcutta he found a bag in a carriage. He asked the driver to take him to the place where he dropped his last passenger. When they arrived and the driver identified the person, Premananda introduced himself and handed over the bag to him. Immediately the gentleman checked the contents and found everything, including 5,000 rupees cash. Overwhelmed, the gentleman saluted Premananda and exclaimed: "Such honesty is only possible for a disciple of Ramakrishna."[92]

One day Haramohan Mittra's mother, a devotee of the Master, came to see Premananda. Because he was very weak, the swami asked his attendant to cover his body with a chadar and sit him up by putting two pillows at his back. After a brief conversation Haramohan's mother left. Curious, the attendant asked Premananda: "This woman devotee is five years older than your mother. Why did you cover your body with a chadar and meet her in a formal way?" Premananda replied: "You see, the Master taught us not to talk with women in a casual way with a bare body. A monk should be very careful."[93]

On 20 October 1917 Shantiram informed his brother Premananda that their mother had been attacked by plague and her condition was critical. Premananda asked his attendant Satyananda to check on his mother, since he had worked for some time in the hospital. After checking her pulse and observing her condition, Satyananda told Shantiram that most probably his mother would pass away that very day. According to Hindu custom, it is very auspicious to die touching the Ganges. So Premananda's brothers, relatives, and Satyananda took Matangini to the bank of the Ganges so she could touch the water. While lying on a cot she continued to repeat the mantram with her rosary. Shortly she said, *"Jai Ramakrishna, Jai Ramakrishna, Jai Ramakrishna"* (Victory to Ramakrishna), and then passed away.[94]

Sometime in March or April 1918, Premananda was sent by his Calcutta doctors to Deoghar, a health resort in Bihar. In the beginning his health improved, but shortly his fever relapsed and he developed stomach trouble. The local doctors took special care of him. In spite of his illness, every day at 11:00 a.m. he would send his attendant to Deoghar station to receive visiting devotees and to arrange for their food and stay. Shivananda came to visit him and remarked, "I see you have opened a hotel here also." "Brother," replied Premananda, "as long as I live my hotel will go with me. I see that the Master brings food, he eats, he feeds. I see that the devotees, God, and the Bhagavata are the same."[95]

One day Premananda expressed a desire to meet the famous yogi Balananda Brahmachari of Deoghar. When this news reached Balananda, he came to visit the swami. Observing Premananda's physical condition, Balananda said: "Sir, if a monk does not have any attraction for his own body, it does not last. If you kindly bring a little attention to your body, it will be cured." Premananda replied: "You see, I don't have any attachment to this body. Now I look upon it like a rotten pumpkin, so my mind does not go to it at all." While leaving Balananda said to the attendant, "His body will not last long."[96]

During this time there was a worldwide influenza epidemic, and many people died. Premananda caught this deadly flu. When the sad news reached Belur Math, Shivananda went to Deoghar and brought Premananda back to Balaram's house. It was Saturday, 27 July 1918. Dr. Bipin Bihari Ghosh, Premananda's cousin, examined him and did not give any hope. His bed was made in the big upper hall, Brahmananda was staying in the next western room, and Turiyananda was downstairs. Turiyananda had had surgery on his leg in Puri; so he could not walk. Premananda wanted to see him, so two monks carried him on a chair to Premananda's room. Turiyananda sat on his bed, held his hand, and both looked at each other. What a scene! Tears began to trickle from their eyes and both remained silent.

When Saradananda came from Udbodhan, Premananda said to him, "You know, I have a great desire to put on a cloth of pure yellow and to eat rice white as jasmine." Saradananda understood. That is a symbolic description of Radha — the aspect of God of which Sri Ramakrishna had said he was a part. Saradananda knew then that Premananda would not live long.[97] The next day Premananda asked his attendant to call Brahmachari Jnana (a disciple of Swamiji) from Belur Math, who was then supervising the monastery. In a feeble voice, Premananda asked, "Jnana, could you do one thing for me?"

"Anything, sir."

"Will you be able to serve the devotees?"

"Yes, sir, I promise I shall do it."

"Remember, let there be no negligence towards the devotees!" Premananda entreated. It was his last wish.[98]

On Tuesday Premananda's condition deteriorated. Brahmananda was gravely pacing on the veranda and engaged his attendant to chant hymns near Premananda. All of a sudden he carried a picture of Sri Ramakrishna to Premananda and said, "Brother Baburam, please look at the Master." Brahmananda tried to suppress his own tears by pressing a cloth on his mouth. He then left the room. After a while Brahmananda returned again and said loudly, "Brother Baburam, Brother Baburam, do you remember the Master?" Premananda opened his eyes, looked with a smile at the oil painting of the Master hanging on the wall, and saluted him with folded hands. He uttered feebly "grace, grace, grace," and then passed away. It was 4:14 p.m. on Tuesday, 30 July 1918. His body was taken to Belur Math and cremated there on the bank of the Ganges.

When the news of Premananda's death reached Holy Mother in Udbodhan, she cried bitterly. She told the devotees: "Baburam was dearest to my heart. All the energy, devotion, and wisdom of Belur Math were embodied in my Baburam and walked there on the bank of the Ganges."[99] Brahmananda cried like a child and then remarked, "Belur Math has lost its mother."[100] M. said, "Sri Ramakrishna's love aspect has disappeared."[101]

Premananda closed his market of love and flew away into the Infinite on two powerful wings: renunciation and love. At the time of his passing, his possessions were an empty canvas bag, a couple of ochre cloths, a short tunic, a chadar, a towel, a pair of slippers, an umbrella, and a few books, including a copy of the Gita. Truly he was Premananda — bliss in love. He was Bliss and he was Love — an all-consuming love that revealed itself in the service of all — it was the burning passion of his life. Towards the end of his life he casually wrote to someone: "I feel a desire now to love everybody. This is a disease which has now possessed me."[102]

5

ॐ

SWAMI YOGANANDA

The temple garden of Dakshineswar was built in 1855 by Rani Rasmani, a wealthy woman of Calcutta. It is a charming place full of trees and flower gardens; and the holy river Ganges flows beside its galaxy of temples. Jogin, a teenaged brahmin boy from the village of Dakshineswar, used to visit this temple garden quite often to bathe in the Ganges or pick flowers for the worship of his family's ancestral deities. His neighbours had told him about Sri Ramakrishna, an eccentric priest of the Dakshineswar Kali Temple. Although he was religious-minded, Jogin had not the slightest interest in seeing the "mad brahmin," as his friends called Ramakrishna. Moreover, Jogin was very shy and avoided meeting people.

One day while young Jogin was picking flowers in the temple garden, he met a middle-aged man walking in the flower garden, and thinking that this man was a gardener, Jogin sought his help. Immediately the man joyfully picked some flowers and gave them to him. Some years later, at the age of sixteen or seventeen, Jogin read an article about the life and teachings of Sri Ramakrishna in *Sulabh Samachar*, a journal of the Brahmo leader Keshab Chandra Sen. He decided to visit the Master. With the journal in hand, Jogin arrived at Sri Ramakrishna's veranda and found the room filled with the Brahmo devotees.[1] He was amazed to find that the man whom he had thought was a gardener and whom his friends called a "mad brahmin" was actually Sri Ramakrishna. Being too shy to enter the room, he stood outside the door attentively listening to the spiritual conversation. Meanwhile, Sri Ramakrishna said to a devotee, "Call those

Swami Yogananda: Alambazar Math, 1896

people inside who are standing on the veranda."[2] The devotee found only Jogin and brought him into the room, where Ramakrishna was explaining the philosophy of love in simple language. Jogin was caught in the spell of his words and sat transfixed.

When the crowd dispersed, the Master walked over to Jogin and asked about his background.

"My name is Jogin," said the boy.

"What is your father's name?" asked Ramakrishna.

"Navin Chandra Roy Chaudhury."

"My goodness!" he replied. "I know your father very well. I used to go to your house quite often and listen to readings from the Bhagavata and other scriptures. Your family members were very respectful towards me."[3]

Thus Sri Ramakrishna talked to Jogin for some time. When Jogin was about to leave, the Master said, "Come again." Jogin agreed. While he was returning home, the boy thought: "This man must be a saint who has seen God. People do not understand that and therefore they laugh at him. How else can one account for such words of devotion, such divine love, and such ecstasy in the name of God? However, let me watch him closely."[4]

The next day Jogin went straight to Sri Ramakrishna, who was glad to see him. The Master recognized him as one of his inner circle and said to him: "It is wonderful that we have come to know each other now. You must come often. You have been born into a noble family and possess many characteristics of spiritual greatness. You will easily advance on this path."[5]

Jogindra Nath Roy Chaudhury was born into a well-to-do aristocratic family at Dakshineswar on 30 March 1861. His father was a pious brahmin who spent long periods of time in spiritual pursuits. He did not pay much attention to managing his properties and, as a result, lost most of them. His only hope lay in his eldest and most promising son, Jogin, who might one day be able to shoulder the responsibilities of the whole family.

However, Jogin developed a religious tendency very early in life. When he was a child of five, he would often be overwhelmed with spiritual feelings. In the midst of play, a serious thought would suddenly possess him and he would lose all interest in the sport. He would withdraw into a quiet corner and, looking at the sky, ask himself: "Where am I? Certainly, I don't belong here. These are not my playmates — I have other friends and companions. I must have come from one of those stars. But which one? I don't know. And why am I here if I belong to another world? Is this all a dream?"[6] Thoughts like these would trouble him, and he would be seized with a longing for familiar regions. As he grew up, however, these boyish imaginations gradually left him.

After his sacred thread ceremony, Jogin began to spend more time in meditation and worship. He would get joy from reading the Ramayana, the Mahabharata, and other scriptures. He was fond of listening to kirtan or devotional singing and to the recitation of the Bhagavata. Sometimes he would help his father pick flowers for worship. It is quite possible that he saw Sri Ramakrishna many times while he was a little boy.

Jogin was sent to a Christian missionary school in Agarpara, a few miles from Dakshineswar. During his final year of school he met Sri Ramakrishna and began to visit him daily. He kept this secret from his parents and friends, thinking that it might create some problems. This contact with Sri Ramakrishna brought about a great change in his thinking; the attainment of God became the sole purpose of his life. Although he knew that his academic studies would ultimately be of financial value to his family, he could not focus his mind on worldly pursuits. He had learned from the Master that one can realize God only through renunciation of lust and gold. He resolved not to marry.

At that time, a hathayogi named Narayan was living in a hut near the Panchavati. He was attracting some people's curiosity by showing them the art of *neti-dhauti*. (*Neti* means gradually swallowing a long, thin piece of wet cloth and then pulling it out; *dhauti* means drinking about a gallon of water and throwing it up. This is how hathayogis cleanse their systems to prevent disease and keep their bodies fit.) After observing the yogi, Jogin felt that lust would not vanish and God could not be realized without practising these hathayoga techniques.

One day Jogin found the Master alone and asked him, "Sir, could you teach me how to conquer lust?" "Chant the name of Hari [Lord], then it will go," answered the Master. This simple remedy did not convince Jogin. He thought that the Master did not know any practical method and had prescribed something useless. "Moreover," he thought, "so many people are repeating the name of Hari. Why does lust not vanish in them?"

The next day Jogin went straight to the hathayogi, and while he sat listening to the yogi, Sri Ramakrishna arrived. The Master took Jogin's hand and asked Jogin to follow him. While they were walking towards his room, the Master said: "Why did you go there? Don't do that. Your mind will only stick to the body if you learn those techniques of hathayoga. It will not thirst after God."

Jogin again doubted Sri Ramakrishna. He thought that the Master had discouraged him from visiting the hathayogi to keep him from running away. However, he thought again: "Why don't I do what he told me to do and see what happens?" Later Jogin said: "Thinking thus, I took the name of Hari with a concentrated mind. And as a matter of fact, shortly afterwards I began to experience the tangible result mentioned by the Master."[7]

After his Entrance examination, Jogin began to live with Sri Ramakrishna for longer periods of time and to spend more time in meditation. He was, however, aware of his family's hardship. One day he said to his father: "It is useless for me to go to school anymore; I shall try to get a job in an office. With your permission I will go to my uncle at Kanpur and try to get a job there."[8] His father consented.

Jogin left for Kanpur, probably in 1884. He tried for several months to get a job but did not succeed, so he spent most of his time in prayer and meditation. His absentmindedness alarmed his uncle, who wrote to Jogin's father, Navin, urging him to arrange for his son's marriage. This is a common way of binding a seeker of God to this mundane world. Navin thought that this would be a wise thing to do and, knowing his son's apathy towards the world, made arrangements for the marriage without telling Jogin, lest the boy run away.

Navin wrote his brother-in-law to send Jogin home on the pretext of his mother's illness. With an anxious heart Jogin rushed to Dakshineswar, but to his great dismay he found everybody jubilant over his forthcoming marriage. He was terribly upset, and he plainly told his father that he wouldn't marry. Navin tried to persuade him, but the boy remained adamant. Navin was in an awkward position, for he had given his word to the bride's father; it would be utterly disgraceful to withdraw now. At last Jogin's mother came to him with tearful eyes and implored her son to marry and save his father's reputation. "Even if you are unwilling, marry for my sake, dear," she said. Jogin was softhearted and gentle by nature; his mother's passionate appeal undermined his firm resolution.[9] Jogin bowed his head before the decree of fate and married a beautiful daughter of Madhusudan Roy, who lived close to Dakshineswar.

People usually get married to find happiness, but Jogin's marriage turned out to be full of misery. With all his gentleness, Jogin had another side to his nature — his strong independence. Forced to marry, he rebelled like a caged lion that desperately wants to be free. When Jogin was taken to the bridal chamber immediately after the ceremony, he began to chant God's name even though the bride's female companions laughed at him.[10]

Jogin and his wife never slept in the same bed. Soon after the wedding, he went to visit his wife's home. After supper, he went to the roof and walked there the whole night instead of going to bed. The next morning he returned home before anyone got up. Later, Swami Vivekananda remarked, "If there is anyone amongst us who has conquered lust in all respects, it is Jogin."[11] Sri Ramakrishna mentioned that six of his disciples, including Jogin, were *ishwarakotis*. (An *ishwarakoti* is a godlike soul who is eternally free from the bondage of karma, and who allows himself to be born simply to do good to humanity.) The Master also declared that Jogin had been Arjuna, the hero of the Mahabharata, in his previous life.[12]

Jogin later described his mental condition: "As soon as I married, the thought came to me that the hope of God-realization was now a mockery. Why should I go to the Master, whose very first teaching was the renunciation of lust and gold? I have ruined my life because of the tenderness of my heart. It cannot be reversed. The sooner I die the better for me. I used to visit the Master daily; but after this event, I stopped going to him altogether and spent my days in utter despair and repentance."[13]

Such news travels fast. Sri Ramakrishna heard about Jogin's marriage and was anxious to see him; he sent for him repeatedly, but Jogin did not come. Everyone said that he had changed since his marriage and that he would not even mention Sri Ramakrishna's name. As Jogin disregarded his repeated summons, the Master hit upon a plan. He knew that before Jogin's marriage, a man from the Kali Temple had given Jogin a few rupees to buy some articles for him. Jogin had sent the articles to the man through a friend, and sent word also that he would soon return the balance of the money. The Master therefore sent this message to Jogin: "What sort of man are you? A man gave you money to buy certain articles, and you have neither returned the balance nor even sent word when you will return it!"

These words touched Jogin's pride and he was grievously wounded. He thought: "The Master considers me to be a cheat even after such a long association! Well, I'll go there today and somehow put an end to the quarrel, and afterwards I will never again turn my steps towards the Kali Temple." In the afternoon, Jogin went to the Kali Temple. He saw from a distance that the Master was standing outside his room, as if in ecstasy, with his cloth under his arm. As soon as he saw Jogin he came forward quickly, saying: "What if you are married? Haven't I too been married? What is there to be afraid of in that? If you have the grace of this place [*meaning himself*], even a hundred thousand marriages will be powerless to affect you. If you want to live a family life and realize God at the same time, bring your wife here once. I will make both of you fit for that. And if you want to renounce worldly life and attain God, I'll make that also possible for you."

Jogin was stupefied. What was this that he had heard? Was it possible? He felt himself suddenly transported from a region of utter despair to one bright with hope. Was this why the Master had accused him — just to make him come to see him? A dead weight was lifted from his heart and he breathed freely again. Jogin bowed down to the Master with tearful eyes. Then the Master, taking Jogin's hand, escorted him to his room. When Jogin referred to the payment of the balance of the money, the Master would not even listen.[14]

The spiritual relationship between the Master and the disciple was reestablished. Ramakrishna reinforced Jogin's spirit of renunciation and the cloud of maya that had been hovering in Jogin's mind disappeared. He began once more to spend time with the Master.

Jogin felt a little guilty because of his behaviour towards his wife and he wanted to do something for her. One day he said to the Master: "Sir, you taught me how to overcome lust. Could you do something for my young wife? What will she do the rest of her life?" Sri Ramakrishna replied with assurance: "Don't worry about your wife. Bring her here once either on Tuesday or Saturday [days considered to be auspicious for worship of the Divine Mother] and the Divine Mother will grant what is right for her." Accordingly, Jogin took his wife to the Master, who accompanied them to the Kali Temple. Jogin and his wife bowed down before the Divine Mother. The Master blessed Jogin's wife, touching her head. He then said to Jogin, "You will not have to worry about her anymore." Jogin realized that the Master had taken on the responsibility of his wife and relieved him of it forever.[15]

Human relationships are very fragile: even a little clash of self-interest can break them. Jogin was deeply involved in spiritual life. His parents upbraided him for his indifference to the world. One day his mother said, "If you don't care to earn money, why did you marry?"

"Didn't I tell you again and again," replied Jogin, "that I had no intention of marrying? But I had to give way to your tears."

"What do you mean?" exclaimed his mother. "How could you marry unless you had the desire to do so?"

Jogin stared at her and remained speechless. He thought: "Gracious God! I committed the act to please my mother, and now she talks like this! Fie on the world! Sri Ramakrishna is the only person I have met whose words and thoughts are in perfect accordance." After that he became disgusted with the world, and found his only solace in the company of Sri Ramakrishna. He spent his days and sometimes nights in the temple garden.[16]

15

In the Company of Sri Ramakrishna

A real teacher practises what he preaches. If his speech and action do not coincide, people do not trust him. Sri Ramakrishna would therefore ask his disciples to test him as money changers test their coins. One evening Jogin decided to spend the night with the Master, with the intention of serving him if needed. Sri Ramakrishna was pleased. After dinner the Master went to bed, and Jogin made his own bed on the floor and slept.

Throughout his life Jogin was a light sleeper. At midnight he woke up and found that the Master was not in his bed. He first checked the water pot which the Master used for washing and found it in its proper place. Then he thought that he might be walking outside, but could not find him there. Suddenly a terrible suspicion gripped his mind: "Has the Master gone to the *nahabat* [concert tower] to be with his wife? Can it be possible that his actions are contrary to his teachings?"

Determined to find out the truth without delay, Jogin went out of the room and stationed himself near the nahabat. But while he waited there and watched the door of the nahabat, he heard the clattering of slippers coming from the side of the Panchavati. Within a few minutes Sri Ramakrishna appeared in front of Jogin and asked, "Hello, why are you standing here?" Embarrassed, Jogin hung his head in shame for having doubted the Master and could not utter a single word. The Master understood everything from the expression on his face. Instead of taking offence, Sri Ramakrishna reassured Jogin: "Well, you are quite right — you must examine a *sadhu* [holy man] by day and by night before believing in him."[17] Though forgiven, Jogin could not sleep anymore that night.

Once Sri Ramakrishna asked Jogin, "What do you think of me?" Jogin replied, "You are neither a householder nor a sannyasin [in any exclusive sense]." He meant that the Master was God — beyond attributes. Ramakrishna was greatly pleased and exclaimed, "What an extraordinary statement you have just made!"[18] Sometimes the Master would ask his disciples to evaluate him in order to check their level of understanding.

Ramakrishna always watched over his disciples' spiritual practices, and also their sleeping and eating habits. He approved of eating a heavy meal at lunch, but did not like his disciples to eat large quantities at night, because he considered night the time for *sadhana* (spiritual practices). One day the Master asked Jogin, "What do you eat at night?" "Bread made from one pound of flour, and one half pound of potato curry," replied

Jogin. Immediately the Master said: "My goodness! I don't need your service. I cannot afford to provide such a large quantity of food every day. You had better eat at home before coming here."[19]

Jogin began to strictly observe the Master's rules regarding eating. He did not even drink water in anyone else's house. One morning he ate a little breakfast at home and then left for Calcutta with the Master. Ramakrishna visited several places, but did not ask Jogin to eat anything as he knew his strict observance about taking food. However, in the evening at Balaram Basu's house, the Master asked Balaram to feed Jogin. The Master knew that Jogin had eaten sweets and fruits as prasad at Balaram's on previous occasions. Balaram immediately took Jogin to the dining hall and fed him sumptuously. Even though the Master frequently passed in and out of spiritual ecstasy, he was able to keep a vigilant watch on the mental and physical conditions of his disciples.[20]

Most artists and scientists are negligent about personal tidiness and external affairs while absorbed in their work. But it is amazing to see that although Ramakrishna was completely oblivious to his body and surroundings during samadhi, he was careful even about trivial details while in the normal plane. One morning the Master left for Balaram's house by carriage with Jogin and Ramlal. When the carriage reached the Dakshineswar gate, the Master asked Jogin, "Did you carry my cloth and towel?" He replied: "I am carrying your towel, but I forgot to bring the cloth. Anyhow, Balaram will be happy to give you a piece of new cloth." The Master said indignantly: "Nonsense! People will say, 'What a hapless fellow has come!' It will cause them trouble and they will be embarrassed. Stop the carriage. Go and bring the cloth." When Jogin obeyed, the Master said: "There is an abundance of everything when a good, fortunate person comes as a guest. Whereas when an unlucky, wretched fellow comes, the host finds great difficulty in accommodating him, particularly if he arrives on a day when there is a dearth of necessities in the household."[21]

It was a great education to live with Sri Ramakrishna: his every action or word carried deep meaning. According to the arrangements of the temple management, every day Sri Ramakrishna was to receive a portion of prasad, food offered to the deities. One morning he found that his share had not been sent to his room. This irregularity disturbed him, so he went to the temple office to inquire about it. The embarrassed temple manager immediately sent the Master's portion to his room. Jogin was surprised at this for he knew that the Master did not care much about eating as he had a very delicate stomach. Moreover he had never seen the Master so upset as he was on that day. After a good deal of reflection, Jogin came to the conclusion that the Master, in spite of his great spirituality, could not overcome the petty tendencies of his priestly class.

Meanwhile, Sri Ramakrishna returned to his room and said to Jogin: "Look here, Rani Rasmani has bequeathed her large estate to the service of this temple so that the offerings may be distributed among devotees and sadhus. That part of the offerings which comes to this room is taken only by devotees who come here with yearning for God, so the gift of Rani Rasmani is turned to good account. But what use is made of the other portion that goes to the priests of this temple? They sell it in the market, and some even feed their mistresses with it! I fight with the temple officials for the share that comes here so that Rasmani's objective may at least be partially fulfilled."[22] Thus Jogin discovered that every act of the Master, no matter how trivial it might appear, had deep significance.

All scriptures teach that progress in the spiritual path is impossible without sincere faith. Knowing this, some people tend to believe in everything and everybody. But Ramakrishna warned his disciples not to believe others blindly. Rather he advised them to use their discrimination both in the spiritual path as well as in worldly matters. Once Jogin went to a shop and bought an iron pan. He appealed to the religious feeling of the shopkeeper and did not examine the pan closely. After returning home he found that the pan had a crack. When the Master heard about it, he reproved Jogin: "Because you are a devotee of God, does that mean that you should be a fool? Do you think any shopkeeper opens a shop to practise religion? Why did you not examine the pan before you purchased it? Never act so foolishly again. When you go out shopping, first determine the usual price of the item by going around to several shops and then thoroughly examine the thing you want to buy. And do not fail to demand the little extras where allowed."[23]

Sometimes when people begin to practise religion, they become so kindhearted that their kindness becomes an obstacle and can even drag them down from the spiritual path. Ramakrishna would instruct such softhearted people to be firm and resolved. One day the Master saw a cockroach in a chest that he used for his clothes. He asked Jogin to take it outside and kill it. But Jogin took it outside the room and let it go. As soon as he returned, the Master asked, "Have you killed it?" "No, sir, I let it go," replied Jogin. Thereupon the Master rebuked him, saying: "I told you to kill the cockroach, but you let it go. You should always do as I ask you to do. Otherwise, later in more serious matters also you will follow your own judgment and come to grief."[24]

On another occasion Jogin was coming from Calcutta to Dakshineswar by boat. One of the passengers, knowing Jogin's destination, began to vilify Ramakrishna: "He is a mere pretender — practising deceit on the public. He eats good food, sleeps on a cozy bed, and turns the heads of schoolboys." Jogin was terribly hurt to hear that man's comment about the Master. At first he wanted to rebuke the man, but his gentle nature prevailed and he thought: "Well, people do not know Sri Ramakrishna, so they have odd ideas about him and criticize him. What can I do?" He kept silent.

Upon arriving at Dakshineswar, Jogin told the Master about the incident. He thought that the Master would simply laugh — as he was indifferent to praise or blame — and the matter would end there. But the Master took it quite seriously and said to Jogin: "That man abused me for nothing and you kept silent! Do you know what the scriptures say? You must cut off the head of him who speaks ill of your guru or at least leave his presence at once. And you did not even protest against these false accusations?"[25] It is amusing and instructive to contrast Sri Ramakrishna's rebuke to Niranjan who, listening to criticism of the Master, was about to sink a boat. The Master trained each disciple according to his temperament.

Jogin learned from the Master to defend the truth. It so happened that a woman of ill fame would come to take her bath in the Ganges at the Dakshineswar temple ghat. On her way back, she would bow down to the Master from a distance and sometimes would talk a little. Some villagers of Dakshineswar noticed it and began to remark about it. Gossip spreads faster than the gospel. Listening to the village gossip, Jogin firmly protested: "The Master's character is pure and stainless. If you have doubts, why don't you investigate?" So a villager secretly went to the woman and asked if the gossip was true. She was shocked and said to the man: "Look, I may make my living in a shameful way, but I am not so mean as to tarnish the character of a god-man. You have no right to spread gossip or vilify the character of my beloved Master." The villager returned to his friends and reported what he had heard from the woman. When Jogin told the Master what had happened, Sri Ramakrishna said: "Some foolish people say so many things. Why do you listen to them?"[26] This time the Master taught Jogin to ignore the endless gossip of worldly people, for otherwise it would drag his mind from God to the worldly plane.

As Jogin was always available, he had to run various kinds of errands for the Master. One day the Master needed some candles for his room, so he asked Jogin to get some from Girish Chandra Ghosh in Calcutta. When Jogin arrived there, he found that Girish was drunk. He told Girish that

Sri Ramakrishna had sent him to get a few candles. Immediately Girish said: "Why a few? Take a box of candles." Girish then began to use abusive words against Sri Ramakrishna, yet from time to time he bowed down to him while facing Dakshineswar. Jogin was scared. He had never come across a drunken devotee. He took the candles, however, and after reaching Dakshineswar, reported everything in detail to the Master. Ramakrishna did not show any indignation towards Girish, rather he said to Jogin: "You saw his bad side, how he scolded me. Did you not also see his good side — how much love and devotion he had for me and how he bowed down to me? Girish is in a special class of devotee — a very high class — but his path is different from yours."[27]

Ramakrishna had a special way of teaching his disciples. He did not teach in a classroom with a curriculum; there was no binding routine nor any book to be read. He put himself on the same level as his young disciples. He was their companion; he talked familiarly with them, without any trace of superiority. The advice he gave them was not his own: it came through his lips from the Mother of the Universe. Sri Ramakrishna enacted the divine play with his disciples in the temple garden of Dakshineswar and demonstrated true spirituality to them by the example of his own life. He taught them how to realize God. He eradicated worldliness from their minds and gave them a taste of divine bliss.

In the middle of 1885 Sri Ramakrishna developed throat cancer, and began to withdraw his divine play from Dakshineswar. His feet also began to swell, and Dr. Mahendranath Pal advised the Master to drink some lemon juice every day. Jogin took the responsibility of supplying fresh lemons from their family garden. The Master took the juice regularly, but one day he could not drink it. Jogin wondered why. Later after investigation he learned that their lemon grove had been leased to a party on that very day and they had lost ownership. As a result, the Master could not drink the lemon juice that Jogin brought without informing the owner, as that would have been considered theft. The disciples were amazed to see how the Master's body and mind were established in truth.[28]

In September 1885 Sri Ramakrishna was taken to Calcutta for treatment and then in December to Cossipore. Jogin followed the Master and served him. It was not so easy to serve Sri Ramakrishna. Once at Cossipore the Master expressed a wish to eat *palo* pudding (a kind of custard made from the zedoary root), and asked Jogin to buy it in Calcutta. On the way Jogin thought that the pudding from the market might be adulterated and that it might aggravate the Master's illness, so he went to

Balaram's house and told everything to the women devotees of the Master. They detained Jogin for lunch and began to make pudding with pure milk. Jogin arrived at Cossipore with the homemade pudding late in the afternoon. Since Ramakrishna could not get the pudding for lunch, he had taken his regular meal instead. He heard from Jogin what had happened, then he said to him: "I wanted to eat the pudding from that particular shop, so I asked you to buy it from there. Why did you bring this pudding, giving trouble to the devotees? Moreover, this pudding is very rich and hard to digest. I shall not eat it."[29] Truly the Master did not touch the pudding at all, and Jogin was extremely embarrassed.

Jogin continued to serve the Master with heart and soul. Since he was very austere and neglected his body, he became sick at Cossipore. The Master was sorry to hear that and asked Jogin to eat at the proper times and take sufficient rest. When he was not serving the Master, Jogin devoted his time to japam and meditation. Another aspect of his nature was his deep feeling for suffering people. Once a man from his village died in a train accident, and his wife and children were left helpless. Jogin mentioned it to his brother disciples, and Tarak immediately gave Jogin forty rupees to take to the family.

In spite of his fatal disease, Sri Ramakrishna gave final shape to his future Order in Cossipore. He made Narendra the leader of his young disciples. One day the elder Gopal brought twelve pieces of ochre cloth and twelve rosaries, which the Master distributed among his disciples, including Jogin. Eight or nine days before his passing away, Ramakrishna asked Jogin to bring the almanac and read the events of each day and the positions of the stars. When Jogin finished reading about 16 August 1886, the Master told him to stop and to put the almanac back in its proper place.[30] Sri Ramakrishna passed away at 1:02 a.m. on the same auspicious day in August that he had selected.

Pilgrimage and Austerity

A few weeks after the passing away of Sri Ramakrishna, Jogin left for a pilgrimage with Holy Mother (Sri Sarada Devi) and her party. First they stopped at Deoghar and then after visiting Varanasi and Ayodhya, they reached Vrindaban, where Krishna had spent his childhood. It was in Vrindaban that Holy Mother had the first direct intimation of her future mission. One day Sri Ramakrishna appeared before her and asked her to give Jogin formal initiation. He even told her the mantram with which she should initiate him. Holy Mother thought it was an hallucination of her own mind, but the vision was repeated the next two days. On the third day she said to the Master: "I do not even speak to Jogin. How can I initiate him?"[31] The Master asked her to have Yogin-ma (a woman disciple of the Master) with her at the time of initiation. Jogin also, in a vision, received similar instructions from the Master. Shortly, the Mother initiated him and Jogin thus became her first initiated disciple.

Later Jogin narrated Holy Mother's days in Vrindaban:

We saw how Holy Mother, even in the midst of her intense grief at the passing away of the Master, fully realized his divine grace and presence at all times. We thought of ourselves as helpless orphans, but the Mother's love became our sheet anchor.

At Vrindaban the Holy Mother had many spiritual experiences. One day her women companions found her absorbed in deep samadhi. They uttered the name of the Lord in her ears and tried to bring her mind down. I repeated the name of Sri Ramakrishna with all my strength; then the Mother seemed to return to the ordinary sense plane. During such periods of ecstasy, her manner of speech, her voice, her way of taking food, her way of walking, and her general behaviour were exactly like those of the Master. We have heard that in deep meditation the worshipper and the worshipped become one. The scriptures mention a spiritual state known as *tadatmya-bhava* — being at one with God. We have read in the Bhagavata how the gopis [shepherd girls of Vrindaban], unable to bear separation from Krishna, became so deeply absorbed in the thought of him that for the moment they forgot their own individualities and behaved as though they were Krishna. In the same manner the Mother, too, forgot her own separate existence and acted just like the Master, feeling her oneness with him. When I asked her some complex questions about spiritual matters shortly after her states of samadhi, she replied in a God-intoxicated mood, very much like Sri Ramakrishna; that is, in the same manner characteristic of the Master, even using his same easy style of expression with metaphors and parables.

We all were surprised to see the spirit of Sri Ramakrishna united with hers. It was unique. We then realized that the Master and the Mother were one in essence, though appearing in separate forms. Is it not said in the scriptures: "Lord, thou art man, thou art woman"? The Master told me many times that there was no difference between him and the Mother.

... [Holy Mother] passed nearly two days in that superconscious state. A great transformation came over the Mother after that experience. Henceforward she was seen to remain always immersed in bliss. All her sorrow and grief and feeling of separation from the Master vanished and a serene, blissful mood took their place. She sometimes behaved like a simple, innocent girl. Sometimes she would express an eagerness to visit the various temples of Vrindaban for *darshan* [seeing the deity] or to visit holy spots on the banks of the Jamuna associated with the divine sport of Krishna and the gopis. She was then in such a blissful state of mind that at times her yearning for Krishna's presence and her utterance of his name with intense love reminded us of Radha. I have heard from her women companions that the Mother at times spoke frankly of herself as Radha. She passed her time in constant meditation and japam and would often go into ecstasy, remaining forgetful of herself for hours together.[32]

After spending about a year in Vrindaban, Jogin went by train to Hardwar along with Holy Mother and her party. On the way, Jogin was suddenly stricken with a high fever. While he was unconscious, a terrible form appeared before him and said: "I would have put an end to your life, but I am helpless. On the order of your guru, Paramahamsa Deva, I am leaving you. However, you must offer some *rasagollas* [juicy cheese balls] to this woman (*pointing to a goddess wearing a red cloth*)." The next morning Jogin's fever abated.

They stayed at Hardwar a few days and visited Brahma-kunda, Chandi Hill, and all the important holy temples at the foothills of the Himalayas. Then the party went to Jaipur to visit the famous Govinda Temple. While visiting the deities, Jogin saw a goddess with a red cloth whom he recognized as the same deity he had seen during his high fever. She was Sitala, the goddess of disease. Jogin bought a half rupee worth of rasagollas from a nearby shop and offered this to the goddess.[33] From Jaipur Holy Mother and her party went to Prayag (Allahabad), the confluence of the Ganges and the Jamuna, and afterwards returned to Calcutta. Holy Mother stayed at Balaram's house for a couple of weeks and then left for Kamarpukur with Jogin and Golap-ma.

Jogin then returned to the Baranagore Monastery, where the young disciples of the Master had joined together and taken final vows of renunciation. Jogin also took formal monastic vows and became Swami Yogananda. His family members found out about it, but were unable to make him return home. Madhusudan Roy, Yogananda's father-in-law, realized his mistake in arranging his daughter's marriage to Jogin, knowing he had monastic tendencies. But Madhusudan was a deeply religious person and accepted it as God's providence. He built a ghat, and adjacent to it a Kali Temple, on the bank of the Ganges near Dakshineswar. Madhusudan spent the last part of his life worshipping the Divine Mother and he engaged his daughter to help him in this service.[34] Yogananda's wife had the blessings of Sri Ramakrishna. She was a highly evolved soul: she lived like a nun and spent most of her time in meditation and austerities. Later, the disciples of Sri Ramakrishna provided for her needs from the Belur Monastery.

In the Baranagore Monastery the disciples studied the Vedanta scriptures as well as the Bible, *The Imitation of Christ*, and other scriptures. One day they read this passage from the Bible: "For there are some eunuchs which were so born from their mother's womb; . . . and there be eunuchs which have made themselves eunuchs for the kingdom of heaven's sake."[35] When someone jokingly called Yogananda a eunuch, he laughingly replied: "You will see — just wait. Jesus left a group of eunuchs who shook the world. We will do the same thing."[36] On another occasion Yogananda mentioned the main teaching of Christ to his disciples: Love one another. "To realize that one sentence is equivalent to studying the whole Bible," said Yogananda.[37]

Yogananda did not care much for studying. He loved to be in solitude, and would practise japam and meditation for many hours. Sometimes he would leave the monastery and practise austerities on the bank of the Ganges. Due to his intense fasting Yogananda's body was lean, but his eyes were bright and luminous. Once some village women who were carrying water from the Ganges saw Yogananda seated under a banyan tree. They were impressed by his appearance, and their love and sympathy welled up for him. They began to inquire about his background, but in order to avoid them, Yogananda replied in Hindi as if he didn't know Bengali. The women thought he was either a Hindustani hemp smoker or a cheat and left.[38]

As is customary for mendicants, he went to beg for food one day and arrived at a thatched cottage in Alambazar. A poor woman was sweeping the house. Seeing the young monk begging food, she angrily said: "Get away from this place! You are a young man, why don't you work and make money? You come in the disguise of a monk at daytime to check the houses and will return at night to steal." Saying this she hit her broomstick on the ground. Yogananda suppressed his laughter; but when he returned to the monastery, he mimicked the woman out of fun. The brothers rolled on the floor with laughter.[39] Yogananda had a good sense of humour, and at the same time he was a serious monk with burning renunciation.

It is good to follow the middle path regarding eating, sleeping, and working. Excessive mortification ruins physical health, and the aspirant cannot continue spiritual disciplines. Yogananda, however, was an extremist. For the sake of God he would have given up everything — even his body. Sometimes he would repeat his mantram day and night almost nonstop, which caused severe headaches. He was then living at Balaram's house in Calcutta. He asked Girish Chandra Ghosh, who knew home-opathy, to give him some medicine. Girish prescribed a medicine and advised Jogin to take light tea and a night's rest. This cured his pain.[40] Swami Shuddhananda, who lived with Yogananda for some time, said: "Jogin Maharaj was so absorbed in meditation most of the time that his face would always look serene and luminous. Even when he would come from his bath, one would feel that he had just come out of his deep meditation."[41]

In November 1888 Yogananda went to Puri with Holy Mother and stayed there three months. Then, in February 1889, he went to Kamarpukur with Holy Mother; she stayed there for a year. During that time Yogananda left on pilgrimage and visited Deoghar, Gaya, Prayag, Chittrakut, and Omkarnath. After returning to Prayag, Yogananda fell ill with chicken pox. When this news reached Baranagore Monastery, Vive-kananda and some other disciples rushed to Prayag and took care of Yogananda until he recovered.

Around this period a crucial incident took place in Yogananda's life, which was later narrated by Shivananda:

Swami Yogananda was a highly evolved soul. He was extremely hand-some and had a manly body. Once he was travelling in Central Province, and he was alone in a train car. At a particular station when the train was about to leave, a beautiful courtesan hurriedly got into the same car with her luggage. As soon as her eyes fell on Yogananda, she was infatuated and begged him, "I offer my everything to you, please accept me." When Yogananda did not respond, she became impatient and threatened him, "If you don't listen to me right now, I shall pull the alarm chain to stop the train, and I shall complain to the guard that you had molested me." She was carrying a bottle of wine in her bag. She began to drink the wine to become more excited, but it had the opposite effect. She became so drunk that she passed out on her seat. When the train reached the next station, Yogananda got off the train unharmed. Look, what grace of the Master! Who else can pro-tect except he?[42]

In 1891 Yogananda went to Varanasi, where he lived in a small cottage in a solitary garden. He spent most of his time in meditation. Once a day he would go out to beg for food; sometimes he would eat dry bread soaked in water for two or three days. What austerity! It ruined his digestive system forever.[43] One night, while he was repeating the name of Sri Ramakrishna, an evil spirit tried to harm him. Immediately he shouted out, "*Jai Ramakrishna*" (Victory to Ramakrishna). Frightened, the spirit said to him: "I shall never again come to disturb you. Henceforth this place is yours."[44] Perhaps it was a haunted place; but by the grace of the Master his life was saved.

In 1892 Yogananda returned to the monastery, which had been moved to Alambazar, and lived there for some months. Then he devoted himself to serving Holy Mother and became her attendant and caretaker until his death. Yogananda was among the three or four monastic disciples of the Master who had free access to Holy Mother. He treasured the following scene of Holy Mother, his mantra-guru, which occurred while he was serving the Master at Dakshineswar: It was three o'clock in the morning. Holy Mother was immersed in meditation on the veranda of the nahabat. A gentle breeze blew away her veil and the light of the full moon fell on her face. Sri Ramakrishna went to the pine grove and the young Jogin carried the Master's water pot. Both saw her in that condition, but she was unaware of it.

Because Yogananda was pure like the ever-free Shukadeva, the Master engaged him to do errands for Holy Mother. "Jogin and Sharat belong to my inner circle," said Holy Mother. "None loved me as did Jogin. If anybody would give him any money, he would save it, saying, 'Mother will use it for her pilgrimage.' The other monks would tease him for staying in this household full of women. He would ask me to address him as 'Yoga.'"[45] Yogananda was so respectful towards Holy Mother that he would not salute her by touching her feet. When the Mother would leave the place, he would touch that spot with his head. Asked about this strange behaviour, Yogananda replied: "What! I don't have the audacity to keep the Mother standing and waiting for me so that I can bow down to her."[46]

Last Years

From 1895 to 1897 Yogananda arranged the birth anniversary festival of Sri Ramakrishna on a large scale at Dakshineswar. In 1898 he organized a similar celebration at Dahn's temple complex of Belur. At that time the name of Sri Ramakrishna was not widely known, but Yogananda had a magnetic personality: he attracted many young volunteers from Ahiritola, Calcutta, and celebrated the Ramakrishna festival with éclat. In 1897, when Swami Vivekananda returned from the West, Yogananda took an active part in organizing the reception for Swamiji that created a sensation all over Calcutta.

On 1 May 1897 Vivekananda inaugurated the Ramakrishna Mission at Balaram's house in Calcutta. He made Brahmananda president, and Yogananda vice-president, of the Ramakrishna Order. When the meeting was over, Swamiji said to Yogananda: "So the work has now begun in this way. Let us see how it succeeds by the will of Sri Ramakrishna."

Yogananda: "You are doing these things by Western methods. Would you say that Sri Ramakrishna left us any such instructions?"

Swamiji: "How do you know that these methods are not in keeping with his ideas? Sri Ramakrishna was the embodiment of infinite ideas: do you want to confine him within your own limits? I shall break those limits and scatter his ideas broadcast all over the world. He never instructed me to introduce worship of him, and so forth. The methods of spiritual practice, concentration and meditation, and the other higher ideals of religion that he taught — those we must realize and teach to all human beings. Infinite are the ideas and infinite are the paths that lead to the Goal. I was not born to create a new sect in this world, too full of sects already. Blessed are we that we have found refuge at the feet of our Master. It is our duty to give the ideas entrusted to us freely to the whole world."

Yogananda did not dissent and so Swamiji continued: "Time and again I have received marks of his grace. He himself is at my back and is making me do all these things."

Yogananda: "Whatever you will, shall come about. We are always ready to follow your lead. I see clearly that the Master is working through you. Still, I confess, doubts do sometimes arise in my mind, for, as we saw it, his method of doing things was so different. I am led to ask myself whether we are not straying from Sri Ramakrishna's teachings."

Swamiji: "The thing is this: Sri Ramakrishna is far greater than his disciples understand him to be. He is the embodiment of infinite spiritual ideas capable of development in infinite ways. Even if one can find a limit to the knowledge of Brahman, one cannot measure the unfathomable depths of our Master's mind! One gracious glance of his eyes can create a hundred thousand Vivekanandas at this instant! But if this time he chooses, instead, to work through me, making me his instrument, I can only bow to his will."[47]

Yogananda was deeply moved and praised Swamiji's greatness.

In time Yogananda's health began to fail. Swamiji took him to Darjeeling and Almora, health resorts in the Himalayan region, and arranged all kinds of treatment for him. In spite of all that, Yogananda's body rapidly deteriorated. It became difficult for him to serve Holy Mother, so he made Brahmachari Krishnalal (later, Swami Dhirananda) his assistant. Swamiji noticed that many women devotees would visit Holy Mother. It was not proper for a young brahmacharin to be around women — although Swamiji had no objection to his serving Holy Mother. Observing the situation, Swamiji asked Yogananda: "As you know, various kinds of women come to Holy Mother. Who will be responsible if this brahmacharin's mind wanders from the spiritual path?" Touching his chest, Yogananda immediately replied: "I will be responsible. I am ready to sacrifice my life for him." It is needless to speak about that Unseen Power that uttered these words through Yogananda's lips as "I."[48]

Yogananda commanded love and respect for his sterling, saintly qualities. But what distinguished him among the disciples of Sri Ramakrishna was his devoted service to Holy Mother. He was one of the first monks to discover the extraordinary spiritual greatness of Mother, hidden under her rural simplicity. Once Saradananda said to Yogananda: "Brother, I do not always understand Swamiji. He speaks in various moods. Whatever stand he takes, he makes so much of it that the others pale into insignificance." Yogananda said: "Sharat [Saradananda's premonastic name], I tell you one thing: Cling to Holy Mother. Whatever she says — that is right."[49] Yogananda then took Saradananda to Holy Mother, and gradually the latter became an attendant of the Mother, remaining so for twenty-one years after Yogananda's passing away.

Yogananda led an ideal life, and he taught by his example. He did not lecture or do any spectacular work. Although married and born into a rich family, he demonstrated how to practise renunciation and purity. He was an uncompromising monk: he shunned everything that took his mind away from the Master. During the last years of his life he would visit Girish and talk about the Master. He presided several times over the weekly meetings of the Ramakrishna Mission. Vivekananda valued his judgment and foresight, so in 1898 he took Yogananda by boat to the new site purchased for Belur Monastery on the bank of the Ganges. Although Yogananda was quite ill, he was very pleased to see the beautiful land that Swamiji had purchased for the permanent home of the Ramakrishna Order.[50]

While Yogananda was bedridden, Adbhutananda came to see him at Holy Mother's house in Bosepara Lane, Calcutta. Yogananda said to him: "This illness will never be cured. The doctors advised me to take pomegranate juice, *luchi* [fried bread], and catfish soup. They have no sense. How can a monk procure such expensive food like that meant for rich aristocrats? They have money and people to prepare such delicacies, but we are monks — we have none except God. We live on alms, so that kind of luxury does not befit us. What do you think?"

Adbhutananda replied: "What do you mean, brother? When one is sick, he needs a special diet; so I don't find any objection to your taking that kind of food."

Yogananda: "I know that. But who will supply it?"

Adbhutananda: "We will arrange everything for you."

Yogananda: "I know that. You see, Holy Mother wants my wife to come and prepare all these things for me. What is your opinion? I am a monk. Shall I have to accept service from my wife? I can't agree to this proposal. My mind is reluctant to yield to it."

Adbhutananda: "When Mother approves it, there should not be any problem."

Yogananda: "Brother, you don't understand. Do you know what people will say? They will say: 'A disciple of Ramakrishna, although a monk, takes the personal service of his wife.' It is not right to give an opportunity for such talk."

Adbhutananda: "Forget it! People say so many things — who cares? If one is true to his religious ideal, no public opinion can do anything. Moreover, who will believe their howling? Brother, please follow what Mother says."

Yogananda: "Whomever I ask about this matter, everyone speaks like you. Nobody understands my feeling. What more shall I say? As much as a person strives to serve me, I know this disease will not be cured."

Adbhutananda: "Brother, don't say that. Everything happens by the will of the Master. If he wants to take you back, none of us can hold you. Again, if he wants to keep you alive for his work, you have no power to stop it. Why are you worried about all these things?"

Yogananda: "Brother, you are right. Let the Master's will be done. I am nobody."[51]

Yogananda knew that he wouldn't live long, and at last he obeyed the Mother's will. His wife served him during the last few days of his life. When Holy Mother requested Yogananda to give some spiritual instructions to his wife, he said: "Mother, I can't do that. You please take care of her and instruct her."[52]

During his last illness Yogananda suffered from fever and blood dysentery. His whole body was emaciated and his voice was feeble. One day he said about the advent of the Master: "There have always been various religious paths, countless scriptures, and holy places in every country. In spite of that why is there a decline in religion? Because in the course of time all ideals become lost. Therefore God incarnates Himself to explain the hidden mystery of religion and to show the ideal."[53] On another occasion he said: "By the grace of the Master I have attained so much knowledge and devotion that I am unable to express it all."[54] When Yogananda's parents came to see him, he said, "I pray — may you attain devotion."

As Yogananda lay ill, Vivekananda said, "Jogin, you get well, let me die instead." "Jogin, you are our crest jewel," said Niranjanananda.[55] One day Girish's sister said to Yogananda: "Jogin, why don't you ask Holy Mother to tell the Master to give you back your health?" Yogananda replied: "Sister, you don't know their ways. They do what is right. My request will not change their will."[56]

Yogananda never prayed to Sri Ramakrishna to cure his disease. He was an illumined soul. He experienced that the Atman alone is real, and the body is made of five elements that disintegrate after death. An embodied being cannot escape pain and misery. So he silently endured his *prarabdha karma* (the result of deeds that were begun in former lives and are now working themselves out in the present one). There is a difference between an ordinary soul and an ever-free soul. The former attains liberation through self-knowledge, but the ever-free soul is the eternal companion of an avatar or divine incarnation.

Six months before Yogananda's death, Sri Ramakrishna appeared before him. Yogananda said: "Master, I don't want to be born again. The lesson of this life is enough for me. Please give me final liberation." The Master replied, "You will have to come once more." "No, I won't come." Yogananda demanded, "Please release me forever." Immediately Sri Ramakrishna disappeared.[57] Yogananda went through six months of physical suffering, hoping that the Master would grant his request.

Knowing Yogananda's resolution, Girish at last said to him: "Brother, don't you know that you have been suffering terribly these last six months? Your pain is causing pain to all of us. Please agree to the will of the Master. Don't refuse to come back with the Master.... Look here, Jogin! Don't seek nirvana. Don't think of the Master as pervading the entire universe, the sun and the moon forming his eyes. Think of the Master as he used to be to us, and thus thinking of him, go to him." At this Yogananda said: "What! I have been suffering in bed for the last six months? All right. Let the Master's will be done. I am his servant. Whatever he asks me to do, I will do." Saying so, Yogananda fully resigned himself to the Master.[58]

Swami Yogananda passed away in samadhi at 3:10 p.m. on 28 March 1899. Before his passing away, he said to Holy Mother, "Mother, Brahma, Vishnu, Shiva, and Sri Ramakrishna have come to take me."[59] In the morning while performing worship, Holy Mother saw that the Master had come to take Yogananda. When Yogananda breathed his last, Brahmachari Krishnalal cried out. Holy Mother was upstairs and she realized what had happened. She also burst into tears and said, "My Jogin has left me — who will now look after me?" Because Yogananda was the first disciple of the Master to die, Mother remarked with a deep sigh: "A brick has slipped from the structure; now the whole thing will come down."[60]

Before the body of Yogananda was taken to Kashi Mittra's cremation ground in North Calcutta, Swamiji waved the light and offered flowers and sweets as a part of the ritual. Swamiji was so stunned that he did not go to the cremation ground. Brahmananda and other disciples and devotees went in a procession and cremated their beloved brother disciple's body on the bank of the Ganges. Grief stricken, Swamiji did not go to Sri Ramakrishna's shrine for three days. He remarked, "A beam is down and now the rafters will fall one after another."[61] Just before Yogananda's death, Shivananda had asked him, "Jogin, do you remember the Master?" Yogananda replied, "Yes, I remember the Master more — even more — much more."[62]

Swami Niranjanananda: Alambazar Math, 1896

6

ॐ

SWAMI NIRANJANANANDA

An eyewitness account is often interesting and convincing. It can portray an event in such vivid detail that it enkindles the human imagination to experience the past as the living present. Swami Adbhutananda, a disciple of Sri Ramakrishna, narrated the following incident: "One day the Master touched brother Niranjan, and for three days and three nights Niranjan did not get one wink of sleep. He had the continuous vision of a mysterious light and kept repeating the Lord's name. His tongue could not stop saying japam for three days. Prior to meeting the Master, Niranjan was employed by spiritualists as a medium for contacting spirits. So one day the Master humourously said: 'Now, my boy, another ghost — the Holy Ghost — is upon you. However much you try, you will not be able to dismiss Him.'"[1]

God acts in mysterious ways. In the early part of 1882, a group of spiritualists from Calcutta heard about Sri Ramakrishna's spiritual power. Spiritualists generally strive for psychic powers and enjoy using them. As it would be a considerable achievement to influence Ramakrishna, they went to the Dakshineswar temple garden to test him. They were told that Ramakrishna had gone for an evening walk to Jadu Mallik's garden house nearby. When they reached Jadu's drawing room and met Ramakrishna, Dr. Pearychand Mittra, the leader of the group, introduced himself and the others, including Niranjan, as spiritualists. Ramakrishna had the power to see inside a person as one sees an object inside a glass case. As soon as he saw Niranjan, the Master remarked, "This boy is very good —

extremely guileless." Immediately Pearychand said: "Sir, he is my nephew. He can mesmerize very well, and he is a wonderful medium." "Shame, shame! Don't get involved in such spooky business," retorted the Master.[2]

Despite this, the spiritualists expressed a desire to use their power to mesmerize Ramakrishna. The childlike Master agreed, regarding this as a mere amusement; moreover, he wished to humble them. Ramakrishna sat on a chair and three spiritualists, including Niranjan and his uncle, began to wave their hands about him. The Master observed their ritual and smiled from time to time. After trying hard for an hour, Pearychand said: "Sir, you are a great soul with a strong mind. We are incapable of mesmerizing you." Then the Master got up and said privately to Niranjan, "Come here often."[3]

Niranjan (Nityaniranjan Ghosh), who later became Swami Niranjanananda, was born in 1862 (probably in August) at Rajarhat-Vishnupur, district 24-Parganas, a few miles from Calcutta. His father's name was Ambika Charan Ghosh. Niranjan was tall and handsome, endowed with a broad chest and beautiful bright eyes. He had a strong, energetic, and athletic physique. His nature was fearless and heroic. In his childhood he was fond of playing with a bow and arrows like the great heroes of the Hindu epics. He had a consummate passion for truth and deep compassion for the poor.

When Niranjan was in his teens, he was sent to his uncle's house at Ahiritola, West Calcutta, for higher education. There he was attracted by the group of spiritualists headed by his uncle, Pearychand Mittra. They made Niranjan their medium; he enjoyed the experience as one enjoys an adventurous game. Niranjan's mind was as powerful as his body. He had developed psychic powers that enabled him to cure illnesses. Once a wealthy man of Calcutta who had suffered from insomnia for eighteen years sought Niranjan's help. The compassionate Niranjan used his miraculous power to cure the man. Later he said, "Finding the man suffering so much in spite of all his riches and wealth, I was seized with a feeling of the emptiness of all worldly things."[4]

The human mind grieves when empty; it always desires to behold an object. Dispassion for the world turns to passion for God. Disillusioned with spiritualism, Niranjan turned to Dakshineswar in his quest for spirituality.

One evening soon after Niranjan had met the Master, he went to Dakshineswar to see him. He found Sri Ramakrishna in his room, surrounded by devotees. The Master was talking about God and how to realize Him; the devotees were spellbound. When all the devotees had left for home, the Master approached Niranjan and expressed his joy at seeing him again. They talked freely for some time. Then the Master said: "My boy, if you allow your mind to dwell on ghosts, you will become a ghost yourself. If you fix your mind on God, your life will be filled with God. Now, which of these are you going to choose?" "Well, of course, the latter," replied Niranjan.[5] Ramakrishna advised him to sever his connection with the spiritualists, and Niranjan agreed to this.

The Master also said to Niranjan: "Look here, my boy, if you do ninety-nine good deeds for a person and one bad, he will remember the bad one and won't care for you anymore. On the other hand, if you commit sins ninety-nine times but do one thing to God's satisfaction, He will forgive all your wrongdoing. This is the difference between the love of man and the love of God. Remember this."[6] As it was getting dark, the Master invited him to spend the night at Dakshineswar, rather than walk the long distance home. Niranjan said his uncle would be anxious and took leave of the Master, promising to come another day.

Niranjan's feet moved towards Calcutta but his mind remained in Dakshineswar. Even at home Ramakrishna occupied all of his thoughts: He felt that the Master himself had possessed him, replacing the spirits. Within two or three days he returned to Dakshineswar. The Master was filled with joy at seeing him. He rushed to Niranjan, and grasping his arms, exclaimed: "O Niranjan, my boy, the days are flitting away. When will you realize God? This life will be in vain if you do not realize Him. When will you devote your mind wholly to God? Oh, how anxious I am for you!" Niranjan was dumbfounded. "What a strange man this is," he thought. "Why is he so concerned about my spiritual welfare?"[7]

Most people of this world have never heard of unselfish and unconditional love. Thus if a person encounters such pure love, he or she tries to find the motive behind it. Niranjan silently questioned the Master's concern for him. In any case, the Master's words appealed to Niranjan more forcibly than any he had ever heard. He spent the night there and also the two following days. When he returned home, his uncle, who had been extremely anxious about him, scolded him and forbade him to visit Dakshineswar. Niranjan felt much aggrieved. Later on, however, his uncle relented and granted him the freedom to visit Sri Ramakrishna whenever he liked.

Ramakrishna recognized Niranjan as one of his inner circle, an *ishwara-koti* — a godlike soul who is perfect from his very birth and is never trapped by maya. Once in a vision Ramakrishna saw the luminous form of Niranjan playing with a bow and arrows. Later he remarked that Niranjan had been born as a partial incarnation of Ramachandra.

The Training of Niranjan

As a good shepherd knows his sheep by sight, so Ramakrishna recognized the intimate disciples who had been born to carry his message. As soon as he met one of them, he would lovingly say, "You belong to this place." He would treat each of them as would a most loving father. Swami Saradananda writes:

Shortly after the arrival of such a devotee the Master would call him aside, ask him to meditate, and then under the influence of divine inspiration he would touch certain parts of his body like the chest or the tongue. By that potent touch the devotee's mind would become indrawn and sense objects would vanish from its perception. His accumulated impressions of the past would be activated and produce spiritual realization in him.... Besides touching the devotees in that way, the Master initiated some of them with mantras.[8]

Niranjan was initiated by the Master with a mantram. He later described this experience:

I was then working in an office. One day I went to visit Sri Ramakrishna at Dakshineswar. He wrote a mantram on my tongue and asked me to repeat it. What an experience! After returning home, even when my eyes were closed, I began to see innumerable fireflies in my room. The mantram was vibrating in my head and in every limb of my body. I wanted to sleep, but I could not stop the repetition of japam. I had previously been unaware of this phenomenon. I became scared and thought that I would go out of my mind. After three days I returned to Dakshineswar and said to the Master, "Sir, what have you done to me?" After listening to my story, he laughed and withdrew the power of the mantram. He then said, "It is called *ajapa japam* [the repetition of japam effortlessly and unceasingly]."[9]

Ramakrishna's teaching varied from person to person. For instance, he scolded the mild-tempered Yogananda because he had not protested some false accusations made against him; but the Master instructed Niranjan differently:

Niranjan was habitually good-natured, but he had a violent temper. One day, when he was coming to Dakshineswar on the public ferry, he overheard some of the other passengers speaking sneeringly of Sri Ramakrishna, saying that he was not a true man of renunciation but a hypocrite who enjoyed good food and every comfort, and whose disciples were gullible schoolboys. Niranjan protested strongly, but the speakers ignored him. At this, Niranjan became enraged, jumped to his feet, and began to rock the boat, threatening to capsize it in midstream. Niranjan was a powerful swimmer; he could easily have swum ashore after carrying out his threat. The passengers were frightened and they begged to be forgiven.

When Ramakrishna heard about this incident, he rebuked Niranjan severely. "Anger is a deadly sin," he said. "You ought never to let it carry you away. The seeming anger of a good man is something different. It's no more than a mark made on water. It vanishes as soon as it's made. As for those mean-minded people who talked against me, they weren't worth getting into a quarrel with — you could waste your whole life in such quarreling. Think of them as being no more than insects. Be indifferent to what they say. See what a great crime you were about to commit, under the influence of this anger! Think of the poor helmsman and the oarsmen in that boat — you were ready to drown them too, and they had done nothing!"[10]

At one time Niranjan was compelled to accept a job with an indigo planter at Murshidabad, more than a hundred miles north of Calcutta. Ramakrishna was aggrieved when he heard of this and remarked, "I would not have been more pained had I heard of his death." A few days later, when he saw Niranjan, he learned that he had to accept the job to maintain his aged mother. With a sigh of relief, the Master told Niranjan: "Ah, then it is all right. It won't contaminate your mind. But I tell you, if you had done so for your own sake, I could not have touched you. Really, it was unthinkable that you would stoop to so much humiliation. Didn't I know that my Niranjan had not the least trace of impurity in him?"

Upon hearing this remark, a member of the audience questioned the Master: "Sir, you are condemning service; but how can we maintain our families without earning money?" The Master replied: "Let him who likes do so. I don't forbid everyone. I say this only to these young aspirants [pointing to Niranjan and others] who form a class by themselves."[11] Ramakrishna did not want his intimate disciples to become slaves of lust and gold.

On 15 June 1884 M. recorded the feelings the Master had for Niranjan in The Gospel of Sri Ramakrishna:

After the music the Master sat with the devotees. Just then Niranjan arrived and prostrated himself before him. At the very sight of this beloved disciple the Master stood up, with beaming eyes and smiling face, and said: "You have come too! (to M.) You see, this boy is absolutely guileless. One cannot be guileless without a great deal of spiritual discipline in previous births. A hypocritical and calculating mind can never attain God.

(To Niranjan) "I feel as if a dark veil has covered your face. It is because you have accepted a job in an office. One must keep accounts there. Besides, one must attend to many other things, and that always keeps the mind in a state of worry. You are serving in an office like other worldly people; but there is a slight difference in that you are earning money for the sake of your mother. One must show the highest respect to one's mother for she is the very embodiment of the Blissful Mother of the Universe. If you had accepted the job for the sake of wife and children, I should have said: 'Fie upon you! A thousand shames!'"[12]

Ramakrishna had two types of teaching. One was for the householders, who are obliged to take care of their families and at the same time practise spiritual disciplines. He reminded them constantly: "First God and then the world." Secondly, he established the monastic ideal for his would-be monastic disciples: "The sannyasi must renounce 'woman and gold' for his own welfare.... The sannyasi, the man of renunciation, is a world teacher. It is his example that awakens the spiritual consciousness of men."[13] Ramakrishna was overjoyed to learn that Niranjan was not attached to women and would not marry. Niranjan told him, "A woman never enters my thoughts." On 15 July 1885, like a proud father, the Master praised Niranjan to the devotees: "Look at Niranjan. He is not attached to anything. He spends money from his own pocket to take poor patients to the hospital. At the proposal of marriage he says, 'Goodness! That is the whirlpool of the Vishalakshi [a stream near Kamarpukur]!' I see him seated on a light."[14]

On that same day, while sitting in his room at Dakshineswar, Ramakrishna was chanting the names of gods and goddesses. M. recorded in the Gospel: "Then he repeated, 'Alekh Niranjana,' which is a name of God. Saying 'Niranjana,' he wept. The devotees wept too. With tears in his eyes the Master said: 'O Niranjan! O my child! Come! Eat this! Take this! When shall I make my life blessed by feeding you? You have assumed this human form for my sake.'"[15] Perhaps this sincere call of the Master reached Niranjan: He resigned from his job and came to visit the Master. In an ecstatic mood, Ramakrishna told him: "You were living in an indigo-house of such a place; on this particular day you rode on your deputy's horse; you stood in such a place with a bow and arrow." Niranjan realized the Master was all-knowing. With tearful eyes he surrendered himself to Ramakrishna, saying, "Sir, all these days I could not recognize you."[16] From that day Niranjan visited the Master frequently.

Sometimes the young disciples would discuss the various riddles of life. Once in Dakshineswar Niranjan and others had a long discussion on free will and predestination. Unable to reach any conclusion, they approached the Master. At first the Master was amused by their naive ideas, but then he commented more seriously:

Does anybody have free will or anything like that? It is by God's will alone that everything has always happened and will continue to happen. Man understands this last of all. Let me give an example of man's free will: It is like a cow tied to a post with a long tether; she can stand at a distance of one cubit from the post or she can go up to the whole length of the tether according to her choice. A man ties a cow with the idea: Let her lie down, stand or move about as she likes within that area. Similarly, God has given man some power and also the freedom to utilize it as he likes. That is why man feels he is free. But the rope is fastened to the post. And remember this: If anybody prays to God earnestly, God may move him to another place and tie him there, or lengthen the tether, or even remove it completely from his neck.[17]

Ramakrishna kept close watch over the disciples' eating, sleeping, and day-to-day behaviour. Since only a good student can be a good teacher, the Master uncompromisingly trained his inner-circle disciples so they could become great spiritual leaders. Self-control and truthfulness are indispensable to spiritual life. Once, on seeing Niranjan take too much *ghee* (clarified butter), which was believed to create lust, the Master exclaimed: "My goodness! You take so much ghee! Are you eventually going to abduct people's daughters and wives?"[18] Another day the Master said to a devotee (*pointing to Niranjan*): "Look at this boy. He is absolutely guileless. But he has one fault: he is slightly untruthful nowadays. The other day he said that he would visit me again very soon, but he didn't come."[19] Hearing this, Niranjan immediately apologized.

In the Service of the Master

In September 1885 Sri Ramakrishna had to move to Shyampukur, Calcutta, for his cancer treatment. Niranjan left home and became the Master's gatekeeper, as he was strong and heroic by nature. There is an interesting story of how Niranjan was fooled by an actress:

In 1884 when Sri Ramakrishna went to see Girish Ghosh's drama, *Chaitanya Lila*, he had been extremely pleased with Binodini, the actress who had played the part of Chaitanya, and had blessed her. She in turn had become very devoted to the Master but could not find another opportunity to meet him. Now, hearing of his illness, she longed to see him again. But the Master's disciples were very strict about visitors. They feared that if Sri Ramakrishna talked too much or if he were touched by impure people his disease would be aggravated [most actresses were prostitutes at that time]. In order to see the Master, Binodini sought help from Kalipada, whom she knew through Girish. One evening, acting on his advice, she dressed herself as a European gentleman and went with Kalipada to the Shyampukur house. Introducing her to Niranjan as a friend of his, Kalipada took her to the Master, who was alone in his room at that time. Sri Ramakrishna laughed when Kalipada told him who this "European gentleman" really was. After praising Binodini's faith, devotion, and courage, the Master gave her some spiritual instruction and allowed her to touch his feet with her forehead. When Binodini and Kalipada had left, Sri Ramakrishna told the disciples about the trick that had been played on them. The Master enjoyed it so much that the disciples could not be angry.[20]

Following his doctor's advice, Ramakrishna moved from the smoggy environment of Calcutta to a garden house at Cossipore on 11 December 1885. Cossipore was then a suburb of Calcutta (but is now within the city) and not very far from the Ganges. The Master was quite happy despite his terminal cancer. On the morning of 23 December Ramakrishna gave unrestrained expression of his love for the devotees. He said to Niranjan, "You are my father; I shall sit on your lap." Touching another devotee's chest, he said, "May your inner spirit be awakened!"[21] By living with the Master, the devotees' own love and devotion also grew by leaps and bounds.

Once Niranjan went back home for a visit. When he returned, the Master said, "Please tell me how you feel." Niranjan replied, "Formerly I loved you, no doubt, but now it is impossible for me to live without you." Then the Master explained to M.: "This illness is showing who belongs to the inner circle and who to the outer. Those who are living here, renouncing the world, belong to the inner circle; and those who pay occasional visits and ask, 'How are you, sir?' belong to the outer circle."[22]

The young disciples took turns around the clock serving the Master. Moreover, they were practising spiritual disciplines according to his instruction. They renounced hearth and home and surrendered themselves to Sri Ramakrishna. The following incident reveals how the Master protected his disciples: One evening Niranjan and a few other disciples decided to get juice from a date palm near the southern boundary of the garden. The Master knew nothing about this. When it was dark, Niranjan and others walked in the direction of the tree. In the meantime, Holy Mother saw the Master running down the steps and through the door. She wondered: "How is it possible? How can one who needs help even to change his position in bed run like an arrow?" She could not believe her eyes, so she went to the Master's room to see if he was there. Ramakrishna was not in his room. In great consternation she looked all around, but she could not find him. At last Holy Mother returned to her room, extremely confused and with much apprehension.

After a while Holy Mother saw the Master running swiftly back to his room. She then went to him and asked about what she had seen. He replied: "Oh, you noticed that. You see, the boys who have come here are all young. They were proceeding merrily to drink the juice of a date palm in the garden. I saw a black cobra there. It is so ferocious and it might have bitten them all. The boys did not know this. So I went there by a different route to drive it away. I told the snake, 'Don't enter here again.'" The Master asked her not to divulge this account to others.[23]

After he had been at Cossipore three or four months, Ramakrishna's body became so emaciated that it was hard to recognize him. But his devotees still hoped that he would free himself from the cancer. During this time the Master told Niranjan: "Look, I am now in such a state that whoever sees me in this condition will attain liberation in this life by the grace of the Divine Mother. But know for certain that it will shorten my life." Upon hearing this from the Master, Niranjan became more vigilant about his guard duty. He sat at the gate day and night with a turban on his head and a stick in his hand to keep outsiders from visiting the Master.[24] Niranjan sometimes had to hurt people, but he accepted this as an unpleasant duty necessary to protect the Master's life.

A mentally-ill woman used to accompany Vijay Goswami to the Kali Temple at Dakshineswar and sing for Sri Ramakrishna. The Master was fond of her singing, but was careful about her as she cherished towards him *madhura bhava*, the attitude of a wife towards her husband. (This is a kind of spiritual relationship that some Vaishnava aspirants adopt towards Krishna.) Once this woman came to Cossipore at noon and wanted to visit the Master. Niranjan stopped her at the entrance. She then became hysterical. Hearing this, the Master asked Shashi to escort her to him, and he blessed her. She then began to make more frequent visits. Niranjan adopted an unbending attitude and prevented her from visiting the Master. Most of the young disciples were very apprehensive because of her unpredictable and seemingly violent behaviour. However, when the woman was finally discouraged, she paid no further visits. Rakhal expressed his sympathy for the woman. He said: "We all feel sorry for her. She causes so much annoyance, and for that she suffers too." Immediately Niranjan remarked, "You feel that way because you have a wife at home." Rakhal replied sharply: "Such bragging! How dare you utter such words before him [Sri Ramakrishna]?"[25] The Master remained silent. He appreciated Rakhal's love and compassion for a suffering soul, as well as Niranjan's faithful service to the guru.

Another day, Ramchandra Datta wanted to visit the Master, but Niranjan stopped him at the gate. Ram was hurt by this because he was one of the Master's prominent lay devotees. He then said to Latu, "Please offer these sweets and flowers to the Master and bring a little prasad for me." Latu was very touched and said to Niranjan, "Brother, Ram Babu is our very own; why are you putting such restrictions on him?" Still Niranjan was inexorable. Then Latu said rather bluntly, "At Shyampukur you allowed the actress Binodini to visit the Master and now you are stopping Ram Babu, who is such a great devotee." This pricked Niranjan's conscience, so he let Ram go to see Ramakrishna. Later when Latu went upstairs, the omniscient Master said to him: "Look, never see faults in others; rather, see their good qualities." Latu was embarrassed. He came down and apologized to Niranjan, saying: "Brother, please don't mind my caustic remark. I am an illiterate person."[26] This shows how the Master taught his disciples to develop close interpersonal relationships.

Once Atul Ghosh, Girish's brother, came to visit the Master and was stopped by Niranjan. Atul was very hurt. Piqued, he took a vow that he would not visit Ramakrishna again unless someone personally came to his house and took him there. One day the Master asked Niranjan to go to Atul's house and bring him to check his health. (Atul, though not a doctor, knew how to check a pulse and evaluate the condition of a disease.) Immediately, Niranjan rushed to Atul and brought him to the Master. Even while he was sick, the Master was training his devotees — sometimes humbling one and sometimes increasing longing in another.[27]

During the winter Ramakrishna would bathe with hot water. One day Niranjan used a lot of firewood to heat a large vessel of water. That waste displeased the Master. But Niranjan was stubborn. He carried the whole vessel of water to the Master and said: "Sir, I don't have enough sense to know how much water you need. Since I have brought it, you will have to use it." The Master was pleased by Niranjan's simple and fearless behaviour.[28]

It is hard for a lover to watch the suffering of his beloved. The real lover wishes he could relieve his beloved's suffering. While serving the Master, Niranjan often worried about him. The Master read his mind and one day asked him, "Niranjan, if I were cured of this disease, what would you do?" With great excitement Niranjan replied, "Master, I would uproot that date palm tree from the garden!" Knowing his heroic nature and his overwhelming love and devotion, the Master remarked, "Yes, you could do that."[29]

The disciples took care of the Master's body, and he in turn took care of their spiritual life. He silently and naturally gave shape to this group of ideal characters. From his birth, Niranjan had been endowed with divine qualities — simplicity, purity, fearlessness, steadiness, truthfulness, and renunciation. When the elder Gopal brought twelve pieces of ochre cloth and twelve rosaries, the Master gave one of them to Niranjan and distributed the rest to other disciples. Thus Ramakrishna sowed the seeds of his forthcoming monastic order.

When Sri Ramakrishna passed away on 16 August 1886, the disciples gathered his relics from the Cossipore cremation ground and put them into an urn. They brought the urn to the garden house and decided to continue their service. But they had no money, so Ramchandra Datta suggested installing the Master's relics at Kankurgachi Yogodyana, his retreat house. Niranjan vehemently protested against this. He, Shashi, and some others secretly transferred the major portion of the Master's relics to a separate urn, which they secretly kept at the house of Balaram Basu, a disciple of Sri Ramakrishna. In the beginning Narendra had yielded to Ram Babu's suggestion, but, learning how his brother disciples felt, he supported their decision. Later, he installed this second urn at Belur Math.

Pilgrimage and Austerity

In December 1886 Niranjan, Narendra, and several other brother disciples went to Antpur, the birthplace of Baburam. There they took the vows of renunciation in front of a sacred fire, not knowing that it was Christmas Eve. Sri Ramakrishna had created the hunger for God in their minds, and they began to spend their days in meditation and austerities. One day Sarada went to bathe in a pond. All of a sudden he slipped from a step and fell into deep water. He did not know how to swim. Immediately Niranjan jumped in and rescued him, ignoring any threat to his own life.

In the early part of 1887 Niranjan joined the Baranagore Monastery and took the final vows of sannyasa with his brother disciples. Vivekananda gave him the name "Swami Niranjanananda." He continued his spiritual disciplines and austerities in the monastery. He also helped perform the worship service, and did most of the laborious work. One day he was carrying some sweets from the market for the Master's offering. A poor woman, holding her little boy in her arms, was walking in the same direction. Seeing the package of sweets in Niranjanananda's hand, the boy cried out, "Mother, I want to eat sweets!" The more she tried to control her son, the more he cried. Niranjanananda gracefully went to the young boy, and placing the packet before him, said, "Please eat these sweets." The poor mother protested: "Father, no. You are carrying these sweets for the Lord. It would be inauspicious if my son were to eat them." Niranjanananda replied: "No, mother, it would be all right. His eating would be the same as the Lord's eating." Handing the packet to the boy, Niranjanananda returned to the market to buy fresh sweets for the Master.[30]

After taking the vows of sannyasa, Niranjanananda went to Puri on a pilgrimage and returned to the Baranagore Monastery on 8 April 1887. The monastery was in very poor condition. Because the disciples could not afford anything better, they were renting a dilapidated house for ten rupees a month. They did not have a suitable altar in the Master's shrine or accessories for worship. Niranjanananda had heard about an aged but expert carpenter in Calcutta and had him make a beautiful altar for the Master. With the help of the devotees, Niranjanananda gradually collected a bed for the Master, utensils, and a Japanese gong for vespers. Niranjanananda planted a bel tree on the spot where the Master's body had been cremated on the bank of the Ganges, and made a marble altar around the tree. He planned to set inscribed marble slabs in various locations connected with Sri Ramakrishna in the Dakshineswar temple garden, but this plan never materialized.[31] Sometimes he would go to Dakshineswar with Swami Virajananda and meditate in the Panchavati or in the Master's room.

Most people in this world live for themselves. But those who live for others really live in the highest sense. There is great joy in sharing and in serving others: Such joy eradicates selfishness and makes a person large-hearted. Whenever there was any problem or illness among the brother disciples or Holy Mother, Niranjanananda would assume responsibility. Niranjanananda nursed Yogananda when he was suffering from smallpox in Allahabad, served Latu when he had pneumonia, and helped both Balaram and Ram up to the time of their deaths. When Girish was passing through a period of depression, Niranjanananda took him to Holy Mother, who lifted his spirits. In 1888, when Holy Mother was living alone at Kamarpukur, Harish, a devotee of the Master who was mentally ill, went there and began to disrupt her peace. Holy Mother subsequently complained to the monks at Baranagore, and both Niranjanananda and Saradananda rushed to Kamarpukur. As soon as Niranjanananda arrived, Harish became so frightened that he hurried off to Vrindaban. Later he recovered from his mental illness.

After Sri Ramakrishna's passing away, his disciples always took special care of Holy Mother, and on the other hand, she looked after their welfare and inspired them. Many years later, referring to the hardships of the disciples, Holy Mother recalled:

What an austere life they led at the Baranagore Monastery! Niranjan and others often starved themselves. They spent all their time in japam and meditation. One day they resolved among themselves: "Well, we have renounced everything in the name of Sri Ramakrishna. Let us see if he will supply us with food if we simply depend on him. Neither will we tell anyone about our wants, nor will we go out for alms." Saying so, they covered themselves with their *chadars* [shawls] and sat down for meditation. The whole day passed. It was late at night. They heard someone knocking at the door. Naren left the seat and asked one of his brother monks: "Please open the door and see who is there. First, check if he has anything in his hand." What a miracle! When the door was opened, they found a man had come from Lala Babu's Krishna Temple near the Ganges with various delicacies in his hand. They were overjoyed and became convinced of the protecting hand of Sri Ramakrishna. They then offered that food to the Master and partook of the prasad. Such things happened many a time.[32]

Denouncing spiritual disciplines and asceticism, worldly people believe that happiness can be derived from worldly possessions and sensual enjoyment. Spiritual people, however, find that happiness and peace come from within by controlling their worldly desires. Enjoyment cannot satiate the desire for enjoyment — it only increases desire, as melted butter intensifies a flame instead of extinguishing it.

In November 1889 Niranjanananda left the monastery on a pilgrimage to practise further austerities. He first went to visit the temple of Lord Shiva at Deoghar, and then proceeded to Varanasi, where he stayed in Banshi Datta's garden house and lived on alms. After that he went to Prayag (Allahabad) at the confluence of the Ganges and the Jamuna rivers. He travelled throughout various parts of India and then went to Sri Lanka. Vivekananda wrote from America on 22 October 1894: "Why doesn't Niranjan learn Pali in Ceylon [Sri Lanka] and study Buddhist scriptures? I cannot make out what good will come of aimless rambling."[33]

However, Swamiji was impressed with Niranjanananda's preaching mission in Sri Lanka. Wherever he went, he would talk about the wonderful life and message of Ramakrishna. When he was in Raipur, an army officer named Suraj Rao met him and was greatly inspired. Suraj later resigned from his job and became a disciple of Swami Vivekananda. Afterwards he became known as Swami Nischayananda. In 1895, before Sri Ramakrishna's birthday, Niranjanananda returned to the monastery, which had been moved from Baranagore to Alambazar in 1892.

With Swami Vivekananda and Others

Gradually the news reached the monastery that Vivekananda would return to India from the West in early 1897. Niranjanananda left for Colombo and received Swamiji there on 15 January 1897. Afterwards he travelled with Swamiji all across southern India as well as in various parts of North India. The brother disciples were thrilled and proud of their leader's success in spreading the message of Vedanta in America and Europe.

In 1898 Niranjanananda went with Swamiji to Almora, then remained there in order to practise further spiritual disciplines. Sudhir, an initiated disciple of Swamiji, joined them. Sudhir was greatly inspired by Niranjanananda, who initiated him into sannyasa on 16 September 1898. Sudhir became Swami Shuddhananda. He and Niranjanananda then went to Varanasi and stayed at Banshi Datta's garden house. They continued their austerities as itinerant mendicants — begging food once a day, walking barefoot without sufficient clothing, sleeping on a blanket without a mosquito curtain, carrying no money, and depending solely on God's will. In Varanasi, Niranjanananda encouraged a group of young men to enter spiritual life and to practise the ideal of service. In 1899 this group observed Sri Ramakrishna's birthday celebration under his guidance. Niranjanananda inspired them to sacrifice their lives for the good of many and the welfare of all. This group later founded the Ramakrishna Mission Home of Service, and some of them received their monastic vows directly from Vivekananda.

After staying a few months at Varanasi, Niranjanananda went to Kankhal, near Hardwar, a place where mendicants live at the foothills of the Himalayas. Sri Ramakrishna had trained his disciples to build character first through practising spiritual disciplines. A person of strong character truly speaks with authority. The monastic disciples had also learned from the Master that in order to teach others one must have no theft or hypocrisy in one's heart. Thought and speech must be united. Religion means the realization of Truth. Renounce everything for God.

The impact of an illumined soul's life is far more profound than the contents of thousands of lectures or books.

When Niranjanananda was in Kankhal, a young man from Varanasi named Kedarnath (later, Swami Achalananda), expressed his desire to become a monk. At first the swami discouraged him, saying that the life of a monk is very difficult. He quoted the passage from the Katha Upanishad: "Like the sharp edge of a razor is that path, so the wise say — hard to tread and difficult to cross" (1.3.14). But it is equally difficult to stay at home when the fire of renunciation burns in one's heart: Kedarnath gave up his job and left home. With Niranjanananda's permission he went to Kankhal in August 1899. Niranjanananda received him cordially, taking him to a dilapidated house where he lived (which is across from the present Mahananda Mission). The next day Niranjanananda gave him an ochre cloth and asked him to repeat the name of Sri Ramakrishna. He taught Kedarnath the basic rule of monastic life: One must live on alms, without possessions, depending on God alone.[34]

After some time Niranjanananda became ill and left for Calcutta. A couple of months later he wrote to Kedarnath: "My physical condition is extremely bad. It would be nice if you would come and give me a little personal service."[35] Kedarnath immediately went to Calcutta to attend Niranjanananda, who was then living in a rented house at Bhavanicharan Datta Lane. Swami Brahmananda and the other brother monks arranged for his treatment and diet. It was a prolonged illness, and at one point he was close to death. Niranjanananda was later moved to another location, Akhil Mistry Lane, where a devotee provided all of his food and paid his medical expenses. Unfortunately, Kedarnath also became ill and had to go to the monastery, which was now located at Belur. He later went back to Varanasi. Then Swami Premananda went to nurse Niranjanananda and he slowly recovered.

Niranjanananda left no writings or any recorded reminiscences; but on 18 December 1946 Swami Achalananda described some of the important characteristics of Niranjanananda's life:

> Swami Niranjanananda believed that Sri Ramakrishna was the infinite God incarnated in human form; and he who took refuge in him would not have to worry in his life.
>
> He had a similarly high estimation of Holy Mother. He believed that by the grace of the Mother, he could do anything.
>
> About Sri Ramakrishna he said: "If anybody came to the Master and said that he wouldn't marry, the Master would dance with joy."

He believed one should sincerely serve the Master — thinking of him as a living, conscious being, our very own. This is the supreme worship. The swami did not put too much stress on rituals and mantras.

He was a strong person and was not afraid of anybody. He considered the Master his only refuge. He appreciated those who had a dauntless nature.

He had tremendous faith in the doctrine of service as established by Swami Vivekananda and he encouraged people to serve human beings as manifestations of God.

He was a man of truth and wanted others also to adhere to the truth. He did not care for people who did not keep their word.

He was extremely generous. Without any misgivings, he would take care of anyone who asked help from him.

He would inspire young people to follow the path of renunciation and again caution them, saying that the path is indeed a difficult one.

He said, "It is important for a monk to live on alms, or *madhukari*." [As a bee collects honey from different flowers, so a monk is supposed to live by begging food from door to door. This is an ancient monastic custom in India.] He himself would collect food like the traditional monks, and then eat it after offering it to the Master.

He used to do physical exercise regularly and he encouraged the young men to keep their bodies strong and active.[36]

Vivekananda went to the West again in June 1899; he returned to India in December 1900. Niranjanananda was delighted to be with Swamiji once more. In January 1902 Swamiji visited Varanasi, where Niranjanananda was then residing. He arranged for Swamiji to stay at Kali Krishna Tagore's garden house. At that time Kakuzo Okakura, the famous Japanese artist, arrived to escort Swamiji to Japan as a royal guest. Due to Swamiji's bad health the visit was cancelled, but Swamiji travelled with him to Bodh Gaya and from there to Varanasi. Swamiji wrote to Mrs. Ole Bull on 10 February 1902: "Mr. Okakura has started on his short tour. He intends to visit Agra, Gwalior, Ajanta, Ellora, Chittor, Udaipur, and Delhi. Niranjan has gone with Okakura."

In the later part of February, when Swamiji became gravely ill, Niranjanananda and Shivananda escorted him to Belur Math. The doctors had been treating Swamiji for diabetes and kidney disease, but at Niranjanananda's earnest request he took ayurvedic medicine for three weeks. During this period, in accordance with the treatment, he did not drink any liquids except a little milk now and then to satiate his thirst.

On Sri Ramakrishna's birthday Niranjanananda became Swamiji's gatekeeper in order to prevent the general public from disturbing him. A young brahmacharin, a disciple of Swamiji, arrived from Mayavati to visit him. Since Niranjanananda did not know the young man, he stopped him at the gate. But while Niranjanananda was talking to someone else, the clever brahmacharin crawled through his legs and entered Swamiji's room. When Niranjanananda heard this from Swamiji, he appreciated the boy's resourcefulness and dedication.[37]

Niranjanananda's character was a mixture of tenderness and sternness. He was an unattached monk and his love for truth was uncompromising. Once a rich man of Calcutta built a Shiva temple in Varanasi, ostensibly to acquire merit. When Vivekananda heard about it, he remarked, "If he would do something to relieve the suffering of the poor, then he would acquire the merit of building a thousand such temples." When Swamiji's statement reached the rich man, he offered a generous donation to the Ramakrishna Mission Home of Service at Varanasi, in a nucleus state at that time. But later, as the rich man's initial enthusiasm waned, he decided to reduce the sum he had originally offered. This breach of promise so offended Niranjanananda's regard for truth that he rejected the offer altogether, even though he knew it would cause great hardship for the institution.[38]

Niranjanananda's devotion to Holy Mother was indeed remarkable. Swami Vivekananda used to say, "Niranjan has a militant disposition, but he has great devotion for Mother so I can easily put up with all his vagaries." In those early days Holy Mother's divinity was not widely acknowledged; even Girish, a great devotee of the Master, confessed his doubt about it. Girish was then passing through a critical time — he had lost his wife and his son, and was suffering from depression. At that time Niranjanananda took him to Holy Mother and later accompanied him to her village of Jayrambati. Girish stayed there for some months with Niranjanananda under the affectionate care of Holy Mother and derived immense spiritual benefit. It was partly as a result of Niranjanananda's active preaching that many devotees came to recognize the spiritual greatness of Holy Mother.

Towards the End

Because he had practised such hard austerity, Niranjanananda's health began to fail. During the last few years of his life he suffered from dysentery. The climate and water of Hardwar are better than those of Belur

Math, so he decided to move there and went to Holy Mother to receive her blessings. This last meeting was deeply moving as Niranjanananda's pent-up devotion for Holy Mother suddenly found expression. No one understood the cause — perhaps he had a premonition that he would not live long. He insisted that Holy Mother do everything for him. He entreated her to cook for him, and feed him as a mother feeds her young child. Holy Mother fulfilled his wishes. Before leaving, he fell at her feet and burst into tears. Then he silently went away, knowing that he would never see her again.

At Hardwar, he lived in a rented house and continued his sadhana. His chronic dysentery was inexorably emaciating his body, but it could not stifle his renunciation. Sri Ramakrishna had enkindled his spirit when Niranjanananda was just in his teens and it continued to shine brightly throughout the remainder of his life. He wished to complete the journey of his life alone. Towards the end, he was stricken with cholera. Like a hero, he took shelter on the bank of the Ganges and surrendered himself to God. When his attendant offered to serve him, Niranjanananda declined. When the attendant nevertheless insisted, he said, "Don't you want me to die in peace?"[39] Then the attendant reluctantly departed. Swami Niranjanananda, a heroic monk of Sri Ramakrishna, passed away in samadhi on 9 May 1904.

Later, Niranjanananda's attendant realized the truth of Sri Rama-krishna's prediction: "Do you know what these youngsters are like? They are like certain plants that grow fruit first and then flowers. These devotees first of all have the vision of God; next, they hear about his glories and attributes, and at last they are united with him. Look at Niranjan. He always keeps his accounts clear. He will be able to go whenever he hears the call."[40]

7

ॐ

SWAMI RAMAKRISHNANANDA

How can one open the door of Truth? Sri Ramakrishna told the secret to his disciples: "The key to this room has to be turned the reverse way."[1] Worldly means are of no avail to one who wants to attain the knowledge of God. Knowledge is of two kinds: "lower" or secular and "higher" or spiritual. Secular knowledge pertains to the world; all book learning and even scriptural knowledge fall into this category. Higher or spiritual knowledge opens the door of Truth. When a person attains this knowledge through spiritual pursuits, he or she transcends the realm of ignorance, or maya, and becomes free forever.

When Swami Ramakrishnananda (then Shashi) was young, he desperately sought higher knowledge from the Bible, from the Hindu scriptures, and also from the lives and teachings of the mystics. He was told by one of his friends that a great amount of wisdom was hidden in the writings of the Sufi mystics. Shashi recalled: "I had heard a great deal about the beauties of the Sufi poets, so I determined to learn Persian in order to be able to read them in the original. I bought several Persian textbooks and began to study most diligently. Often when I was at Dakshineswar I would go off to some corner with my books instead of staying to serve Sri Ramakrishna. One day he called me and I did not hear him. He had to call a second [and a third] time. When I came to him, he asked, 'What were you doing?' I told him. He said, 'If you neglect your duty in order to learn Persian, you will lose what little devotion you have.' Not many words, but they sufficed. By that time I had purchased fifteen or twenty rupees' worth of books, but I threw all of them into the Ganges."[2]

SWAMI RAMAKRISHNANANDA

Shashi Bhusan Chakrabarty was born at 4:56 a.m. on Monday, 13 July 1863, in Ichapur Village (Hooghly District, West Bengal). He was the eldest of eight children. His father, Ishwar Chandra Chakrabarty, was a court pandit of Raja Indra Narayan Singh of Paikpara, North Calcutta. Ishwar Chandra was well versed in Tantra scriptures and disciplines, and was a disciple of Jaganmohan Tarkalankar, a famous tantric saint of Bengal. A great devotee of the Divine Mother, Ishwar Chandra would sometimes practise *sadhana* (spiritual disciplines) at night in the cremation ground, which is considered to be an auspicious place for tantric sadhana. It is said that one night he saw the Divine Mother in the form of a little girl, who directed him to follow her and then disappeared into the temple. His wife, Bhavasundari Devi, was a guileless, pious woman. She was so shy that she would put a veil over her face even in front of her son Shashi.

Shashi was brought up in spiritual surroundings by his orthodox brahmin parents. Ishwar Chandra worshipped his family deities daily and he performed an elaborate Kali worship once a year. When he was a boy, Shashi learned ritualistic worship from his saintly father. During the annual autumn worship of Mother Durga, Shashi would perform the worship service — ritual, japam, meditation, chanting — for twenty-four hours at a stretch without leaving his seat. Physical discipline alone cannot account for such a feat of endurance: Only Shashi's orthodox upbringing, tremendous willpower, deep spiritual absorption, and divine intoxication can explain this phenomenon.

After finishing his education in the village school, Shashi went to Calcutta for higher English education. He lived with his cousin Sharat (later, Swami Saradananda) who was almost his contemporary. He passed the Calcutta University Entrance examination, and, as he was a brilliant student, won a scholarship. He passed his First Arts examination from Albert College, then entered the Metropolitan College (now Vidyasagar College) for his B.A. He had a wonderful academic record in college; his special subjects of study were Sanskrit and English literature, mathematics, and philosophy. During their college days both Sharat and Shashi became members of the Brahmo Samaj and were inspired by the lectures of Keshab Chandra Sen, the great Brahmo leader. For a certain period Shashi privately tutored Keshab's sons.

With Sri Ramakrishna in Dakshineswar

Shashi and his young friends first heard about Sri Ramakrishna from Keshab, who spoke highly of the saint of Dakshineswar to his congregation.

The young boys said to each other: "If Keshab Chandra Sen, whom we honour so much, shows such great reverence for this *paramahamsa* [an illumined soul], there must be something extraordinary in him."[3] Shashi later recalled:

> It was really Keshab Chandra Sen who may be said to have discovered Sri Ramakrishna and made him known to the world. At that time Keshab was the most prominent figure in Calcutta. His church was always crowded, and many young men were his ardent admirers. It was indeed impossible not to be moved by him. When he stood in his church, dressed in his white robe, and talked with God, the tears streaming down his face, there was not a dry eye in the whole congregation. He was a really great soul and a true devotee.[4]

Hunger for God made young Shashi restless. Keshab inspired him immensely but could not fully satiate his spiritual hunger. One day in October 1883, Shashi, Sharat, and some of their friends went to Dakshineswar to visit Sri Ramakrishna. They found the Master seated on his small couch. He received the boys with a smile and asked them to sit on a mat on the floor. He then asked their names and where they lived, and was pleased to know that they belonged to Keshab's Brahmo Samaj.

At first sight Sri Ramakrishna recognized Shashi and Sharat as his own. Sensing their spirit of renunciation, the Master said: "Bricks and tiles, if burnt with the trademark on them, retain those marks forever. Similarly, you should enter the world after advancing a little in the path of spirituality. Then you will not sink in the mire of worldliness. But nowadays parents get their boys married while quite young, and thus pave the way to their ruin. The boys come out of school to find themselves fathers of several children. So they run hither and thither in search of a job to maintain the family. With great difficulty perhaps they find one, but are hard pressed to feed so many mouths with that small income. They become naturally anxious to earn money and therefore find little time to think of God."[5]

"Then, sir, is it wrong to marry? Is it against the will of God?" asked one of the boys. The Master asked him to take a certain book down from the shelf and directed him to read a particular passage that quoted Christ's opinion of marriage: "For there are some eunuchs, which were so born from their mother's womb; there are some eunuchs, which were made eunuchs of men; and there be eunuchs, which have made themselves eunuchs for the kingdom of heaven's sake. He that is able to receive it, let him receive." The Master then asked him to read Saint Paul: "I say therefore to the unmarried and widows, it is good for them if they abide even as I. But if they cannot contain let them marry: for it is better to marry than to burn."

Someone interrupted, saying: "Do you mean to say, sir, that marriage is against the will of God? And how can His creation go on if people cease to marry?" Sri Ramakrishna smiled and said: "Don't worry about that. Those who wish to marry are at perfect liberty to do so. What I said just now was between ourselves. I speak on what I have got to say; you take as much of it as you like and no more."

Sri Ramakrishna asked Shashi whether he believed in God with form or without form. Shashi replied frankly, "I am not certain about the very existence of God, so I am not able to speak one way or the other!"⁶ This simple and direct reply pleased the Master very much. When the boys took leave of him, the Master said to Shashi, "Please come again and alone."⁷

After the first meeting Shashi felt an irresistible attraction for Sri Ramakrishna, and he began to visit him frequently. "After I had listened to Sri Ramakrishna," he later recalled, "I had nothing more to say. I did not have to talk. Often I would go to him with my mind full of doubts which I wished him to clear away. But when I reached the temple I would find his room full of people and would feel very much disappointed. As soon as he saw me he would say, 'Come in, sit down. Are you doing well?' Then he would return to his subject but invariably he would take up the very doubt that was troubling my mind and clear it away completely."⁸

Sri Ramakrishna always tested the genuineness of his disciples, using various methods, before accepting them into his inner circle. Long after Sri Ramakrishna's passing away, Shashi told the following incident to Swami Paramananda, who related it to his American disciples years later:

When Swami Ramakrishnananda first came to Sri Ramakrishna, he wanted to touch Sri Ramakrishna's feet that he might take dust off them, for in India, in relation to the holy, this is considered the greatest blessing. But Sri Ramakrishna withdrew his feet. Swami Ramakrishnananda thought that it was because he was unworthy. Afterwards Sri Ramakrishna told him that it was only to increase his yearning. A small soul, full of pride and egotism, would have felt injured, but a big soul is only filled with greater longing.⁹

On the very first day Ramakrishna recognized that Shashi and Sharat belonged to his inner circle. On 23 December 1885 the Master said to M.: "When God assumes a human body for the sake of His devotees, many of His devotees accompany Him to this earth. Some of them belong to the inner circle, some to the outer circle, and some become the suppliers of

His physical needs. . . . The Divine Mother used to reveal to me the nature of the devotees before their coming. In a vision I saw that Shashi and Sharat had been among the followers of Christ."[10]

One day while Shashi was hurriedly passing through the Master's room looking for a particular object, Ramakrishna said to him, "Whom you are looking for, he is here — here — here."[11] Immediately Shashi's eyes fell on the blissful form of the Master; he then realized that Sri Ramakrishna was the polestar of his life.

Gradually, Shashi became acquainted with Narendra and other young disciples of the Master. One day Shashi and Sharat visited Narendra in his home and talked about the Master for many hours. Narendra told Shashi and Sharat: "He is bestowing love, devotion, divine knowledge, liberation and whatever else one may desire, on whomsoever he likes. Oh, what a wonderful power! He can do anything he likes."[12]

Observing that other disciples were experiencing ecstasy and devotion, one day Shashi prayed to the Master for those spiritual experiences. The Master said to him, "If you have that experience, you won't be able to serve me." "Then I don't need it," replied Shashi. "I don't care for that ecstasy which will take away my opportunity to serve you."[13] Another day Shashi noisily ripped a piece of cloth in the Master's presence, startling him. Because of Ramakrishna's experience of oneness, when the cloth was being torn, he felt as if his own chest were being torn as well. When a person is highly spiritually evolved, his physical and mental systems become very sensitive. The Master did not like his disciple's rough action, so he said to him: "What are you doing? Never tear the cloth in that way. The serpent power [kundalini shakti], which is within me, may snap at you. Be careful."[14]

From his boyhood, Shashi cherished a great regard for religious books. He was a keen student of the Bible and *Chaitanya Charitamrita* (Life of Chaitanya), and had studied many lives of the mystics. He was a strict follower of religious disciplines. After studying Chaitanya's life he resolved to be a vegetarian for the rest of his life. Sri Ramakrishna also advised him to eat only vegetarian food and to observe the caste system; this later helped him to work among the orthodox people in South India.[15] The Master demanded from his disciples physical as well as mental cleanliness. One day he said to Shashi, "Please scrape your tongue daily, otherwise I won't eat from your hand."[16]

It takes more time and effort to prepare a delicious dish than it does to eat it. Similarly, preparation and training are very important for God-realization, which may dawn on a person in the twinkling of an eye. It is therefore important to learn how a god-man like Sri Ramakrishna trained his disciples. This can be discovered from the records and reminiscences of disciples like Shashi, who recalled:

It was only on Sundays that there was a crowd at the temple. On other days the Master was left alone with his few chosen ones. Not everyone could stay with him — only those whom he chose to have. And why did he keep them? In order that in one night he might make them perfect. Just as a goldsmith gives shape to a lump of gold, so he would mould them in such a way that their lives would be transformed; they would never forget the impression he had stamped on them.

Sri Ramakrishna possessed the peculiar power to discern at once whether a man was fit to serve him or not. Sometimes people would come and want to stay with him, but seeing their unfitness he would tell them with childlike frankness, "You had better go home." Occasionally there would be a feast and the Master would sit with his disciples; sometimes a man would come whose character was blemished but who would sit with him in the attempt to appear good. At once Sri Ramakrishna would discern his character and say: "Here is a man who is not pure. He will spoil my children." Without hesitation he would send him away. When he was alone with his special disciples, they would sing and talk and play together. If a visitor came, he would tell him, "Go and have a bath, eat something, and rest awhile." About two o'clock he would begin to talk, and he would go on teaching for five or six hours continuously. He would not know when to stop.

Sometimes the Master would wake at four in the morning, and he would call the disciples who were sleeping in his room, saying: "What are you all doing? Snoring? Get up, sit on your mat, and meditate." Sometimes he would wake up at midnight, call them, and make them spend the whole night singing and praising the name of the Lord.

All the disciples were still at a malleable age, in their teens or early twenties — two were scarcely sixteen — and the Master played with them as if they were little children. He was very fun-loving and was discovered near the Panchavati one day by a visitor, playing a game of leap-frog with his boys. Sometimes he would send them into peals of laughter by his mimicry. Then again he would be grave and wake them long before the dawn and make them sit in meditation on the mats on which they had been sleeping. Again at the evening hour he would tell them to go to the banyan tree and meditate.

The Master said, "If you will practise even one-sixteenth part of what I have practised, you will surely reach the goal." That sixteenth part of individual striving, however, was essential. He could not impose realization as one pastes a picture on a page. Someone said to him once,

"You have the power by a touch to make a man perfect, so why do you not do it?" "Because if I did," he answered, "the person would not be able to keep perfection. He must grow to it and be ready to take it."

His method was peculiar. He did not tell a man to give up everything. On the contrary, he would say: "Go on, my children, and enjoy all you wish. The Divine Mother has given this universe for your enjoyment. But as you enjoy remember always that it does not come from yourself but out of the Mother's bounty. Never forget Her in your pleasure, but always recognize that it is from Her." In this way, by becoming mindful of the Mother, the person would gradually lose all taste for the pleasures of the senses.

The Master never told us that anything was "wrong." On the contrary, he used to say: "Go and have a good time. The responsibility will be mine." He knew there was nothing wrong in the pleasures of the world — that by tasting them his children would come to realize their worthlessness and would be satisfied only with higher pleasures. He was not merely the helper of the good, he was also the helper of the wicked. He tolerated and loved both. He wanted his children to always be happy. And if one of us came with the least shadow on his face, the Master could not bear that — he would at once scold us.

Just by looking at a man he could tell what that person was fit for. If he saw that he was falsely leading a religious life, he would say to him, "Go and get married." If he saw that a man was ready to renounce, he would not ask him directly to give up, but he would direct his mind in such a way that the man would, of his own accord, renounce. He used to say that by seeing even one corner of a man's toe, he could make out just what sort of man he was.

At one time there was a very poor boy who used to come almost daily to Sri Ramakrishna, but the Master would never take any of the food he brought. We did not know why. Finally one day Sri Ramakrishna said: "This poor fellow comes here because he has a great desire to be rich. Very well. Let me taste a little of what he has brought." And he took a small quantity of the food. The boy's situation began to improve immediately, and today he is one of the most prosperous men of Calcutta.

There was one boy who often came to Dakshineswar to see the Master. One day the Master took him into the temple and, touching his heart, gave him a vision of the Divine. Afterwards he explained that the boy would not be able to realize God in this life, but he wished to show him what he would attain in his next birth so that he might be encouraged to struggle for it. I remember that once he took the karma of a certain devotee on himself and suffered from a serious bodily disorder for six months.

"God may come at any time," he would say, "but this need not frighten us. When the king wishes to visit one of his servants, he knows the servant will not have soft cushions and the proper things with which to receive him, so the day before he comes, he sends other servants to cleanse everything and prepare for his reception. Similarly, God, before He comes to the heart, sends servants to make it ready for His coming. And who are those servants? Purity, chastity, humility, loving-kindness. Or again, as in the east the red glow in the sky tells us that the sun is about to rise, so just by looking at a man one can tell whether God will come soon to him."[17]

Sri Ramakrishna trained his disciples to be great teachers of the world. He first asked them to realize God, and then, once they had His command, to teach people. Otherwise the teachings would not be effective. Shashi narrated how Sri Ramakrishna questioned a pandit in Dakshineswar:

"Have you a commission from the Lord? Has He commanded you to teach?" When the pandit admitted he had not, Sri Ramakrishna said: "Then all your lectures are worthless. People will hear you for a time but it will not last." What he said proved to be true. Soon the pandit lost all his popularity, everyone began to criticize him, and he had to give up. Then one day he came to Dakshineswar and prostrated before Sri Ramakrishna, saying: "All this while we have been chewing the chaff and you have been eating the kernel. We have been content with dry books while you have been enjoying life."[18]

A person who sees faults in others does not realize that those faults are within. What is inside comes outside; fault-finding is very injurious to spiritual life. Shashi recalled:

The Master never condemned any man. He was ready to excuse everything. He used to tell us that the difference between man and God was this: If a man failed to serve God ninety-nine times, but the hundredth time served Him with even a little love, God forgot the ninety-nine times he had failed and would say, "Oh! My devotee served Me so well today." But if a man served another man well ninety-nine times and the hundredth time failed in his service, the man would forget the ninety-nine good services and say, "That rascal failed to serve me one day." If there was the least spark of good in anyone, Sri Ramakrishna saw only that and overlooked all the rest.[19]

Love manifests through action, manner, and feelings. A real lover always takes the position of a giver; the lover enjoys giving everything — body, mind, possessions, wealth — to the beloved. Like his cousin Sharat, Shashi was not well-to-do. He knew that the Master was very fond of ice, so he bought a big piece and carefully wrapped it with paper and then with a towel so that it would not melt. He walked over six miles from Calcutta to Dakshineswar. It was a hot summer day and the scorching sun blistered his body. When the Master saw him, he began to say, "Ah! Ah!" as if he were in pain. When Shashi asked him what was the matter, the Master said that as he looked at Shashi's body, his own began to burn. The Master was overwhelmed by Shashi's sincerity and love. Strange to say, the ice did not melt at all on the way.

Last Days With the Master

For almost two years Shashi regularly visited the Master at Dakshineswar and acquired great spiritual treasures from him. In the middle of 1885 Ramakrishna developed throat cancer and the devotees arranged for his treatment in Shyampukur, Calcutta. Holy Mother took the responsibility of cooking special food for the Master and some young disciples began to nurse him under Narendra's leadership. Shashi would eat at home, then serve the Master at night. Shashi was then preparing for his B.A. examination. His parents had great expectations for him because he was their eldest son and a brilliant student.

Now Shashi faced a great dilemma: Should he serve his guru or build his career through study? His discriminating mind selected the first one. He stopped going home, gave up his studies, and became a full-time attendant of the Master. An old neighbour of Shashi asked him, "Why don't you serve your guru after the examination?" Shashi replied: "Sir, could you give me any guarantee that I shall not die before that examination?"[20] When his father begged him to return home, he replied: "For me the world and home are both like a place infested with tigers."[21] His father even used a mantram to get his son back home, but this failed. It is said that on one occasion Shashi's father criticized Sri Ramakrishna in front of him. Immediately Shashi was ready to stab him, saying, "Who is my father?" Ishwar Chandra was pleased with his son, and said to him, "Yes, your devotion to your guru is genuine."[22]

The doctor advised the devotees to move Sri Ramakrishna from smoggy, congested Calcutta to a clean, quiet country place. Accordingly, the Master was taken to the Cossipore garden house on 11 December 1885. Shashi followed the Master like a shadow. All of the attendants were great devotees, but Shashi's devotion was special. He was the very embodiment of service. He was convinced that service to the guru was the highest form of religion. He practised no spiritual discipline, knew no other asceticism, travelled to no holy places. Forgetting his personal comfort, food, or rest, he was always ready to serve the Master. His life's purpose was to alleviate the Master's suffering. Indeed, he would have given his life if he thought that would cure him. Everyone marvelled at his indefatigable energy, his endurance, and his boundless love for the Master.

Love is reciprocal. Ramakrishna poured his fountain of love into his disciples and captivated them forever. It was winter when the Master arrived at the Cossipore garden house. Once, in the middle of a cold night, Shashi left the Master's room to clean the commode; he wore only a thin cloth. On his return he saw that Ramakrishna, who was very sick, had somehow crawled across the room and was reaching up for a shawl that was hanging on a clotheshorse. At this painful sight Shashi thought to himself: Alas! In my hurry I forgot to cover him sufficiently, so perhaps he is cold and is trying to get a shawl. "What are you doing, sir?" Shashi asked him in a scolding tone. "The air is very chilly, and you should not be up. Why did you not ask me for the shawl?" Filled with love and concern, the Master held out his shawl, and then said in a feeble voice: "I felt cold as you went out almost barebodied on such a cold night, so I picked up this shawl for you. Please take this."[23] Shashi was overwhelmed.

One winter day the Master expressed a wish to eat *jamruls* (star apples). It is a juicy tropical fruit, only available in summer. Shashi knew that the Master was a man of truth and that such a person's wish could not go unfulfilled. Moreover, the scriptures say that nature fulfills all the wishes of a knower of Brahman. The heroic devotee Shashi inquired and discovered that someone had a jamrul tree that produced fruits out of season. He collected some jamruls and offered them to the Master. The Master asked him with wonder, "Where did you get jamruls in this season?"[24] Shashi told him, and he was happy to serve the Master.

Sometime in the middle of January 1886, the elder Gopal wanted to distribute twelve pieces of ochre cloth and rosaries to some monks. Pointing to his young disciples, the Master said to him: "You won't find better monks than these. Give your cloths and rosaries to them." Instead, Gopal offered them to the Master and he himself distributed them among his young disciples. Shashi got an ochre cloth, the garb of a monk, from the Master. Thus Sri Ramakrishna himself founded his monastic order.

Shashi, Niranjan, and others kept vigilant eyes on the Master so that outsiders might not disturb him. During this time a woman who was mentally ill had been troubling everyone in order to see the Master. She was very unpredictable. Sometimes she would cry and shout. From time to time she would enter the Master's room without notice and disturb his rest.

"If she comes again," said Shashi, "I shall shove her out of the place." The Master tenderly said: "No, no! Let her come and go away."[25]

Even when he was on his deathbed, the Master continued to teach his disciples that the highest truth cannot be experienced without renunciation and purity. On 22 April 1886 M. recorded in *The Gospel of Sri Ramakrishna*:

> In the evening Rakhal, Shashi, and M. were strolling in the garden at Cossipore.
>
> M.: "The Master is like a child — beyond the three gunas."
>
> Shashi and Rakhal: "He himself has said that."
>
> M.: "He said, 'In such a state of mind one sees God constantly.' In him there is not the slightest trace of worldliness. His mind is like dry fuel, which catches fire quickly."
>
> Shashi: "He described the different kinds of intelligence to Charu. The right intelligence is that through which one attains God; but the intelligence that enables one to become a deputy magistrate or a lawyer, or to acquire a house, is a mean intelligence. It is like thin and watery curd, which merely soaks flattened rice but does not add any flavour to it. It is not like thick, superior curd. But the intelligence through which one attains God is like thick curd."
>
> M.: "Ah, what wonderful words!"
>
> Shashi: "Kali said to the Master: 'What's the good of having joy? The Bhils [a savage tribe] are joyous. Savages are always singing and dancing in a frenzy of delight.'"
>
> Rakhal: "He [*meaning the Master*] replied to Kali: 'What do you mean? Can the Bliss of Brahman be the same as worldly pleasure? One cannot enjoy the Bliss of Brahman unless one completely rids oneself of attachment to worldly things. There is the joy of money and sense experience, and there is the Bliss of God-realization. Can the two ever be the same? The rishis enjoyed the Bliss of Brahman.'"[26]

Sri Ramakrishna lived at the Cossipore garden house for the last eight months of his life, and during this period Shashi hardly went out. During the Chariot Festival of Lord Jagannath, the Master asked Shashi to go out and see the festival. At first, Shashi declined, unwilling to leave him alone on his sickbed. But when the Master insisted, he went to a place close to the garden to see the festival. At the festival, Shashi purchased for only two pice a small knife to cut lemons for the Master. The Master was delighted to see the knife, and said: "You should not fail to visit such festivals and make some purchase however small. Poor people prepare so many things on these special occasions and bring them to the fair for sale with the hope of earning something. Try to keep up the ancient traditions as far as practicable and encourage others to do so."[27]

Shashi's life was a glowing example of the "servant" attitude towards God. He forgot hunger and thirst, sleep and rest, and above all his body. At times the Master had to tell him: "Please go and eat; now I am all right. I don't need you at present." Sometimes Shashi would fan the Master nonstop for hours. Feeling Shashi's aches himself, Ramakrishna would take the palm-leaf fan from his hand and give it to Latu. Towards the end of his life the Master said to Shashi: "Look, you boys have tied me with this loving service. If you let me go, then only can I go."[28]

On 16 August 1886 Sri Ramakrishna passed away. Shashi left this graphic account of the Master's last day:

We all thought he was better because he ate so much more supper than usual, and he said nothing of going. In the afternoon [actually eight or nine days earlier] he had asked Jogin to look in the almanac and see whether it was an auspicious day. Also he had been telling us for some time that the vessel which was floating in the ocean was already two-thirds full of water, and soon the rest would fill up and plunge into the ocean. But we did not believe that he was really going. He never seemed to mind the pain. He never lost his cheerfulness. He used to say that he was all well and happy, only there was a little something here [pointing to his throat]. "Within me are two persons," he would declare. "One is the Divine Mother, and the other is Her devotee. It is the devotee that has been taken ill."

When Sri Ramakrishna gave up his body I think it was the most blissful moment of his life. A thrill of joy ran through him. I myself saw it. I remember every incident of that last day. Our Master seemed very well and cheerful. In the afternoon he talked for fully two hours to a gentleman who had come to put some questions to him about yoga. A little later I ran some seven miles to bring the doctor. When I reached the doctor's house he was not there, but I was told that he was at a certain place, so I ran another mile and met him on the way. He had an engagement and said he could not come, but I dragged him away just the same.

On that last night Ramakrishna was talking with us to the very last. For supper he had drunk a half glass of payasam [pudding] and seemed to relish it. There was, no doubt, a little heat in the body, so he asked us to fan him, and some ten of us were all fanning at once. He was sitting up against five or six pillows which were supported by my body and at the same time I too was fanning. This made a slight motion and twice he asked me, "Why are you shaking?" It was as if his mind were so fixed and steady that he could perceive the least motion. Narendra took his feet and began to rub them and Sri Ramakrishna was talking to him, telling him what he must do. "Take care of these boys," he repeated again and again as if he were putting them in Naren's charge. Then he asked to lie down.

Suddenly at one o'clock [actually 1:02 a.m.] he fell towards one side. There was a low sound in his throat, and I saw all the hairs of his body stand on end. Narendra quickly laid his feet on a quilt and ran downstairs as if he could not bear it. A doctor, who was a great devotee and who was feeling his pulse, saw that it had stopped and began to weep aloud. "What are you doing?" I asked, impatient with him for acting as if the Master had really left us.

We all believed that it was only samadhi, so Naren came back and we sat down, some twenty of us, and began repeating all together: "Hari Om! Hari Om!" In this way we waited until between one and two the next day. Still the body had some heat in it, especially around the back, but the doctor insisted that the soul had left it. About five o'clock the body had grown cold, so we placed it on a cot, covered it with garlands, and carried it to the burning ghat.[29]

It was hard for Shashi to believe that the Master had left his physical form. With tearful eyes he sat near the funeral pyre with a palm-leaf fan in his hand. Sharat and Naren sought to console him. Latu took him by the hand and tried to lift his spirits a little, but he remained motionless with grief. Then Shashi collected the ashes and bones of the Master and put them in an urn. He placed the urn on his head and carried it to the garden house, where it was kept on the Master's bed.

The next day, Ramchandra Datta, a prominent householder devotee of the Master, came to the Cossipore garden house and asked the disciples to return to their homes. He also told them of his plan to enshrine the relics of the Master at his garden house at Kankurgachi and establish a monastery there. Shashi and Niranjan were shocked and refused to accept the idea. They told him that they would not give him the relics, and that they would continue the worship service of the Master. Naren tried to pacify them: "Brothers, it is not good to quarrel over this urn. We have no monastery ourselves, and Ram Babu is willing to give the title of his garden house in the name of the Master. It is a good proposition. We should begin his worship there. If we can build our characters according to the Master's ideal, we will have achieved the purpose of our lives."[30]

At last Shashi and Niranjan consulted with Naren and other disciples and quietly put the larger portion of the relics into an urn secretly kept at Balaram Basu's house; the remaining portion was given to Ramchandra Datta. Then on 23 August 1886, Krishna's birthday, the disciples and devotees of Sri Ramakrishna formed a procession and walked from Ram's house to Kankurgachi, singing devotional songs the entire way. Shashi carried the urn with the Master's ashes on his head. During the consecration ceremony, as they were covering the urn with earth, Shashi cried out, "Oh, the Master is in pain!"[31] The devotees wept as they listened to Shashi's words.

At the Baranagore and Alambazar Monasteries

Shashi reluctantly returned home, but his mind was preoccupied with the Master. His parents were happy to have him back. But who can change Divine Providence? One evening early in September Sri Ramakrishna appeared before Surendra Mittra and said: "What are you doing here? My boys are roaming about, without a place to live. Attend to that, before anything else." Surendra immediately rushed to Naren's house and told him what had happened. He promised to offer the same amount of money that he used to give for the Master's expenses in Cossipore. Naren and the disciples were then able to rent a house in Baranagore at ten rupees per month and thus establish the first Ramakrishna Math.

It was an abandoned, dilapidated two-storeyed building, infested with snakes and said to be haunted by ghosts. The ground floor was dark, damp, and unfit for habitation; so those rooms were used as the kitchen and for storage. Shashi was once bitten by a snake in one of those dark rooms. They set up a shrine in an upstairs room: The relics of Sri Ramakrishna were brought from Balaram's house, and a picture of the Master was placed on the altar. The articles that the Master had used at Cossipore were also preserved in the shrine room. Shashi kept the memory of the Master ablaze in the monastery by his wholehearted dedication and devoted service. His scrupulous precision and regularity of service made everyone feel the living presence of the Master.

From 1886 to 1897 Shashi kept a constant vigil over the Master's relics, seldom visiting any holy place or leaving the monastery overnight. Because he came from an orthodox brahmin family, he performed the Master's worship as one serves a living human being. He would get up at 4:00 a.m., and after washing would enter the shrine to rouse the Master from his bed. He would then offer a twig for a toothbrush and water to rinse his mouth. Next he would offer some sweets made from coconut and a glass of water for breakfast, and tobacco to smoke. He never allowed his brother disciples to help him. Afterwards he would pick flowers, sweep the shrine, wash the worship vessels, and make the necessary preparations for worship. He would then go to the nearby market to buy groceries. Shashi always bought the best produce for the Master; although he did not have much money, he had a rich heart. People would comment that it was hard to find nice things at the market because of these monks. After returning from the market he would help the cook cut vegetables, and then he would go to bathe in the Ganges and bring holy water for worship. Afterwards he would perform rituals and offer cooked food to the Master.

In the evening he would conduct the vesper service, waving a light, fanning the Master, and singing with the disciples the vesper song of Vishwanath in Varanasi:

> *Jai Shiva Omkara, Bhaja Shiva Omkara,*
> *Brahma Vishnu Sadashiva,*
> *Hara Hara Mahadeva!*

Swami Virajananda (a monastic disciple of Vivekananda), later recalled:

Oh, how wonderful was the *arati* [vespers] of Shashi Maharaj. It was really a sight for the gods. Enveloped within the smoke of burning incense and drowned in the music of drums and cymbals, he would wave a *chamar* [a fan made of a yak's tail] towards the end of the arati. Intoxicated with God-consciousness he would repeat, "*Jai Gurudeva! Jai Gurudeva!*" (Victory to the Guru), in a crescendo of divine abandon and would dance from one side of the hall to the other rhythmically pacing the floor. What a unique feeling of ecstatic love would course through the hearts of men witnessing it can better be imagined than described. The whole building would be in a tremor. With a heavenly glow on his face he looked the very embodiment of the God of Fire. The hand of the drummer would get benumbed and would refuse to move. The spectators would watch from the adjoining room and join him, all repeating in chorus, "*Jai Gurudeva! Jai Gurudeva!*" They too would dance in rapture and fervour. Then all would prostrate themselves before the deity and recite in chorus this verse from the *Guru Gita*: "I bow down to the adorable guru who by the collyrium of knowledge, opened my eyes, blinded by the disease of ignorance."

After this, the last part of a hymn composed by Swami Abhedananda would be sung: "Let our salutations be to Ramakrishna, the taintless, eternal, of universal form, God incarnate out of mercy for his devotees, and adorable Lord of all."

Finally the evening service would end with the words, "*Jai Sri Gurumaharaj ki Jai!*"[32]

In December 1886 Shashi and some other disciples went to Antpur, the country home of Baburam. Inspired by Narendra, they took informal vows of monasticism during a nightlong vigil around a sacred fire. Later they discovered that their vigil had taken place on Christmas Eve. A month later they took formal monastic vows by performing the traditional *viraja homa* ceremony in Baranagore. Narendra gave the name "Swami Ramakrishnananda" to Shashi, knowing that his devotion to the Master was second to none.

It is extremely important for future generations to know every detail of the beginning of the Ramakrishna Movement: how the Master's disciples faced hunger, pain, poverty, and persecution, and how they overcame them by the power and grace of the Master. The financial help of Surendra Mittra and a few other devotees was not sufficient to maintain the monastery. The young monks had to survive on the most meagre food, they had very little clothing, and they slept on the floor under a single big mosquito curtain for want of separate bedding. During this trying period, Ramakrishnananda worked as a teacher in the Baranagore High School for two hours daily after lunch, foregoing his rest. He continued this for three months to support the monastery. The young monks went out daily by turns for alms and became the target of taunts and pity from the local people. The food they collected was not even sufficient for the day. Some days they lived only on rice with a pinch of salt; it was a festive day when they got a vegetable curry.

One day four monks went out for alms, but unfortunately received nothing. The monastery store was also empty. Ramakrishnananda was anxious and disturbed, thinking that the Master would have to starve that day as there was nothing to offer to him. Giving up the desire for food, the brother disciples became absorbed in devotional singing. Ramakrishnananda then secretly went to the house of a friendly neighbour and said to him, "Brother dear, today nothing has been obtained from begging. Could you give me a few handfuls of rice, some potatoes, and a little *ghee* [clarified butter]?" Although other members of his family were not sympathetic to the young monks, he gave Ramakrishnananda a half pound of rice, some potatoes, and a little ghee. The swami gladly cooked that food and offered it to the Master. He then mixed it together and made some balls, which he carried to the hall and put one in the mouth of each monk. That small amount of sanctified food appeased their hunger, and they were touched by Ramakrishnananda's love and concern. With delight they asked, "Brother Shashi, where did you get such delicious food?"

Many years later Vivekananda recalled:

Oh, what a steadfastness to the ideal did we ever find in Shashi! He was a mother to us. It was he who managed our food. We used to get up at three o'clock in the morning. Then all of us, some after bathing, would go to the shrine and be lost in japam and meditation. There were times when the meditation lasted to four or five o'clock in the afternoon. Shashi would be waiting with our dinner; if necessary, he would, by sheer force, drag us out of our meditation. Who cared then if the world existed or not![33]

Love removes friction and factions. The disciples often had differences of opinion about how they should perform their work, but not in their goal — God-realization. Swami Adbhutananda reminisced:

Once there was a heated exchange of words between the brother disciples in connection with the shrine. It began when a householder devotee said: "You fellows do nothing but act as priests to the photograph of the Master, burning incense and waving lights before it, just as orthodox priests do before the stone image of Goddess Sitala."

This remark upset Brother Shashi very much and he said sharply: "The money of such a householder should not be touched with a barge pole! It is cursed."

Brother Loren [Vivekananda] used to be amused when he saw Shashi angry. He told him, "All right then, go and beg food for your Master." "Very well," responded Shashi, "and I will not touch a bit of your money either! I will beg in order to feed my Master." Loren said with a smile, "And I suppose you will offer him *luchis* [fried bread] that you get by begging?" Undaunted Shashi replied, "Yes, I will offer him luchis; and moreover, I will serve those offered luchis to you to gulp down afterwards."

Then Loren pretended to get angry: "No, by no means will I allow luchis to be offered to him while we have nothing to eat! Such a Master should be thrown out. If you won't do it, I am going to throw him out myself!" Saying this, he sprang up and started towards the shrine. Shashi said something in English and ran after him.

When I saw what was happening, I tried to intercede. I told Loren, "Brother, why are you opposed to Shashi's desire to serve the Master luchis? Let him go his own way and you yours." Loren returned, "Keep quiet, you fool." A harsh retort was about to come out of my mouth, when Brother Loren laughed such a laugh that Shashi too began to laugh. A few minutes later, we were all sitting together making arrangements for the Master's worship.[34]

Swami Adbhutananda spoke of another incident about Ramakrishnananda's uncompromising attitude of service to the Master:

One day Brother Shashi asked the old swami [Swami Satchidananda] to put a fresh twig, stripped of leaves and bark, in the shrine early in the morning to be offered to the Master for use as a toothbrush. The old swami did not know that one end of the twig was to be gently beaten to soften the fibres and make them brushlike. He brought a whole twig, unbeaten, as most people would use. During the breakfast offering Shashi saw this, and he rushed up to the old swami and scolded him bitterly: "You rogue, you have caused the Master's gum to bleed today. I will teach you a good lesson." I cried out to the old swami: "Don't just stand there looking at him, brother. Run away!" So he fled and the situation calmed down immediately. Shashi got another twig, properly beaten to soften the fibres, and threw away the first one.[35]

Christmas Eve was always celebrated at the Baranagore Monastery. Some Bengali Christians from the Salvation Army knew that the disciples of Sri Ramakrishna had love and admiration for Jesus Christ, so they would visit the monastery often with the ulterior motive of converting the monks. One day they audaciously made a proposal of conversion to Ramakrishnananda and others, saying that none but Christ could grant salvation. Ramakrishnananda, who was well versed in the Bible, argued with the Christian missionaries vehemently and proved the fallacy of their dogmatic statement. After losing the debate, the shrewd missionaries tried to tempt those monks, saying that if they became Christians they would be provided with European wives! At this affront Ramakrishnananda flew into a rage, scolded them severely and asked them to leave. After this they never returned to the monastery.

Sometimes young students would come to the monastery and some even stayed during their vacations. Ramakrishnananda would inspire them and teach mathematics to those who were deficient in that subject. One of the students, Haripada (later, Swami Bodhananda), recalled:

> One day Swami Ramakrishnananda explained to us the technique of self-confidence: "If anybody asks you if you can give talks on the Gita, don't say, 'I don't know the teachings well enough to give talks on them.' Shake off this false timidity and say, 'Yes.' That assertion will be honest and truthful. On the contrary, if you hesitate and say, 'I know a little,' many people will believe that and that will be wrong. Have courage and confidence in your ability. Make the resolve, 'I can do it and I will do it,' and through the grace of the Master you will succeed."[36]

Beginning in 1887 some of the Master's disciples began to travel as itinerant monks; they practised austerities in the Himalayas and other holy places of India. Between their travels, sometimes they would return to the monastery. During this period Ramakrishnananda never went out; to serve Sri Ramakrishna was his great pilgrimage. In February 1892 the Ramakrishna Monastery was moved from Baranagore to Alambazar, not far from the Dakshineswar temple garden. The Alambazar Monastery was a large two-storeyed building with a number of rooms and pillared verandas; there were also a lawn and a pond in the compound. During its occupation by two previous tenants a few suicides had occurred in the house, and the rumour had spread that the house was haunted. For that reason the monks got it at a low rent of ten rupees per month.

Ramakrishnananda set up the shrine and followed the same routine as in Baranagore. One summer night when he was lying in his room and fanning himself with a palm-leaf fan, he felt that the Master too must be suffering from the heat. At once he entered the shrine and stood near the bed of the Master, fanning him till dawn. Once Girish Chandra Ghosh, a devotee of the Master, remarked: "Shashi is *asana-siddha* [perfect in sitting]; otherwise it is impossible for anyone to worship Mother Jagaddhatri at a twenty-four hour stretch sitting in one place."[37] Later someone asked Ramakrishnananda how he was able to do it. He replied modestly, "Devotion can accomplish anything."[38]

Everything is not in books: A good student learns by watching his or her teacher. Ramakrishnananda was a wonderful trainer of the soul, and to live with him was an education. Swami Satchidananda, who was the swami's helper for some time in Alambazar, recalled:

One day Swami Ramakrishnananda told me, "Before you sweep the room, first sprinkle a little water on the floor, otherwise the dust will go on the body of the Master." Another day he asked me to prepare betel-rolls for the Master; he chewed one and said, "You have put in too much lime. It will burn the Master's mouth." He entrusted me to put the Master to bed, to fan him for some time, and drop the curtain. When I went to take my supper, he asked, "Have you dropped the curtain?" "Yes, swami," I replied. Afterwards he never asked me to put the Master to bed, because I had not fanned the Master for a sufficient time. One morning he went to prepare *halua* [farina pudding] for the Master, and found the pan dirty. When he learned that Latu Maharaj had fried gram with oil and chili in that pan, the swami scolded him, but later he felt pained because he had hurt his brother.

Very early in the morning he would accompany me to pick flowers from the neighbours' gardens. After returning he would put the flower basket near the shrine and pray with folded hands: "Master, give us a piece of land. I shall plant various kinds of flowers and use them for your worship." One day I plucked flowers, and he became mad at me when he saw the quantity was not enough. Another day he told me, "You go to Dakshineswar temple garden and pick jasmine, and I shall make a garland for the Master." I went to Dakshineswar for a couple of days, but the gardeners forbade me to pick flowers. When I reported this to the swami, he asked M. to get permission from the temple manager so that we could pick flowers from the temple garden. Swami Yogananda suggested buying flowers, but the swami did not agree.

Sri Ramakrishna used to chew some spices, so Swami Ramakrishnananda used to keep those spices in a small bag near the Master's bed. He used to dry them after washing them, and clean them one by one so that there would not be any tiny stone particles in them. He would check my cleaning and ask me not to hurry. While in Dakshineswar Sri Ramakrishna would bathe in the fresh water of the Ganges, so as a part of ritualistic worship the swami would give a bath to him in the same way. Observing that I told him, "It destroys my faith in the Ganges, because her water to me is always pure whether it is old or fresh." But he insisted: "We must give a bath to the Master daily with fresh Ganges water. If it is difficult for you, you will not have to do it. I shall bring the water when I go for a bath in the Ganges."

Sri Ramakrishna's personal articles were kept in a broken tin trunk. On a special occasion, I opened it to get some stone bowls and found that some mice had soiled them. When I told him what had happened, he asked me to clean those bowls and use them. He was very sad. On the same day he went to a nearby shop, bought a big trunk and transferred everything into it and locked it. One night the swami could not sleep because he was shivering from cold. He thought perhaps he had forgotten to put the quilt over the Master's picture. He immediately opened the shrine and found that his guess was correct. He covered the Master's picture with the quilt, then slept peacefully. One day in the living room after lunch, he was reading the chapter on *moksha* [liberation] from the Mahabharata, and others were talking loudly. I told them, "It is not proper to make noise while the Master is resting." "You are right," said Swami Ramakrishnananda. From then on he never allowed anyone to make noise there.[39]

Ramakrishnananda was learned and devotional, but he was not a gloomy ascetic. After dinner he would dramatically read Mark Twain's *The Innocents at Home* and *The Innocents Abroad*. He would roar with laughter as he read them, and the others would laugh along with him. He enjoyed solving mathematical problems; sometimes after his noon rest he would work on the mathematics on a slate or piece of paper. Often for inspiration he would read the episode of Rishabha Deva from the Bhagavata, and comment: "The spiritual state of Rishabha Deva is extraordinarily high and may be compared to that of a paramahamsa." He also translated the teachings of Sri Ramakrishna from Bengali into Sanskrit verses and got them serially published in *Vidyodaya*, a Sanskrit journal. Ramakrishnananda never had an idle moment, as he had a wide range of interests.

In September 1893 Swami Vivekananda represented Hinduism at the Parliament of Religions in Chicago and became a celebrity. People's attention then fell on the Alambazar Monastery, and gradually the monks' financial problems decreased. In 1894 the disciples and devotees arranged the birth anniversary of Sri Ramakrishna on a grand scale in Dakshineswar. On this occasion Ramakrishnananda danced in ecstasy and chanted the Master's name. The devotees and visitors were overwhelmed by his devotion. In 1895 Vivekananda wrote to Ramakrishnananda, asking him to come to America and assist in the Vedanta work, which he could not handle alone. Ramakrishnananda agreed, but Dr. Salzer, a German homeopath, advised against it because the cold climate of America would aggravate Ramakrishnananda's troublesome skin condition. Ramakrishnananda dropped the idea and carried on his usual work in the monastery.

In February 1897 Vivekananda returned to Calcutta from the West, and stayed with his Western disciples at Gopallal Seal's garden house, which was near the monastery. He spent most of the time with his brother disciples at Alambazar and discussed their future work with them. One day some pandits from West India came to the Alambazar Monastery to test Swamiji's knowledge of the Vedas. While this discussion was taking place, Ramakrishnananda was seated in the shrine in meditation posture, counting his beads. He was praying wholeheartedly to the Master, he said later on, so that Swamiji might come out victorious in the debate. Such was his love for Vivekananda![40]

One day Ramakrishnananda asked Swamiji, "How can one be a good preacher?" Swamiji first touched his hand to his head and said, "One needs good intellect." Then touching his face, he said, "One should have good looks." Touching his lips, he said, "One should have a sweet tongue." Touching his chest, he said: "One should have a broad, catholic heart, otherwise people won't listen to you. I achieved more through my loving heart than through my sharp intellect." At last, pointing to his sex organ, he said: "One should have self-control. This chastity is the most vital aspect in a preacher's life."[41]

As Ramakrishnananda was extremely orthodox, Swamiji asked him one day: "Shashi, I want to put your love for me to the test. Can you buy for me a piece of English bread from a Muslim shop at the corner of

Chitpore Road?"[42] An orthodox Hindu would not even touch that kind of food. Without any hesitation, Ramakrishnananda obeyed the order of their beloved leader. Then Swamiji put him to a second test. In March 1897, before going to Darjeeling for a change, Swamiji called aside Ramakrishnananda and said: "I have given word to my friends at Madras that I shall very soon send one of my brother disciples there. I have selected you. You are to go to Madras and found a monastery there in the name of our beloved Master."[43] Ramakrishnananda neither raised any objection nor pleaded any excuse. In the last part of March 1897 he left for Madras by ship with Swami Sadananda, a disciple of Vivekananda, and arrived there in April. Thus came to an end his vigil over the Master's remains. He was assigned to work in a new place among unknown people.

In Madras

Returning from America in January 1897, Vivekananda stopped at Colombo in Sri Lanka, and some important cities in South India. In Madras he stayed for nine days in Castle Kernan, which was known as the Ice House because it had been constructed by an American company to store ice on the seashore. Swamiji created great enthusiasm among the people in Madras, and they asked him to send one of his brother monks to start a monastery there. With Ramakrishnananda in mind, Swamiji told them, "I shall send you one who is more orthodox than your most orthodox brahmins of the South and who is at the same time incomparable in performing worship, scriptural knowledge, and meditation on God."[44]

Ramakrishnananda was cordially received by the Madrasi devotees of Vivekananda. They first rented Flora Cottage, located on the same road as the Ice House. Shortly afterwards, Biligiri Iyengar, a prominent lawyer and the owner of the Ice House, offered the first floor of that castle to Ramakrishnananda to start his work. Because the disciples had learned from the Master, "First God and then the world," Ramakrishnananda first set up the shrine in a room and installed a picture of the Master that he had carried from Calcutta. He then began to conduct worship service as he had before; in addition, he started to give classes on the Upanishads, Gita, and Bhagavata. At one time, he gave eleven classes a week in different parts of the city, travelling by *jutka*, a narrow, uncomfortable, horse-drawn carriage. Sometimes he would return to the monastery after an exhausting day of classes and lectures to find that there was no food for supper.

Ramakrishnananda's life exemplified the teaching of the Gita, "You are entitled to work, but never to its fruits." Swami Shankarananda recalled:

One afternoon it was drizzling and the sky was overcast with clouds. A hackney carriage came in time to take the swami to his class. The swami asked a brahmacharin [*probably Shankarananda himself*] to accompany him that day. The carriage arrived in George Town, where the swami used to hold one of his classes. . . . There was no one else in the room. The swami waited for about a quarter of an hour but no one turned up. He then opened his Upanishad and began to read and explain with all ardour and amiability. After an hour he stopped, closed his book and said to the brahmacharin, "Well, let us go." The brahmacharin followed him to the carriage which was waiting. On the way he asked the swami, "How is it that you gave the class for fully one hour though nobody turned up." The swami replied, "I have not come to teach anybody. I only fulfill the vow I have taken."[45]

Like all pioneers, Ramakrishnananda faced various difficulties. He received very little financial help from the devotees, and he lived alone for most of the first four years. It was a strenuous life: He had to perform the worship, give classes, cook, and do all the household duties. In addition, he was trying to inspire and train some young people. In his inaugural lecture on "Necessity of Religious Education in Youth," he said: "Religion takes a man to God by making God of a man. . . . Religion is the highest chemistry, for it analyzes the compound man into the elements, ego and nonego, the self and the nonself, the soul and the body. Religion is the burning furnace in which is burnt up all the dross of his heart." He then concluded: "The heart of a young man is very pure, so it is a fit reservoir for religion to flow in and every young man therefore is a fit candidate for a place in the heavenly office of religion."[46]

He tried to spread the teachings of Sri Ramakrishna among his students, and reminded them that purity and renunciation are essential in spiritual life. He boldly declared that "God and Mammon" cannot be worshiped simultaneously. This made a few city leaders nervous, as they were afraid that their boys would shun family life and become monastics. They threatened to withdraw financial support if Ramakrishnananda did not change the mode of his teaching.

As a true disciple of Sri Ramakrishna he could not compromise the truth; he privately said to an ardent devotee: "Am I to preach other than what I learned from my Master? Certainly I won't do that. I don't care a fig for the bigwigs. They are at liberty to do whatever they like. If I am ousted today from this castle, I shall very gladly find accommodation in a room of one of my students' houses. I am a sannyasin and do not know where my next meal will come from."[47] Because he was in debt, Ramakrishnananda went to a publisher of the Upanishads in Madras and told him: "I shall translate Upanishads for you. Please give me some money."[48] Realizing Ramakrishnananda's financial difficulties, the publisher arranged a monthly subscription for the fledgling monastery. The raja of Ramnad also began to send some money on a regular basis; thus the Master provided Ramakrishnananda's bare necessities.

In June 1899 Vivekananda left Calcutta for America a second time, with Swami Turiyananda and Sister Nivedita. They wished to visit Madras but were not allowed to land; there was a plague in Calcutta and the ship was quarantined in the Madras harbour. This was a great disappointment to the whole city. The boat was anchored far from the wharf, and friends and devotees who had gathered in large numbers to meet Swamiji, had to take small boats to the ship. Ramakrishnananda took a boat with some devotees; he had bought thirty pounds of flour and prepared single-handedly various kinds of salty (nimki) and sweet (gaja) snacks for Swamiji, which he carried with him in several large cans. Swamiji greeted him and talked to him, leaning from the deck. He had brought a big jar of Ganges water for Ramakrishnananda. The food, fruits, flowers, and other presents, were drawn up in baskets, and the Ganges water was lowered to them in the same basket.

Prevented from touching Swamiji's feet, Ramakrishnananda said to his companion: "Please ask the boatman to take us right around the steamer. Let us at least make a pradakshinam [a religious rite to encircle the deity] of the two great souls whose feet we have not been able to touch today."[49] When the boatman grumbled, Ramakrishnananda offered him some extra money, thereby fulfilling his wish.

Vivekananda returned from the West in December 1900. In December 1901 Ramakrishnananda visited Vivekananda at Belur; the monastery had been moved there from Alambazar in 1898. It was Ramakrishnananda's first visit to the new monastery. He was happy to see the permanent home of the Master on the bank of the Ganges, and also to visit Swamiji, whose health was not good. On 2 January 1902 Swamiji initiated Brahmachari Basanta (who was with Ramakrishnananda at Madras) into sannyasa, naming him Swami Paramananda. Swamis Ramakrishnananda and Paramananda returned to Madras in the middle of January 1902.

On the night of 4 July 1902, Ramakrishnananda called Satchidananda loudly, "Dinabandhu! Dinabandhu!" "What happened?" asked

Satchidananda. "I saw Swamiji standing before me and he said to me, 'Look here, Shashi, I threw away this body like spitting out spittle,' and he spat twice or thrice."[50] Both swamis could not figure out the meaning of that vision, and neither of them got any more sleep that night. The next day Ramakrishnananda received a cable from Belur Math with the sad news of Vivekananda's passing away. The swamis cried for their beloved leader and arranged for a big memorial meeting in Madras.

Swami Shankarananda reminisced:

One summer morning (between 1902 and 1903) Swami Ramakrishnananda returned from his classes by 10:30 a.m. in a hackney carriage. After entering his room he stripped himself, sat on the edge of his cot and began to fan himself. Seeing him in such a plight owing to the summer heat the brahmacharin began to fan him from behind. After a minute or so the swami threw away his fan and with clenched fists threw out his arms as if to fight with somebody. He began to say, "It is for you that I suffer so much. See, what suffering I go through." The next moment he fell flat on the floor with outstretched hands and joined palms, and began to rub his face on the carpet, saying, "No brother, no brother, excuse me, excuse me. What you have done is perfect. It is all right, it is all right." He got up with flowing eyes and blissful countenance and cast a divine look around before he sat again. All this was with Swami Vivekananda, who had sent him to Madras to live the life as moulded by Sri Ramakrishna.[51]

Swami Vishuddhananda wrote in his memoirs:

Once I saw Swami Ramakrishnananda praying before an oil painting of Swami Vivekananda after his return from a lecture tour. I overheard his fervent prayers as he bowed down before him: "O my beloved brother, you are verily the accredited representative of Sri Ramakrishna and it is you who have sent me over here to propagate his message. I am only carrying out your commands. I beseech you to see to it that no pride or self-esteem enters my heart, no thirst for name or fame disturbs my mind. All the burden and the responsibility that you have placed upon me are verily yours. Bless me so that I may carry on the work of our Master only as an instrument in his hands and that I may offer all the fruits of work unto him. Guide me always in the right path." What a glorious example of self-surrender and dedication to God and his work![52]

There is a saying, "One should adore the children of the guru like the guru." Ramakrishnananda's love and esteem towards his brother disciples almost bordered on worship. Once the swami was in Ernakulam,

South India, and stayed with Mr. Duraiswami Aiyar, a prominent lawyer. Upon entering the house, Ramakrishnananda told Mr. Aiyar: "I have heard that Swami Vivekananda stayed in your house in his itinerant days. This is a holy place. I wish to see first the exact place or room where he stayed." Mr. Aiyar replied, "He was seated, when he came in, even where we stand now." At once Ramakrishnananda rolled on the floor and kissed the ground, for to him the very dust of the place where his leader had been was sacred.[53]

Perfection in life comes from good and systematic training. Several monks who lived with Ramakrishnananda from 1897 to 1910 were unanimous in their opinion that the swami was a strict disciplinarian and a hard taskmaster. Ramakrishnananda established the routine in the Madras Monastery. All the monks got up at 5:00 a.m. and practised meditation in their rooms. The swami opened the shrine and performed the morning service and food offering. Then he returned to his room and recited the Chandi, the Gita, and the *Vishnusahasranama*. After half an hour, one monk removed the food tray from the shrine, another monk cleaned the shrine and worship vessels, and another monk fixed the breakfast. After breakfast Ramakrishnananda and some of the monks cut vegetables; while they worked, one monk read a scripture and the swami then explained its meaning. Punctually at 11:00 a.m. Ramakrishnananda went to the shrine to perform the daily worship. After the food offering at 12:30 p.m., the shrine was closed. After lunch, the monks rested. At 3:00 p.m. they went to Ramakrishnananda's room. There, one of the monks read the *Chaitanya Charitamrita* (Life of Chaitanya) and the swami explained it with parallel examples from the life and teachings of Sri Ramakrishna. Punctually at 4:00 p.m. the shrine was opened. In the evening there was a vesper service. At 8:30 p.m. food was offered to the Master and at 9:00 p.m. the shrine was closed. After supper, Ramakrishnananda told stories about the Master and Swamiji with his natural enthusiasm.

Only a person who loves has a right to govern or punish. Ramakrishnananda had a loving mother's heart, but he could not tolerate any kind of mistake or dereliction of duty. He expected the monks to be precise and prompt in action, and punctual and attentive in their habits, or else he would scold them severely. He was famous for rebuking and correcting the monks. Once Ramakrishnananda scolded Swami Sharvananda so severely that he almost broke down because he had never been so severely reprimanded. Seeing him weeping, Ramakrishnananda told him affectionately: "Do you know what Sri Ramakrishna used to say? A blacksmith first puts a lump of iron into the fire; when it becomes red hot, he puts it on the anvil and beats it into shape. That is how an unformed lump of metal is shaped into a useful article! All of you are like that unformed lump, and it is for your good that you are put to the forge and beaten into shape on the anvil by such scoldings."[54] Indeed, his method was that of the sledgehammer blow of the blacksmith. Many came, but only a few genuine ones withstood his test.

P. M. Mudaliar recalled:

He was a strict disciplinarian though he heeded not external respect and regard. He used to correct such of the habits of students as are obstructive to spiritual progress. Once a student was found sitting in his class with his chin resting on the palm of his hand. He at once said, "Do not sit like that; it is a pensive attitude." Another day one student was found gently shaking his legs while sitting on a bench, and the swami said to him, "Stop shaking, it is not good and conducive to well-being." Whenever any student drank water while standing, he would enjoin him to sit and drink. He was taking so much interest in the spiritual welfare of his students and even regulated their habits![55]

The storyteller plays an important role in spreading the Indian religious tradition. In an informal setting, people absorb spirituality unconsciously from the teacher. "Every night after food," said Swami Shankarananda, "all brothers used to come to Swami Ramakrishnananda, who would talk to them on various subjects till it was time to retire. Sometimes he would talk about the Master's physical formation, how his soles and palms were soft and had a reddish tinge, and so on; how he was careful about every little thing that was in his room at Dakshineswar and how he had taught his disciples to keep things in their proper places after using them. He was always carefully watching over them and knew whatever doubts and misgivings arose in their minds. He would correct them as suited each of them without letting any of them know; but they would very soon feel ease and tranquillity restored and the absence of any mental struggles. Sometimes the swami would talk about the funny expressions and gestures the Master used to make or the mimicry of other persons at Dakshineswar, even without any reservation with regard to the use of abusive language."[56]

Castle Kernan came up for auction after the death of Mr. Biligiri Iyengar in 1906. A devotee tried to acquire the house for Ramakrishnananda, but he was outbid by a rich landlord. When the auction was going on, Ramakrishnananda was seated on a bench in a corner of the compound; from time to time a devotee reported the progress to him. He calmly said to the devotee: "Why do you worry about it? What do we care who buys or who sells? My wants are few. I need only a small room for Sri Ramakrishna. I can stay anywhere and spend my time in talking of him."[57] As anticipated, the swami had to move out of the main building and temporarily take shelter in the gatehouse of the same compound.

Within five years of his arrival in Madras, Ramakrishnananda became well known in the city, and his work was appreciated by many. Beginning in 1898 Ramakrishnananda began to celebrate the birth anniversary of Sri Ramakrishna on a large scale, and many local people attended. The swami and the devotees deeply felt that a permanent home for the Master was needed. In 1902 they had raised 4,100 rupees for their building fund; and in 1906 a student of the swami donated a piece of land on Brodies Road in the Mylapore area. On an auspicious day, Ramakrishnananda conducted the religious ceremonies, and Swami Abhedananda, who was visiting from the U.S.A. at that time, laid the foundation stone. The building was constructed at the cost of 5,500 rupees; the swami dedicated it on 17 November 1907 and moved into the new ashrama shortly afterwards.

Ramakrishnananda was as elated as a child and said to a devotee: "This is a fine house for the Master to live in. Realizing that he occupies it, we must keep it very clean and pure." Later the swami humorously said: "I was in Triplicane [Castle Kernan] and Parthasarathi [Krishna] subjected me to many trials; but now Kapaleeswara [Shiva] has drawn me to him. You know he is the Lord of *bhikshus* [mendicants] as his name means, and he is sure to protect me hereafter."[58]

P. M. Mudaliar recalled Ramakrishnananda's love for Christ:

He was very orthodox, yet he possessed a tolerant heart. Once he had occasion to go to Saidapet in response to a dinner invitation by a student of his. Swami Paramananda and myself accompanied him. After partaking of dinner towards the evening, we went to Saint Thomas Mount, which was not far off from Saidapet. We ascended the mount and saw a church at its summit. The pastor of the church, who was informed of the swami's desire to see it, was courteous enough to open its gates. We all entered the church and to our amazement the swami went straight to the altar, knelt before it as a Christian would do and prayed.[59]

Sister Devamata [Laura Glenn, an American devotee] wrote in *Days in an Indian Monastery*:

He knew the Bible from cover to cover and expounded it in a spirit and with an understanding which are rare even in Christian countries. . . . When Good Friday came, he talked on the Crucifixion. . . . My whole being was stirred by the living reality of his words and as we drove home I asked how he could make them so real and living. He sat silent for a moment, then he said quietly and simply: "My Master used to tell me that in a previous life Saradananda and I were Christ's disciples."[60]

Service and Devotion to the Master

Ramakrishnananda's service to Sri Ramakrishna is now legendary in the Ramakrishna Order. He was an active, intelligent, independent, dauntless, heroic devotee of the Master. Swami Bodhananda recalled:

Indeed, his method of service had its own character. Those who had the privilege of observing the details of his daily service at the chapel can testify to this fact. His making of the bed, putting on the mosquito curtain around its frame after the evening service, his offering of flowers on the sacred remains and the slippers, his vesper service, his ecstatic dance while chanting the hymns of Shiva and Guru, his waving of the big fan on the bed on hot nights, his cooking the meals for the offering, his deftness, neatness, promptness, and thoroughness in every detail left an indelible impression on the mind of the beholder. The whole spectacle was exalting, thrilling, and stirring. Even the hardest heart would be moved with his superhuman devotion.[61]

Brahmachari Tejnarayan (later, Swami Sharvananda) was sent from Belur Math to assist Ramakrishnananda in Madras. As soon as he arrived Ramakrishnananda asked him what he had brought for the Master. When Tejnarayan replied that he had nothing, the swami said in a convincing tone: "Whenever you come from outside to the monastery, you must bring something for the Master." Then Ramakrishnananda learned that Tejnarayan had some leftover mangoes and sweets in his basket, which he had gotten for his journey. Immediately Ramakrishnananda said, "Never mind, bring those mangoes and offer them to the Master." When Tejnarayan informed him that he had already eaten from that stock, the swami asserted: "That does not matter. Fruits can be washed and offered, even if the first portion has been used by others."[62]

One day Ramakrishnananda pointed to the picture of the Master in the shrine, and said to Tejnarayan: "Look here, my boy, don't consider that a mere picture of Sri Ramakrishna. He is actually present here. Try to feel his living presence and do your services accordingly."[63] His way of expression was unique. One day he said casually: "You people call the Master an avatar, or divine incarnation. Do you have any idea of what an avatar is?" Then he expressed it in the language of mathematics: "Swami Vivekananda and all his lectures and writings plus all the disciples of the Master and their works plus the infinite — are equal to Sri Rama-krishna."[64]

Devotion is contagious. Shankarananda recalled Ramakrishnananda's mode of devotion: "While making *pranams* [salutations] to the Master, the swami would either fall flat with his folded palms outstretched or stand and put his palms together over his heart and would press together his teeth so hard they clattered, and his whole frame would become stiff, his head down to the neck would show a slight tremor. After pranams one could see his eyes slightly reddened and a heavenly glow suffusing his face with an expression of blessedness."[65]

Although Ramakrishnananda was a Vedanta monk, he was a staunch dualist in his belief in the purifying power of *prasad*. He always gave a little prasad to everyone who would visit — even in those difficult days at the Baranagore Monastery — even if it were only a bit of sugar candy or some sweets offered to the Master, kept for that purpose. The swami firmly believed that whosoever partook of a little prasad of Sri Rama-krishna would be purified of all sins and blessed with faith and devotion. In Madras he used to offer coconut sweets or sugar candy to every visitor and insisted that the monks distribute prasad among the devotees without fail.

One generally does not vent anger upon a stranger; during times of anguish and suffering one releases frustration and anger upon those one knows and loves. One evening a few devotees came to the monastery to meet Ramakrishnananda, but he was in the shrine. They overheard him talking with someone loudly in angry tones: "You have brought me here, an old man, and left me helpless. Are you testing my powers of patience and endurance? I will not go and beg hereafter for my sake or even for yours. If anything comes unasked, I will offer it to you and share the prasad. Or, I will bring sea sand for offering to you and I shall live upon that."[66] Later they realized that the swami was quarrelling with his beloved Master.

Swami Sharvananda recalled another touching incident. Once there was no food in the temple storeroom to offer Sri Ramakrishna at 4:00 p.m. At 3:00 p.m. the matter was brought to Ramakrishnananda, and it greatly upset him. He took it as a test from the Master. He did not become angry with the monks for not informing him beforehand; his ire and grievance were solely turned against the Master. He burst out: "You want to test me? I will eat sand and do Swamiji's work here. Sirrah! You are testing me, I know. But you should also know my grim resolve. I would rather die and perish here than budge an inch from this place. Do your worst, if you will!" His face became ruddy and glowed in terrible anguish and fervour; he began to pace back and forth in the hall. It was a tense half hour. At 3:30 p.m. someone knocked at the front door. Mr. Kondiah Chetty, an old student of the swami, came with some flour, ghee, sugar candy, and dried fruits. He also offered five rupees as a donation. The swami burst out in childlike glee, and bade the monks to bring two stoves, and made some nice preparations for the offering. At 4:00 p.m. the refreshment was offered to the Master as usual.[67]

Love cannot be defined. A real lover gets joy and finds fulfillment in life by serving and giving his everything to the beloved. Ramakrishnananda kept the Master alive in his mind through his intense love. One day he was resting when all of a sudden he had a desire to feed Ramakrishna hot luchis, which was his favourite dish. Immediately Ramakrishnananda got up and made the dough, then he fried luchis. He placed a plate in front of the Master and carried hot, crispy luchis to him one after another, as if the Master were eating and enjoying his favourite dish.[68]

Ramakrishnananda was very mindful that nothing should be offered to the Master either too cold or too warm, especially milk. Shankarananda recalled: "One day when all other offerings had been carried to the shrine, the swami came to take the milk from the kitchen. He cautiously clasped the hot bowl between his palms and with a grave and attentive face began to move towards the shrine with steady and measured steps. The bowl was almost full. After he had gone a few steps a little of the milk spilt on the floor. At once his teeth clattered and in a suppressed voice he said: 'He will have warm milk! He will have warm milk!'"[69] He made that remark to the Master; perhaps he was mad at himself for spilling the milk. On another occasion he tested the warmth of the milk by dipping his finger into it and burned his finger. Placing the milk bowl before the Master he said in a complaining tone, "You want to drink warm milk and my finger is burnt."[70]

The first building of the Madras Monastery cracked in several places within a couple of years of its construction. When it rained, water would come down through the fissures in the roof. At such times Ramakrishnananda would go into the shrine to see whether water was leaking through the ceiling. One night it began to drip inside the shrine too, right on Sri Ramakrishna's picture. The swami stood there holding an umbrella till the night passed and the rain stopped. He did not remove the picture to a safer side because that would wake his Master from sleep at an untimely hour, which would be wrong.[71]

Swami Sharvananda recounted this incident:

One sultry evening after supper Shashi Maharaj laid himself down on the cot and I was massaging him as usual. It must have been 11:00 p.m. and the heat was oppressive. He suddenly got up, tied his cloth round his waist and went into the shrine. He bade me also to follow. He stood with a fan near the cot on which Sri Ramakrishna's picture was laid for the night's rest and began to fan him. He asked me to fan Swamiji's picture which was kept on a pedestal. He went on fanning for nearly an hour, and then gently walked out of the shrine. His whole behaviour could not fail to engender the feeling in my heart that Sri Ramakrishna was actually present there, sleeping there on the cot, and we were serving him.

Then he went out of the room and stood on the veranda outside the building. I brought a chair for him and he sat on it. I started fanning him. Shashi Maharaj did not speak a word, as if his mind were soaring high to some transcendental region. He suddenly turned towards me and exclaimed: "You see, my mind is soaring in the heights. If I sit now, I can fall into samadhi immediately." I kept quiet and wondered at the sublimity of the situation. It must have been about 2:00 a.m. when he got up and said, "Now let us go and retire." It was a memorable night for me to witness such a sublime spectacle.[72]

With Brother Disciples and Holy Mother

Love unites and hatred separates. Unselfishness creates harmony, and selfishness, disharmony. Joy and peace reign in the community where people have mutual love and respect, feeling and concern for one another. Sri Ramakrishna bound his disciples with a cord of love, and turned their minds to one ideal, one goal. In 1906, when Swami Premananda came to South India for a pilgrimage with his mother, Ramakrishnananda made all the arrangements for them and even travelled with them. During that same year, Ramakrishnananda went to Colombo to receive Abhedananda, his brother disciple, who was visiting India for the first time since going to America. The swamis then travelled to various places in Sri Lanka and South India. Abhedananda lectured in many places and laid the foundation stone of the Bangalore Ashrama.

At Ramakrishnananda's fervent request, Brahmananda, the spiritual son of Ramakrishna and the president of the Order, visited Madras in October 1908. Ramakrishnananda accommodated Brahmananda (called "Maharaj" by the devotees) in his room, which was renovated especially for that purpose. He said: "The Master and his son will stay inside. I will stay out in the entrance hall and serve them. What more do I want?"[73] He told the South Indian devotees: "You have not seen the Master — be content to see Maharaj."[74] V. Krishnaswami Iyer asked Ramakrishnananda whether the new swami would give any lectures in Madras. Ramakrishnananda smilingly replied: "What is there in lectures? He never gives lectures. Men such as he can impart religion by a mere look or touch."[75]

Three days after Brahmananda's arrival, Ramakrishnananda went to Sister Devamata and asked her to buy certain things for Maharaj. Then he asked, "Sister, what do you think of our president?" She replied, "I think he is very wonderful, but I am a little afraid of him." Ramakrishnananda leaned forward in his chair and whispered, "So am I."[76]

After staying some days in Madras, Ramakrishnananda accompanied Brahmananda on a pilgrimage in South India. First the swamis went to Rameswaram, on the coast of the Indian Ocean, and stayed three days as the guests of the raja of Ramnad. After their arrival both swamis went to visit Lord Shiva, and then returned to the palace. Brahmananda scolded the devotees who were busy unpacking the luggage: "Can't these things wait? You have come here to worship the Lord and that is what you should attend to first."[77] On the second day Brahmananda and Ramakrishnananda worshipped the Lord in a ceremonious way with Ganges water that Maharaj had brought from Varanasi.

On the way to Madras from Rameswaram they stopped at Madurai to visit the famous Meenakshi Temple, and stayed three days. In this temple Brahmananda had a wonderful vision that the living image of the Mother Meenakshi was coming towards him. Realizing that Maharaj was in ecstasy, Ramakrishnananda supported him for nearly an hour in the midst of a large crowd. He himself chanted the glory of the Divine Mother with tearful eyes. Afterwards the swamis came out of the shrine. In the front hall of the temple Ramakrishnananda saw an image of Shankara, the great teacher of Vedanta, and he moved forward to touch his feet with his head, but the priests obstructed him. He pushed them aside, saying, "Who can prevent my worshipping the Great One?"[78] His overwhelming devotion silenced the priests, and he fulfilled his wish.

Sometimes it is extremely difficult to understand what is in the minds of illumined souls. One day in Madras, Brahmananda asked C. Ramaswami Iyengar to get a picture of a South Indian dancing girl. The devotee was puzzled. But he purchased it and gave it to Ramakrishnananda, who was also unaware of the purpose behind it. He immediately hid the picture so that others might not misunderstand Brahmananda, and he asked Mr. Iyengar not to talk about it unless Maharaj asked for the picture. However, Brahmananda asked about the picture and learned that Mr. Iyengar had given it to Ramakrishnananda. Maharaj did not like this interference. He became very cool and stopped talking to Ramakrishnananda, which was unbearable for him. Meanwhile, Maharaj asked his attendant to consult the almanac to fix a date for his leaving Madras. Ramakrishnananda could not bear the situation anymore; he prostrated at Maharaj's feet and said: "Pray, be not angry with me. I am an unworthy and insignificant servant. At a mere nod of your head, a hundred Shashis can be called forth." Immediately the face of Brahmananda was lit up with a smile and the cloud of misunderstanding disappeared from them. Of course, the picture was handed over to Maharaj.[79]

Later the mystery of that picture came to light. One of Brahmananda's Calcutta disciples was suffering from lust, and he had confided this to his guru. Maharaj took the picture of that beautiful girl, signed "Swami Brahmananda" on it, and sent it to the devotee. The intention was that whenever the disciple looked at that girl with lust, his guru's face would appear in his mental eye and his lust would disappear.[80]

Shankarananda recalled another incident, which he had heard from Swamis Ambikananda and Dhirananda and which was later verified by Ramu, a devotee: "Ramu had brought for Maharaj some pictures of dancing girls and other pictures which he had asked Ramu to get a few days before. Maharaj wanted to send them to Aparesh Mukherjee who was writing a new drama, *Ramanuja*, so that he could give South Indian stage-effects in dress, pose, and so on. It was at Swami Brahmananda's suggestion that Aparesh had begun the dramatization of the life of Ramanuja, though it was staged much later.[81]

It is interesting to observe how great souls differ in their opinions on work, and how quickly they are able to reconcile their differences. When the *Inspired Talks* of Vivekananda was first published by Madras Math, Brahmananda took an interest in it and said that a copy should be sent to *The Hindu* of Madras and, after the review appeared in that daily, another copy should be sent to the *Bombay Chronicle* with a copy of *The Hindu* review enclosed. Ramakrishnananda, however, differed on this point: He wanted to send copies to both newspapers simultaneously for review. Brahmananda suddenly withdrew his suggestion and said: "Well, you are in charge of this Math, and you are a scholar. It is all your business. I see it was wrong on my part to interfere in this matter." Saying this, Maharaj became indifferent, and sent a letter to a devotee in Puri fixing the date of his departure from Madras. Ramakrishnananda kept quiet for a couple of days, but he could not bear the indifference of his beloved brother anymore. One morning he knelt before Brahmananda and said with folded hands: "Maharaj, I have fallen from your grace. If you do not bestow your blessings upon me, who will? What am I without your grace? Men like me may be created by the hundreds out of dust by your wish. Will you not forgive me?" Immediately the brothers reconciled and everything went on as usual.[82]

In order to invoke the living presence of the Master, Ramakrishnananda wanted Brahmananda to conduct the worship service at least once. One day Brahmananda passed near the shrine after his bath; Ramakrishnananda stood in his way with folded hands and beseeched him to enter the shrine and offer worship to the Master. Maharaj was not accustomed to performing formal ritualistic worship and asked to be excused, but it was of no avail. He had to comply with the request of his beloved brother monk; and when Maharaj entered the shrine, Ramakrishnananda quietly closed the door, and nobody knew what transpired there.[83]

The disciples loved one another greatly. Once at Madras Ramakrishnananda received a letter with the news that Brahmananda was ill. During the worship service, he addressed the picture of Sri Ramakrishna, "If you do not cure Maharaj, I shall throw you away into the sea."[84]

It was mainly due to Ramakrishnananda that the message of Sri Ramakrishna spread far and wide in South India. He believed strongly that the whole of the South would be sanctified by the touch of the blessed feet of the Holy Mother and Swami Brahmananda. He therefore worked hard to arrange their visits on a grand scale in spite of insufficient funds. In February 1911 Holy Mother went to Madras and stayed for a month in a two-storyed house that Ramakrishnananda had rented near the monastery. He also arranged for Mother's pilgrimage to Madurai and Rameswaram, and accompanied her and her party. Holy Mother later said: "Shashi procured for me one hundred and eight bel leaves made of gold to worship Shiva at Rameswaram."[85]

After Rameswaram, Holy Mother visited the Bangalore Ashrama. Observing the exuberant devotion of the local devotees, Holy Mother said to her attendant: "What a pity I do not know their language! They would feel peace of mind if I could say a few words." As her words were translated to the devotees in English, they said: "No, no. This is very nice. Our hearts are filled with joy. There is no need of spoken words."[86] One evening Holy Mother and a couple of her companions climbed a hillock behind the monastery to look at the sunset. As soon as Ramakrishnananda heard of this, he exclaimed in a spiritual mood, "Indeed, the mother has become *parvata-vasini* [the dweller on the mountain, an epithet of Mother

Durga]!" He hurried to the place, prostrated himself before her, and recited a hymn to the Divine Mother. Truly the disciples demonstrated how to love and serve the Master and Holy Mother. This education in devotion is part of their legacy to future generations.

As a Preacher and Writer

In addition to scholarship, an ideal preacher should have passion, burning faith, personal experience, renunciation, purity, and dependence on God. Ramakrishnananda was endowed with all of these. It is said that whenever Ramakrishnananda lectured, he carried in his pockets pictures of Sri Ramakrishna and of Holy Mother. He would touch these pictures as he lectured. He would say: "Whatever the Master makes me speak, I speak like a gramophone. I don't claim any personal credit from it."[87]

From 1897 to 1911 Ramakrishnananda travelled all over South India, preaching the Hindu religion and philosophy as well as the message of Sri Ramakrishna. In 1902 or 1903 he went to Trivandrum as a guest of Kalipada Ghosh and stayed for a month; he lectured there and also at other places in Kerala. One day Ramakrishnananda went to visit the Padmanabhaswamy Temple of Trivandrum. As he was about to enter the inner sanctuary, a priest asked him if he was a brahmin. Ramakrishnananda did not answer him directly, but started reciting a Sanskrit hymn in a solemn voice: "No man am I, no god, no yaksha; neither am I brahmin, nor kshatriya, nor vaishya, nor shudra; no brahmacharin am I, nor householder, nor forest-dweller, nor mendicant. I am the Self, the pure consciousness."[88] His melodious voice and serene look overwhelmed the priest and the others, and none barred his way.

In 1903 Ramakrishnananda visited Bangalore and Mysore and lectured extensively. In 1905 Ramakrishnananda went to attend the seventy-second birth anniversary of Sri Ramakrishna in Bombay. One day he told the local devotees that even the direct disciples could not fully fathom the greatness of the Master. He said: "Do you think it is we who are preaching his wonderful life and message? Far from it. The Master himself is doing it in mysterious ways. Wherever we go to preach about him we find that the field is already prepared. Some are blessed by him in dreams; some get spiritual initiation directly from him; some are attracted by the quality of his teachings, which clothe the highest truth in simple language and parables; and some are inspired by seeing and hearing his disciples."[89]

In March 1905 Ramakrishnananda went to celebrate the Ramakrishna festival in Burma, at the invitation of the Rangoon Ramakrishna-Sevak-Samiti. Every day he performed worship, lectured, and talked about the Master. On the festival day the swami walked four miles to pick *nageswar champa* flowers, which were the Master's favourite. Sharat Chandra Chattopadhyay, the celebrated Bengali novelist (then an unknown young man) accompanied Ramakrishnananda on this walk. Sharat had read Darwin, Tyndall, Mill, and other Western thinkers and considered himself an atheist. On the way, Sharat asked: "Why do you worship so much?"

Swami Ramakrishnananda: "Because I derive immense joy from it."

Sharat: "Is ritual then the highest form of worship?"

Swami: "To see God everywhere is the highest worship; the second best is meditation; the third, prayer and japam; and the last, external worship."

Sharat: "Then why do people perform such pompous worship?"

Swami: "Worship is not at all an external affair; it comes from the heart. Ordinary people perform worship either to escape from the displeasure of God or in expectation of fulfilling some desires. All these are low motives. Real worship is not done till devotion overflows the heart and tears roll down from the eyes for a glimpse of God."

During his short stay in Rangoon, Ramakrishnananda visited some important places of interest, including the Buddhist pagodas. One moonlit night he went to see the Shwedagon Pagoda, which was situated in a suburb of the city. There he met an Irish Buddhist monk. This monk was very impressed when he heard the swami's talk on the following day.

Irish Monk: "All the religions in the world are insubstantial and narrow; Buddhism alone is true and catholic. That is why half of humanity follows this path; and for that very reason I have adopted it."

Swami: "We respect all the current religions of the world, as all of them are equally true and have the same goal in view."

Irish Monk: "Who is the propounder of this doctrine?"

Swami: "Sri Ramakrishna, the divine incarnation of this age, lived and taught this wonderful gospel."

Irish Monk: "What is the specialty of his teaching?"

Swami: "He realized and preached the harmony of religions. Buddha, Christ, Muhammad, and other world teachers — each proclaimed that the religion taught by him is the only way to salvation. The difference between Sri Ramakrishna and other prophets is that he himself preached no new religion, but practised all religions in his life and experienced the universal truth underlying them all. His message can be summed up in the sentence: 'As many faiths so many paths.'"

Another day, knowing Sharat's atheistic attitude, Ramakrishnananda said to him: "Atheists are in the core of their hearts true theists as they are always searching for God, though indirectly. Can they be atheists whose minds are busily engaged in the search for God?"

Sharat: "Could you tell me, swami, why this disbelief assails us?"

Swami: "This disbelief is a great obstacle in spiritual life. It is not only an obstacle but a disease. One will have to clear up the past life tendencies ingrained in the mind by practising spiritual exercises and good deeds. He on whom faith descends is very fortunate. He needs nothing else. Faith in God is a precious treasure. Our disease is desire, and the remedy is spiritual discrimination. God has given us the power to discriminate between the eternal and the evanescent. If we forget Him, we shall be nowhere."

Sharat: "Why do we not see God?"

Swami: "Sri Ramakrishna used to say, 'There are pearls lying on the oceanbed. If you want them, dive deep to the bottom. You can't get them if you float and swim on the surface. God does exist, and if you wish to see Him you must undergo a regular course of spiritual discipline for a certain period.'"

Sharat: "If God always thinks of the welfare of human beings, why then have they so much misery?"

Swami: "God is all-auspicious and all-powerful. Whatever He does is always for the good of all beings. Our parents wish for the welfare of their children, but they are not all-powerful. Endowed with these two qualities, if God allots sorrow and suffering to anyone then know for certain that it is His blessing in disguise. What we call misery is in fact His kindness. We forget God in our greed for transient pleasures. So He makes us remember Him by these little miseries. His kindness is expressed through both favourable and unfavourable circumstances. When He adorns our coveted playhouse of life with wife, wealth, friends, fame, and so on — it is the *pleasant* kindness of God. But when He takes them away one after another, makes us shed tears and drags us forcibly towards Him — it is His *unpleasant* kindness."[90]

Sharat had a long conversation with the swami on various topics, which is recorded in *The Story of a Dedicated Life*. The influence of Ramakrishnananda's visit and lectures took shape twenty years later in the form of two beautiful institutions: The Ramakrishna Mission Hospital and the Ramakrishna Mission Library and Cultural Centre.

Ramakrishnananda was a powerful orator, a delightful conversationalist, and also a serious writer. He was such an erudite scholar that he could lecture and write in three languages: English, Bengali, and Sanskrit. He could also speak Tamil, the local language of Madras. He translated some teachings of Sri Ramakrishna into Sanskrit while he was in the Alambazar Monastery; he also wrote a beautiful Sanskrit hymn on Swami Vivekananda; in addition, he composed Sanskrit mantras for the brahmacharya vows of the Ramakrishna Order. Further, he introduced and systematized the ritualistic worship of Sri Ramakrishna, which is now more or less followed by the centres of the Order.

He contributed many articles to the Bengali *Udbodhan* magazine, and wrote *Sri Ramanuj Charit* in Bengali, an authoritative life of Ramanuja, the propounder of the qualified-monistic Vedanta. (This book has been translated into English.) He also translated some of the writings of Vivekananda from Bengali into English and vice versa. He had so much regard for Swamiji that when he heard that Pandit Pramathanath Tarakabhusan had corrected Vivekananda's Sanskrit compositions, he became upset and commented: "Those words were composed by a *rishi* [a seer of truth]."[91]

Ramakrishnananda's main works in English are: *God and Divine Incarnation*, *The Message of Eternal Wisdom*, *Sri Krishna: Pastoral and King-maker*, *For Thinkers on Education*, *The Ancient Quest*, *Sri Ramakrishna and His Mission*, and *Search After Happiness*.

As a Monk and Teacher

Sri Ramakrishna used to say: "The sannyasin, the man of renunciation, is a world teacher. It is his example that awakens the spiritual consciousness of men."[92] Ramakrishnananda was a sannyasin of spotless character. He once said to an American devotee: "Man must give up everything to God, then alone he thrives.... If you study all the personal religions, you will find that all preach renunciation. Renunciation is their fundamental teaching."[93]

Another time he explained the mystery of renunciation: "Those who give up the world for spiritual life are giving up the uncertain for the certain, the passing for the permanent. All our power comes from renunciation. Only when we have given up our lives do we begin to live. At present we are like prisoners. We may get a glimpse of freedom now and then but the world falls upon us when we are off our guard and drags us back once more into our prison cells. As soon as a man finds out, however, that these little pleasures of the flesh are nothing compared with the infinite pleasures of the spirit, he wants to renounce; not for the sake of renunciation, but because he has found something better. He has realized the hollowness of the enjoyments of the world and can be satisfied only with higher enjoyment. Renunciation means giving up a lesser thing for a greater."[94]

Selfishness is sin; unselfishness is the first milestone on the path of spirituality. A selfish person may perhaps enjoy comfort and health, but a sannyasin can never afford to be selfish. Ramakrishnananda said: "So long as we are selfish our work must be fruitless. We may deliver fine lectures, we may gain name and fame, but the actual results will be nil. The moment, however, that our little self disappears, at that moment our real work begins. Then we may live an obscure life and go nowhere, but we shall accomplish wonders.

"When we drop the ego from our consciousness and live in God, we have unlimited power. God is the only existence that is real; all other existences are unrealities behind which God exists as the reality. This maya is so irresistible and it is this maya which makes us selfish. Only when God is gracious to us can we lift the veil and get a glimpse of Him. Then all selfishness drops off.

"The word 'selfishness' is not always understood. When by 'self' I understand the body or the little self and I do something for that self, I am selfish. But there is a Self which is beyond this physical body; when I do something for that Self, that is worshipping God. The man who lives in that higher Self is never selfish. Try to feel God inside yourself and you will overcome all selfishness. When you live constantly in the presence of Divinity, the ego loses its power; but so long as the ego rules a man, he is a bond-slave. All your anxieties and worries come from egotism and selfishness. Let go of your little self and they will all disappear."[95]

Sister Devamata wrote about Ramakrishnananda's concept of religion: "If Swami Ramakrishnananda was a conservative in his mode of worship, he was essentially a liberal in his religious conviction. Tolerance, universality of outlook, freedom from all prejudice — these formed the keystones of his thought structure. Religion he defined as 'the struggle of spirit against matter,' and he gave welcome to whatever helped in the struggle. When someone came with words of condemnation on his lips, I heard him say: 'Never find fault with any form of religion. Differences are all in the external customs. That which makes up the external is the shell. It may be hard and rough and perhaps not to our liking, but it holds a valuable kernel. The kernel of every religion is God. To whatever religion a man belongs, he has to worship the same God. The essential parts of religion are everywhere the same. It is only in the nonessential parts that differences are found. Various religious beliefs and doctrines are merely partial reflections of Truth, but because they have that little reflected light of Truth in them, we take them to be the whole Truth. Religion may be defined as giving God His due. "God alone is the proprietor of this universe, God alone is the proprietor of myself" — recognizing this and then giving up all to Him, that is religion. Wishing to keep all for yourself is irreligion. Throw away the idea of "me and mine," giving up all to God — this is the essential of every religion.'"[96]

Only a spiritual person can create a spiritual atmosphere where one can feel peace, joy, and harmony. On the other hand, wherever worldly people go they carry with them a worldly atmosphere: They talk about politics, food, enjoyment; they gossip with delight. Ramakrishnananda could not bear such people. If any visitor read a secular book or newspaper in the ashrama, he would scold him, saying, "You can do that anywhere. Here you should try to think of God."[97]

His whole mind was always saturated with thoughts of God. One day he said to Sister Devamata: "A man who has realized God must keep on realizing Him all his life. To realize God is the aim of every human being whether he knows it or not. No man who has not true love towards God can be religious. Religion begins with attraction to God and no soul will ever find real satisfaction until he has reached God. All bondage comes to an end when man realizes Him.

"The realization of God cannot be attained in a haphazard way. There is a regular method. First you must hear, then you must understand what you hear, and from understanding you go on to realization. You must know the light is there, otherwise you may go in the opposite direction to find it. Next, you must hear from a teacher how to do it. Then you must understand clearly just what it is; and when you have understood, realization will come."[98]

To realize God one needs a pure mind, and the mind becomes pure through unselfish action. Karma yoga, or unselfish action, is sometimes confusing to people. To explain this, one day Ramakrishnananda told Sister Devamata: "Work for others is self-amelioration. We need to serve others in order to lift ourselves up out of the state of degradation and selfishness into which we have fallen. We should be grateful to the needy for making it possible for us to raise ourselves. That is the only real good that comes out of all that we do for others; we merely better ourselves."[99]

According to Vedanta philosophy the microcosm and macrocosm are not different; they originate from the same substance. Ramakrishnananda embodied this philosophy: In addition to religion and philosophy, he had a wide range of knowledge in physical science and mathematics. Once he said: "Actually time, space, and causation are not separate entities outside; they all exist in me, that is, in my mind. The whole universe is inside man.

"Science is the struggle of man in the outer world. Religion is the struggle of man in the inner world. Science makes man struggle for Truth in the outside universe, and religion makes him struggle for Truth in the inner universe. Both struggles are great, no doubt, but one ends in success and the other ends in failure. That is the difference. Religion begins where science ends. The whole scientific method is based on observation and experiment; but the moment man realizes that there is something beyond observation and experiment he will give them up and leave material science behind. Science will always have to deal with finite bodies, and God is infinite."[100]

A real lover always thinks of the beloved, and would never do anything to displease the beloved. The stories of Ramakrishnananda's love for Sri Ramakrishna are now legends in the Order. Once he told Sister Devamata: "The true devotee never thinks of himself. He is so full of the thought of God that his own self is forgotten. This body is only an instrument, a passive instrument, and an instrument really has no existence of its own, for it is wholly dependent on the one who uses it. Suppose a pen were conscious, it could say, 'I have written hundreds of letters,' but actually it has done nothing, for the one who holds it has written the letters. So because we are conscious we think we are doing all these things, whereas, in reality we are as much an instrument in the hand of a Higher Power as the pen in our hands, and He makes all things possible."[101]

Life means struggle. Only two types of people do not struggle: the dead, and the illumined who have transcended the pairs of opposites. One day someone complained about dryness in spiritual life. "That very complaining," Ramakrishnananda answered, "shows that their devotion is strong, even though they may not seem to express it so well as at other times. The very fact that they are restless proves that this dryness of heart is an unnatural condition for them, just as the fish feels dryness and jumps about when it is out of water, water being its natural element. Their devotion is not lessened in any way. So long as the hunger for devotion to God is there, a man is steady in devotion."[102]

In spiritual life, where self-effort ends, self-surrender begins. A real monastic always surrenders himself to God and depends on his own Self. Sister Devamata recalled: "Shortly before I left Madras, as we were driving back from the city one evening, I expressed regret that I was leaving when he had so few to help him. The answer that came was direct and uncompromising: 'I do not need anyone to help me. I am all full of God. What need have I of anyone else? If He sends people to help me, I am satisfied. If He does not send, I am satisfied. I know that whatever He sends is for my good and is the best thing for me.'"[103]

It is exhilarating to live with a God-intoxicated person: That person showers divine bliss, which makes worldly intoxication seem dull and boring. Sister Devamata wrote in her *Days in an Indian Monastery*: "One imbibes what one lives with. One's habit of thought is determined by the trend of one's conversation.... Swami Ramakrishnananda once said to me: 'Mind is like a big mirror which gives a perfect reflection but which has been so thickly covered with dirt that nothing can be seen in it. The more you can rub off that dirt the more you will be able to see yourself in it. The more you can remove the least speck of dust the more you can get a perfect image of your true Self. What is the dirt that hides the image? Selfish desires. Be free from every selfish desire. That is purity. Purity means singleness. Desire is a very dangerous thing. Sometimes we think we have killed all selfish desires; but somewhere in our mind there lingers some remnant; and as from a spark left in the corner of the hearth may come again a big fire, so out of that small remnant may spring a huge fire of desire.'

"One evening someone asked Swami Ramakrishnananda how one should practise meditation. His answer was: 'Meditation means complete self-abandonment. Meditation requires complete annihilation of self-consciousness. You know that before a great light, lesser lights disappear; so before the effulgent glory of God, the little glory of the ego will completely vanish, as stars vanish when the sun rises. You must therefore practise the presence of God inside you. You may say, "I cannot see Him with these eyes of mine. I cannot hear Him with these ears. How then am I to perceive Him?" You can never perceive Him in this way. To go to the Creator you must throw aside these instruments which take you directly to the creation. You must go beyond your mind and senses, then meditation will come of itself. This is the only way to get inner vision. These senses are made for the creation, not for the Creator.'"[104]

Last Days

Ramakrishnananda's life was short but eventful. For fourteen years he worked hard to spread the message of Sri Ramakrishna and Swami Vivekananda in South India. He burnt his energy quickly. In April 1911, shortly after the Holy Mother's departure for Calcutta, Ramakrishnananda became seriously ill with diabetes and tuberculosis. He said that the cause of this breakdown was that "Madras life was too strenuous." Due to overwork and lack of proper food, he had literally worked himself to the point of death. Ramakrishnananda was too humble to take credit for the success of the Madras centre. He said: "It is no credit of mine. The Master's grace and Swamiji's command are mainly responsible for the success of my work in the South."[105]

At the request of the devotees, Ramakrishnananda moved to Bangalore Ashrama for a change in climate and rest. Unfortunately, the bracing climate of Bangalore failed to improve his health, and the local doctors diagnosed his disease as galloping tuberculosis. Brahmananda and Saradananda asked him to go to Calcutta for better treatment. Ramakrishnananda left for Calcutta in June 1911 via Madras. Brahmananda was then at Puri, but when he received a cable from Madras he hastened to the railway junction at Khurda Road to meet his sick brother. As soon as the train arrived, Brahmananda entered the rail car and was shocked on seeing Ramakrishnananda's emaciated body. Brahmananda exclaimed: "Shashi, what is this? Shake it off!" Ramakrishnananda prostrated before him and replied, "Raja, that is possible only through your blessings."[106] Maharaj asked him to follow the advice of the doctors implicitly. This was their last meeting.

On 10 June 1911 Ramakrishnananda arrived in Calcutta. He was accommodated in the Udbodhan Office and placed under the treatment of noted physicians. In spite of the best treatment possible and careful nursing his condition gradually deteriorated. But Ramakrishnananda's mind dwelt on his guru. One day Kaviraj Durgaprasad Sen, who had treated Sri Ramakrishna, asked the swami, "Do you see such things as a crematorium or a *tulsi* [basil] grove in your dreams?" Ramakrishnananda replied, "No, I don't see them; but I frequently see the Master, Holy Mother, Swamiji, Dakshineswar, and so on, in my dreams."[107]

Ramakrishnananda had dry skin because of an excessive bile secretion in his system, and he suffered from a burning sensation in his body. His attendants had to fan him almost continually. He would roll on the bed restlessly and pray, "Victory to the Master! Victory to my guru!" His desire for food was almost gone. He ate very little: In the morning he would eat a few pieces of cream-cracker biscuits soaked in milk and at noon a few morsels of rice with milk. Saradananda often sat by his side at mealtime and persuaded him to eat a little more. One day Ramakrishnananda said: "Brother Sharat, my eating is being gradually stopped. The Divine Mother does not allow me to eat anymore. Please don't take the trouble of coming to me during my mealtime."[108]

Premananda visited him quite often. One morning he came and gave some instructions to Ramakrishnananda's attendants regarding his service, but Ramakrishnananda did not like this and scolded Premananda. However, when Premananda left, the swami stopped eating and began to cry. Later, at Ramakrishnananda's request, his attendant brought Premananda back from Balaram's house. Putting his head at Premananda's feet, Ramakrishnananda began to sob like a child. "What happened, brother?" Premananda asked. Ramakrishnananda replied, "Brother, I lost faith in the Master, please kick my face." Premananda said: "It is impossible for me to believe that Shashi has lost faith in the Master. It is beyond imagination!" Ramakrishnananda said: "The Master showed me your greatness and who you are! And I became rude to you — that proved I lost faith in the Master." Premananda asked him to eat his meal, and fed him with his own hand.[109]

One day Ramakrishnananda's younger brother came to see him. Ramakrishnananda told him to remind their mother to make an offering to the Divine Mother that she had promised when Ramakrishnananda was three years old. Upon returning home, the swami's brother learned from their mother that it was true, and he immediately fulfilled his dying brother's wish. Another day his mother, Bhavasundari, came to see him. He leaned his head towards her, and said, "Mother, put your palms on my head and bless me."[110] And she blessed her loving son.

Ramakrishnananda's condition rapidly worsened, and he began to cough up blood. He lost sleep at night; his body was reduced to a skeleton. One day, unable to bear the physical pain, he asked his attendant to bring down the picture of Sri Ramakrishna from the wall. Holding it, he said plaintively: "Master, why do you put me to all this suffering? I have committed no sin consciously with this body. Why then is all this suffering allotted to me?" Then he immediately begged forgiveness for blaming the Master: "Master, I made mistakes. Please forgive me."[111] He then asked his attendant to put the picture of the Master in its proper place.

Sometimes he would forget his suffering and would passionately talk about the Master for a long time. When the attendant would ask him to keep quiet, the swami would reply, "When I talk about the Master, I lose body consciousness, and even the death-pain becomes insignificant."[112] During his last days he became inspired when he talked about Christ, and he would relate how Sri Ramakrishna had regarded him as Christ's companion in his previous life. He also recalled how the Master received the vision of Christ while he was in samadhi, and the very body of Christ had entered into his own. Even in delirium Ramakrishnananda would utter the divine names: "Durga, Durga; Shiva, Shiva; Sri Guru, Sri Guru."

One morning at 9:00 a.m., a couple of days before his passing away, the swami was lying down with closed eyes. His attendant was silently seated nearby. All of a sudden Ramakrishnananda got up and told the attendant: "The Master, Mother, and Swamiji have come. Please offer them an *asana* [prayer rug]." The attendant was dumbfounded. Again the swami repeated: "Can't you see? The Master has come. Spread the carpet and set three bolsters." The attendant followed his order. Ramakrishnananda with folded hands bowed down thrice, and then watched something unseen, without blinking. After a while he said: "They left. Now take away the carpet and bolsters."[113]

Towards the end Ramakrishnananda expressed a desire to see Holy Mother, who was then at Jayrambati, her birthplace. Swami Dhirananda was sent to bring her, but she could not come, perhaps for two reasons: first, she knew that it would be unbearable for her to witness Ramakrishnananda's death; second, there was not enough room in Udbodhan for her to stay. However, the swami was blessed with a vision of Holy Mother on his last night of earthly life. Ramakrishnananda exclaimed, "Ah, Mother has come."

On the morning of his last day, Pulin Mittra, a famous singer and disciple of Brahmananda, came to see him. Ramakrishnananda expressed his vision in a Bengali line, *Pohalo dukha rajani* (the night of misery is over), and asked Pulin to take it to Girish Chandra Ghosh, the great dramatist and disciple of the Master, to compose a song. Girish recalled: "By the grace of Sri Ramakrishna, I completed the composition immediately. Pulin Mittra sang it before him. He was greatly moved and was satisfied with the composition."[114] Here is a translation of the song composed by Girish:

The night of misery is over.
The terrible nightmare of ego is gone forever.
The illusion of life and death is no more.
Lo, the light of knowledge is dawning, and the Mother Divine is
    smiling.
The Mother is bestowing the boon of fearlessness.
Sing victory in a loud voice.
Proclaim the conquest of death by blowing the trumpet.
Let the name of the Mother vibrate all over the world.
The Mother says: "Weep no more. Look at the feet of Ramakrishna.

Then all worries will vanish, all pain will go.
Son, look at my side: The Saviour of the world is standing with his
eyes full of grace and compassion."

Pulin sang this song for a long time and Ramakrishnananda listened with rapt attention. It seemed that the song gave him peace because it tallied with his vision. After this he desired to hear another: *A Song on Samadhi* composed by Swami Vivekananda. Pulin sang that also. Ramakrishnananda was in an ecstatic mood that whole morning. Doctor J. N. Kanjilal checked him and found him in better condition. He drank a little sanctified water that had been offered to the Master, and for the last three hours of his life he was in samadhi. At 1:00 p.m. he began to perspire, his face flushed, the hair of his body stood on end, and his gaze was fixed between his eyebrows. Swami Ramakrishnananda left his body while in samadhi at 1:10 p.m. on Monday, 21 August 1911.

The brother disciples and other monks began to chant the name of Sri Ramakrishna, and they observed that the hair on Ramakrishnananda's body remained erect for a long time. Later his body was brought down from the first floor, and Sister Nivedita bowed down to the departed monk. He was decorated with flowers and garlands and then was carried in a procession. The air was laden with the fragrance of flowers, perfume, and incense. A *sankirtan* party (a group of singers) led the procession. It first stopped at the Cossipore garden house, then at the Cossipore cremation ground, and, crossing the Ganges, at last it reached Belur Math. Ramakrishnananda's body was cremated on the bank of the Ganges at the southeast corner of the Vivekananda Temple.

When the news of his death reached Holy Mother, she remarked with tearful eyes: "Alas, Shashi is gone. My back is broken." After receiving the sad news at Puri, the grief-stricken Brahmananda exclaimed: "The guardian angel of the South has passed away. The southern side is, as it were, covered with darkness." The Hindu community of Madras convened a memorial meeting and paid their homage to Ramakrishnananda, who had sacrificed his life for their spiritual development.

Sister Devamata wrote: "What Saint Paul declared in his Epistle to the Galatians, 'Yet not I, but Christ liveth in me,' perfectly described Swami Ramakrishnananda's attitude towards himself and towards that one whom he called guru. He was dead wholly to himself and alive only in Sri Ramakrishna."[115]

8

ॐ

SWAMI SARADANANDA

As a garland-maker picks many flowers of different colours and creates a beautiful wreath, so Sri Ramakrishna chose his disciples from the companions of previous divine incarnations and trained them to carry his message of religious harmony in this present age. On 23 December 1885 Sri Ramakrishna remarked about Shashi and Sharat: "In a vision I saw that Shashi and Sharat had been among the followers of Christ."[1]

Pointing to his foremost disciple Peter, Christ said, "Upon this rock I will build my church." Later on, Peter's unshakable faith, indomitable energy, and unflinching love for his Lord gave a tremendous impetus to early Christianity. Just as Peter supported the early Christian church, Sharat carried the heavy responsibility of the young Ramakrishna Movement for over thirty years. Sharat was completely unaware of his future role when, one day at Dakshineswar Sri Ramakrishna sat upon his lap in an ecstatic mood and later explained to the curious devotees, "I was testing how much weight he could bear."[2]

Sharat Chandra Chakrabarty was born in Calcutta at 6:32 p.m. on Saturday, 23 December 1865. The house where he was born, 125 Amherst Street, was later demolished by the Calcutta Corporation in order to extend Harrison Road, now Mahatma Gandhi Road. His father, Girish Chandra Chakrabarty, and mother, Nilmani Devi, were devout Hindu brahmins and quite well-to-do. They had a large family and were partners in Druggist's Hall, a large foreign-medicine pharmacy.

SWAMI SARADANANDA, C.1903

Sharat was very quiet and gentle, which was construed by some as signs that the boy was not intelligent. At an early age, observing his mother worshipping the family deity, he developed a strong religious inclination. At the age of thirteen, like all brahmin boys, he was invested with the sacred thread, and he regularly practised japam and meditation. He memorized many hymns about various gods and goddesses, which he would recite to his young friends. Sharat was admitted to Albert School and later to Hare School; he was a good student and scored at the top of most of his school examinations. He took a leading role in his school's debating society and developed a strong body by exercising regularly and eating well.

Sharat was born with a warm, loving, and unselfish heart. He was extremely courteous and was incapable of using harsh words or of hurting anybody's feelings. His generosity was such that he saved his pocket money to help his poor classmates buy books, paper, pencils, and so on. Sometimes he would give his used clothes, sweaters, and shoes to his poor friends. Once he discovered that one of his neighbour's maidservants had been stricken with cholera and that her master, fearing contagion, had moved her up to the roof and left her to her fate. Sharat rushed to the dying woman and did what he could for her. When she died, he made all the necessary arrangements for her last rites.

Shashi, a cousin of Sharat, was studying and living with Sharat's family. While they were in school, Shashi and Sharat were greatly influenced by the Brahmo leader Keshab Chandra Sen. They attended his services, studied the Brahmo Samaj literature, and practised meditation according to its tradition. In 1882 Sharat passed the Entrance examination and then in 1883 he was admitted to Saint Xavier's College. Father Laffont was then the principal of that college. Charmed by Sharat's deep interest in religion, the noble principal began to tutor him in the Bible and Christianity.

In the Company of Sri Ramakrishna

In October 1883, Kaliprasad, a mutual friend of Shashi and Sharat, read Keshab Chandra Sen's article about Sri Ramakrishna in the *Indian Mirror*. He suggested to his friends that they all visit this saint of Dakshineswar. All agreed. One afternoon the group of boys arrived at Dakshineswar and found the Master seated on his small couch. He received them all with a smile and asked them to sit on the mat. He then asked their names and where they lived, and was pleased to learn that they belonged to Keshab's Brahmo Samaj.

At first sight, Sri Ramakrishna recognized Sharat and Shashi as his own. Sensing their spirit of renunciation, the Master said: "Bricks and tiles, if burnt with the trademark on them, retain those marks forever. Similarly you should enter the world after advancing a little in the path of spirituality. Then you will not sink in the mire of worldliness. But nowadays parents get their boys married while quite young, and thus pave the way to their ruin. The boys come out of school to find themselves fathers of several children. So they run hither and thither in search of a job to maintain the family. With great difficulty perhaps they find one, but are hard pressed to feed so many mouths with that small income. They become naturally anxious to earn money and therefore find little time to think of God."

"Then, sir, is it wrong to marry? Is it against the will of God?" asked one of the boys. The Master asked him to take a certain book down from the shelf and directed him to read a particular passage that quoted Christ's opinion of marriage: "For there are some eunuchs, which were so born from their mother's womb; there are some eunuchs, which were made eunuchs of men; and there be eunuchs, which have made themselves eunuchs for the kingdom of heaven's sake. He that is able to receive it, let him receive." The Master then asked him to read Saint Paul: "I say therefore to the unmarried and widows, it is good for them if they abide even as I. But if they cannot contain let them marry: for it is better to marry than to burn."

Someone interrupted, saying, "Do you mean to say, sir, that marriage is against the will of God? And how can His creation go on if people cease to marry?" Sri Ramakrishna smiled and said: "Don't worry about that. Those who wish to marry are at perfect liberty to do so. What I said just now was between ourselves. I speak on what I have got to say; you take as much of it as you like and no more."[3]

Sri Ramakrishna set the fire of renunciation in the minds of Sharat and Shashi. When they were about to leave, the Master asked them to visit him alone. Sharat began to visit the Master on a regular basis on Thursdays, a college holiday. On 26 November 1883 Sharat arrived at Dakshineswar by boat with two of his friends and found that the Master was about to leave for Calcutta to attend the Brahmo Festival at Mani Mallik's house. Ramakrishna was pleased to see them and asked his attendant Baburam to give them the address so that they could attend the festival. Sharat wrote of the festival:

We saw a wonderful scene. We felt that high waves of heavenly bliss were flowing in the room. All were completely lost in the *kirtan* [devotional singing]. They were laughing, crying, and dancing. Some, unable to control themselves, fell on the ground. Overwhelmed with emotion, others acted like madmen. The Master was dancing in the centre of the God-intoxicated group, now rhythmically going forward with rapid steps and again going backward in a similar way. In whichever direction he would move, the people as if enchanted, would make room for him.

An extraordinary tenderness, sweetness, and leonine strength were visible in every limb of the Master's body, and his face shone with a divine smile. It was a superb dance! In it there was no artificiality or affectation, no jumping, no unnatural gestures or acrobatics. Nor was there seen any absence of control. Rather, one noticed in the Master's dancing rhythmical and natural gestures and movements of limbs. It seemed as if an overflow of grace, bliss, and sweetness surged from within, like a big fish happily swimming all over a vast, clear lake, sometimes slowly and sometimes fast. It was as if the dance was the dynamic physical expression of the surge of the blissful ocean of Brahman, which the Master was experiencing within. As he danced this way, sometimes he lost outward consciousness and sometimes his cloth fell. When that happened, someone would fasten it tightly around his waist. Again, if he saw someone lose normal consciousness, imbued with spiritual emotions, he would touch that person's chest and bring him back to consciousness. We felt a current of divine bliss emanating from the Master and spreading in all directions, making it possible for the devotees to see God face to face.... Afterwards the Master told all of us that one could attain supreme peace if one could raise the mind from sense objects to God.[4]

One day at Dakshineswar, the Master was praising Ganesha, the god of success, for his great filial love and absolute purity of heart. Sharat was present in the audience. He said at once: "Sir, I like the character of Ganesha very much. He is my ideal." "No," the Master immediately corrected him and said: "Ganesha is not your ideal. Your ideal is Shiva. In you lie dormant the attributes of Shiva. Always think of yourself as Shiva and me as your Shakti [power]. I am the ultimate repository of all your powers."[5] It is amazing how this mystical utterance of the Master was fulfilled later in Sharat's life!

Sharat was tremendously attracted to the Master. Not only did he visit Ramakrishna regularly, but he also began to stay at night at Dakshineswar in order to practise spiritual disciplines under his guidance. The Master would awaken his young disciples at midnight and send them to different spots in the temple garden. Once Sharat could not concentrate, and reported it to the Master. Immediately the Master pressed his index finger in between Sharat's eyebrows, and his mind became calm like the flame of a lamp in a windless place.[6]

Before coming to Dakshineswar, Sharat had met Narendra at a mutual friend's home in Calcutta, without knowing who he was. Sharat's first impression was that Narendra was conceited and had bad manners. Later, during his second or third visit, Sharat heard the Master praise a young man named Narendra so highly that he became interested in meeting him, not realizing this was the same person he had already met and disliked. Pointing to the young disciples the Master said:

These boys are good. This boy has passed one and a half examinations [Sharat was preparing for his First Arts examination]; he is polite and calm. But I have not seen another boy like Narendra. He is as efficient in music, vocal and instrumental, as in the acquisition of knowledge, in conversation as well as in religious matters. He loses normal consciousness in meditation for whole nights. My Narendra is a coin with no alloy whatsoever: toss it up, and you hear the truest sound. . . . He goes to the Brahmo Samaj also and sings devotional songs there; but he is not like other Brahmos. He is a true knower of Brahman. He sees Light when he sits for meditation. Is it for nothing that I love Narendra so much?

Curious, Sharat asked, "Sir, where does Narendra live?" The Master replied, "Narendra is a son of Vishwanath Datta of Simla, Calcutta."[7] After returning to Calcutta, Sharat went to visit Narendra and was amazed to see the same boy whom he had previously met. From then on they became close friends. They visited each other and talked long hours about the Master and spiritual life. Narendra told Sharat and Shashi about his experience with the Master: "He is bestowing love, devotion, divine knowledge, liberation and whatever else one may desire, on whomsoever he likes. Oh, what wonderful power! He can do anything he likes."[8]

When the Master heard from Sharat about his meeting with Narendra and the development of their close friendship, he was overjoyed. He remarked in his homely way, "A housewife knows which lid will go with which cooking pot."[9]

One day Sri Ramakrishna became a *kalpataru* (the wish-fulfilling tree) and fulfilled the wishes of his disciples. Some asked for devotion, some knowledge, and some liberation. Seeing Sharat silent, the Master asked him: "How would you like to realize God? What divine vision do you prefer to see in meditation?" Sharat replied: "I do not want to see any particular form of God in meditation. I want to see Him in all beings. I do not like visions." The Master said with a smile: "That is the last word in spiritual attainment. You cannot have it all at once." "But I won't be satisfied with anything short of that," replied Sharat. "I shall strive my best until I am able to attain it." At last the Master blessed him, saying, "Yes, you will attain it."[10]

Sri Ramakrishna kept a vigilant eye on his disciples. Observing Sharat's spirit of nonattachment, the Master asked him, "Whom do you love most of all?" "Well, sir," answered Sharat, "I don't think I love anyone." At this the Master indignantly said: "Oh, what a dry rascal! Fall either into one pit or the other — into the pit of filth or into the pit of gold!"[11] But who is foolish enough to want to fall into the pit of filth? If one has love in one's heart for one's fellow beings, one can easily divert it towards God.

Once the Master sang a Brahmo song to Sharat and told him, "Assimilate any one of these ideas and you will reach the goal." The song runs as follows:

Thou art my All in All, O Lord! — the Life of my life, the Essence
    of essence;
In the three worlds I have none else but Thee to call my own.
Thou art my peace, my joy, my hope; Thou my support, my
    wealth, my glory;
Thou my wisdom and my strength.
Thou art my home, my place of rest; my dearest friend, my next
    of kin;
My present and my future, Thou; my heaven and my salvation.
Thou art my scriptures, my commandments; Thou art my
    ever-gracious guru;
Thou the Spring of my boundless bliss.
Thou art the Way, and Thou the Goal; Thou the adorable One,
    O Lord!
Thou art the Mother tender-hearted; Thou the chastising Father;
Thou the Creator and Protector; Thou the Helmsman who dost
    steer my craft across the sea of life.[12]

In 1885 Sharat passed the First Arts examination. His father wanted him to study medicine so he could work with him at his pharmacy. Although Sharat had no interest in becoming a doctor or a pharmacist, he took Narendra's advice and enrolled in Calcutta Medical College. Sharat knew that the Master would not accept food from the hands of lawyers or doctors. Moreover, the Master was very fond of Sharat's sister's cooking, and Sharat would carry the food she prepared for him to Dakshineswar. When the Master learned about Sharat's admission to the

Medical College, he said clearly, "If you become a doctor, I shall not be able to eat food from your hand."[13] Sharat was in a dilemma, but the ever-gracious Master removed it shortly afterwards.

Sharat could not bear a casual, haphazard way of doing things; he was quite alert and methodical about everything, traits which he learned from the Master. In 1885 Sharat went with the Master to attend the festival at Panihati, which he recorded graphically in *Sri Ramakrishna, The Great Master*. After taking leave of the Master, when Sharat reached the ferry that would take him back to Calcutta, he remembered that he had left his shoes near Ramakrishna's room. He immediately rushed back to pick them up. Learning the cause of his return, the Master said: "My boy, always remember things and never leave anything behind. All the fun and joy of attending the Panihati festival would have been marred if you had gone home and found that your shoes were missing, and you did not know where you had left them."[14]

Sharat bowed down to Sri Ramakrishna, and as he was about to leave again, the Master asked: "How did you enjoy the day? It was a veritable fair of Hari's name. Wasn't it?" Sharat agreed. Then the Master praised the younger Naren: "That dark-complexioned boy has been visiting this place only for a short time, and already he is having ecstasies. . . . He is a good boy. Please go to his house one day and talk to him. Will you?" Sharat replied, "But, sir, I like no one as much as I do the elder Naren [Vivekananda], so I don't feel any inclination to visit the younger Naren." The Master scolded him, saying: "You, brat, are very one-sided! It is a sign of small-mindedness. As the flower tray of the Lord contains various kinds of flowers, so he has all kinds of devotees. It is a sign of narrowness if one cannot mix and have joy with all. You must one day visit the younger Naren. Won't you?" Sharat promised to visit him and left.[15]

After a few days Sharat went to visit the younger Naren and had a wonderful conversation with him, which solved a great problem of his life. In passing, the younger Naren had said: "Brother, whatever the Master asks us to do is for our good; otherwise, what self-interest does he have?" Immediately Sharat realized why the Master had insisted that he visit the younger Naren. The Master's every word and action had some deep meaning. Sharat then gave up his study of medicine, so that he could serve the Master wholeheartedly.[16]

After the Panihati festival Sri Ramakrishna developed throat cancer; in September 1885 he had to move to Shyampukur, Calcutta, for treatment. Some prominent doctors began treating him; and the young disciples, including Sharat, devoted themselves to nursing the Master under Narendra's leadership. The doctors cautioned the disciples that Ramakrishna's cancer would be aggravated if he talked often or merged frequently into samadhi, so the disciples kept a vigilant watch over him.

Nevertheless, one day the Master began to teach Sharat about meditation and posture. Sharat later wrote:

Sitting in the lotus posture, placing the back of the right hand on the palm of the left hand and then raising both to the level of the chest, he said with his eyes closed, "This is the best posture for all kinds of meditation on God with forms." Again seated in the same posture, he placed his right and left hands on his right and left knees respectively, and touched the tips of the thumb and the index finger of each hand while the other fingers remained straightened. Then fixing his gaze between the eyebrows, he said, "This is an excellent posture for meditation on the formless God."

Saying so the Master went into samadhi. Shortly afterwards he forcibly brought his mind to the normal plane of consciousness, and said: "I couldn't show you more. As soon as I sit in that way, the mind gets stimulated and becomes absorbed in samadhi; and the air current moves upward and hits the wound of the throat. That is why the doctor advised me to avoid going into samadhi."

Sharat humbly said: "Sir, why did you show me all those techniques? I didn't ask you." The Master replied: "That is true. But it is hard for me to remain quiet without telling and demonstrating some spiritual matters to you all."[17] Sharat was touched by the Master's infinite compassion for him.

On 11 December 1885 Sri Ramakrishna had to move to the Cossipore garden house, close to the Ganges; the air there was not polluted as it was in Calcutta. In the beginning Sharat served the Master while staying at home, but later he moved to Cossipore. Sharat's father was alarmed. He felt that his son had been brainwashed by Sri Ramakrishna. He begged Sharat to be guided by their family guru, Jaganmohan Tarkalankar, a famous pandit and tantric yogi. When Sharat did not respond, Girish hit upon another plan to bring his son back home. He went to Cossipore with Jaganmohan, requesting him beforehand to ask some difficult, esoteric questions of Sri Ramakrishna in front of Sharat. He thought that if the Master could not answer those questions, Sharat would come back to his senses and return home. But the result was the reverse. After talking briefly, Jaganmohan realized the greatness of the Master, and told Girish privately, "I will never advise Sharat to give up such a guru."[18]

Girish's hopes were dashed, but he still did not give up. He thought that perhaps marriage could bind Sharat to the world. Another day he went to Cossipore and told Sri Ramakrishna, "Sir, if you ask Sharat to marry, he will." Immediately Sharat said: "Do you think I shall obey if the Master asks me to marry? In no way shall I deviate from my duty, even if the Master requests me to do so." Ramakrishna said to Girish with a smile: "Did you hear what Sharat says? What else can I do?"[19] Once Sri Ramakrishna remarked: "Mahamaya does not trap those who are around me."

Sharat was the eldest son and the centre of his family's attention because of his maturity and intelligence, and his loving and steady nature. Gradually Sharat's mother and brothers became devotees of the Master and visited him in Cossipore. One day Charu Chandra, one of Sharat's younger brothers, came to see the Master. Ramakrishna was pleased to meet the boy. "He is a fine boy," said the Master to Sharat, "a little more intelligent than you. Let me see if he has good or bad tendencies." So saying, he took Charu's right hand into his own and weighing it said, "Yes, he has good tendencies." He then asked Sharat: "Shall I draw him? [That is, draw his mind away from the world and turn it towards God.] What do you say?" Sharat replied, "Yes, sir, please do so." Sri Ramakrishna thought for a while and said: "No, no more. I have taken one, and if I take this one also, your parents, especially your mother, will be very grieved. I have displeased many a Shakti [woman] in my life. No more now."[20]

In spite of his illness, the Master gave Charu some spiritual instructions and told him: "That intelligence is the right one which helps one to realize God. And that intelligence is inferior which brings worldly prosperity."[21] He asked his attendant to give the boy some refreshments and send him back home.

Day and night in Cossipore Sharat witnessed the final divine play of Sri Ramakrishna. On 1 January 1886 the Master went for his last walk in the garden and again became a *kalpataru* (wish-fulfilling tree). He blessed many devotees, saying, "Be illumined." Sharat and Latu were then busy cleaning the Master's room but saw that historic event from the roof. Later when somebody asked Sharat why he did not go to the Master for blessings, he replied: "I did not feel any necessity for that. Why should I? Was not the Master dearer than the dearest to me? Then, what doubt was there that he would give me, of his own accord, anything that I needed?"[22]

Sometime in the middle of January, the elder Gopal wanted to distribute twelve pieces of ochre cloth and twelve rosaries to some monks. Pointing to his young disciples, the Master said to him: "You won't find better monks than these. Give your cloths and rosaries to them." Instead, Gopal offered them to the Master and he himself distributed them among his young disciples. Sharat received an ochre cloth, the garb of a monk, from the Master. With a view to teaching them to rely on God and to purge pride from their minds, one day the Master asked the disciples to beg food from door to door like traditional monks. Later Sharat told one funny incident. When he appeared in front of a house and asked for alms, an old lady came out and indignantly said to him: "You have such a strong body, why are you living on alms? Can you not get a job as a tram conductor?" Saying so, she shut the door.[23]

Days of Austerity and Travelling

After Sri Ramakrishna's passing away on 16 August 1886, the disciples had to return to their respective homes. Sharat's parents were happy to have him back, but his mind was not at home. He could not succeed in concentrating on his studies; the blissful form of the Master appeared in his mind and he cried when he was alone. However, within a couple of months, the Ramakrishna Monastery was established at Baranagore with the generous help of Surendra Mittra. Sharat began to visit the monastery off and on, sometimes spending the night. His father advised him to put his mind on his studies, but it was to no avail. Then Sharat's desperate father locked him in a room. As an obstructed river flows more vigorously, so this confinement increased his renunciation and longing. The unperturbed Sharat was waiting for a call from the Master. One day his younger brother Prakash furtively unlocked the room; Sharat silently walked out of the house and went straight to the monastery.

During December 1886 Sharat and some other disciples went to Antpur, the country home of Baburam. Inspired by Narendra, they took informal vows of monasticism during a night-long vigil around a sacred fire. Later they discovered that their vigil had taken place on Christmas Eve. A month later they took formal monastic vows through the *viraja homa* ceremony in Baranagore. Narendra gave the name "Swami Saradananda" to Sharat. During this period Saradananda's parents, sensing that he had gone beyond their recall, visited Baranagore to give him their blessings.

God makes everything favourable for one who loves Him. After cutting all family ties, Saradananda became absorbed in spiritual disciplines. Sometimes Vivekananda and Saradananda would spend the whole night in japam and meditation at the Cossipore cremation ground, where the Master's body had been cremated. Also Saradananda would sometimes go to Dakshineswar and practise sadhana in the Panchavati grove. On 9 April 1887 Vivekananda said to M.: "The Master has given me charge of Sharat. Sharat is now yearning for God; the kundalini is awakened in him."[24]

Luxury and comforts are obstacles to spiritual life, because they invariably prevent the aspirant from moving forward. Poverty and struggle act as friends. The disciples of the Master faced dire poverty in the monastery. They had very little food to eat and sometimes they starved. However, the Master had given them a taste of divine bliss, which helped them to transcend physical sufferings. In the monastery everybody carried out their respective responsibilities; Saradananda would help with the household duties, such as cleaning the rooms, washing the dishes, and so on.

Saradananda learned from Vivekananda how to sing and play drums (tabla), and he had a sweet, melodious voice, which from a distance could be mistaken for that of a woman. One night, while Saradananda was singing, some young neighbours thought they were hearing a woman's voice. With a view to exposing the monks' hypocrisy, they scaled the boundary wall and entered the monastery. After discovering the truth, they were ashamed and sincerely apologized to the monks. When Saradananda would recite the Chandi (the glory of the Divine Mother) and other hymns with his melodious voice, even bystanders felt spiritually uplifted. Even in advanced age, he would sing one or two devotional songs on the occasion of the Master's or Swamiji's birthday.

After Sri Ramakrishna's birthday in March 1887, Saradananda went with Premananda and Abhedananda on a pilgrimage to Puri, a place sacred to Jagannath (Krishna). At that time there was no railroad to Puri, so they walked three hundred miles. They stayed six months at the Emar Monastery in Puri and practised austerities. They regularly visited the Jagannath Temple and attended the famous Chariot Festival. Saradananda later reminisced: "I would look at the image of Chaitanya without blinking. The seaview would make my mind limitless. Sitting on the seacoast at Swargadwara I would spend the night fearlessly. I lived by begging food from *Anandabazar* [the temple food market]."[25]

When Saradananda returned to Baranagore after this pilgrimage, he became more indrawn; his body was emaciated and his face was aglow with devotion. During this period the disciples were restless to achieve the highest spiritual experiences, so they travelled to various holy places of India and from time to time they would return to the monastery for a break. Probably in the fall of 1889, Saradananda left for a pilgrimage with Vaikunthanath Sanyal, a householder disciple of the Master. First they visited the Vishnu Temple of Gaya and then Bodh Gaya, where Buddha attained illumination.

From Gaya, Saradananda and Vaikuntha reached Varanasi, the abode of Lord Shiva, and became the guest of Pramadadas Mittra, a rich devotee and a famous Sanskrit scholar. Within a week they visited the important shrines of Varanasi and then left for Ayodhya, the birthplace of Ramachandra. Afterwards they went to Hardwar and Rishikesh, in the foothills of the Himalayas, two of the most important places for ascetics. On 31 December 1889 Saradananda wrote to Pramadadas from Rishikesh: "It is a beautiful place. The mountain stands on its north and east sides and below flows the Ganges. It seems this place is the meeting point of heaven and earth. It is said that once the great sage Vyasa practised austerity here with 60,000 disciples. I heard that some holy people live here, but so far I have not seen an exalted one. Truly speaking, after seeing the Master, our eyes are spoiled. We have never seen that spirituality in any place, and we don't expect to either."[26] As the climate was good and food was available, Saradananda continued his sadhana in Rishikesh. One day he told Vaikuntha: "By the grace of the Master henceforth I have separated myself from the mind. The vagaries of the mind will not be able to delude me anymore; I am, as it were, the witness."[27]

On the day of *Shivaratri* (the spring festival of the Lord Shiva) Saradananda and Turiyananda went to visit Nilkantheshwar Shiva, sixteen miles from Rishikesh. It was on a remote hill in a jungle full of ferocious animals. On their way back that evening they lost their way. They decided to take two separate routes, so that both lives would not be endangered at once. Luckily, Turiyananda reached a solitary ashrama, and the next morning he and another monk went out to locate Saradananda. After a long search they saw him meditating, seated on a piece of rock. When he was asked why he did not try to find shelter, Saradananda replied, "When death is certain, it is better to die chanting God's name without being anxious."[28]

On 12 April 1890 Saradananda, Turiyananda, and Vaikuntha left Rishikesh for Gangotri (the source of the Ganges), Kedar, and Badri — three important holy places located in the interior part of the Himalayas, at high altitudes. Each swami carried two blankets, personal clothing, one stick, and no money. They began their journey barefoot on the trail. At that time travelling in the Himalayas was not only very difficult but also dangerous. Some days they had to go without food and some days without shelter. However, this pilgrimage was full of thrilling experiences for them.

On the fourth day Saradananda developed a blister on one foot, and it became difficult for him to walk. He asked his companions to reach the nearest village before evening and try to get help for him, while he waited for them by the side of the road. When they left, Saradananda began to

21

crawl towards the village. In the meantime, the workers of Kalikamli Baba's Ashrama, who provided free food to mendicants, were carrying food on their horses along that same road. They put Saradananda on a horse and dropped him off at the nearest village. Saradananda arrived just as Turiyananda and Vaikuntha were planning to rescue him. All were happy and realized the grace of the Master. They stayed in the village temple for three days while Saradananda recovered. At last they reached Gangotri and stayed three days at Kalikamli Baba's Ashrama.

From Gangotri they wanted to take a shortcut to Kedar, but they did not know the way. So they hired a guide, offering him a cloth as payment, since they had no money. The guide went with them for a distance and then disappeared. They walked for three days along the jungle path without food. Turiyananda ate some soft leaves and began to vomit. In the afternoon there was rain; they could do nothing but sit helplessly for meditation under the sky, covering their bodies with blankets. By the grace of the Master, the rain stopped within ten minutes and they reached a farmer's cottage. The next morning they followed a group of hill people who were going in the same direction. Turiyananda and Vaikuntha went first and Saradananda followed them. While walking down a one-mile slope, Saradananda saw an old woman who was losing her balance because she did not have a walking stick; he gave his own stick to her, risking his life. When they reached the bottom of the slope, Turiyananda noticed that Saradananda had no walking stick, and he was told that it had been given away to an old woman.

The local group changed direction, but Saradananda and his party continued their journey towards Kedarnath. On their way they crossed a small stream with a terrible current. While crossing Saradananda fell into the stream, and immediately Turiyananda and Vaikuntha extended their sticks to rescue him. Then they reached a village, Buro Kedar, and that night got a full meal from the villagers. Finally, after passing through all these hardships, Saradananda wanted to test whether the Master was with him or not. He thought: If anyone feeds me *luchi* (fried bread) and *halua* (farina pudding) tomorrow, I shall believe that the Master is with me.

The next morning Saradananda went alone to visit the village marketplace. All of a sudden, a shopkeeper called to him, "Hello, holy man, have some refreshment." Saradananda replied: "I have two more companions. Please give me whatever you want, and I shall share with them." "No, you eat first," said the shopkeeper. "I shall arrange for them later." The shopkeeper then served him hot fried bread and farina pudding. When Saradananda asked for food for his companions, the man refused to give anymore. Saradananda told the whole story to Turiyananda and Vaikuntha, and knew without a doubt that the Master was with him.[29]

From this village Turiyananda left alone for Rajpur, in the foothills of Mussorie, to practise austerities. Saradananda and Vaikuntha visited Kedarnath on 4 May 1890, then Tunganath and Badrinath, and finally Almora. After arriving at Almora on 12 August 1890, Saradananda wrote a detailed letter to Pramadadas about their journey. At Tunganath they had passed sleepless nights because of the cold. It snowed on them in Kedarnath, and the panoramic view and the perpetual snow range of the Himalayas charmed them. In Badrinath they bathed in the hot springs and visited the cave of the sage Vyasa, where he had compiled the Vedas.

Saradananda met Vivekananda and Akhandananda at Almora and then on 5 September they all left for another journey towards Garhwal. Akhandananda had a high fever and bronchitis, and a doctor advised him to go down to the plains. So the brother disciples arranged for Akhandananda's treatment at Dehra Dun, and then left for Rishikesh to practise austerities. Later Saradananda and others met Akhandananda at Meerut, and stayed there for several weeks. In February 1891 Saradananda unexpectedly met Swamiji at Delhi. Then after visiting Etawah, Mathura, Vrindaban, and Prayag, Saradananda and Vaikuntha reached Varanasi in April 1891.

In Varanasi they continued their sadhana and lived on alms. During this time, Dinu (or Dinanath), an earnest elderly devotee, came to Varanasi in search of a guru. He was so impressed by Saradananda that he took sannyasa vows from him and became Swami Satchidananda. Sometime in June, Saradananda, Abhedananda, and Satchidananda circumambulated the holy city Varanasi as an austerity. Eventually they all became sick. Saradananda first got a fever and then was attacked by dysentery; he was nursed by Satchidananda. During this pilgrimage he always carried a picture of Sri Ramakrishna, which he gave to Satchidananda. Finally, in September 1891, Saradananda returned to the Baranagore Monastery.

After recuperating from dysentery, Saradananda went to Jayrambati, the birthplace of Holy Mother, to attend the Jagaddhatri worship. He stayed there a few weeks and contracted malaria. He suffered a long time even after returning to Baranagore. In 1892 the Ramakrishna Monastery was moved from Baranagore to Alambazar, close to the Dakshineswar temple garden. Saradananda decided to perform some sadhana at the Panchavati, where the Master had practised various kinds of disciplines. Later Saradananda reminisced: "I would beg for uncooked food from

Dakshineswar village, and cook it myself in an earthen pot. Offering it to the Master, I would eat once a day, and practise japam and meditation day and night."[30]

In 1893 Vivekananda represented Hinduism at the Parliament of Religions in Chicago, and the news of his success reached the brothers at Alambazar. Saradananda again left for pilgrimage, this time to West India, and visited Jaipur, Pushkar, Mount Abu, Dwaraka, Prabhas, Junagad, and Chittor. After returning from the pilgrimage, he nursed Abhedananda, who was seriously ill from a severe infection in his feet. Abhedananda recuperated after three months under Saradananda's care. Saradananda also took care of Yajneswar Bhattacharya, a householder devotee of the Master, who was dying from tuberculosis. Forgetting himself, Saradananda served everyone throughout his life like a loving mother.

A person becomes great through his actions, dedication, unselfishness, and self-control. One day Saradananda saw muddy footprints on the floor of the shrine at Alambazar Monastery. He learned that the cook had made them, and he called for him loudly, as if he were going to burst with fury. As soon as the cook appeared, Saradananda controlled his temper and calmly said, "You can go."[31]

In Europe and America

After spreading the message of Vedanta in America and England for several years, Vivekananda desperately needed an assistant to continue the momentum. He wrote Saradananda and asked him to come to England. In the beginning Saradananda was reluctant, but then he went to Holy Mother and sought her advice. The Mother told him: "My son, be not afraid. You should go to the West. The Master will protect you, and will be with you wherever you go."[32]

In March 1896 Saradananda left for England and arrived there on 1 April. On the way his ship was buffeted by a hurricane in the Mediterranean Sea. "All the passengers were in a great panic," the swami recalled. "Some were crying; some were running here and there in fear; some were shaking out of nervousness. The whole scene was frightening, but I was not afraid in the least. My mind was as steady and calm as the needle of a compass."[33] When the ship stopped at Rome, he went to visit Saint Peter's Cathedral. Standing in front of the sanctuary, his mind became absorbed in his previous incarnation, and he lost outer consciousness for some time. (Ramakrishna had said that he and Shashi had previously been companions of Christ.)

In London Saradananda was the guest of Mr. E. T. Sturdy, a Vedanta student. Vivekananda arrived there at the end of April. The two swamis had not seen each other for a long time; Saradananda told Vivekananda all the news of their brother disciples at the Alambazar Monastery and of their activities in India. It was a most happy occasion.

From May 1896 Vivekananda began his whirlwind activity in London — five classes a week, Jnana Yoga lectures on Sundays, and meeting new people. Saradananda attended Swamiji's lectures and learned how to lecture in the West, as he had no previous experience in public lecturing. In London, at Swamiji's behest, he gave some classes on the Gita. His first task was to supply materials about the life of Sri Ramakrishna to Professor Max Müller, the famous German orientalist. Years later, Saradananda recalled:

> At the invitation of Max Müller, Swamiji went to Oxford and stayed in his home as a guest. Max Müller wrote an article in the *Nineteenth Century* on Sri Ramakrishna entitled "A Real Mahatman." He asked Swamiji to furnish him with enough material for a book so he could write about Sri Ramakrishna in greater detail. Swamiji agreed to help. When he returned, he asked me to undertake the job forthwith. I worked hard and gathered all the incidents in the life of the Master and the teachings of the Master and showed the manuscript to Swamiji. I thought Swamiji would edit it and make extensive corrections. He didn't do that. He simply changed a few words for fear of exaggeration and sent the whole manuscript to Professor Müller. As I remember, Professor Müller incorporated the complete manuscript in his book [*The Life and Sayings of Sri Ramakrishna*] and published it without making any alterations.[34]

Vivekananda established the Vedanta Society of New York in 1894. Towards the end of June 1896 he asked Saradananda to go to America with J. J. Goodwin, his English disciple and stenographer, to carry on the Vedanta work. Saradananda was nervous about lecturing, but Swamiji encouraged him: "Look, I have already lectured there. You just teach them a little Gita and Upanishad, and answer their questions. That is all."

After arriving in New York, Saradananda was introduced by the president of the Vedanta Society and gave his first talk. While Saradananda was lecturing, Goodwin sat in the back, laughing. This made the swami nervous, thinking that he was not lecturing well. When the lecture was over, he asked Goodwin why he was laughing. "You were speaking well," answered Goodwin, "that's why I was laughing."[35]

Saradananda's sweet and gentle personality and his masterly exposition of the Vedanta philosophy proved attractive at once. He was invited to be one of the speakers at the Green Acre Conference of Comparative Religions in Maine, where he lectured on Vedanta and held classes on yoga. After the sessions closed, Saradananda lectured in Brooklyn, New York, and Boston. At the Brooklyn Ethical Association he lectured on "The Ethical Ideas of the Hindus." Everywhere Saradananda went he made friends and won staunch followers of Vedanta. Finally he settled down in New York to carry on the Vedanta work in an organized way.

Once in New York a woman sought the swami's help regarding some terrible psychic experiences: At night the furniture of her room moved around, the windows flew open, she felt an unknown presence, and some formless being lifted her body a few inches off the floor. After reflecting a few moments, Saradananda said: "I am glad you have come. But if you ask my opinion, I will say that these experiences are the result of a weakened state of mind. Please train your mind firmly to think thoughts that are wholesome, good, and beneficial. By invigorating thoughts alone, these occult phenomena and psychic experiences can be averted."[36] The swami gave her some spiritual instructions and asked her to meditate daily and read inspiring books. This eventually solved her problems.

Saradananda had a wonderful sense of humour. Once the swami was staying as a guest at Ridgely Manor, the country home of Mr. Francis Leggett, then president of the Vedanta Society. Every morning Miss Josephine MacLeod, Mr. Leggett's sister-in-law, would ask the swami, "Did you sleep well?" It so happened that one Sunday while Saradananda was lecturing, Miss MacLeod fell asleep. Then, while shaking hands after the lecture, he asked, "Did you sleep well?" Both laughed heartily.

Saradananda used to hold classes regularly in Montclair, New Jersey, where he would stay at the home of Mr. and Mrs. Wheeler. Swami Atulananda, a Western monk, wrote in his book *With the Swamis in America*:

> An interesting incident took place when Swami Saradananda was living at this happy home. The swami had often spoken about Sri Ramakrishna and one day he produced his Master's photograph and showed it to the lady of the house. "Oh, swami," she exclaimed, "it is the same face!" "What do you mean?" said the swami. And then she told him that long ago, in her youth, before she was married, she had had a vision of a Hindu and that it was the same face that now she saw in the photograph. "It was Sri Ramakrishna," she said, "but I did not know it until now. I was so much impressed and charmed at the vision at the time, that I remember the face very distinctly, and I have been going about here and there ever since I had the vision,

wherever I heard that a Hindu had come to America, but I was always disappointed, not finding the same face. And now at last I see that it was Sri Ramakrishna."[37]

Referring to this incident, Saradananda later recalled: "The Master chooses his own men and women. We are mere instruments in his hands. It is a privilege to work under his banner. In America he had already prepared the ground for me; I was not alone. He brought to me men and women of exalted character who helped me in our work and bore great love for our Master."[38]

Mrs. Ole Bull of Boston, who immensely helped Vivekananda's Vedanta work in the West, invited Saradananda to her home. She also introduced the swami to her influential friends, such as Professor William James and other academics at Harvard University. Mrs. Bull often said that Swamiji was like the brilliant scorching sun and Saradananda, the cool, refreshing moon.

Saradananda lectured at the Free Religious Association in Boston on "Sympathy of Religions"; he lectured at the Cambridge Conferences also. It is a great loss that only one of the swami's lectures was recorded, "The Vedanta: Its Theory and Practice." Dr. Lewis G. Janes, director of the Cambridge Conferences, wrote to the editor of the *Brahmavadin* in appreciation of Saradananda's work:

> In Cambridge, the classes in the Vedanta philosophy, constituting a single feature in the broad field of comparative study outlined for the Cambridge Conferences, attracted large and intelligent audiences, in part made up of professors and students of Harvard University. The swami's exposition of the principles of the Advaita doctrine, in just comparison with other views which are held in India, was admirably lucid and clear. His replies to questions were always ready and satisfactory.... In Boston, Waltham, and Worcester, Massachusetts, Swami Saradananda conducted a series of lectures which were largely attended and which everywhere manifested a sustained interest in his subject."[39]

Just at this time when Saradananda was at the height of his usefulness in America, Vivekananda recalled him to India to help him organize the Ramakrishna Mission at Belur. After having stayed two and a half years in America, he sailed with Mrs. Ole Bull and Miss MacLeod for India on 12 January 1898, handing over the responsibility of the Vedanta Society to Abhedananda. Saradananda reached London on 20 January and Paris on 21 January. He admired the art, music, and other creative talents of the French people. The following are a few entries from his diary:

Saturday, 22 Jan. 1898: Paris — the theatre — Sarah Bernhardt as the
blind wife — La Belle Paris — the artistic in French life — the Notre
Dame — Theatre Renaissance — La Villa Morte.

Sunday, 23 Jan. 1898: Left Paris at 8:00 p.m. In the train from Paris to
Naples. Madeleine Church. Acquaintance with Mr. Niblack, the American Embassy. A ride of two nights and one day to Rome from Paris.

Tuesday, 25 Jan. 1898: Arrival at Rome early in the morning. The Hotel
Continental. St. Peter. View from the top of the Mount Janiculum. The
Catacomb of Saint Sebastian. The theatre at night — Signora Elinora
Duse, the great actress. Santa Scolla — the Sistine Chapel — the mas-
terpieces of Michael Angelo. The Moses.

Wednesday, 26 Jan. 1898: Colosseum in the morning.

Thursday, 27 Jan. 1898: The morning in the Vatican library and the
Sculpture Gallery at the Vatican. St. Peter for the last time.[40]

The party left Rome for India via Naples and Brindisi, Italy. They
arrived in Calcutta on 8 February 1898; Swamiji and other monks went to
Howrah Station to receive them.

Back to India

On 3 February 1898 the Ramakrishna Monastery was moved from
Alambazar to Nilambar Mukherjee's garden house in the village of Belur,
and a nearby plot of land was purchased on the bank of the Ganges,
where the permanent home of the Order could be built. Under Vivekananda's direction, the brother monks took the responsibility of levelling
the ground, then building living quarters and a shrine. Saradananda was
entrusted to oversee the office and supervise foreign visitors. He also
organized plague relief in Calcutta. During August and September he
gave a series of lectures in Bengali at Albert Hall in Calcutta, which was
later published in Gitatattwa. In October he received a cable from Swamiji,
who was then travelling with the Western devotees and had become very
ill in Srinagar, Kashmir.

Saradananda immediately left for Rawalpindi by train, and then took
a tonga (horse carriage) to Srinagar. On the way a terrible accident took
place: Suddenly there was a landslide in front of the carriage, and the
horse began to run down the road frantically. While trying to gain control of the carriage, the coachman muttered to himself, "I will see whether
Allah protects me this time." Then another carriage came from the opposite direction around a turn, and the startled horse jumped in the air. One
of the carriage wheels bounced against a rock, and the carriage rushed

towards a ravine several thousand feet deep. The luggage was thrown off, a dislodged boulder crushed the horse to death, the coachman fell from the carriage and lost consciousness — but luckily the carriage was stuck in a tree before it could fall into the ravine. Throughout all this, Saradananda remained calm. He jumped from the carriage into thorny bushes; he hurt his feet, but was otherwise unharmed. He rescued the coachman, took him to the nearest village, and then left for Srinagar by another carriage.[41]

In Srinagar Saradananda served Swamiji until he recovered from his illness; then the whole party went to Lahore. Swamiji asked Saradananda to show his Western devotees the holy places of North India, and then left for Belur Math with his disciple Sadananda. Saradananda and others returned to Calcutta in November. Saradananda was present when Swamiji installed the relics of Sri Ramakrishna in Belur Math on 9 December 1898. On 7 February 1899 Swamiji sent Saradananda and Turiyananda to West India to preach and collect funds. After visiting Kanpur, Agra, Jaipur, Ahmedabad, Limbdi, Junagad, and Bhavnagar, they returned to Belur Math on 3 May, after having received a cable from Swamiji who planned to leave for the West again on 20 June 1899.

As General Secretary of the Ramakrishna Order

Vivekananda framed the rules and regulations of the Belur Monastery, and asked Saradananda and other brother disciples to implement them and train the young monks accordingly. With the vision of a seer, Swamiji knew that Saradananda would play an important role in the life of the organization he founded to fulfill the mission of the Master. Saradananda was endowed with remarkable devotion and steadiness, sound judgement and a tender heart, and also was acquainted with Western methods of organization. Swamiji made Brahmananda the president (spiritual head), and Saradananda the general secretary (executive head), of Ramakrishna Math and Mission. For nearly three decades (1898-1927) Saradananda was the chief organizer of the Ramakrishna Order in its manifold activities.

Saradananda was a born leader. He always considered the youngest member of the Order his equal and was perfectly just and democratic in his dealings. Whenever there was a lack of servants in the monastery, he would offer to share the menial and domestic chores along with the younger members. He never judged anyone or anything without considering all sides. Hasty judgements or decisions were foreign to his nature. This of course stood him in good stead as the executive head of the Order. Everyone was sure to get a hearing from him. He never listened to slander: He followed Swamiji's instruction "to allow slander to enter one ear only to throw it out by the other."[42]

When Swamiji left for America, Saradananda put his mind to training the young monks. He gave classes on the scriptures, and inspired them to practise japam and meditation more intensely. Once he decided to conduct an uninterrupted meditation from 11:00 p.m. to 7:00 a.m.: Each monk was to meditate for an hour in the shrine, one after another. Someone said that might disturb the Master's sleep. Saradananda replied: "In Dakshineswar we have seen that the Master would sleep for only a short time. Moreover, we are going to meditate in the shrine and not in his bedroom."[43] Sometimes he would ask the monks to beg for food, cook it under a tree, and then eat after offering it to the Master. The disciples of the Master created an intense spiritual atmosphere in the monastery that even a stranger could feel.

In December 1899 Saradananda was invited to give lectures in East Bengal (now Bangladesh). He lectured at Dhaka and Narayangunj, and visited the saintly Durga Charan Nag, a great devotee of Sri Ramakrishna. On 4 January 1900 he went to Barisal and stayed eight days. He was received by Ashwini Kumar Datta, a great leader and devotee of the Master. Saradananda gave several lectures in Brajamohan College: among them were "Vedanta, the Universal Religion," "Origin and Development of Religion," and "Synthesis of Jnana, Karma, and Bhakti."

Ashwini Datta was a famous orator in Barisal, but while speaking he would move his hands and head in an effort to convince the audience. Someone observed that Saradananda spoke without moving his hands and asked about it. The swami replied: "To move one's hands and use facial gestures are great arts of oratory, and most speakers use those tools to make their lectures impressive. But Swamiji did not like it. He said: 'During a lecture one should remove one's ego and stand in front of the Master humbly and calmly. He will make you speak whatever he wants, and he himself will listen to it. Thus when one speaks surrendering fully, then only that lecture carries the message of God.'"[44] Then Saradananda told the devotees that previously he had had that bad habit, but Swamiji had corrected him in London.

One day some devotees asked him to talk about Sri Ramakrishna. Saradananda said with a smile:

It is futile to try to understand the Master as long as one has a little bit of ego. The more I grow, the more I see that I could not understand the Master. Only Swamiji and Nag Mahashay understood him to some extent. We are his servants; we are just trying to obey his orders. I shall understand him when he makes me understand out of his mercy. I get scared when I speak about the Master. Even Swamiji said, "Unknowingly trying to make the Master great, I may make him small." When a person like Swamiji speaks this way, what to speak of others! Meditate on the Master, and he will undoubtedly reveal himself unto you. Have faith. How little we have understood the Infinite Master!

Saying so, Saradananda's voice choked, his body became motionless, tears rolled from his half-closed eyes, his breathing stopped, and a divine beauty reflected on his face. The audience was dumbfounded. After a while, saying "Ramakrishna, Ramakrishna," the swami came back to external consciousness.[45]

Saradananda returned to Belur Math on 13 January 1900. A gentleman who had seen Sri Ramakrishna a couple of times, once came to Belur to meet Saradananda. The swami cordially received him, because he had seen the Master. But the gentleman said: "What good is there in seeing Sri Ramakrishna! Even the boatmen and carriage drivers have also seen him." Immediately Saradananda gravely said: "Whatever you have just said to me, never utter that again. You are talking about the boatmen and others; do you know what happened to them at the moment of death? What do you know about the results of seeing the Master? Have you not heard that even Pratap Hazra [a hypocrite who lived at Dakshineswar during the Master's time] breathed his last, seeing the Master?"[46]

In November 1900 Saradananda decided to practise tantric sadhana under the guidance of his uncle, Ishwar Chandra Chakrabarty, who was an adept tantric. He received permission from Holy Mother and Brahmananda and then began to spend long hours in japam, meditation, and tantric rituals. This sadhana unveiled to him the mystery of Shakti worship, which is the realization of the Divine Mother in all; and eventually it helped him to be the caretaker of Holy Mother and to write the life of the Master. Saradananda wrote in the dedication of his beautiful Bengali book *Bharate Shakti Puja* (Mother Worship in India): "By whose gracious glance the author has been able to realize the revelation of Divine Motherhood in every woman — to Her lotus feet the work is dedicated in all humility and devotion."[47]

Vivekananda returned unexpectedly to Belur on 9 December 1900; after his second visit to the West he was not well. Owing partly to this and partly to the fact that he wanted to see the work progress as quickly as possible during his lifetime, he was now and then very severe in his dealings with brother disciples. During this time no one dared go near Swamiji except Saradananda, whose steadiness and mental poise could freeze anybody's hot temper. Once Swamiji sent Saradananda to Calcutta on an errand. When he learned that it had not been done, he rebuked him with harsh language. Saradananda remained as motionless as a statue. When tea was served, he began to drink it as if nothing had happened. Disappointed, Swamiji commented: "Sharat's veins carry the blood of fish; it will never warm up."[48] Observing that Saradananda was free from anger, Swamiji teased him at other times, "Your veins carry frog's blood, or the blood of sand fish." Swamiji knew that this noble evenmindedness is necessary for the head of a monastic order.

Vivekananda passed away on 4 July 1902, and the responsibilities of organizing and managing the growing work of the Order fell on Saradananda. But Saradananda always consulted with Brahmananda, the president, when making any decision on serious matters. Since 1898 Trigunatitananda had edited and managed the Bengali magazine *Udbodhan*, which had been started by Swamiji. In December 1902, when Trigunatitananda left for America to take over for Turiyananda, his editorial and managerial duties fell on Saradananda. To keep the financially troubled magazine alive, Saradananda planned to move it to a house in Calcutta, where the magazine office would be downstairs, and the shrine and Holy Mother's residence would be upstairs.

Holy Mother in Udbodhan and Jayrambati

Only a few disciples of Sri Ramakrishna had free access to Holy Mother. Until his death in 1899, Yogananda had been the Mother's caretaker; then Trigunatitananda looked after her. When Trigunatitananda left for America, Saradananda took over the responsibility until Holy Mother passed away in 1920. It hurt Saradananda when he found that Mother had no place of her own, either in Calcutta or in Jayrambati. In Calcutta she lived either in a rented house or in a devotee's home, and in Jayrambati she lived with her brother's family. She therefore had no freedom to conduct her spiritual ministry. It was Saradananda, though a monk, who borrowed money to build a house for the Mother, which also would be used for the *Udbodhan* office. This building is now called "Udbodhan," or "Mother's House." The publication office was moved to the new building towards the end of 1908, and Holy Mother moved in on 23 May 1909. Some years later, Saradananda had a house built in Jayrambati for the Mother.

Once Holy Mother said: "I shall be able to live at Udbodhan as long as Sharat is there. I do not see anyone who can be responsible for me after that. Sharat can, in every respect. He is the man to bear my burden."[49] From 1904 to 1920, in spite of his diverse activities and heavy duties in connection with management of the Ramakrishna Math and Mission, the swami poured his heart and soul into serving Holy Mother. He also looked after the welfare of her relatives, nursed her dying younger brother, and made provisions for her niece Radhu's future financial security. He accompanied the Mother on her several pilgrimages and often visited her at Jayrambati, especially when she was ill.

During his stay in Calcutta, Saradananda personally looked after her; and wherever she went, he always took care of her needs and finances. Saradananda's devotion to the Mother has become legend in the Ramakrishna Order. Holy Mother used to speak of him as her Vasuki, a mythical snake, who protected her with his thousand hoods. "Wherever water pours, he spreads his umbrella to protect me," she said.

Swami Nikhilananda recorded some glimpses of Saradananda's memorable service to Holy Mother:

> To attend Holy Mother, with her eccentric relatives, was a delicate and difficult task. As she herself put it: "I shall have no difficulty as long as Sharat lives. I do not see anybody else who can shoulder my burden." If anyone spoke of her going to Calcutta when the swami was not there, she would say: "I simply cannot think of going to Calcutta when Sharat is not there. While I am in Calcutta, if he says that he wants to go elsewhere for a few days, I tell him: "Wait awhile, my child. First let me leave the place and then you may go." The swami sometimes sang to entertain her, and when her body was burnt with high fever he placed her tender hands on his bare body and thus cooled her. Her confidence in the swami was total.
>
> Saradananda called himself the Mother's "doorkeeper," and he felt proud of the position. From his small room at the left of the entrance to the Mother's house in Calcutta he kept an eye on the devotees who went upstairs to salute her. It was not an easy task. Once a devotee walked a great distance to come to Udbodhan and was very hot. It was about three in the afternoon. Holy Mother had just returned from a devotee's house and was resting. Saradananda said to the devotee: "I won't allow you to go up now; Mother is tired." With the words "Is she just your mother?" the visitor practically pushed him aside and went to the Mother. Very soon he felt repentant for his rash act and prayed that he might avoid the swami while going out. He also told the Mother about his improper conduct but was reassured by her.

Sheepishly he came down the stairs and found Saradananda seated in the same place. He asked his forgiveness for the offence. Saradananda embraced him and said: "Why do you talk about offending me? Can one see Mother without such yearning?"

On another occasion, when the Mother was ill, a devotee came to her and prayed for initiation. She asked him to come a few days later. But as he insisted she asked him to speak to Saradananda about it. "I do not know anybody else," he insisted again. "I have come to you; please initiate me." "What do you mean?" the Mother replied. "Sharat is the jewel of my head. What he says will be done." The devotee went to the swami, who fixed a day for his initiation.

In spite of all Holy Mother's affection and confidence in him, Saradananda was the very image of humility. A disciple of the Mother on one occasion took the dust of his feet, perhaps with a little show, as the swami was about to begin his daily duties. The swami said: "Why such a big salutation? What is the idea?" "Sir, why do you say that?" the disciple replied. "Whom else should I salute but you?" The swami said: "I am seated here awaiting her grace by whom you have been blessed. If she wishes, she can this very moment seat you in my place." When Saradananda prostrated himself before the Mother, as a witness observed, it was an unusual sight. He melted, as it were, on the ground before her. He showed that with his salutation he offered at her feet his body, soul, and everything.

For over fifteen years Saradananda had the unique privilege of being close to Holy Mother and looking after her needs. How small he felt in her presence! Once he remarked: "What can we understand of Mother? This, however, I can say: I have never seen such a great mind; and I do not hope to see one. It is not within our capacity to comprehend the extent of Mother's glory and power. I have never seen in anyone else such attachment; nor have I seen such detachment. She was so deeply attached to Radhu. But before her death she said: 'Please send her away.' Radhu lost all attraction for her."

A devotee once said to Saradananda that he could easily believe in the divinity of Sri Ramakrishna; at least he cherished that faith. But he could not comprehend Holy Mother as the Divine Mother. The swami replied: "Do you mean to say that God married the daughter of a woman who maintained herself by gathering cow dung?"[50]

As a Writer

In 1909 Saradananda began to write his monumental work *Sri Sri Rama-krishna Lilaprasanga* in Bengali, which has been translated as *Sri Ramakrishna,*

The Great Master. It is not only an authentic, interpretive biography of the Master, but also a classic in Bengali literature. It consists of five volumes and took nearly ten years to complete. Saradananda gave three reasons for this great undertaking: First, he wrote it to repay the money that he had borrowed to build Holy Mother's house in Calcutta and to publish *Udbodhan*. Second, he wished to publish an accurate and complete account of the Master's life. As an editor of *Udbodhan*, he had to correct and rewrite many articles about Sri Ramakrishna that were full of misinformation. As an eyewitness to the Master's life, he could not bear that any untruth be told about the Master. Third, he tried to justify the philanthropic activities of the Ramakrishna Mission and also remove the misunderstanding about Ramakrishna's teaching, "Serve human beings as God." M., the recorder of *The Gospel of Sri Ramakrishna*, had commented that the monastic disciples changed the focus of the Master's teaching, which according to M. was God-realization and not social services. Of course, M. later changed his mind in 1912, when Holy Mother visited the Ramakrishna Mission Home of Service in Varanasi and said, "The Master is ever-present in this place, and Mother Lakshmi always casts Her benign glance upon it."[51]

Once Girish Chandra Ghosh had asked Vivekananda to write a biography of Sri Ramakrishna. Swamiji declined, expressing his inability, "Shall I make the image of a monkey while trying to make that of Shiva?" On another occasion Swamiji said, "Sharat will write."[52] Later Girish asked Saradananda to write about Sri Ramakrishna's divine life, his sadhana, and his message. Otherwise, in the future some less adept people might present the Master in a narrow, incorrect way, which might eventually form a cult and defeat the purpose of his incarnation. There was cause for such apprehension: It was well known that Girish had given his "power of attorney" to the Master, who took complete responsibility for him. Some people began to imitate this and deceive themselves, because they did not understand the importance of self-surrender. Saradananda first wrote "Sri Ramakrishna as a Guru," the third and fourth parts of *Lilaprasanga*, and then wrote the rest. In the beginning of the third part, Saradananda explained the mystery of the "power of attorney" that the Master had accepted from Girish. Before publication, Saradananda read the chapter to Girish who wholeheartedly approved it.

Once a monk asked Saradananda to write a life of Sri Ramakrishna that would contain all the stories about him. The swami replied: "Is it so easy to write about the Master? One should not undertake such work without having his command. If I get his command, I shall try." Some years later when *Lilaprasanga* was published, the same monk asked Saradananda whether he had received the command before writing the book. He avoided the question, saying, "That is none of your business."[53]

One day, Asitananda, an attendant of Saradananda, worked up the courage to ask the swami if he had experienced nirvikalpa samadhi. "Did I waste my time cutting grass [i.e., living meaninglessly] when I lived in the company of Sri Ramakrishna?" Saradananda replied. When the attendant pressed him for details, the swami said: "Read the chapter on samadhi in *Sri Ramakrishna, the Great Master*. I have not written anything about samadhi without experiencing it myself."[54]

Christopher Isherwood, the author of *Ramakrishna and His Disciples*, wrote:

> Although Saradananda did not begin his work until more than twenty years after Ramakrishna's death, there is no doubt of its authenticity. Many of those who had known Ramakrishna were then still alive, and Saradananda carefully compared his memories with theirs. *The Great Master* has also the value of having been written by a monastic disciple, who has actually shared the extraordinary experiences he describes. "Nothing beyond my spiritual experience has been recorded in the book," Saradananda once told a questioner. This seemingly cautious answer is in fact a claim so tremendous that it silences all suspicion of boastfulness; a man like Saradananda could not have made it unless it was literally true.[55]

Having the permission and blessing from Holy Mother, Saradananda began to write *Sri Sri Ramakrishna Lilaprasanga*. He collected all information about Holy Mother in the book directly from her. When the Mother was in Calcutta, Saradananda used to read the manuscript to her, as it was then published serially in the *Udbodhan*. When she was in Jayrambati, someone else would read it to her. She commented: "Everything has been written correctly in Sharat's book." Once a learned disciple of the Mother said, "Mother, what a wonderful book Sharat Maharaj has written!" The Mother replied, "Yes, it needs learning and intellect to understand Sharat's book."[56]

In 1925 during the Chariot Festival in Puri, Saradananda talked about the adverse conditions in which he wrote the *Lilaprasanga* in Udbodhan:

> Holy Mother was living upstairs along with Radhu; I was surrounded by devotees and I had to keep the accounts also; the burden of the loan for the house was on me. I used to write the *Lilaprasanga* sitting in the small room downstairs. Then nobody dared to talk to me, as I had no

time to chat for a long time. If anybody would ask anything, I would say, "Be quick," and finish the talk briefly. People would think that I was egotistic. I could not write much about the devotees [except Gopal's Mother and Vivekananda], because there was so much material to write about the Master. When the mind was ready, only then could I write.[57]

The Bhagavad Gita says, "He who finds action in inaction, and inaction in action, he is a perfect yogi" (4.18). Amidst the hectic surroundings and crowds, Saradananda continued his serious writing project. One day some young monks were talking loudly and laughing in the Udbodhan office, adjacent to the swami's room. Golap-ma, an attendant of Holy Mother, scolded them: "Shame on you! Mother is upstairs and Sharat is doing serious work, and you boys are making such great noise!" Overhearing Golap-ma's loud voice, the swami said to her: "Well, Golap-ma, please don't give your ears to them. It is the nature of the boys to behave like that. I am so close to them, but I don't listen to what they are talking about. I have told my ears, 'Don't listen to anything that is unnecessary.' So my ears are not listening to them."[58] Saradananda had total control over his senses.

Moreover, his life was extremely disciplined and he followed his routine strictly. After having his morning bath, Saradananda would go to the shrine and bow down to the Master and then to Holy Mother. At 7:00 a.m., he would come downstairs and write for hours sitting in the same place. He had no time to stretch. As a result, in later years the circulation in his legs was greatly impaired, and they would sometimes tremble. In between his writing sessions he would drink tea and smoke his hubble-bubble. He would have lunch at 1:30 p.m., and after that he would rest for an hour and a half. He wrote again until evening, and then he would meet the devotees. Sometimes he would go to Belur Math and stay for a couple of days.

In his memoirs, Swami Nikhilananda wrote about an important incident:

Before we left for Varanasi [in 1925], Swami Shuddhananda asked Swami Saradananda in front of me to finish the Cossipore chapter of the *Lilaprasanga* [which would describe Sri Ramakrishna's last days]. He said that he had some notes but he was not well enough to write the article. Swami Shuddhananda then said: "You can dictate it and Nikhilananda will write it." He said he would see what could be done. I believe he took his notebook with him. He did not feel well in Varanasi, so nothing was done. When we were leaving for Puri, Swami Shuddhananda reminded him about the article and again asked him to dictate the whole thing to me. Then the swami made the following significant remark: "When Holy Mother was alive I felt a great deal of inner strength and began to write the *Lilaprasanga*. She died and I felt as if all my powers were gone. Then I saw Swami Brahmananda and began to feel strong again. When he died I felt as if my brain was completely paralyzed. I simply cannot finish the book." Then he added: "When I began to write the *Lilaprasanga* I thought I understood the Master. But now I clearly see that the life of the Master is very deep. I was merely hovering over the top branches; the root is far beneath the ground."[59]

Neither M. nor Saradananda recorded the last days of Sri Ramakrishna. Perhaps it was not the will of the Master. In 1925 when a disciple asked him to complete the Master's life, Saradananda said humbly: "Perhaps it will never be completed. I am not getting any inspiration from within. The Master made me write whatever he wanted. Now when I read the *Lilaprasanga*, I wonder, have I written all these things? I have no more inclination to do anything. It seems that the Master is doing everything."[60]

An Ideal Karma Yogi

A real karma yogi is fearless and is not concerned about others' criticism. He works for God and depends on His will. As the karma yogi has no selfish motives, he cannot be affected by praise or blame. Krishna said in the Gita, "They are wretched who seek the results of their actions." Saradananda was a role model for leading a balanced life. His character was a perfect blend of the four yogas: he was a jnani (man of wisdom) and attained nirvikalpa samadhi; his devotion for the Master, the Mother, and Swami Vivekananda was profound; he was a perfect yogi — even a thousand problems could not perturb the equanimity of his mind; and he was an ideal worker who offered his body, mind, and soul to carry out Sri Ramakrishna's mission.

Once Holy Mother said to one of her disciples: "Look at Sharat! He works so much, he faces so many problems, yet he remains calm and never complains. He is a *sadhu* [holy man]. Why does he undergo all these things? If he wishes he can remain absorbed in God day and night. It is only for your good that he is living on this earthly plane."[61] Another time Swamiji said, "The Master brought Sharat for his work."

As the general secretary of the Ramakrishna Order, Saradananda had to face problem after problem. He was a wonderful troubleshooter. In 1909 Devabrata Basu and Sachindra Nath Sen, two young revolutionaries who were fighting to free India from the British, were convicted in the Maniktala Bomb Case, but later they were found not guilty and released by the court. They then joined the Ramakrishna Order, took initiation from Holy Mother, and after their final vows they became Swamis Prajnananda and Chinmayananda. Swamis Atmaprakashananda and Satyananda had also been revolutionaries. To accept them into the Order was to invite the wrath and suspicion of the British government and the police. But to refuse admission to a sincere spiritual aspirant simply because of his past conduct would be sheer cowardice. Saradananda accepted them all and boldly faced the police and the government.

Although the Ramakrishna Order has never involved itself in politics, the presence of the former revolutionaries brought police surveillance upon the Order. When Atmaprakashananda joined the Udbodhan centre in 1912, the police learned about it and summoned Saradananda and Atmaprakashananda for questioning. The police official did not offer a chair to Saradananda nor speak courteously to him. But Saradananda gently assured the police official that the young men who joined the Order had given up all political activities. While returning to the monastery, Atmaprakashananda said in an aggrieved tone: "Swami, I am extremely sorry. It is for my sake that you have had to put up with an insult unworthy of your position." "Who can insult me?" Saradananda replied. "If my mind does not accept the rudeness, how can I be insulted? Have I kept anything for myself? I have already offered body, mind, and soul at the blessed feet of our Lord, where there cannot be any room for good and bad, honour and dishonour. Be at ease. You need not worry on my behalf."[62]

The problems continued. Most of the revolutionaries had been inspired by the patriotic lectures and writings of Vivekananda. When they were arrested, the police found Vivekananda's books in their homes. So the British government was very upset about the publications of the Ramakrishna Mission. In Dhaka on 11 December 1916 Lord Carmichael, the governor of Bengal, made some damaging remarks during his Durbar speech about the Ramakrishna Mission, which had a devastating effect on its activities. The general public became afraid of supporting the Mission, as they feared that they might be tortured or harassed by the government. Moreover, the British government had the full power to curb the philanthropic activities of the Mission.

During this crisis, Saradananda stood calmly at the helm of the Ramakrishna Mission. Wishing to remove this doubt and misunderstanding, on 23 January 1917 Saradananda wrote a memorandum, containing twelve points, to Lord Carmichael. On 2 March Mr. Gourlay, the governor's secretary, and Mr. Denham, the police chief, came to Belur Math to meet with Saradananda. On 10 March Saradananda was invited to the

Governor's house, where he talked with Lord Carmichael for an hour. On 26 March the governor withdrew his statement, a rare event during the British rule in India. The letter he wrote to Saradananda follows:

Dear Sir,

I thank you for having come to see me and for the trouble you have taken to tell me about the origin of the Ramakrishna Mission, and its aims and objects.

I read with great interest the memorial which the Mission authorities submitted to me some time ago. I regret very much to hear that words used by me at the Durbar in December last regarding the Mission should have led in any way to the curtailment of the good religious, social, and educational work the Mission has done and is doing. As you, I know, realize my object was not to condemn the Ramakrishna Mission and its members. I know the character of the Mission's work is entirely non-political, and I have heard nothing but good of its work of social service for the people. What I wanted to impress upon the public is this: Charitable and philanthropic works such as the Mission undertake is being adopted deliberately by a section of the revolutionary party as a cloak for their own nefarious scheme and in order to attract to their organizations youths who are animated by ideals such as those which actuate the Mission, with the intention of perverting these ideals to their own purposes, and with this object unscrupulous use is being made of the name and reputation of the Ramakrishna Mission.

I have full sympathy with the real aims of the true Ramakrishna Mission and it was this abuse of the name of the Mission I wish to prevent. I hope the words I used will help the Mission to guard against the illegitimate use of its name by unscrupulous people.

Yours very sincerely,
(Sd.) Carmichael[63]

When this letter was published in the newspapers, the cloud of misunderstanding and the public's fear dissipated; the police surveillance was also withdrawn. In 1919 Lord Ronaldshay, the new governor of Bengal, came to visit Belur Math. Saradananda cordially received him and with all humility untied his shoes before taking him to the shrine. The governor expressed his gratitude and learned from Saradananda about the history and activities of the Ramakrishna Mission.

Whenever any distinguished guest or foreign visitor came to visit Belur Math, Saradananda would go from Udbodhan (Calcutta) to receive them. Although Brahmananda had a gigantic spiritual personality, when these important visitors came, he became as nervous as a child. In 1911 Madame Emma Calvé, the famous French opera singer and a devotee of Swamiji, visited Belur Math. Saradananda cordially received her and introduced her to Brahmananda. Calvé came with an interpreter because she did not know English well. Saradananda first took her to the small shrine built in memory of Swamiji on the actual spot where his body had been cremated. She sat down in a meditation posture and prayed before the engraved emblem of Vivekananda. Saradananda then escorted her to the Master's shrine. She knelt down before the image of Sri Ramakrishna and paid her respects. Calvé said to Saradananda: "Swamiji used to repeat a nice chant that starts with, 'Lead us from darkness to light.' Would you kindly repeat the whole chant if you know it? I am eager to hear it."

Immediately Saradananda chanted with his sweet, melodious voice: "*Asato ma sadgamaya. Tamaso ma jyotir gamaya. Mrityor ma amritam gamaya. Avir avir ma edhi.*" (Lead us from the unreal to the Real. Lead us from darkness to Light. Lead us from death to Immortality. Light us through and through.) When she was about to leave the shrine, Sharat Chakrabarty, a disciple of Swamiji, asked her to sing a song as an offering to the Master. Gladly, Calvé sang a song in French. Her magnificent voice charged the atmosphere with joy and beauty. After she left, Saradananda made a comment: "Look at the influence of Swamiji! Living in affluence and luxury, still she could not forget him."[64]

Miss Laura Glenn (later, Sister Devamata), an American devotee of Swamiji, had not been able to see Saradananda in America. However, when she moved to India, she met the swami at Udbodhan. She wrote in her memoirs about Saradananda:

I saw at once why he had called forth so much love wherever he went in the West. He seemed to possess an exalted gentleness, a graciousness and courtesy which made a direct appeal. His was the highest breeding of all — the breeding, not merely of manner or of culture, but of spirit. It was the outgrowth of Divine, rather than of human, relations....

His life was lived in a little room across the hall from the Udbodhan office. In the far inner corner of the room, beside a long open window opening on a central court, he sat cross-legged, with a small writing desk in front of him. Hour after hour he wrote articles for the magazine, a book of his own, official letters or letters to friends. He was always a generous correspondent. Visitors came and he would lay down his pen or pencil, only to pick it up again as soon as they were gone. When daylight dimmed and the lamps were brought, the little desk was pushed to one side, and pen, pencil and thought grew still....

I did not see Swami Saradananda during the closing years of his life; but letters from him and from other swamis of the Order kept me in touch with him and I could discern from what was written how gradually he was drawing away from the outer world into his inmost being. As the days went by, fewer and fewer were the hours given to earthly tasks; more and more were the hours devoted to super-earthly communion, until his life became unbroken meditation and he was gone. No disciple ever served his Master's cause with greater fervour and steadfastness than did he.[65]

Once Swami Pavitrananda talked to Saradananda about a conflict regarding work, "Swami, I work but I don't feel that I am working for the Master." Saradananda calmly asked, "Don't you think that it is not your work?" "Yes, I do. It is not my work. I am just following your order. I do whatever you have asked me to do." "That is enough," he replied.[66]

Swami Nikhilananda recalled:

I am active by nature. One day Swami Saradananda said to me: "It is good to be active but it depends on several factors. Your health must be good and you must be able to get along with fellow-workers. But suppose you have injured one of your limbs, then it would be difficult for you to work. Therefore I request you to cultivate the habit of reading. Even that is not enough. Suppose you become blind. Therefore it is good that you also practise meditation so that if you cannot read or work at least you can meditate."[67]

The secrets of Saradananda's great success in his active life were his humility and his respect for the human dignity of others. In 1918 Umananda wrote from Vrindaban to tell Saradananda that he was coming to Calcutta to see him. But the letter was somehow misplaced. When Umananda arrived, Saradananda reprimanded the younger monk for leaving the centre without previously writing to him; and although Umananda said that he had written, the swami did not believe him. Later, when Saradananda discovered the letter, he tearfully regretted his conduct. He approached Brahmananda, then president, with the request that he should be relieved of the secretaryship of the Order. Saradananda told him the whole story and lamented: "He was right; I scolded him without reason. I must send for him and beg his forgiveness." Brahmananda asked him not to go so far. But Saradananda could not rest until he actually apologized to the monk for his mistake and begged his forgiveness.[68]

Saradananda knew human nature very well. Those monks who were unbalanced or who had been rejected by other centres, would take shelter in Udbodhan with Holy Mother and Saradananda. The swami adopted three basic methods to make these monks work: He gave them freedom, he put his trust in them, and finally he poured his love and affection on them. He was *ajatashatru*, a person whose enemy has never been born. In 1919 the head of a centre had problems with his monastic workers and Saradananda wrote to him: "Each soul is eternally free, so each person desires to be free in every respect of his life. A real leader never obstructs others' freedom; rather, he teaches how one should enjoy freedom properly even in the field of action." In another letter he wrote: "The causes of friction and factions in the monastery are: anger, hatred, intolerance for others' mistakes, incompatibility between the mind and the speech [meaning, taking the course of untruth and duplicity], and above all, an effort to control the monks through tricks and politics instead of unselfish love."[69]

Once Saradananda advised a devotee: "If you want to work, depend on God and stand on your own feet. Don't depend on any human being — even myself. If nobody comes forward to help your work, resolve to do it alone, even at the cost of your body. When you have such courage, strength, and dependence on God, only then are you eligible to do work."[70]

Stories of Saradananda's loving heart are unending. Under his guidance the Ramakrishna Mission usually took the field promptly whenever there were famines, floods, epidemics, earthquakes, or other natural disasters. Although he could not personally go to the field of action, Saradananda's heart shed tears of blood at the suffering of the people. He prayed to the Master with heart and soul to mitigate their sufferings. He wrote in detail to Holy Mother, whom he looked upon as the Divine Mother Herself, and begged her to bless the people and alleviate their suffering. His outward bearing seemed stern and grave, but inside he was tender and full of compassion.

"Service to man is service to God." This message of Vivekananda was exemplified in Saradananda's life. He acted as the mother of the Order. Whenever Holy Mother or any of the direct disciples were sick, he was always present to look after their treatment. Once when Brahmananda was living in Belur Math he was suffering from an abscess and needed minor surgery. Saradananda accompanied Dr. Kanjilal (a devotee and disciple of Holy Mother) from Calcutta, and they left for the monastery by boat. In the middle of the Ganges, a heavy storm arose and the country boat began tossing violently. Saradananda was calmly smoking his hubble-bubble, but the panicky doctor could not control himself. Angrily he threw the hubble-bubble into the Ganges, and told Saradananda: "You are a strange man! The boat is about to sink, and you are enjoying your smoke!" The swami calmly said, "Is it wise to jump into the water before the boat sinks?" He then advised the boatman to put the sail down. Gradually the storm subsided and the boat safely reached the Belur ghat.[71] This incident indicates that the knower of Brahman conquers the fear of death, and that nothing in this world can perturb him.

As a Spiritual Teacher

Only a *jivanmukta* (one who is liberated-in-life) can be a real teacher. He is free, so he can teach others how to be free. In the language of the Gita, Saradananda was *sthita-prajna*, a man of steady wisdom. To those who knew him intimately, he seemed almost perfect with his deep spirituality, intellectual acumen, and above all, his wonderful, pure character. He was equally great in the graces of head, hand, and heart. This unique synthesis, apart from his intense spirituality, was the main quality that made him irresistibly attractive. Saradananda was the refuge of the sick, mentally disturbed, disobedient, rejected, dejected, and fallen. His love for them was not mere passive tolerance, but was silently active and positive in result. The secret was that, along with loving patience, his behaviour with all was actuated by his consciousness of the inner divinity of each person. Thus, like a good teacher, he helped forlorn people regain their self-confidence.

Beginning in 1920 with Holy Mother's passing away, Saradananda underwent several heavy bereavements. Before she left, Holy Mother said to one of her disciples, "My child, I am leaving Sharat behind." Saradananda recorded in his diary: "July 20, Tuesday — Holy Mother in peace and glory of *mahasamadhi* at 1:30 a.m. July 21, Wednesday — Procession to Belur Math via Baranagore at about 10:30 a.m., and the *yajna* [oblation in fire] at about 3:00 p.m. A heavy shower ended the ceremony at about dusk. August 1, Sunday — Special *puja* of the Ramakrishna Order at Belur and Calcutta Maths on account of the ascension of Holy Mother."[72]

In 1922 Swamis Brahmananda and Turiyananda passed away. Saradananda felt an emptiness; he became more indrawn. He told the monks: "Mother and Maharaj [Brahmananda] have left. Now you take the responsibility and get involved in the activities of the Order. I no longer have any enthusiasm or inclination to work."[73]

However, with Brahmananda's passing away, the position of president became open. According to the rules of the Order, an election was held and the monks cast their votes. There were two nominees: Swami Shivananda and Swami Saradananda. When the election was over, it was found that Saradananda had received ninety-five percent of the votes. When his name was announced as the president, he declined, saying: "Swamiji appointed me the secretary. I shall never give up that post." He himself proposed Swami Shivananda's name as the president of the Order, and remained as secretary until the end.[74] After Holy Mother and Brahmananda's passing away, Saradananda began to give initiation to spiritual aspirants, and administered sannyasa and brahmacharya vows to the monks.

Swami Aseshananda recalled:

Some days he would cut short his meditation in order to prepare himself to initiate disciples. Before giving the mantram, he always did some simple worship of Sri Ramakrishna and Holy Mother, using flowers, sandalpaste, leaves, and grass. He told us: "It is not easy to give initiation. You will have to work for your disciples. An illumined guru has to perform special japam for their inner growth and spiritual welfare. The relationship between the guru and disciple is established by God. The real guru has to take the burden of his disciples. He works for them through silent prayer and meditation. He has no rest until all of them have become illumined." It reminds me of the beautiful statement of Christ that a good shepherd has no rest until the last sheep has been brought to the fold.[75]

To Saradananda, work was worship. Once he said: "All through my life I worked, envisioning the faces of the Master and Swamiji. I had no time to pay any attention to others' opinions."[76] His health began to fail, partly from overwork and partly from taking on the bad karma of his disciples. Some monks asked him to refrain from giving initiation. The swami replied: "Do not say that. I consider myself blessed that people come to me to hear the Lord's name. It is not they but I who have to be thankful for this. I am fortunate indeed that I have been given the privilege of telling them of the Lord."[77]

The mark of a real teacher is that he is completely truthful. Whatever that person says, he does. Once when a young monk was going to Belur Math from Calcutta, Saradananda told him to inform Premananda that he would visit the monastery in the afternoon. A terrible thunderstorm arose in the afternoon. When it stopped, the swami left for Belur, crossing the Ganges by ferry and then walking a few miles. He arrived in the monastery after Premananda had finished his supper and was relaxing on the veranda. "Is there any emergency today that you have come to

Belur in this bad weather?" asked Premananda. "No," replied Saradananda, "but I sent word to you in the morning that I would be in the monastery, so I have come." Premananda remarked: "Like guru like disciple. If any word would come from the lips of the Master, he always kept it."[78]

Doubt is a horrible disease of the human mind. An illumined teacher always tries to remove the doubts of his disciples. In 1925 two young scientists came to Calcutta to visit Saradananda at Udbodhan. One of them asked, "Does God exist?" "Yes," replied the swami.

> Scientist: "What is the proof?"
> Saradananda: "The words of the rishis [seers of truth]. After experiencing God, they proclaimed that God exists."
> Scientist: "There is a possibility of their making mistakes."
> Saradananda: "Is it possible that all sages have made mistakes?"
> Scientist: "I won't believe without experiencing God myself."

"Very well," said the swami. "Is it possible that you will only believe after seeing everything yourself? Suppose you have never been in England. You will have to know about England from those who have visited it. Although you have not seen it, you can't deny the existence of England. Likewise, God exists; you will have to trust the judgement of those who have seen Him. After seeing God, Ramakrishna said to all: 'I have seen God. You can also see Him through spiritual disciplines and longing.' In this scientific age, the Master came to dispel the doubts of the people by demonstrating religion." The young scientists were convinced and accepted Saradananda's words.[79]

Once a disciple asked Saradananda: "X. instructs his disciples not to practise japam without taking a bath, etc. Are such observances compulsory?"

Saradananda: "The Master came to make religion easy. People were being crushed under the weight of rules and regulations. To repeat the Lord's name or to worship Him, no special time or place is necessary. In whatever condition one may be, one can take His name. The Master never gave too much importance to these external observances. As to means, adopt whichever suits you best. If you like God with form, that will also lead you to the goal. If you like God without form, well and good; stick to it and you will progress. If you doubt His very existence, then better put the question to Him thus: 'I do not know whether You exist or not, whether You are formless or have form. Do please grant that I may know Your real nature.'"[80]

Disciple: "Have any realized God through mere work?"

Saradananda: "Through selfless work the mind gets purified. And when the mind becomes pure, knowledge and devotion arise in it. Knowledge is the very nature of the Self, but being covered with ignorance, it is not manifest. The object of selfless work is to remove this covering. As a matter of fact, knowledge dawns as soon as the mind becomes pure. In the Mahabharata you have the story of the chaste woman who attained knowledge by serving her husband and by performing her other household duties. In the Gita also you find, 'By work alone King Janaka and others attained perfection' (3.20). Not one but many attained perfection through work, for the text adds 'and others.'"[81]

Disciple: "I am trying to follow all your instructions, but somehow I find that I am not quite at home in my spiritual practices. Sometimes they seem mechanical — as if there is no life in them."

Saradananda: "If you follow the same routine every day it is only natural that you should feel so sometimes. But then on those days when you like any particular portion of the sadhana, devote yourself to that and let the other parts go. In this way you may perhaps be neglecting particular practices for three or four days at a stretch. But that does not matter. When you renew these practices you will find delight in them.

"Before you meditate, think of the Master. If you do that you will see that whatever you do will yield good results. Sometimes think that he is in everything and he exists everywhere. That you are, as it were, immersed in him even as a pot is immersed in the ocean. Think thus: 'That Supreme State of the all-pervading Deity the sages realize for all time, like the sky extending as far as sight can go.' He knows everything about you. You cannot hide anything from Him. He knows even your inmost thoughts.

"Of course one is much benefitted by regular practice. If one practises regularly for some time every day, one gains strength and finds pleasure in spiritual practices."

Disciple: "I have read much about the Master. Through books I have been able to know much about his life. Yet when I think of his life I do not find joy in it. Why is it so?"

Saradananda: "To find joy in anything the brain and the heart must unite. Through mere intellectualism one does not get joy. Everything becomes lifeless. If what you have read about the Master appeals also to your heart, only then will you delight in thinking about his life. He will then seem to be living."[82]

Whenever there was an opportunity, young monks would ask questions of Saradananda either about their spiritual problems or about the Master's teachings. In January 1925, when Saradananda was visiting Varanasi, some monks asked him the following questions:

B.: "Swami, the Master has exhorted us to 'make the thought tally with speech.' What does it mean?"

Saradananda: "That you must be sincere, that your inner life should tally with the outer."

B.: "It is naturally so. Whatever we speak we think in our mind."

Saradananda: "Do you think it is so easy? We chant the name of the Lord very superficially. We say, 'O Lord, I am Your servant and You are my Master; I have renounced everything for You; I call You, Lord, please grant me Your vision.' And at the same time we are harbouring bad thoughts in the mind. It does not work. As you speak, so you must think. In other words, while you take the name of the Lord think of Him alone."

S.: "The Master used to say, 'Having the knowledge of nonduality your own, you can go wherever you like.' What does it mean?"

Saradananda: "Not 'go wherever you like,' but 'do whatever you like.' He meant evidently that after attaining Supreme Knowledge one cannot commit any evil deed. How can one who has realized God or attained knowledge through discrimination, renunciation, love, devotion, and purity, do mischief? Therefore, after attaining nondual knowledge whatever a person does, it must be good."[83]

K.: "Swami, we do not see God. How can we love Him without seeing Him? How can we love a Being who is unseen and whose very existence is doubtful?"

Saradananda: "Act according to the instructions of the guru. If you can strictly follow what the guru has prescribed for the realization of God, everything will be smooth at last. Meditation comes afterwards. If one fails to meditate, one should go on repeating the mantram very earnestly. (To B.) Do you follow what the guru has instructed you? Who practises even half of what the guru has instructed? If you practise, surely you will get the result. Do you know purascharana of the mantram? It means a mantram becomes conscious (kinetic) when you repeat it one hundred thousand times a day. The repetition of the mantram in a proper spirit even once purifies the mind. Instantly the mind fills with delight and becomes blissful."[84]

Disciple: "What is the meaning of our mantram?"

Saradananda: "'May God who is the creator, sustainer, and dissolver of the universe, remove my sorrows.' This is the significance of all mantras. Have faith in God; otherwise even thousands of explanations will be of no use. Pray to Him and love Him."[85]

Saradananda had experienced the truth, so his words were very convincing. Many monks and devotees would come to him to solve their spiritual as well as other problems. Swami Saradeshananda recalled:

Once there was a discussion in front of him about a popular religious teacher. This teacher used to have ecstatic moods but his character was very bad, scandalous. Many people were attracted to him at first, but later on some of them, after coming in closer contact with him and getting to know of his private life, began to circulate the true stories. One of our brother monks even then expressed his appreciation of the teacher's ecstatic moods, although he knew his character to be very bad. Swami Saradananda, hearing the monk's praise, began to scold him with strong words: "Do not think that only ecstatic moods indicate a very high state in religious life; pure character alone is the basis of religious life. Without pure character who can retain all these ecstatic moods? Ecstatic moods cannot endure without a pure, good character."

On another occasion I asked him the real meaning of God vision, or realization: Is it seeing something with the physical eyes externally or feeling something inside our inner self? He replied: "It is the realization, feeling something inside our inner self, but you know when we see something with our eyes or hear something with our ears, we become firmly convinced about its existence. But inner realization gives us an even greater conviction of the true eternal reality. That is realization — God vision."[86]

Last Years

Saradananda is a glowing example of a person who could keep his mind in God, or the Self, and at the same time his hands at work. A real yogi regards the Self as actionless even while being engaged in action. Activity belongs to the body, the senses, and the mind, and does not affect the unchanging Self. The Gita says, "Great is the man who controls the senses with his mind and engages them in selfless actions" (3.7).

Monks tend to go into seclusion for meditation, giving up action. To them Saradananda said: "Remove your doubt forever, my boys, and remember what I say today. Those who will attain the summum bonum here will also attain it there, and those who will not attain it here will never attain it there."[87] (By *here* and *there* the swami meant work and seclusion.) On another occasion, while in Puri, he told a monk who was not well but nonetheless was anxious to return to work in his centre: "Look, after doing such voluminous work in my life I have this knowledge that we do nothing; we are mere instruments. Everything happens according to the will of the Master. Previously I used to think that without me this particular work would suffer. During my absence who would do this work? Now I see for want of anybody, the Master's work will not stop."[88]

"In his dealings with us younger monks," writes Swami Aseshananda, "the swami's love and forgiveness were limitless. One day when I was with him at Puri, he told me he couldn't find the beads that he usually kept in a drawer. 'They belonged to the Holy Mother and I kept them after her mahasamadhi,' he said. 'They were strung on a golden thread. Probably somebody came and took them on account of the golden thread while we were away seeing Lord Jagannath at His temple.' I was concerned. I thought perhaps I had accidentally thrown the rosary into the sea along with the flowers after evening worship. I returned to the beach and searched for a long time but found nothing. The swami consoled me: 'One by one everything is going away. This is the will of the Mother. What can be done? Don't worry.'"[89]

As Saradananda grew older, he could no longer personally look after the health of the sick monks and devotees, but still he showed his concern and gave his love and sympathy to all. One hot summer day after lunch Saradananda left Udbodhan alone, which was unusual, so his attendant (Aseshananda) followed him. Saradananda tried to discourage him from following: He was going to visit Khokani, a Parsee devotee who was dying from advanced tuberculosis, and he was concerned about his attendant's health. Observing the attendant's earnestness, Saradananda allowed him to come along. They reached Ezra Street in Central Calcutta, where the devotee was living on the second floor of a house. Khokani was overjoyed seeing the swami, but he continually coughed. He was not careful about sanitary rules; he used his hands instead of a handkerchief when he coughed. Nevertheless, Saradananda sat on his bed and comforted him by putting his hand on his head and caressing it.

Khokani asked his brother to buy some fruits and sweets for Saradananda. When the fruits arrived, without washing his hands, Khokani peeled the fruits, sliced them, and then offered them to the swami on a plate. His attendant protested: "Khokani, the swami has just finished his meal. I don't think he will be able to take anything now." But when Khokani insisted, Saradananda took a few slices of fruits and sweets to fulfill the desire of a dying devotee. He then meditated a little and took leave. On the way back, the attendant said: "Swami, you should not have taken those fruits. I have heard that tuberculosis is very contagious. Your life is precious to all of us." Saradananda gently replied, quoting Sri Ramakrishna, "No harm will come if one accepts the food given with a loving heart."[90] Within a few days Khokani died.

Holy Mother used to visit Jayrambati often. Many times, Saradananda would go there to take care of the Mother and her relatives. Once she said to Swami Parameshwarananda, her attendant in Jayrambati: "My child, after I leave this body, many devotees of our Master will come here. You should all do something so that they are properly taken care of. It will hurt me to see them go elsewhere for food and shelter during my absence. It will be good if a temple is built and an accommodation for monks and devotees is arranged, where they will meditate and think of God with simple living and high devotion, away from the noise and cares of the world. That will please me immensely."[91] When Saradananda learned of Holy Mother's wish, he felt that his duty towards Holy Mother was not yet finished. Under his guidance, a temple was built on the spot where the Mother's body had been cremated in Belur Math; it was dedicated on 21 December 1921. Another temple was built on the spot where Holy Mother was born in Jayrambati, and it was dedicated on a grand scale on 19 April 1923. Saradananda was in a high spiritual mood because his task was done. With great joy he initiated many people and gave the vows of sannyasa and brahmacharya to some monks. (During Holy Mother's centenary in 1953, the front hall of the temple was extended and a marble statue of the Mother was installed on the altar in place of her oil portrait.)

After returning to Calcutta from Jayrambati, Saradananda became more absorbed within himself. Some of the entries of his diary indicate that he was having divine communion and various visions: "Dec. 12, 1923 — 1st day of communion. Jan. 4, 1924 — 2nd day of communion. Jan. 17, 1924 — 3rd vision of Divine Mother. Jan. 31, 1924 — communion poor. Feb. 8, 1924 — The circle of communion began again. Feb. 10, 1924 — Intense communion touching centre — massage. Repeated vision of the Divine Mother continues which culminated on Feb. 19. Feb. 19, 1924 — communion —'you in me.'"[92]

In 1924 Yogin-ma and Golap-ma passed away. They were devotees of the Master and close companions of Holy Mother. Grief for these dear ones deeply affected Saradananda, and physical illness made him too tired to carry out the duties of the Order. In November 1924, at the request of the monks and devotees, he left on a pilgrimage to Bhubaneswar, Puri, and Varanasi for several months. He wrote a letter to a monk: "Now I am almost retired from my work. In the future if I get any command from the Master to do something, I shall resume my work with zeal and I am sure that the Master will endow me with strength also. If not, then know that whatever I am supposed to do is over."[93]

Saradananda was extremely conscientious. Although he felt that his work was almost finished, he thought about how to guide the Ramakrishna Math and Mission so that the activities and the spiritual current of the Order might flow in the right direction. In 1926 he convened the first convention of the Ramakrishna Math and Mission in Belur Math, which was attended by many monks and devotees from all over the world. The convention began on 1 April 1926 and continued till 8 April. Saradananda was the chairman, and he gave two important and inspiring speeches: "Ramakrishna Mission: Its Past, Present, and Future" (1 April) and "The Ideas, Ideals, and Activities of the Ramakrishna Mission" (3 April). Both of these precious speeches were published in *Ramakrishna Math and Mission Convention 1926*.

Here is an excerpt from Saradananda's first lecture, which was also the welcoming address to the delegates:

It seems to be the invariable rule that every new movement should pass through the stages of opposition and indifference before its principles are accepted by society and humanity at large. And as human nature is the same everywhere, we find this rule displayed alike in the East and the West. The more radical the ideas of your reform movement, the more vehement will be the opposition. People will say the principles of the movement will ruin the very foundation of everything that is good and useful. But if the movement has real life in it and is based on the essential truths governing human nature, it will survive, grow, and win over the hearts of people despite the opposition. Outside opposition actually helps concentrate the energies of the movement and stimulates the expression of the fundamental truths on which it stands; so we cannot say the process of opposition is all bad, after all.

After a period the opposition wears away and gives place to indifference, when those who first opposed the movement begin to say that after all there is nothing so very new in it: "For have we not in such and such passages of our old histories and scriptures a mention of the principles which it preaches? This is sufficient proof that our forefathers knew these principles and carried them into practice long ago, so we need not think much of it." During this second stage the movement spreads unhindered far and wide and finds secure footing in due time through the recognition of its existence and utility by society.

At the end of the second stage, we find the movement accepted by public opinion; the ranks of its members swell rapidly with this social acceptance and recognition.

However, the third stage, complete public acceptance, is not to be regarded as the millennium. Security of position brings a relaxation of spirits and energy, and the sudden growth of extensity quickly lessens the intensity and unity of purpose that were found among the early promoters of the movement. In place of outside opposition we find the mushrooming of internal opposition due to the varied opinions of its members and later, in place of the former spirit of sacrifice for truth, a struggle to maintain the secure social position by compromising truth with half truths and clinging more to the appearance than to the spirit of things.

If the leaders of the movement are not watchful or neglect to find remedies to check these evils, you can well imagine the result. First and foremost, the unifying bond of love within the movement slackens from the pressure of selfish motives and the members, losing sight of the welfare and improvement of the movement as a whole, detach themselves into groups with a view to improving and making permanent these separate groups that are unrelated to the whole. This process of disintegration goes on dividing the work to pieces. In the course of time disobedience to superiors, vanity, indolence, and a whole host of other faults crop up within the work to ruin it forever....

Hold fast to God, for God contains the stored-up energy — the kundalini — behind every movement; judge yourself and others by God's effulgent light. The spirit of rededication will make the convention a success....

I welcome you with all my heart in the name of our Master, our illustrious leader, the Swami Vivekananda, and our late revered president, the best beloved of the Master, the Swami Brahmananda.[94]

Saradananda's speeches were considered to be the guidelines of the Ramakrishna Order. The by-product of the convention was the appointment of a Working Committee for the control and conduct of all the activities of the organization. The farsighted Saradananda realized that Sri Ramakrishna's direct disciples were passing away one after another, so the next generation should come forward to take responsibility. This Working Committee was evidently his last legacy to the Order. After that he did not take an active part in its operation.

The saying, "Absolute power corrupts absolutely," lost its meaning in the case of Swami Saradananda, the executive secretary of the Ramakrishna Math and Mission. On his last birthday, in 1927, Saradananda went to Belur Math, where the monks and devotees paid homage to him. When a devotee placed a beautiful garland around his neck, the swami smilingly said: "I am a doorkeeper of the Mother's house. You are decorating me with a garland? Does a doorkeeper deserve such an expensive garland?"[95] All laughed, and at the same time got a glimpse of his humility.

During his last years Saradananda was in poor health. He suffered from diabetes, rheumatism, and high blood pressure. In spite of these physical ailments, he spent long hours in japam and meditation. His doctor, D. P. Ghosh, suggested that he reduce his meditation time, otherwise it would damage his health. The swami remarked: "What am I to do in old age? Here sitting quietly I repeat the name of the Lord. Nobody will do anything. At least by seeing me they may be inclined to do something."[96]

When one of his attendants asked him what need there was for a man like him to meditate so long, thus impairing his health, he said: "The call has come. I am preparing for the great journey. Now meditation is the food of my life, and chanting His name, the source of my delight."[97]

In early August 1927 Saradananda went to Belur Math to attend a trustee meeting. He greeted the monks joyfully and had lunch with Shivananda. While leaving for Udbodhan he said to Shivananda, "Mahapurush, my body has deteriorated; it seems it will not last long."[98]

On 6 August 1927 Saradananda followed his regular routine of taking his morning bath, meditating three hours in his room, and then going to the shrine to prostrate before the pictures of the Master and Holy Mother. On that day he stayed in the shrine for half an hour; then came near the exit door and again returned to the shrine. He repeated this unusual behaviour a few times. Standing in front of Holy Mother's picture he silently prayed, perhaps requesting her to take her tired son back. When he finally came out of the shrine, Saradananda's face was glowing with joy and serenity.[99] It is said that during her last illness, Mother once remarked: "I am tired of this life. I shall now depart with Sharat in my arms and take him wherever I go."

After lunch Saradananda rested a little, and in the afternoon he answered his mail, dictating letters to his attendant and then signing them. The last sentence of his last letter was: "He who surrenders, the Master will definitely protect him, protect him, protect him."[100]

After vespers, Swamis Haripremananda and Aseshananda went to Saradananda's room and found him half reclining on his bed, struggling to get up but unable to do so. It was 8:30 p.m. He said to his attendants: "Don't tell anybody. Make no noise. I will go downstairs to meet the devotees soon."[101] But he felt dizzy and laid down on the bed. His forehead began to perspire. He asked his attendant to rub his head with a little medicated oil and prepare an ayurvedic medicine. Very soon three doctors came, examined him, and declared that the swami had had a stroke. One doctor suggested that an icepack be put on Saradananda's head. Three kinds of medication — allopathic, homeopathic, and ayurvedic — were tried with no visible results.

The sad news spread. Monks and devotees came from all over India to visit him. Saradananda retained consciousness throughout, but his speech was impaired. A few days later the swami could only smile in response to Dr. Ghosh's question, "Swami, do you want to drink tea?" Another day he used his left hand to drink sanctified water from a spoon. Thus the swami passed thirteen days.

Saradananda's condition was rapidly deteriorating and he had a temperature of 105 degrees. The doctors lost all hope and indicated that the final moment was imminent. Friday, 19 August 1927 was the birth anniversary of Sri Krishna. About 1:00 a.m. the monks began to chant "Hari Om Ramakrishna." At 2:34 a.m. Swami Saradananda, the great yogi and beloved disciple of Sri Ramakrishna, breathed his last. At that very moment in Belur Math, Shivananda heard the familiar and sweet voice of Saradananda, "Tarak-da, I am going to Kashi [Varanasi]."[102] At noon Saradananda's remains were taken from Calcutta to Belur Math and cremated there.

Life inspires life. Swami Saradananda led a pure, serene, dedicated, and harmonious life, a source of inspiration for future generations. Swami Nikhilananda wrote in his reminiscences: "Whenever I think of Swami Saradananda I remember the following verse of the Bhagavad Gita: 'Not the desirer of desires attains peace, but he into whom all desires enter as the waters enter the ocean, which is full to the brim and grounded in stillness' (2.70)."[103]

In his early days with Sri Ramakrishna, the young Sharat asked a blessing that he might see God in every being. The Master blessed him, saying, "Yes, you will attain it." The following incident indicates how that blessing was fulfilled towards the end of his life: "One of the devotees who was nurtured by Swami Saradananda's loving care one day remarked, 'Swami, why do you love us so much?' Swami Saradananda did not say anything. After a few days when that devotee came to Udbodhan, the swami said: 'A few days ago I went to Belur Math and prostrated before Sri Ramakrishna. The Master appeared before me and said, "You love all because you find me in all." That is the answer I would give today.'"[104]

Courtesy: Vedanta Society of Northern California

SWAMI TURIYANANDA: SHANTI ASHRAMA, C.1901

9

ॐ

SWAMI TURIYANANDA

One morning before daybreak in North Calcutta, a teenage boy was bathing in the Ganges when he saw something floating near him. Some people on the shore saw it too, and shouted: "Crocodile! Crocodile! Come out quickly!" The boy immediately rushed towards the shore; but he stopped while still standing in the knee-deep water and thought to himself: "What are you doing? You repeat day and night, 'Soham! Soham!' [I am He! I am He!] And now all of a sudden you forget your ideal and think that you are the body! Shame on you!"[1] He immediately went back into the deep water and continued his bathing. Fortunately, the crocodile had left.

This fearless boy was Harinath Chattopadhya, who would grow up to become Swami Turiyananda. He was born on 3 January 1863, in North Calcutta. Harinath's father, Chandranath Chattopadhya, was an ortho-dox brahmin who worked for a British firm in Calcutta. Chandranath was known for his piety, courage, and power to foretell the future. He had three sons and three daughters; Harinath was the youngest child. When Harinath was three years old, his mother, Prasannamayi, died from a rabid jackal's bite while protecting him. As a result, he was brought up by his sister-in-law. His father died when he was twelve. While Harinath was crying bitterly just before his father's death, his sister asked Chandranath to say some words of consolation to him. "What is there to say?" the dying man replied. "Hari belongs to the world and the world belongs to Hari."[2] This prophecy became true.

357

From his very boyhood, Harinath was drawn to the brahmin ideals of orthodoxy and asceticism. After he was initiated into the Gayatri mantram during his sacred thread ceremony, he would bathe three times a day, practise japam and meditation regularly, sleep on the floor, and eat simple vegetarian food. He used to wrestle in a gymnasium and could do 100 push-ups and 500 knee-bends at a stretch. Thus he trained his body so that it could bear severe austerity in the future. Moreover, he strictly practised continence and told his friends that he would never marry.

Harinath began his education in the Kambuliatola Bengali School, where he studied Bengali and Sanskrit literature. Then he went to the General Assembly, a school run by Christian missionaries. Although he was quite orthodox in many respects, he was without sectarian narrowness. He always attended the classes on the Bible, which the other Hindu boys avoided. Any kind of religious book fascinated him. He was also interested in the study of the Upanishads, and he committed to memory the Chandi, Gita, *Vivekachudamani*, and many mystical couplets of Tulasidas. Sometimes in the evening, sitting on the bank of the Ganges, he would recite the scriptures and cry for God.

In his teenage years, Harinath began to feel intense renunciation and a desire to avoid worldly life. He and his friend Gangadhar, who later became Swami Akhandananda, went to the Sarvamangala Temple on Chitpore Road to visit a holy man who had occult powers. People flocked to him to receive his blessings so that their diseases would be cured, or to have their futures foretold. Harinath started to visit him every evening. One day the holy man asked him, "What do you want?" "I want to practise spiritual disciplines and to realize God," replied Harinath. The holy man was highly pleased. He said: "Wonderful! Surely you will succeed, my boy. But the time has not yet come. You continue your sadhana at home."[3] Around that time, some people came to Harinath with a proposal of marriage — but they never visited him again after hearing his fiery words of renunciation.

In the Company of Sri Ramakrishna

Harinath met Sri Ramakrishna for the first time at Dinanath Basu's house in Baghbazar, Calcutta. He was then thirteen or fourteen years old. Harinath watched as Hriday helped Ramakrishna get down from a horse carriage; the Master was in ecstasy. Later, Harinath wrote about this first impression: "The Master appeared very thin. He had a shirt on, and his cloth was securely tied around his waist. One of his feet was on the step of the carriage, and the other was inside. He was in a semiconscious state. When he got down, what a wonderful sight! There was an indescribable radiance over his face. I thought: 'I have heard from the scriptures about the great sage Shukadeva. Is he the same Shukadeva?'"[4] Then Ramakrishna was taken to the second floor of Dinanath Basu's house and Harinath followed him. Regaining a little consciousness of the outer world, the Master saw a portrait of Mother Kali on the wall. He bowed down to Her and then thrilled the audience by singing a song describing the oneness of Krishna and Kali.

This first meeting with the God-intoxicated saint left a deep impression on Harinath's mind. As he was inclined to Shankara's nondualistic philosophy and a life of renunciation, austerity, and continence, he did not feel that it was necessary for him to become a disciple of Sri Ramakrishna, who was a devotee of the Divine Mother. However, after two or three years (probably in 1880) Harinath went to Dakshineswar and visited the Master again. Observing some auspicious signs in him, the Master asked him to come on weekdays, when there would not be many people present.

Gradually, Harinath became familiar with Ramakrishna and began to ask all sorts of personal questions. "Sir," he asked one day, "how can one become free from lust completely?" Sri Ramakrishna replied: "Why should it go, my boy? Give it a turn in another direction. What is lust? It is the desire to get. So desire to get God and strengthen this desire greatly."[5] Sri Ramakrishna's way of teaching was simple, natural, and very effective. He did not ask his disciples to mortify themselves. He said, "The more you go towards the east, the farther you will be away from the west." The more you increase your love for God, the more your lust, anger, and jealousy will decrease.

Another day, Harinath said to Sri Ramakrishna that he was not at all interested in women; in fact, he could not bear them. To this the Master replied: "You talk like a fool! Looking down upon women! Why? They are the manifestations of the Divine Mother. Bow down to them with respect. That is the only way to escape from their snares."[6] These fiery words permanently changed Harinath's attitude towards women.

Young Harinath received specific instructions on meditation and other spiritual disciplines from the Master. "Sir," he asked one day, "how does one become aware of the dawn of knowledge?" Sri Ramakrishna replied: "A man does not jump about when he gets illumination. Outwardly he remains as he was; but his entire perspective of the world is changed. The touch of the philosopher's stone converts a steel sword into gold. It retains its former shape, but it can no longer kill — it has become soft."[7]

Like a true Vedantin, Harinath plunged into the study of Vedanta scriptures and discussions; as a result, he could not visit Ramakrishna for some time. Such absences did not go unnoticed. When Harinath's friends visited Dakshineswar, the Master learned from them that he was absorbed in the study of Vedanta day and night. When Harinath went to Dakshineswar a few days later, the Master said: "Hello, I hear that nowadays you are studying and discussing Vedanta philosophy. That is good, of course. But tell me, what is the teaching of Vedanta? Is it not that Brahman alone is real and the world unreal? Isn't that its substance? Or does it say something else? Then why don't you give up the unreal and cling to the real?"[8] This was a turning point in Harinath's life. He realized that mere study and discussion would have no effect until he directly experienced the truth that "Brahman alone is real and the world unreal."

One day, the Master said to Harinath: "What is there in the scriptures? They are like sheets of paper with a shopping list on them. The list is useful only to check off the items once purchased. When you have done that, the list is thrown away. So you should check your knowledge, your devotion, and consult the scriptures to see whether they agree. It is said, 'When you have knowledge of the Absolute, the scriptures are worth only a straw.'"[9] A few days later, Sri Ramakrishna went to Balaram's house at Calcutta and sent for Harinath. The Master greeted him cordially and continued his talk to the devotees: "Nothing can be achieved — neither knowledge, nor devotion, nor vision — without God's grace. Well, is it an easy matter to realize that lust and gold are unreal and to have the firm conviction that the world is eternally nonexistent? Is it possible without His compassion? Can a man have that conviction through his own effort? A man is after all a tiny creature, with very limited powers. What an infinitesimal part of truth can he grasp by himself!"[10] While talking about God's grace, the Master went into ecstasy.

Harinath felt as if these words had been directed to him, for he had been straining every nerve to attain illumination by his own efforts. After a short while, the Master regained his normal consciousness and began to sing a song based on the *Uttara Rama Charitam*, where Hanuman tells the sons of Rama:

> O Kusa and Lava, why are you so proud?
> If I had not let myself be captured,
> Could you have captured me?

While Ramakrishna sang, tears rolled down his face, literally wetting the ground. Harinath later remarked: "I was deeply moved. That very day the Master deeply imprinted on my mind the fact that one cannot attain God through self-effort, by performing sadhana. Only if God reveals Himself is it possible to attain Him."[11]

Once Harinath said to the Master that his goal was to attain nirvana (liberation) in this very life. For this the Master reproached him: "Those who seek nirvana are selfish and small-minded. They are full of fear. They are like those parcheesi players who are always eager to reach home. An amateur player, once he sends his piece home, doesn't like to bring it out again. Such players are unskilled. But an adept player is never afraid of coming out again, if by doing so he gets the opportunity to capture an opponent. Then he rolls the right number and returns home once more. It seems that whenever he rolls the dice, the right number comes up for him. So do not fear. Play without any fear." Harinath asked with wonder, "Does it actually happen?" "Of course it happens," replied the Master. "By Mother's grace everything takes place."[12]

Sri Ramakrishna's life was his message. Harinath later recalled his days with the Master:

Ah, those days at Dakshineswar were like heaven itself! From morning till one o'clock in the afternoon everyone would be busy picking flowers and making other preparations for worship until the poor were fed. In the meantime Sri Ramakrishna would discuss spiritual subjects, and the devotees would listen to him with rapt attention. Even his fun and jokes were related to God. There was no other topic. Everything culminated in his samadhi [transcendental state of consciousness]. After lunch, Sri Ramakrishna would rest for a short period and again would speak on spiritual matters. At vesper time he would go to the temple of Mother Kali and fan Her a little. He would become God-intoxicated there and would return to his room reeling in a state of ecstasy. He used to ask those of us who were practising spiritual disciplines under his guidance, "Tell me, do you feel divine inebriation when you meditate in the mornings and evenings?" At night Sri Ramakrishna slept very little. He used to get up and wake those who were sleeping in his room, saying: "Don't sleep too much! Wake up and meditate!" Again he would lie down a short while, and then rise before dawn and chant the name of the Lord in his inimitable sweet voice. The disciples would sit and meditate in their own way. Now and then the Master would go to them and correct their posture.

An hour of congregational singing in the company of the Master would fill us with such exuberant joy that we would feel transported, as it were, into an ethereal region. But now, even meditation fails to evoke that celestial bliss, or even a semblance of it. That bliss would stay with us continuously for a week. We used to feel intoxicated, though we did not know why or how. Who would believe it? It is difficult to convince anyone. Yet I must speak out. The ordinary man seeks nirvana because he has suffered. But he does not know the tremendous joy in divine communion.[13]

To live with Sri Ramakrishna was a great education. He taught his disciples how to attain perfection in samadhi as well as in service. Harinath later recalled:

One day at Dakshineswar the Master said to me: "Go to the Panchavati. Some devotees had a picnic there. See if they have left anything behind. If you find anything, bring it here." I went and found an umbrella in one place, a knife in another place, and some other articles. I gathered them up and took them to the Master. The knife had been borrowed from him. I was just placing it on the shelf when he said: "Where are you putting it? No, not there. Put it underneath this small bedstead. That is where it belongs. You must put everything in its proper place. Suppose I need the knife during the night. If you put it anywhere you please, I will have to go around the room in the dark, stretching out my arms in search of it, wondering where you put it. Is such service a service? No! You do things as you like and thereby only cause trouble. If you want to serve properly, you should completely forget yourself."[14]

As Sri Ramakrishna tested his disciples, so the disciples verified the genuineness of their guru. One day Harinath arrived at Dakshineswar when the Master was having his dinner. He saw that a number of bowls containing various cooked items were placed before him. Harinath thought that this kind of luxurious eating was unbecoming to a holy man. The Master said at once: "Well, the tendency of my mind is always towards the Infinite. It is by such rajasic devices that I hold it down to the lower planes. Otherwise I could not talk with you."[15] Harinath was dumbfounded. Another time, at Balaram's house, Sri Ramakrishna was illustrating his teachings with some very apt tales. Harinath was surprised at the spontaneity with which these stories cropped up in his talk, and he asked, "Sir, do you prepare your similes before you go out?" The Master replied: "No. Mother is always present. Wherever I am, Mother supplies me with ideas."[16]

After attaining illumination, Sri Ramakrishna waited for his disciples nearly twenty-five years. During the last few years of his life, when his young disciples joined him, the Master poured all his spiritual treasures into them and bound them with love. He hastened to train his disciples so that they could carry his message to the world. Once he said to Harinath: "I want to see you quite often, for I know you are dear to the Lord. Otherwise why should I spend my time on you? You can't give me anything worth even a cent; and when I go to your house, you can't even spread a torn mat for me to sit on. Yet I love you so much. Don't forget to come here, because here you will get everything that is needed for your spiritual life. If you can find elsewhere opportunities for God-realization, you may go there. What I want is that you should realize God — that you should transcend the misery of the world and enjoy divine bliss; that you should attain Him in this life. The Divine Mother tells me if you only come here, you will realize God without any effort. That is why I ask you to see me so often." Saying these words, Sri Ramakrishna was overcome with emotion and began to shed tears.[17]

Since he was visiting Dakshineswar frequently, Harinath came to know other young disciples of the Master. He was very close to Narendra. Their approaches to spiritual life were by no means identical, yet Narendra appreciated Harinath's renunciation, scriptural knowledge, and brahminical orthodoxy. One day both were walking to Calcutta from Dakshineswar. On the way, Narendra said to Harinath, "Tell me something." "What shall I tell you?" replied Harinath. Then Harinath quoted a verse from Shiva Mahimnah Stotram: "If the goddess of learning were to write eternally, having the largest branch of the celestial tree for Her pen, the whole earth for Her paper, the blue mountain for Her inkpot, and the ocean for Her ink, even then, O Lord, Thy attributes could not be fully described." Then Narendra shared his understanding of Sri Ramakrishna, "He is LOVE personified."[18] Harinath thus discovered that they had identical views about the Master.

On 24 May 1884 Harinath again visited Sri Ramakrishna at Dakshineswar. He said to the Master, "Well, why does it take many people such a long time to realize God?"

Master: "The truth is that a man doesn't feel restless for God unless he is finished with his enjoyments and duties."

Harinath: "Why is there so much suffering in the world?"

Master: "This world is the *lila* [divine play] of God. It is like a game. In this game there are joy and sorrow, virtue and vice, knowledge and ignorance, good and evil. The game cannot continue if sin and suffering are altogether eliminated from creation. In the game of hide-and-seek one must touch the 'granny' in order to be free. But the 'granny' is never pleased if she is touched at the very outset. It is God's wish that the play should continue for some time."

Harinath: "But this play of God is our death."

Master (*smiling*): "Please tell me who *you* are. God alone has become all this — maya, the universe, living beings, and the twenty-four cosmic principles. 'As the snake I bite, and as the charmer I cure.' It is God Himself who has become both vidya and avidya. He remains deluded by the maya of avidya, ignorance. Again, with the help of the guru, He is cured by the maya of vidya, Knowledge."[19]

On 14 July 1885 Harinath met Sri Ramakrishna at Balaram's house in Calcutta. The Master said to him: "You see, in one form He is the Absolute and in another He is the Relative. What does Vedanta teach? Brahman alone is real and the world is illusory. Isn't that so? But as long as God keeps the 'ego of a devotee' in a man, the Relative is also real. When He completely effaces the ego, then what *is* remains. That cannot be described by the tongue. . . . As long as a man analyses with the mind, he cannot reach the Absolute. Atman cannot be realized through this mind; Atman is realized through Atman alone. Pure mind, Pure Buddhi, Pure Atman — all these are one and the same.

"Just think how many things you need to perceive an object. You need eyes; you need light; you need mind. You cannot perceive the object if you leave out any one of these three. As long as the mind functions, how can you say that the universe and the 'I' do not exist? When the mind is annihilated, when it stops deliberating pro and con, then one goes into samadhi, one attains the knowledge of Brahman."[20] Thus the Master taught Harinath the intricate aspects of Vedanta.

His six years' association with Sri Ramakrishna convinced Harinath that the Master was an incarnation of God. Hence, when the Master was suffering from cancer, he could not believe that disease would really overcome him. Harinath took it as a part of the Master's play, because he had heard from him many times, "Let the body and the affliction take care of themselves; O my mind, you dwell in bliss."

One day at Cossipore Harinath asked, "Sir, how are you?" The Master replied: "Oh, I am in great pain. I cannot eat anything, and there is an unbearable burning in my throat." Harinath knew that a knower of Brahman is beyond the pairs of opposites, pleasure and pain. He understood that the Master was testing him, so he said to him humbly, "Sir, whatever you may say, I see you as an infinite ocean of bliss." At this, Sri Ramakrishna said with a smile, "This rascal has found me out."[21]

Years of Wandering and Austerity

Sri Ramakrishna passed away at the Cossipore garden house on 16 August 1886. The disciples then moved to Baranagore and founded the Ramakrishna Monastery there. In the early part of 1887, they took their monastic vows under the leadership of Swami Vivekananda. Harinath became Swami Turiyananda. Then Swamiji read and explained to his brother disciples two chapters from the Brihadaranyaka Upanishad (Antaryami Brahman 3.7 and Maitreyi Brahman 4.5), where renunciation and the greatest truths of Vedanta are discussed. They all plunged into the quest for the Supreme without concern for hardship.

Everyone without exception, sometime or other, passes through a "dark night" in spiritual life. In this period, the spiritual aspirant encounters subtle, unseen enemies, such as lust, anger, greed, delusion, pride, and jealousy. It is outright warfare. After joining the monastery, Turiyananda passed through such a dry spell. He described it later on: "When I was young and living in the Baranagore Math, once I had a very despondent mood. I could not meditate. I was then pacing back and forth on the roof. Then suddenly there was a rift in the cloud, and out came the full moon in all its majesty. All darkness was dispelled, and the whole landscape was flooded with light. As soon as I saw that I thought: See, the moon was there all the time but I could not see her. So the Atman is also ever present, shining in its own glory, but I did not see it. The cloud of ignorance stood between the Atman and my intellect overshadowing my mind. And at once I felt strong again, my doubts all gone."[22]

There are some monks who feel bound even in a monastery, so they travel from place to place. In 1889 Turiyananda left the Baranagore Monastery and went to Rishikesh, where the ascetics live in the foothills of the Himalayas. In the summer of 1890, he and Swami Saradananda went to Gangotri, the source of the Ganges; from there they visited Kedarnath, in the Himalayas, the famous place sacred to Lord Shiva. It was a difficult journey. They lost their way in a jungle and spent three days without food.

Turiyananda then decided to practise sadhana alone at Rajpur, on the Mussoorie Hill of Dehra Dun. Here a police officer thought that Turiyananda was an anarchist posing as a holy man, and asked him all sorts of questions. The swami replied fearlessly, showing his displeasure. At this the police officer said: "How dare you talk that way! Are you not afraid of the police?" Turiyananda immediately burst out: "I afraid! I am not frightened even of Yama, the god of death, what to speak of the police?"[23]

The officer then realized that the swami was a genuine monk, and later became his devotee.

In Rajpur, Turiyananda met Vivekananda and some other brother disciples; then they all went to Rishikesh. In Rishikesh Swamiji became very sick. Turiyananda nursed him and prayed to the Master for his life. Then they went to Meerut and stayed six weeks until Swamiji recovered fully. When Swamiji left for Delhi alone, Turiyananda and Brahmananda made a pilgrimage to Jwalamukhi in the Kangra valley. Jwalamukhi is one of the fifty-one holy shrines of the Divine Mother, although it does not have any image of the goddess. Afterwards they visited Gopinathpur, Baijnath, Pathankot, Multan, Gujranwala, Montgomery, and other places. Brahmananda then became sick, so they went to Bombay via Karachi by steamer.

In Bombay they again met Vivekananda, who was then getting ready to go to America to represent Hinduism at the Parliament of Religions in Chicago. Every evening many people would come to Swamiji to listen to his spiritual discourses. However, one evening Swamiji was not well, so he asked Turiyananda to speak to the devotees. When the talk was over, Swamiji said to Turiyananda: "Why did you talk to these householders about fiery renunciation? You may be a monk, but they have families. You ought to have told them something that would be useful to them. They will be terrified to hear such things, and their minds will be disturbed." Turiyananda apologized, saying, "I thought that you were listening, so I spoke about something inspiring."[24] He then realized that one should keep one's audience in mind before one speaks.

From Bombay, Turiyananda and Brahmananda went to Mount Abu, Pushkar, Jaipur, and Vrindaban. In Vrindaban they practised severe austerities for six months. According to Indian custom, a monk begs for his food from door to door. Turiyananda had to beg from nearly thirty houses to get one meal. One day, he thought: "What am I doing? I am a vagabond. Everybody is working, producing something, whereas I am doing nothing." He was hungry and exhausted, and fell asleep under a tree in the Keshi ghat of Vrindaban. There he had a vision: He saw himself outside of his body, and he was looking at himself while he slept. He saw his body expanding and expanding, until there was no end to it. The body became so large that it covered the entire world. Then he addressed himself: "Oh, you are not a vagabond. You are one with the universe. You are the all-pervading Atman." So thinking, he jumped up and felt very happy. His despondency was at an end.[25]

Once Turiyananda said: "Though I travelled much, I also studied much all along. At Vrindaban I studied a great deal of devotional scriptures. It is not good to wander much if you do not at the same time continue your spiritual effort."[26]

Towards the end of 1893, Turiyananda and Brahmananda heard about Swamiji's success in America. In 1894 they left Vrindaban to visit Lucknow and Ayodhya, and in 1895 they returned to the monastery, which had been moved to Alambazar. They received many inspiring letters that Swamiji wrote from America, asking his brother disciples to organize the Ramakrishna Order. He suggested that Turiyananda give classes on the scriptures to the monastics in the mornings and evenings, which he agreed to do. In 1896 Turiyananda took the responsibility of performing worship when Ramakrishnananda was sick. But Turiyananda's natural trend of mind was always pulling him back to a life of austerity and wandering; after a stay of little more than a year, he left the monastery.

Turiyananda first went to Allahabad, the confluence of the Ganges and Jamuna. Then he travelled towards Narmada, a favorite place of hermits, on foot via Chitrakut, Rewa, and Jabbalpur. He carried no money, lived on alms, and slept wherever he could. Later Turiyananda said: "One night in Ujjain, I was sleeping under a tree. A storm came, and suddenly someone touched me. I got up and at once a branch fell on the spot where I had slept."[27] Sri Ramakrishna had saved his life. He then visited the holy places in West India. He found that the mountain region of Girnar had an atmosphere conducive to meditation, so he settled down there in a cave.

After some months Turiyananda travelled to Uttarkashi via Delhi, Hardwar, and Rishikesh. In this Himalayan region, he became ill. Day by day his sickness grew worse. Finally he thought it wise to consult a doctor and started towards a village to find one. On the way he suddenly remembered a verse that is applicable to a holy man if he falls ill: "For the sick monk, the medicine is the Ganges water and Lord Narayana is the doctor." He felt ashamed to seek an ordinary doctor; it was as if he had almost lost faith in God. Instead of going to the doctor, he went to the riverside. He sipped a little Ganges water, repeated the Lord's name, and returned to the cottage. Sure enough, soon after that he was cured.

Turiyananda later recalled: "I lived happily in the Garhwal Hills, totally forgot the existence of the world, and aimed only at God-realization.... Oh, those days are coming to my mind. While I lived at Srinagar ghat, I used to rise very early and bathe. Then I would sit in meditation and afterwards read. At eleven, I would rise and procure some food in an hour. Then I would again begin meditation and japam. And thus I spent every day. It was there that I committed eight Upanishads to memory. I would meditate on every verse I read, and what an indescribable joy it was! I used to read the commentary of Shankara and the gloss of Jnanananda. And much further light used to come through meditation."[28]

Vedanta says that a knower of Brahman becomes fearless. Fear originates from duality. Because an illumined soul experiences the nondual Brahman, he can never fear anyone. Once while in the Himalayan region in Tihiri-Garhwal, Turiyananda was living in a thatched hut that had a broken door. One night he heard the villagers cry, "Tiger! Tiger!" He immediately put some bricks behind the door to protect himself. Just then he remembered a passage from the Taittiriya Upanishad that declares that even at the command of Brahman the god of death does his duty like a slave. His awareness of the Atman awakened, and defeated the body idea. He kicked the piles of brick away from the entrance, and sat for meditation.[29] Fortunately, the tiger did not show up.

It is very helpful for spiritual aspirants to hear about the struggles and experiences of the mystics directly from them. Some mystics are reticent; fortunately, Turiyananda was very frank about himself. He said: "Formerly my nerves were very fine, and I had great powers of explaining things. Whenever anyone asked me a question, I could see everything from its very origin to its outer expression — I could see from what motive he spoke and why. And there was a flood of light in a single word of mine.

"I used to observe absolute silence during the Navaratri. I would feel a sort of intoxication and the mind would be one-pointed. I have done what one being born a man should do. My aim was to make my life pure. I used to read a great deal, eight or nine hours daily. I read many Puranas and then Vedanta, and my mind finally settled on Vedanta."[30]

Towards the latter part of 1896, Turiyananda returned to Calcutta. Not long after, Vivekananda returned from the West, and founded the Ramakrishna Mission on 1 May 1897. In 1898 a plot of land was purchased at Belur on the bank of the Ganges for the headquarters of the Ramakrishna Order. After the inauguration of the monastery, Swamiji made some basic rules for the monks. One rule was that every monk was supposed to come to the shrine for meditation at 4:00 a.m.

One morning Turiyananda was ill and could not attend the meditation. Later, he told Swamiji that he was feverish and had a cold. Swamiji scolded him: "Shame! Shame! Still you are concerned about your body!" Turiyananda was one of the most austere monks amongst the disciples of the Master. He kept quiet. Then Vivekananda calmly explained: "Do you know why I scold you all? You are the children of Sri Ramakrishna. People will learn by observing your lives. It hurts me when I see in you anything short of the ideal. If they find any laxity in you, they will become all the more lax themselves. As the Master used to say, 'If I do sixteen parts, you will do one-sixteenth.' Similarly if you do one-sixteenth, they will do one-sixteenth of the one-sixteenth. If you do not do that one part even, where will they stand?"[31]

Turiyananda travelled to various places in India with Vivekananda. Once, in Darjeeling, Swamiji said to Turiyananda: "Brother Hari, I have made a new path and opened it to all. Up till now it was thought that liberation could be attained only by meditation, repetition of God's names, scriptural discussion and so forth. Now young men and women will attain liberation by doing the Lord's work."[32]

However, the path of action is not for everybody: Turiyananda wanted to pass his days in spiritual disciplines. But Vivekananda intervened: "Brother, can't you see I have been laying down my life, inch by inch, in fulfilling the mission of the Master, till I am on the verge of death? Can you merely stand looking on and not come to my help by relieving me of a part of my great burden?"[33] Turiyananda could not refuse their leader's entreaties.

In America

In June 1899 Turiyananda left for England and America with Vivekananda and his Irish disciple, Sister Nivedita. On the boat to England, Turiyananda asked Nivedita to teach him Western customs. She explained with an illustration. Picking up a knife, she held the sharp edge in her hand and gave the handle to Turiyananda, saying, "Swami, whenever you give something to someone, always take the inconvenient and unpleasant side yourself, and give the convenient and pleasant side to the other."[34]

After visiting England, the two swamis left for America on 16 August 1899. Soon after their arrival in New York, they went to Ridgely Manor, the Leggett family's country home, where they rested for a few weeks. Then one day Vivekananda told Turiyananda: "Brother, I don't have any money. I am going to San Francisco. Now you find a means of supporting yourself." This was a shock to Turiyananda, as he was fresh from India. Swamiji told him: "Don't be frightened when I say you have to conduct classes and lectures. Whatever you say will do good to the people. Show them what spirituality is."[35]

Turiyananda moved to Mrs. Wheeler's residence at Montclair in New Jersey, forty miles from New York City, where there was a Vedanta

Society led by Abhedananda. Mrs. Wheeler was a student of Swami Saradananda and had a considerable spiritual background. Her home was open to the disciples of Sri Ramakrishna, and there the swami got a closer view of American family life. Mr. Wheeler was a Christian Scientist, but he was sympathetic towards Vedanta. The swami began to give classes at Montclair, and conducted services in New York on Saturdays and Sundays, when Abhedananda was not in the city. The students of the New York Vedanta Society accepted Turiyananda with love because of his simple, meditative nature.

Gurudas (later, Swami Atulananda), a Western student of Turiyananda, wrote, "He talked with fire and enthusiasm, and he would lose himself entirely in his subject, forgetting everything else for the time being." Turiyananda was an illumined monk — full of purity and renunciation. He was a constant source of inspiration to the students. One day while walking on the street in New York, he shouted to Gurudas: "Be a lion! Be a lion! Break the cage and be free!"[36]

Turiyananda carried on the Vedanta work in New York for a year; during that time Vivekananda preached in California. Turiyananda startled the sophisticated Western audience with the bold, uncompromising message of Vedanta: "Brahman alone is real, everything else is unreal; the human soul is that Brahman. We are bound by the delusion of ignorance. Tear away the delusion and be free. All power is within you, for you are the Atman. Assert your divine nature."[37]

After the lecture, a timid young woman told Turiyananda that she could not understand how the soul could be God and the world unreal. "It took me many years to realize this," replied the swami, "but once it is realized the work is done." Then the lady began to speak in praise of Christianity as being so much easier to grasp. "Yes," the swami admitted, "Vedanta is not an easy, comfortable religion. Truth is never cheap. So long as we are satisfied with glass beads we don't search for diamonds. It is hard work to delve into the earth, remove the stones and rocks, and go to great depths to find the precious stone. Vedanta is the jewel among religions."[38]

Students of the New York Vedanta Society found that Turiyananda was an inexhaustible mine of spiritual wisdom. While walking, eating, or sitting, his spiritual conversation flowed like a perennial spring. Once he was asked: "Swami, how is it possible for you to always speak of holy subjects? Don't you ever get exhausted?" Turiyananda replied: "You see, I have lived this life from my youth; it has become part and parcel of me. And Divine Mother keeps the supply filled up. Her store can never be exhausted. Whatever goes out, She at once fills up again."[39]

Turiyananda was a living example of Vedanta. Sometimes the students would try to find ways to give the swami a break from his rigid routine. One evening Gurudas said: "Swami, there is a fine concert tonight. It is an oratorio and you will like it. You have never heard our Western music. Let us go." "But why should you care for those things?" the swami remarked. "You have had enough of that now. Let us stay here and read something nice and have good talk. These amusements we must give up now if we want Mother."[40] He had no curiosity for new things or any desire for sightseeing. He was perfectly happy and contented within himself.

Turiyananda never hesitated to correct the shortcomings of his students in a bold and straightforward way, for which he was sometimes very much misunderstood. Once, observing their discontent, the swami said: "Yes, you people in the West always try to cover up and hide your mistakes. But how can the wound be treated unless the bandages are removed? You hide your real character behind a smooth and polite exterior, but the sore festers in the heart. The guru is the physician, and once the disease is diagnosed he must not fear to apply the lancet, if necessary. Sometimes a deep clean incision is the only remedy. You are so sensitive, always afraid of being scolded or exposed. When I flatter a little, you say, 'Swami is so wonderful,' but when I utter a harsh word you run away."[41]

It is true that Eastern and Western upbringing and culture are different, so it is natural that misunderstandings sometimes develop between the two. But Turiyananda was a great yogi. When the students complained that he did not understand them, the swami replied: "I know you better than you know yourself, because I can look deep into your mind. What is hidden to yourself, is revealed to me. In time you will realize that what I tell you is true."[42]

Women have consistently played a vital role in Western society's religion and social activities. Mrs. Wheeler introduced Turiyananda to various distinguished people and organizations. She induced the swami to accept an invitation from Dr. Lewis Janes to speak at the Brooklyn Ethical Association. In the early part of December 1899, at the invitation of Dr. Janes (who was the president of Cambridge Conferences) Turiyananda went to Cambridge, Massachusetts, to deliver a lecture on Shankaracharya before the Conference members. Actually, Turiyananda read a paper (later published in the *Prabuddha Bharata*, December 1913) and talked about Vedanta.

From Cambridge, Turiyananda went to Boston and became the guest of a wealthy woman, who helped him with the Vedanta work there. Unfortunately, she was quite bossy. Once she had a difference of opinion with the swami, and said to him, "If you do not accept my viewpoint, I shall stop helping you." Turiyananda calmly replied: "I am a monk. God will help me. I shall not mind at all if you throw me out on the streets of Boston." The woman then realized her mistake, and continued to help him. Later, when Turiyananda was in Los Angeles, a similar incident happened. He was the guest of a woman who owned a large oil company. She wanted to control Turiyananda and tried to curb his freedom. Turiyananda boldly said to the woman, "Madam, you have helped me with a few dollars, but that does not mean I have sold my head to you."[43] Turiyananda was truly a free soul; he was guided only by God.

From December 1899 to May 1900 Vivekananda conducted Vedanta work extensively in California, and founded the Vedanta Society in San Francisco. When the members requested a resident swami, Swamiji promised that he would send Turiyananda to them. While leaving San Francisco, Vivekananda said to the students: "I have lectured to you on Vedanta; in Turiyananda you will see Vedanta personified. He lives it every moment of his life. He is the ideal Hindu monk, and he will help you all to live pure and holy lives."[44]

Considering the big city with all its comforts unsuitable for spiritual practice, some of the students wanted a quiet spot where they might devote themselves to a life of renunciation. Miss Minnie C. Boock, a student of Vedanta, offered a property of 160 acres in northern California for a retreat. When Vivekananda arrived in New York in June 1900, he accepted her offer and asked Turiyananda to take up the project. He was hesitant to assume the responsibility. Swamiji said, "It is the will of the Mother that you should take charge of the work there." Turiyananda jokingly remarked: "Rather say it is *your* will. Certainly you have not heard the Mother communicate Her will to you in that way. How can we hear the words of the Mother?" "Yes, brother," said Swamiji with great emotion, "yes, the words of the Mother can be heard as clearly as we hear one another. It only requires a fine nerve to hear the words of the Mother."[45] When Turiyananda agreed to the proposal, Swamiji said: "Don't trouble yourself about lecturing. You just live the life. Be an example to them. Let them see how men of renunciation live."[46]

Shanti Ashrama

On 4 July 1900 Turiyananda left New York by train, along with Swamiji and Miss Boock. This was the last time the two brother disciples would be together. Just before Swamiji got off the train at Detroit, Turiyananda asked for advice regarding his future work. Swamiji said: "Go and establish the ashrama in California. Hoist the flag of Vedanta there. From this moment destroy even the memory of India. Mother will do the rest."[47] Turiyananda arrived in Los Angeles on 8 July 1900. He became the guest of Miss Boock's sister in Alhambra, and later went to the Mead sisters' house in Pasadena. Then, after a couple of weeks, he moved to San Francisco, where he was cordially received by the members of the Vedanta Society. They told him what Vivekananda had said, "I will send you a real Hindu monk, who lives what I talk about." Turiyananda responded, "I am a row boat: I can take two or three to the other side of this ocean of the world. But Swamiji is an Atlantic liner: he can take thousands."[48] While he was in San Francisco, he gave some lectures and conducted meditations in the mornings.

On 2 August he left for the new retreat with a dozen enthusiastic men and women. They travelled by train to San Jose, then by four-horse stage to Mount Hamilton (Lick Observatory), and thence by private horse carriage some twenty-two miles over narrow mountain roads to the San Antonio Valley.

Ashrama life began under primitive conditions — no running water, no electricity, and no bathroom facilities. There were snakes, scorpions, and tarantulas all around. They had to bring water from a distance of six miles, and lived on vegetarian food. Moreover, there was no market nearby. Turiyananda found himself in a wilderness, with all these people depending solely upon him. He felt disheartened. He complained to the Divine Mother: "Mother, what have You done? What do You mean by this? These people will die. No shelter, no water — what shall they do?" Mrs. Agnes Stanley immediately said to him: "Swami, why are you dejected? Have you lost faith in Her? You have less faith than even Baby [Ida Ansell]." So saying, she emptied her purse in his lap.

Turiyananda now caught a glimpse of the enterprising American mind. These students came from the old pioneer stock and were not about to be cowed by hardships. Turiyananda was delighted to hear the bold words of his student. He said to her: "You are right. Mother will protect us. How great is your faith! Your name henceforth will be Shraddha [one who has firm faith in God]."[49]

The ordeals and hardships continued in that remote, rugged mountain area. The students, however, had a wonderful teacher of Vedanta, who had the power to raise their minds to a higher realm of spirituality where they could lose body consciousness. In the beginning they had only one small cabin and a shed, and their first meal was boiled rice and brown sugar. After supper they gathered round a campfire, and the swami chanted: "We meditate on the adorable and effulgent light of Brahman who has produced this universe. May He enlighten our understanding."

Turiyananda named the retreat "Shanti Ashrama," the abode of peace; everyone worked hard to create a spiritual atmosphere there. First, they built the meditation cabin, and gradually added more cabins for the ashrama members. Although there was an informal daily routine in the ashrama, one day someone suggested that formal rules be set. Turiyananda replied: "Why do you want rules? Is not everything going on nicely and orderly without formal rules? Don't you see how punctual everyone is — how regular we all are? No one ever is absent from the classes or meditations. Mother has made her own rules. Let us be satisfied with that. Why should we make rules of our own? Let there be freedom, but no license. That is Mother's way of ruling. We have no organization, but see how organized we are. This kind of organization is lasting, but all other kinds of organization break up in time. This kind of organization makes one free; all other kinds are binding. This is the highest organization; it is based on spiritual laws."[50]

Every morning at five o'clock, Turiyananda would waken the members of the retreat with his melodious chanting. He and the men would then take their baths at a well, some distance from the main camp. This routine was followed both in summer and winter. In winter they would build a fire in the meditation room and meditate there for an hour, but in summer they meditated under the trees. When they entered the shrine, everyone carried a cushion to sit on and removed their shoes. Turiyananda would enter last of all, and would glance around to see that the students had all come and were in their places along the walls. He would chant in Sanskrit before and after meditation, which created a deep spiritual atmosphere.

After meditation, the women would prepare breakfast. The men would be engaged in different chores, such as carrying water from the well, chopping wood, planting vegetables, and building wooden cabins. Turiyananda took a lively interest in everything, and he participated heartily in the work. At 8:00 a.m., breakfast was served in the canvas dining tent. The swami would talk on various subjects and everyone joined in the conversation. But Turiyananda never allowed them to drift away from their main topic: spiritual life. After breakfast, all attended to their respective duties. They met again at 10:00 a.m. for a one-hour Gita class, which was followed by one hour of meditation. At 1:00 p.m. they had lunch; then the students were free for some time. Those who wanted tea could have it at 4:00 p.m. At 7:00 p.m. supper was served; and at 8:00 p.m. they started their two-hour evening meditation. At 10:00 p.m. all retired to their tents.

Turiyananda kept a watchful eye on all the students and their activities. He was often seen with some disciple or other, giving advice or having fun. In the kitchen one day the swami found a woman tasting the food to see whether salt had been added. "During the cooking process, we do not taste the food in India," he told her, "because it is offered to the Lord. We do not cook for ourselves or the family. We cook food as an offering to God. After we have offered it to Him, it is distributed among the members of the family. So we keep our kitchen and everything connected with it very clean and holy. We take our bath, say our prayers and put on a clean cloth before we enter the kitchen. Every act of our life must be made án offering to God, then we shall advance spiritually."

Whenever flowers were presented to the swami, he would place them before the picture of Sri Ramakrishna in the shrine, without smelling them, and without any comment. Gurudas asked, "Don't you care for flowers, swami?" "Oh, yes," he said, "otherwise how could I offer them to the Master? But we never smell flowers before offering them to God."[51]

Once a young woman came to Shanti Ashrama. She had heard that in the forest retreats in India, the students serve the teacher: "Let the student, fuel in hand, approach a guru who is well versed in the Vedas and always devoted to Brahman" (Mundaka Upanishad, 1.2.12). She therefore went into the forest, gathered a few sticks of dry wood, and went to Turiyananda's tent. The swami heard her approach, and said, "Yes, come in." She entered, laid the wood before him, and sat down. Turiyananda understood the meaning at once, and was touched at the simplicity and humility of this highly cultured young woman.[52]

Sometimes Turiyananda would speak about Sri Ramakrishna's great love and childlike simplicity. One day he said in a hushed voice: "Once our Master told us that he had other disciples who spoke a different language, who had different customs, somewhere far away in the West. 'They also will worship me,' the Master said. 'They also are Mother's children.' You are those disciples," Turiyananda said very solemnly. "Mother has revealed it to me."[53]

A real Vedantin is supposed to transcend body consciousness and be immersed in the Atman. Physical pain and mental affliction should not perturb him. One day in the meditation cabin, a poisonous beetle bit Turiyananda's hand. Without even opening his eyes to see what had bitten him, he flicked the insect aside and continued with his meditation. Slowly his hand began to swell; by the following morning, his whole arm was badly swollen, which caused the students great anxiety. The nearest doctor was fifty miles away, and they had no transportation except a horse and a two-wheeled cart. Then something like a miracle happened. A young doctor from New York arrived in the evening, after having walked fifty miles. He immediately opened his kit, lanced Turiyananda's hand, and applied the necessary remedies. The students were greatly relieved. In this incident, they observed Turiyananda's power of forbearance. This doctor later became one of Turiyananda's most earnest disciples.

In Shanti Ashrama, the students learned the profound truths of Vedanta from Turiyananda. One day he said to them: "You are always speaking of being good. That is your highest ideal. We in India want *mukti*, liberation. You believe in sin, so you want to conquer sin by being good. We believe ignorance to be the great evil, so we want to conquer ignorance with *jnana*, wisdom. And jnana is mukti. 'Know the truth,' Jesus said, 'and the truth shall make you free.'"[54]

Another day, someone asked the swami why there was so much evil in the world. He replied: "Tulasidas says, 'To the good the world is full of good; but to the bad the world is full of evil.' The world is neither good nor bad. What I call good, you perhaps call bad, and the reverse. Where is the standard? The standard is in our own attitude toward life. Each one has his own standard. And with increased experience and insight, the standard changes. The pity is that we still recognize evil. When we become perfectly good ourselves, the whole world will appear good. We see only the reflection of our own minds. See the Lord always in everything, and you will see no evil. A suspicious mind sees evil everywhere; a trusting mind sees only good."[55]

In her memoirs, Ida Ansell described how Turiyananda taught practical Vedanta. She was entrusted with the duty of taking notes of the swami's class talks. One time her pencil was dull, so she sharpened it with a blunt knife. As a result, the point was jagged and asymmetrical. Turiyananda happened to notice this. He picked up the pencil and, with the same knife, carefully whittled the jagged wood into a smooth, symmetrical point. Handing it back to her, he said: "Make every act an act of worship. Whatever you do, do it as an offering to the Mother and do it as perfectly as you can."[56]

Turiyananda hated procrastination. He once quoted a proverb: "Whatever you have to do tomorrow, do today; whatever you have to do today, do this minute."

In community life, there are always occasions when differences of opinion lead to fault-finding. Turiyananda noticed this in the ashrama community, and remarked one day: "We are like dogs in glass houses, barking at our own reflections. We see another's *sushupti* [deep sleep], not our own. We should be strict with our faults and lenient with the faults of others."[57]

"Sincerity," Turiyananda told the students, "is the backbone of spirituality. One should practise it in one's actions and thoughts. There should be no disagreement between what one feels and what one says; and at the same time, one should not be cruel or unkind when one adheres to truth. Make your heart and tongue one." Then he quoted a Sanskrit proverb: "Say what is kind, but not what is untrue. Say what is true, but not what is unkind." Finally, he chanted a beautiful verse from the Mundaka Upanishad: "Truth alone triumphs, not falsehood. The path by which the sages reach perfection is the path of truth. There is no other way to freedom — no other way" (3.1.6).[58]

In Shanti Ashrama, Turiyananda freely distributed the greatest spiritual treasures of India to his American students. He asked them to preserve these teachings. Gurudas recorded in his memoirs some immortal teachings of Vedanta, taught by Turiyananda:

"Be yourself, and be strong. Realization is only for the strong, the pure, and the upright. Remember that you are the Atman. That gives the greatest strength and courage. Be brave; break through the bondage of maya. Be like the lion; don't tremble at anything. Swamiji has taught you that every soul is potentially divine. Realize your own divinity, then you will realize that all souls are divine. A cloud obscures the sun. We say, 'There is no sun.' But the sun always shines. So the cloud of ignorance makes us believe that we are weak human beings. But the sun of the Atman is always shining. Remove the cloud of ignorance, and the Atman will reveal itself in your heart. When you realize that, then you are a man. Otherwise you are not different from beasts."

And when asked how this can be realized, he answered, "Through meditation. Meditation is the key that opens the door to Truth. Meditate, meditate! Meditate till light flashes into your mind and the Atman stands self-revealed. Not by talk, not by study — but by meditation alone the Truth is known."[59]

It was in this same spirit of trusting in God alone that the swami was very strongly opposed to all planning. There also he used almost the identical language: "Why do you plan? Why are you scheming? Why do you look so far ahead? Let Mother plan. Her plan comes true.

Human planning is all in vain if She does not consent. She knows what will happen. The future is an open book to Her. Live in the present; make the best of your time and opportunities. Don't think of the future. Know for certain that Mother's will shall come to pass. Trust in Her. Only try to love Her sincerely. Give yourself to Her. Let Her do with you as She wishes." But on one occasion he added, "Trusting in Mother does not mean idleness. Try to know Her will, and then be up and doing like a man. Don't you see, I am never idle. The mind must be occupied in someway or other. If you don't do physical work you must use your mind — read, study, or meditate. And don't spend your time in idle gossip. Gossip breeds mischief. If you talk, talk of the Lord."

Of reading, Swami Turiyananda gave us the advice to read only books written by men of realization. When he found a lady student studying a book of New Thought, he told her, "Go to the source. Don't waste your time reading the ideas of every fool who wants to preach religion. There are thousands of books on religion. You cannot read them all. Therefore select the best. Only those who have realized the truth can speak with authority. Otherwise it is the blind leading the blind. Both come to grief; both fall into the ditch. Only the true guru can lead us right, and the true guru is he who knows Brahman."[60]

Once a student versed in Christian Science asked: "Is it not our duty to keep our body healthy?" "Yes," said the swami. "But from the highest standpoint, the body itself is the great disease. We want to go beyond the idea of body and to realize that we are the Atman. It is the love for our body that stands in the way to our realization of that higher state where we can say: 'I am not this body. I am the Atman. The body is an illusion.' As long as we love the body we cannot realize the Self, and we shall be born again and again. But when we love the Atman then we become indifferent towards the body. And when all love for the body goes, liberation will come very soon."

One of the students was psychic. One day Turiyananda found her practising automatic writing. Making her mind passive, she sat with a pencil in her hand, and automatic writing would begin. The hand would begin to move and write, and our friend would see afterwards what was written. In that way beautiful things would be written on the paper. But when the swami saw her thus engaged, he rebuked her severely. "What is this foolishness?" he called out. "Do you want to be controlled by spooks? Give up that nonsense. We want mukti, liberation. We want to go beyond this world and all worlds. Why should you want to communicate with the departed? Leave them in peace. It is all *maya*. Get out of maya and be free!"

To live with Swami Turiyananda was a constant joy and inspiration. It was also an education, for one was learning all the time. And we all felt that spiritual help came through him. Sometimes gentle, sometimes the "roaring lion of Vedanta," the swami was always fully awake. There was not a dull moment in the ashrama.[61]

One morning some students were talking about the various reasons they had for coming to the ashrama, when the swami happened to pass and asked what they were talking about. When they told him, he said: "If you fall into the river, jump in, or are thrown in, the result is the same — you get wet. Whatever the reason, now there is no escape. You have been stung by the cobra and you must die."[62] Another time, when there was talk of the possibility of someone leaving, the swami said: "Where will they go? Vedanta is the essence of religion. When you have seen the full moon in all its glory, who cares to look at a candle?"[63]

In San Francisco and Oakland

Turiyananda left Shanti Ashrama on 10 January 1901, and went to San Francisco for treatment of gallstones and other complications. A female student served the swami with great devotion, but she found it a difficult task to care for him. He appeared stubborn, seemed to want his own way in everything, and found fault even in small matters. She did not realize that Turiyananda was training her by curbing her sensitive ego.

One day when Turiyananda reprimanded her, she wept. Noticing this, the swami immediately changed his tone. With all gentleness, he said: "You don't know that we are accustomed to act like this in India. We scold those whom we love for their own good. We never utter a harsh word to people to whom we are indifferent. We try to improve those whom we love. What does it matter whether I am in good health or in ill health? I have come to this country for your good and not for mine."[64]

During February and March 1901, at 770 Oak Street in San Francisco, Turiyananda conducted a meditation class every day at 10:00 a.m.; and on Tuesdays and Thursdays he gave lectures on the Gita and Raja Yoga. One day a student asked, "Sir, what is attachment?" The swami replied, "It is made up of the ideas of 'I' and 'mine.'" Another asked, "What are the necessary conditions to establish Shanti Ashrama on a permanent basis?" "There are many conditions," the swami answered. "The desire for liberation and a dedicated life — if these two are there, that is enough."[65]

Once a woman told Turiyananda that her husband was not sympathetic to her desire to attend the classes, so she was attending against his wishes. "It is the duty of the wife to attend to her husband and to be obedient," Turiyananda told her. "Don't come here so often. Come occasionally. Try to explain to your husband what you are learning. Pray to the Mother. Everything will be all right."

But her husband did not pay any attention to her words. At that time, most Americans had a very poor opinion of the Hindus: they believed that mixing with the holy men of India was contrary to social etiquette. One day, seeing that the woman was unable to change her husband's attitude, Turiyananda said to her, "I would like to see your husband."

"Sir, it is better that you do not go," she protested. "It is quite possible that my husband will behave rudely towards you."

The swami, however, went to her house and met her husband. Strangely, just a handshake removed all the man's antagonism, and he began to behave like a devotee. From then on, there were no more obstacles to the woman's coming to the Vedanta Society.[66]

For seven weeks, on Friday nights and Saturday mornings, Turiyananda held classes in the house of Mrs. F. S. Rhodehamel in Oakland. The whole house would vibrate with the swami's chanting, "*Hari Om, Hari Om.*" In these classes, the swami tried to lead away from the mere intellectual satisfaction of philosophic probing. He said: "No matter about philosophy, or even the Gita. The thing to do is to *know Mother*. That is the whole of religion. Nothing else counts. Take all your troubles to Mother. She will right all wrongs." "How will She right wrongs, swami?" asked someone. Turiyananda replied: "By drawing you close to Her. When you know Mother, nothing else matters."[67]

In spite of his ill health, Turiyananda gave lectures and classes in and around San Francisco for a few months, and then returned to Shanti Ashrama for a period of five months. The mental strain of constant teaching and training took a toll on his body and nerves. His mind was clear, but his health broke down. It became evident that he needed rest.

Knowing of Turiyananda's poor health, Vivekananda wrote to the president of the Vedanta Society of San Francisco and asked him to send the swami back to India. Turiyananda also expressed a desire to see Swamiji again. The Society decided to give him a first-class passage for India, in the hope that the long sea voyage and his meeting with Swamiji would have a beneficial effect on his health, and that he would come back to Shanti Ashrama with renewed zeal and strength.

Gurudas later wrote about Swami Turiyananda's last days in Shanti Ashrama: "One evening, just after dusk, when I entered the little cabin we shared together, the swami told me of a vision he had had. The Divine Mother had come to him and had asked him to remain in the ashrama. But he had refused. Then She told him that if he stayed in the ashrama the work would grow rapidly, and many beautiful buildings would be erected. Still he had refused. At last She showed him the place full of disciples. 'Let me go to Swamiji first,' he had said. And the Mother with grave countenance vanished from his sight.

"The vision had left him unhappy and disturbed in mind. 'I have done wrong,' he said with a sigh, 'but it cannot be helped now.'"[68] Turiyananda had fully surrendered himself to the Divine Mother, yet he refused Her command. Why? Nobody knows. It will always remain a mystery.

Before his departure, Turiyananda called Gurudas to his cabin and gave him final instructions: "I leave you in full charge. I have told you everything. You have seen how I have lived here. Now try to do the same.... Depend on Mother for everything. Trust in Her, and She will guide you. One thing remember: Never boss anyone. Look upon all alike, treat all alike. No favourites. Hear all, and be just."

Then the swami began to chant, "Om, Om, Om." His body rhythmically rocked to and fro. After a few moments he suddenly stopped, and straightening himself, said with great force: "Control your passions, anger, jealousy, pride. And never speak ill of others behind their backs. Let everything be open and free. When anything has to be done, always be the first to do it. Others will follow. But unless you do it first, no one will. You know how I have done all kinds of physical work here only for that reason."

Gurudas asked, "But what about the classes, swami? What shall I teach? I am a student myself."

Turiyananda replied, "Don't you know yet, my boy, that it is life that counts? Life creates life. Serve! Serve! Serve! That is the great teaching. Be humble. Be the servant of all. Only he who knows how to serve is fit to rule. But you have studied many years; teach what you know. As you give out, so you will receive."

"Swami," Gurudas ventured, "when you are gone we will be like sheep without a shepherd." "But I will be with you in spirit," Turiyananda said solemnly.[69]

Turiyananda left Shanti Ashrama in late May of 1902, and set sail for India from San Francisco on 6 June. He had stayed two years and nine months in the United States; of this, about eighteen months had been spent at Shanti Ashrama.

Return to India

The first leg of Turiyananda's trip, from San Francisco to Burma, was uneventful. He was very eager to see Vivekananda again. Tragically, however, during the voyage from Rangoon to Calcutta he learned from a fellow passenger's newspaper that Swamiji had passed away on 4 July 1902. It was a terrible shock, and it completely changed his plans for future work. He decided that he would not return to the West, but instead would spend the remaining part of his life in meditation and austerity. Burning with renunciation, he threw his expensive Western clothes and his precious watch into the ocean. He lost all interest in work, and even in the bare necessities of life.

When his boat reached Calcutta on 14 July, Saradananda and a number of monks came to the pier to receive Turiyananda and bring him to Belur Math. When Turiyananda disembarked, he put his arms around Saradananda and burst into tears. Turiyananda lived with other disciples of the Master at Belur Math for about three months. He never boasted of his work in America. If anybody praised him, he would say, "The Master does his own work, we are just his instruments."

He wrote to Ida Ansell from Belur Math on 20 September 1902: "The blow was too severe and I have not recovered from its shock. One redeeming feature is that Swamiji has got the rest he needed so badly. What he has done for the world, let the world realize that and be benefitted by for ages. He gave his body in samadhi and it was not an ordinary death. It was conscious passing out. Of course, it is calamitous to us, but we must learn to submit to Mother's will."[70]

Towards the end of October 1902, Turiyananda moved to Vrindaban. Having taken up active work only at Swamiji's request, he now returned to his first life — a life of contemplation. Brahmananda sent Brahmachari Krishnalal (later, Swami Dhirananda) to serve Turiyananda. For a few days, Krishnalal cooked food for him, but Turiyananda preferred to lead the life of a traditional monk and live on alms. In the latter part of 1903, Brahmananda joined Turiyananda and lived at Vrindaban for a couple of months.

In Vrindaban, Turiyananda gave classes on the Bhagavata; two Vaishnava monks used to attend this class. They lived together, and would quarrel. One day the swami said to them: "If you are of such different temperaments and are always quarrelling, why can't you live apart? What is the meaning of being together and yet fighting?" These words surprised the monks, and they replied: "Sir, we did not expect to hear such a thing from you. Being such a great monk, how can you suggest that we shun the company of the holy? We may quarrel, but if a monk deprives himself of the company of another monk, with whom should he live?"[71] These words immensely pleased Turiyananda and he began to show more affection towards them.

Turiyananda was very frank and truthful. But his candour in pointing out a person's defects often proved painful. One day he came across this verse of the Bhagavata: "Realizing the universe as one in the aspect of Purusha and prakriti, never praise or blame the action of others" (11. 28. 1). Then he read the commentary on that verse: "If accidentally the teeth bite the tongue, hurt and cut it, do people take a piece of stone and break the teeth? No, because the teeth belong to the same person to whom the tongue belongs. Since the one Lord who is in me also resides in others, it is improper to find fault with them."[72] This teaching made a deep impression on Turiyananda; thereafter, he became gentler in correcting those in his charge.

In the Himalayas

In 1905 Turiyananda's health broke down due to his severe austerities, and he had to leave Vrindaban. He went to Advaita Ashrama at Mayavati in the Himalayas, where he stayed a few months and regained his health. Then he visited Almora, Nainital, Hardwar, Rishikesh, and at last settled in Uttarkashi in 1906. There is heavy snowfall in this area, and the ascetics who live there are compelled to go down to Rishikesh during the winter months. But Turiyananda decided to stay in Uttarkashi, despite the snow.

Devigiri, a well-known monk, used to look after the poor mendicants in Uttarkashi. He learned that Turiyananda was a close friend of his guru Swami Vijnanananda of Tihiri. Before leaving the place, he said to Turiyananda: "Sir, this is the first time you are staying in this region during the winter. You are unaware of how cold it gets, and what hardships you will have to face. It is extremely necessary to keep some food in reserve for the intensely cold days when it is impossible to go out for alms. Please accept something."[73] Having been requested many times, Turiyananda agreed to accept some rice, flour, and lentils from Devigiri. There was no bed in his hut, so Devigiri spread some dry grass on the ground under Turiyananda's blanket.

The swami would arise at three o'clock in the morning to perform his morning ablutions. He then remained absorbed in meditation until noon. Afterwards, he took his bath and ate some rice and milk — his only meal of the day. When Devigiri was there, the swami would discuss with him the Karika of the Mandukya Upanishad. Turiyananda was fond of this verse: "There is no dissolution, no birth, none in bondage, none aspiring for wisdom, no seeker of liberation, and none liberated. This is the absolute truth" (2.32). Recalling his association with Turiyananda, Devigiri later said: "How shall I describe him? Only on rare occasions do we come across such a great Vedantin and a man of renunciation. He was an illumined soul and worthy of respect."[74]

After spending nine months in Uttarkashi, Turiyananda went on pilgrimage to Kedarnath and Badrinath, two great shrines high in the Himalayas. Later, he told about his experiences on the way to Kedarnath. He and two other swamis had gone for days without food when they were caught in a snowstorm. They were ready to give up their lives in meditation; but, by the grace of God, they found a miserable hut where they spent the night. The following day they reached a village and got food.

In Kurukshetra and Nangol

In 1907 Turiyananda went to Kurukshetra, about eighty miles from Delhi, to attend a religious festival in connection with the solar eclipse. Brahmachari Gurudas came from America and joined him. It was evening when they arrived by train, and the place was crowded with fifty thousand people: they could not find a place to stay. A woman gave them some food and they spread their blankets on the open ground to sleep. At midnight, it started to rain. Turiyananda and Gurudas rushed to a nearby shed, already filled with pilgrims, and squeezed themselves inside, against the pilgrims' protests.

Recalling this night, Gurudas later wrote: "The swami said, 'We are on the battlefield of Kurukshetra, where Sri Krishna preached the Gita.' Then he began to chant the second chapter of the Gita from memory. A few pilgrims came and listened. He chanted in a loud voice with much feeling.

"The swami had just finished chanting when a gentleman approached us. He scowled and said, 'What are you doing in my shed?' The swami replied, 'We are sannyasins; we are taking shelter here.' 'Who is the sahib?' he asked, pointing at me. (We learned later that he suspected me of being an English spy in disguise.) The swami told him who I was and that I had come to see the *mela* (fair) and bathe in the holy water of Kurukshetra. At this the man became quite amiable and said: 'You may both stay here as my guests. I will supply you with food.' He called a servant and told him to place some straw under our blankets. Then, saluting us very humbly, he went away. When he was gone, the swami said to me, 'See how Mother plays. Now we can be at peace.'"[75]

They stayed in Kurukshetra for nine days. Gurudas later wrote of another incident that happened there: "One day two gentlemen came to us and began to talk to Turiyananda. The swami spoke of the highest Vedanta, 'I am not the body, the mind, or the ego; I am only the eternal Atman,' and so on. Those gentlemen would not accept that. One of them asked, 'Well, swami, if you are not the body, can you put your hand in this fire?' The swami jumped up and said: 'Yes, I can do it. Even if I put my hand into the fire, I will not be burned; but the body will get the burn.' Then the other gentleman, thinking that they were going too far, dissuaded the swami."[76]

Shankara said: "If you want to attain liberation, shun the crowd like a poisonous snake." It is a journey from the alone to the alone. When the solar eclipse festival was over, Turiyananda looked for a solitary place where he could remain absorbed in God-consciousness. Alone, he went to Karnavas, Ahar, Mandu, Pushpabati, and at last settled temporarily in Gadamukteshwar on the Ganges, in the Meerut district. He arrived there sometime in November 1907 and stayed till the end of 1908. In 1909 he went to Nangol, a small village on the Ganges about sixty miles below Hardwar, and stayed there until the first part of 1910. It is surrounded by forests, and wild beasts roam there freely. The ascetics live in small huts on the bank of the Ganges, and go to the village once a day to beg for food. Every afternoon, they would assemble at Turiyananda's place to hear him explain the Hindi Ramayana of Tulasidas.

Living in the lap of luxury, and without shedding a tear, one cannot realize God. Turiyananda demonstrated through his life a glowing example of a true seeker of God. In Nangol, his spiritual adventure reached its climax. Transcending the body idea and forgetting food and clothing, he remained absorbed in the thought of God.

His clothes were completely worn-out, yet he did not ask for a cloth from anyone. Mostly, he stayed in his hut naked. One day he found a piece of cloth near the cremation ground; he used that as a loincloth.

One day a monk arranged a feast at his cottage and invited other mendicants. Swami Gangananda went there and later told Turiyananda about the greediness of an old monk. Turiyananda scolded Gangananda: "Why are you criticizing that old monk? Your boat is in the middle of the turbulent river. Don't see fault in others, rather see your own defects. He who sees fault in others is guilty."[77] Turiyananda was quite outspoken, but he meant well. If one loves a person, one can tell him a harsh truth. Another day, a young man said: "I don't believe in the holiness of the Ganges." Turiyananda replied: "You are now young and healthy. Why would you believe all those things? When your blood circulation slows down, you will feel the necessity of believing in the Ganges."[78]

25

One early morning Turiyanada went out for his morning ablutions. He saw a big tiger seated above a rock looking around. From a distance they looked at each other, and then after a while the tiger left. Turiyananda's burning renunciation made him fearless. Hunger and thirst, disease and death, cannot overpower a knower of Brahman.

During the early days in Nangol, Turiyananda had an attack of malaria, and his body became extremely emaciated. In spite of this, he still went to the village to beg for food. One day he was extremely weak and fell down while crossing the river. When he entered the village wearing his wet cloth and looking for food, an old woman showed her sympathy and inquired about his health. Turiyananda replied: "I am trying to forget the body, and you are reminding me of it by asking about my welfare. Please don't ask about my health anymore."[79] Although he was in such a bad state of health, he did not let the swamis at Belur Math know about it. At last Swami Kalyanananda, a disciple of Swamiji and the head of Kankhal centre, learned about Turiyananda's condition from a devotee. Kalyanananda immediately sent Brahmachari Gangaram to serve him.

Seeing Turiyananda's serious condition, Gangaram wanted to inform Belur Math. However, the swami warned him: "Take care. If I learn that you have written any letter, then even in this state of health I will leave this place."[80] Then he said, "Ganges water is the medicine and the Lord is the physician." Later, in February or March 1910, Kalyanananda himself went to Nangol and brought Turiyananda to Kankhal for treatment.

In Kankhal, Almora, and Puri

An easygoing life is not for mystics. They know that in order to have divine communion, one must transcend body consciousness. That is why they neglect their bodies, and as a result, they must face the consequences. But God takes care of them; He uses them to teach people how to reach Him. Turiyananda gradually began to recuperate in Kankhal.

Gurudas had been living in Varanasi since the Kurukshetra pilgrimage. On 7 April 1910 he went to Kankhal with Premananda to see Turiyananda, who was very happy to see them. However, when Premananda wanted to take Turiyananda to Belur Math, he declined because he was too weak to move.

In spite of his illness, Turiyananda was always ready to speak about God and spiritual life. A brahmacharin once asked, "Maharaj, what is a good subject for meditation?" "Any subject that appeals to you," the swami replied. "All lead to the same goal." Then he explained the relationship between the guru and the disciple: "The guru should hold the disciple through love. He should not bind him, but give him full freedom. His aim should be to dispel delusion, to clear the vision.... The disciple should obey through love, not from fear. That would be slavery."[81]

Gurudas wrote in "Days with Swami Turiyananda at Kankhal":

I spoke about Lady Minto's visit to Belur Math. She had asked the monks there what Sri Ramakrishna taught. One had answered, "He taught from the Hindu scriptures." When the swami heard this, he said: "His words were scripture. He taught more even than the scriptures. But he himself used to say that everything he taught could be found in our scriptures."

"Did not his teachings differ somewhat from Shankaracharya's maya theory?" I asked.

"Yes," he replied. "Shankara taught only one phase, how to get freedom, nirvana. Our Master first made one free and then taught how one should live in the world. His touch would make one free. But those who follow his instructions also get free. His words have such *shakti* [power]. Be free first. Do away with name and form and the entire universe. Then see Mother in all. Then be Her playfellow."

When I came to his room again, he began at once, "What we know we must bring into practice, at least once. But Sri Ramakrishna practised everything three times. Through practise new knowledge comes. Do something, practise! Bondage and freedom are both in the mind. Atman is beyond mind."

Towards evening a party of pilgrims came to see the swami. One of the men wanted to know something about the swami's experiences in the West. The swami smiled and said: "The West is materialistic, the land of enjoyment. But there are many good things. The food is superior. Everything is done in a scientific way, even cooking. And sanitation is much better. They are strong and healthy people. The women have much more freedom, and they are all educated. There is more privacy in the West, and their dress is fit for action. Here everything is for inaction. We are not so energetic. Even the humblest servant is treated with respect. Work is not disgrace. A man is a man, no matter what his occupation is. But he must obey the laws of society. There are no outcasts and no *don't-touchism*."[82]

Turiyananda remained in Kankhal for some months; then, in the latter part of 1910, he went to Belur Math. One morning Turiyananda was seated on the eastern veranda of the monastery, facing the Ganges. While he was talking to some devotees, M., the recorder of *The Gospel of Sri Ramakrishna*, came and greeted him. Then M. asked Turiyananda: "You have performed so many austerities. Tell us please what we should do."

The swami quoted a Hindi couplet: "A person desiring wealth lies at the door of a rich man although he is often kicked by him. Yet he never leaves the rich man's door." Then he commented: "Live in the world, remembering the Lord constantly. What else is there to do? In the world there are always happiness and misery, dangers and difficulties. We should see that we do not forget Him."[83]

In early 1911, after a short stay at Belur Math, Turiyananda went to Puri. He consulted a doctor there, who discovered that he had diabetes. Brahmananda was also in Puri, and he always enjoyed Turiyananda's company. There is a Hindi saying, "When an ass meets another ass, they kick each other; and when a holy man meets another holy man, they only talk about God."

Although Turiyananda's health slightly improved in Puri, he had some trouble with his eyes. The doctor prescribed eye drops. One morning, as soon as his attendant, Sharvananda, put eye drops in his eyes, he cried out: "I think you have given me the wrong medicine. See what you have used!" The attendant was shocked when he discovered that it was diluted nitric acid. Filled with remorse and fear, he began to tremble and cry while someone else washed the acid out of the swami's eyes. Turiyananda remained calm and composed. He was the embodiment of forbearance. He later consoled his attendant: "You see, as soon as you put the drops in my eyes, I felt a terrible burning sensation covering my whole body. I thought: 'O Mother, what can I do if You want to take away my eyes? May Your will be done!'"[84] Brahmananda also prayed. By the Master's grace, his eyes were saved.

On 21 December 1911 Brahmananda and Turiyananda left Puri for Belur Math; then they went to Varanasi on 20 March 1912. After staying a few months in Varanasi, they went to Kankhal for Durga Puja (worship of the Divine Mother). The puja was performed at the Kankhal monastery, and Turiyananda chanted the Chandi. He knew the Chandi by heart, and it took him only an hour to recite the whole text.

From 1912 to 1914, Turiyananda lived in Dehra Dun, Rishikesh, Varanasi, Kankhal. Wherever he stayed, he conducted classes on the scriptures and trained monks and devotees. Turiyananda was a spiritual dynamo. He often mentioned this great saying of the sage Vyasa, "He who wishes to think upon the Lord after all his duties have been finished is like the fool who wishes to bathe in the sea after the waves have subsided."[85] Because Turiyananda had diabetes, the doctor advised that he stay in a cool place. On 8 April 1915 he left for Almora, a small resort town in the Himalayas. During his itinerant days, Vivekananda had expressed a wish to have a retreat centre in Almora. Shivananda and Turiyananda therefore fulfilled his wish, and the Ramakrishna Cottage came into existence. It is a wonderful place for practising spiritual disciplines.

From Almora, Turiyananda wrote many inspiring letters to the monks and the devotees. On 8 July 1916 he wrote: "'The ever-free Atman takes a human birth in order to taste the bliss of liberation-in-life, and not for the fulfillment of any worldly desires.' I can hardly convey to you what wonderful joy and light dawned on me when I first read this verse of Shankara. Then the purpose of life shined forth before me, and all problems were solved automatically. I realized: The purpose of human birth is nothing but tasting the bliss of jivan-mukti, or freedom while living. Truly there is no cause for the ever-free Atman to assume a human body, except that it likes to enjoy the freedom while in the body."[86]

The Ramakrishna Cottage was dedicated on 22 May 1916 with a ritual worship of Sri Ramakrishna. Turiyananda's health deteriorated, so he left Almora on 5 December 1916 for Belur Math via Lucknow and Varanasi. On 4 June 1917 he went to Puri, where Brahmananda joined him from South India.

One day Turiyananda went to the Jagannath Temple. As he was going up the entrance stairs, he suddenly saw Sri Ramakrishna, with a garland of flowers around his neck, coming down the steps towards him. Turiyananda rushed forward and prostrated. But when he stretched out his hands to touch the Master's feet, he could not see him anymore. Then he remembered that the Master was no longer living in the body. Turiyananda concluded that Sri Ramakrishna, whom he believed was an incarnation of Lord Jagannath, had graciously appeared before him in a vision.[87]

He had many kinds of mystical experiences in Puri. He later said: "In the Jagannath Temple at Puri, suddenly a sound came to my ears and my heart was filled with a great joy — so much so that I felt like I was walking on air. The sound continued in various strains. My whole mind felt attracted. I then remembered what I had read of *anahata dhvani* [music of the spheres as it is called], and I thought it must be that."[88] Another day he had a vision of Swamiji merging into the ocean.

Turiyananda's diabetes became worse. One time he was so ill that he was on the verge of death. Swamiji appeared before him and said: "Brother Hari, where are you going? Your time has not yet come." Another time, Turiyananda fell into a coma and the doctors lost hope. All of a sudden, he opened his eyes, looked at Swami Shankarananda, who was seated next to him, and said, "I am not going this time."[89] The doctor did some surgery on his boils. Turiyananda recovered somewhat and returned to Calcutta on 10 November 1917 with Brahmananda and Saradananda. He stayed at Balaram's house, where he could get medical help more easily than he could at Belur Math.

One time an abscess formed on Turiyananda's leg, and an English surgeon was consulted. He agreed to do the surgery, but pointed out that Turiyananda might become lame. When the swami heard about it, he said: "I don't want to live as an invalid, completely depending on others. If that is to be the case, better I die." The news reached Holy Mother. She sent the following message to Turiyananda through her attendant: "Why do you wish to give up the body? Being alive permits you to do the Master's work. Don't wish for death."[90]

In later years Turiyananda underwent several surgeries, but he never allowed the doctors to use chloroform. He simply withdrew his mind from the body like a yogi; he showed no sign of pain during surgery. The swami spent most of the winter of 1917 at Udbodhan, Holy Mother's Calcutta residence. Just before leaving Udbodhan, he bowed down to Holy Mother and said: "Mother, with your blessings I have regained my health. Except for your grace I would have left this world."[91] From Udbodhan Turiyananda went to Belur Math for a short period, and afterwards he stayed at Balaram's house nearly ten months.

Last Days in Varanasi

On 4 February 1919 Turiyananda left for Varanasi, "the city of light," and lived there until the end of his life. During his last three and a half years, the swami inspired many monks and devotees. Many of his conversations are recorded and translated in *Spiritual Talks*. He would meditate early in the morning, then after a little walk he would eat his breakfast. He was a serious reader, and would share with others his wisdom and spiritual experiences. Turiyananda had very little body consciousness: when asked how he was, he would quote the Master's words, "Let the body and the affliction take care of themselves; O my mind, you dwell in bliss."

According to the Vedantic tradition, an illumined soul is free from desires, so he is not subject to rebirth. But Sri Ramakrishna said that even after attaining full knowledge, a person may take a birth again if he wishes. A scholarly monk once objected to this view, and Turiyananda told him: "Knowledge is knowledge. People do come back even after realization.... To be born for a selfish purpose [i.e., to enjoy sense pleasures] alone deserves censure. But certainly there is nothing wrong in a person's being reborn without any selfish desire."[92] Ever-free souls assume human births in order to do good to humanity.

Part of the afternoon routine was that someone would read the Bhagavata or some other religious book in the swami's presence. He would then explain the passage and answer questions. Following the reading, in the early evening, the swami usually took a walk on the veranda. Afterwards he sat out in front of his room and devotees would gather to receive his spiritual instructions and to listen to his reminiscences of Sri Ramakrishna and Vivekananda.

Turiyananda always tried to inspire the young novices with the ideals of monastic life. One needs courage and self-confidence in order to lead that life. One day Turiyananda quoted this verse from the Gita, "Let a man be lifted up by his own Self; let him not lower himself; for he himself is his friend, he himself is his enemy" (6.5). Then he commented: "Who is your best friend? No one but the Self, the Atman. If we do not know Him, the Atman may even seem to be our enemy. There is no saviour in this world for any of us except the Atman. We have to take refuge in Him alone."[93]

One day, encouraging a young man to live a contemplative life, Turiyananda remarked: "Musk grows in the navel of the musk deer; but the animal does not know it. Hence it becomes mad in the search for its perfume, running here and there; but all in vain. Similarly we run about and exhaust ourselves — till we gain the knowledge of the divinity that is always within us."[94]

A person who has experienced the Atman can separate himself from body consciousness. He then watches his own body like a witness. In Varanasi, when a doctor operated on Turiyananda's finger, the attendant asked, "Don't you feel any pain?" The swami replied: "Look, the mind is like a child; we must hold it tight. But like a youngster it will go on crying 'Let me go! Let me go!' Once in the midst of surgery I let my mind get loose. Immediately I felt intense pain. The surgery was not finished. So I had to catch hold of the mind once more." Turiyananda was silent for some time. Then he continued: "Do you know how it is? In the Bhagavad Gita we read: 'Wherein established in the bliss of his inmost being he is not shaken even by the heaviest sorrow' (6.22). This verse is explained by Shankara as follows, 'A man of realization is not shaken even by the pain caused by the application of a sharp weapon.' Two ideas are brought out here. First, Shankara shows that a perfect yogi has extraordinary control over his mind. Secondly, he shows that such a man remains in a state far beyond the control of nature."[95]

The doctors who came in contact with Turiyananda became his devotees. One day Dr. Suresh Bhattacharya said to the swami: "I have been reading *The Gospel of Sri Ramakrishna*; the more I read it, the newer it seems to me. I understand it much better now; and it strikes me that probably I did not read the book carefully enough the previous time. It is amazing!" The swami answered: "Yes, whatever the Master practised and whatever he realized, all this he expressed in simple language. Therefore his words are so clear and so touching. But they are very deep. Even now when we read the *Gospel*, each time we feel we understand it better."[96]

During the summer of 1921, Turiyananda's suffering continued to increase. Now it was skin trouble on his back. Swami Saradananda came to Varanasi from Calcutta with Dr. Kanjilal to see his brother monk. The same year the best surgeons of Varanasi operated on Turiyananda, removing a large carbuncle and much of the tissue surrounding it. In mid-1922, he suffered from another carbuncle. This operation was the last one. Turiyananda's entire back became infected, and gangrene set in: The doctors lost hope.

Swami Turiyananda passed away at 6:45 p.m. on 21 July 1922. The night before his death, he said to his attendants, "Tomorrow is the last day." Towards the end, he chanted, "Om Ramakrishna, Om Ramakrishna." Then he asked an attendant to help him sit up. With folded hands he saluted the Master, and then drank a little holy water. He then summed up his life's experience: "Everything is real. Brahman is real. The world is real. The world is Brahman. The life force is established in Truth. Hail Ramakrishna! Hail Ramakrishna! Say that he is the embodiment of Truth, and embodiment of Knowledge."[97] He then recited an Upanishadic mantram along with Akhandananda: "*Satyam jnanam anantam Brahma*" (Brahman is Truth, Knowledge, and Infinity). Slowly he closed his eyes, as if merging into Brahman.

Sri Ramakrishna had once remarked about Turiyananda, "He comes of that transcendent region whence name and form are manufactured."[98]

Swami Turiyananda justified his name, which means "transcendental bliss." Truly he tasted the bliss of transcendental Brahman, and he shared that with each and all. He was a true mystic, and silently transformed many lives in the East and the West. Turiyananda was indeed an awakener of souls. His fiery words to his students were: "Clench your fists and say: I will conquer! Now or never — make that your motto, even in this life I must see God. That is the only way. Never postpone."[99]

10

ॐ

SWAMI ADBHUTANANDA

The natural inclination of most mystics is to remain in undisturbed communion with God, unknown to the world. And yet their lives can tell us more about God than can whole libraries on religion, philosophy, and theology. They do not preach religion: sometimes they teach through silence, and sometimes through only a few words. Those who are really seeking God will be drawn to these mystics as bees are drawn to sweet-smelling flowers.

Swami Adbhutananda, familiarly and affectionately known as Latu Maharaj, was a true mystic. Through the careful training and divine influence of his guru, Sri Ramakrishna, this unsophisticated village boy became an illumined saint. His brother disciple, Swami Vivekananda, once said: "Latu is Sri Ramakrishna's greatest miracle. Having absolutely no education, he has attained the highest wisdom simply by virtue of the Master's touch."[1] Swami Turiyananda also said of him, "Many of us had to go through the muddy waters of intellectual knowledge before we attained God, but Latu jumped over them like Hanuman. [According to the Hindu epic Ramayana, Hanuman went to Sri Lanka to search for Sita by jumping over the ocean from India.] His life teaches us how to live in God without touching the dirt of the world."[2]

Latu's lack of formal education made him unique among Sri Ramakrishna's direct disciples. Perhaps because his mind was uncluttered by intellectualism and not trained to doubt, he absorbed the instructions of his guru with unquestioning simplicity. Once the Master told him in an ecstatic mood, "One day the gems of the Vedas and Vedanta will pour

SWAMI ADBHUTANANDA: ALAMBAZAR MATH, 1896

forth from your lips."[3] Thus Latu was commissioned and blessed by his teacher. This prophecy later came to be fulfilled to the letter. It would seem as though Sri Ramakrishna intended to demonstrate to the modern world through Latu that God can be realized without the study of books and scriptures, that spiritual wisdom comes not through intellectualism but through inner realization.

Although, as mentioned before, the natural tendency of mystics is to remain hidden, unseen, and unheard, the spiritual traditions of the world show us that God loves to play and manifest Himself through these saints. Their life stories are also a great inspiration for humanity. Once Sharat Chandra Chakrabarty, a learned disciple of Vivekananda, asked Latu for permission to write his biography. Immediately Latu said: "Sir, please do not write anything about me. I am an insignificant person. If you wish to write anything, then write about Sri Ramakrishna and Swami Vivekananda. That will benefit humanity."[4]

Early Life

Relatively little is known about Latu's childhood. Like many other mystics, he was very reticent about himself. If anyone asked him about his childhood he would say: "Do you mean to leave God aside to talk about this insignificant person? Don't be silly."[5] This would be followed by a stern silence, and the subject would be abandoned.

What little is known about Latu's childhood has been pieced together from comments he let slip from time to time. He was born in northeastern India in the Chapra district of Bihar, probably sometime just after the middle of the nineteenth century. He was given the name Rakhturam, which means "O Rama, be thou the protector of this child." His father was a poor villager, and although both of his parents worked hard, they could barely provide one good meal a day for the family. Both his father and mother died before Rakhturam was five years old. He was left in the care of an uncle who was very affectionate towards him, and had no children of his own.

Growing up in the village, Rakhturam led a carefree life, often spending his days with other boys who were tending cows and sheep in the fields. Sometimes he would wander off alone, even to other villages, and then his uncle would have to search for him. Once in later years he gave a glimpse of the mood of this period of his life: "I used to wander freely with the cowherd boys. How simple and guileless they were! You can't have real joy unless you are like that."[6]

Rakhturam's uncle, although not as poor as his parents, had a tendency to spend beyond his means, and this finally led him into debt. He was ultimately forced to sell his house and all his possessions to his creditors. Hoping to find a means of livelihood in the city, Rakhturam and his uncle travelled several hundred miles to Calcutta on foot, arriving virtually destitute. Fortunately, they knew Phulchand, a village neighbour, who worked in the Calcutta office of Dr. Ramchandra Datta. Through this friend, Rakhturam was hired as a servant in Ramchandra's house.

Although the actual date of his arrival in Calcutta is not known, Rakhturam was young when he came to the city. He proved to be an energetic and faithful servant. He did the household shopping, carried Ramchandra's lunch to his office, took the children to the park to play, and did all sorts of odd jobs around the home. Despite his busy schedule, he also used to find time for wrestling and other physical exercises.

Rakhturam had a natural frankness and honesty that were enhanced by his youth and lack of sophistication. Ramchandra came to trust him. Once a friend of Ramchandra suspected that Rakhturam had stolen some coins from the household shopping money. Wanting to protect Ramchandra, the friend asked Rakhturam, "My boy, tell me honestly — how much did you pocket today?" Rakhturam retorted sharply, "Sir, I am a servant, not a thief!" The boldness of this reply offended the man and he complained to Ramchandra. But Ramchandra supported the boy and said: "He is not a thief. Whatever he needs he asks from my wife."[7]

First Meetings with Sri Ramakrishna

Rakhturam became known as "Latu" in his new Calcutta surroundings, and he was called by that name thereafter. Sri Ramakrishna, with his village accent, would affectionately call him "Leto" or "Noto." In later years Swami Vivekananda, listening to Latu's words of wisdom, would address him playfully as "Plato." In return, Latu would call Vivekananda by his premonastic name, Naren — but with his Bihari accent he pronounced it "Loren."

Sri Ramakrishna lived at the Dakshineswar temple garden, a few miles north of Calcutta on the eastern bank of the Ganges. After completing many years of spiritual practices, he began to long for devotees and disciples to whom he could give his teachings, the fruits of his realization. Gradually, the disciples began to gather. Ramchandra Datta, Latu's employer, was one of the first disciples to come to Sri Ramakrishna. Having a devotional nature, Ramchandra loved to speak about the

Master, which enkindled Latu's passionate love for God. One day Latu heard Ramchandra repeating some of Sri Ramakrishna's teachings: "God sees into the mind of a man, without concern for what he is or where he is. He who yearns for God and wants none other than God — to such a man God reveals Himself. One should call on Him with a simple and innocent heart. Without sincere longing, none can see God. One should pray to Him in solitude and weep for Him; only then will He bestow his mercy."[8] These words impressed Latu greatly, and he could sometimes be found lying covered with his blanket, quietly wiping tears from his eyes. However, he never told anyone why he was weeping.

Latu eagerly waited for an opportunity to see Ramakrishna. One Sunday (either in late 1879 or early 1880), while Ramchandra was getting ready to go to Dakshineswar, Latu asked him: "Would you take me with you? I want to see Sri Ramakrishna." Observing Latu's earnestness, Ramchandra agreed.

When the Master saw Latu, he asked Ramchandra: "Ram, did you bring this boy with you? Where did you get him? I see some holy signs in him." Ramakrishna asked Latu to sit down, and began to speak about ever-free souls: "The knowledge of those who are ever-free souls only needs to be unveiled, as it were. They are like underground springs which remain covered until a stonemason digging in the earth removes a particular rock. Then the water begins to flow." Saying this, he touched Latu, and the boy went into an ecstatic state. Tears trickled from his eyes and his lips began to quiver with emotion. This continued for an hour. At last the Master touched Latu and he slowly returned to a normal state of consciousness.[9]

Ramakrishna asked his nephew Ramlal to give some prasad to Latu and then sent him to visit the Kali Temple. From the very beginning the Master recognized Latu's divinely pure nature, which he had verified by touching him. When Ramchandra and Latu were about to return to Calcutta, Ramakrishna said to the former, "Please send Latu here from time to time."

Latu's body returned to Calcutta but his mind remained in Dakshineswar. After his first meeting with the Master, Latu began finding it difficult to work for Ramchandra with his earlier enthusiasm. After a few weeks, in February 1880, Ramchandra expressed a desire to send some sweets and fruits to the Master. Latu immediately said, "Sir, I will carry your things to the Master." Latu walked six miles alone to Dakshineswar with sweets and fruits. He met the Master on the garden path and bowed down to him, jubilant. He then visited the temple deities and returned to the Master. When Sri Ramakrishna asked him to have lunch there, he declined. Because he was a strict vegetarian, he was afraid to eat the non-vegetarian meal in the temple dining hall. The Master informed him that vegetarian prasad was available from the Vishnu Temple and that prasad is always pure. However, Latu expressed a desire to eat the Master's prasad. Ramakrishna smiled and told Ramlal, "Look, this boy is so smart that he wants food from my share!" When Ramakrishna had his lunch, he gave some food to Latu from his plate.

Latu stayed at Dakshineswar the whole day and listened to the talks of the Master with other devotees. In the evening when he was about to return to Calcutta, the Master said: "Don't go on foot. Take some coins from here and get a seat in a boat or carriage." Latu replied that he had coins, and he even jingled them in his pocket. The Master smiled at Latu's guilelessness. "Come again," said the Master.[10]

After this second visit Latu almost lost interest in his job, but he continued to do his duties. Ramchandra and his wife observed the change in Latu. One day Ramchandra mentioned this to Ramakrishna. The Master told him: "It is understandable that Latu should act like this, for he longs to come here. Send him again sometime." Ramchandra sent Latu to Dakshineswar the next day. A doctor had just come to see Ramakrishna and had advised him to leave the Calcutta area for some time for a change of climate. This meant a visit to the village of Kamarpukur, the Master's birthplace, sixty miles northwest of Calcutta. Seeing Latu the Master said: "Leto, do not let your visits to this place [meaning himself] affect your work. Ram is giving you shelter, food, clothing, and whatever else you need. It is not right for you to shirk your duties in his house. Be careful that you are not ungrateful."

At this reproof tears came to Latu's eyes. He said: "I don't want to have a job anymore. I only want to stay here and serve you."

"But if you stay here, who will work for Ram's family?" answered Ramakrishna gently. "Ram's family is my family also."

Latu, now beginning to weep, replied: "No, I shall never go back there again. I want to stay here."

"But I will not be here," said the Master. "I am going to Kamarpukur. When I return, then you can come."

Unwillingly Latu returned to Calcutta. This time he had heard a beautiful teaching that the Master had given to a devotee; it was also applicable to himself: "Do all your household duties, but keep your mind in God. Serve your wife, son, father, mother as your very own, but always know that they are not yours. Though a maidservant works in her rich master's house, her mind is on her home and family in the country. She looks after her master's young children, saying to them, 'my Hari, my Ram,' yet in her heart of hearts she knows that they are not hers."[11]

Latu came to Dakshineswar to visit the Master on another day, only to find that he had left for Kamarpukur. However, this news did not lessen his tremendous longing to see the Master. He sat on the bank of the Ganges and started to weep. He had heard from someone that Sri Ramakrishna was ever-present at Dakshineswar and that anyone who called on him would see him. Holding steadfastly to this idea, the boy sat there from midday until evening. Ramlal, the Master's nephew, was employed as a priest in the Kali Temple at that time. He noticed Latu in the temple garden. In his own words: "As many times as I said to Latu, 'The Master has gone home,' so many times did he repeat, 'No, you do not understand; the Master is definitely here.' I found I could not convince the boy, so I went to the temple to conduct the vesper service. When it was over, I returned to the spot where I had left Latu, taking with me some prasad for him to eat. There I discovered him bowing down and touching his forehead to the ground. Mystified, I kept quiet. After a moment or two, when the boy rose and saw me standing before him, he seemed surprised and asked me: 'Ah! Where has the Master gone?' Dumbfounded, I gave him the prasad and went back to the temple."[12]

After eight long months, Sri Ramakrishna returned to Dakshineswar. One day Ramchandra again sent Latu to the temple garden with some fruits and sweets for the Master. It was evening, and Ramakrishna asked Latu to stay the night. After supper, at the Master's request, Latu began to massage his feet. Kedarnath Chatterjee, a devotee who was there at the time, recalled the following conversation:

Sri Ramakrishna asked Latu: "Do you feel sleepy?"
Latu: "No, sir."
Master: "Are you afraid of anything?"
Latu: "No, sir."
Master: "Is your mind upset?"
Latu: "No, sir."
Master: "Are you sure you aren't sleepy?"
Latu: "Yes, sir."
Master: "Then why are your eyes like that?"
Latu: "I don't know."

After a while Latu began to weep. Ramakrishna asked: "Why are you weeping? What has happened to you? Tell me." Then turning to Kedarnath, he said: "Look at this boy. He is weeping and won't tell me anything." Kedarnath said: "It is your play, sir. You have transmitted spiritual power to him and he is in an ecstatic mood."

Latu stayed at Dakshineswar for three days. On the third day the Master told him: "Ram is getting worried about you. It is time for you to go home." Latu replied readily: "My master won't be angry with me if I stay. He has already hired another servant who does all the work." "What's that?" responded the Master. "You are going to stay here and still receive a salary from Ram? If you are paid by someone, you must also work for him. I have never heard of anyone serving one person and taking money from another." Just at this point in the conversation, Ramchandra and his wife entered Sri Ramakrishna's room. The Master turned to them and said: "Look at this boy. When I say to him, 'Go home,' he laughs and tells me, 'If I stay here my master won't be angry. I don't want to leave.' What is all this? Why should he stay here and forget his duties? Come now, Ram, you try to convince him of what I say."

"Sir," replied Ramchandra, "you have turned this boy's head with your love. Now why are you giving me unnecessary trouble?" Then the Master said with a smile: "What nectar has drawn this boy here? I know nothing of it."

This time Latu returned to Calcutta. However, as much as Ramchandra's wife tried, she could not change his mind. "I don't want to work here anymore, nor take any money from you," Latu stated assertively. "Please tell Ram Babu that from now on I want to stay at Dakshineswar." Ramchandra's wife asked him, "But who will feed and clothe you at Dakshineswar?" "I shall serve the Master," replied Latu, "and get prasad to eat from the temple there, and you will give me a cloth to wear." "But if you are not working here," she pointed out, "why should your master [Ramchandra] give you a cloth?" Latu answered: "Why, Ram Babu loves me. Won't he give me a cloth?" Ramchandra's wife laughed, marvelling at Latu's simplicity and guilelessness.[13]

With Sri Ramakrishna in Dakshineswar

In June 1881, Hriday, a nephew of Ramakrishna who had served and attended him for many years, left Dakshineswar. Ramchandra immediately sent Latu to serve the Master in his place. Two days later Ramchandra himself came to Dakshineswar, and the Master said to him: "Permit this boy to stay here. He is a very pure soul."[14] Ramchandra willingly agreed.

At Dakshineswar Latu began a life of rigorous spiritual discipline under the Master's guidance, coupled with continual service to him. He patterned his life on absolute obedience to his guru. There are many incidents illustrating his uncompromising directness and fervour both in serving the Master and in his spiritual struggles.

The Master once said to Latu: "Be careful about wine and about lust and gold. These things are obstacles that create doubts about God. A person who meditates after taking intoxicants and a yogi who is attached to women are both hypocrites and only deceive themselves."

Latu himself said later: "One day I was going from Dakshineswar to Ram Babu's house in Calcutta. There was a wine shop at the Cossipore Road junction, and when I passed that place, my mind became restless, although I did not know why. When I returned to Dakshineswar, I told the Master about it and he said: 'The odour of the wine caused restlessness in your mind. Avoid it from now on.'" Latu followed the Master's instructions literally, and one day Ramchandra spoke to the Master about it: "Sir, what have you asked Latu to do? In order to follow your advice, he walks eight miles to Calcutta [the normal distance is four miles] by some roundabout route." The Master said: "I don't remember telling Latu to do such a thing." "You asked him to avoid the smell of wine," said Ramchandra. "As a result, not only will he not go near a shop where it is sold, he will not even walk down a street where such a shop is located. He takes some other route."

Ramakrishna then told Latu: "Leto, I asked you not to smell wine; I didn't forbid you to walk down the street where it is sold. It won't hurt you to pass near the shop. Remember this [*pointing to his own body*], and no intoxicant will be able to disturb you."[15]

Latu would never begin the day without first seeing Ramakrishna and saluting him. One morning for some reason he did not see the Master when he first woke up; so he shouted, "Where are you?" "Wait a minute — I am coming," Ramakrishna answered. Latu kept his hands tightly pressed to his eyes until the Master came. Then he took away his hands and bowed down to his feet. Another morning when he did not see the Master right away, Latu again called for him to come to the room. But this time the Master answered by asking Latu to come outside. Latu walked out on the western veranda and saw the Master in the flower garden. Latu asked him, "Sir, what are you doing?" "Yesterday a devotee brought a pair of sandals for you," answered the Master, "and I can find only one of them. A jackal may have taken the other, so I am looking for it." Latu said in a plaintive tone: "Sir, please come here. Don't search for that sandal."

26

"But I shall feel sorry if you can't wear these new sandals," replied the Master, "since it was only yesterday that the devotee brought them." Latu anxiously said: "Sir, please stop. If you keep looking for my sandal, it will be harmful for me. My whole day will be spent in vain." (The disciple is expected to serve the guru. The reverse is not only unusual, but is even considered inauspicious for the disciple.) Ramakrishna responded: "Do you know what day is really spent in vain? That day when the Lord's name is not chanted."[16]

As Latu had received no formal schooling, Ramakrishna hoped that he might acquire at least a rudimentary education, so he tried to take him through the Bengali alphabet himself. Showing him the first few letters, the Master carefully gave Latu their proper pronunciation and asked him to repeat them. But Latu was from Bihar, and his pronunciation was quite different from that of a Bengali. Ramakrishna corrected him repeatedly with much amusement, but the result was always the same. Both the Master and Latu began to laugh, and the lesson was stopped for that day. The experiment continued for three days, after which Ramakrishna gave up in despair and told Latu, "No more book-learning for you."[17] Thus ended Latu's education.

Sri Ramakrishna always stressed the necessity of harmonizing the various paths to God. At one time he told a group of disciples: "Don't be one-sided. Our attitude towards the Lord must be symphonic in nature, made up of many instruments. It is a feast of many dishes." The Master took great pains to develop this ideal in the lives of his young disciples. He led them through the four yogas — the paths of discrimination, devotion, unselfish action, and meditation. At the same time, he would select a particular yoga most suitable to the temperament of an individual disciple and recommend that path in order to awaken the disciple's spiritual energy.

Sri Ramakrishna knew that Latu was of an emotional nature; therefore he encouraged him to take part in kirtan, devotional singing. The following incident was related by Ramlal:

One day some devotees from Konnagar came to Dakshineswar and began to sing the Lord's name in the Master's presence. The Master and Latu joined in the singing. It was the first time that I had seen Latu join in a group such as this. He was seated in a corner, but when the Master called him, he at once came forward and soon started to dance. In time, however, he became tired and lay down. The Master saw this and began to sing *Ram Nam* [the glorious name of Lord Rama] as he danced around Latu's prostrate body. Never before had I heard the

Master sing Ram Nam so sweetly. One of the devotees from Konnagar became overwhelmed by the mood of the singing, and, with great
emotion, fell at the Master's feet."[18]

Latu was always eager to serve his guru. One day he learned that the
Master had expressed a wish to have a picture of Sri Chaitanya for his
room, and the next day he went to Ramchandra in Calcutta to obtain one.
When the Master saw the new picture in his room, he asked: "Did Ram
mind your asking for this picture? Did you ask for it in my name?" "No,"
replied Latu, "I didn't mention your name. I simply asked him for a picture of Chaitanya." "Oh, indeed!" said the Master. "And what was his
reply?" "He advised me to go to mother [Ramchandra's wife] and ask for
one." "Good," said the Master. "You should never ask for anything in my
name."[19] (According to the scriptures, it is not good for yogis to accept
gifts. This frees the yogi from being influenced by the giver and also from
any obligation to him.)

One night Latu was fanning the Master. He had worked hard all day
and felt drowsy; but despite his sleepiness, his service to the Master did
not slacken. Observing this, the Master asked him half-jokingly and half-
seriously, "Leto, can you say whether God sleeps or not?" The question
surprised Latu and he answered that he didn't know. Then, more seriously, the Master continued: "Everyone in the world sleeps, but God
does not; for if God slept, the universe would be plunged into darkness
and would dissolve. God must remain awake day and night taking care
of his creatures, so that they can sleep without fear."

Latu was amazed. "Do you mean that God takes care of his creatures
while they are sleeping, and that they accept service from Him, their Creator?" "Yes," said the Master, "that is right. He lulls His creatures to sleep
and stays awake to watch over them."[20]

One incident in particular reveals Latu's direct and uncompromising
approach to spiritual life. He fell sound asleep early one evening at Dakshineswar. Ramakrishna noticed his disciple sleeping and not only woke
him, but rebuked him sharply: "If you sleep in the evening, when will
you meditate? You should meditate so deeply that the night passes unnoticed. Instead, your eyelids are heavy with sleep at this auspicious time.
Did you come here only to sleep?"

That was enough. The Master's scolding caused a veritable upheaval
in Latu's mind. In his own words: "How can I express the deep sorrow
that seized me at the Master's words! 'What a wretch I am,' I said to myself,
'that having the rare blessing of such holy company, I should be wasting
my time.' I started to whip my mind. Mercilessly, I splashed water on my

eyes and began to walk briskly along the bank of the Ganges. When my body became overheated, I returned and sat near him. Again I dozed, and again I went out for a walk. Thus I fought the whole night. The struggle continued the next night also. It was a terrible fight. Sleep would overcome my eyes during the day, but I did not give up. The battle went on day and night. Finally, night sleep came under control, but not day sleep."

After two years of struggle, Latu conquered sleep and never again slept at night. Swami Saradananda wrote: "Latu was invariably seen praying and meditating the whole night and sleeping during the day. His life was a literal example of the teaching of the Gita: 'In that which is night to all beings, the man of self-control is awake; and where all beings are awake, there is night for the sage who sees (2.69).'"[21]

"He who has controlled the tongue, has controlled all other senses," says the Bhagavata. In the early days at Dakshineswar, Latu used to wrestle and had a large appetite. One day he went to a devotee's house in Calcutta and ate an exceptional quantity of food. The next day in front of the Master that devotee praised Latu's power of consuming food. Later, the Master told Latu privately: "Look, it is not good to eat excessively by competing with others. During lunch, you may eat as much as you wish; but at night, don't eat too much." Latu obeyed his Master's advice. Gradually he reduced his meals to such an extent that his body became emaciated. The Master observed this and told Latu: "Look, you have gone to the other extreme. Please eat the amount that will keep your body in fit condition. Otherwise, if you eat too little you won't be able to focus your mind during meditation."[22]

Brahmacharya, or continence, is indispensable in spiritual life. Ramakrishna told his disciples: "When a man succeeds in the conservation of his sexual energy, his intellect reflects the image of Brahman, even as a glass gives a perfect image when its back is painted with mercury solution. The man who carries this image of Brahman in his heart is able to accomplish everything—he will succeed wonderfully in whatever action he engages himself."[23] Sri Ramakrishna advised his householder disciples to lead a normal family life while practising self-control. But the Master cautioned those who wanted to become monks to be careful about women. He told Latu: "If you want to realize God, you will have to be a brahmacharin. Without practising brahmacharya, or continence, one cannot concentrate steadily on God. From brahmacharya comes intellectual conviction and then comes faith in the power of Brahman. Without this faith, one cannot feel that he lives in Brahman. . . . Practise japam and meditation day and night. This is the way one can get rid of attachment for lust and gold."[24]

Sri Ramakrishna was extremely frugal and did not approve of his disciples' extravagance. Latu recalled: "Once in Dakshineswar the Master asked a devotee to light the oil lamp in his room. The devotee used four match sticks, yet still couldn't light the lamp. The Master then got down from his cot and lighted the lamp himself. He said to the devotee: 'Hello, the householders save their hard-earned money and give it to the monks. Is it proper to misuse their money?' Another day I was about to use a match stick to ignite his tobacco, and he scolded me, 'Go to the kitchen, and get fire from there.'"[25]

It is amazing how Sri Ramakrishna used small things to teach his disciples. One day after the midday meal, the Master asked Rakhal to prepare some betel-rolls (betel is chewed after meals in India). Rakhal replied that he did not know how to make betel-rolls. "How strange," said the Master. "Does one have to be trained as an apprentice to learn to make betel-rolls? Go and prepare some and bring them here." Rakhal did not make a move. This annoyed Latu. He told Rakhal: "What is the matter with you? Won't you do what he says? And you are arguing with him! You are not behaving properly!"

Latu's angry words provoked Rakhal, who blurted out: "If you think that is so, why don't you go and do it yourself? I won't do it. I have never made a betel-roll in my life." By this time Latu's anger had reached a high pitch, and he went on saying many things inarticulately in his half-Bengali and half-Hindi language.

The Master enjoyed the commotion and called his nephew Ramlal: "Come and see the fun! Just see the fight between these two." Then he added, "Well, Ramlal, tell me who is the greater devotee, Rakhal or Latu?" Ramlal understood the point and said, "I think Rakhal is the greater of the two." This remark threw Latu into a fit of rage and he stammered out: "Ah! What a verdict! He disobeyed the Master and yet he is a greater devotee!" Latu's fury made the Master laugh and he said: "You are right, Ramlal. Yes, Rakhal's devotion ranks higher. Just see how easily he is smiling and talking." Pointing to Latu he added: "And how terribly angry he is! A real devotee — can he show anger before the Lord? Anger is satanic. Anger makes love and devotion take wing." Latu was cut to the quick. He was filled simultaneously with shame and pique, and tears came to his eyes. He said to the Master: "I will never again be angry before you. Please forgive me."[26]

Religion means realization of God. Ordinary teachers *teach* religion; but teachers like Buddha, Christ, or Ramakrishna could *give* religion. Years later Brahmananda narrated how the Master roused Latu's spiritual consciousness one day:

> Following the Master's instructions, Latu woke us one particular morning for meditation. It was not yet dawn. After washing quickly, we sat down to do japam. The Master said to us, "Dive deep today — repeating the Lord's name with devotion." Then he began to sing, "Wake up, O Mother Kundalini, wake up," and went around and around us. He continued as we did our japam. All of a sudden, without any apparent cause, my whole body shook violently. At the same time, Latu uttered a cry. The Master placed his hands on Latu's shoulders and held him, saying: "Don't get up. Stay where you are." I could see that Latu was feeling great pain, but the Master refused to let him get up. After some time, I saw that Latu had lost normal consciousness. The Master was still singing the same song and continued singing it for more than an hour. Thus even through songs he would transmit spiritual power to us.[27]

Ramakrishna knew the tendencies of his disciples and would send them to different temples or spots in the temple garden of Dakshineswar to practise meditation. Ramlal told the following story:

> One day at noon the Master sent Latu to one of the Shiva temples to meditate. Late afternoon came and Latu still had not appeared, so the Master sent me to see about him. When I entered the temple, I saw Latu sitting motionless, deep in meditation and bathed in perspiration.
>
> When I told the Master what I had seen, he himself went to the temple, taking a fan with him. He asked me to bring a glass of water. When I entered, I saw the Master fanning Latu. Latu began to tremble. The Master said: "My boy, it is twilight. When will you set the lamps and light them?" At the sound of the Master's voice, Latu slowly began to regain consciousness. He opened his eyes and seemed puzzled to see the Master before him.
>
> "You have perspired a great deal," the Master said. "Rest a bit more before you leave your seat." By this time Latu was fully conscious of what was going on. "What are you doing, sir!" he cried. "Won't this disgrace me? It is I who should be serving you." With great affection the Master said: "No, my boy, it is not you I am serving, but the Lord Shiva inside you. He was uncomfortable in such unbearable heat. Did you know that He had entered you?" Latu replied: "No, I knew nothing. I was gazing at the *lingam* [the image of Shiva] and saw a wonderful light. I remember only that the light flooded the whole temple. After that I lost consciousness."[28]

Ramakrishna used to describe the signs of a man who is advanced in meditation: Birds will settle on his head, taking him to be some inert thing; a snake will glide over his body and he will not know it; his meditation will continue without a break in all circumstances — with eyes shut or open, while talking or walking or engaged in any work. The elder Gopal, another disciple of the Master, related this incident: "One day Latu was meditating on the bank of the Ganges. He used to choose a seat above the level to which the water rose during flood tide. However, that day the water rose unusually high, up to where he was sitting in meditation, and continued rising. Latu was so absorbed that he did not feel the water. I anxiously reported the matter to the Master. He came hurriedly, waded out to where Latu was, and brought him back to normal consciousness."[29]

Another day during meditation, Latu lost outer consciousness, fell flat on his face, and began to make a noise. The elder Gopal noticed this and immediately informed the Master. Sri Ramakrishna rushed to Latu and helped him to lie down on his back. He then put his knee on his chest and began to massage him. Gradually Latu returned to a normal state of consciousness. The Master asked: "Haven't you seen Mother Kali today? Don't talk about it. If you speak out, people will create a furore here." Latu kept quiet. From then on, whenever Latu meditated, his eyes, face, and chest turned red.[30]

One night the Master said to his young disciples: "What is the matter with you? Have you come here to sleep?" He then gave specific instructions to each disciple and sent them to different places in the temple garden. Ramakrishna sent Latu to the beltala, where he had practised tantric sadhana. At midnight, Latu became immersed in deep meditation and could not move from his seat. In the morning, Ramakrishna did not find his attendant in his room, so he went to look for him in the beltala. He found Latu there, guarded by two dogs as he meditated. Slowly Latu regained outer consciousness, saw the Master in front of him, and bowed down to him. While returning to his room, the Master said to Latu: "I saw two *bhairavas* [guardian spirits] protecting you disguised as two dogs. You are very fortunate! The Divine Mother sent those spirits to protect you."[31]

While he was in the temple one evening, Latu found that he could not meditate; he returned to the Master's room feeling discouraged. The Master asked, "Why have you come back so soon?" "I couldn't concentrate my mind on japam." "Why not?" "I don't know," answered Latu. "On other days when I sit for japam and meditation, I see something and the mind gets concentrated. But today nothing appeared. I tried hard to concentrate, but I failed." He added: "On my way to the temple the thought came to me — if Mother would appear to me and offer a boon, what should I ask for?"

Immediately the Master said: "There's the trouble. Can one do japam with the mind full of desires? Never let that happen again. When sitting to meditate one should not ask for anything. . . . If Mother ever insists on giving you something, then ask only for devotion to Her. Never ask for wealth, power, sense pleasures, or anything else."[32]

Latu was extremely fortunate that he got the opportunity to live with Ramakrishna and serve him for over six years. Sri Ramakrishna taught Latu various spiritual disciplines. One day while Latu was massaging Ramakrishna's feet, the Master asked, "Do you know what your Lord Rama is doing now?" Latu was dumbfounded and kept quiet. The Master said, "Your Lord Rama is now passing an elephant through the eye of a needle." Latu understood that Ramakrishna, out of compassion, was pouring spirituality into him. Later, Latu reminisced: "Did you know that the Master snatched me from the snares of the world? I was an orphan. He flooded me with love and affection. If he had not accepted me, I would have been like an animal, spending all my days working like a slave. My life would have been worth nothing. I am an unlettered man. He used to tell me: 'Always keep your mind spotless. Don't allow impure thoughts to enter it. If you find such desires tormenting you, pray to God and chant His name. He will protect you. If the mind still will not remain calm, then go to the temple of the Mother and sit before Her. Or else come here [pointing to himself].'"[33]

Latu was quite outspoken, but the Master taught him to be humble and not to hurt anyone. Once at Dakshineswar a devotee did not behave well and Latu got irritated and scolded him harshly. The Master observed everything. When the devotee left, Ramakrishna told Latu: "It is not good to speak harshly to those who come here. They are tormented with worldly problems. If they come here and then are scolded for their shortcomings, where will they go? In the presence of holy company never use harsh words to anyone, and never say anything to cause pain to another. Tomorrow, you go to him and apologize, so that he may forget what you said to him today."

So the next day Latu visited the devotee, with his pride humbled. He spoke to him sweetly. When he returned, the Master asked, "Did you offer him my salutations?" Amazed at his words, Latu said that he had not. Then the Master said, "Go to him again and offer him my salutations." So again Latu went to that devotee and conveyed Ramakrishna's salutations. At this the devotee burst into tears. Latu was moved to see him weeping. When he returned this time the Master said, "Now your misdeed is pardoned."[34]

Sarada Devi (Holy Mother) used to live in the *nahabat* (concert tower) at Dakshineswar, where she cooked for the Master and for the devotees. The Master knew that she was alone and needed some help. One day, seeing Latu meditating on the bank of the Ganges, Ramakrishna said to him, "Look here, Leto, the one on whom you are meditating is now sweating over the flour." (Evidently the Master meant Sarada Devi, whom he regarded as identical with the Divine Mother Kali. Latu had been meditating on Kali.) He then took Latu to the nahabat and said to Holy Mother: "This boy is a pure soul. He will knead the flour and flatten the chapatis for you. Whenever you need any help, please ask him."[35] Thus Latu became a member of Holy Mother's household.

It was great fun to live with Sri Ramakrishna. Not only was he a spiritual guide to his disciples, but he would also join them in picnics, go to the theatre with them, or watch their frivolous games, as M. described in *The Gospel of Sri Ramakrishna*:

> The devotees were engaged in a game of golakdham. [This is a game in which the player tries to get to "heaven" by passing through different "planes"; but with each false step he falls into a particular "hell."] Hazra joined them. The Master stood by, watching them play. M. and Kishori reached "heaven." Sri Ramakrishna bowed before them and said, "Blessed are you two brothers." He said to M., aside, "Don't play anymore." Hazra fell into "hell." The Master said: "What's the matter with Hazra? Again!" No sooner had Hazra got out of "hell" than he fell into it again. All burst into laughter. Latu, at the first throw of the dice, went to "heaven" from "earth." He began to cut capers of joy. "See Latu's joy!" said the Master. "He would have been terribly sad if he hadn't achieved this.... This too has a meaning. Hazra is so vain that he thinks he will triumph over all even in this game. This is the law of God, that He never humiliates a righteous person. Such a man is victorious everywhere."[36]

On 14 December 1883 Ramakrishna told Latu and other devotees the story of a little boy named Jatila, who was afraid to go to school through the forest. But his poor mother made him go, and told him to call on Brother Madhusudan (Krishna) for help. Whenever Jatila called on Krishna, he appeared before the boy and escorted him in the forest. This story created a tremendous longing in Latu's mind. He realized that God answers sincere prayer. M. recorded in the *Gospel*: "At three o'clock in the morning M. left his seat. He proceeded toward the Panchavati.... Suddenly he heard a distant sound, as if someone were wailing piteously. 'Oh, where art Thou, Brother Madhusudan?' The light of the full moon streamed through the thick foliage of the Panchavati, and as he proceeded he saw at a distance one of the Master's disciples [Latu] sitting alone in the grove, crying helplessly, 'Oh, where art Thou, Brother Madhusudan?' Silently M. watched him."[37]

The grace of the guru was Latu's only refuge. He did not read any books, but day and night he saw the blazing life of his Master and heard his teachings. Once he said: "I saw the Master in samadhi many times, but one day I saw his beautiful unique form. His body complexion was changed, and his face radiated fearlessness and compassion. I shall never forget that form of the Master."[38]

On 3 August 1884 Latu and M. both had the opportunity to see the Master's divine form, about which M. recorded in the *Gospel*: "Presently the Master left them, going in the direction of the pine trees. After a few minutes M. and Latu, standing in the Panchavati, saw the Master coming back toward them. Behind him the sky was black with the rain-cloud. Its reflection in the Ganges made the water darker. The disciples felt that the Master was God Incarnate, a Divine Child five years old, radiant with the smile of innocence and purity.... The presence of this God-man charged the trees, shrubs, flowers, plants, and temples with spiritual fervour and divine joy."[39]

When God incarnates as a human being, he behaves accordingly. Like other human beings, he has hunger and thirst, suffering and sickness; and at the same time he can transcend body consciousness at any time. Once the Master had an accident in Dakshineswar, and his arm was broken. Dr. Madhusudan set it with a splint and put a bandage around it. Latu served the Master day and night. When the devotees came to see Ramakrishna, he jokingly said to them: "Hello, Ram says that I am an avatar. What do you say? Have you ever heard that an avatar's arm had been broken?"

Latu recalled:

Sometime after the Master hurt his arm, Tarak came to Dakshineswar from Vrindaban. When he noticed the bandage on the Master's arm, he asked, "What happened to your arm?" The Master replied: "I was going to take a look at the moon, when my feet tripped over a low railing and my arm was broken. The suffering has not stopped." "Is it a dislocation or a fracture?" Tarak asked. "I don't know," said the Master. "These people have simply bandaged my arm. I like to chant the Mother's name with my mind at ease — but just see the trouble now. They won't even let me undo the bandage. Is it possible to call on the

Mother in such a painful state? Sometimes I think, what nonsense this bandage is! Let me break all these bonds and merge in the Divine. Then again I think, no, this is just another aspect of the divine play. There is also some joy in this."

Tarak told the Master, "By your mere wish you can be cured." "What!" exclaimed Ramakrishna. "Can I cure myself by only a wish?" Then he paused a moment and added: "No. Suffering from this affliction is good, for those who come here with desires will see the condition I am in and will go away. They won't bother me." Then he said, "Mother, you played a clever trick." At that he started to sing. Soon he went into samadhi.[40]

At Shyampukur and Cossipore

In the middle of 1885 Ramakrishna's throat became sore. This was the first indication of cancer. To conveniently treat him, the devotees moved Ramakrishna from Dakshineswar to Shyampukur, in North Calcutta. Latu was his personal attendant, so he went with him. Between his duties, Latu continued his spiritual disciplines and quite often experienced ecstasy.

Dr. Mahendralal Sarkar, an eminent scientist, was the Master's physician. He believed spiritual ecstasy to be a kind of nervous debility. On 25 October 1885 Narendra sang a few devotional songs to the Master when Dr. Sarkar was present. M. later recorded:

A strange transformation came over the devotees. They all became mad, as it were, with divine ecstasy. . . . The younger Naren and Latu went into deep samadhi. The atmosphere of the room became electric. Everyone felt the presence of God.

Master: "You have just noticed the effect of divine ecstasy. What does your 'science' say about that? Do you think it is a mere hoax?"

Doctor: "I must say that this is all natural, when so many people have experienced it. It cannot be a hoax."[41]

Ramakrishna stayed at Shyampukur for three months, and then moved to Cossipore on 11 December 1885. Gradually the Master's body became weak, making it impossible for him to walk to the toilet. He asked Latu to clean his commode. With great joy Latu replied: "Master, whatever you will order me to do, I will do. I am your sweeper and servant."[42]

Later, Latu reminisced about the Cossipore days: "Serving the Master was our worship. We didn't need any other spiritual disciplines. The Master taught us: 'During worship, one should think that his Chosen Deity is in front of him: You are washing His feet, bathing Him, decorating Him, feeding Him, and placing Him in your heart, offering flowers at His feet.' At Cossipore we did that to the Master."[43]

In the early part of 1886 the elder Gopal expressed a desire to distribute twelve ochre cloths and twelve rosaries to some monks in the area. The Master said to him: "Offer those cloths and rosaries to these young disciples. Each one of them is equivalent to a thousand monks." Gopal handed them over to the Master, and he gave one ochre cloth and a rosary to Latu and the remaining ones to others.[44]

Latu earlier had had various kinds of spiritual experiences — such as ecstasy and visions of divine forms or light — but he experienced the highest samadhi at Cossipore. He later narrated to a devotee: "You see, it is nothing spectacular to see light during meditation; it only strengthens faith. When body consciousness goes away and the mind becomes pure, one realizes a realm behind the light, which neither can be known through the intellect nor can it be expressed by words. One day at Cossipore I was rubbing the Master's head, then that transcendental realm opened to me. My senses failed to grasp that Infinite, but I realized It through and through."[45]

Shashi later testified: "One day the Master asked Latu to rub his head. After a while I noticed that Latu's hand stopped, his body became motionless, and he was absorbed in deep meditation. I called him a couple of times and even touched his body, but did not get any response. The Master said to me: 'Don't disturb him. Is his mind in this world?' Then without disturbing Latu, I began to rub the Master's head."[46]

Sri Ramakrishna passed away on 16 August 1886. Latu vividly described that day and the days that followed:

> Every night, just before going to bed, the Master would say, "*Hari Om Tat Sat* [Verily, the Lord is the only Reality]." That last night he uttered this as I was fanning him. It was nearly 11:00 p.m. Then he heaved a sigh and seemed to go into samadhi. Brother Loren asked us to chant "Hari Om Tat Sat." We continued to chant until 1:00 a.m., when the Master came down from samadhi. Then he ate a little farina pudding which Shashi fed him. Suddenly, he went into samadhi again. Seeing this, Loren grew worried. He called Gopal Dada and asked him to get Ramlal Dada.
>
> Gopal Dada and I left immediately for Dakshineswar, and Ramlal Dada came back with us. He examined the Master and said: "The crown of his head is still warm. Please call Captain [Vishwanath Upadhyaya, the Resident of the Nepalese Government in Calcutta, and a devotee of the Master]."

Holy Mother was unable to restrain herself. When she came to the Master's room, she cried, "O Mother Kali, what have I done that You have left us?" Seeing the Mother weeping, Baburam and Jogin went up to her, and Golap-ma took her to her room.

Shortly after that Captain arrived. He asked us to rub the Master's body with *ghee* [clarified butter]. Shashi rubbed his body and Vaikuntha massaged his feet, but it was to no avail. Early that morning Doctor Mahendra [Mahendralal Sarkar] came to examine the Master and said, "He has given up the body."

In the meantime, the Calcutta devotees had received the news, and one after another they began to arrive. A photograph [actually two] was taken of the Master with the devotees. By that time it was afternoon.

The Master's body remained on a cot, beautifully decorated, until it was carried to the cremation ground at Cossipore. Ram Babu told me to stay at the garden house until Akshay Babu returned from the cremation ground. So I stayed there while the others went. Only once did I hear Holy Mother weeping; after that she was silent. Never have I seen a woman with such strength.

That night I went to the cremation ground. I saw many people sitting quietly on the bank of the Ganges. Shashi was near the funeral pyre with a fan in his hand, and Sharat was with him. Both Sharat and Loren sought to console Shashi. I took him by the hand and tried to lift his spirits a little, but he remained motionless with grief. Then Shashi collected the ashes and bones of the Master and put them in an urn. He placed the urn on his head and carried it to the garden house, where it was kept on the Master's bed.⁴⁷

The disciples continued to worship Ramakrishna's relics. However, Ramchandra wanted to enshrine the relics of the Master at his garden house at Kankurgachi and establish a monastery there. Some disciples refused to accept this idea. Narendra settled the matter by sharing some of the relics with Ramchandra, who installed them at Kankurgachi on Krishna's birthday, 23 August 1886. Latu attended that consecration ceremony.⁴⁸

Pilgrimage to Vrindaban

On 30 August 1886 Holy Mother left for pilgrimage along with Lakshmi (Ramakrishna's niece), Golap-ma, M.'s wife, Kali, Jogin, and Latu. They first stopped at Deoghar to visit the temple of Lord Shiva, and then went to Varanasi. Latu met Swami Bhaskarananda, a well-known scholar and monk, who told him: "Don't waste your time roaming about; sit down in one place and call on Him. Then you are sure to get the Lord's grace."⁴⁹

The party stayed three days at Varanasi, and then after spending one day at Ayodhya (the birthplace of Sri Rama), they went to Vrindaban. Balaram Basu, a devotee of the Master, arranged for their stay in his retreat house. Latu visited different temples of Vrindaban with the Holy Mother.

At Vrindaban, there were no fixed times for Latu's meals. He would come at odd hours to Mother or her companions and ask for something to eat. Sometimes he would feed the monkeys his own bread, and would ask for more food. The other women were understandably annoyed by this, but the Mother was forgiving and never scolded him for his childlike behaviour. She asked her companions to keep Latu's meals well-covered in a certain place so that he might come at any time and take his meals as he liked. Sometimes Latu would disappear for a few days, which caused anxiety to Holy Mother; but suddenly he would appear again and inform her that he had been on the bank of the Jamuna. His unusual manner of living was not controlled by any rules or routine.

At Baranagore Monastery

After Sri Ramakrishna's passing away, Narendra and some of the other disciples established the first Ramakrishna monastery at Baranagore, which is between Calcutta and Dakshineswar, and is very close to the Ganges where the Master's body was cremated. The rent was very low because it was an old, dilapidated building, and it had the reputation of being haunted. In January 1887 Narendra and some other disciples took formal monastic vows. At Baranagore Monastery they studied the scriptures, practised severe austerity and meditation, and thus prepared themselves to be world teachers.

Either in the last part of January or in early February 1887, Holy Mother heard that Ramchandra's daughter had died in a fire, and she immediately sent Latu to Calcutta to his previous employer. He stayed there for a few days and then went to the Baranagore Monastery. As some disciples had already taken monastic vows, Vivekananda asked Latu to also take vows. Latu agreed at once. According to custom, before the sannyasa ceremony one performs one's own *shraddha* ceremony (funeral rites), thus severing all ties with the world and ensuring liberation for one's family. During the shraddha ceremony, Latu followed his own unconventional method. Instead of repeating the Sanskrit mantras, he simply evoked his departed ancestors in his own guileless way and offered food and other articles to them, saying, "Father dear, do come here; take your seat; accept my worship; take this food and drink," and so on.

Latu's whole life was extraordinary. His single-minded approach to God was wonderful in every way, and he was unique among the disciples of Sri Ramakrishna. Vivekananda therefore gave him the monastic name Swami Adbhutananda, meaning, "He who finds bliss in the wonderful nature of the Atman." Henceforth we shall call him "Latu Maharaj" instead of Latu or Adbhutananda, as he is well-known by that name. ("Maharaj" is a term of respect commonly used in addressing a monk.) After he became a sannyasin, Latu Maharaj stayed at Baranagore Math (monastery) for a year and a half. In later years he would tell many stories about the early days at the monastery:

Shashi's performance of the vesper service was something worth seeing. Everybody could palpably feel the Master's presence. Brother Kali [Abhedananda] composed the mantras for the Master's worship, and ever since then the worship has been conducted with these mantras. In those days we loved each other so dearly that if perchance someone got angry with someone else, that anger did not last long. Very often our topic of conversation would be the Master's transcendent love. If one person said, "He used to love me the most," another would at once contradict him and say, "No, he loved me the most." One day during such a discussion I told them: "The Master did not leave any property behind and still your squabbling seems unending. The Lord alone knows whether you would have gone to court if he had left any property." There was an outburst of laughter at my remark.

I noticed that everyone at the Math was studying hard. One day I asked Brother Sharat [Saradananda]: "Why do you read so many books? All of you are finished with school, yet you study so hard! Are you to appear for an examination?" Sharat replied, "Brother, without serious study how are we to understand the subtle matters of religion?" I rejoined that the Master had talked so much about these subtle matters, and I had never seen him reading books. Sharat said: "His case is completely different. He himself said that the Divine Mother used to provide him with heaps of knowledge. Have we reached that stage, or can we ever hope to reach it? We have to read in order to acquire such knowledge."

I did not leave the matter there, but replied, "The Master said that we get one conception of the truth through studying books and quite another by spiritual experience." Then Sharat said, "But didn't he say that those who would be teachers will have to study the scriptures as well?" Then I realized that men understand differently according to their mental constitutions and that the Master taught each one according to his own nature. From then on I kept quiet.[50]

Recalling the days at Baranagore Math, Swami Ramakrishnananda spoke of the intensity of Latu Maharaj's meditation: "We often had to call Latu back to normal consciousness and virtually force him to take food. There were many days when we called him again and again but with no response, so we would place his food in his room and leave. The rest of the day would pass. When we went to call him for supper, we would find the noon meal still where it had been placed, untouched and stale, and Latu lying down in the same straight posture as before, completely covered with a thick cotton chadar. We had to resort to many tricks just to force a little food down his throat."[51] Thus a mystic transcends body consciousness through love and longing for God.

Once Swami Saradananda told Mahendranath Datta how Latu Maharaj would pass the night at Baranagore: "You see, at night that rascal Leto doesn't sleep at all. During the first part of the night he pretends to be asleep and even snores; but he keeps his rosary with him, and when the others are asleep he sits up and starts counting his beads. One night I heard the ticking of beads and thought a mouse might have come in the room. When I gave a rap the sound stopped. A little later the ticks began again. This went on for a while, and I began to suspect that it might not be a mouse. The next night I stayed awake and was very watchful. The moment I heard the first tick, I struck a match and found Leto sitting up, counting his beads. Then I laughed: 'Ah, you mean to surpass us all! While we are sleeping, you are counting your beads!'"[52]

A monk does not respect another monk if he lacks spirituality. From the following stories told by Swami Turiyananda, it is clear that he had great regard for Latu Maharaj:

Many of the brother monks were leaving the monastery at Baranagore to practise austerity. I too felt an urge to meet holy men in other places of India. As I was thinking this over, a voice said from within me, "Where will you find such a sadhu as he?" Startled, I turned my gaze and saw Latu Maharaj lying down covered with a thick cloth, deep in meditation. Immediately the thought came, "Where, indeed, will I find a sadhu like him?" The very same moment Latu Maharaj spoke out: "Where will you go? It is better to engage yourself in tapasya here." That time I stayed at the monastery.

Another day in the course of conversation on spiritual things I remarked, "The Lord is free from faults such as partiality, cruelty, and the like." Latu Maharaj did not say anything then, but after the gentleman to whom I was talking had gone, he said: "What a statement you made! You mean that the Lord is like a little child and you, like a mother, have to go to His defense?" I tried to vindicate myself and said: "If He did whatever came to His mind He would be a capricious despot. Is He like the Czar of Russia? He is kind and benevolent." Latu Maharaj blinked and said: "It is very good of you to save your Lord from criticism! But won't you admit that even the despotic czars are guided by Him?" What a wonderful light he threw on the issue! His words remained with me as if they had been chiseled permanently in stone.[53]

Days of Austerity

"If a man worships me," says Krishna in the Gita, "and meditates upon me with an undistracted mind, devoting every moment to me, I shall supply all his needs" (9.22). Latu Maharaj surrendered himself to Sri Ramakrishna wholeheartedly. After the Master's passing away, he went through various kinds of sadhanas; he explained, "It is he who is taking me by the hand through all these disciplines."

From 1886 to 1912, when he moved permanently to Varanasi, Latu Maharaj lived almost entirely in the Calcutta area, not far from the places where Ramakrishna had stayed and often visited. Yet even in the city he lived the life of a wandering monk, unattached to people or places. Until 1903, when he took up residence at Balaram Basu's house, there was no one place that he called home. Sometimes he stayed at the homes of various householder devotees of the Master, but most often he could be found living simply on the bank of the Ganges. He would get food, a few coins, or minimal necessities from different devotees, and they in turn felt blessed to serve this holy man. Sometimes he stayed at the Alambazar Monastery and then the Belur Monastery. (The Ramakrishna Math was moved from Baranagore to Alambazar in 1892 and finally to Belur in 1898.) Once a devotee came to Latu Maharaj and asked him not to beg for alms anymore, but allow the householder disciples to supply his needs. At first Latu Maharaj objected, saying that it was part of the monk's way of life to beg for his food. But when he found out that his brother disciple Swami Brahmananda had encouraged the devotee to ask this of him, he relented. From then on, he accepted service from the devotees, but never anything more than was absolutely needed.

Once Girish Chandra Ghosh remarked to a devotee, "If you want to see a monk such as the Gita describes, go and see Latu." The devotee did not know what Girish meant. Girish said: "I see you have not read the second chapter of the Gita. The nature of a man of steady wisdom is described there. You can see all those qualities exemplified in Latu's character."[54] To quote from the Gita: "When a man completely casts off all the desires of the mind, his Self finding satisfaction in Itself alone, then he is called a man of steady wisdom. He who is not perturbed by adversity, who does not long for happiness, who is free from attachment, fear, and wrath, is called a man of steady wisdom" (2.55-56).

A true mystic loves to live alone, without any possessions, and without depending on anyone except God. That is why, between 1893 and 1894, Latu Maharaj left the monastery and began to live on the bank of the Ganges. The following incident was narrated by an eyewitness:

Latu Maharaj used to tie some dry gram [chickpeas] in the corner of his towel and leave it to soak in the Ganges. He would eat it after it had softened. One day, as usual, he put the gram to soak with a brick on top of it to hold it in place. It was ebb tide then. He sat for meditation and became so absorbed that he did not notice when the tide had changed. [In the Ganges the tide changes every six hours.] When he returned to normal consciousness, he found the river at full flood tide. His gram! There was no way of knowing whether the cloth had been swept away. He sat still. What could he do? When the tide had gone out again, he found his piece of cloth with the gram exactly where he had placed it. He picked it up and started eating.[55]

In later years Latu Maharaj would speak of these days in Calcutta:

I used to stay on the bank of the Ganges and live on *puris* [fried bread] and potato curry or fried gram. One day during that time Shantiram Babu [Premananda's brother] urged me to stay with his family. I told him politely: "You know, Shanti Babu, I have no fixed hours for bathing, eating, and so on. Why should you trouble yourself unnecessarily because of me? I am quite happy with my puris and curry from the market." Do you know what he said? "Ours is such a big family and we have so many expenses that even if a pound of wheat were wasted, would it be noticed? And you don't need to worry — they will bring your meals to your room at noon and at night, and you can eat at your own convenience. There will be no trouble for you or for us." I didn't have the heart to say no to him.[56]

One day I was sitting rather absent-mindedly on a boat loaded with straw at Baghbazar, North Calcutta. The crew did not notice me, and I was not aware of when the boat weighed anchor. I realized what was happening only after the boat had gone up the river some distance past Dakshineswar. I asked the boatmen to help me, and they let me off the boat. On the way back to Calcutta, I stopped at the Dakshineswar temple garden, and Ramlal Dada fed me sumptuously.[57]

Latu Maharaj used to spend his days at a bathing ghat near a Shiva temple and his nights on the terrace of the *chandni* (porch) at Baghbazar ghat, where he practised japam and meditation. When someone asked him how he spent his days when it rained, Latu Mahraj replied: "Well, near the ghat there used to be many empty railway cars. I would get into one. When the rain stopped, I would get out again. Once I got into a car and did not notice when it was hooked up to the engine and pulled away. The next day several porters came and asked me to leave the car. I asked them where I was, and they told me I was at Chitpore. What could be done? I had to walk back to the Baghbazar ghat. Since then I stopped taking shelter in railway cars. When it rained I would leave the terrace and take shelter in a corner of the chandni. The police at the chandni knew me and would not trouble me."[58]

Latu Maharaj once told a devotee:

Don't think that once a spiritual aspirant has experienced samadhi, he can have it thereafter any number of times or whenever he wants it. There are many aspirants who have tasted it but once. There are many more who cannot reach it even once in a whole lifetime. The Master has given me endless grace. After making me struggle for only eight years, he graciously lifted me up to that state again. One day, I was seated on the bank of the Ganges, when I saw a light coming out of the waters of the river. It grew in size until at last it filled the sky, the earth, and the space between them. Inside that infinite effulgence there were numberless other lights. Looking at this, I lost myself completely. I do not know what happened next. However, when I returned from that wonderful realm, I remained in a state of ecstatic joy. What bliss! It cannot be expressed in words. The heaviness of my heart had disappeared completely. I felt that the whole world was saturated with bliss and bliss alone.[59]

During his stay in Calcutta, Latu Maharaj made several pilgrimages to other parts of India. In 1895 he visited Puri, the holy place of Lord Jagannath (Krishna). In 1897 he was among the party that went with Vivekananda to Kashmir and other holy places of North and West India. Then in 1903 Latu Maharaj made a second pilgrimage to Puri. In later years he talked about the time he spent in Puri:

The Lord Jagannath in Puri is a living presence in the form of a simple wooden image. He appears to each person according to his particular spiritual mood and level of attainment. I prayed to Him: "Lord, please show me that beautiful form of yours which you showed to Chaitanya that made him shed profuse tears in ecstasy. What do I know of you? Please bestow your grace on me." Surrendering in this way, I stayed there and waited. Then one day he answered my prayer.

When I went to take leave of Lord Jagannath, I asked for two blessings: First, that I would not have to wander here and there, but could settle in one place and plunge into meditation on the Lord; and second, that whatever I ate I would be able to digest.

A devotee asked the reason for the second request and Latu Maharaj answered: "Don't you understand? A monk lives on alms, and thus he must maintain his body on all kinds of food taken at irregular hours. If his digestion is not good, his health will break down, and then his spiritual practices will suffer a setback. That is why I asked for such a boon."[60]

With His Brother Monks

Ramakrishna bound his young monastic disciples with love, and they always loved one another. When Latu had pneumonia at Baranagore, his brother disciples nursed him like loving mothers. Similarly Latu Maharaj took care of them.

Latu Maharaj heard from Holy Mother about Vivekananda's success in the Parliament of Religions in Chicago in 1893. Girish Ghosh said: "Latu would often come to my place and listen eagerly to every word about Swamiji's triumphant activities in America. His attitude was like a child's, full of faith and enthusiasm. When I told him that Swamiji's speech had been considered the best, he laughed gleefully like a boy and said: 'It is bound to be so. Didn't the Master say that in him eighteen powers were working in their highest form? It cannot be otherwise. Can the Master's prediction be false?' One day he was so beside himself with joy that he cried out: 'Please write to him, "Fear not, the Master is protecting you."'"[61]

Vivekananda returned to Calcutta from the West on 18 February 1897. All of the disciples and devotees of Ramakrishna went to meet Swamiji at Pasupati Basu's house in Baghbazar, except for Latu Maharaj. Swamiji inquired about him and then located him in the large crowd outside the house. Later Latu Maharaj said to a devotee:

When Swamiji returned from the West, some of his Western disciples were with him. Thinking Swamiji might have developed some sort of egotism at having Westerners as his disciples, I did not go to meet him. But Swamiji sought me out and talked with me. He asked me, "All the others came; why didn't you come?" I replied: "You have Western disciples now, men and women. I wondered whether you would remember me." He caught hold of my hand and said, "You are my same old Brother Latu, and I am your same old Brother Loren." Then I knew that he regarded us the same as before, that fame and position had not lessened his love for us. He invited me to eat with him and to sit by his side. I then had no doubt that Swamiji's mind was not tarnished by pride. Moreover, I noticed that soon after his arrival in Calcutta, he got rid of his expensive Western clothes and put on a two-rupee chadar [a cloth worn as a shawl] and two-and-a-half rupee shoes as before. He threw his tremendous name and fame to the four winds.

About ten days after Swamiji's arrival in Calcutta, they organized a huge meeting in the courtyard of the palace of the Raja of Shobhabazar. That was the first time that I heard Swamiji lecture. I found that his power to inspire people had increased enormously, for I saw that the audience became intensely inspired as he spoke.[62]

On 1 May 1897 Vivekananda established the Ramakrishna Mission at Balaram's residence in Calcutta. Latu Maharaj was present at that meeting, and he recalled: "Brother Jogin told Swamiji: 'Holding meetings, delivering lectures, philanthropic activities — these are Western ideas that only lead to development of the ego. Did the Master teach us these things?' Swamiji grew very serious and said: 'How do you know that these are not the Master's ideas? Infinite are his ideas. Do you want to limit him within the bounds of your narrow intellect? I will not allow that. I will break down any limitations and broadcast his liberal ideas to the world. He never asked me to preach the worship of his photograph! Meditation, prayer, and realizing his high, noble, life-giving ideals in our own lives and also transmitting these ideas to the wide world are what he taught us.'"[63]

Latu Maharaj was a contemplative, not an active person; so one day he asked Swamiji humbly: "Brother, why have you started all these activities? Won't these interfere with our meditation and prayer?" Swamiji smiled at him and said:

How would you understand why I am introducing all this work? You are a dumbbell. At the sight of *ka* you shed tears like Prahlada [a devotee of Krishna, who remembered Lord Krishna at the sound of the first letter of his name, *ka*]. You are all devotees. What do you understand of this? You can only whine like babies. You think you can attain liberation through crying, that on the last day the Master will come to take you to heaven, and there you will enjoy to your heart's content! And those who are studying the scriptures for knowledge, who are working to educate people in the path of righteousness and serve the diseased and distressed, will all go to hell because all these works are maya. What a grand idea! — that to do good to mankind is an unnecessary bother and that one cannot attain God through these troublesome activities. This is your view, isn't it? As if God-realization were very easy — you call on God and here He comes! Does God appear before the man who merely places his picture on an altar and throws a few flowers before Him? Tell me that.[64]

Latu Maharaj was dumbfounded. Another brother disciple lisped a few words in continuation of Latu Maharaj's thought and got a cutting snub. Swamiji continued: "Ah, what you call devotion is sentimental non-sense that only weakens man. Who cares for that kind of devotion? I have no faith in that devotion which makes a person so selfish, so busy with his personal liberation, that his heart does not feel for others.... You know, one day I foolishly asked the Master for this kind of devotion and liberation, and he rebuked me and called me selfish and small-minded. Should I be misled by your words? I will work as he has told me." After this, Vivekananda burst into tears and left the room. The brother monks realized Vivekananda's greatness and why the Master had made him their leader. The next day Latu Maharaj privately told Swamiji: "Brother, I am a fool. Please don't take my words to heart."[65]

In 1897 Latu Maharaj went on a tour of North India with Vivekananda and other monks. They visited Almora, Ambala, Amritsar, Kashmir, Lahore, Dehra Dun, Delhi, Alwar, Khetri, and Jaipur. Latu Maharaj later narrated an incident that took place in Almora. One day Swamiji saw a Muslim fakir on the street and immediately gave him two rupees. When Latu Maharaj inquired about Swamiji's charity to that stranger, he replied: "That fakir once saved my life. I was lying unconscious from hunger on a road in this town, and it was he who fed me a cucumber and brought me back to consciousness. What do you think, Leto? Could I ever repay that debt with a few coins?"[66]

While they were in Kashmir, Swamiji rented a houseboat. The boat-man and his family used one corner of the boat as their home. Latu Maharaj was not prepared for this. He was the first of the party to get onto the boat, but the moment he saw a woman on board, he jumped out again. Swamiji understood the situation, but no matter how much he tried to persuade him, Latu Maharaj insisted that he must not share a boat with a woman. At last Swamiji said: "I am here with you. What is there to fear? Nothing will happen to you." Only then did Latu Maharaj agree.[67]

One day Swamiji, in fun, asked the boatman's young daughter to carry a betel-roll to Latu Maharaj. Latu Maharaj was surprised when he saw the girl: He immediately jumped into the icy water, even though he could not swim. Swamiji, who was watching from a distance, had not anticipated such an extreme reaction. He rushed to the spot and, with the help of the boatman, pulled Latu Maharaj from the water.[68] Latu Maharaj later realized that Swamiji had played a practical joke on him. Although to a sophisticated person such behaviour might seem extreme, Latu Maharaj's sincerity and simplicity caused him to live out every principle of a monk's life to its fullest degree.

Another day while they were in Kashmir, Swamiji asked Latu Maharaj to buy some cooked rice and meat for him. At that time Latu Maharaj had given up eating meat. Thinking that Swamiji might insist that he should also eat meat, he said, "I am happy to buy rice and meat for you, but mind you, I won't eat it myself." Swamiji told him that he did not have to buy it, but Latu Maharaj went to the shop anyway and bought the food for Swamiji.[69]

During this stay, Swamiji went to visit a very ancient temple in the area. When he returned, he remarked that the temple was probably about three thousand years old. Latu Maharaj asked him how he knew this. "It is not possible for me to explain it to you," said Swamiji jokingly. "If you had had a little education, however, I might make an attempt." Latu Maharaj replied: "I see! Now I understand the depth of your scholarship. It is so deep that it cannot rise to explain this to a fool like myself!" This made everyone present roll with laughter.[70]

Latu Maharaj recalled: "One day in Delhi a man came to Swamiji and asked, 'Sir, I practise so much japam and meditation, but I still do not see the light.' Swamiji replied: 'You are reciting prayers and hymns in Sanskrit without knowing the meaning, like a parrot. Instead, pray to God with real longing in your mother tongue. Then you will see the light.'"[71]

At Khetri Latu Maharaj talked with Raja Ajit Singh, who was a disciple of Swamiji. Latu Maharaj spoke with such intelligence that the raja had no idea that he had no formal education. In fact, he enjoyed talking to Latu Maharaj so much that he mentioned it to Swamiji. One day the raja brought out a globe and started pointing out the various countries. Latu Maharaj had never seen a globe before. Swamiji understood the situation immediately and came forward to his brother disciple's help, giving such a turn to the conversation that the raja could not know that Latu Maharaj had had no schooling.[72]

At the beginning of 1898 Vivekananda, Latu Maharaj, and the rest of the party returned to Calcutta. Soon after this, property was purchased at

Belur on the bank of the Ganges. The headquarters of the Ramakrishna Order was built here. During this period Latu Maharaj stayed at Nilambar Babu's garden house, which was close to the new property. Brahmachari Hariparvat recalled:

I saw Latu Maharaj at Nilambar Babu's garden house. At that time Sharat Maharaj had just returned from the West and was staying at the monastery. He looked very smart and kept his room and belongings very tidy. Latu Maharaj used to go in and begin to upset the orderliness by moving a book from the desk to the bed, hiding the inkpot in the corner, and so on. It almost became a routine with him. Sharat Maharaj's bed sheet was sparkling white. Sometimes Latu Maharaj would deliberately drag his dusty feet across the clean bed and then lie down and roll on it, laughing all the time. Sharat Maharaj would ask, "What are you doing, Brother Latu?" Latu Maharaj would laugh and say, "Nothing — only testing whether you remember our old ways of life and seeing how Westernized you have become." At this Sharat Maharaj would laugh also.[73]

The day before the Kali Puja celebration in November 1898, Holy Mother visited the site of the new Belur Math, blessing the grounds with her presence. Latu Maharaj reminisced: "That day Mother visited the Math grounds and worshipped the Master herself. Each of the disciples took the dust of her feet, and then they collected it and put it in a casket. This is worshipped even today at the Math. Mother was pleased to see the Math premises. Observing that the pinnacles of the Dakshineswar Kali Temple could be seen from there, she remarked: 'How nice. People coming here will see Dakshineswar too and will remember the Master's divine play.'"[74]

"We were all present on the consecration day [9 December 1898]," said Latu Maharaj. "Brother Vivekananda carried the urn containing Sri Ramakrishna's relics to the monastery shrine on his own shoulders. He himself performed the worship, and when it was over he addressed a few words to us: 'Today the Master has been installed here. Brothers, let Sri Ramakrishna be our guide. He wants only three things from us — purity, simplicity, and catholicity. Do not fail to live up to these three ideals. All faiths and sects must be respected and harmonized here; none should be considered subordinate to any other.'"[75]

When a board of trustees was established for the Ramakrishna Order early in 1901, Vivekananda asked Latu Maharaj to become one of the trustees. But Latu Maharaj refused: "I don't want position or authority. Please, brother, don't get me involved." "Brother Latu," Swamiji said, "please obey me. Put your name down as a trustee. Don't refuse." Brahmananda also urged him to do the same, but Latu Maharaj remained firm and said, "I don't want to be entangled in anything."[76]

When Vivekananda left for the West in June 1899, Latu Maharaj moved to Upendra Mukherjee's Basumati Press office in Calcutta. Upendra was an ardent devotee of the Master, and he invited Latu Maharaj to stay at his place as long as he liked. Later a devotee asked, "Why of all places, Maharaj, did you choose to stay at a printing press office?"

Latu Maharaj: "What is wrong with that? It was very comfortable at night. I used to spread my blanket on the big wooden boxes which held the paper and lie down in comfort."

Devotee: "But it must have been noisy, Maharaj."

Latu Maharaj: "Yes, that is true. But it didn't disturb my meditation. A few employees respected me and served me well, and Upen Babu loved me dearly. So I stayed there."

Devotee: "It is because you used to associate with printers that respectable people did not come to you. I have heard that they were all ruffians."

Latu Maharaj: "Yes, I associated with them; but why should people think they were ruffians?"

Devotee: "Many of them were of bad character and were addicted to drinking and gambling. Isn't this true? Why should you keep the company of people like that?"

Latu Maharaj: "But they were not hypocrites."[77]

Latu Maharaj divided men into two categories — those who were free from any pretense and those who were hypocritical. He showed love and sympathy for simple and unostentatious people, but would keep learned hypocrites at a distance. Sometimes he would cook some food and feed the poor press workers. During the day he stayed on the bank of the Ganges and at night at the press. Once in the dead hours of night, Latu Maharaj was heard shouting at the top of his voice: "Shut up, you devil! You dare to threaten me, a child of Sri Ramakrishna? Your tricks and threats are useless — be sure of that!" Hearing him roaring like this, the workers in the adjacent rooms ran to where he was and found him seated in the heroic posture. (This sitting posture is done by keeping the knees together, spreading the legs and resting them at the side of the hips.) His eyes were fixed and blazing with vehemence. Finding him in such a terrifying mood, one of the compositors asked, "Maharaj, to whom are you shouting in the dead of the night? We don't see anyone here."[78] Latu Maharaj did not reply. It is hard to guess what was going on in his mind then; it may be that he was fighting against some kind of temptation, which naturally comes to a yogi.

Swami Vivekananda returned from the West on the evening of 9 December 1900, arriving in Belur Math unannounced. All the monks were overjoyed to see their beloved leader. On that particular evening Latu Maharaj was seated alone on the bank of the Ganges at Belur Math. A devotee told Latu Maharaj about Swamiji's arrival, but he did not move. Instead, he said to the devotee: "Why be so excited? This is a good hour for meditation. Sit down right here. Look, how calm is the Ganges! Meditate." After Swamiji had finished his meal, he came to the ghat to see Latu Maharaj. They embraced each other. After exchanging a few words, Swamiji said: "Leto, what's the matter? Everyone came to meet me except you. Are you annoyed with me?" "Why should I be annoyed?" replied Latu Maharaj. "My mind wanted to be here, so I was here." "I heard that you have not been staying at the monastery. How have you maintained yourself?" asked Swamiji. Latu Maharaj replied: "Upen Babu helped me. On days when food didn't come unasked for, I used to stand near his shop. He would understand at once and give me some coins." At this Swamiji gazed upward and said, "O Lord, bless Upen." After a few more minutes of conversation, Swamiji retired inside the monastery. Latu Maharaj remained sitting where he was and soon became absorbed in meditation.[79]

Swamiji made a rule at the monastery that the monks must get up at 4:00 a.m. and, after washing quickly, sit down to meditate in the shrine. The next morning a bell was rung and everyone was expected to rise. Latu Maharaj said later: "I didn't like the rule, so without telling anyone, I decided to leave the monastery. That morning, as I was leaving with my cloth and towel, Swamiji stopped me and asked, 'Where are you going?' I said, 'To Calcutta.' 'Why?' Then I told him: 'You have recently returned from the West and are introducing new rules and regulations. It will not be easy for me to abide by them. I do not have that degree of control over my mind that it will quiet down to meditate when a bell is rung. Who knows when my mind might become absorbed? I have not yet reached that state. If you can do it, that is fine.'

"Then Swamiji said: 'All right. You can go.' But I had hardly reached the gate when he called me back and said: 'You don't have to observe this rule. You should do as you like. These rules are meant for the novices.' I said, 'I am glad you said that.'"[80]

Another time Latu Maharaj said: "Swamiji wanted to see the monks strong and healthy, so he made a rule that everyone should do physical exercises with dumbbells. I was at the monastery then. I went to him and asked: 'Brother, what is this? Are we to do physical exercises at this age? That is impossible for me.' Swamiji broke into laughter and did not say anything."[81]

Although Latu Maharaj could not read the scriptures himself, he showed great interest in hearing them and would ask others to read to him. Swami Shuddhananda recalled: "I remember an occasion when I slept in the same room with Latu Maharaj. At midnight he got up and said, 'Sudhir, Sudhir, read the Gita.' So I read the Gita to him that night." On another occasion, Latu Maharaj went with Shuddhananda to listen to a class by Pandit Shashadhar on the Katha Upanishad. The pandit read the verse: "The Purusha, no larger than a thumb, the inner Self, always dwells in the hearts of men. Let a man separate Him from the body with perseverance, as one separates the tender stalk from a blade of grass" (2.3.17). As Latu Maharaj heard this passage, he cried out repeatedly, "Sudhir, the pandit said right." He must have reached that state himself, otherwise he could not have understood that abstruse Sanskrit passage.[82]

Sometime in 1902 Swamiji told Latu Maharaj: "Leto, what do you think? This is just the beginning. The people of Europe and America are now starting to appreciate the greatness of our Master. After a couple of years they will accept his ideas. Now they are only a handful, but later hundreds will come. Then you will understand what this Vivekananda had done." Latu Maharaj listened to Swamiji and then said quietly: "Brother, have you done anything new? Haven't you walked the same path that the other great teachers have travelled — Buddha, Shankara, and so on?" Swamiji said: "You are right, my dear Plato. I have only followed in their footsteps." Then Swamiji folded his hands and saluted the ancient teachers.[83]

On 4 July 1902 Vivekananda passed away. Latu Maharaj was then at Balaram's house, but did not go to Belur Math to see Swamiji. The following morning he left Balaram's and went to Haramohan's house. No one knew what was on his mind. However, a couple of days later, someone said to him: "Maharaj, everyone went to Belur Math to see Swamiji except you. People made some remarks about it." With a heavy heart, Latu Maharaj replied: "Let them talk. Will their talk heal my pain? They do not know how much my Brother Vivekananda loved me! I will miss his great love for me. His love for me was second only to the Master's. Now he is gone." Latu Maharaj could not speak anymore.[84] It seems that the reason he did not choose to see Swamiji's body was that a terrible grief tore his heart, which he did not want to publicly display.

At Balaram's House in Calcutta

Sometime in 1903 Balaram Basu's family invited Latu Maharaj to live in their house in Baghbazar, Calcutta. They kept a room on the ground floor available for monks who needed shelter and food, and from time to time some of Sri Ramakrishna's monastic disciples would stay there. At first Latu Maharaj refused the offer, saying that his hours were so irregular that he would be an inconvenience to the household. But the family insisted that having him at their house could only be a blessing, not an inconvenience, and that arrangements could be adjusted to his way of life. Latu Maharaj finally consented. He ultimately stayed at Balaram's nine years (1903 to 1912) without a break.

Although he was living in a devotee's home, he continued to lead the same austere life as before. Sister Devamata recalled: "My first meeting with Latu Maharaj was in Calcutta at Balaram Babu's house.... Latu Maharaj was a person of few words. He was also a person of few needs. His room bore witness to it. It lay immediately to the right of the house entrance; the door was nearly always open; and as one passed, one could see the large empty space with a small thin mat on the floor, at the far end a low table for a bed; on one side a few half-dead embers in an open hearth, and on them a pot of tea. I suspect that that pot of tea represented the whole of Latu Maharaj's concession to the body."[85]

How does an illumined soul live in this world? Shankara says in the *Vivekachudamani*: "Sometimes he appears to be a fool, sometimes a wise man. Sometimes he seems splendid as a king. Sometimes he wanders calmly, and sometimes behaves like a motionless python, which waits for food to come to it. Sometimes he is honoured, sometimes insulted, sometimes unknown. That is how the illumined soul lives, always absorbed in the highest bliss" (Verse 542).

Latu Maharaj's life testifies to the validity of the scriptures. In most people's eyes, he was inactive; but in fact, he was extremely active. His mind was thinking of God almost all the time. He would spend most of the day alone; but for a little while in the mornings and evenings people could come to see him, and he would talk with them about spiritual matters. People from different walks of life — judges, doctors, teachers, learned monks, and householders — would come to this unlettered monk for peace and wisdom. His teachings were simple, fresh, inspiring, convincing, and practical — and they all came from his experience.

Once a devotee asked, "How can one overcome lust?" Latu Maharaj replied: "Keep a picture of Sri Ramakrishna with you. Whenever lustful feelings arise, you should look at the picture intently. You will find that the senses will gradually be gathered in and the mind will be freed from lust."[86]

A sinner becomes sinless by associating with the holy. Once a devotee had done something wrong and was feeling very bad about it. When Latu Maharaj heard this, he called for the devotee to come and see him. He told the devotee: "Look here, my son, just because you have made one or two mistakes, you should not give up your spiritual practices and brood over your lapses and feel hopeless. To err is human. Call on God. He will give you the strength to overcome weakness and destroy your delusion. He is the compassionate one. However great your sins might be, the current of His mercy will not be kept from you. How little is your sin, and yet you are so depressed!... Do you know what Brother Vivekananda used to say? 'Don't worry about a little spot of ink on the body. It is nothing. If one bathes in God's infinite ocean of mercy, the stains of a thousand inkspots will be washed away.' So I am telling you, do not grieve. Pray unceasingly. Your bad tendencies will go away in a short time."

Yet the devotee was so ashamed of his conduct that he could not raise his head. Seeing this, Latu Maharaj said: "Before he commits a sin, a man's conscience fills him with shame, yet he brushes it aside. But divine law is such that after the sin is committed, shame overwhelms him again, and he cannot raise his head in front of others."

Even these words could not shake the devotee free from his sense of guilt. Latu Maharaj continued: "What are you ashamed of, my son? The Lord has seen everything you have done. You cannot hide anything from Him. Since He knows all of it, why should you still be so melancholy? Instead, engage yourself in harder spiritual disciplines, keep the company of holy men, and come here now and then." These words helped the devotee regain his mental strength, and he began to practise spiritual disciplines more vigorously.[87]

Once two Western women came to see Latu Maharaj at Balaram's house, and discussed the humanitarian activities of the Ramakrishna Mission. They were atheists, but they believed in doing good works for the benefit of humanity. Chandrasekhar Chatterjee acted as interpreter.

First lady: "To do good to others is life's ideal — we agree with you on this point. But you give a higher place to God than to philanthropy, and we do not agree with that. God cannot be perceived, and there is no proof of His existence. We don't understand why you want people to have faith in this unknown entity first and then to do good to others."

Latu Maharaj: "Those who try to serve humanity without believing in God cannot keep it up for a long time. After a while the question crops up, 'What shall I gain from this?' And once this question arises, one begins to lose interest. Those who want to serve others will have to make personal sacrifices. You must realize that the desire to sacrifice for the sake of others cannot come unless one believes in God."

Hearing this, both ladies laughed and the second one remarked, "That is no explanation."

Latu Maharaj: "Will you please tell me why you want to do philanthropic work?"

Second lady: "We do philanthropic work because it does good to others."

Latu Maharaj: "But can you tell me what I shall get from it? Why should I work for the benefit of others?"

First lady: "Because we live in society, we have obligations to our fellow human beings, and fulfilling those obligations is our religion. Our ideal is to alleviate suffering."

Latu Maharaj: "There is a higher ideal than what you have just said, and that is the realization of God. Those who strive for it are heroes. To do good to others is, after all, only a social activity; it has nothing to do with God-realization. Moreover, philanthropic works may bring good to others, but what about you? Can you explain to me what benefit working for others will bring you?"

At this point, both of the ladies were puzzled. Latu Maharaj continued: "You see, there is a loophole in your argument. All arguments are invariably fallacious. Only if you admit the existence of God does everything become meaningful. When we bring God into our lives, distinctions lessen and we feel that all people are our own. On the physical plane there is a difference between myself and others, but on the spiritual plane we are the same Satchidananda (Existence-Consciousness-Bliss Absolute). From that standpoint no one can help another — one is only helping oneself. The key to our philanthropy is this: In doing good to others, we try to forget the apparent distinctions between ourselves and other people. The welfare of others is my welfare — that is our attitude. Who does not want his own good? If you believe in God and then serve society, you can never feel any resentment. . . . People may get social merit through philanthropic activities, but if their egos are involved in those activities, they will not get any spiritual merit. Even the result of a good action turns into a bondage if it is done with ego. On the other hand, unselfish action destroys the bondage of action and brings liberation to humanity."[88]

It is difficult to understand the moods of an illumined soul. Although his behaviour may sometimes seem strange to others, there is likely to be a deeper meaning behind what he does. Latu Maharaj would sometimes appear whimsical — his moods would change without warning. One day he got the idea of brass-plating Sri Ramakrishna's wooden cot, which was still in his room at Dakshineswar. He told a devotee about the idea, and the devotee agreed to finance the project. A few days later the devotee came to confirm the plans, but Latu Maharaj had changed his mind. He said: "Our Master could not touch metal. To brass-plate the cot wouldn't be right, so let us drop the matter."[89]

Although he generally scorned money, one day Latu Maharaj asked a devotee to write a letter to Abhedananda in America, asking him to send some money to pay for his cataract operation. The devotee wrote accordingly. One of Abhedananda's American devotees sent him some money. Another time Latu Maharaj decided that he wanted to own a watch, so he sent a letter to Abhedananda, asking for one. Sometime later he received a package from Abhedananda with the tail of a rattlesnake enclosed in it instead of the hoped-for watch. Latu Maharaj expressed his boyish annoyance in his reply: "I wanted a watch, and you have sent me the tail of a rattlesnake!"[90]

One of the qualities of a highly-evolved soul is simplicity; and simplicity is one of the most difficult qualities to imitate, for it is spontaneous. With Latu Maharaj, as with other holy men, one never knew what response he might make or what he might say, but it would always be straight to the point. Once a devotee came to visit Latu Maharaj in Calcutta after having attended the birth anniversary festival of Sri Ramakrishna at the Belur Monastery. He came with several friends. Latu Maharaj asked him, "How much did you give as an offering to the Lord in the shrine?" The devotee told him what he had given. Then Latu Maharaj asked about his friends. When he heard that they had not offered anything, he smiled, "Your friends want religion by 'bearing post.'" The devotee did not understand. Latu Maharaj explained that they wanted their letters to reach their destination without putting any stamps on them; thus the recipient must pay the postage. The devotee remarked, "Maharaj, you have coined a wonderful phrase."

Latu Maharaj continued: "So many people [five thousand, as reported by the devotee] took prasad at Belur Math and most of them did not donate anything. Is it good to take prasad without having offered something to the Lord? The monks do not have any money. Whatever the devotees offer to the Lord is again spent for the devotees. How much of it is used to feed a few monks? The Master used to say that one should make an offering when one visits a holy place."[91]

A Sanskrit poet once said that the ideal human character is as strong as a thunderbolt and as soft as a flower. Latu Maharaj's outward manner was stern and sometimes even forbidding, but once a person was allowed past that gruff exterior, he would find that inwardly the swami was sweetness and tenderness itself. In fact, when he was in a mood to talk, he would be very free and sociable. Even children liked to be with him and would play with him, climbing on his shoulders. Once Premananda told one of Latu Maharaj's close devotees: "You have nothing to fear. You have received the grace of Latu Maharaj. Such a loving monk is rarely seen. By the very touch of the air he moves in you will be purified and blessed."[92]

He was especially kindhearted to people who were genuinely suffering. Once a drunkard came to Latu Maharaj at midnight and, in his drunken state, insisted on offering the swami some food, so that afterwards he himself could take it as prasad. The man was rather belligerent, but Latu Maharaj quietly accepted the food, and the man went away satisfied. Latu Maharaj commented: "Such people want a little sympathy. Why should we not give it to them?"[93]

One day a devotee arrived to visit Latu Maharaj with his clothes thoroughly drenched from the rain. Latu Maharaj offered him one of his cloths to wear. The devotee was dismayed at the idea of wearing a monk's ochre cloth. But Latu Maharaj insisted, pointing out that if he fell sick from the exposure and wetness, he might not be able to work at his office and his situation would be worse than ever.[94]

Although many lives were changed by coming into contact with Latu Maharaj, he did not consciously accept any disciples. Latu Maharaj used to say: "Do you think that one man whispers a mantram into the ear of another, and then he becomes the guru and the other fellow his disciple? And does the disciple attain illumination immediately? Is it that easy? The guru can give a lot of advice, but everything is in the hand of God, just as the lawyer says that he has pleaded his case as best he can, now everything is in the hands of the judge."[95]

On another occasion he said: "Do you think that a monk is your sweeper who will keep sweeping your mind for you day after day? He may clean your mind once; after that it is up to you to keep it clean. If you don't have any motivation, what can a monk do? Can a holy man erase your past impressions, or do you think he will carry you to the Lord on his shoulders? He will show you the path, but you will have to walk it yourself. That is the only way to reach God."[96]

Sometimes Latu Maharaj would teach through jokes and stories and sometimes through scolding or silence. One day a devotee said to him:

"Maharaj, your scoldings are like chocolates in the shape of bayonets, they are so sweet and loving. Parents scold for the good of their children, but your scoldings are sweeter still, for parents could never give us so much love."[97]

In 1907 Holy Mother spent a few days at Balaram's house. One day she stopped for a minute at the door of Latu Maharaj and asked, "How are you, Latu, my child?" He always remembered the days at Dakshineswar when he had rendered personal service to her. "Go away," he said. "You are an honourable lady. Why have you come to the outer apartment to speak to me? Please go upstairs right away. I will not speak to you here. You could have sent for me, and I would have gone to see you. I am your servant, you know." Holy Mother laughed and left.

Every day Holy Mother sent a little prasad for Latu Maharaj, who visited her infrequently. When Holy Mother was leaving for Jayrambati, the devotees went upstairs to take the dust of her feet; but Latu Maharaj remained in his room. He began to pace back and forth and muttered: "Who is mother or father to a monk? He is free from all maya." The Mother stopped in front of his room and heard him still repeating those words. She said: "My child, you don't have to accept me." Latu Maharaj sprang from his room and fell at her feet, weeping without restraint. Holy Mother's eyes, too, became moist. Then Latu Maharaj began to wipe her tears with his cloth. He said: "You are going to your father's house, Mother; don't weep. Sharat will bring you back. Is it proper for one to cry when one departs?" Latu Maharaj's childlike simplicity, naturalness, and devotion to the Mother deeply moved all those who were present. "Is Latu an ordinary person?" the Mother once said to a monk. "It will do you good if you live with him."[98]

Latu Maharaj esteemed women greatly. He once told a group of male devotees: "Some men abuse women, but you should never raise your hand against them. You do not know how much they bear — they are forbearance itself. If you abuse them, where shall they turn? They are aspects of the Divine Mother, and if the Mother is insulted, the Lord is displeased. Thus your well-being lies in making them happy."[99]

It is amazing how Latu Maharaj, without ever studying Vedanta philosophy, would answer abstruse questions about Vedanta. One day Shashadhar Ganguly, a teacher from Malda, asked him, "Can the Atman be an object of knowledge?"

Latu Maharaj: "An object is something that cannot be known without the help of something else, but the Atman is self-revealing. So you cannot say the Atman is an object of knowledge."

28

Shashadhar: "Then why should we want to know the Atman?"

Latu Maharaj: "Because the Atman is our real nature."

Shashadhar: "If the Atman is our real nature, then why are we not aware of it?"

Latu Maharaj: "Listen, can anyone deviate from his real nature? If he does, it cannot be called his real nature; for it is changeable. Man's real nature is covered by a dense cloud of ignorance, and consequently he appears to be something different, but that does not mean he has deviated from his real nature.... Haven't you seen those polishing shops at Mechuabazar in Calcutta where they have glass jars filled with coloured liquids? The metal worker takes a tarnished brass pot and dips it into a jar, and instantly all the tarnish goes away and the pot starts to glitter. Then he dips it into another jar and it turns a golden colour. Similarly, dip your mind in the jar of the Lord's name, and all the unclean stuff will be washed away. Then dip it in the jar of the Lord's grace. You will see how beautifully your real nature will shine forth."[100]

In June 1911, after a number of years of strenuous work in Madras, Ramakrishnananda fell ill and returned to Calcutta. Latu Maharaj visited him almost every day. Soon after Ramakrishnananda passed away in August, Latu Maharaj began to talk about going to Varanasi and living there for the remainder of his life. When he told this to Girish Ghosh, the latter protested, "O sadhu, you are going to leave Calcutta, but who will let you go?"[101] Latu Maharaj dropped the idea, but took it up again after Girish's death in 1912.

In October 1912 Latu Maharaj left Balaram's house for Varanasi; he never returned to Calcutta. On the eve of his departure, just before getting into a carriage, he looked intently at the room where he had stayed for so many years. Then he said, "Maya, maya, maya," and saluted the Lord. At the Howrah Railway Station he was met by a devotee who was extremely downcast at his departure. Latu Maharaj reassured him: "Look here, my boy. Don't feel sad at my leaving. Over there flows the Mother Ganges, who saves the souls of the fallen and the forlorn. Sit on her bank as often as possible. People say that the company of holy men purifies one; so does the company of Mother Ganges. Meditate there. Pray and count your beads. You will see — your mind and body will become purified. Whenever restlessness strikes you, go there and sit quietly, and you will find that your mind will calm down. As you watch the waves of the Ganges, the waves of your mind will be calmed."[102]

At Varanasi

Latu Maharaj spent the last eight years of his life in the holy city of Varanasi. He first stayed at Ramakrishna Advaita Ashrama and later at different locations. As was characteristic of him, he was so often absorbed in meditation that he rarely had a fixed time for meals. Biharilal Sarkar, a district court judge of Calcutta and a staunch devotee of Latu Maharaj, visited him frequently. Biharilal wrote: "There was such irregularity in his daily life that one could not say whether he was living in a city or in a forest. Today he might take his meal at 10:00 p.m., tomorrow at twelve midnight, and the next day at 3:00 a.m. His routine was very uncertain. His attendant had to be always alert for the moment when he would get up from meditation and ask for a meal to be prepared. Perhaps at 1:00 a.m., all of a sudden, he would start to scold no one in particular for no reason. Others might wonder, but those who lived with him knew that he was struggling to bring his mind down from a high spiritual plane."[103]

A devotee who saw Latu Maharaj undergoing such spiritual practices at Varanasi once said to him: "Maharaj, you have seen Sri Ramakrishna and you served him for a long time. You have practised so much austerity on the bank of the Ganges in Calcutta. Why are you practising such rigorous austerity now in your old age?"

Latu Maharaj replied: "You know, merely seeing the Master and serving him are not enough for the attainment of the Highest. It is not that easy. Both self-effort and divine grace are necessary to realize God. Without self-effort how can one attain grace? You will have to work hard for even a little grace. Is it easy to hold onto the Lord's grace? Has grace a limited dimension that achieving it will make an aspirant quiet forever? Grace is infinite. Who knows in how many ways He will show His grace?"[104]

In Varanasi, Latu Maharaj continued to teach whoever came to him. He distributed his hard-earned spiritual treasures without reservation. A householder devotee of the Master once conveyed his love to Latu Maharaj in a letter. Latu Maharaj remarked: "Is it so easy to convey love to a person? A lot of spiritual discipline is needed to be able to really transmit love. What do ordinary people know about love? Only God can truly love, and only illumined souls are really able to transmit love." On another occasion he said: "Your love springs from worldly attachment. Dogs play together and also fight for food among themselves. Your love is like that. You people embrace each other and exchange sweet words, but the moment someone encroaches upon your self-interest, you become angry and are ready to hit him. Don't express that kind of love."[105]

One day some devotees were talking about worship. Latu Maharaj told them: "Do you know what worship is? Everything belongs to the Lord, so what is there to offer to Him? But the Master used to tell us: 'Once a rich man went to visit his orchard. He saw the gardeners busy with their work. The caretaker approached him and presented him with a ripe papaya, saying: "Sir, I picked this ripe fruit for you yesterday. Please accept it." Now the owner knows that the garden, the trees, the fruit all belong to him; but won't he appreciate the love and thoughtfulness of the caretaker? Worship is like this.'"[106]

Another devotee asked a common question: How can we love God or surrender to Him, without seeing Him? Latu Maharaj answered:

Don't you send your application for a job to the manager of a company without ever having seen him? Your interview with the manager depends upon sending your application to him. You write the application thus: "Sir, please appoint me for the job; I shall be extremely happy to serve you; I promise my unswerving obedience to you," and so on. And you write all this without having seen the manager, don't you?

Similarly, you can send an application to the Lord. However, this application is not to be written on paper, but on the pages of one's mind: "O Lord, may I never forget Your name. I take refuge in You. Please assign me to Your service and destroy my ego and doubts. You are my master, guru, father, mother, and all in all. I am Your child. Make me Your instrument. Do not delude me with Your bewitching maya. O my sweet Lord, I have not seen You; I have only heard Your name. Please make me Your own." You will have to pray like this daily. Only then will He choose to bestow His grace on you.[107]

Towards the end of Latu Maharaj's life, a devotee asked him, "Do you feel now that the world is a burden?" He answered: "Look, when you dive deep into the Ganges, though there are thousands of pounds of water above you, you don't feel that weight. Similarly, if you plunge into God's creation yet still hold onto Him, you will not feel its burden. Then the world becomes a place of merriment."[108]

His Passing Away

During his last days, Latu Maharaj seemed to be gradually withdrawing from the world. He wanted to speak with people less and less, and when he spoke it was generally of higher things. His body, which had once been remarkably strong, had been gradually weakened by age and by the effects of years of intense spiritual disciplines and his indifference towards the physical world. During the last few years he suffered from diabetes and minor physical ailments. Sometime in the last year of his life he developed a blister on his leg. He did not take care of it properly, and eventually gangrene set in. A devotee brought a doctor from Calcutta who operated on the wound and temporarily arrested the infection. The devotee stayed and nursed Latu Maharaj for a few weeks following the operation. One day, noticing an element of pride in the devotee, Latu Maharaj said to him: "Although you are serving me, do not boast of it to others. Remember that one should serve God, the guru, and the sick with great love and humility."[109]

During this time, Turiyananda, who was staying at the Ramakrishna Mission Home of Service at Varanasi, would often come to visit him and would sit by him silently for an hour or so. One day a devotee asked the swami: "Maharaj, why do you sit there silently like that? Latu Maharaj does not talk to you." Turiyananda replied: "Latu Maharaj is almost always in deep meditation. How can he talk with me? So I sit in silence for some time and then leave, having enjoyed his holy company."[110] Saradananda also came from Calcutta to visit him. He took the dust of Latu Maharaj's feet and then asked him, "Hello, sadhu, how are you?" Latu Maharaj replied, "It is troublesome to have a body." Later, another monk asked Saradananda, "Maharaj, why did you make salutation to Latu Maharaj?" The swami replied: "Latu Maharaj came to the Master before any of us. He is the most senior among the monastic disciples. Why shouldn't I salute him?"[111]

Latu Maharaj gradually severed the bonds of human relationships. Many a time the devotees heard him saying, "I have given up such-and-such a person's maya." They did not understand what he meant. On being asked, he replied: "Shall I have to carry the burdens of the devotees always? When I withdraw my mind from the world, I do not think of them."[112] Thus we see that although he did not formally accept disciples, he would share deeply in the joy and suffering of others.

Latu Maharaj said one day: "There are three possible relationships one can have with God: 'My God,' 'I am God,' and 'I am God's.' The last one is best, because it does not tempt pride."[113] Another day he spoke of Mahavir (Hanuman), the great devotee of Lord Rama: "In order to test Mahavir's devotion, Rama once asked him, 'How do you think of me?' Mahavir replied: 'Lord, while I identify myself with the body, I am Thy servant. When I consider myself as an individual soul, I am a part of Thee. And when I look upon myself as the Atman, I am one with Thee — this is my firm conviction.'"[114]

Eventually gangrene developed in the blister again. The doctors operated several times on successive days, but this time unsuccessfully, and the disease took its course. Latu Maharaj passed away in the holy city of Varanasi at 12:10 p.m. on Saturday, 24 April 1920.

On 12 May 1920 Turiyananda wrote to Miss Josephine MacLeod, an American devotee of Vivekananda:

> I am extremely sorry to let you know that Swami Adbhutananda — Latu Maharaj — is now no more. He breathed his last on the 24th of April. His passing away was indeed wonderful. He entered a meditative state from the first moment he fell ill, and remained absorbed in that state until he gave up the body. He had developed a small blister on his right ankle that developed into gangrene. All the best local medical help was requisitioned but to no avail and in ten days he expired. He showed no signs of pain during his illness. But the wonder of all wonders was that after his death when his body was placed in a sitting position to conform with some of the funeral rites, we found him looking so beautiful, so serene, so full of peace and bliss. His face beamed with light and an intelligence unspeakable, as if he were taking leave from his friends for the last time with an exhortation of affectionate benediction. Really, it was a sight for the gods to see.
>
> We chanted the name of the Lord for three hours and then took his body decorated with flower garlands, sandalpaste, etc., in procession to the Ganges side and carried [it] to Manikarnika by boat to be immersed in the holy water of the Mother Ganges after due performance of the last rites necessary for the occasion of *jala* [water] samadhi.
>
> Latu Maharaj entered into eternal peace and another son of Sri Ramakrishna joins him, making us feel poorer for this irreparable loss. Indeed, we have lost a spiritual giant in the person of Latu Maharaj, whose illiteracy and unsophisticated life helped him most to become what he was — a genuine and ardent devotee of Sri Ramakrishna.[115]

At the threshold of Latu's spiritual life, the Master had said to him (*pointing to himself*): "Here God alone exists. Do not forget this." "How can I forget someone who loves me so much?" answered Latu.[116] He did not forget. Throughout his life, his mind was filled with the thoughts of Sri Ramakrishna, and he would sometimes reveal to others the substance of these thoughts. Latu Maharaj completely fulfilled the name "Adbhutananda," one who enjoys the wonderful bliss of Brahman.

Michelet wrote in *The Bible of Humanity*, "Man must rest, get his breath, refresh himself at the great living wells, which keep the freshness of the eternal." Swami Adbhutananda was one such fountainhead of spirituality.

11

ॐ

SWAMI ABHEDANANDA

Ascertaining what is right and what is wrong is a great dilemma in human life. Sometimes people try to hide their mistakes by keeping quiet, concealing the truth, philosophizing and excusing improper conduct, or arguing to defend their actions. This is the nature of weak people. That person is truly great who does not hesitate to confess a mistake and tries to correct it immediately. Sometimes students do not see their own mistakes, so a real teacher always comes forward to correct them.

Kali was serving his guru, Sri Ramakrishna, during his last illness at the Cossipore garden house. There were two ponds in the compound, stocked with plenty of fish. Kali was a good angler. One day he caught some fish, and news of this reached the Master. In the evening when Kali was serving him, the Master asked, "Is it true that you have been catching many fish with a fishing rod?" "Yes, sir." The Master said, "It is a sin to catch fish with a fishing rod, for thereby living beings are killed."

In defense Kali quoted from the Gita: "He who thinks that the Self is the slayer as well as he who thinks that the Self is slain is ignorant, for the Self neither slays nor is slain" (2.19). He further added, "So why should it be a sin to catch fish?"

Ramakrishna smiled and tried to make Kali understand through various arguments. He said, "When a person attains true knowledge, he does not take a false step." Suddenly the Master began coughing and there was a trace of blood in his sputum. Frightened by this, Kali told him: "Sir, talking

SWAMI ABHEDANANDA

will aggravate your cancer. Please do not talk anymore." But the Master said: "I consider you to be one of the most intelligent of the boys. You will understand if you meditate on what I have said."

According to Ramakrishna's instructions, Kali meditated for three days and realized the meaning behind his statement. He went to the Master and said: "Sir, I have now realized why it is wrong to catch fish. I shall not do it again. Please forgive me." The Master was very pleased to hear this. He said: "It is deceitful to catch fish in this way. Hiding a hook inside bait and hiding poison in food offered to an invited guest are sins of the same kind." Kali humbly accepted what the Master said and felt his infinite compassion. Ramakrishna continued: "It is true that the Atman does not die nor is It killed. But he who has realized this truth is the Atman him self, so why should he have the tendency to kill others? As long as the tendency to kill remains, he is not identified with the Atman nor does he have any Self-knowledge. That is why I say that when one attains true knowledge one does not take any false step. You should realize that the Atman is beyond the body, the sense organs, the mind, and the intellect, and that It is the witness of phenomena."[1] The Master's words penetrated Kali's heart and he realized the truth.

Kali Prasad Chandra was born on Tuesday, 2 October 1866, at 21 Nimu Goswami Lane, Ahiritola, North Calcutta. His father, Rasiklal Chandra, was an English teacher in the Oriental Seminary. His first wife died, leaving a son and a daughter. This son's name was Biharilal; he later became a Christian. At the request of friends and relatives, Rasiklal married Nayantara Devi, a gentle and spiritual girl who was fourteen years old. She was an ideal wife. In the course of time she had nine children: the first five of them died at an early age; of the remaining four, Kali was the second. Before Kali was born, Nayantara prayed to the Divine Mother Kali for a son. When the child was born, she gave him the name "Kali Prasad," or the blessings of Mother Kali.

In 1871, at the age of five, Kali was admitted to Govinda Seal's nursery school, where he studied for two years. He learned the alphabet, heard stories from the Ramayana and the Mahabharata, and began to memorize Sanskrit verses on morality and ethics. He then joined Jadu Pandit's Banga Vidyalaya, and in the evening he would go to a Sanskrit school at Hatibagan, where he studied Sanskrit grammar. Kali was a bright student and a voracious reader. During this period, along with his regular courses, he studied classical Sanskrit literature, including the *Hitopodesha*, *Raghuvamsham*, *Kumarasambhavam*, *Shakuntala*, and *Bhatti-kavyam*. He learned prosody and could compose verses in Sanskrit. At the age of ten Kali was admitted to the Oriental Seminary, the well-known high school where his father taught English.

One needs sound health in order to practise spiritual disciplines. Although from his boyhood Kali was more interested in developing his intellect, he did not neglect his health. He swam regularly in the Ganges with his friends and exercised daily in a neighbourhood gymnasium. However, once Kali had read Herbert Spencer's *Education*, in which the author claims that those who do vigorous physical exercise do so at the expense of their brains, he stopped going to the gymnasium.

Kali had studied Wilson's *History of India* and there had learned about Shankaracharya, the great exponent of Vedanta. Shankara's life and works inspired young Kali and thenceforth he cherished a desire to become a pandit and philosopher like him. Kali took a drawing class in school and within a year excelled. The teacher praised his skill and prophesied a bright future for him, but one day Kali told the teacher that he would not come to the drawing class anymore because he had decided to become a philosopher. Kali's teacher tried to convince him that it was better to be a painter than a philosopher. But Kali replied: "No, sir. A painter studies the surface of things but a philosopher goes below the surface and studies the causes of things. So I want to be a philosopher."[2]

Kali had been extremely inquisitive from his boyhood. To satisfy his hunger for knowledge, he would ask his father various questions that surprised the wise English teacher. In addition, Kali would use his savings to buy books instead of refreshments. Kali had a remarkable memory and keen power of concentration: He learned to fish, shop, cook, work with wood, garden, bind books, and so on. When he was fourteen he found a copy of the Bhagavad Gita in his father's study and began reading it. But his father told him that it was too difficult a book for one so young; taking the book away from Kali, he hid it in his room. When his father left the house, Kali searched for the book and located it. In the dead of night when everybody was asleep, he read the Gita by the light of an oil lamp.

In the 1880s Calcutta was the capital of India, and the city pulsated with cultural activities as well as political and religious movements. Kali attended the lectures of Surendranath Banerjee, a great national leader; Keshab Chandra Sen and Pratap Chandra Majumdar, the famous Brahmo leaders; and Reverend Kali Charan Banerjee, a Christian evangelist. At that time Hindu leaders were working to protect their religion from the onslaught of Christian propaganda. In 1882-83 Pandit Shashadhar Tarkachudamani, a well-known scholar, began to interpret Hinduism from the scientific point of view, and gave a series of lectures on the six systems of Hindu philosophy. Kali regularly attended those lectures in Albert Hall. One day he expressed a desire to learn the *Yoga Aphorisms* of Patanjali from him, but Shashadhar told Kali that he had no time and referred him to another renowned scholar, Kalibar Vedantavagish.

Kali's desire to learn the scriptures was phenomenal. He went to Vedantavagish, who was then translating Patanjali's *Yoga Aphorisms* from Sanskrit into Bengali. Vedantavagish told Kali that he had no spare time to teach him the *Yoga Sutras*; but he could explain the sutras to him in the mornings while his attendant gave him an oil massage before his bath. Kali began to visit the pandit every morning; while he read the aphorisms, the pandit would explain them. Thus he completed his study of yoga philosophy.

Kali then bought a copy of *Shiva Samhita* and learned the disciplines of hatha yoga, kundalini yoga, pranayama, and raja yoga. He had a desire to be absorbed in samadhi through *khechari mudra*, a special technique of hatha yoga; but he was told not to practise any of the methods described in hatha yoga treatises without being properly instructed by a competent yogi.

With Sri Ramakrishna at Dakshineswar

The scriptures did not quench Kali's thirst for knowledge, so he desperately searched for a spiritual teacher. In June 1884 Kali went to Dakshineswar and met Sri Ramakrishna. In his autobiography, he describes their first meeting:

I became restless to find a guru who could teach me yoga. I confided my desire to my classmate Yajneshwar Bhattacharya, who was very fond of me. Yajneshwar told me: "I know a wonderful yogi. His name is Sri Ramakrishna Paramahamsa, and he lives in Rani Rasmani's temple garden in Dakshineswar. He has no pretensions. Many respectable people visit him, and he sometimes comes to Calcutta. Perhaps he can fulfill your desire to learn yoga." My joy knew no bounds when I heard this from Yajneshwar, and I at once resolved to meet Sri Ramakrishna, though I had no idea where Dakshineswar was.

One Sunday morning I started for Dakshineswar by asking directions from people on the street. I crossed the Baghbazar bridge and walked north on the Barrackpore Trunk Road. It was quite a distance. I then asked a person on the road about the temple garden of Dakshineswar. He told me: "You have gone the wrong way. The Kali Temple is on the bank of the Ganges." Finally I reached the temple garden at eleven o'clock. When I asked about Sri Ramakrishna, a temple worker informed me that he had gone to Calcutta that morning. I was exhausted, having walked all that way barefoot in the sun. Disappointed, I sat on the steps of Sri Ramakrishna's northern veranda and wondered how I could ever go back to Calcutta. I was hungry and thirsty, I was dead tired, I had no money, I had not informed my family as to where I was going, I had no acquaintance in Dakshineswar, and moreover I had no strength to walk back to Calcutta. I began to cry.

Just then another young man arrived and asked me about Sri Ramakrishna, and I told him that he had gone to Calcutta. The young man was also disappointed. We then talked and got acquainted with each other. On inquiry I learned that his name was Shashi. He advised me about my circumstances, saying, "Have a bath in the Ganges, take prasad, and then return to Calcutta after a rest." Later in the afternoon, when I expressed my intention to return to Calcutta, Shashi told me: "You should not return home without seeing the Master. Is there any certainty that such an opportunity will come again in your lifetime? Since you have come to see him with so much difficulty, it is better for you to wait." I knew my parents would be worried about me because I had not told them where I was going. Understanding how I felt, Shashi said to me: "Look, brother, I have also come here without informing my parents. Don't worry. We shall stay here tonight. The Master will positively return from Calcutta by late evening, as he never stays overnight at any devotee's house in Calcutta."

Shashi showed me around and in the evening took me to the Kali Temple to attend the vesper service. I felt tremendous peace and joy. Ramlal, the Master's nephew, gave us some luchis and sweets for refreshments. We waited on the northern veranda for the Master's arrival. Finally a horse carriage arrived at the northeastern corner of the Master's room, and Shashi and Ramlal went to receive the Master. My heart was beating hard. I stood where I was, motionless. After getting down from the carriage, Sri Ramakrishna said, "Kali, Kali, Kali," entered his room, and sat on his small cot.

Ramlal and Shashi informed the Master about me while I waited on the veranda. Then Ramlal came out and said that the Master was waiting for me. I entered the room and bowed down to him. The Master asked about me and I told him: "I have a desire to learn yoga. Will you kindly teach me?" The Master kept quiet for a while and then said: "It is a good sign that you have a desire to learn yoga at this young age. You were a yogi in your previous life. A little was left for perfection. This will be your last birth. Yes, I shall teach you yoga. Rest tonight and come to me again tomorrow morning."

The next morning Ramlal told me the Master was waiting to see me. Entering his room I bowed down to him. He then asked me what I was studying, and I replied, "I am now in the Entrance class [tenth grade]." "Very good," said the Master. Then he took me to the northern veranda. He asked me to sit on a cot. When I was seated in the lotus posture, the Master asked me to stick out my tongue. As soon as I did that, he wrote a mantram on it with the middle finger of his right hand and advised me to meditate on Kali, the Divine Mother. I did what he said. Gradually I lost outer consciousness and sat in deep meditation. I felt an unspeakable joy within. I don't know how long I stayed in that condition. After some time the Master touched my chest and brought me back to outer consciousness. He then asked me what had happened, and I told him about my blissful experience during meditation. He was very pleased. Afterwards the Master instructed me on meditation and sang these lines of a mystical song:

> When will you sleep in the divine chamber
> With the clean [good] and the unclean [evil]?
> When these two wives are friendly to each other,
> Mother Shyama will be within your reach.

The Master further told me to meditate every morning and again at night and to report to him my visions and spiritual experiences. Then the Master asked me to go to the Kali Temple and meditate there. When I returned from the temple the Master gave me prasad and asked me to visit him again. He even offered to provide my fare if I could not get it from home. In the meantime a devotee had arrived by carriage from Calcutta to visit the Master, and the Master asked me to return home with that devotee. On my way back home I thought of the Master's overwhelming love and compassion.[3]

Meanwhile, a great commotion erupted at Kali's home when he had not returned by Sunday afternoon. His mother cried, thinking that he might have drowned in the Ganges. His parents searched for him in every possible location. At last his mother remembered that recently Kali had inquired about the temple garden of Rani Rasmani, so she asked her husband to go to Dakshineswar. The next morning Rasiklal reached Dakshineswar and learned from Sri Ramakrishna that Kali had already left for Calcutta. While leaving Dakshineswar Rasiklal said to Ramakrishna: "Sir, Kali is my son. Please advise him to get married and become a householder." "Your son is a great yogi," replied Ramakrishna. "As he does not want to get married, what good would it be to force him to marry?" Rasiklal said, "It is the supreme dharma for a son to serve his parents."[4] Ramakrishna kept quiet. With great relief, Rasiklal returned home.

Spiritual life is not always smooth and easy. Without exception every seeker of God faces internal as well as external obstacles. After his first visit Kali had felt an attraction for the Master, and whenever he could he went to see him in Dakshineswar. His father did not approve of these frequent visits, and he locked the main door of the house so that Kali could not go to Dakshineswar. One afternoon someone left the door unlocked; Kali ran to the Ahiritola ghat and went to Dakshineswar by boat. That night he stayed with the Master.

Kali began to practise spiritual disciplines under the Master's guidance and through his grace was blessed with many wonderful visions of gods and goddesses. One day while meditating at home, Kali saw various gods and goddesses and divine incarnations — Krishna, Christ, Chaitanya, and others — merge one by one into the luminous form of Sri Ramakrishna. He hastened to Dakshineswar and narrated this experience to the Master. To this Sri Ramakrishna said: "Ah, you have seen *Vaikuntha* [the abode of Vishnu]! Henceforth you will no longer have these visions. You have risen to the formless state."[5] This proved to be true. From then on, during meditation Kali's mind was absorbed in the infinite — the vastness of the Impersonal Brahman, rather than divine forms. After this vision Kali was fully convinced that the Master was an avatar, as he later wrote in a Sanskrit hymn to Ramakrishna.

Ramakrishna trained each disciple separately. As Ramakrishna did not teach through books or through any set curriculum, it is important to learn from each disciple how he was trained. Kali wrote in his autobiography:

> Whenever I went to Dakshineswar I would give personal service to the Master. I would carry his towel and water pot when he went to the pine grove to answer the calls of nature. Sometimes the Master would walk around the Panchavati with his hand on my shoulder. I also went with the Master to Girish Ghosh's Star Theatre to see the *Chaitanya Lila* and *Prahlad Charitra* plays. Every Saturday and Sunday devotees would gather at Dakshineswar to see the Master. I also began visiting him on Saturday afternoons, returning to Calcutta the following day with some devotees. Thus I became acquainted with other disciples of the Master.
>
> I would really feel immense bliss in my heart to hear the teachings of the Master. When in ecstasy, he would sometimes laugh, sometimes

cry, sometimes dance, and sometimes go into samadhi. Again at other times he would joyously sing in his melodious voice the songs of Ramprasad, Kamalakanta, and other mystic composers. Occasionally he would sing kirtan, depicting Radha and Krishna's divine play in Vrindaban. Sometimes while describing the divine play of Rama and Sita, he would, like the great saint Tulasidas, float in an ocean of bliss. The spirit of the harmony of religions was reflected in Sri Ramakrishna's everyday life, and he constantly taught his followers the liberal, universal message, "As many faiths, so many paths."

Ramakrishna also used to teach us to chant "*Haribol, Haribol,*" [literally, "chant the name of the Lord"] loudly while clapping our hands. When somebody asked him the reason for clapping one's hands, he said: "As the birds of the tree fly away when one claps one's hands loudly, so the sinful thoughts of the mind go away when one chants God's name while clapping one's hands." Every evening in Dakshineswar the Master would sit on his bed facing the north and repeat, "Haribol, Haribol" while clapping his hands. Sometimes he would repeat "Hari is my guru, my guru is Hari." "O Krishna, O Krishna." "O Govinda, you are my life and soul." "Not I, not I — but Thou, Thou." "I am an instrument, you are the operator." Then he would go into ecstasy. In that state he would importune Mother Kali, but his words would not be audible to us. Watching his God-intoxicated state we were amazed. We felt that the Master was in communion with the Divine Mother, that he was talking to Her, and that the Mother was answering his questions. We realized that Sri Ramakrishna was not a human being. He was God.

Ramakrishna taught us to practise japam and meditation every morning and evening. About meditation, he sometimes referred to his naked guru Tota Puri's illustration, telling us, "Tota used to say that if a brass water pot is not cleansed every day, stains accumulate on it; likewise, if the mind is not cleansed by meditation every day, impurities accumulate in it."

Sometimes while teaching us, the Master would tell us about his own sadhana. He said: "When I meditated I became like a motionless stone image. Sometimes birds sat on my head, but I could not feel them." In fact, during deep meditation, when the mind becomes still and motionless, one does not notice if flies or mosquitoes sit on the body. The Master used to say that this is a sign of a concentrated mind.[6]

Whenever Ramakrishna visited the devotees' homes in Calcutta, Kali would go there and listen to the Master's wonderful conversations. On 3 July 1884 he went to Balaram's house in Baghbazar, where the Master had gone to attend the Chariot Festival of Jagannath (Krishna). Kali recorded the event:

Many devotees were present and Vaishnav Charan sang kirtan:
O tongue, always repeat the name of Mother Durga!
Who but your Mother Durga will save you in distress? . . .
As soon as Sri Ramakrishna heard a line or two of the song he went into samadhi. Then the Master sang, "O Mother, for Yashoda Thou wouldst dance when she called Thee her precious 'Blue Jewel'. . ."
In the meantime a small decorated chariot of Lord Jagannath had been brought to the upper veranda, and the Master pulled it along with the devotees. While pulling the chariot the Master sang:
Behold, the two brothers [Gauranga and Nityananda] have come,
Who weep while chanting Hari's name. . . .
He sang again:
See how all Nadia [the birthplace of Gauranga] is shaking
Under the waves of Gauranga's love! . . .
It was a divine sight! The Master sang and danced in ecstasy, and the devotees joined him. Afterwards the Master sat in the big hall and told Pandit Shashadhar: "This is called *bhajanananda*, or the bliss derived from the worship of God. Worldly people enjoy pleasure derived from lust and gold, and devotees attain the bliss of Brahman through the worship of God." Thus the devotees passed joyful days with the Master.[7]

Ramakrishna was very fond of ice cream. One hot summer day in April, a Calcutta devotee brought some ice cream for him, which he relished like a young boy. Coincidentally, from then on he had a sore throat. At first he ignored it, but it was finally diagnosed as cancer. Several doctors were consulted who prescribed various medicines. Despite his illness, Ramakrishna continued to teach his disciples. In the month of Jaistha (May-June) 1885 Kali went with the Master to attend the Vaishnava festival at Panihati where he witnessed the Master in samadhi during kirtan.

It was the Master's last outing. After this trip his pain increased and was unrelenting. He had great difficulty swallowing, eating, and talking. Kali recalled:

One day Golap-ma said to the Master: "Dr. Durga Charan of Calcutta is a reputable physician. Perhaps he can find some remedy for you." Immediately the Master agreed to visit him. That night I stayed at Dakshineswar. Latu and Golap-ma were also there. The next morning the Master, Golap-ma, Latu, and I went to Calcutta by boat. After landing there, we rented a horse carriage and went to the doctor's office at Beadon Square. Out of his mercy the Master asked me to sit next to him, and Golap-ma and Latu sat on the opposite seat.

The doctor examined the Master's throat and prescribed some medications. Then we went to the Ahiritola ghat and rented a boat for Dakshineswar. It was about 1:30 p.m. and none of us had had any food. The Master was hungry. He asked the boatman to anchor the boat at the Baranagore ghat and then asked me to buy some sweets from a nearby market. Golap-ma had four pice with her which she gave me. I immediately went to the market and bought some *chanar murki* [small, sweet cheese balls]. The Master took the packet of sweets from my hand and joyfully ate them all. He then threw the empty packet into the Ganges and drank some water from the river with his hands. He showed his satisfaction. The Master knew that the three of us were hungry, but without sharing any sweets he had eaten everything. It was amazing! As soon as his hunger was relieved, our own stomachs felt full. We looked at each other silently. Then the Master smiled and like a boy began to make jokes — which he continued all the way to Dakshineswar. We all got out of the boat, and later the three of us discussed what had happened and realized that it was a miracle.

A similar event occurred when Krishna was alive and enacted his divine play. When the five Pandavas and their wife Draupadi were living in the forest during their exile, the sage Durvasa went to their cottage with his twelve hundred disciples and asked for food. According to the custom guests had to be fed, for otherwise it would be very inauspicious. Durvasa and his disciples went to the river for a bath, and while they were gone, the helpless Draupadi called on Krishna to come to the rescue. Krishna came and asked Draupadi for some food. There was nothing but a few particles of rice and a little spinach at the bottom of a cooking vessel. Krishna ate this and drank a glass of water and by doing so, filled the stomachs of Durvasa and his disciples. So it is said, "If God is pleased the whole world becomes pleased." That day I realized this truth by observing Sri Ramakrishna's life.[8]

At Shyampukur and Cossipore

In September 1885 Ramakrishna was taken from Dakshineswar to 55 Shyampukur Street in Calcutta, in order to have his cancer treated. Several reputable physicians, notably Dr. Mahendralal Sarkar, attended him; Holy Mother took the responsibility of preparing his diet; and the disciples, including Kali, nursed their guru around the clock. Kali recalled:

One day the Master was in deep samadhi, seated on his bed like a wooden statue. He had no outer consciousness. Dr. Mahendralal Sarkar checked his pulse and felt no throbbing. He then put his stethoscope on the Master's heart and did not get a heartbeat. Next, Dr. Sarkar touched the Master's eyeballs with his finger, but still the Master's outer consciousness did not return. The doctor was dumbfounded. After some time the Master returned to the normal plane of consciousness and began talking with the doctor about God.

It may be asked why the Master had cancer. It is really difficult to answer this question. Once while staying at the Shyampukur house the Master said: "The Divine Mother has shown me that people are getting rid of their sins by touching my feet. I am absorbing the results of their sinful actions, so I am suffering from this terrible cancer." This is called "vicarious atonement."[9]

Sri Ramakrishna lived in the Shyampukur house for three months. However, instead of abating, his disease worsened. Because the air in Calcutta is very polluted, the doctors advised that he be moved to the country. After searching for a place, the devotees found a spacious garden house in Cossipore, a suburb of Calcutta, which they rented for eighty rupees per month. On 11 December 1885 the Master was taken there, accompanied by Holy Mother, Golap-ma, his niece Lakshmi, and his young attendants. One day the Master told his disciples: "This cancer in my throat is a ruse. It is because of this that you have gathered together."[10]

Holy Mother prepared for the Master a special diet, with Golap-ma and Lakshmi helping her. Gradually the number of attendants increased, so a brahmin cook and a maidservant were hired. Narendra created a schedule so that everyone could take turns serving the Master. Kali would attend him two hours during the day and again two hours at night. The Master would sit on a small stool on the terrace while Kali bathed him with warm water.

After a few days in Cossipore the Master felt a little relief. The large room on the upper floor of the house was used as the Master's bedroom; to the south of that was an open terrace over the portico. The Master used to stand on the open terrace and gaze at the trees and creepers in the garden. The fresh air proved to be beneficial for his health, and this raised the devotees' hopes that he might completely recover.

One day Kali's father came to Cossipore and told Ramakrishna that his wife was crying bitterly for her son; he requested the Master to send Kali home for a visit. Ramakrishna immediately sent Kali home; his parents were delighted to see him. Kali wrote in his autobiography:

With tears in her eyes my mother asked me to have supper and to stay for the night. But within half an hour I felt uncomfortable at home. I felt as if I were in hellfire. My heart was restless and thoughts of the Master haunted me. I tried to control my desire to run away from home, but failed. After hurriedly eating some refreshments, I said goodbye to my parents and returned to Cossipore. The Master was surprised to see me and asked, "Did you not go home?" "Yes, sir. I did." "Your parents must have asked you to stay at home. Why did you not stay?" "I did stay." "How long?" "For half an hour." "But why did you return?"

"I went with the idea of staying at home tonight. My parents also begged me to stay. But I felt great agony while I was there. My mind longed to return to you. While there I felt as if I were in hell, so I ate a few sweets and hurried back here after saying goodbye to them. My mind was pacified only after arriving back here."

With a faint smile the Master said to me affectionately: "Very well! There is no doubt that you will have peace here." In fact I always felt peace and joy when I was around the Master. Parental affection seemed insipid compared to the Master's pure love.[11]

Sometime in the middle of January 1886, the elder Gopal wanted to distribute twelve pieces of ochre cloth and twelve rosaries to some monks. Pointing to his young disciples, the Master said: "You won't find better monks than these. Give your cloths and rosaries to them." Instead, Gopal offered them to the Master and he himself distributed them among his young disciples. Thus Sri Ramakrishna himself started his monastic order. Kali was among those who received an ochre cloth, the garb of a monk, from the Master.

It is an ancient Indian custom for monks to live on alms. One day the Master asked his disciples to go out and beg for food. This act helps eradicate the ego and teaches one to depend solely on God. Narendra, Niranjan, Kali, and Hutko Gopal first went to Holy Mother and asked for alms, chanting this hymn on the goddess Annapurna:

> O Parvati, the goddess of food, whose store is overflowing,
> O beloved of Shankara, give me alms so that I may attain
> knowledge and wisdom.

The merciful mother, taken by surprise, gave them a handful of alms. They then went from door to door begging for food. Some gave them rice, some gave vegetables or fruit. Some scolded them, saying: "You young fellows, are you not ashamed to beg for food disguised as beggars? Go away and find a job." Some remarked: "These young men are robbers. They have come to get information so that they can return at night and rob us." The young disciples endured all kinds of criticism. When at last they returned to the Master with their alms, he was very pleased. Holy Mother cooked a portion of the food. After partaking of it, the Master remarked: "The food obtained from begging is pure. It is not defiled by anyone's selfish desire. I am very pleased to eat it today."[12]

Narendra was extremely worried about the Master's physical condition. One winter night when he was pacing in the Cossipore garden with Sharat, Kali, Niranjan, and the elder Gopal, he expressed his thoughts to them: "The Master is suffering from a terminal disease. Who can say if he has not made up his mind to give up his body? While there is still time, let us make as much spiritual progress as we can by performing service, meditation, and devotional exercises. Otherwise, when he passes away, there will be no limit to our repentance. To postpone calling on the Lord till desires are fulfilled! This is exactly how our days are passing, and we are getting more and more entangled in the net of desires. It is these desires only that lead to destruction and death. So let us give up desires."

Shortly afterwards Narendra saw a dry heap of grass and some broken tree branches and said: "Set fire to it. Holy men light *dhunis* [sacred fires] under trees at this time. Let us also light a dhuni and burn up our desires." A fire was lit, and they meditated for a few hours, mentally offering their worldly desires into the blazing fire. It gave them tremendous peace and joy. At 4:00 a.m. they extinguished the fire and went to their beds.[13]

The disciples learned a scientific religion from their Master: One must first experiment with the truth, then verify it, and at last accept it. One day Narendra was having a discussion with Kali, Jogin, and Tarak on Hindu prejudices about food and the knowledge of Brahman. He said: "After attaining Self-knowledge, food can be taken from anyone's hand. Then one cannot look down upon anyone. As long as prejudices persist, Brahman has not been fully realized." Except for Narendra, none of them had ever eaten Muslim food. "Come, let me break your prejudices today," Narendra said to his brother disciples. In the evening Narendra took Kali and others to a Muslim restaurant on Beadon Street and ordered chicken curry. After dinner they returned to Cossipore. Later that night Kali related the whole story to the Master who laughed heartily and said: "It is all right. You are now free from all prejudice."[14]

When Kali was not serving the Master, he would meditate and study Eastern and Western philosophy. Once he was reading John Stuart Mill's logic, philosophy, and essays on religion. One night, seeing him reading in his room, the Master asked, "My boy, what are you reading?" "It is an English book on logic that teaches how to make arguments about the existence of God," replied Kali. "Very well," Ramakrishna replied. "It is you who have introduced the habit of reading among the boys. You should know that book-learning is of no value. If you want to kill yourself, a nail-cutter can serve the purpose. But if you are to kill others, you need swords, shields, and other weapons. Study is necessary for that purpose. Those who will teach people are to read books."[15]

It was March 1886. During *Shivaratri* (the spring festival of Lord Shiva) the disciples of Ramakrishna observed a fast and a vigil, worshipping the Lord four times throughout the night. During the break after the first worship, all left the room except Narendra and Kali. Suddenly Narendra wanted to use Kali to test his power to transmit superconsciousness. He said to Kali, "Please touch me for a while." A little later another disciple entered the room and found Narendra in deep meditation and Kali seated, touching Narendra's right knee, his hand rapidly trembling. After a few minutes Narendra opened his eyes and inquired, "How did you feel?" Kali replied, "I felt as if a current were entering into me, just as when one holds an electric battery, one's hand trembles all the while."[16]

During the second worship Kali went into deep meditation and lost outer consciousness. His body became stiff, and his neck and head were a little bent. After the last worship Shashi came to the worship room and informed Narendra that the Master wanted to see him. As soon as Narendra entered the room, the Master said: "Well, you are frittering away your power before you have accumulated enough. Gather it first and then you will understand how much of it you should spend and in what way. Mother will let you know. Do you understand what great harm you have done to that boy by infusing your idea into him? He had been following a particular line for a long time. All is spoilt now. Well, what's done is done. Never do it again. However, the boy is lucky."[17] Narendra was dumbfounded.

From that time onward, Kali defended his actions through nondualistic Vedanta. Studying the *Ashtavakra Samhita* and practising discrimination between the real and the unreal through the "*neti neti*" (not this, not this) process of nondualistic Vedanta, Kali began to argue against others' ideas about blind faith in God. When the elder Gopal reported to Ramakrishna that Kali had become an atheist, the Master smiled. However, when Kali was serving the Master one night, he said, "Hello, I hear you have become an atheist." Kali kept quiet. The Master questioned him further: "Do you believe in God? Do you accept the validity of the scriptures?" "No, sir," replied Kali. To this the Master said, "If you had said this to another holy man, he would have slapped your face." "Sir, you are free to do so. As long as I do not realize that God exists and that the Vedas are true how can I blindly accept these things? If you kindly enlighten me and give me spiritual insight, I shall accept them all." Kali's sincerity impressed Ramakrishna who said with delight: "A day will come when you will know and accept everything; but don't be one-sided. I don't care for one-sidedness."[18]

One can refute another's ideas but one cannot refute another's experience, just as the taste of sugar's sweetness cannot be nullified by arguing against it. Sri Ramakrishna knew that words were not enough to convince his disciple, so he began to resolve Kali's doubts and misconceptions about Brahman by giving him his own experience of cosmic consciousness. Kali wrote in his autobiography:

> One afternoon, while the Master was lying on his bed, a man was pacing back and forth outside on the green lawn of the garden house. The Master said to me: "Please ask that man not to walk on the grass. I am in great pain, as if he were walking on my chest." I was amazed when I heard his words and actually saw the man on the grass. I hurriedly went outside and asked the man not to walk on the grass. Then the Master was relieved.
>
> Pandit Shashadhar had great love and respect for Sri Ramakrishna. One day he came to see the Master at Cossipore when the cancer was in an advanced stage. Shashadhar said to the Master, "Sir, if you put your mind on your throat a little, your cancer will surely be cured." The Master answered, "How can the mind that I have already offered to the Lord be diverted again to this body of flesh and blood?" But still Shashadhar pleaded, "Sir, when you talk to the Divine Mother, please ask Her to cure your cancer." Then the Master replied: "When I see the Mother of the Universe, I forget my body and the universe. So, how can I tell the Mother about this insignificant body of flesh and blood?" The pandit was dumbfounded. We too remained still. No one spoke a word.[19]

At one time the main topic of discussion and meditation among the disciples in their leisure hours was the life and teachings of Buddha. Narendra was well-versed in Buddhism, and his enthusiasm was contagious. On the wall of the meditation room, the vow of Buddha was inscribed in bold letters: "Let my body dry up on this seat; let my skin, flesh, and bones be dissolved; without realizing that Enlightenment which is difficult to attain even in aeons, I won't let the body move from this seat."

One day, Narendra, Kali, and Tarak secretly planned to visit Bodh Gaya, where Buddha had attained nirvana. They left one evening without informing the Master. Tarak provided the passage money. They crossed the Ganges and took a train from the Bally Station. After arriving in Bodh

Gaya they went to the temple and recited, "I take refuge in Buddha." While they meditated under the Bo tree, Narendra had a vision of light, and he felt the presence of Buddha. Kali wrote: "A current of peace seemed to be flowing all over my body. Brother Tarak also remained absorbed in deep meditation."[20] They stayed in Bodh Gaya three or four days and at last returned to Cossipore. Sri Ramakrishna was happy to see them return. He remarked: "Go around the world, and you will find that true religion does not exist anywhere. Whatever of spirituality there is, it (*pointing to his own body*) is all here."[21]

M. recorded the attitude of Kali at that time in *The Gospel of Sri Rama-krishna*:

> Shashi: "Kali said to the Master: 'What's the good of having joy? The Bhils [a savage tribe] are joyous. Savages are always singing and dancing in a frenzy of delight.'"
>
> Rakhal: "He [*meaning the Master*] replied to Kali: 'What do you mean? Can the Bliss of Brahman be the same as worldly pleasure? Ordinary men are satisfied with worldly pleasure. One cannot enjoy the Bliss of Brahman unless one completely rids oneself of attachment to worldly things. There is the joy of money and sense experience, and there is the Bliss of God-realization. Can the two ever be the same? The rishis enjoyed the Bliss of Brahman.'"
>
> M: "You see, Kali nowadays meditates on Buddha; that is why he speaks of a state beyond Bliss."
>
> Rakhal: "Yes, Kali told the Master about Buddha. Sri Ramakrishna said to him: 'Buddha is an Incarnation of God. How can you compare him to anybody else? As he is great, so too is his teaching great.' Kali said to him: 'Everything, indeed, is the manifestation of God's Power. Both worldly pleasure and the Bliss of God are the manifestation of the Power.'"
>
> M: "What did the Master say to that?"
>
> Rakhal: "He said: 'How can that be? Is the power to beget a child the same as the power through which one realizes God?'"[22]

One day Vijaykrishna Goswami, a religious leader and devotee, came to Cossipore to see Sri Ramakrishna. While there he spoke highly of a great hatha yogi whom he had met in a cave of the Barabar Hills in Gaya. Having heard about the yogi, Kali desperately wanted to see him. He collected his train fare, and without telling anybody, left for Gaya. From the Gaya Station he walked eight miles and reached a village at the foot of Barabar Hills, where he passed the night in an inn meant for pilgrims. There he met a monk of the Dashnami-Puri sect and copied from his note-book the monastic vows of Shankara's order (*viraja-homa mantras* including the *presh mantram* [a special mantram], *math* [monastery], *madi* [sect], and *yogapatta* [name]).

The next morning Kali got directions to the yogi's cave, but the villagers warned him not to go to the hatha yogi because his disciples threw stones at anyone who tried to go there. But Kali was adamant about meeting the yogi, so he took a back route through the jungle and began to climb. At last he suddenly appeared at the entrance of the cave where the yogi was seated with his disciples in front of a dhuni fire. They were about to attack Kali, but he quickly bowed down to them, saying, "*Om namo Narayanaya.*" Since Kali wore a monk's ochre robe, they also saluted him. They asked him questions and learned that he knew the sannyasa mantras. It was divine providence that he had learned these mantras at the pilgrim's inn just the previous night.

Kali asked the yogi to teach him hatha yoga, pranayama, and other yoga techniques. But after interviewing him, Kali realized that he was not a perfected yogi. He knew only a few techniques of pranayama that had been mentioned in *Pavana Swarodaya* (a book on breathing exercises). Moreover, Kali noticed that one of the yogi's disciples was suffering from asthma. At that moment the compassionate form of Sri Ramakrishna appeared in his mind, and he realized that he had made a great mistake. Kali was now trapped: He wanted to leave but the yogi did not approve, and he was afraid to run away because the disciples might kill him. In the afternoon Kali pretended that he was going to bring water from outside the cave, and then began to run down the hill. The disciples started to throw stones at him, but fortunately he reached the village without injury. The next morning he took a train back to Cossipore. When Kali told Ramakrishna about his adventure, instead of becoming angry, he smiled and blessed him. At this, Kali realized the greatness of his guru.[23]

Sri Ramakrishna passed away at 1:02 a.m. on 16 August 1886. In his autobiography Kali wrote a detailed account of the Master's death. Here are some excerpts: "We saw the Master suddenly merge into samadhi as usual. His eyes remained fixed on the tip of his nose. Narendra began to chant 'Om' aloud, and we all joined him. We expected the Master to come back from samadhi soon and regain normal consciousness. . . . But as the whole night passed and his outer consciousness did not return, we lost hope and were at a loss about what to do. . . . Gradually the news of the Master's passing away spread and people began to flock to the Cossipore garden house."[24]

At 10:00 a.m. Dr. Mahendralal Sarkar came, and after checking the body declared that Ramakrishna had breathed his last. In the afternoon the Master's body was carried by his disciples to the Cossipore cremation ground. His relics were collected in an urn and brought to the garden house. The disciples decided to continue to serve the Master through regular worship, but they had no money and no means of support. Moreover, Ramchandra Datta proposed that the young disciples return to their homes and the Master's relics be installed in his Kankurgachi Yogodyana. The disciples were helpless to prevent him from doing this. However, they took the main portion of the relics and put it in another urn that they secretly kept in Balaram's house, hoping one day to install it on the bank of the Ganges and build a temple there. On the birthday of Krishna, 24 August 1886, part of Sri Ramakrishna's relics was carried in procession by his disciples and devotees and ceremoniously installed at Kankurgachi Yogodyana.

At Baranagore Monastery and Itinerant Days

A couple of weeks after the passing away of Sri Ramakrishna, the grief-stricken Holy Mother left for a pilgrimage accompanied by Golap-ma, Lakshmi, M.'s wife, Kali, Jogin, and Latu. They first stopped at Deoghar and then, after visiting Varanasi and Ayodhya, arrived at Vrindaban. The party stayed at Kala Babu's kunja, Balaram Basu's retreat house. Once Ramakrishna had told Kali, "There is a partial manifestation of Krishna in you."[25] During his stay in Vrindaban, he visited many temples and meditated on Krishna for long hours. Kali was very austere and adventurous. He decided to circumambulate Vrindaban with other Vaishnava pilgrims. It took 21 days to walk the 168 miles.

One evening early in September 1886, when Kali was in Vrindaban, Ramakrishna appeared before Surendra Mittra in Calcutta and said: "What are you doing here? My boys are roaming about, without a place to live in. Attend to that, before anything else." Surendra immediately rushed to Narendra's house and told him what had happened. He promised to provide the same amount of money that he had formerly given for the Master in Cossipore. Narendra and the other disciples rented a house in Baranagore at ten rupees per month and established the first Ramakrishna monastery.

The Baranagore Monastery was an abandoned, dilapidated two-storey building, infested with snakes and said to be haunted by ghosts. The rooms on the ground floor were dark, damp, and unfit for habitation, so they were used as the kitchen and for storage. Shashi was once bitten by a snake in one of those dark rooms. The monks set up a shrine in an upstairs room — the relics of the Master were brought from Balaram's house, and a picture of Sri Ramakrishna was placed on the altar. The articles that the

Master had used at Cossipore were also preserved in the shrine room. Shashi kept the memory of the Master ablaze in the monastery with his wholehearted dedication and devout service to the Master. His scrupulous precision and regularity of service made everybody feel the living presence of the Master.

As soon as Kali heard about the Baranagore Monastery he returned to Calcutta and joined the brotherhood. The southernmost room of the second floor was used for meditation and study, and was known as Kali Tapasvi's Room ("*tapasvi*" means one who performs "*tapas*," austerity), since Kali secluded himself there during most of the day. An ascetic by nature, he ate vegetarian food, wore no shoes, and shunned peoples' company. He spent his time in meditation, studying the scriptures, and composing some Sanskrit hymns on Sri Ramakrishna and Holy Mother. One day Kali visited Holy Mother at her residence at Nilambar Babu's house in Belur, and read a hymn that he had composed about her: *Prakritim paramam abhyam varadam*, etc. (O Divine Nature Supreme! Remover of all fears, giver of all boons, etc.). After listening to the hymn, Holy Mother blessed him, saying, "May Saraswati, the goddess of learning, sit on your tongue."[26]

When someone in the Baranagore Monastery complained that Kali was not taking any responsibility for the household work, Narendra said, "Let one of the brothers be a scholar and I'll do the dishes myself." One day Mahendranath Datta, one of Narendra's brothers, was shocked when he saw Kali lying like a dead person in the sun on the dusty floor of the veranda. Jogin told him with a smile: "He is not dead. The rascal meditates that way."[27] Sometimes the disciples would tease and make fun with each other. Ramakrishna had given them the taste of true spirituality; he did not care for "dry monks."

Poverty and hardship could not dampen the spirit of the disciples. They had mutual love, respect, and deep understanding. One night Kali was shivering with cold and could not sleep, as none of them had warm clothing or sufficient blankets. They used to sleep on the floor of a big room under a single mosquito curtain. When Kali told Narendra about his suffering, Narendra got up at 2:00 a.m. and made hot tea for his brother. He told Kali, "Enjoy this hot cup of tea and get rid of the cold." He also teased him, "This hot cup of tea seems to me more concrete than your blessed theory of Advaita, don't you think so, Kali?"[28] Love and service bring solidarity to the Order, not rules and regulations.

Kali was well versed in both Eastern and Western philosophies, and enjoyed discussions with Narendra. Latu recalled:

Brother Kali was often busy studying the scriptures and other books. During rare leisure moments he would debate with Brother Loren [Narendra]. Loren used to silence him very easily, but one day Kali cornered Loren in an argument so well that Loren could not give a reply. Then Loren said: "Let us stop here today. Tomorrow we shall start again from this same point." Brother Kali was very happy for the time being. But the next day Loren began giving new arguments that refuted Kali's points, and Kali had to admit he was beaten. "I couldn't defeat Loren for a single day!" he said regretfully. But I told him: "Brother, it is bound to be so. Brother Loren is our leader. How can you surpass him?"[29]

One day Narendra proposed to the brotherhood that they all take the vows of sannyasa according to scriptural injunction. All agreed. When Kali told them that he had a copy of the viraja-homa mantras, which he had gotten from a monk in Gaya, his brothers were excited, knowing that this was the Master's divine grace. In the third week of January 1887, they took final monastic vows by performing the traditional viraja homa in front of the Master's picture. Narendra gave Kali the name "Swami Abhedananda."

In March 1887 Swamis Abhedananda, Premananda, and Saradananda went to Puri for a pilgrimage and stayed six months in the Emar Monastery. They lived on the prasad of Jagannath, practised spiritual disciplines most of the time, and attended the Chariot Festival of Jagannath. On their way back to Calcutta they visited the Sun Temple of Konarak, the Lingaraj Shiva Temple in Bhubaneswar, and the Buddhist caves of Udaygiri-Khandagiri. In 1888 Abhedananda went with Vivekananda and others to Allahabad to look after Yogananda, who was then suffering from smallpox.

On 5 February 1889 Abhedananda travelled with Holy Mother and her party to Kamarpukur and Jayrambati via Antpur. He stayed with the Mother for some time in Jayrambati and then decided to travel to the pilgrimage sites of North India. Holy Mother approved of his pilgrimage. Swami Nirmalananda expressed a desire to travel with Abhedananda; depending on God alone, they started their journey. Both swamis resolved that they would not carry any money or pass the night in anyone's house. They would go barefoot, and wear only loin cloths. They also decided to live on alms that they would beg once a day. As itinerant monks, they carried only a blanket, a water pot, a staff, and an extra loin cloth. They walked twenty to twenty-five miles a day.

After walking over five hundred miles, the swamis reached Gazipur, near Varanasi. There they met Sisir Chandra Basu, a judge of the Gazipur court who was then translating into English Panini's Sanskrit grammar and

Shankara's commentary on the Isha Upanishad. Abhedananda helped the judge with that project. At that time Hariprasanna (later, Swami Vijnanananda), a disciple of Sri Ramakrishna, was working as an engineer in Gazipur. He was delighted to see the brother monks and showed both swamis around the place. One day Hariprasanna introduced Abhedananda to another famous Sanskrit scholar who was a dualist. A day was set for a debate between the dualist pandit and the nondualist Abhedananda. It lasted for an hour, and Abhedananda defeated the pandit, greatly pleasing Hariprasanna and Nirmalananda. In Gazipur, Abhedananda met Pavhari Baba, a great yogi and knower of Brahman who lived in a cave. Abhedananda talked with him about God and was extremely impressed with the yogi.

From Gazipur the swamis went to Varanasi, the abode of Lord Shiva and Mother Annapurna. They visited the temples, circumambulated the holy city, and met Swami Bhaskarananda and Trailanga Swami, two great saints of Varanasi. After staying a few days, they went to Ayodhya, the birthplace of Ramachandra. Then after visiting Lucknow they arrived at Hardwar-Rishikesh, the abode of ascetics in the foothills of the Himalayas. Abhedananda built a thatched hut in Rishikesh like other monks, begged for his food once a day, and practised spiritual disciplines. From Rishikesh he walked hundreds of miles in the high altitudes of the Himalayas and visited Devaprayag, Joshimath, Badrinath, Kedarnath, Uttarkashi, Gangotri, and Jamunotri. In those days it was not easy to travel to those difficult, inaccessible places. The swami wrote in detail about his Himalayan travel in *My Life-Story*.

At last Abhedananda and Nirmalananda returned to Rishikesh. Abhedananda never cared for an easygoing life and always kept himself busy either practising meditation or studying the scriptures. During his stay in Rishikesh, he studied the *Brahma Sutras* with Shankara's commentary under Dhanaraj Giri, the abbot of Kailash Math who was an authority on the six types of Indian philosophy. Later when Vivekananda visited Rishikesh and asked Dhanaraj Giri about Abhedananda, the latter remarked, "Abhedananda — an extraordinary intellect!" During his stay in Rishikesh, Abhedananda became ill with bronchitis and a high fever. Fortunately, at that time Turiyananda and Saradananda were there; they took care of their brother disciple and later, in March 1890, sent him back to Varanasi for further treatment. Abhedananda gradually recovered and returned to the Baranagore Monastery.

This time he did not stay in the monastery long, as he wanted to travel to other holy places in India. It is amazing how Abhedananda travelled to so many places in India on foot like a true sannyasin, without money or possessions. He first went to Gaya and then Varanasi, Prayag, Agra, Delhi, Jaipur, Udaipur, Khetri, Mount Abu, and Girnar. In Porbandar he heard that Vivekananda was in Junagad; he went there and was delighted to see Swamiji. From Junagad Abhedananda went to Dwaraka, Krishna's kingdom on the coast of the Arabian Sea. A Gujarati devotee bought a ticket for him so that he could travel to Bombay by ship.

From Bombay Abhedananda went to Mahabaleswar, where he again met Vivekananda. Abhedananda continued his journey towards Central India and visited Pune, Baroda, Nasik, and Dandakaranya, a place connected with Ramachandra. Then he travelled to some important holy places in South India: Rameswaram, Madurai, Trichinapalli, Tanjore, Kumbhakonam, Kanchi, and Pakshitirtham. He had various spiritual experiences, visited many temples and places of interest, and met a number of mystics and pandits. Finally Abhedananda returned to Calcutta via Madras by ship.

In 1892 the Ramakrishna Monastery was moved from Baranagore to Alambazar, not far from the Dakshineswar temple garden. The Alambazar Monastery was a large two-storey building with a number of rooms and pillared verandas. There was a lawn and a pond in the compound. A few suicides had occurred in the house during the occupation of the two previous tenants, and the rumour had spread that the house was haunted. For this reason the monks were able to rent it for a mere ten rupees per month. Ramakrishnananda set up the shrine and followed the same routine that had been established at Baranagore. By the grace of the Master, the living conditions in the Alambazar Monastery were considerably improved.

Ramakrishnananda and Saradananda cordially received Abhedananda and arranged a private room for him in the monastery. The monks and devotees named it "Kali Vedanti's Room" because he spent most of the time there practising meditation and studying Vedanta. Some days after his arrival at Alambazar, Abhedananda became terribly ill due to an infection in his feet. His body became swollen and his feet were full of festering boils. The physicians found that Guinea worms had penetrated his feet when he walked barefoot in Gujarat.

Abhedananda wrote in his autobiography: "The doctor operated on my feet seven times and I was bedridden for four months. I shall never forget Saradananda's untiring, selfless service to me, as he constantly attended me without caring for food or sleep. Later Niranjanananda came and began to nurse me. I lost my power to walk. After three months I began to recuperate. Leaning on Saradananda's shoulder, I would walk a few steps a day like a child. Gradually I regained my strength to walk. I shall never forget the love of my brother disciples."[30]

In September 1893 Vivekananda represented Hinduism at the Parliament of Religions in Chicago and became internationally well known. Reports of the Parliament were published in Indian magazines and newspapers. The brother monks at the Alambazar Monastery were not at first clear about the identity of Vivekananda, as they knew him as Vividishananda. (He had taken the name "Vivekananda" at the request of Raja Ajit Singh of Khetri before leaving for America.) However, a letter from Swamiji, six months after the Parliament, removed all doubts and they were proud of their leader's achievement.

When people are possessed with jealousy, they cannot discriminate between truth and untruth. But "truth alone triumphs." Observing Vivekananda's success, the Christian missionaries and the Brahmo leader Pratap Chandra Majumdar began to slander him by telling the American people that he was not a true representative of Hinduism. In response to this false propaganda, Vivekananda wrote his brother monks at Alambazar: "Hold a public meeting in Calcutta approving of my activities in America and mentioning that I am accredited to represent Hinduism and send a letter of thanks to Dr. Barrows [chairman of the Parliament] with a copy to me."[31]

Immediately Abhedananda, Ramakrishnananda, and Saradananda organized a big public meeting in Calcutta. Abhedananda temporarily moved to Balaram's house, so that he could easily make contact with prominent religious leaders, distinguished scholars, high government officials, writers and journalists of high repute, and other eminent community leaders. The monastic disciples and the devotees of Sri Ramakrishna took special interest in this "sacred task," but Abhedananda took the lead. Most of the dignitaries invited agreed to attend the meeting, and the Honourable Raja Peary Mohan Mukhopadhyay promised to preside. The raja was impressed by the newspaper clippings about Vivekananda in America which stated: "After having him we feel how foolish it is to send missionaries to this learned nation." He remarked: "India should remain eternally grateful to him for the highest honour accorded to him in America as a representative of the Hindu religion."[32]

A very large public meeting was held on 5 September 1894 in the Calcutta Town Hall. The resolutions of the meeting were unanimously carried and were forwarded to Swami Vivekananda, Dr. John Henry Barrows, and Mr. Merwin-Marie Snell (president of the scientific section).

Here is an excerpt from the resolution: "This meeting desires to record its grateful appreciation of the great services rendered to the cause of Hinduism by Swami Vivekananda at the Parliament of Religions at Chicago, and his subsequent work in America."[33]

Physically exhausted from his work, Abhedananda obtained permission from his brother disciples to go for rest and meditation in Nainital and Almora, two Himalayan resorts. He took some Sanskrit and English books with him, which he read between periods of meditation. After some months he returned to Alambazar Monastery.

In England and America

In June 1896 Vivekananda sent Saradananda from London to America to keep the Vedanta movement there alive; in July he sent a cable to Ramakrishnananda: "Send Kali immediately to London to assist me in my work here. I am arranging his passage."[34] Accordingly, Abhedananda left for London in the middle of August 1896 and arrived there towards the end of September. On the way he suffered from seasickness and the lack of proper vegetarian food. Abhedananda missed Vivekananda and Mr. E. T. Sturdy at the dock, but reached Miss Henrietta Müller's residence at Wimbledon. Swamiji was worried at first but later was overjoyed when he saw that Abhedananda had arrived safely. The two brothers exchanged their news after many years of being apart. Swamiji arranged to buy new clothes for Abhedananda, showed him around London, and introduced him to his friends and devotees.

Gradually Abhedananda became acquainted with Western culture and way of life. A month after his arrival Vivekananda announced that Abhedananda would speak on Hinduism. At first Abhedananda was nervous and reluctant to speak, but Swamiji heartened him with inspiring words: "Depend on the Master who has ever given me strength and courage in all the trials of my life. . . . 'Out of the fullness of the heart the mouth speaketh.'" These words comforted him and gave him courage. Abhedananda based his lecture on the *Panchadashi*, an authoritative text on Vedanta. On 27 October 1896 he gave his maiden speech before the learned audience of the Christo-Theosophical Society at Bloomsbury Square in London. Vivekananda was highly pleased and said, "Even if I perish on this plane, my message will be sounded through these dear lips and the world will hear it."[35]

Vivekananda was fully confident that even in his absence Abhedananda would be able to carry on the Vedanta work in London. Swamiji entrusted him with his classes on Vedanta and Raja Yoga and left for India in December 1896. For one year Abhedananda continued to give classes and lectures in different churches and religious and philosophical societies in London and its suburbs. During his stay in London, the swami became acquainted with many distinguished savants, including Max Müller and Paul Deussen. Abhedananda's eloquence, his lucid exposition of Vedanta philosophy, and his depth of spiritual realization made a profound impression on his audiences.

To establish the Order's work in India, Vivekananda called Saradananda back from America. He asked Abhedananda to carry on the Vedanta work in the United States, so on 31 July 1897 Abhedananda left for New York and arrived there on 9 August. He was the guest of Miss Mary Phillips, the secretary of the Vedanta Society of New York, which Vivekananda had founded in 1894. On 25 August a reception for Abhedananda was given by the Society.

Abhedananda did not confine himself to New York City; he travelled and gave talks in various places along the East Coast — Philadelphia, Washington, Virginia, and New Paltz in New York state. He returned to New York City on 19 September. Saradananda was then preaching in the Boston and Cambridge areas, and preparing for his return to India. On 27 September he came to New York and met Abhedananda. Both brothers were happy to see one another after a long time; they exchanged their news and experiences in the Western work. They met again at Mrs. Wheeler's residence in Montclair, New Jersey. One day Abhedananda went to meet Thomas Edison, the famous scientist and inventor. They talked about Vedanta and India, and Mr. Edison showed the swami his laboratory.

Abhedananda started a lecture series at Mott Memorial Hall in New York, which was rented by the Vedanta Society. On 29 September 1897 he gave his first lecture, "What is Vedanta?" Edward Emerson, a close relative of Ralph Waldo Emerson, presided over the meeting. About this first lecture, Swami Atulananda, a Western monk, wrote in *With the Swamis in America*: "Punctually at three o'clock a swami entered the hall. He was dressed in a robe and turban of an orange colour. He went straight to the platform and without a moment's delay began to deliver his lecture.... The discourse was lucid, convincing, and impressive. There was not much flourish, not much eloquence, hardly any gesticulation. It was a straightforward, well-reasoned-out exposition of Vedanta philosophy, delivered in a calm, dignified manner.... Young, tall, straight, good-looking, the swami had his appearance in his favour.... I was told that the swami

I had listened to was Swami Abhedananda, another disciple of Sri Rama-krishna."[36]

On 2 October 1897 Abhedananda began giving classes on Viveka-nanda's *Raja Yoga* twice a week, on Wednesdays and Saturdays. After the peace chant from the Upanishads, Abhedananda would meditate for a while and the students joined him. The class would last for an hour and after that he would invite questions. On Mondays he conducted lectures and classes at Montclair, New Jersey as well. The swami stayed at the Brook-lyn residence of Sister Ellen Waldo (a relative of Ralph Waldo Emerson).

During this time the Vedanta Society of New York was moved to 117 Lexington Avenue, because its previous location had become surrounded by gambling and crime. The Society's activities — lectures and classes, instructions and interviews — at the centre and in the homes where Abhedananda visited, were carried on for over twenty years under his able direction. The publication department was organized and a monthly bulletin was issued early in 1905 as an independent source of contact to particularly serve those who lived outside the centre's vicinity. The swami worked very hard; he slept very little, as he spent most of the night writing his books, the sale of which eventually made the Society self-supporting.

It is said that libel and slander, censure and criticism are the ornaments of those who pave the way for truth. Attacks from backbiters and fault-finders make a pioneering soul more strong and determined. When Abhedananda became popular in New York, some Christian missionar-ies could not bear it. Out of jealousy some fabricated scandalous stories to defame the swami's character. Undaunted, Abhedananda paid them no heed; he continued to work with his usual vigour and sangfroid.

Abhedananda later told his disciples how he faced the trials and tribu-lations in his life: "When I was in America, I would try to forget my sorrows and sufferings by singing or praying to the Master. I would spend my time practising japam and meditation, or studying books. There was none with whom I could open my heart, so I lived in my own world. . . . If a person upholds the truth, he encounters more obstacles; but one should never give up the truth. One should hold the post [i.e., God] with might and main. Don't you see how I have confronted the storms of obstacles? I don't care even if the whole world stands against me. I am holding onto the Master."[37]

From October 1897 to April 1898 Abhedananda continued giving his lectures and classes in New York and gradually more people came to know about the Society. On 3 January 1898 Mr. Francis Leggett, a wealthy friend of Swamiji, invited Abhedananda to his home and introduced him to Miss Emma Thursby, Miss Adams, and other Vedanta students and friends. On 12 January Abhedananda saw Saradananda off for his return trip to India with Mrs. Ole Bull and Miss Josephine MacLeod. On 25 January Abhedananda was invited for dinner by Reverend Heber Newton, a nationally well-known minister of All Souls' Episcopal Church in New York. Reverend Newton was a liberal and powerful man, and was attracted to the universal message of Vedanta and Indian philosophies. They became good friends and Reverend Newton often sent his followers to listen to Abhedananda.

On 6 April Mr. Leggett introduced Abhedananda to Dr. Elmer Gates, a famous scientist and psychologist, who was then doing research on the relationship between physical science and mental science. Dr. Gates was impressed when he spoke to Abhedananda about raja yoga, which he considered to be very rational and scientific. He invited Abhedananda to his laboratory in Chevy Chase, near Washington D.C. During the swami's summer recess in May, he went to Dr. Gates' house and stayed a couple of days; he also gave a few talks. Abhedananda expressed a wish to meet the president of the United States. Mr. Urgin, a member of the House of Representatives, arranged his meeting with President McKinley on 19 May 1898. The president received Abhedananda cordially and inquired about the Vedanta movement in the United States and also British rule in India. Abhedananda also met John G. Brady, the governor of Alaska, who invited him to visit Alaska during the summer.

From Washington D.C. Abhedananda went to Cambridge, Massachussetts, to attend the Cambridge Conference at the invitation of Dr. Lewis G. Janes. He stayed with Dr. Janes at the home of Mrs. Ole Bull, who was then in India. Abhedananda was then the guest speaker at the annual festival of the Free Religions Association, held on the evening of 27 May 1898 at the Parker Memorial Building. In introducing Abhedananda Dr. Janes said: "Something of the thought that came into the Transcendentalist movement, consciously or unconsciously, I am sure, came from the old home of our Aryan brothers in India, something indirectly through Germany, something directly, I know not how, into the heart and mind of Emerson. It gives me great pleasure to welcome our brother from India, Swami Abhedananda."[38] The swami spoke on Transcendentalism.

Abhedananda stayed nearly a month in Cambridge and Boston, where he met several famous intellectuals, such as professors Lanman, Royce, Shaler, and William James, the author of *The Varieties of Religious Experience* and *Pragmatism*. Professor James invited Abhedananda to speak in his house on "Unity in Variety." A discussion followed for four hours and at last Professor James conceded the validity of monistic philosophy.

In 1898 Abhedananda said in his lecture "The Ideal of Vedanta and How to Attain It":

> The ideal of Vedanta is to solve the problem of life, to point out the aim of human existence, to make our ways of living better and more harmonious with the universal Will that is working in nature, to make us realize that the will which is now working through our bodies, is, in reality, a part and parcel of that universal Will. . . . Its ideal is to show us how we can live in this world without being overcome by sorrows and misery, without being afflicted by sufferings and misfortunes that are sure to fall on every human being in some way or other; how to conquer death in this life, how we can embrace death without being frightened in the least. And above all, the chief object of Vedanta is to make us live the life of unselfishness, purity, and attain to perfection in this life. . . . The mission of Vedanta is to establish that oneness and to bring harmony, peace, toleration amongst different religions, sects, creeds, and denominations that exist in this world.[39]

Abhedananda lectured before the Outlook Club, a women's group in Lynn, Massachusetts, and tried to remove misunderstandings about the position of women in India. In this lecture the swami clearly outlined Vedanta:

> This religion of Vedanta is not confined to any particular book. It includes all scriptures and all the teachings of all great prophets who flourished at different times, in different countries. It is based on science, philosophy, and logic. It harmonizes with the ultimate conclusions of modern science. As truth is the goal of all science and philosophy, so the same Truth is the goal of Vedanta. Modern science has discovered nothing that opposes the conclusions of the Vedanta philosophy. Vedanta is a philosophy and a religion at the same time. It recognizes each of the different stages, such as dualistic, qualified nondualistic, and nondualistic. In short, it is the Universal Religion. It embraces Christianity and points out its fundamental basis. It recognizes Jesus as the Son of God.
>
> Professor Max Müller says: "Vedanta is the most sublime of all philosophies, and the most comforting of all religions. It has room for almost every religion; nay, it embraces them all."[40]

In August 1898 Abhedananda lectured at the Green Acre Conference in Maine. Miss Sarah Farmer was the founder of this "popular summer school for the study of things pertaining to higher life." Dr. Lewis G. Janes, who was the president of the Brooklyn Ethical Association, conducted this school of comparative religions. Vivekananda had lectured and conducted a summer retreat there in 1894, and Saradananda had spoken there in 1896-97.

Neglecting his health, Abhedananda continued to preach and became sick. Knowing that the swami was not well and that he ate only vegetarian food, Dr. Janes told him: "That will not do for you here. When you go to Rome, do as the Romans do. You have a mission in your life, so you must take proper nourishing food, otherwise you will be sick."[41] Holy Mother also learned about his illness and she advised him to take fish and not to mortify his body with severe austerities.

After staying four weeks in Green Acre, Abhedananda returned to New York and continued his preaching as usual. On 4 March 1900 the *New York Herald* reported on how Abhedananda trained the American children: "Every Saturday afternoon a class of young boys and girls gathers together in the rooms of the Vedanta Society in East Fifty-fifth Street, to speak an hour or so with Swami Abhedananda and drink in the teachings of the Hindu philosophy, which is expounded to them in the most fascinating way. The young people come in with beaming, expectant faces, and draw their chairs around the handsome Oriental figure of the swami, who sits in the circle wearing a robe of rich red, and holding in his hand an ancient Sanskrit book, the *Hitopadesha*, or book of 'good counsels.' This book is one of the oldest pieces of literature in the world. It dates back to the thirteenth century B.C. and is the source of all of our fables of animals, our tales and fairy stories."[42]

On Easter Sunday, 2 April 1899, Abhedananda initiated six students into the vows of brahmacharya; Gurudas (later, Swami Atulananda) was among them. In April Abhedananda went to Worcester, Massachusetts, and gave a lecture entitled "Hindu Religion." On 7 May he spoke on "Immortality" at the Cambridge Conference. This time he lectured in many places in the northeastern United States, and also visited Niagara Falls. In August 1899 Abhedananda was invited to lecture before a Spiritualistic Camp Meeting at Lily Dale, near Chattaqua in New York State. He spoke on "Reincarnation" to an audience of 7,000. On 4 August he attended a seance, where he saw automatic typing on a typewriter. In his famous book *Life Beyond Death* he narrated some of his experiences in communicating with departed spirits.

When Vivekananda returned to America for the second time with Turiyananda on 28 August 1899, Abhedananda was again busy with the Green Acre Conference. Vivekananda and Turiyananda went to Mr. Leggett's country home at Ridgely Manor in Stone Ridge, New York. On 7 September Abhedananda received a cable from Vivekananda asking him to come to Ridgely, and the next day he travelled there from Boston. Abhedananda was delighted to see Swamiji and Turiyananda and gave them the news of all his activities. He stayed with them for ten days and then returned to New York City. On 7 November Vivekananda attended a reception given by the members of the Vedanta Society.

The Vedanta Society of New York was legally registered as an organization on 28 October 1898 and Mr. Francis Leggett became its president. At that time Abhedananda was lecturing regularly in a rented place, the Assembly Hall at 109 East 22nd Street. On 15 October 1899 the Society's office and library were established at 146 East 55th Street, through the cooperation of students and friends. The lectures were then held in Tuxedo Hall at 59th Street and Madison Avenue. In May 1900 the Vedanta Society was moved to 102 East 58th Street, which became its headquarters. In July 1900, before leaving America for the last time, Vivekananda gave a few lectures in the Society and complimented Abhedananda: "I am very happy to see that the Society has a house of its own."[43] (Actually, it was a rented house in a good neighbourhood. Later, the Society bought a house.)

From 1901 onwards Abhedananda's audiences increased to 600, and the number of students in his yoga class increased so much that he had to give the class twice a day. To accommodate the overflowing audiences, the Society rented Carnegie Lyceum for Abhedananda's lectures. The *New York Sun* described Abhedananda's lecture given on the first Sunday of 1901:

> Swami Abhedananda lectured in the Carnegie Lyceum yesterday afternoon on the "Religious Need of the Twentieth Century." He spoke of tuning the molecules of the brain cells to harmonize with the vibrations of the Cosmic Mind, and so gaining power, and he said that the mind and matter were not dual entities, but the subjective and objective manifestations of the unknown.
>
> "The twentieth century needs a religion," he said, "with no scheme for salvation, no need for heaven or hell, no fear of eternal punishment. The twentieth century needs a religion free from sacerdotal institutions and free from all books, scriptures, and personalities. The twentieth century needs a religion with a concept of God, not personal, not impersonal but beyond both, a God whose supreme aspect will harmonize with the ultimate Reality of the universe. The twentieth century religion must accept the ultimate conclusions of all the philosophies of the world."[44]

On 22 June 1901 Abhedananda left New York City for Buffalo, New York to see the Pan American Exposition. After visiting Cleveland and Chicago he went to San Francisco. On 1 August 1901 the *San Francisco Chronicle* published this news: "Swami Abhedananda, who arrived here on Monday from New York, was the guest of honour at a reception given last evening at the residence of Dr. M. H. Logan. The swami is a dignified intellectual-looking East Indian.... He speaks English fluently, and his thoughts as he gives them utterance are so framed as to form an axiom."[45]

On 6 August Abhedananda left for Shanti Ashrama, a Vedanta retreat near the San Antonio Valley on Mount Hamilton, twenty miles from Lick Observatory. It was a quiet place and favourable for spiritual disciplines. Turiyananda and Brahmachari Gurudas received him cordially; but Abhedananda stayed there for only four days as water was scarce and the facilities were insufficient. From Shanti Ashrama Abhedananda returned to the San Francisco area, giving a lecture on "Vedanta Philosophy" on 6 September at the University of California at Berkeley. Abhedananda said: "On one side, Vedanta philosophy gives expression to the highest ideal of all philosophy, and on the other, it gives a foundation to a system of religion which is the most rationalistic of all systems and it harmonizes with the ultimate conclusions of modern science and philosophy."[46]

From San Francisco Abhedananda went to Los Angeles, and then returned to New York on 7 October 1901, after visiting Yosemite Falls, Salt Lake City, Colorado Springs, Chicago, Toronto, and Thousand Island Park, New York. He continued giving lectures and classes as usual. During the summer recess, Abhedananda travelled to various places on the East Coast, and then left for a European tour on 7 August 1902. He landed at Liverpool, England, and then went to Glasgow, Scotland. After visiting a few places in England, Abhedananda crossed the English Channel and travelled extensively in France and Switzerland. He returned to New York in the early part of October 1902.

After the summer recess, Abhedananda arranged a memorial meeting for Swami Vivekananda, who had passed away at Belur Math on 4 July 1902. Abhedananda read letters from Saradananda and Premananda regarding Swamiji's death; Mrs. Ole Bull, Miss Josephine MacLeod, and others paid their homage to Vivekananda.

The annual meeting of the Society was held on 22 January 1903. The progress report was good; the Society was sound financially and membership had increased. On 15 May, when the summer recess had begun, Abhedananda left for Europe and travelled widely in Italy, Switzerland, and Belgium. He returned to New York on 6 October 1903.

Because the Vedanta movement was growing rapidly in the United States, the Ramakrishna Order sent Swami Nirmalananda to America to help Abhedananda. Nirmalananda arrived in New York on 12 November 1903 and began to give classes in December. On 4 May 1904 the Society was moved to 62 West 71st Street. The building had a spacious hall that could accommodate 300 people. On 24 May 1904 Abhedananda went to Saint Louis, Missouri, to attend the World's Fair, where he arranged for an exhibition of Vedanta literature in the Book Fair. He also gave a lecture at the Webster Groves Society on "Indian Women," and took a boat trip on the Mississippi River. On 16 June he returned to New York.

On 28 June 1904 Abhedananda again left for Europe. He reached Holland on 8 July, and visited various places in Amsterdam. From there he went to Munich, then the capital of Bavaria. During his European tours, he visited museums and places of historical importance, and sometimes climbed mountains, as he was very fond of adventure. On 16 October he returned to New York after visiting Paris and London.

The year 1905 was significant for the Vedanta Society. On 30 January another Vedanta Centre was inaugurated in Brooklyn, which Nirmalananda took charge of. On 1 February Abhedananda left for Toronto and lectured at the Historical Society. He was interviewed by a reporter of the *Toronto News*, met many distinguished people, and then after visiting Niagara Falls, returned to New York on 7 February. On 27 March he went to Washington D.C. to form a Vedanta Society; he returned to New York on the following day.

On 29 June Abhedananda and Professor Herschel C. Parker of Columbia University, then president of the New York Vedanta Society, went for a long tour from Alaska to Mexico. They reached Alaska via Toronto, Fort William, Winnipeg, and Vancouver. In Alaska they were Governor Brady's guests. The Governor's sister showed them the deserted homes of Native Americans and other important sites. On the way to Mexico, they saw the Portland Fair in Oregon, met Swami Trigunatitananda in San Francisco, and visited Swami Satchidananda in Los Angeles. They also visited the Grand Canyon in Arizona, and at last reached Mexico City on 14 September. It was there that Abhedananda met a Spanish gentleman who had read his books and who surprised the swami by showing him a copy of *Reincarnation* that he kept in his pocket. He asked Abhedananda to stay longer in Mexico, give a course of lectures, and establish a centre. Abhedananda returned to New York on 27 October via Saint Louis, where he gave an informal talk on Vedanta to an audience of fifty people.

On Tuesdays during the fall he lectured at The Brooklyn Institute of Arts and Sciences on "India and Her People," and on Sundays in New York he gave a lecture series on "The Great Saviours of the World." In this series he pointed out:

> If we cannot recognize the divinity in the prophets of other nations, in the saviours of other people, then we have not realized the divinity of our own prophet and have not understood the eternal Truth of the unity of Divine Being under the variety of names and forms. If a mother cannot recognize her son when he changes the colour of his garment or puts on the dress of a foreigner, I am sure that she is not a true mother. Similarly, I am sure that the Christian who sees divinity in Christ alone and does not recognize his own Master when he comes in the form of Buddha or Krishna, has not realized the divinity of Jesus the Christ. . . .
>
> All these prophets, these messengers of God, are great. Each one was commissioned by the Almighty to deliver His message. Each one of them was a glorious Son of God, a perfected soul, manifested for the good of humanity to establish righteousness and to destroy evil.[47]

Six Months in India

On 27 January 1906 Nirmalananda returned to India, and on 15 April Swami Bodhananda was sent to New York to assist Abhedananda. Then, after working and travelling ten years in the West, Abhedananda felt an urge to visit India for a short period. The swami left New York on 16 May 1906 and after changing ships at London, landed in Colombo, Sri Lanka on 16 June. Ramakrishnananda, Paramananda, Barrister Thyagaraja, and Angarika Dharmapala, the Buddhist representative at the Chicago Parliament of Religions, received him at the port. On 18 June the local Vivekananda Society honoured him with a grand reception. There Abhedananda was delighted to meet Ananda Coomaraswami, who later became a great exponent of Indian arts. After visiting the Tooth Temple of Buddha in Kandy and the Bo tree in Anuradhapuram, all three swamis arrived at the South Indian port of Tuticorin.

Abhedananda gave many lectures on this tour, and he received a warm welcome wherever he went. From Tuticorin Abhedananda and his party went to Tinnevelly and then to Madurai, Trichinapalli, Padukota, Tanjore, Kumbhakonam, and at last arrived at Madras on 15 July. The citizens of Madras gave him a wonderful reception and then, after resting for a few days, the swami and his party visited Bangalore, Mysore, and the

Sringeri Math, which had been established by Shankara. After travelling in South India, Abhedananda reached Puri on 23 August by train from Madras. Brahmananda, Shivananda, and Premananda received him at the station and then, after visiting the Lord Jagannath, they arrived at Shashi Niketan.

On 9 September Abhedananda and other swamis arrived at Howrah Station where a large crowd, including several prominent people of Calcutta, were waiting to welcome him. He stayed in Calcutta for a week and a memorable reception was given for him at the Town Hall on 12 September. In reply, Abhedananda paid a glowing tribute to Swamiji:

> Swami Vivekananda was not an ordinary man. He was the patriot-saint of modern India; he may be called an incarnation of divine wisdom in this age of commercialism. It was he who turned the table of commercialism in a foreign land like America. . . . He was the pioneer, the first preacher, the first Hindu sannyasin who went to the United States, carrying his Master's message and the gospel of Truth as taught by our ancient rishis. Vivekananda represented the Vedic religion, the *Sanatana Dharma*, which we may call a universal religion. He achieved great success because he preached nothing but the Eternal Truth.[48]

Abhedananda was happy to see M. and other devotees of the Master. One day he visited his mother and went to Kalighat to offer worship with her. He then went to Belur Math and stayed with his brother disciples until 4 October. Abhedananda was delighted to attend Durga Puja after many years. Knowing the need for more swamis in the West, the Belur Math authorities decided to send Paramananda to America with Abhedananda. On 5 October Abhedananda and Paramananda left for Bombay by train. On the way they stopped at Patna, Varanasi, Allahabad, Agra, Alwar, Ahmedabad, and finally arrived at Bombay on 30 October 1906.

Back in America (1907-1921)

On 10 November 1906 Abhedananda and Paramananda left Bombay and arrived in New York during the early part of 1907. When he returned to America, Abhedananda reorganized the activities of the Society. He sent Bodhananda to take charge of the Pittsburgh (Pennsylvania) Vedanta Centre and engaged Paramananda to conduct services at the New York Centre. He kept himself free to lecture in various places, as well as to revive the Vedanta movement in London. During the birthday celebration of Sri Ramakrishna, Abhedananda said:

The keynote of the life teachings of Buddha was active self-sacrifice, while the mission of Krishna to the world was to teach divine love. The great work of Ramakrishna was to bring the message of harmony. He came not to reform but to unite. He pointed out the wondrous fact that the religions of the world are not antagonistic in themselves, but that they are essentially one. Behind all religious doctrines and dogmas the Master discovered one grand eternal truth. History has no record of such a saint.[49]

On 2 March 1907 a house was purchased for the Vedanta Society at 105 West 80th Street in New York City. It was a five-storey building with two rooms on each floor. The rooms on the ground floor were converted into a single room that served as the lecture hall. Some of the upstairs rooms were rented to others in order to maintain the Society. During this time the members of the Society decided to establish a retreat site for students of Vedanta. Accordingly a plot of 370 acres was bought in the Berkshire Hills, not far from the picturesque little village of West Cornwall, Connecticut. It was 107 miles from New York and it took about four hours to reach. The Berkshire Retreat was duly inaugurated by Abhedananda in March 1907, and he remarked, "The ashrama looks like Fairyland."

On 26 June 1907 Abhedananda left for London, leaving Paramananda in charge of the Society. In the second week of July the swami began his classes on yoga and lectures on Vedanta in different locations around London. He returned to New York on 6 September 1907. On 29 January 1908 Abhedananda left for London. Sister Nivedita, Vivekananda's Irish disciple, visited Abhedananda many times and discussed the difficulties of her work in India. On 1 July he inaugurated the Vedanta Society at 22 Conduit Street. Sister Nivedita spoke first, then Abhedananda lectured on the history and objectives of Vedanta philosophy. During this trip the swami visited Paris for several days and then returned to New York on 21 August.

In September 1908 Abhedananda went on a lecture tour in Chicago and then Denver, Colorado. He returned to New York on 24 October. Towards the end of 1908, one of his disciples, Sister Avavamia, founded a Vedanta Society in Sydney, Australia. Paramananda started a Vedanta Centre in Boston, thus managing two centres. When not travelling, Abhedananda stayed either in New York or at the Berkshire Retreat.

On 29 February 1909 Abhedananda returned to London. After staying there for a month, he travelled to Paris and founded a Vedanta Society. After a month of giving lectures and classes, Abhedananda returned to London on 6 May. On the following day Frank Dvorak, the celebrated

Czechoslovakian artist, came to the Vedanta Centre to see Abhedananda. At Abhedananda's request, Dvorak later painted oil portraits of Rama-krishna and Holy Mother, which are still preserved in the Ramakrishna Vedanta Math in Calcutta. Abhedananda returned to New York on 26 June. Another of Abhedananda's important contributions was an Indo-American Club, which the swami formed in New York in 1909 so that Indian students could get together and come in close contact with American friends.

For most of 1910 and 1911 Abhedananda lived in the Berkshire Retreat and only occasionally was he in New York. He lectured regularly on Sundays and gave classes on yoga and meditation. Abhedananda's long absences from New York caused the income of the Society to drop, and most of the rooms had to be rented out to meet the expenses. Meanwhile Paramananda permanently moved to Boston; Abhedananda moved permanently to the Berkshire Retreat on 5 May 1911. On 12 June he wrote to Brahmananda and asked him to send another swami for the New York Society. Accordingly in 1912 Bodhananda was appointed the head of the New York Vedanta Society.

From 1912 to 1919 Abhedananda lived mostly in the Berkshire Retreat, and occasionally went out for a lecture tour. Mrs. Mary Le Page (Sister Shivani) wrote in her book *Swami Abhedananda in America*:

This ashrama in the Berkshires! Three hundred and seventy acres of rolling pasture lands and hills, a brook and several springs. Two old New England houses needing only renovation and some remodelling; barns, carriage house, sheds, all made to fit the purpose the swami had in mind. . . . The place within a few years was self-supporting; feed for stock raised on the place. Fruits of many kinds, and a splendid kitchen garden kept the table well supplied for summer guests who came and went the season long. The place was kept very plain, everything simple, and the swami's routines for the workers mainly voluntary and in line with training and aptitudes. There always was to be found among the students someone who had training as carpenter, or knew something of the trades. The place was kept in good repair without hired labour. Always there was hard work to be done, always some addition being made, some project under way, nothing ever finished. Season after season the work went on. If ever karma yoga maintained a school for study such was here.[50]

Abhedananda was not only highly intellectual, a great orator and prolific writer, but he was also a hard-working, practical person. He taught his students to harmonize action and contemplation in their lives. There are many interesting entries in his diary of 1912: "I planted with Le Page and Whitnie Alaska peas, cauliflower, and cabbage seeds in the garden; started the engine with Le Page and it worked all right." "Washed the dogs and cleaned their houses." "Held classes in the evening." "Worked with Frank at the stable." "Picked pears and apples and packed them." "I worked on the chicken house foundation with Whitnie in the evening." "Started the engine at 1:30 p.m. and cut wood until 2:30 p.m."[51]

In February 1913 Abhedananda went to Jacksonville, Florida, and gave three lectures in a Methodist church, and then went to Atlanta, Georgia, to deliver several lectures at the Psychological Society, Unitarian Church, and Ethical Society. In Atlanta the swami said: "Vedanta is the most ancient and the most modern of philosophies. Vedanta stands for no special creed, philosophy or religion, but teaches accumulated wisdom. It stresses the Delphic oracle of Socrates: 'Know thy Self.' It teaches that all progress is the evolution of God involved in man. Evolution presupposes involution."[52] For the next few years Abhedananda mainly stayed in the Berkshire Retreat and did lecture tours in Los Angeles, San Francisco, Minneapolis, Denver, Hartford, and other places.

Swami Prajnanananda recorded his reminiscences of Abhedananda in *Mon O Manush*:

> In 1915 I [Abhedananda] was in London. On 6 May I went to the booking office to purchase a ticket from London to New York on the *S.S. Lusitania*. While I was in that office, a mysterious thing happened. I was about to buy the ticket, but immediately I heard a clear voice forbidding me to buy it. I was dumbfounded. I thought it might be a freak of my mind. I looked around but couldn't find anybody. So again I went to the counter and the same thing happened. Then I decided to return to the apartment without buying any ticket. However, I planned to buy the ticket the following day. The next morning I saw in the newspaper in big letters "S.S. Lusitania Is No More." I was overwhelmed. Tears rolled down my cheeks. I realized that the Master had saved my life.[53] [On 7 May 1915, during World War I, this British liner was destroyed by a German submarine in the Atlantic Ocean, near the Cork coast of Ireland. One thousand one hundred ninety-eight passengers died.]

In the early part of 1919, Abhedananda, with Brahmananda's approval, decided to return to India. He began to wind up his American work; he sold the Retreat and all its furnishings. On 15 December 1919 he moved to New York, where Bodhananda and the devotees gave him a farewell reception. On 21 December Abhedananda arrived in San Francisco. He lived there for a year, lecturing regularly and helping Prakashananda to organize the Vedanta Society after the death of Trigunatitananda. On 21 December 1920 he left for Los Angeles and lectured there till 19 June 1921, when he returned to San Francisco. Abhedananda finally left America on 27 July 1921.

Abhedananda had gathered tremendous experience from travelling and lecturing extensively in Europe and America for twenty-five years. Since his arrival in the West in 1896, he had crossed the Atlantic Ocean seventeen times and had carried the message of Vedanta to innumerable people. His writings also had made a tremendous impact on the Western mind. On the eve of his departure from San Francisco, the swami said: "The East and the West will unite — such is God's will. The signs of the times greatly encourage me, and my visit and prolonged stay in this country have clearly convinced me that it is possible to make the world our home, and to love all as brothers and sisters. God's spirit is working everywhere. Blessed is he who sees the work, and realizes the Divine Spirit."[54]

Back to India

"I sailed from San Francisco," wrote Abhedananda, "and crossed the Pacific Ocean, breaking my voyage at Honolulu, where I was a delegate from India at the 'Pan-Pacific Educational Conference.' Then I came to Japan and studied Japanese culture, philosophy, and religion; I stopped at Shanghai, Hong Kong, Canton, Manila, and Singapore, where I delivered the message of Vedanta philosophy in popular lectures. From Singapore I was invited to Kualalumpur in the Malaya States, where I gave a series of lectures on Confucianism, Buddhism, and Taoism before Chinese and Hindu audiences. From there I was invited to Rangoon, where after delivering several public lectures on the 'Message of Buddha' and 'Religion of the Hindus,' I returned to Calcutta."[55]

On 10 November 1921 Abhedananda reached Calcutta and then went to Belur Math by car. It was noon, and the shrine was closed, but a monk opened it so that Abhedananda could bow down to the Master. Brahmananda and Shivananda were in South India, but Saradananda came the next day from Udbodhan to greet his brother disciple. On 25 December a civic reception was given for Abhedananda at the Calcutta University Institute. On 10 January 1922 Abhedananda went to Jamshedpur and gave three lectures at the Tata Institute: "Universal Religion," "Progressive Hinduism," and "Message of Vedanta." On 13 February Abhedananda went with Shivananda to Dhaka and Mymensingh in Bangladesh, where he gave several lectures. Abhedananda returned to Calcutta on 26 February. Meanwhile Brahmananda had become seriously ill and was dying from diabetes and cholera. Abhedananda visited him frequently at Balaram's house in Calcutta; Brahmananda passed away on 10 April 1922.

It was during this period that a new chapter of the Ramakrishna Order began: Shivananda was elected president of the Order. On 24 April 1922 Abhedananda left for a lecture tour and pilgrimage to Shillong and Guwahati in Assam, and after returning to Calcutta he left for Tibet on 14 July. On the way he stopped at Varanasi, Lahore, Rawalpindi, and Srinagar. He met the maharaja of Kashmir, who arranged his trip to Tibet. He left Srinagar on 1 August. Abhedananda recorded in his diary: "I went to Tibet and Kashmir crossing the Himalayas on foot, to study the manners, customs, the Buddhistic philosophy, and Lamaism which prevail among the Tibetan Lamas. I went along Yarkand Road, the highway to Europe, and stopped at Leh, the capital of Ladak in western Tibet. My destination was the Hemis Monastery, which was about twenty-five miles north of the city of Leh."[56]

Abhedananda was interested in visiting the Hemis Monastery, because he had read N. Notovitch's *The Unknown Life of Christ*, which was based on a Tibetan manuscript preserved in this monastery. Abhedananda had some pages translated with the help of a lama, and later he wrote in detail about his journey and research on Christ in his famous book *Journey into Kashmir and Tibet*. The entire trip took nearly three months, and he returned to Srinagar on 29 October. After visiting Rawalpindi, the ancient city of Takshashila, Lahore, Rishikesh, Hardwar, and Varanasi the swami arrived at Calcutta on 11 December 1922.

In Calcutta and Darjeeling

"In 1923 after returning from Tibet," wrote Abhedananda in his diary, "I established the Ramakrishna Vedanta Society in Calcutta of which I am the president. In 1924 I opened a branch of this Society at Darjeeling under the name of Ramakrishna Vedanta Ashrama."[57] Why did Abhedananda move from Belur Math to Calcutta? Moni Bagchi wrote in *Swami Abhedananda: A Spiritual Biography*:

When he returned from America, he returned with a huge number of books and furniture and a pile of his manuscripts relating to his innumerable speeches and writings, which were to be processed before publishing in book form. Those things remained almost unpacked for want of adequate space in the monastery of Belur. The Ramakrishna Mission headquarters in those days had a limited number of rooms and it became difficult to provide Abhedananda with a suitable and even a sizeable space.... It was at this time that Swami Abhedananda held consultations with Swami Shivananda and Swami Saradananda and proposed to them that since there was difficulty of accommodation at the headquarters of the Mission, it would be proper for him to shift to Calcutta and settle there and to carry on his own activities. It is on record that both Shivananda and Saradananda had given their consent to this proposal, and accordingly efforts were being made from the beginning of 1923 to find a suitable house for Swami Abhedananda in Calcutta.

Yet there were other reasons for his choice of Calcutta as the centre of his future work. It could be safely presumed that when he returned to India from America, he must have had some plans of his own, the realization of which needed a separate establishment, if not altogether a separate organization outside the Order. He was one of the trustees of Belur Math and as such there was no question of his disassociating from the parent body.[58]

Abhedananda remained a trustee of the Ramakrishna Math and Mission all through his life, but his organization gradually became separated from the Ramakrishna Order. On 20 February 1923 Abhedananda moved to a rented house at 45B Mechuabazar Street (now Keshab Sen Street), in Calcutta; and again on 1 May to 11 Eden Hospital Road. He set up the shrine for Sri Ramakrishna, conducted lectures and classes, initiated some disciples, and exchanged views with prominent national leaders. His dynamic personality kept him active till the end of his life: He continued his lecture tours in various places of India and began to publish his writings. *The Complete Works of Swami Abhedananda* comprise eleven volumes and are published by the Ramakrishna Vedanta Math, Calcutta.

On 9 May 1923 Abhedananda visited Darjeeling, a Himalayan resort where many wealthy people go for their summer holidays. He stayed there for a couple of months, and was greatly benefitted by the beauty of the place and its invigorating climate. The following year, on 18 October 1924, he returned to Darjeeling and bought a cottage on a piece of land below the railway station. There Abedhananda established the Ramakrishna Vedanta Ashrama, with an attached primary school, a charitable dispensary, and memorial building in the name of Sister Nivedita, who had died there in 1911. The whole hill town felt Abhedananda's presence during his two months' stay there; thus many national leaders, such as Mahatma Gandhi, Chittaranjan Das, Lord Lytton (then the governor of

Bengal), the nawab of Dhaka, and others came in contact with· him. Abhedananda told Gandhi: "You are doing the work started by Ramakrishna and Vivekananda along the lines of removing untouchability and encouraging cottage industries. Therefore I bring to you blessings."[59]

On 1 August 1925 the Ramakrishna Vedanta Society in Calcutta was moved from the flat on Eden Hospital Road (which had become insufficient) to 40 Beadon Street, a commodious four-storey building. On 3 January 1926 Abhedananda wrote in his diary: "At noon Swami Shivananda and Swami Saradananda made a friendly call in a Ford car on their way to an invitation for a feast. We had a nice talk quietly. They showed their sympathy and cooperation with the works of our Society. They took a light refreshment and stayed for an hour."[60]

In 1926 Abhedananda started *Vishwavani*, a monthly Bengali journal to disseminate the ideas of Vedanta. His life was full of various activities both in Calcutta and Darjeeling, such as writing books and articles, giving public lectures and classes on the scriptures, meeting visitors, and inspiring some young men to adopt the life of renunciation. Abhedananda wanted to·have a permanent home for the Society, so in 1929 a plot of land was purchased at 19 Raja Rajkrishna Street in North Calcutta. It took several years to build the house; during this period the swami lived mainly in Darjeeling. Towards the end of 1934 he moved into the Society's new house and began to supervise the construction of the Master's shrine, which was dedicated on Sri Ramakrishna's birthday, 2 March 1937. While installing the picture of Sri Ramakrishna, the swami prayed: "Master, please dwell here to do good to humanity as long as the sun and moon exist."[61]

In March 1937 the centenary celebration of Sri Ramakrishna was coming to a close in Calcutta. Abhedananda and Vijnanananda were then the only two surviving monastic disciples of Sri Ramakrishna. On 1 March the Parliament of Religions was held at the Town Hall in Calcutta. Brajendra Nath Seal, an eminent scholar and philosopher, and a classmate of Vivekananda, inaugurated the parliament but invited Abhedananda to preside over it when he had to leave because of ill health. Abhedananda introduced himself: "I stand here not as a delegate from any institution, not as the president of the Ramakrishna Vedanta Society of Calcutta, but as the humble child of Sri Ramakrishna."[62] The next day the swami read a paper about Sri Ramakrishna; it was his last public lecture. He said: "For the first time it was demonstrated that all religions were like so many paths leading to the same goal, that the realization of the same Almighty Being is the highest ideal of Christianity, Mohammedanism, Judaism, Zoroastrianism, Hinduism, as well as of all other religions of the world.

Sri Ramakrishna's mission was to proclaim the eternal truth that God is one but has many aspects, and that the same one God is worshipped by different nations under various names and forms; that He is personal, impersonal, and beyond both; that He is with name and form and yet nameless and formless."[63]

On the occasion of Sri Ramakrishna's centenary celebration, All India Radio in Calcutta broadcast Abhedananda's five-minute talk about Ramakrishna in Bengali. It is the only available recorded voice of a disciple of Ramakrishna, and it is the most precious verbal testimony about the Master. Translated, this testimony states:

> Om, salutation to Bhagavan Ramakrishna. During the nineteenth century, Western materialism was deluging India. The Christian missionaries, through brainwashing, were trying to create confusion and hatred in the minds of the Hindus regarding their religion. It was then that Ramakrishna appeared to revive the moribund condition of the Sanatana Dharma [eternal religion].
>
> He was born in a remote village of Bengal. He had no formal education. But he experienced the Imperishable Brahman and became a great teacher. He did not care for dry scriptural arguments. He solved the problems of life through his spiritual power. He said: "The nature of all human beings cannot be the same. It is natural to be different." He respected all beings and worshipped the God of different religions. After experiencing the truth of unity in diversity, Ramakrishna proclaimed: "As many faiths, so many paths. All religions are true."
>
> The Master's renunciation was phenomenal. While living in Dakshineswar and at the Cossipore garden, we saw that he could not touch money or any metal. He perceived the manifestation of the Divine Mother in all women.
>
> Ramakrishna told us: "He who was Rama and he who was Krishna, is now Ramakrishna in this body." Pointing to himself, the Master further said: "I will be worshipped in the homes of many people."
>
> Salutations to Ramakrishna, the perfect embodiment of the Eternal Truth that manifests Itself in various forms to help mankind. He is an incarnation of the Supreme Lord and is worshipped by all. Peace, Peace, Peace.[64]

In the early part of May 1937 Abhedananda left for Darjeeling, his favourite place. There, amidst nature's panoramic beauty and silence, he would remain absorbed in meditation, study, and writing. Most of his books and profound writings were done there. He would get up early in the morning and meditate; then, facing the peaks of the Himalayas, he would take his breakfast. Afterwards he would go for a long walk, alone, and then from 9:00 to 11:00 a.m. he would write. After his bath, he would meditate for another hour and then have lunch. After lunch he would read a newspaper, usually the *Statesman*, and then would take some rest. Again he would write from 3:00 to 5:00 p.m., and then go for a walk. In the evening he would meet devotees and visitors and talk to them on various topics.

After dedicating the shrine of Sri Ramakrishna on 29 August 1937, Abhedananda left Darjeeling on 21 September. It had been his last visit. On the way to Calcutta the Darjeeling Mail was derailed, and Abhedananda strained his heart as he hurriedly left the train. Completely exhausted, he returned to the Ramakrishna Vedanta Math in Calcutta. From then on his health began to fail, and water began accumulating in his system. Several prominent doctors treated his dropsy, but in the end he was under the care of Kaviraj Vimalananda, an ayurvedic physician.

His life's work done, he silently began to prepare himself for his final journey. On his seventy-third birthday he said to one of his disciples: "I am only an instrument in the blissful sportive play of the Master, and the moment my life's mission is over, I shall not wait even for a second longer."[65] Once Swami Brahmananda had remarked: "When Kali reduces his external activities, people will realize the manifestation of his spiritual power."[66]

Abhedananda was virtually bedridden for the last year and a half of his life. Even in that condition, every night after supper his disciples would read the manuscript of his lectures and he would dictate corrections. On 14 January 1938, in spite of his severe illness, he went to Belur Math to attend the dedication ceremony of Sri Ramakrishna's marble statue in the new temple. While Vijnanananda was installing the relics of the Master in the altar, Abhedananda stood motionless, listening to the monks singing a hymn he had composed for the Master during his Baranagore days. It was his last visit to Belur Math.

Abhedananda had played his part in the divine drama of Sri Ramakrishna. Gradually the great yogi made himself ready to return to his beloved guru. One day he said to a disciple, "My body belongs to the Master." Towards the end he indicated that his body should be cremated at the Cossipore cremation ground after his death. On 7 September 1939 he followed his regular routine, but in the evening he had a high temperature that continued the whole night. His disciples served him around the clock. In the morning he felt a little better, and asked his attendant to give him a glass of water. He sat on his bed and lay down after drinking the water. Swami Abhedananda passed away shortly after, at 8:16 a.m. on Friday, 8 September 1939.

The news of his death spread throughout the city and an announcement was broadcast by All India Radio. The devotees and monks of Belur Math and all other ashramas flocked to see Abhedananda at the Ramakrishna Vedanta Math. His body was carried in procession and cremated at Cossipore cremation ground. His disciples followed his last request: "Make a little place for me at the feet of the Master."[67]

Towards the end of his life, this great austere Vedantin Abhedananda told his disciples: "Tapasya or austerity enhances willpower. Have self-confidence. Have faith in yourself. Think: I am a child of Immortal Bliss. The infinite power is playing within me. If you have this conviction, you will conquer the world."[68]

SWAMI TRIGUNATITANANDA: SAN FRANCISCO

12

ॐ

SWAMI TRIGUNATITANANDA

T his story begins with the loss of a gold watch. Sarada Prasanna, the son of a rich landlord, was admitted to the Metropolitan Institution in North Calcutta when he was in the seventh grade. For four years Sarada studied in that school, where M., the recorder of *The Gospel of Sri Ramakrishna*, was headmaster. Sarada was a talented boy, and his teachers expected him to achieve a brilliant score in the Entrance examination and thereby obtain a scholarship; Sarada was also contemplating his bright future. But who can change Divine Providence? On the second day of the examination, someone stole Sarada's gold watch while he was having refreshments. Sarada was extremely upset; he felt that because of his carelessness a highly valuable thing had been stolen. He could not concentrate on the remaining subjects of the test, and he failed to place in the first division.[1]

The loss of the gold watch caused Sarada prolonged agony. M., who was very fond of Sarada, noticed his depression and on 27 December 1884 brought him to Dakshineswar. This was Sarada's first visit to Sri Ramakrishna. There is no record of what the Master said to him that day, but the *Gospel* entry indicates that Sri Ramakrishna talked about some important aspects of human life. Referring to Bankim Chandra Chatterjee's famous novel *Devi Chaudhurani*, the Master said: "People like the author of this book believe that knowledge is impossible without the study of books. In order to know God one must read books! But if I want to know Jadu Mallik, must I first know the number of his houses and the amount of money he has in government securities? Do I really need all this information? . . . He who seeks God plunges headlong; he doesn't calculate about how much or how little he needs for the protection of his body. . . . It is the pure mind that perceives God, and at that time this ordinary mind does not function. A mind that has the slightest trace of attachment to the world cannot be called pure."[2] The Master's teachings worked on Sarada's mind. He came to realize that spiritual treasures were far more valuable than a gold watch. This seemingly trivial incident was the turning point of his life.

Sarada Prasanna Mittra, who later became Swami Trigunatitananda, was born in the village of Naora (Paikhati), 24-Parganas, at 9:26 p.m. on Monday, 30 January 1865. His parents believed that he was born to them through the grace of the Divine Mother Durga; therefore they named him "Sarada," another name for Durga. The astrologer who drew up his horoscope said that Sarada was born at an auspicious time, and predicted that he would be a great yogi and a man of wisdom. Sarada's maternal grandfather, Nilkamal Sarkar, was a powerful and wealthy landlord of Paikhati. Sarada's father, Shivakrishna Mittra, was also a rich landlord who moved the family to a home in Nandan Bagan, Calcutta, when Sarada was three years old.

Shivakrishna was a religious man who spent most of his time in worship and the study of the scriptures; he therefore raised his son in a spiritual atmosphere. Sarada had such a wonderful memory that he memorized 108 hymns and salutation mantras on different gods and goddesses before he was fourteen. He could also chant the Gita, the Chandi, and the Upanishads in a melodious voice. He was pure, simple, and religious-minded even as a boy. His contact with Sri Ramakrishna when he was nineteen further stimulated his religious spirit.

Meetings with Sri Ramakrishna

In Sarada's home there had always been servants and maids who did all the household work. As a result, Sarada considered himself above menial tasks. However, one hot day when Sarada arrived at Dakshineswar, Ramakrishna said to him, "Please bring some water and wash my feet." Many of Sarada's friends were standing nearby, making the situation all the more embarrassing. Sarada's face flushed with humiliation. He did not know what to do. But the Master repeated the request, and Sarada felt compelled to obey. He later said that the Master thus forever broke down his aristocratic pride and implanted in his mind the spirit of service.[3]

In April 1885, a few months after he first met the Master, Sarada entered Metropolitan College. He made good marks in the first year and was recognized as a brilliant student. But as his visits to Dakshineswar became more and more frequent, he began to show a growing indifference to secular learning. Quite often he would miss classes in order to be with the Master. Sri Ramakrishna gave spiritual instructions to this sincere young disciple, fed him, and asked Holy Mother to pay his carriage fare. Whenever Sarada came to Dakshineswar, Holy Mother would keep money on the step of the nahabat as she knew Sarada had come surreptitiously, eluding his father's watchful eyes. One day Sri Ramakrishna sent Sarada to Holy Mother for spiritual instruction and mentioned her infinite power, quoting a Bengali couplet:

Radha's infinite power of maya is beyond description,
Millions of Krishnas and Ramas evolve, abide, and dissolve in it.[4]

Although Sarada was Ramakrishna's disciple, Holy Mother later gave him formal initiation. As far as the record shows, Jogin and Sarada were the only two monastic disciples of Sri Ramakrishna who were initiated by Holy Mother.

Ramakrishna taught householders and monastics differently. Sarada wrote: "Without self-control householders can never be true to their ideals. Sri Ramakrishna used to say to all, including the householders: 'Have the knowledge of oneness first, and then do your work'; 'Hold fast to the pole [i.e., God], and then go on whirling'; 'Keep the greater part of your mind fixed on God and with the rest attend to your ordinary rounds of duty.' With these and many other beautiful similes he used to teach householders how they should lead their lives."[5] Sarada wrote later in an article "Brahmacharya": "The only way to conquer lust is to look upon all women as your own mother, as images of the Divine Mother. . . . Sri Ramakrishna used to say, 'When a man succeeds in the conservation of his sexual energy, his intellect reflects the image of Brahman, even as a glass gives a perfect image when its back is painted with silver nitrate. The man who carries this image of Brahman in his heart is able to accomplish everything — he will succeed wonderfully in whatever action he engages himself.'"[6]

Of Sarada's many wonderful experiences associated with the Master, one stands in marked relief. One of the last vestiges of the ego to be removed is sexual desire; with all its subtle ramifications. Years of practice and asceticism are often necessary for its eradication. Sarada had set his will to conquer this great foe, but the task seemed impossible. However, one day as he sat in meditation, he felt the Master's grace within and the idea of sex disappeared like a mirage, never to return.

Sarada's frequent visits to Dakshineswar alarmed his parents. They secretly arranged his marriage, thinking this might divert his mind. M. recorded in the *Gospel*, on 14 July 1885:

> Master (*to Sarada*): "Why don't you come to Dakshineswar? Why don't you see me when I come to Calcutta?"
>
> Sarada: "Nobody tells me about it."
>
> Master: "Next time I shall let you know. (*To M., smiling*) Make a list of these youngsters." (*M. and the devotees laugh.*)
>
> Sarada: "My relatives at home want me to marry. (*Pointing to M.*) How many times he has scolded me about marriage!"
>
> Master: "Why should you marry just now? (*To M.*) Sarada is now in a very good state of mind. Formerly he had a hesitant look; now his face beams with joy."[7]

In September 1885 Ramakrishna was moved from Dakshineswar to Shyampukur in Calcutta for cancer treatment, and in December 1885 he was moved again to Cossipore. Sarada continued his visits to the Master, serving him during his last days. Sometimes he stayed overnight, enduring his father's scoldings. On 3 January 1886 Sarada's mother told him that his father had finalized arrangements for his marriage. Sarada was stunned. He could not believe it. He hurried to his room, and after thinking about his future, wrote a short note: "My respected parents, I will not marry. I have no desire to be trapped in the meshes of maya. In whatever direction my eyes go, I am going." He put the note on his desk and left at 11:30 a.m. He first went to Cossipore, and after receiving the Master's blessings, left for Puri (300 miles away) on foot. He had not told the Master that he had run away from home.

Meanwhile Sarada's parents discovered that he was missing and began to search for him. Finally they went to the Master and learned what had happened. After a few days Sarada wrote to them from Panshkura, Midnapore: "Respected parents, I am your ungrateful son and have caused you so much pain. Please forgive me. Millions of people in our country are suffering — under such circumstances that it is hard for me to live idly at home. Don't worry about me. I am fine. Please don't come here to get me because I shall leave this place as soon as I mail this letter."

After travelling to various places, Sarada reached Puri via Bhadrak, Orissa. His parents had also departed for Puri. They arrived there on Wednesday, 27 January 1886, and found Sarada. They were overwhelmed with joy. Sarada narrated his journey to his parents:

After writing to you I began to walk and did not get any food for two days. I was hungry and exhausted. I expected to find a village before evening, but unfortunately I reached a dense forest. I followed a zigzag path for some time and then I was lost in darkness. I began to chant Sri Ramakrishna's name and prayed to God for help. Without finding any way out, I climbed up a big tree and fell asleep on its branch. Suddenly I heard a man's voice, saying: "Hello, holy man. Here are some sweets. Please come down and appease your hunger." After a short while he brought a jug of water and disappeared in the darkness. I was impressed with his sympathy and received that food and drink as the grace of the compassionate God. At daybreak I searched for that man in the forest, but I couldn't find any human being or any village nearby.[8]

When Sarada had left Cossipore, Tarak gave him five rupees, knowing he was penniless. But in spite of all hardships, Sarada didn't spend the money. Such was his spirit of renunciation! He wanted to experience the divine promise, "Lo, I am with you always."

Sarada stayed in Puri with his parents for some days and visited all the important temples. He returned to Calcutta with them only one month before the First Arts examination. Knowing that Sarada was willing to take the examination, Shivakrishna met the principal of the Metropolitan College and arranged everything. Although Sarada had not touched his books for almost a whole year, he passed the examination creditably with only one month's preparation.

To worldly people spiritual life is distasteful, and to spiritual people worldly enjoyments are disgusting. It is not possible to force a worldly person to be spiritual or a spiritual person to be worldly. In spite of his persistent efforts, Shivakrishna failed to stop Sarada's visits to Ramakrishna at Cossipore. But when Ramakrishna passed away on 16 August 1886, Sarada's father smilingly remarked, "I repeated the mantram regularly at Kalighat, so I got the result."[9] In other words, he probably prayed for the Master's death. What a terrible attachment to his son! Shivakrishna believed that he would get Sarada back after Sri Ramakrishna's passing away, but things did not work out that way.

Austerity at Baranagore Math

After the disciples of Ramakrishna lost their beloved Master, they rented a dilapidated house at Baranagore with the help of Surendra Nath Mittra. This house became the first Ramakrishna Monastery. Sarada continued to visit the brother disciples, although his parents strongly disapproved. They feared he might leave home and become a monk. Before Christmas 1886, the disciples decided to visit Antpur, the birthplace of Baburam. Narendra secretly sent a messenger to Sarada with news of the forthcoming trip to Antpur. Sarada immediately left home, joined the group, and went with them to Antpur. There, on Christmas Eve, the disciples took vows of renunciation in front of a sacrificial fire: They vowed that they would never go back to family life. Their Master had enkindled the fire of renunciation and the burning desire for liberation in their hearts. One day while they were at Antpur Sarada went to bathe in a pond, but he did not know how to swim. Suddenly he slipped from a step and fell into deep water. Immediately Niranjan dove into the water and rescued him. On another day the disciples arranged the Hara-Gauri Festival, dressing Sarada as Shiva and Gangadhar as Gauri. These young disciples had learned from their Master how to make spiritual life enjoyable.

After a week the disciples of Ramakrishna returned to Baranagore; Sarada stayed in the monastery rather than returning home. Sarada's elder brother, Binay, secretly arranged an esoteric sacrificial ceremony to try to turn Sarada away from spiritual life. Twelve brahmins performed the ceremony for one month and twelve days. At the end of this time they told Binay: "It is impossible to bring your brother back to the world. He is praying intensely to realize God by embracing monastic life. Therefore, this sacrifice is not capable of bringing a pure soul to the lower plane." Binay had spent four thousand rupees for the ceremony, but to no avail. At last he went to the disciples of Ramakrishna and asked them to send Sarada back home. In all likelihood they refused, preferring to let Sarada decide where to live. A month later Sarada heard about his brother's machinations. He became disgusted and stopped visiting home completely.[10]

In January 1887 Sarada and other disciples performed the *viraja homa*, a special fire sacrifice, in front of Sri Ramakrishna's picture and took their final monastic vows. Swami Vivekananda gave Sarada the name "Swami Trigunatitananda." Vivekananda later teased him about his long name and asked him to shorten it, so "Trigunatita" became what he was usually called.

In the Baranagore Monastery the disciples began intense spiritual practices. They would also go on pilgrimages. One day Vivekananda asked Saradananda to visit Navadwip, the birthplace of Chaitanya, on foot. Saradananda immediately prepared to walk the sixty miles to Navadwip alone, without taking any money. However, Swamis Shivananda and Trigunatita found out about it and went along with him. At noon, after they had walked for some time, Trigunatita disappeared. Saradananda and Shivananda sat under a tree to wait for him and contemplated begging for some food in a nearby village. In the meantime, Trigunatita appeared and told them: "It is noon. After finishing my bath, I satisfied my hunger." When asked how, Trigunatita replied: "I ate some tender grass and then drank some water."[11] Both the swamis were dumbfounded.

Trigunatita's eating habits were very unusual! Once while at Baranagore Monastery Trigunatita suffered from stomach trouble. Swami Brahmananda sent him to Dr. Bepin Ghosh, a cousin of Swami Premananda, for treatment. The doctor was a devotee and knew Trigunatita well. He wanted to serve him before proceeding with the examination, so he said, "Please tell me what you would like to eat." "*Rasagollas*" (cheese balls soaked in syrup), the swami replied. Dr. Ghosh offered him two rupees' worth of rasagollas, more than two dozen, which Trigunatita finished very quickly. Then the doctor said, "Please tell me why you have come to me today." Trigunatita replied, "I have stomach trouble, so Swami Brahmananda sent me to you for treatment." "My goodness! Why then did you eat those rasagollas?" "You offered them with love, so what else could I do?" answered the swami.[12] The doctor then gave him medicine.

Trigunatita had a strange capacity for food. He could eat an enormous amount of food, and again, he could fast for days at a stretch. About his eating habits, Premananda said: "He had an occult power. Once I thickened seven and a half seers of milk [two gallons approximately] and served him the whole quantity. He ate it all without stopping. On another occasion he stayed under the bel tree of Belur Math for several days, eating only one banana a day."[13] Once Premananda's mother invited three of the Master's disciples to Balaram Basu's house. She cooked various dishes, but because of unavoidable circumstances only Trigunatita was able to go there. She was unhappy that much food would be wasted. However, Trigunatita began to eat and gradually finished the entire quantity. Premananda's mother was frightened, thinking that the swami would be sick. The next day, when she saw the swami well, she remarked: "It is amazing how Sarada eats! He has travelled over many mountains and learned many mantras so he can make any amount of food vanish. Otherwise it is not possible for a human being to eat so much."[14]

Trigunatita's self-control was also phenomenal. Once he decided to reduce his food intake. He began to eat two ounces of rice and two ounces of chilies each day, and he continued this regimen for a month.[15] Another time, while staying at Balaram's house, he went with Brahmananda and two other disciples to a devotee's house where they were unexpectedly served a meal. After returning to Balaram's house, Brahmananda realized that Balaram would be upset if the food he planned to serve was wasted. Trigunatita said to him: "Don't worry. I shall finish the food." Even though he had just eaten a regular meal, he consumed the food meant for four persons.[16]

He had very little body consciousness. Sometimes in the winter he would cover his body with a piece of thin cloth, and sometimes with two blankets. Once he was suffering from blood dysentery and living on barley water. When he went to a devotee's house, however, he was able to eat a large amount of sweets. He later told the doctor, "This excessive eating has cured my disease." Another time when he was shivering with fever, he bathed with cold water, ate a sumptuous meal, and recovered completely.[17]

Like his food habits, Trigunatita's actions and behaviour were unusual and sometimes not understandable to others. He had indomitable energy and was undaunted by any situation. He was sceptical about the existence of ghosts; he had visited a number of haunted houses and found nothing to substantiate claims of ghostly inhabitants. This aroused in him a determination to see a ghost, should one really exist. Someone told him about an old empty house near Baranagore Monastery where he could see a ghost at midnight. Without telling anyone, Trigunatita went there before midnight and waited for the ghost. Suddenly he saw a faint light appear in the corner of the room. The light grew brighter until, in the centre of the light, there appeared an eye. It approached him with deadly malevolence. The swami felt his blood dry up in his veins and his body wither like a green tree before a forest fire in the sinister light of that eye. He was about to faint, when all of a sudden Sri Ramakrishna appeared. Holding his hand, the Master said: "My child, why are you so foolishly taking chances with certain death? It is sufficient for you to keep your mind fixed on me." With those words, the Master disappeared. Trigunatita's spirit at once revived and he left the house, his curiosity about ghosts satisfied forever.[18]

During his sadhana at the Baranagore Monastery, he had a great desire to perform some tantric rituals at midnight in the cremation ground. He knew that Vivekananda wouldn't give him permission to do this, so one night while the others slept, Trigunatita silently prepared to leave for the cremation ground. To his utter astonishment and disappointment, he heard Vivekananda calling out, "Where are you going?" Trigunatita stood speechless. Vivekananda went on to say: "Sri Ramakrishna appeared to me in my sleep and told me where you were going. He said that you should not go, that he has done all these things for us, and that it is quite sufficient for us to keep our minds fixed on him." Of course, this was the end of his attempt to practise tantric sadhana.[19]

Trigunatita was an extremist by nature. Once he decided to repeat his mantram day and night. His goal was "God-realization or death by starvation." Shivananda was very concerned about this young brother monk, and tried to persuade him to come out of his room. Trigunatita did come out, but he refused to eat. At last, it was decided that while Trigunatita ate, Shivananda would touch him and repeat a mantram on his behalf. Thus he hurriedly took his meal and continued his japam.[20]

When Trigunatita studied the Vedanta scriptures, he put his whole mind and all his energy into it. He forgot food and drink, sleep and surroundings. When it was dark, he would bring his mind back to the world and light a lantern. He would study Sanskrit literature and European philosophy until midnight. He practised spiritual disciplines with steadfast devotion, and he never lost his temper if scolded or criticized.

Trigunatita's father again tried to bring him back home, and asked him to finish his B. A. degree. Trigunatita refused, and instead left for Puri on 26 February 1887, along with some brother disciples. In Puri he practised Vaishnava sadhana with all the traditional face and body marks; he wore a tulsi rosary around his neck and also carried a picture of his Chosen Deity. After some time he returned to Baranagore.[21]

In *The Gospel of Sri Ramakrishna*, M. recorded Trigunatita's mental condition while he was at the Baranagore Monastery:

7 May 1887
Narendra was in charge of the members of the monastery. [Sarada] Prasanna had been practising austere sadhana for the past few days. Once Narendra had told him of his desire to fast to death for the realization of God. During Narendra's absence in Calcutta, Prasanna had left the monastery for an unknown destination.

Narendra (*to M.*): "You see what a lot of trouble I am in! Here, too, I am involved in a world of maya. Who knows where this boy has gone?"

Prasanna had left a letter for Narendra. This was the substance of the letter: "I am going to Vrindaban on foot. It is very risky for me to live here. Here my mind is undergoing a change. Formerly I used to dream about my parents and other relatives. Then I dreamt of woman, the embodiment of maya. I have suffered twice; I had to go back to my relatives at home. Therefore I am going far away from them. The Master once told me, 'Your people at home are apt to do anything; never trust them.'"

8 May 1887

There was a big plot of wooded land to the west of the monastery compound. M. was seated alone under a tree, when suddenly Prasanna appeared. It was about three o'clock in the afternoon.

M.: "Where have you been all these days? Everyone has been so worried about you. Have you seen the brothers? When did you arrive?"

Prasanna: "Just now. Yes, I have seen them."

M.: "You left a note saying that you were going to Vrindaban. We were terribly worried about you. How far did you go?"

Prasanna: "Only as far as Konnagar."

Both of them laughed.

M.: "Sit down. Tell me all about it. Where did you stop first?"

Prasanna: "At the Dakshineswar temple garden. I spent one night there."

M. (*smiling*): "What is Hazra's present mood?"

Prasanna: "Hazra asked me, 'What do you think of me?'"

Both laughed.

M. (*smiling*): "What did you say?"

Prasanna: "I said nothing."

M.: "Then?"

Prasanna: "Then he asked me whether I had brought tobacco for him."

Both laughed.

Prasanna: "He wanted me to wait on him." (*Laughter.*)

M.: "Where did you go next?"

Prasanna: "By degrees I got to Konnagar. I spent the night in the open. I intended to proceed farther and asked some gentlemen whether I could procure enough money there for a railway ticket to the up-country."

M.: "What did they say?"

Prasanna: "They said, 'You may get a rupee or so; but who will give you the whole fare?'"

Both laughed.

M.: "What did you take with you?"

Prasanna: "Oh, one or two pieces of cloth and a picture of the Master. I didn't show the picture to anybody."

Rakhal was seated in Kali Tapasvi's room. Prasanna sat near him. M., too, was there.

Rakhal (*to Prasanna*): "Where do you want to go, running away from here? Here you are in the company of holy men. Wouldn't it be foolish to run away from this? Where will you find another like Narendra?"

Prasanna. "My parents live in Calcutta. I am afraid of being drawn by their love. That is why I want to flee to a distant place."

Rakhal: "Can our parents love us as intensely as Gurumaharaj [*meaning Sri Ramakrishna*] did? What have we done for him, to deserve all this love? Why was he so eager for our welfare in body, mind, and soul? What have we done for him, to deserve all this?"

Prasanna (*to Rakhal*): "Don't you yourself feel like running away from here?"

Rakhal: "Yes, now and then I have a fancy to spend a few days on the bank of the Narmada."

Tarak and Prasanna were talking in the room of the "danas." He too was trying to persuade Prasanna to live there.

Prasanna: "I have neither jnana [knowledge] nor prema [love]. What have I in the world for a support?"

Tarak: "It is no doubt difficult to attain jnana; but how can you say you have no prema?"

Prasanna: "I have not yet wept for God. How can I say I have prema? What have I realized in all these days?"

Tarak: "But you have seen the Master. And why do you say that you have no jnana?"

Prasanna: "What sort of jnana are you talking about? Jnana means Knowledge. Knowledge of what? Certainly of God. But I am not even sure of the existence of God."

Tarak: "Yes, that's true. According to the jnani, there is no God."

M. (*to himself*): "Ah! The Master used to say that those who seek God pass through the state that Prasanna is now experiencing. In that state sometimes one doubts the very existence of God."

Narendra and Prasanna were talking in the meditation room. Rakhal, Harish, and the younger Gopal were seated in another part of the room.

Narendra was reading from the Gita and explaining the verses to Prasanna:

The Lord, O Arjuna, dwells in the hearts of all beings, causing them, by His maya, to revolve as if mounted on a machine. Take refuge in Him with all thy heart, O Bharata. By His grace wilt thou attain Supreme Peace and the Eternal Abode. Relinquishing all dharmas, take refuge in Me alone. I shall liberate thee from all sins. Grieve not.

Then he said to Prasanna: "Surrender yourself at His feet. Resign yourself completely to His will."

Narendra said to Prasanna: "Don't you remember Sri Ramakrishna's words? God is the hill of sugar and you are but an ant. One grain is enough to fill your stomach, and you think of bringing home the entire hill! Don't you remember what the Master said about Sukadeva? Even Sukadeva was a big ant at the most. That is why I scolded Kali, saying: 'You fool! Do you want to measure God with your tape and foot-rule?'

"God is the Ocean of Mercy. Be His slave and take refuge in Him. He will show compassion. Pray to Him: 'Protect me always with Thy compassionate face. Lead me from the unreal to the Real, from darkness to Light, from death to Immortality. Reveal Thyself to me and protect me always with Thy compassionate face.'"

Prasanna: "What kind of spiritual discipline should one practise?"

Narendra: "Repeat His name. That's enough."

Prasanna: "How are we to know that God is kind?"

Narendra: "The Vedas say, 'That which is Thy compassionate face.' John Stuart Mill said the same thing. He said, 'How much kindness must He have, who has implanted kindness in the hearts of men.' The Master used to say: 'Faith is the one essential thing. God exists. He is very near us. Through faith alone one sees Him.'"

Prasanna: "Sometimes you say that God does not exist, and now you are saying all these things! You are not consistent. You keep changing your opinions."

All laughed.

Narendra: "All right! I shall never change what I have just said. As long as one has desires and cravings, so long one doubts the existence of God."[22]

Obstacles in spiritual life are not always bad: First, they reveal the evil nature of maya; second, they create intense longing for the goal. If there is no obstruction to its flow, the river stagnates and eventually dies. Similarly, when one's spiritual life passes through test after test, one achieves experience and strength, leading ultimately to fulfillment. Trigunatita's parents and other family members tried their utmost to stop his spiritual journey, but his guru's grace helped him to overcome the obstacles they set in his way. If a person has sincere love for God, He makes everything favourable. Although Trigunatita was a monk, he had love and respect for his parents. After his father's death on 9 November 1888, he took his mother and younger brother Ashutosh to Holy Mother. Ashutosh became a disciple of Holy Mother and served her in Udbodhan. Trigunatita's mother died on 29 November 1895.

Pilgrimage

A real monk always thinks of Brahman and the teachings of Vedanta. He is content with the food that chance brings him, and he roams the world with a joyful mind. Trigunatita had a desire to visit the holy places throughout India. Sometime in 1891 he left for Varanasi and visited the temples of Lord Vishwanath and Mother Annapurna. There he met Pramadadas Mittra, a great Sanskrit scholar and a good friend of Vivekananda. From Varanasi he went to Chunar and visited the temple of the Goddess Durga. It was a solitary place on the top of a hill. He lived there a few days, but could not stay long as there was no food available nearby. Then he visited Kali and the eight-armed goddess Durga at Vindhyachal. Afterwards he went to Prayag (Allahabad), the confluence of the Ganges and the Jamuna, where he suffered from fever for twelve days. In this holy city Trigunatita attended Durga Puja, the autumn worship of the Divine Mother, as well as Ramlila, a performance on the divine life of Ramachandra.

Trigunatita then went to Kanpur, a historical place, and Vithur — also called Brahmavarta — an ancient Hindu holy place. There he saw the marble seat of the Creator, Brahma, as well as the ashrama of Dhruva, and the hermitage of the sage Valmiki. He then travelled to the ancient city of Etawah where he visited the ashrama of Khatkhatia Baba, a great soul, and he also met his brother disciple Swami Akhandananda. Both swamis then continued on to Agra where they visited the Taj Mahal. From Agra they journeyed to Mathura, the birthplace of Krishna, and Vrindaban, where Krishna had spent his boyhood. They stayed at Kalababu's Kunja (a family retreat of Balaram Basu), attended the festival of lights at Govardhan Hill, as well as the Raslila, and the food festival of Yatipur. They also visited Shyam-kunda, Radha-kunda, and other holy places.

In December 1891 Trigunatita resumed his journey. He went first to Bharatpur, then visited Madanmohan Temple in Keroni, and again met Akhandananda at Pushkar. They climbed the Savitri Hill and visited the Brahma Temple. Afterwards they reached Ajmir, where Trigunatita was sick for more than two weeks. When he recovered, a devotee bought a train ticket for him and he left for Chittor alone. After visiting various places, he arrived at Dwaraka, a place where Krishna had lived on the coast of the Arabian Sea. Then he went to Porbandar, or Sudama Puri, by boat and found lodging at the Hatkeshwar Shiva Temple. There he met some monks who were planning to visit Hinglaj, a difficult pilgrimage in the western desert of India.

The group of monks thought it would be easier if they could go to Karachi by boat and then by camel to Hinglaj. But who would bear the expenses? They heard of a learned Bengali monk living with the Dewan of Porbandar, so they decided to go with Trigunatita, as he was Bengali, to ask the monk for financial help. This learned monk turned out to be Swami Vivekananda, who was surprised to see Trigunatita there. When Swamiji learned the cause of his visit, he said to him: "I can't ask for money from anybody. Whatever you have, give to them." However, when the Dewan heard about it, he fulfilled the wish of the pilgrims.

Trigunatita talked to Swamiji for a long time and then returned to the Hatkeshwar Temple. The next day, when he was about to leave with the other monks, Swamiji came and took him to his residence. Trigunatita stayed with the Dewan and Vivekananda a couple of days and then, at Swamiji's request, went to Junagad where he lived with Haridas Vihari-das, the Dewan of Junagad, for several days. Then after visiting several other places, he returned to the Ramakrishna Monastery, which had been moved from Baranagore to Alambazar.

Trigunatita began to help his brother disciples with the household duties of the monastery. He had tremendous concentration and perseverance. Whatever he undertook he would steadfastly continue until the work was completed. He was curious about astrology and palmistry and would study those subjects day and night; he could forecast a person's future by seeing his horoscope. After staying in the monastery a year, he went to Darjeeling. A few months later he returned to Calcutta and then left for Almora, in the Himalayan region.

Pascal, the famous French philosopher, said of God, "Thou wouldst not have looked for Me, if thou hadst not found Me." Trigunatita tried to satisfy his insatiable desire to see the Lord by visiting holy places. In 1895 he left for Tibet to visit Mount Kailas and Manas Sarovar (a holy lake). It was the most difficult pilgrimage anyone could undertake, but Trigunatita's indomitable spirit carried him through thick and thin. It was June or July when he went and the snow had just begun to melt; he was overwhelmed by the panoramic beauty of the Himalayas.

One evening he found himself on the bank of a river with no way to cross except by going over an old ruined dam. There was enough moonlight to see, so he decided to cross the river by jumping from one rock to another. When he reached the middle, a thick patch of cloud covered the moon, obscuring his vision. He was completely helpless. One false step meant that he would be carried away by the swift current of the icy water. He began to chant the name of Sri Ramakrishna. All of a sudden he heard a voice say, "Follow me," and he went forward. Before he knew it, his feet touched the firm ground of the other shore. Just then the clouds disappeared and the moon shone forth with all her former brilliance. He did not see anyone around. He realized that his Master's grace and protection were still with him.[23]

While travelling in the Himalayas, Trigunatita came across a village with an old, dilapidated temple on its outskirts. Itinerant mendicants generally love to stay overnight in such temples. However, at sunset the villagers closed the temple gates and asked him to leave. They told him that with the approach of dusk, dense clouds of mosquitoes would descend on the temple compound and anyone who remained at night would surely bleed to death. Some unfortunate travellers had died that way in the past. Therefore, the gates were always closed at night. Trigunatita decided to stay at the temple that night in spite of the warnings. The villagers closed the gates and left.

Scarcely had the sun disappeared below the horizon, when a cloud of mosquitos descended upon the compound. Never before had he undergone such horrible torture. Protected only by a thin blanket, he either crouched in a corner or rushed hither and thither trying to escape their onslaught. There was no escape, no refuge anywhere. He prayed to the Master and endured the pain with his superhuman willpower. At daybreak the mosquitos quickly disappeared. The anxious villagers opened the gates and were surprised to see the swami still alive. However, he had to stay in the village for a week to recover from the mosquito bites.[24]

On another occasion he lost his way at night in the pouring rain. Overcome by hunger and weariness, he lay down to sleep in the rain by the side of the road. Without knowing it he had come near a railway station. At that time a railway porter with a lantern was returning home, and he noticed Trigunatita's pitiable condition. He took the swami to his home, gave him a dry cloth for the night, fed him, and arranged for a place for him to sleep. When Trigunatita left the next morning, he blessed the porter.[25]

Trigunatita had an analytical mind and was very sceptical regarding undue claims of miraculous power. Once in his travels he came to a place where a small spring flowed over the top of an overhanging rock. Nearby lived a fakir who claimed to be able to make the water flow at will — for a small sum of money. Many people paid to see the water flow at the fakir's command, but Trigunatita was not so easily convinced. When the visitors left, the swami climbed up around the rocks and discovered an intermittent spring. Thus the inquisitive mind of the swami tested every claim to the supernatural.[26]

In Calcutta and with Swami Vivekananda

After returning from pilgrimage in the latter part of 1895, Trigunatita stayed at the Calcutta residence of Dr. Shashi Bhusan Ghosh to recuperate from his many illnesses. He then began to write accounts of his travels in Tibet, which were published serially in the *Indian Mirror*, starting 22 December 1895. He began to study Vedanta literature extensively and gave classes at various places in Calcutta on the Gita and the Upanishads. He inaugurated three centres in Calcutta to teach morality and spirituality to young people. He also thought of starting a Bengali magazine to propagate Vedic culture and the message of Sri Ramakrishna. In January 1896 Vivekananda wrote to him from America: "Your idea for the paper is very good indeed. Apply yourself to it heart and soul." However, the paper, *Udbodhan*, was not started until 1899.

During his stay in Calcutta, Trigunatita developed a fistula, which needed surgery. Dr. Matilal Mukherjee of Baranagore informed the swami that since the operation would take some time and would be painful, he would use chloroform to put him to sleep. Trigunatita told the doctor to do the surgery without chloroform and that he would endure the pain. The surgeon was amazed but agreed to perform the surgery as he requested. He spent half an hour removing the fistula, cutting nearly six inches. The surgeon and nurses did not see any change in Trigunatita's face — he was as calm as if he were in deep meditation.[27]

Vivekananda returned from the West in January 1897, and in May established the Ramakrishna Mission in Calcutta. In 1898 a plot of land, along with a house, was purchased at Belur and the monastery was moved there in 1899. Swamiji made a rule that any monk who didn't go to the shrine for meditation at 4:00 a.m. would have to beg for his food outside the monastery that day. Once Shivananda and Trigunatita were late getting to the shrine and Swamiji asked them to live on alms that day. When they came back with food from Belur village, Swamiji joyfully took a portion of it.[28] The brother disciples obeyed Swamiji's orders as they had Ramakrishna's.

Another morning at Belur Math, Swamiji was going to the shrine for meditation and found that Trigunatita was in bed with a high temperature. Swamiji said to him: "Get up. Let us go for meditation. If you meditate, your fever will disappear." Akhandananda was nearby and he thought that perhaps Swamiji was joking. But he was not joking! Swamiji took Trigunatita's hand and pulled him to the Master's shrine. There they meditated for a couple of hours. It is said that after that meditation Trigunatita's temperature returned to normal.[29]

To spread the message of Sri Ramakrishna in Bengali, Swamiji asked Trigunatita to start the magazine that he had thought of in 1896. Vivekananda contributed one thousand rupees that Josephine MacLeod had given him; Haramohan Mittra donated another thousand. These contributions enabled Trigunatita to buy a press and inaugurate the publication of *Udbodhan*. Trigunatita rented a couple of rooms at Combuliatola Lane, Calcutta, for the magazine, labouring on this pioneering job alone, without any previous experience. His main assets were his sincerity, patience, perseverance, and above all, his love for the ideal. As he had no monastic assistants at first, Trigunatita was the editor, proofreader, manager, and supervisor of the press; and when the typesetters were sick, he had to compose the type also.

Sometimes he would go door to door to collect subscriptions, in addition to eliciting articles from various writers. Since his funds were limited, he didn't travel by tram; instead, he would walk ten miles a day, then eat one meal at a devotee's house at noon, and eat some puffed rice in the morning and evening. He slept one hour a day, between 3:00 and 4:00 a.m. To avoid sleep he would splash cold water on his eyes or read the proofs at night while standing. Over and above all this, if any of his press workers were sick, he would nurse them. When he was sick, he would lie down and cover himself with a blanket for a while, then continue his regular work the next morning.[30]

Thus in January 1899, the biweekly (later monthly) magazine came into existence. Swamiji named the magazine *Udbodhan*, "The Awakening." Sharat Chandra Chakrabarty, a disciple of Swamiji, recorded the following in his *Talks with Swami Vivekananda*:

Disciple: "Sir, it is impossible for any other man to exert himself as Swami Trigunatita is doing for the magazine."

Swamiji: "Do you think these monastic children of Sri Ramakrishna are born simply to sit for meditation under trees lighting dhuni-fires? Whenever any of them will take up some work, people will be astonished to see their energy. Learn from them how to work. Look, Trigunatita has given up his spiritual practices, his meditation and everything, to carry out my orders, and he has set himself to work. Is it a matter of small sacrifice? He will not stop short of success!"

Disciple: "But, sir, it looks rather odd in our eyes that monks in ochre robes should go about from door to door as the swami is doing."

Swamiji: "Why? The circulation of the magazine is only for the good of the householders. The masses will benefit by the spread of these new ideas in the country. Do you think this unselfish work is in any way inferior to devotional practices? Our object is to do good to humanity."

Disciple: "Sir, the other day I saw that Swami Trigunatita worshipped the photograph of Sri Ramakrishna in the press room before beginning to work, and he asked for your blessings for the success of the work."

Swamiji: "Well, the Master is our centre. Each one of us is a ray of that light-centre. So Trigunatita has started the work by worshipping the Master — he did the right thing....Tell him when you go that I am exceedingly delighted with his work. Give him my loving blessings."[31]

Trigunatita edited and managed the *Udbodhan* for four years. Later Swami Shuddhananda was engaged to assist him. Trigunatita was methodical, frugal, and bore responsibility without complaint. His love for the ideal never allowed him to be discouraged. In spite of his heavy workload, he remained cheerful. He kept a picture of Mother Durga on his desk. The Divine Mother endowed him with both physical and mental strength. Once at Balaram's house, where he used to stay at night, he carried a tin of kerosene oil (weighing nearly fifty pounds) from the first floor to the second floor with one finger. He was short and heavyset and would sometimes put a book on a high stool and read standing the whole night.

With Holy Mother

When Holy Mother was living at Nilambar Babu's garden house in Belur (from 1894 to 1895), Trigunatita was her attendant. He would spread a white cloth under the shefalika flower tree (an autumnal white fragrant flower) so that the blooms might not fall in the dust. Holy Mother would use those flowers for her morning worship. He was extremely thoughtful and resourceful in every action.

After Swami Yogananda's death in March 1899, Trigunatita took charge of Holy Mother's physical needs in addition to editing the *Udbodhan*. His zeal to serve her appeared to be almost an obsession. In October 1899 Holy Mother was going to Jayrambati in a bullock cart via Burdwan. It was past midnight. Trigunatita was walking in front of the carriage as her bodyguard, with a heavy stick on his shoulder. Suddenly he saw a wide breach in the road made by a flood. At once he realized that when the carriage came to the opening, it would either be overturned or receive a terrific jolt, not only disturbing the Mother's sleep but possibly hurting her physically. Immediately he laid his large body in the breach and asked the driver to drive the vehicle over him. Luckily, Holy Mother awoke before this happened. She took in the situation, and rebuked her disciple for his rashness.[32]

While returning from Jayrambati, Trigunatita stopped at Baidyabati and went to a hotel for a meal. The owner told him that the rate was six pice per meal. The swami said to him that he was a good eater and would be glad to pay extra for his meal. But the owner declined to receive any extra money from a monk. The swami was hungry and began to eat his meal — mainly rice and *dal* (lentil). The waiter went on serving Trigunatita until there was no cooked rice and dal left in the hotel. The poor hotel keeper, approaching the swami, said: "Father, please leave now. I can't feed you anymore. You will not have to pay anything." Trigunatita blessed the hotel keeper and left. He later greatly enjoyed narrating this incident.[33]

Trigunatita's love for and faith in Holy Mother was phenomenal. Once Yogin-ma, a disciple of Sri Ramakrishna, asked the swami to buy some hot chilies for Holy Mother. In his eagerness to get the hottest possible, he walked through many markets from Baghbazar to Barabazar (four miles), tasting all the hot chilies by chewing one of each, until his tongue became red and swollen. At last he found the hottest ones at Barabazar and brought them to the Mother. When Holy Mother heard about it, she said, "What devotion to the guru!" Later when Trigunatita went to America, he sent money regularly for Holy Mother's personal service.[34]

In America

By 1902 Swami Turiyananda had worked strenuously for three years in America. When his health broke, he decided to return to India. Dr. M. H. Logan, the president of the Vedanta Society of San Francisco, wrote to Vivekananda and asked him to send another swami. Swamiji asked Trigunatita to replace Turiyananda. Trigunatita handed over charge of the *Udbodhan* to Swami Shuddhananda and began to make the necessary arrangements for his departure. Meanwhile, Vivekananda passed away on 4 July 1902. Despite this tragedy, Trigunatita sailed for the United States in the early part of November via Colombo and Japan, and arrived in San Francisco on 2 January 1903. Believing, in his simplicity, that there might not be any vegetables in America, he went fully prepared to live on bread and water. He was determined to remain a vegetarian at all costs. He found afterwards, of course, that vegetables and cereals of all kinds were available in America in great abundance.

Trigunatita was well received by Dr. Logan, Mr. and Mrs. C. F. Peterson, and other members of the Society. He began lecturing at the Petersons' house, but it could not accommodate the large crowds. So in March 1903, the Society rented a commodious house at 40 Steiner Street, where Trigunatita and the Peterson family could live and he could conduct the services. Trigunatita gave classes on the Gita on Monday evenings and on the Upanishads on Thursday evenings; he lectured in the morning and evening on Sundays. Music, of course, was part of every service.

In 1904 some students invited Trigunatita to start a Vedanta centre in Los Angeles, nearly 500 miles south of San Francisco. The swami began the work there, but later found it difficult to manage both places; so he asked for an assistant from India. The authorities of Belur Math sent Swami Satchidananda, who received a hearty welcome in San Francisco and then, under Trigunatita's guidance, started the work in Los Angeles. But after only a year, Satchidananda was compelled to return to India because of poor health.[35]

In the same year, the work in San Francisco had grown to such proportions that Trigunatita felt the Society should have a suitable building of its own. With Trigunatita, to think was to act, and a committee was at once appointed to look for a suitable site. Soon a meeting of all the members was called, the funds were quickly raised, and a plot of land was purchased on the corner of Webster and Filbert Streets. On 25 August 1905, with appropriate ceremonies, the cornerstone was laid. The swami placed in it pictures of Sri Ramakrishna, Holy Mother, and others within a metal box. Regarding the future of the temple, Trigunatita said, "I shall not live to enjoy; others will come later who will enjoy"; and, referring to his own participation, he boldly proclaimed: "Believe me, if there is the least tinge of selfishness in building this temple, it will fall; but if it is the Master's work, it will stand."[36] It is amazing that the terrible earthquake and fire of 1906, which destroyed much of San Francisco, did no damage to the temple. This was the first Hindu Temple in the Western world. It was dedicated on 7 January 1906 and the first services were held there on Sunday, 15 January 1906.

Trigunatita was ingenuous. He planned the temple himself, combining ideas from a Hindu temple, a Christian church, a Muslim mosque, and an American residence. It was designed by the architect Joseph A. Leonard, in a style generally called Pointed Architecture of Grecian and Roman origin. All the mouldings, ornaments, and the arches of the veranda are of Moorish style. The points of the domes, towers, and pinnacles, directed upwards to the sky, have a religious meaning — moving towards God, or rising higher and higher until we reach the very highest.[37]

Shortly after the dedication of the temple, Trigunatita was inspired to start a monastery for the young American students. He recruited ten and put them on the third floor and in the tower rooms on the roof. The young men were all engaged in various occupations and continued to earn their own living, contributing their share of the expenses of the monastery, until such time as each might be ready, in the swami's judgement, to take first monastic vows.

These young men were subjected to strict discipline. They had to rise early in the morning, meditate regularly, and do household duties such as cleaning, sweeping, and gardening. Trigunatita taught them that all works connected with the temple were holy, and if performed in the right spirit, would purify their minds and advance their meditation. He himself joined the students in doing the household work; over and above that, he cooked all the meals so that the young men might eat pure, sattvic food, which is essential for spiritual growth. The meals began with a chant and ended with a few minutes of silent meditation. Each student in turn read from one of the scriptures of the world. This was followed by questions, with answers by the swami. Every meal indeed became a sacrament.

Trigunatita was fond of teaching by means of forceful maxims. When someone at the table recited the great watchword of the American Republic, "Eternal vigilance is the price of liberty," he made him repeat it. Some of the mottoes hanging in every room of the monastery were: "Live like a hermit, but work like a horse"; "Do it now"; "Watch and pray"; "Do or die — but you will not die."[38] The swami believed in singing as a devotional exercise, and led his young male disciples in hymns and chants up on the roof of the temple, or down by the harbour in the early morning, astonishing the fishermen and sailors.

Trigunatita was an uncompromising ascetic. He taught his students through personal example more than through words. He was a consistent example of regularity and punctuality. He would go to bed last and rise before any of the other members of the monastery. His office was his bedroom, and he had no bed: He would spread one blanket on the carpet, put another blanket over himself, and use the upper part of his right arm as his pillow.[39] The swami strongly believed that through discipline one can form a strong character, which is absolutely essential as a foundation for spiritual life. To the earnest disciple he would say: "I don't mind if I break every bone in your body if I can drag you up to the shores of the ocean of Immortality and throw you in. Then my work will be finished."[40]

Swami Atulananda left this eyewitness account:

Swami Trigunatita was a man of austere type. When he first came to San Francisco, he fasted once for three days — maybe to accumulate power to carry on the work. He was a strict disciplinarian. Once on Sri Ramakrishna's birthday he spent fifteen hours in worship from 6:00 a.m. to 9:00 p.m. and delivered three lectures, all without leaving the platform.... He was a very jolly type of man and very active too. He encouraged others also to follow a tight routine — meditation, study, work, and so on. At lectures there would be no chairs on the platform. He had a desk only and, when speaking, he used to lean on it.

He ran a bookstall and he himself kept the accounts. One day he found the account five dollars short. He was worried, and for days together he worked, trying to make the account balance. Then at long last he wrote at the bottom of the page: "Five dollars short. However, let it go." In that way he tallied the account. He wouldn't take any-body's advice. Once he had to purchase a suit. He went to the market and the trade people sold him a cheap suit. When he came home Mrs. Peterson said, "Oh, swami, what have you done? It is the kind of thing that race track people wear. You cannot go out in this dress." Then a compromise was worked out in which the swami was permitted to wear the suit only at home. Another day he purchased a dark red col-lar, put it on, and came home all the way feeling quite proud of it. Seeing him with that collar, Mrs. Peterson exclaimed, "Oh, what have you done? These collars are used by gamblers. You cannot use it. I am going to hide it."[41]

Trigunatita had an undaunted personality. He boldly faced all the challenges of his life. In the anteroom next to the monastery kitchen there were several strings stretched across one end from wall to wall. Dangling from these were a number of lifelike spiders of different sizes and kinds. The young members were curious about it. First they thought they were there simply as decoration, but later Trigunatita revealed the mystery behind the spiders. Once while bathing in the Ganges he had been trapped by a swarm of water spiders. He had received such a shock that to overcome that phobia, or rather to make sure that it no longer existed, he hung up the artificial spiders where he could see them a number of times each day.[42]

Trigunatita also started a convent as a separate community at the earnest entreaties of some women disciples who wanted to live a life of discipline under his guidance. They did their cooking and household work in the spirit of worship and service to humanity, and faithfully adhered to the established rules. These women were all self-supporting, working in the daytime outside and then doing their duties in the convent in the morning and evening. In spite of their hard work, they were happy as they felt they were on the path that would lead them to God-realization. Trigunatita sensed that the convent might be the seed of spiritual awakening among American women, but for a number of reasons it came to an end in 1912.[43]

The life of Trigunatita was one long sacrifice, and those who were privileged to be in his presence found that their doubts and troubles melted away like snow before the sun. He veritably radiated holiness, for he always lived in the consciousness of the Divine Mother. However, he was overworked and his health was failing. So in April 1906 Swami Prakashananda was sent to assist him. The new swami took over the cooking and other monastery responsibilities, and he won the hearts of the members of the Society with his gentle and loving disposition. Nevertheless, the membership of the monastery began to dwindle for various reasons from 1913 on until finally, after the death of Swami Trigunatita, it was closed in 1915.

One of the members of the monastery, a Hungarian named Joseph Horvath, was a printer; this gave Trigunatita the idea of starting a printing press in the temple basement. A complete printing outfit was secured, and Mr. Horvath devoted all his time to the swami's publication projects.

In April 1909 Trigunatita started a monthly magazine called *Voice of Freedom*. This magazine served as a channel through which the message of Vedanta reached many souls who could not attend the swami's lectures. Within three years the magazine was an established success with a growing list of interested friends and subscribers. The swami wanted to blend the thoughts and culture of the East and the West through this magazine. It was mentioned in the prospectus of the first issue (April 1909): "This periodical is called *Voice of Freedom* because when Freedom is realized, its *voice* and power reign supreme everywhere, whether in heaven or on earth, or beyond; in every age, whether within the span of history, or before or after. The idea of freedom is inborn in man."

By a special arrangement with M., Trigunatita published an American edition of his *Gospel* in 1912, which was circulated widely. In 1914 Mr. Horvath left for Hungary to visit his parents and no one could be found with the necessary experience to take his place. However, Trigunatita managed to print the *Voice of Freedom* with the help of another member of the society. The *Voice of Freedom* continued until March 1916, one year after Trigunatita's death.

While Vivekananda was in America from 1899 to 1900, one of his disciples, Minnie C. Boock, offered as a gift for the work a tract of land, 160 acres in the San Antonio Valley. This remote property is eighteen miles southeast of Mount Hamilton, California, the site of the world-famous Lick Observatory. Swamiji accepted the offer and sent Turiyananda to build a retreat for the American Vedanta students. Turiyananda began the work with the help of a dozen students, and named the retreat Shanti Ashrama. However, he had to return to India in 1902 and Gurudas (later, Swami Atulananda) was temporarily placed in charge of the ashrama. When Trigunatita came to San Francisco, he took charge of Shanti Ashrama, but Gurudas continued to manage it.

Atulananda reminisced: "I lived with Swami Trigunatita at Shanti Ashrama. For one month every year he used to come there with his students, thirty or forty in number, men and women both. He separated men from women. Of course, even before, men and women used to live in separate tents. There were separate bathrooms for the two sexes. But the swami effected separate dining tables also. We used to make fun of it."[44]

Trigunatita planned a rigorous schedule for the retreat. From 3:45 a.m. to 10:00 p.m. the students were busy with chanting, meditation, and scripture classes, along with chopping wood, carrying water, cooking, cleaning, and maintenance. They were also placed on a strict vegetarian diet. The swami provided plenty of relaxation in between periods of work. Wednesday and Saturday afternoons were declared holidays, and a stream of genuine fun and merriment relieved the students from any monotony or strain that might have resulted from the rigorous routine. At night Trigunatita would tell stories about Sri Ramakrishna, as well as stories about his own life, ranging from his adventures in eating, travelling, and seeing ghosts, to visions of God. On the full-moon night the swami would hold a *dhuni* fire ceremony (a ritual where an aspirant pours oblations into the fire, signifying the destruction of his ego and worldly desires) on a hill under the open sky, and the students would sit around the fire and spend the whole night in spiritual practices.[45]

Those who had the privilege of attending the classes at Shanti Ashrama could hardly forget their unique experiences. They were surcharged with the spirituality of Trigunatita. On the top of the meditation cabin was a wooden flag bearing the inscription "Om Ramakrishna," carved in relief by Trigunatita himself. The same inscription appeared on a flagpole on the Dhuni Hill and on the entrance gate to the Shanti Ashrama. The swami, in spite of his rheumatism and other physical troubles, kept the spirit of Vedanta and Sri Ramakrishna alive in the minds of his American students.

Apart from Shanti Ashrama, Trigunatita had a master plan for a Vedanta colony with a temple, library, orphanage, hospital, and an area where members could retire and live comfortably in their old age. For this purpose he bought 200 acres of fertile land on the outskirts of Concord, one and a half hour's drive from San Francisco. He kept twenty-five acres for the Society, and the rest was distributed among the members who wished to settle in the colony. Some members built houses, sunk wells, planted orchards, and started crops. In addition to his regular duties in San Francisco, the swami went to the colony once every week to supervise its progress and inspire its members. Improvements continued until January 1914, but unfortunately after his passing away the colony project came to an end.[46]

In 1915 the Panama-Pacific International Exposition was held in the Marina district of San Francisco, just inside the Golden Gate and only three blocks from the temple. In preparation for the great event, Trigunatita had purchased the national flags of various countries for display, and had also installed a new system of electric lights that could be seen from the Exposition grounds and made the Hindu Temple look like a fairyland at night. Trigunatita also got permission from the city of San Francisco to build a garden around the temple. An ornamental lattice iron fence atop the wall protected the plants and flowers from passers-by. Statues and other decorative features made the garden one of the attractions of the neighbourhood and even today the Hindu Temple is a landmark in San Francisco. Unfortunately, the swami did not live to see the opening of the Exposition.[47]

Trigunatita was not a cloistered monk. He personally knew many distinguished people of San Francisco and neighbouring cities. They came to know him either through the business of the Society or through his lectures and classes. He was a likable person and made friends with unknown neighbours as well as with the mayor of the city. With his students he acted like an affectionate mother as well as a chastising father. He expected the best from them and trained them to give public speeches. Trigunatita gave the following instructions to help his students prepare for a lecture:

1. The lesson or lecture is to be taken sincerely and faithfully as a spiritual service and religious practice for one's own spiritual advancement.
2. Sit in a sincere and prayerful mood.
3. Make the mind blank. Drive off all the desires and thoughts of the secular side of work.

4. Meditate on God.
5. Then meditate on the subject intensely.
6. Then offer the lesson or lecture as a sacred sacrifice to God.
7. Bow down in the spirit of thankfulness to God and ask for his blessing.
8. Finally, when you come to the platform to speak, remember that you are talking to God. God is the only audience.[48]

Trigunatita was a man of truth. Once he was invited to dinner by a noted clergyman. This man was a good friend and an admirer of the swami. After dinner the clergyman asked the swami, "Is the food all right?" The swami was reluctant to say anything. When the host insisted on knowing Trigunatita's opinion, he replied: "It is hard for me to tell you the harsh truth. Truly, I don't relish this kind of food." The clergyman was a little shocked, but he appreciated Trigunatita's frankness and love for truth. He said to the swami: "I know you will not deviate from truth, even for the sake of social etiquette or friendship. But let me tell you, if you are invited by somebody in the future, please don't say such a harsh truth; otherwise, they will criticize you." Rather than be put in that position again, from that time on the swami never accepted another dinner invitation.[49]

Towards the End

For the last five years of his life, Trigunatita continuously suffered from rheumatism and Bright's disease. However, he continued to follow his routine punctually, did not deviate from his strict diet, and would not reduce his workload. As a result, his health broke down even further. Once he told a disciple: "A number of times during moments of excruciating pain, I would think, 'Let the body go, and end it all.' But I could not do it — the thought would come that the Mother's work must go on, and I set my will to force the body to carry on. This body has become a mere shell and may go to pieces at any time. For three years now I have held the body together by sheer force of will."[50]

In December 1914 Trigunatita asked one of his disciples to comment on his lectures. When the disciple pointed out to him that his voice quivered during the lecture, he replied, "I have tried my utmost to control it, but as I go onto the platform, my Divine Mother appears to me and fills me full of such feelings of love that it is sometimes difficult for me to articulate."[51]

Trigunatita must have had a premonition of his end. On 24 December 1914 he said to a young disciple: "I want you to promise me that if anything should happen to me in the near future you will see to it that after my death my brain is removed and presented to a scientific institution to be preserved in alcohol for analysis."[52] It was his belief that the brain of a yogi would be found to differ in size and structure from that of a worldly person, and that when this was demonstrated the scientific world would be compelled to acknowledge it. Thus he planned that even in death his body might serve the truth.

On Friday, 25 December 1914 Trigunatita conducted the all-day Christmas Service from 6:00 a.m. to 9:00 p.m. This consisted of three lectures (at 11:00 a.m., 3:00 p.m., and 6:00 p.m.), chanting and singing, reading and exposition of the scriptures. It was a divine experience for those privileged to be present on that day when the advent of Jesus Christ, an incarnation of God, was celebrated by a direct disciple of Sri Ramakrishna, another incarnation of God. The floral decorations, the illumination of Christ's picture, the fragrance of incense, the devotional songs and instrumental music, and the holy presence of the swami created an uplifting atmosphere. As on other occasions, the swami did not leave the platform even for a moment during the whole day. How he mastered his physical ailments and made his pain-racked body endure the fifteen hours, only he could say.[53]

Two days later, on Sunday afternoon, 27 December 1914, Trigunatita was lecturing from the podium of the Hindu Temple in San Francisco. All of a sudden a young man in the front threw a bomb onto the pulpit; there was an explosion and a cloud of dense blue smoke obscured the platform. When the smoke cleared it was found that the young man, a former student of Trigunatita named Louis Vavra, had been killed, and that the swami had received severe injuries. He was taken at once to the Affiliated Colleges Hospital. On his way to the hospital, the swami inquired, "Where is Louis, poor fellow!" Sometime previously Trigunatita had observed the young man's unbalanced mental condition and had recommended that he find a job in the country, where the surroundings would be soothing. Even in the midst of excruciating pain the swami's mind was filled with pity for his mentally ill student.[54]

A number of devotees visited Trigunatita daily and reported his progress to the temple. In addition to regular nurses a male attendant was appointed to lift and carefully move the swami's heavy body. One nurse made a comment, "I have never seen such a calm, uncomplaining, and enduring patient in my life." From his hospital bed, the swami asked Mrs. Peterson to arrange the repair of the damage to the temple. Accordingly, she collected the funds and his wishes were carried out. The doctor gave

Trigunatita a high dosage of sleep medication to reduce his pain, and as a result he was not always conscious. Although he received the best medical care, the infection that resulted from his wounds could not be abated.

On the afternoon of 9 January the swami told one of his young disciples that he would leave his body the next day, which was the birthday of Vivekananda, according to the Indian lunar calendar. And as he foretold, Swami Trigunatitananda, the great yogi and disciple of Sri Ramakrishna, passed away at 7:30 p.m. on 10 January 1915. As the news of his death spread, a large number of people, including the Catholic, Protestant, and Jewish religious leaders of San Francisco came to pay homage to the swami. His body was cremated according to his wishes at Cypress Lawn Cemetery. One year later, on 13 April 1916, Swami Prakashananda carried Swami Trigunatitananda's relics to Shanti Ashrama and installed them on the top of the highest hill, Siddha Giri, the "Hill of Realization."[55]

Swami Trigunatitananda's ashes remain as a mute symbol of his vanished form, but his immortal message lives on after him: Work hard. Discipline yourself. Build your character. Endure to the end. Realize your Self. And be free.

13

ॐ

SWAMI ADVAITANANDA

The scriptures say, "Tormented by three kinds of suffering — physical and mental, terrestrial, and supernatural — people inquire about religion as an antidote to sufferings." Bliss is inherent in human beings; therefore they cannot bear pain, for it is foreign to their true nature. However, sometimes grief plays an important role in human life: It makes people understand the impermanency of the world. Nothing makes life so empty as the loss of a mother in one's infancy, the death of a father in boyhood, or the loss of a spouse in old age.

Gopal Chandra Ghosh of Sinthi, Calcutta, lost his wife when he was fifty-five years of age. Brokenhearted and unable to bear his overwhelming grief, Gopal went to a friend, Dr. Mahendra Pal of Sinthi, for consolation. Mahendra was a devotee of Sri Ramakrishna, so he suggested that Gopal see the Master at Dakshineswar, thinking that holy company might assuage his grief. Sometime in March or April of 1884, Mahendra accompanied Gopal on a visit there. Mahendra told the Master about his friend's condition. Generally Ramakrishna felt an affinity with his disciples at first sight, but he treated Gopal like a stranger. Gopal also did not see anything extraordinary about the Master. After returning home, still deeply depressed, Gopal decided not to visit Ramakrishna again. Mahendra told Gopal: "Look, holy people sometimes do not like to be caught easily. They test our sincerity through indifference. Please visit the Master frequently."[1]

33

SWAMI ADVAITANANDA: BELUR MATH

The second time Gopal went to Dakshineswar, Ramakrishna, like a good physician, gave him an infallible antidote for his grief. Speaking of God, he lifted Gopal's mind, uprooting his worldly ties and attachments. Gopal learned from the Master that the world is unreal, like water in a mirage, and that dispassion is the only medicine which will counteract grief and delusion. The Master's words on the impermanency of the world appealed to Gopal and made a lasting impression on his mind. He returned home and seriously began to think of renouncing the world to search for God. He was attracted to the Master, and soon returned to Dakshineswar. Gopal later narrated what happened after his third visit: "The Master possessed me. I would think of him day and night. The pang of separation from the Master gave me chest pain. No matter how hard I tried, I couldn't forget his face."[2]

Gopal Chandra Ghosh was born in 1828 at Rajpur (Jagaddal) in 24-Parganas, nearly twenty-five miles north of Calcutta. Very little is known about his family except that his father's name was Govardhan Ghosh. Gopal moved to Sinthi, a northern suburb of Calcutta, in order to work for Beni Madhav Pal. Beni Pal also lived in Sinthi and had a household goods shop at China Bazar, Calcutta. He was a Brahmo devotee and used to invite Sri Ramakrishna to his beautiful garden house during the spring and fall festivals of the Brahmo Samaj. According to M., the recorder of *The Gospel of Sri Ramakrishna*, Gopal first met the Master sometime in the latter part of the 1870s. M. recorded three visits of the Master to Beni Pal's garden house in great detail: 28 October 1882; 22 April 1883; 19 October 1884. Gopal probably saw Sri Ramakrishna in the crowd during festival time, but this did not leave any deep impression on his mind. Moreover, Gopal was a self-effacing person and did not try to put himself in the limelight.

In the Company of Sri Ramakrishna

As he had no family ties after the death of his wife, Gopal moved from Sinthi to Dakshineswar to serve the Master. Ramakrishna accepted Gopal as his disciple and would address him as "the elder Gopal" or "Overseer." The other disciples called him "Gopal-da" (Gopal, the elder brother), since he was eight years older than Ramakrishna. The Master introduced him to Holy Mother, who needed a person who could shop and run errands for her. Ramakrishna praised Gopal's managerial capacity in household affairs and his sweet behaviour with people. One way to judge a person's internal nature is to watch his external actions: If he is organized outside that indicates he is organized inside also. Gopal was neat and clean, and by temperament methodical and orderly.

A few days after becoming acquainted with the Master, Gopal felt intense renunciation and expressed his desire to go for a pilgrimage. On 5 April 1884, M. recorded the following conversation in the *Gospel*:

> Master (*to the elder Gopal*): "Do you intend to go on a pilgrimage now?"
> Gopal: "Yes, sir. I should like to wander about a little."
> Master (*to the elder Gopal and the other devotees*): "As long as a man feels that God is 'there,' he is ignorant. But he attains knowledge when he feels that God is 'here.'
>
> "A man wanted a smoke. He went to a neighbour's house to light his charcoal. It was the dead of night and the household was asleep. After he had knocked a great deal, someone came down to open the door. At the sight of the man he asked, 'Hello! What's the matter?' The man replied: 'Can't you guess? You know how fond I am of smoking. I have come here to light my charcoal.' The neighbour said: 'Ha! Ha! You are a fine man indeed! You took the trouble to come and do all this knocking at the door! Why, you have a lighted lantern in your hand!' (*All laugh.*)
>
> "What a man seeks is very near him. Still he wanders about from place to place."[3]

It is not known whether the elder Gopal went on a pilgrimage or not. Perhaps he gradually became close to the Master and decided to serve him. In spite of his age, Gopal tried to keep the same pace as the other young disciples. When Narendra would sing to the accompaniment of the *tanpura* (a stringed instrument) in the Master's room, Gopal would play the *tabla* (drums). As a newcomer, he was absorbing Sri Ramakrishna's teachings and way of life. One day Dr. Mahendra Pal came to visit Gopal and the Master in Dakshineswar. They left his room through the western door and stepped onto the garden path. They saw a woman sweeper coming towards them, carrying on her head a tub of excrement from a privy, about five or six yards away. When the Master saw her, he prostrated before her, stretching fully on the ground, saying, "Mother, who can do this work except you?"[4] In this way the Master taught his devotees not to look down upon anybody.

Ramakrishna disliked carelessness in people. If a person is forgetful in minor things, he will be forgetful in the vital aspects of life. On 25 May 1884 Sri Ramakrishna went to the Panchavati, where arrangements had been made for *kirtan* (devotional singing). Gopal carried an umbrella for the Master. Suddenly there was a rainstorm. The Master returned to his room with the devotees, and the musician continued her songs there.

"Have you brought the umbrella?" the Master asked Gopal.

"No, sir," Gopal replied, "I forgot all about it while listening to the music." Gopal rushed to the Panchavati and brought back the umbrella.

The Master said: "I am generally unmindful about the world, but not to that extent. Rakhal also is very careless. Referring to the date of an invitation, he says 'the eleventh' instead of 'the thirteenth.' And Gopal — he belongs in a herd of cows!"[5] (The word *gopal* also means "herd of cows.")

Sometime in 1885 Gopal felt the need for initiation from the Master, but because he was bashful he could not ask for it in front of others. Moreover, Ramakrishna did not give any formal initiation to his disciples. He would transmit spiritual power to them in other ways — such as touching them, or writing a mantram on the tongue, or whispering a mantram in the ear, or singing a song, or just through a glance. Latu described the following incident: "Once, before the noon meal, the Master was walking alone in the temple garden of Dakshineswar. Gopal-da took the opportunity to express his desire for initiation to the Master. I saw from a distance that Gopal-da knelt down on the ground and, holding the feet of the Master, began to cry. The Master lifted him up from the ground holding his arms. Gopal-da was still crying profusely. What the Master said to him, I did not hear. Since that time I have noticed Gopal-da chanting God's name every evening in front of the Krishna Temple."[6]

In September 1885 Ramakrishna moved to Shyampukur in Calcutta for cancer treatment and Gopal accompanied him. He served the Master like a nurse, giving him medicine and a proper diet. Usually Holy Mother prepared the Master's food and carried it to his room. Gopal acted as Holy Mother's messenger; he was free with her, and she did not cover her face with a veil in front of him. When the doctor prescribed any special diet for the Master, Gopal would note down the details and convey them to Holy Mother. When the food was ready, she would send Gopal or Latu to inform the Master. The devotees and disciples would immediately leave the room and Holy Mother would bring the food. The Master took his meals twice daily: a little before midday and shortly after sunset. Holy Mother would wait in his room until he had finished his meal, then she would take back the cups and plates.

On 11 December 1885 Ramakrishna moved to the Cossipore garden house from Shyampukur. Gopal continued his usual duties. M. wrote in the *Gospel*: "On the morning of 23 December Ramakrishna gave unrestrained expression to his love for the devotees. Touching Kalipada's chest, he said, 'May your inner spirit be awakened!' He stroked Kalipada's chin affectionately and said, 'Whoever has sincerely called on God or performed his daily religious devotions will certainly come here.' In the morning two ladies received his special blessings. His love this day really broke all bounds. He wanted to bless Gopal of Sinthi and said to a devotee, 'Bring Gopal here.'"[7]

In Cossipore, Narendra began to practise intense spiritual disciplines. One night he said to the elder Gopal and Sharat: "The Master's disease is extremely serious. May he not intend to lay down his body! Strive your best for spiritual enlightenment through service to him and prayer and meditation while there is yet time. Otherwise, after his passing away, there will be no end to your repentance."[8] On 4 January 1886 Narendra said to the Master, "I intend to light a fire under the bel tree of Dakshineswar and meditate."[9] The Master suggested that he practise meditation under the Panchavati because the authorities of the powder magazine, which was adjacent to the Dakshineswar garden, wouldn't allow fire so close. Gopal was in the Master's room; he got permission to accompany Narendra and they left for Dakshineswar at 9:00 p.m.

It was common among the disciples of Ramakrishna to practise japam and meditation the whole night under his guidance. The burning fire of renunciation that the Master instilled in their hearts destroyed all their worldly desires. They forgot their body consciousness, their careers, and their family obligations: They loved their Master wholeheartedly and were carried away with divine intoxication by his grace. They served the Master day and night along with their practice of spiritual disciplines.

Gopal was responsible for giving medicine to the Master. One day the Master noticed that the time for taking medicine had passed, so he asked another disciple, "Where is that old man?" When the Master learned that Gopal was sleeping, he said joyfully: "Oh, how many sleepless nights he has passed! Let him sleep. Please don't call him. You had better give me the medicine today."[10]

Gopal used to wash the Master's cancerous sore daily with a special solution made from margosa leaves boiled in water, which is considered to be antiseptic. One day when Gopal touched the sore, the Master cried out with pain. Gopal said sadly: "Sir, what can I do? If I wash, you will get pain, so let me not do it." "No, no, you go on washing. Look, I have no more pain," the Master replied as he withdrew his mind from that spot. Gopal was then able to wash the area carefully, and the Master remained silent and cheerful as if Gopal were washing someone's else's wound.[11] Another day at Cossipore, Gopal inadvertently breathed on the Master's food plate. As a result, the Master could not offer the food thus defiled to the Divine Mother — and he never ate any food without offering it first to Her.[12] The Master had to be served again with fresh food. After that Gopal was extremely careful while nursing the Master.

Once Holy Mother recalled a significant incident that took place when the Master lay ill at Cossipore. A number of his disciples, including Gopal, were taking turns attending to his needs. But one day, instead of serving the Master, Gopal went off somewhere to meditate. He meditated for a long time. When Girish Babu heard about this, he remarked: "The one upon whom Gopal is meditating with closed eyes is suffering on a sickbed, and fancy, he is meditating upon him!" Gopal was sent for. When he arrived the Master asked him to stroke his legs. Then he said to Gopal: "Do you think I am asking you to stroke my legs because they are aching? Oh, no! In your previous births you did many virtuous acts; therefore I am accepting your service."[13]

Sri Ramakrishna made his life a model for his disciples to follow. Gopal, though older than the other disciples, tried very hard to follow the ideal the Master set for them. Even his brother disciples praised his sincerity, love, and steadfast dedication to the Master. One day he heard the Master say, "Never tell a lie — even jokingly or casually."[14] Gopal followed this teaching to the letter and encouraged others to do the same. Once a doctor prescribed the juice of three lemons for the Master's upset stomach, and Gopal was entrusted to collect them. Instead of only three he brought several additional lemons, but the Master accepted only three and asked him to return the extras. Gopal realized that the Master was an embodiment of truth and his speech and action were always congruous.

Every year during *makar-sankranti* (an auspicious day in the middle of January) monks and pilgrims from all over India go to Gangasagar, the confluence of the Ganges and the Bay of Bengal, for a holy bath. Many pilgrims go by boat from the Jagannath ghat of Calcutta. Gopal had a little money and wanted to acquire virtue by offering cloths to holy people on that auspicious day; so he bought twelve pieces of cloth and twelve rosaries of rudraksha beads to distribute among the monks. He dyed the cloths in the ochre colour himself. When the Master heard about it, he said to Gopal: "You will attain a thousand times more virtue if you present those ochre cloths and rosaries to my children rather than giving them to the monks of Jagannath ghat. Where else will you find such all-renouncing monks? Each of them is equal to a thousand monks."[15] This changed Gopal's mind.

On Tuesday, 12 January 1886 (makar-sankranti), Gopal gave the ochre cloths and rosaries to the Master, who touched them and sanctified them with a mantram. He himself then distributed them among his young disciples. They put on the ochre cloths and saluted the Master. Sri Ramakrishna was pleased to see them in monastic cloth and blessed them. The disciples who received the ochre cloths were: Narendra, Rakhal, Niranjan, Baburam, Shashi, Sharat, Kali, Jogin, Latu, Tarak, and Gopal. The twelfth cloth and rosary, according to the Master's instruction, were set aside for Girish Ghosh. Later Girish touched them to his head and felt the Master's special blessing. In this sense it may be said that the Ramakrishna Order was founded by Sri Ramakrishna himself, although it did not come into official existence until after his death.

On the evening of 6 May 1886, Narendra and Gopal were meditating in a room. Suddenly Narendra felt as if a lamp had begun to burn behind his head. The light grew more and more intense, until it seemed that the lamp itself burst. Narendra went into nirvikalpa samadhi. When after a while he became partly aware of his surroundings, he felt that he had somehow lost his body and was nothing but a head. "Where is my body?" he shouted. Surprised, Gopal came near him. "Where is my body?" Narendra repeated. Touching him, Gopal said: "It is here, Naren. Can't you feel it?" But Narendra continued to cry out for his body until Gopal, alarmed, ran to tell the Master what had happened. Ramakrishna did not seem at all surprised. "Let him stay like that for a while," he said calmly. "He's been bothering me long enough to put him into that state."[16]

Sri Ramakrishna passed away at 1:02 a.m. on 16 August 1886. At first the disciples could not ascertain whether the Master had died or gone into samadhi. Immediately Narendra sent Gopal and Latu to Dakshineswar to bring Ramlal, the Master's nephew, thinking that he could determine the Master's condition. When Ramlal arrived, he found that the crown of the Master's head was warm. Several doctors were informed, and at last Dr. Mahendralal Sarkar declared that Ramakrishna had passed away. After the cremation that afternoon, all the disciples left for home except Gopal, Latu, and Tarak, for they had no place to go. Within a few weeks the Baranagore Monastery was established with the help of Surendra Nath Mittra, a well-to-do devotee of the Master. Gopal joined the other disciples, took the final vows of sannyasa, and became Swami Advaitananda.

Austerity and Pilgrimage

Advaitananda lived for a while at the Baranagore Monastery. He helped his brother monks with household work, and played tabla when Vivekananda sang. Sometimes the young monks would tease him or make him the subject of practical jokes. Most of the disciples slept in one large room as they did not have many rooms. One night when Advaitananda went to the bathroom, Akhandananda replaced his pillow with a brick. When Advaitananda returned, he discovered his brick-pillow. He smiled and said to Akhandananda: "Ganga [the premonastic name of Akhandananda], I know you have done this mischief. Brother, I shall use your precious gift tonight as my pillow." Akhandananda was very touched. Immediately he threw away the brick and brought back the pillow. With an apology, Akhandananda said, "Brother, you are a real monk — free from anger and ego."[17]

While living at the Baranagore Monastery, Advaitananda visited many holy places in India. He left the monastery towards the end of 1887 and went to Varanasi, where he stayed in a cottage of Banshi Datta's garden house and lived on alms. He devoted most of his time to spiritual disciplines and made considerable progress. Sometime in the middle of 1888 he went to Kedarnath and Badrinath, two holy pilgrimage sites in the remote Himalayas. There he met Akhandananda, whom he had not seen in a long time, and burst into tears of joy. After that he stayed for some time in Vrindaban and practised austerities. On 25 March 1890 he went to Gaya with Holy Mother, who performed rites for the departed ancestors of her family. In the same year Advaitananda met Vivekananda and six other brother disciples in Meerut. The brother monks remained together a few weeks, then began to travel again in different directions. Advaitananda left to attend the Kumbha Festival at Hardwar with Akhandananda.

At last Advaitananda returned to the old cottage of Banshi Datta's garden house in Varanasi. He decided to spend the remaining part of his life in this abode of Lord Shiva. Swami Virajananda, a disciple of Vivekananda, left this account of Advaitananda:

In September 1895 I stopped at Varanasi on my way to Vrindaban and stayed with Gopal-da at Banshi Datta's house. His room was small, but neat and clean. He was very methodical and economical. Very early in the morning, even in the cold winter, he would bathe in the Ganges and return to his cottage chanting the Sanskrit hymns on gods and goddesses. He practised japam and meditation until 9:00 a.m., and then he would go to beg alms from door to door. He was extremely punctual about his spiritual disciplines, eating, sleeping, walking, and other activities. Though his belongings were very few, everything was kept in its proper place. This indicated his great taste and orderliness. In the afternoon during our walk, he would show me the important places of Varanasi. Gopal-da, Swami Satchidananda, and I circumambulated Panchakoshi [the holy city of Varanasi] in four days and covered forty-four miles. We walked until noon and then we cooked, ate, and took rest. At night we slept under a tree by the side of the road.[18]

Advaitananda passed five years in Varanasi practising austerities and forgetting the mundane world. He took care of whoever came to Varanasi and would show that person the temples of the City of Light. In spite of his old age he was healthy. However, once while walking through the street barefoot, a thorn pricked his foot, giving him a great deal of pain. On 13 August 1896 Swami Shivananda wrote to Pramadadas Mittra of Varanasi: "Our old swami [Advaitananda], who is now at Varanasi, has written that a thorn has pricked his foot and is causing a lot of pain. He has had surgery twice and is still bedridden. Please inquire about him immediately and help him in any way possible. He is now staying at the residence of Sagar Chandra Sur, which is behind the Cooch Bihar Kali Temple. Awaiting your early reply."[19] Advaitananda slowly recovered through the loving service of devotees.

Advaitananda travelled extensively all over India. In 1897 he visited Raipur, Central India, with Nabai Chaitanya of Konnagar. Then he went to Kanyakumari, Rameswaram, and other holy places of South India. In 1899 he visited Kamakhya and Darjeeling; and in 1900 he went to Dwaraka and other holy places of western India.

At Belur Math

In 1897 Vivekananda returned from the West and established the Ramakrishna Mission. He wanted to do some philanthropic work for the regeneration of India's poor. For that reason he recalled those brother disciples who were practising austerities in various parts of India. Advaitananda responded to Swamiji's call: He left Varanasi and went to Alambazar, where the monastery had been moved in 1892. In the early part of 1898, a plot of land was purchased at Belur on the bank of the Ganges for the permanent home of the Order, and Advaitananda was entrusted to make the land ready for construction. The site had previously been used as a dock for repairing boats and steamers, and the landscape was uneven. On 13 February the Ramakrishna Monastery was moved from Alambazar to Nilambar Babu's garden house, just south of the new property.

Although he was the oldest of the group, in carrying out responsibilities he was second to none. Early in the morning after breakfast he would go to the new plot and engage the Santal tribal labourers who had been hired to level the ground. He scolded them if he found any dereliction of duty. Sometimes Vivekananda would visit the grounds and talk to the poor labourers. He loved to hear the stories of their lives and hardships and sometimes would arrange a feast for them. Once their leader said to Swamiji: "O dear swami, don't come to us when we work — our work stops when we talk to you. Later the old father [Advaitananda] scolds us." Swamiji was touched by his words. Then he said: "No, no, he will not say anything. Tell me something about your part of the country."[20] Thus Swamiji came to know about their culture and way of life.

Pioneering work is always difficult. Advaitananda worked until noon; then he took his bath in the Ganges and sitting under a tree he ate his lunch, which had been sent from the monastery. Apart from levelling the ground and other construction work, Advaitananda started a vegetable garden and a dairy farm. Swami Adbhutananda recalled about the early days: "Without Gopal-da the monks of Belur Math would not have had vegetables along with their rice. He worked so hard to produce various kinds of vegetables in the monastery garden."[21]

In spite of all their hardships, there was fun and laughter among the brother disciples. Swami Vijnanananda related the following incident:

Gopal-da and Swami Nityananda were together at Belur Math along with several monks and brahmacharins. Nityananda asked the young monks, "Brothers, come with me and till this plot of land; I shall grow eggplant and potatoes." The young monks immediately started the project. Gopal-da noticed it. He went to them and said: "Oh, how hard you are working here! One should not load such a strenuous task on the young ones. You boys, come with me." Gopal-da took them to his plot and said to them with affection: "Now, brothers, dig this plot for a flower bed. The soil of the other plot is harder than this plot." Swamiji and other monks had a hearty laugh when they heard the story of Gopal-da's loving sympathy for the young monks.[22]

Once Advaitananda went to visit Holy Mother in Calcutta. Mother was happy to see the old swami, her devoted attendant. While eating prasad, Advaitananda inquired about Mother's rheumatic pain. She replied: "That rheumatic pain is my constant companion. It will not leave me in this life. However, how are you?" "I also suffer from rheumatic pain," answered Advaitananda. "But I work hard. I don't get much help from the boys. I am growing various kinds of vegetables — okra, eggplant, plantain, and so on — in the monastery garden. As a result, nowadays we seldom buy vegetables. Sometimes I send some vegetables to you." Holy Mother: "My son, you are an old-timer; your life is different from the modern boys who generally don't care for household matters. The monastery is like a family home, where you need food, clothing, and other necessities. Without these things how can you live there? So it is your duty to take care of the Master's children."[23]

The young novitiates, who came from modern schools and colleges, could hardly rise to Advaitananda's standard of perfection regarding work, and for that reason they had a very hard time with him. Many of them received mild scoldings from the old swami, but they took his criticisms more as a token of affection than as any indication of bitterness. One day he had a revelation, which he described later: "The Master has shown me that it is he who is manifested through all. Then who is there to blame or whom to criticize?"[24] After this experience Advaitananda ceased finding fault with anyone, however great might be the latter's errors. Turiyananda once said: "We are much indebted to Gopal-da, because we learned the secret of work from him. He was organized and concentrated in everything he did. And he was very methodical in his habits. Until his last day he regularly practised meditation."[25]

Although Vivekananda was thirty-five years younger than Advaitananda, Advaitananda had tremendous love and respect for Swamiji because the Master had made him the leader of the disciples. On the other hand, Swamiji also had affectionate regard for Advaitananda. Once Swamiji composed a comical verse to tease Advaitananda, but that really indicated in what great esteem the old swami was held by all. Swamiji had an idea that the monks of the Ramakrishna Order should know the Sanskrit scriptures, so he asked Advaitananda to study *Laghu Kaumudi* (Sanskrit Grammar). The swami took this request as a command and obeyed it with love.

Swamiji used to tease this old waggish monk, "You are like an old bull; breaking off your horns, you have joined the young calves."[26] One day Swamiji said: "Gopal-da, you are getting old day by day. Be careful. Now you must start taking milk and fruits, which will give you new life and then your bones will not be rusted. After all, you are the oldest among us, so tomorrow we shall wash you ceremoniously with milk." The next day Swamiji and other monks poured ten seers of milk on Advaitananda's head and then washed him with Ganges water. Afterwards a new cloth was offered to him and he was given various kinds of nutritious food. Swamiji joyfully said to him, "Brother, from today you are the abbot and the responsibility of the monastery is yours."[27] It was all done in fun. When one of Swamiji's pet ducks suffered for a week and then died from shortness of breath, Advaitananda said to him, "Sir, it is no use living in this *kaliyuga* [the dark age] when ducks catch cold from rain and damp and frogs sneeze!"[28]

In 1901 Swamiji made Advaitananda one of the trustees of the Ramakrishna Math and Mission; later he became the vice-president. When Vivekananda died on 4 July 1902, Advaitananda first checked his pulse and then said to Swami Nirbhayananda: "Alas! What are you looking at? Hurry to Dr. Mahendranath Mazumdar [of Baranagore] and bring him here as soon as you can."

After Vivekananda's passing away, the banner of Sri Ramakrishna was carried by his other disciples. They shaped their lives according to the spiritual ideals of the Master; they also helped others to put these ideals into practice for their physical, mental, and spiritual advancement. There is a saying, "An organization succeeds not because it is big or because it is long established, but because there are people in it who live it, sleep it, dream it, and build a future for it."

Advaitananda made strenuous efforts to mould his life according to the example of the Master and would sometimes express disappointment that he fell so short of his ideal. But this feeling of inadequacy indicated his real spiritual height. He had keen powers of observation like Sri Ramakrishna. He forbade the monks to bang doors or tear a new cloth with a shrill noise, as the Master could not bear it. He kept himself busy in the service of Sri Ramakrishna and couldn't bear lazy people. Because of his age and temperament he did not engage in public activities such as relief work and preaching; his monastic life was therefore uneventful. In spite of that, he definitely set an example for all and he was a source of inspiration to many.

Even in his old age he would get up early and sit for meditation and japam. He suffered from rheumatic pain, so according to the doctor's instructions, he would do regular exercises in his room. Then he would go to the shrine to bow down to the Master. He prayed: "Master, I am doing exercise for this body. I have done enough, now release me."[29] Afterwards, he would supervise the activities of the monastery. Swami Premananda would do the ritualistic worship in the shrine. When he went to Calcutta for other work, Advaitananda would perform the ritual.

In the afternoon he would go for a walk and advise the caretakers of the garden and dairy if they had any problems. At that time the young monks had to do everything in the monastery; Advaitananda helped them by sharing his experience with them.

Advaitananda loved to do his own work. If anyone offered any personal service, he would decline. His attitude was that a monk should be self-reliant, depending only on God and no one else. He was fond of music and would play tabla when the brothers sang devotional songs. Sometimes when he had a little leisure, he would copy the scriptures in his beautiful handwriting. He used to chant the Gita every day. For his daily chanting he copied five different Gitas. Perhaps he had no money to buy a book.

Humour breaks the barrier of age and eradicates monotony, sadness, and gloom from life. For example, a sad countenance was an offense against the rules of the Franciscan Order: The brothers were expected to turn a smiling face to God and to humanity. They were to make the Lord glad by their gaiety and not weary Him with whining and lamentation. The monks of Sri Ramakrishna also did not care for religion that was obsessed with fear or brought gloom to life. They learned from the Master that humour has its place in religion, and the bliss that they experienced was expressed in their lives. Advaitananda had a wonderful sense of humour and loved to tease the brothers. For example, he disliked tea while Swami Subodhananda loved it; so one day he said to Subodhananda, "Look, don't drink tea; you will get blood dysentery." But Subodhananda asserted emphatically, "Gopal-da, each drop of tea produces a drop of blood." "All right, brother, drink more," Advaitananda said jokingly. All laughed.[30]

Towards the End

In late 1909, Advaitananda, an all-renouncing sannyasin of the Master, made himself ready to depart from this world. He had suffered from stomach trouble off and on, and towards the end he had a fever. Dr. Matilal Mukhopadhyay of Ghusuri, Howrah, was his physician and all the monks served their old brother with loving care. One day the swami stood in front of Sri Ramakrishna's picture and prayed, "Master, please release me from this pain." The Master soon answered the prayer of his old disciple. Swami Premananda later said: "Before his death Gopal-da saw the Master carrying a mace on his shoulder. He then asked, 'Master, why are you carrying the mace on your shoulder?' The Master replied: 'I am Gadadhar [literally, "Upholder of the Mace," an epithet of Lord Vishnu. Gadadhar was also Sri Ramakrishna's childhood name]. In this age I shall rebuild after destroying everything.'"[31] Truly, Sri Ramakrishna was born in this modern time to destroy doubt and delusion from the minds of the people.

Advaitananda passed away at 4:15 p.m. on Tuesday, 28 December 1909. Until the end he was fully conscious, chanting the name of Sri Ramakrishna. As soon as Premananda put a little *charanamrita* (sanctified water) in his mouth, he breathed his last. Premananda wrote a vivid account of his death in a letter: "Gopal-da has gone to the abode of the Master. He had a little fever and nobody realized that he would leave the body so soon. During his last moments his face looked so beautiful! It is a wonderful play of the Master's devotee! At that time Dr. Matilal Mukhopadhyay was present. Gopal-da drank a little lemon juice and milk. He greeted Mati Babu [Dr. Mukhopadhyay]. Smiling, he left the body."[32] He was then eighty-one. His body was cremated at Belur Math on the bank of the Ganges.

Swami Advaitananda started his spiritual journey late, but his sincerity and steadfast devotion to the Master brought fulfillment at the end of his life. Sri Ramakrishna made him a role model for elderly seekers of God. He will be remembered by the Ramakrishna Order for his cheerful manner and methodical ways, his self-reliance, his untiring zeal in every work he undertook, and his implicit devotion to the Master and his cause.

SWAMI SUBODHANANDA

14

ॐ

SWAMI SUBODHANANDA

rue religion is always simple; it is realized only by those who are simple themselves. Cunning, calculating people may be successful on the worldly plane, but not on the spiritual one. To know spiritual truth, one should approach childlike mystics, not theologians or philosophers. The latter interpret the truth according to their own understanding and make simple things complicated. Intellectual gymnasts enjoy skim milk, but the childlike mystics enjoy cream. Christ said in the Bible, "Except ye be converted, and become as little children, ye shall not enter into the kingdom of heaven."[1] Subodh (later, Swami Subodhananda) was one such guileless divine child. Sri Ramakrishna used to call him *Khoka*, "little boy"; he behaved like a boy all through his life and became a great mystic.

Subodh Chandra Ghosh was born on 8 November 1867 at 23 Shankar Ghosh Lane, Calcutta. His father, Krishnadas Ghosh, and mother, Nayantara, were devout Hindus, and his family owned the Siddheswari Kali Temple of Thanthania. (When Sri Ramakrishna first came to Calcutta in 1852, he often visited this temple as he stayed nearby.) Although Krishnadas was a traditional Hindu, he was closely associated with the Brahmo Samaj, a socioreligious organization. He would take his children to the Brahmo Samaj services and buy religious books for them. In the evening Subodh's loving mother would tell him stories from the Bhagavata, the Ramayana, and the Mahabharata; these stories created a religious inclination in him from his very childhood. "When I was young, I used to read

34

the biographies of holy people and would observe how their lives were transformed,"[2] Subodh said later.

When Subodh was a young boy, he was afraid of riding in a boat because he did not know how to swim. He was also afraid of the dark, so he would sleep in his grandmother's room. However, he had a premonition that he would not live at home and would travel alone like an itinerant monk. He therefore tried his utmost to conquer this fear of darkness. One dark evening Subodh and other children of the family were playing noisily in their bedroom. To stop the noise, Subodh's mother covered herself with a blanket and came into the room to frighten them. When they all cried out, she removed the blanket. When Subodh saw that it was his mother, he resolved that he would never again be afraid of the dark.

From childhood Subodh was calm, simple, and sweet. At the same time, he was quite outspoken. He was sent to Albert Collegiate School where he was recognized as a brilliant student; he was gifted in mathematics and scored high marks in the class. After being promoted to the seventh grade, he joined the Hare School. When he was in the eighth grade, his father suggested that he marry. Subodh's family was rich, and at that time it was quite common for boys and girls to get married in their teens. However, Subodh said to his father, "Please don't insist that I get married." "Why?" his father asked. "Study well and get good results on your examination. Then we shall arrange your marriage with a girl from an aristocratic family." Subodh protested: "If you force me to marry, I shall obey you. But I will leave home; family life is not for me. Please don't entangle me." His father replied, "All right, let us not talk about it now."[3] Subodh realized that if he received good marks on the examination, his father would arrange his marriage. Accordingly, Subodh did not try very hard, and fervently prayed to God that the examination results would be bad. And he actually did get poor marks. The teachers suggested that he stay in the eighth grade another year, but Subodh moved to Vidyasagar's School where M., the recorder of *The Gospel of Sri Ramakrishna*, was the headmaster.

His failure in the examination had the desired result: His father lost interest in Subodh's marriage. Sometime in 1885 Krishnadas told his son about Sri Ramakrishna and his meeting with Keshab Chandra Sen. Subodh had read about the Master in the Brahmo journals. One day Krishnadas presented a book to him, *Sri Sri Ramakrishna Paramahamser Ukti* (The Sayings of Sri Ramakrishna) compiled by Suresh Chandra Datta in December 1884. Subodh was so deeply impressed with the book that a great desire arose in his mind to meet Sri Ramakrishna. When he told his father of this desire, he was promised a trip to Dakshineswar on a holiday with the rest of his family.

In the Company of Sri Ramakrishna

When a person knows the location of a hidden treasure, it is impossible for him to be patient. Similarly, Subodh became restless to see the Master. He could not wait for a holiday. So one morning in August of 1885 he started for Dakshineswar with his friend Kshirod Chandra Mittra. However, they did not know where Dakshineswar was, except that it was situated on the bank of the Ganges and north of Calcutta. They walked quite a distance and lost their way. Subodh was worried because he had not gotten permission from his family, but Kshirod asked him to be patient. They arrived at Ariadaha and asked a man the way to the Dakshineswar temple garden. The man pointed out a short-cut over the ridges of a paddy field, and soon Subodh and Kshirod reached Dakshineswar.

Subodh thought that a paramahamsa was some sort of magician. He had never before spoken to a sadhu or monk, so he said to Kshirod: "You must go first and talk to the holy man. I don't know the proper etiquette." Kshirod agreed. They entered the room and saluted Sri Ramakrishna with folded hands. Kshirod went to the Master, who was seated on his bed. Subodh remained at the threshold. "Where do you come from?" asked Sri Ramakrishna. "From Calcutta," Kshirod replied. Pointing to Subodh the Master said: "Why is that gentleman standing so far away? Come nearer." This encouraged Subodh to move closer. "Do you not belong to the family of Shankar Ghosh?" asked the Master. Subodh was surprised and said, "Yes, sir, but how did you know it?" "When I was staying at Jhamapukur," said the Master, "I often visited your home as well as your Kali Temple at Thanthania. That was before you were born. I knew you would come. Well, the Divine Mother sends here those who will attain spirituality. You belong to this place." "Sir, if I belong to this place, why did you not call me earlier?" asked Subodh. The Master replied, "Look, everything happens at the right time."[4]

Sri Ramakrishna held Subodh's hand and closed his eyes for a few minutes. At last he said: "You will attain the goal. Mother says so." He asked Subodh to sit on his bed. "No, sir," said Subodh, "I can't sit on your bed. This is my school clothing; it is not fresh. Moreover, I have touched people on the way and my feet are dusty." The Master forced him to sit on his bed, saying: "You are my very own. What does it matter whether your cloth is clean or not?" After a while Subodh sat on the floor. Immediately the Master asked his nephew Ramlal to spread a carpet for the boys and then inquired, "How have you come to Dakshineswar?" Since the Master's loving care and affection had removed Subodh's shyness and uneasiness, he promptly replied, "We have come on foot." "My goodness! You have covered such a distance on foot?" the Master asked, surprised. "How did you find out about me?" Subodh replied: "I am impressed by reading your teachings. They are really remarkable. You are such a great man and so famous! Therefore, we have come to see you."

These words brought on a sudden change in Ramakrishna's mood. With a humility that amazed the boys, he said, "Ah, I am lower than a worm. Name and fame! Ridiculous! Really, I am more insignificant than a worm." After a while the Master said to Subodh: "Mother sends here those who will receive Her grace. Come here on Tuesdays or Saturdays. Many people from your part of town come here on those days. Come with them." Subodh said: "No, sir, that will not do: My relatives will find out that I am coming here. Please tell me what you want to say now." "I cannot take back my words, my child," said the Master. "If I say I shall go to a certain place on such and such a day, I must do so in spite of rain or thunderstorm. Even if I don't like it, Mother drags me there. I have said those words, so do come on Tuesdays or Saturdays."

Subodh agreed, and finding it was getting late, asked leave to go home. "Have some refreshments," the Master said. "It is not necessary, sir. We shall eat at home," Subodh replied. "No, have some sweets and water, and then go," said the Master, and he asked Latu to serve them. When they finished their refreshments, the Master again said: "Your home is quite a distance from here; moreover, you are too young to walk. Why don't you go by boat or share carriage? I shall give you the fare."

Subodh: "I don't know how to swim. We can't go by boat."

Ramakrishna: "Then go by carriage."

Subodh: "No, sir, we shall walk."

Ramakrishna: "Look, my child, your feet will be tired from covering such a distance."

Subodh: "Sir, we are young [he was then seventeen]; if we do not walk now, then when shall we walk? Moreover, you are a holy man; where will you get money?"

Ramakrishna (*with a smile*): "Some people donate money for this place. You will not have to worry about that. Please take some money and go by carriage."

Since Subodh was inexorable, the Master said to Kshirod, "You take the money and go by carriage." But Subodh interrupted and told his friend: "Don't accept the money. We shall go on foot." Without insisting further the Master said, "Come again either on Tuesday or Saturday." Both took the dust of the Master's feet and left for home.[5]

Subodh's parents had not seen him since that morning and they were extremely anxious. They told their friends and relatives that Subodh was missing and they all began to search for him. When Subodh returned home in the afternoon, he learned of the commotion he had caused. His grandmother brought sweets for him and the women of the family bombarded him with questions. He told his weeping mother that he had been to Dakshineswar to meet Sri Ramakrishna.

On the following Saturday Subodh and Kshirod fled from school and hurried to Dakshineswar. The Master's room was crowded with visitors. Peeping through the door, the boys saluted Sri Ramakrishna with folded hands. When he caught sight of them he raised his hand as a signal for them to stay outside. The Master asked the audience to wait and then went out to greet them.

It was about 3:00 p.m. Sri Ramakrishna asked Rakhal to bring some Ganges water, with which he washed his hands. He then took the boys to the stairs leading to the Shiva temples at the south of his room. He sat cross-legged on the floor, and asked the boys to sit down also. He then bade them unbutton their shirts and stick out their tongues. The Master first wrote something with his finger on Kshirod's tongue and stroked his body from the navel to the throat. He did the same to Subodh, saying, "Awake, Mother, awake!" Then he told them to meditate.

The Master's magic touch awakened Subodh's latent spirituality. No sooner had he begun to meditate than his whole body trembled, and he felt a current rushing along his spinal column to his brain. An ineffable joy overwhelmed him, and he saw a strange light within him in which the forms of numerous gods and goddesses flashed. His meditation deepened, and the boy lost all sense of personal identity. When he regained consciousness he found the Master stroking his body in the reverse direction, from the head downwards. "Well," he said, "have you practised meditation at home?" "Very little, sir," replied the boy. "I used to think a little of gods and goddesses since I heard of them from my mother." "Ah," said the Master, "that's why you could concentrate so easily." Then he asked Kshirod if he had seen or felt anything. When the boy replied in the negative, the Master said, "All right, you will do so later on."

Sri Ramakrishna then told them to go to the Panchavati and meditate while he returned to his room. They did not know where the Panchavati was, so they went to the Kali Temple for meditation. Afterwards, they went to the Master's room. When they took leave of him they were given some refreshments; he again asked them to take carriage fare, but they declined. The Master said to Subodh: "There is a teacher who lives near you named Mahendra [M.]. He often comes here and is a good man. Go to see him now and then, and also come here."[6] Subodh made no reply because he was not certain that he would be able to see M.

Like a child, Subodh would freely discuss his personal problems with the Master. One day, when Subodh informed the Master about his fear of ghosts, Sri Ramakrishna pressed his thumbnail between Subodh's eyebrows. From then on he would see a soft light over his forehead and that permanently destroyed his fear of ghosts. As he was close to his mother, he told her about his vision of light. She said: "My son, you are fortunate, but don't divulge it to others. You will lose it if you do so."[7] (Tradition says that one should not divulge one's spiritual experiences to anyone except the guru, otherwise one may not have the experience again.) But Subodh answered: "What harm could it do me, mother? It's not the light I want, but That which it comes from."

Subodh lost interest in his studies. He preferred to be with Sri Ramakrishna and to spend time in meditation, prayer, and repeating the name of God. Some days he was late in returning from Dakshineswar, and his private tutor had to wait for him. One day the tutor indignantly said to Subodh: "You are neglecting your studies. If you are not punctual, the next time I shall report it to your father." Subodh replied: "What will my father do? He does not read; it is I who am supposed to read. If I don't have the desire, none can force me to read. But please come as usual. I shall study whenever I have time and the inclination." The tutor was surprised, and out of duty, reported the incident to Krishnadas. The anxious father remarked: "It is a matter of concern; but it is better not to put too much pressure on him. I have noticed that whatever he reads, he reads attentively."[8]

M. visited the Master at Dakshineswar on 31 August 1885, and Sri Ramakrishna said to him: "Two boys came here the other day. One of them was Subodh. He is Shankar Ghosh's great-grandson. The other, Kshirod, is his neighbour. They are nice boys. I told them I was ill and asked them to go to you for instruction. Please look after them a little." M. replied: "Yes, sir. They are our neighbours."[9] After returning home, M. sent a letter of invitation to Subodh; the boy, however, did not go, thinking it meaningless to receive spiritual instruction from a householder.

After a few days, Subodh again went to Dakshineswar and the Master introduced him to Shashi and Sharat. He also asked them to visit each other so that his young disciples would know each other well. Subodh said to them: "I shall visit your homes, but you should not come to our house. That may make my father mad at me."[10] The Master was extremely careful not to upset his boys' parents, because that might disrupt their mental peace. However, he was impressed with Subodh's frankness and common sense. Ramakrishna had been diagnosed as having throat cancer. As it developed he could not speak much, so he asked Shashi and Sharat to introduce Subodh to Narendra whom he had made the leader of the young group.

After some time the Master asked Subodh, "Mahendra's house is very close to yours, then why did you not call on him?" Subodh replied: "He hasn't been able to renounce his family. What could I learn about God from him?"[11] Immediately the Master said with a laugh, "O Rakhal, did you hear what this rascal Khoka said?" He was pleased to see Subodh so stern in his renunciation; but he said: "He won't talk about himself; he will only tell you what he has learned from me. Don't hesitate to go to him." After a couple of days when Subodh finally went to see M., he relayed this conversation in his blunt way. M. said humbly: "It is quite true. I am nobody, but I live beside the ocean of knowledge and bliss, and I keep a few pitchers of that water with me. When a guest comes, I offer that to him. What else am I to talk about?"[12]

M. continued talking and shared his experiences with his young student: "You see, after I met the Master, all my university education became insignificant. When I got my degrees, I felt I had learned everything in this world. But after I talked to the Master, I realized that all my academic knowledge was nothing but ignorance. 'That knowledge is true knowledge which removes ignorance and helps one to attain Brahman': This one sentence of the Master's removed my pride of learning. I wondered how people could become proud of these trivial university degrees!"[13] After some pleasant hours Subodh took his leave. Thus did Sri Ramakrishna seal the bond of friendship and love among his disciples.

Sri Ramakrishna was finishing his divine play at the temple garden of Dakshineswar. He put all his energy into training the young boys. Sometimes Subodh would arrive at Dakshineswar at noon, having walked all the way from school in the hot sun. He had a strong desire to serve his guru. While fanning the Master, he would feel that all his fatigue had gone. The Master could not bear for Subodh to fan him while standing, so he asked him to sit on his bed and fan him. Like a loving father, at times the Master took the palm leaf fan himself and fanned Subodh. Sometimes he would talk to Subodh about japam, meditation, and *brahmacharya* (celibacy), and would also test his faith and devotion. On one occasion, the Master touched Subodh's body and blessed him: "Today I have taken away the lust from your mind."[14]

In the beginning Subodh did not accept the Master as an avatar, or divine incarnation. One day the Master asked him, "What do you think of me?" Subodh replied: "People say many different things about you. I won't believe any of them until I find clear proof."[15] At this the Master, who was egoless, said: "Very well. As a money changer checks a coin, likewise accept me after testing."[16] In a letter written many years later, Swami Subodhananda said of Sri Ramakrishna and Holy Mother: "If they don't want to reveal themselves, who can recognize them?"[17] As he grew closer and closer to the Master, his conviction in Sri Ramakrishna's divinity gradually gained strength. One day when the Master advised Subodh to practise meditation, he replied: "Sir, I won't be able to do that. If I have to practise meditation, why should I come to you? I may as well go to some other guru."[18] Understanding his inner feeling, the Master said: "All right, you will not have to practise meditation. But think of me in the morning and evening."[19]

It was not easy to live with Sri Ramakrishna: He could see the inside and outside of his disciples like a person sees books inside a glass bookcase; none could hide anything from him. The Master would correct their shortcomings and guide them along the right path. He taught them how to do household duties as well as how to see God everywhere. His room was always neat and clean. Though his belongings were very few, they were nicely arranged in their respective places. The garden paths outside his room were also swept regularly. If any of his disciples inadvertently spat on the path, he cautioned him: "Hello! What have you done? The Divine Mother walks here. Don't desecrate the garden path. Please bring some Ganges water and wash that spot."[20]

One evening Subodh observed the devotees dancing and singing *kirtan* in the Master's room at Dakshineswar. They were overwhelmed with devotion. Sri Ramakrishna himself joined them and his ecstasy surcharged the whole place with heavenly bliss. The devotees were beside themselves with joy: Some were crying, some laughing, some dancing. Others were transfixed like motionless statues, and some began to roll on the floor. Subodh was very sceptical about this kind of emotional display. Still, he waited there to know the truth from the Master. When all the devotees had left, the Master came to Subodh and asked: "Hello! It is late and you are still here?" "Sir, I have a question," said Subodh. "Who had real ecstasy in the kirtan today?" The Master thought a while and then said, "Today Latu alone had the fullest measure of it; others had sprinklings."[21]

Subodh learned from Ramakrishna various aspects of spiritual life, which he later related to the devotees: "One day I asked the Master: 'I have read about gods and goddesses in books and heard about them from various people. Can one really see them?' Sri Ramakrishna replied: 'One can see God as one sees two persons talking together or walking. But one should call on God from the bottom of one's heart. Pray and cry for Him. Demand His vision from Him as children demand toys from their parents with loud cries. Remove all worldly desires from the mind. Always remember: I have a Mother and I am Her son.'"[22] On another occasion the Master said: "Those who shall attain spiritual experience will feel comfortable with my ideas and teachings. . . . He who has faith in me, has faith in God; and, again, he who does not have faith in me, does not have faith in God either."[23]

Although Subodh did not live with Sri Ramakrishna all the time like some of the other disciples, he observed the Master's life minutely and served him whenever he got the opportunity. He later narrated the following:

The Master had special devotion for Mother Ganges. He used to say, "*Ganga-vari Brahma-vari*" (The water of the Ganges is as pure as Brahman). If anybody was overwhelmed with grief or affliction or delusion, he would tell him, "Go and drink a little Ganges water, you will be all right." It was amazing to find that the person would get the desired result.[24]

The Master's feet were extremely tender and delicate. He could not wear regular shoes. We had to place cotton padding inside the shoes so he could use them. . . .[25] In the earlier part of his life the Master used his golden amulet, but later he could not touch anything metallic. Someone had to carry the water pot for his washing.

I have seen something wonderful in the Master. His room would be packed with people, and they would have many questions in their minds. Yet in a single talk he would answer all of their unspoken questions.

Once Keshab Chandra Sen invited the Master to his house, and secretly offered flowers with sandalpaste at his feet. Then he said, "Sir, please don't tell this to anybody, otherwise people will say that I have worshipped a human being." The Master's nature was like that of a child. He told Vijaykrishna Goswami and an official of the temple: "Look, Keshab has offered flowers at my feet and requested me not to tell anyone. Please don't tell it to others."[26]

Sometimes the Master would say, "The Divine Mother Herself has come to visit the world in human form [*meaning himself*]; when people of all sects assemble here, this body will not last."[27]

One day while walking in the Panchavati at Dakshineswar, the Master went into ecstasy. Then, facing the northwest, he pointed to himself and said, "Look, the Mother is saying that the more a person thinks of me, the more quickly he will understand the highest truths of religion." Again, pointing to the northwest, he said, "I shall be born again in that direction, then many people will attain knowledge."[28]

On another occasion the Master told me about himself: "This body is a cage of flesh and bone, but the Mother is playing inside it. . . . He who was Rama and Krishna is living in this body."[29]

Ramakrishna would freely talk to the disciples about the struggles and experiences of his spiritual journey. He saw the Divine Mother in all women; as a result no woman could tempt him. Once the Master said to Subodh: "During my sadhana I was in a God-intoxicated state. One day, while I was picking grass sitting under the Panchavati in Dakshineswar, a beautiful young woman came and stood behind me, trying to draw my attention. I was unaware of her presence. After waiting for a long time, she felt neglected and said to me: 'Hello, sadhu, I have been standing behind you for a long time — neither did you look at me nor talk to me. I have visited many ashramas. Wherever I went, everyone eagerly talked to me or asked me to stay in the ashrama. You are a wonderful detached monk. You didn't look at me even once!'"[30] Subodh learned a lesson; and he later told this incident to M.

Subodh's contact with the Master has not been extensively recorded in *The Gospel of Sri Ramakrishna* or *Sri Ramakrishna, the Great Master*, because he visited the Master secretly on weekdays so his parents would not know about it. Sometimes he would run away from school and return home before evening after visiting the Master in Dakshineswar.

In September 1885 Sri Ramakrishna moved to Shyampukur in North Calcutta for cancer treatment. Whenever he found any opportunity, Subodh would visit the Master. On Kali Puja day in 1885, Subodh met M. at 9:00 a.m. in their family temple where the latter had come to offer worship at the Master's behest. Subodh was sad because he could not go with M. to visit the Master on that auspicious day. M. consoled him: "Don't feel bad. Today is Kali Puja — an auspicious day. Please make yourself cheerful." Subodh then told M. his plan: "Tonight, when everyone will be busy in their temple's worship service, I shall secretly visit the Master."

On that particular night there was a special worship at the Shyampukur house, and the devotees worshipped the Master as the Divine Mother. In the darkness of the early morning hours, Subodh speedily reached the Master and surprised him. "My goodness! Where did you come from?" asked Sri Ramakrishna. Subodh humbly replied: "Yesterday I couldn't come with M. to see you; since then my heart has been restless to see you. I didn't sleep at all last night. Now after seeing you I feel peaceful." The Master joyfully told his attendants: "Listen to what this boy says! He was longing to see me and so spent a sleepless night! Please give him some prasad." When Subodh returned home, his mother asked: "Where have you been? I thought you were sleeping somewhere in the house." Subodh replied: "I went to see the Master at Shyampukur. Please don't tell the others."[31]

During one visit, knowing about the recent aggravation of the Master's throat pain, Subodh simply said: "Sir, you used to live in a damp room in Dakshineswar. As a result, it seems you have a sore throat because of the cold. Please take tea. Whenever we have sore throats, we drink tea and the soreness goes away. If you want, I can bring some good tea from my home." Immediately the childlike Master called Rakhal and said: "Look, I want to drink tea. This boy says that I will be cured if I drink tea." Rakhal said: "Sir, tea is very hot; it may aggravate your throat. You may not be able to bear it." "No, then it is not necessary," said the Master. He consoled Subodh, "Hot tea will not suit me."[32] Subodh was moved by the Master's childlike nature.

On 11 December 1885 Sri Ramakrishna was moved from Shyampukur to Cossipore. One day the Master asked Subodh to copy a devotional song, *Sitapati Ramachandra Raghupati Raghurai*, etc., composed by Saint Tulasidas, but he declined by saying that his handwriting was not good enough. The Master insisted: "Please copy that song. It does not matter whether your writing is good or bad." When the boy still would not agree, the Master said: "You are really a dumbbell. Neglecting your studies, you only played with your friends." Being thus reprimanded, Subodh smiled. The Master also laughed and then said, "My boy, aren't you upset that I scolded you?" Subodh replied, "Sir, even your scoldings are sweet."[33] The Master then joyfully called his other disciples and said: "Boys, listen to what this boy says. He says that even my scoldings are sweet." Before he left, the Master blessed Subodh by touching his head.

Subodh narrated the following incident about Sri Ramakrishna's last illness: "It was extremely difficult for the Master to talk. One day I said to him: 'Sir, if you wish you can get well. Please cure yourself.' The Master then asked me, 'Do you really believe that?' 'Yes, I do believe that,' I replied. 'What you have said is true,' the Master said. 'But I shall not try to save this body, which is made out of flesh and bone, blood and marrow. Whatever is created is subject to destruction.' Then he said to me, 'Promise that you will never ask me this again.' Thus the Master made me promise."[34]

One day at Cossipore Subodh privately asked the Master to bless him so that he could realize God. Ramakrishna affectionately patted his back thrice and said: "Yes, yes, you will realize God; and in the future many people will learn from you."[35]

Sri Ramakrishna passed away on 16 August 1886. When Subodh heard of the Master's death, he cried out while holding his mother, and then fell unconscious. His father ordered that water be splashed over his head and face to return him to consciousness. Subodh did not go to Cossipore either because of his family's resistance, or because he thought that the grief and pain would be too much for him to bear. He was then nineteen years old.

Days of Austerity and Travelling

From his very birth Subodh was endowed with passion for God and dispassion for the world. After his guru's passing away, the fire of renunciation was enkindled in his heart. Without the Master he felt empty, and his home became a prison to him. It is said that when Holy Mother moved from Cossipore to Balaram's house in Calcutta, Subodh visited her every day. Subodh tried to finish his education, but as soon as he would open a book, he would see the Master standing in front of him. He slept very little and felt no inclination to eat. He would spend a long time in meditation in the temple that belonged to his family.

When Holy Mother was staying at Kamarpukur after a pilgrimage, Subodh went to visit her. He was happy to see the birthplaces of Ramakrishna and Holy Mother. After receiving Holy Mother's blessings, Subodh returned to Calcutta. It soon became unbearable for him to stay at home, so one day he simply walked away. He first went to the family temple and prostrated before the Divine Mother to ask Her blessings. He felt that the Mother smiled and told him: "Don't be afraid. I am always with you."[36]

Subodh crossed the Ganges and started walking on the Grand Trunk Road, which led to Varanasi some 500 miles away. His longing was so intense that he felt his life was useless without God-realization. If anyone asked about his home or family, he would say that he had none in this world. Later he narrated the story of this journey in a letter: "For the sake of my mental peace I left home. I began my journey heading towards the western part of India on foot without carrying any money with me. If anybody wanted to talk to me on the way, I would talk only of God. As a result, no worldly thought would enter my mind. Sometimes I stayed at night under a tree or in a meadow or on the bank of a river. At noon I ate whatever I got by begging from door to door like the mendicants. I had no extra clothing or shoes or umbrella. In the rain my clothes would get wet and they would eventually dry from my body heat."[37] Thus he reached Varanasi. After visiting Lord Vishwanath and Mother Annapurna in their respective temples he felt some degree of peace. Meanwhile, his relatives found out where he was and brought him back to Calcutta.

It is difficult for a free bird to live in a cage. Ramakrishna had given Subodh a taste of renunciation and divine bliss: He could no longer live at home. He joined the Ramakrishna Monastery at Baranagore. Performing the traditional *viraja homa*, Subodh took final monastic vows and became known as Swami Subodhananda. As he was one of the youngest among the disciples, he was known as "Khoka Maharaj" in the Ramakrishna Order. Swami Vivekananda and others lovingly called him "Khoka," which means "little boy." About his days in Baranagore, Subodhananda said: "Swamiji and others were engaged in deep meditation and japam. I used to wash the dishes, sweep the floor, and do all sorts of household work." He was reluctant to say anything about his personal experiences. Once when someone asked whether his kundalini had awakened, he replied, "Yes, sometimes I feel a tickling sensation rising from the bottom of the backbone towards the head."[38]

In spite of hardship and poverty in the Baranagore Monastery, the disciples of Ramakrishna lived in a joyful mood. Ramakrishna had joined them together like a pearl necklace and had united them in their one goal — God-realization. They dived deep in the realm of spirituality and at the same time made their lives joyful with fun and jokes.

At night when all were asleep, Latu would practise meditation under his mosquito curtain. Subodhananda knew this. Mischievously, he put a wet cloth on the top of Latu's curtain. As the water began to drip, Latu became frightened — the Baranagore Monastery was haunted. After discovering the mischief-maker, Latu exclaimed: "Sharat! Look, this rascal Khoka is frightening me!"[39]

In December 1889 Subodhananda and Brahmananda went to Varanasi to practise austerities. They stayed at Pramadadas Mittra's garden house and lived on alms like other itinerant monks. In the early part of 1890 they went on a pilgrimage to Omkarnath and Panchavati in Central India; Bombay, Dwaraka, Girnar, Pushkar in West India; and later to Vrindaban, the playground of Krishna. Subodhananda and Brahmananda stayed in Vrindaban from the first week of February to the middle of April 1890, practising various spiritual disciplines. As Subodhananda was very fond of tea, he would go for tea every day to the cottage of Vijaykrishna Goswami, a saintly devotee of Ramakrishna. While they had tea, they would often speak of the Master. One day Vijaykrishna said, "I have never seen another person like him [Sri Ramakrishna]." On another occasion he said: "I have come across some illumined souls who have attained perfection in their respective moods and faiths, but I have never seen anyone; except Sri Ramakrishna Paramahamsa, who attained perfection in all moods and in all faiths. This is something new in the history of the world."[40]

During his stay in Vrindaban, Subodhananda circumambulated the playground of Krishna — a distance of 168 miles. He covered this long journey alone without any belongings. One day a woman saw him, and inflamed by lust, attacked him from behind. Frightened, he prayed to the Master aloud for protection. Immediately, the woman fell on the ground, unconscious.[41]

From Vrindaban, Subodhananda left for a pilgrimage in the Himalayas. He visited the holy shrines of Kedarnath and Badrinath. While he was practising austerities in Hardwar, the following incident occurred:

> I had been suffering from fever for two months. I was so weak that I could not lift my water pot to pour water into my mouth. One night when I went near the water pot to quench my thirst, I fell down on the floor unconscious. When I regained consciousness, my feelings were hurt and I cried: "Master, I am suffering terribly. There is none to look after me. You didn't give me sufficient strength even to drink a glass of water by myself." Thinking thus I fell asleep. Then I saw [in a dream or vision] the Master stroking my body with his hand, and he said: "Why are you anxious? Don't you see I am always near you? What do you want — attendants or money?" I replied: "I don't want either of those things. I can't avoid disease as long as I have a body. May I never forget you: that is all I want. Be with me wherever I go."
>
> Early in the morning I heard a voice from outside, "Swami, please open the door." I got up and opened the door. A young monk told me: "Please tell me what you need. I shall beg food for you." I said to him, "I don't want anything." When I asked how he knew about me, he said that he had arrived there a couple of days earlier to perform a religious rite at the Brahmakunda. The previous night Mother Durga had appeared to him in a vision and said, "You will get more virtue

by serving that sick monk in the cottage than by performing this religious rite." So early in the morning he came to my cottage and realized that his vision was true. Tears trickled from my eyes. I controlled myself and asked the young monk to let me live alone.

On the same day another monk received fifty rupees by money order. He came to me and said: "You are suffering from fever. You need food and medicine. Please use this money." I declined his offer. Early the next morning the young monk came again and told me that at night Mother Durga had exhorted him to serve me as before. Then I told him politely that I really didn't need any service and that perhaps Mother Durga had asked him to serve someone else. The young monk left. Then I prayed to the Master: "Please don't tempt me anymore. I am glad that you have crushed my pique." The young monk also came on the third day, but never again.[42]

When Subodhananda was practising austerities in Gaya he had a life-threatening experience which he later described: "It was the month of August. I saw a person wade through the Phalgu River and reach the other side. It was waist-deep, so I decided to cross. My companion knew how to swim, but I didn't. Suddenly the river swelled with a strong current because of heavy rain. When I had crossed a certain distance, I suddenly found myself in throat-deep water. I realized that there was very little chance of saving my life so I said to my companion: 'I don't know where this current will take me. There is little chance for my life. Please convey my salutations to my brother disciples.' Then I prayed to the Master, 'Please accept my last *pranam* [salutation].' As soon as I said that, I was completely submerged. I felt that someone held my hand and pulled me through that gushing stream to the other side of the river."[43]

During his itinerant days, Subodhananda would sometimes sleep under a tree by the side of a road. The ground was his bed, and his arms were his pillow. He described one night's experience while he was passing through Bihar or Uttar Pradesh: "Once on my way I slept under a banyan tree at night. After a while I had a dream. I saw an old woman telling me: 'You get up. Because of you the snakes are unable to get out of their holes. Go forward a little, and you will find a police station. You can spend the night there.' 'Will they allow me to stay?' I asked her. She said: 'Yes, they will allow you to sleep there. When you knock at their door, they will ask, "Who are you?" Say to them, "I am a mendicant."' I awoke and according to the instructions of the old woman, I got shelter in the veranda of the police station. The next morning I went to check the ground under the banyan tree and found many holes. The local people told me that the place was infested with cobras." Someone asked the swami, "Who was that woman?" After a brief silence, the swami replied, "It was the Divine Mother."[44]

Once Subodhananda was passing through Mongher in Bihar. He was very hungry and exhausted. He sat down by the side of the road and asked some cowherd boys to pick some peas from the nearby field. Seeing them in his field, the farmer chased the boys and they ran back to the swami. Subodhananda calmly said to the farmer: "Brother, please punish me. It is I who asked these boys to pick peas for me, so the fault is mine." The farmer was very impressed with Subodhananda's simplicity and humility; he told him to take as many peas as he needed. But Subodhananda refused his offer. In the meantime, a man brought various kinds of food for the swami; he ate some and distributed the rest among the boys.[45]

It is difficult to record Subodhananda's travel accounts chronologically since he travelled often and alone throughout many parts of India, leaving no records. He visited some important holy places of South India, such as Kanyakumari, Rameswaram, Madurai, and Madras. He learned a little of the Tamil language and later would tell devotees about South Indian folklore and religious traditions.

In 1897 Subodhananda gave a lecture to the Young Men's Hindu Association in Madras on "Sannyasa and Brahmacharya," which was published in the November 1898 issue of *Prabuddha Bharata*. Following are some excerpts:

> Sannyasa is the renunciation of all selfish motives and desires. Before I explain what sannyasa is, I should speak to you about brahmacharya; for unless the latter is realized, no sannyasa or renunciation is possible. The observance of brahmacharya requires strict regulation of one's diet, habits, and thoughts. Of all the injunctions prescribed for this stage, the greatest stress is laid by the scriptures upon the complete mastery of the sexual instinct. Nothing should be sensed or done by the aspirant that might directly or otherwise tend to arouse the animal in him or her. In this way one is directed to bring one's mind under full control. He who is not a slave to his senses and mind, but on the contrary has made them his slaves, is a true brahmacharin. All the religions of the world preach this brahmacharya and sannyasa, both of which have one and the same end in view, namely, to lift the mind up from all sensual concerns towards God. When the mind reaches God it enjoys divine bliss. . . .
>
> Our Master used to say that if we wanted to pass a thread through the eye of a needle all the scattered fibres of the thread should be brought to a point and then alone could we make it go through the

needle; otherwise, if the fibres were allowed to point in all directions they would prevent the thread from passing through the eye; similarly, if we want to lift our mind up towards God, we must bring it back from all external things and concentrate it on one point....

Our Master says that as rain water does not stand upon high ground but always seeks the lowest level, similarly, those who are puffed up with vanity cannot retain any faith in themselves, for faith always seeks the hearts of the humble and the meek.

As long as there are quarrels among different individuals and sects, they do not rise up to realize the highest truth. When truth shines, the darkness of ignorance and its crew of narrowness, bigotry, and fanaticism that deluge the earth with murder and bloodshed, shall all vanish. "My God is the true God, your God is false," are the words of men groping in the darkness of ignorance. Once Keshab Chandra Sen, the leader of the Brahmo Samaj, asked our Master, "Since there is only one God, how is it that there are so many sects quarrelling with one another?" The Master replied: "You see, people always quarrel over their lands, properties, and other things of the world, saying, 'This land is mine, and that is thine.' In this way they divide this earth in various ways by drawing lines of demarcation to distinguish their respective properties; but no one ever quarrels about the open space that is above the earth, for that belongs to none, as there can be drawn no lines on it to distinguish one's property from that of another; similarly, when the mind rises above all worldly concerns he can have no occasion to quarrel, for then he reaches a certain point which is the common goal of all." When a man realizes God he cannot quarrel, but when he is below the right mark, that is, when he is distant from God, he is more or less given to quarrelling, although you may have many occasions for it, and thus at last end all these disagreements by realizing universal harmony and agreement, which are only to be found in God, who is both within and without you.

In 1892 the Ramakrishna Monastery was moved from Baranagore to Alambazar, near Dakshineswar. Between his travels, Subodhananda lived in the monastery with his brother disciples. The monastery was in an extremely poor financial condition. One day Saradananda and Subodhananda went to Girish Chandra Ghosh, a bohemian devotee of the Master as well as a great actor and playwright. When Girish was approached for money, he bluntly said, "Where is any money?" Subodhananda replied jokingly: "Sharat Maharaj will grab you and I shall take the money, breaking your box." Girish extended his hand to Subodhananda and said, "First try to bend my finger." Girish was extremely strong. When Subodhananda failed to bend his finger, Girish said to his secretary, "Abinash, whatever money I have in the box, please give everything to the monks." Girish fed the swamis and told Subodhananda: "I am a wild horse; only the best jockey can handle me. Khoka, I see you will be able to deal with me."[46]

With Swami Vivekananda and Others

After Vivekananda returned from the West in 1897, he founded the Ramakrishna Mission. He asked his brother disciples to propagate practical Vedanta as taught by Sri Ramakrishna for the good of humanity. Before this, most of the disciples had either lived in seclusion and practised spiritual disciplines, or had wandered throughout the country as itinerant monks. Swamiji wanted his brother disciples to become accustomed to speaking in public, so he persuaded them to give weekly lectures by turn in the Alambazar Monastery. When Subodhananda's turn came he tried in vain to be excused. The other monks thought that this was very funny and gathered eagerly in the hall to watch Khoka make a fool of himself. At last Subodhananda mounted the platform — miserable and unwilling — and opened his mouth to speak. But before he could say a word, the building began to vibrate and rock, and trees crashed down outside: This was the devastating earthquake of 12 June 1897. The meeting was dissolved. Swamiji humourously said, "Well, Khoka, you have made an earth-shaking speech!"[47] All laughed, including Subodhananda.

Swamiji noticed that Subodhananda avoided women; he didn't even talk to them. One day Swamiji said: "Khoka, women devotees come to hear about the Master; please talk to them. If you avoid them, where will they go? They are the manifestations of the Divine Mother. Treat them as your mother or daughter." From then on, Subodhananda would associate with women and address them as "Mayi" or "Mother."[48] When Vivekananda's Western women devotees came to Belur Math, he would send Subodhananda to look after them and supply their needs. Once Subodhananda said to Swamiji: "Please excuse me. I can neither speak English properly nor can I understand their language." Swamiji said: "You will not have to worry about that. When they tell you 'Thank you,' you say to them, 'I don't care.'" However, when Subodhananda followed Swamiji's instruction, the women devotees were puzzled. They laughed when they discovered that it was Swamiji's mischief.[49]

From his boyhood, Subodhananda loved to drink tea. One night at Belur Math, Vivekananda was meditating in his room; Brahmananda and Subodhananda were sleeping in the next room. When Swamiji finished his meditation, he woke up Subodhananda and asked if he would mind bringing him a pipe to smoke. Subodhananda did so, and Vivekananda was so pleased that he exclaimed impulsively, "Any boon you ask for shall be granted!" "What could I possibly ask for?" said Subodhananda. "The Master gave us everything we need." But Brahmananda said, "No, Khoka, ask for something." So Subodhananda considered carefully and then said, "Grant me this — that I may never, for the rest of my life, miss my daily cup of tea." Many years later, Subodhananda was asked whether this boon had really been granted. He answered that it had and that the tea had sometimes arrived without his expectation, just as he was about to go to sleep at night.[50]

Subodhananda was among the first group of trustees of Belur Math appointed by Vivekananda in 1901; later he was elected treasurer of the Ramakrishna Math and Mission. His love for Swamiji was second only to his love for the Master. Swamiji also had great affection for him. Sometimes when Swamiji would become so serious that none of his brother disciples dared to approach him, it was left to Khoka Maharaj to go and interrupt his mood.

Subodhananda narrated the following incident: "One night Swamiji was reading a book while lying on his stomach. He was extremely serious. The dinner bell was rung, but he did not hear it. We were all waiting for him. When nobody dared to call him, Swami Brahmananda asked me to call Swamiji. I silently went to his room, looked at the page number, and abruptly closed the book. Swamiji said angrily: 'Khoka, you rascal! Why did you close my book? Now how shall I know where I was reading?' I immediately opened the book and showed him the exact place. Then I said: 'Please come for supper. The food will be cold and all are waiting for you.' He then came to the dining room and ate with us."[51]

Subodhananda was very fond of travelling. Between his stays at Belur Math in 1899 he visited Almora, Mayavati, and again Kedarnath and Badrinath. The next year he went to Navadwip (the birthplace of Chaitanya), Darjeeling, and Kamakhya in Assam. In 1902 he revisited Mayavati and was there when Swamiji passed away. In 1905 he went to Almora again to recover from kalaazar (a serious infectious disease). As a trustee of the Ramakrishna Order, he shouldered the responsibility for philanthropic activities with his brother disciples. During the plague epidemic in Calcutta in 1899, he worked hard to relieve the suffering of the helpless, panic-stricken people. He had a very tender heart, and sometimes begged money from others to help poor patients with food and medicine. One family near Belur Monastery was saved from starvation by the swami's kindness. Whenever he heard that anyone was sick or needed help, he would immediately go to his or her aid.

In 1908 there was a great famine in the Chilka region of Orissa. Subodhananda threw himself heart and soul into the relief work. He collected and distributed rice, lentils, and clothes among the famine-stricken people. He worked day and night without caring for his own food or rest, and became sick as a result. Sri Ramakrishna appeared before him and said, "You will not have to do this work anymore."[52] However, Subodhananda continued the relief work until the condition of the people improved.

Subodhananda was extremely devoted to Holy Mother. He visited Jayrambati in 1891 with Girish Chandra Ghosh and Swami Niranjanananda. In 1911 when Holy Mother visited Belur Math after her pilgrimage to South India, Brahmananda arranged a grand reception for her. The shrine was decorated, and monks and devotees stood in line as Holy Mother walked slowly onto the monastery grounds. Brahmananda announced that no one should break the line and rush to take the dust of her feet. Suddenly, however, somebody came from behind the line, took the dust of Mother's feet and disappeared into the crowd. Amused, Brahmananda cried out: "Who is he? Catch him!"[53] Everyone laughed, seeing Subodhananda's childlike nature.

Once Subodhananda was going to Calcutta from Belur Math by steamer. On the way, a few young men from Bali started criticizing Vivekananda. Subodhananda boldly told them: "Do you give any donation to Belur Math? If so, please stop it from today. What will you gain by criticizing Swamiji? Neither will your criticism make Swamiji's hands fall off, nor will your praise help him grow two more hands." When he heard that those young men did not help Belur Math, the swami said: "Then why do you criticize unnecessarily? Can you appreciate the monks? You work like slaves under English officers and you are supposed to flatter them; if you make any mistake, they will kick you out with their boots." A few days later, one of those young men came to Belur Math and apologized to Subodhananda: "Maharaj, the other day out of sheer ignorance, we did wrong. Your words came true. One of us was kicked out of the office by an English officer."[54]

Subodhananda's love and respect for Swamiji was phenomenal. Once in Varanasi, Swami Raghavananda asked him: "Maharaj, who is greater — Trailanga Swami or Swamiji?" Subodhananda replied: "Trailanga Swami is the greatest among men, but Swamiji is Shiva Himself. If anybody criticized Swamiji before the Master, he would say, 'Here the Lord Shiva has been criticized, please sprinkle a little Ganges water.'"[55]

As a Guru, and Trips to East Bengal

Subodhananda's unassuming nature and plain clothing hid the fact that he was a great soul and a disciple of Sri Ramakrishna; but his renunciation and simple, joyful face attracted devotees. In the monastery he wore an ochre cloth, a T-shirt, and a pair of slippers. He washed his own clothes, and ate with the other monks on the floor of the dining room.

Subodhananda was reluctant to give spiritual instructions to devotees. If anybody approached him for initiation, he would say: "What do I know about initiation? I am a Khoka. You go to Swami Brahmananda or Holy Mother — they are highly spiritual." Once Holy Mother said: "Why does Khoka not initiate people? As long as the Master's disciples are alive, let the people receive their grace."[56] He also received a command from the Master to instruct people. In 1915 Subodhananda began to initiate devotees privately.

Once in later years some devotees from East Bengal came to Swami Shivananda, then the president of the Ramakrishna Order, and invited him to Dhaka. The swami was not well, so he asked Subodhananda to go instead. Subodhananda replied: "Oh, no, I can't go there. There are many big rivers in East Bengal and I am afraid to cross them."[57] Knowing his nature, Shivananda did not press him any further at that time. However, on 7 May 1924, Subodhananda went to dedicate the Ramakrishna Temple at Sonargao, Dhaka, at the behest of Shivananda. "People of East Bengal," said Shivananda, "are greatly devoted to Sri Ramakrishna. Please initiate them." Subodhananda obeyed and initiated many people, even children. After returning to Belur Math, he informed Shivananda that he had initiated one and all, including children. Shivananda asked, "How will the children practise meditation and japam?" He replied, "You ordered me to initiate everybody, so I deprived none."[58]

Subodhananda was extremely self-effacing and did not consider himself to be a guru. Once a woman disciple asked him: "Swami, I don't know the Gayatri mantram or ritual or chanting. People practise the Gayatri thrice a day. Could you teach me all those disciplines?" Subodhananda said humbly: "Mother, I don't know all those things either. You see, I am a Khoka. I have given you what I have received from the Master, what I have known from my own experience, and what has kept me in a blissful state. Please control your mind and practise japam and meditation."[59]

In 1925 Subodhananda again went to East Bengal, and gave initiation to many people, even outcasts. His affection for them was no less than his affection for the highly cultured people of society. Once in Baliati Ashrama he gave a lecture for ten minutes on "Sri Ramakrishna and the Harmony of Religions" in front of a thousand people. He was fond of talking about the Master and taught people from his own experience: "Pray to God sincerely, then you will see him. Sincere prayer means: Tell the Lord your pain and your problems with tears in your eyes. Ask him for faith and devotion. Always remember that you are a companion of Sri Ramakrishna's companion. Make your mind strong." When someone asked him how to control lust, he replied: "The more you go towards the east, the farther you are from the west. Don't pay any attention to lustful thoughts; just move towards God. After some days you will see that lust has unconsciously disappeared from your mind. Without the will of the Divine Mother nothing will happen. Surrender to Her. Out of mercy She will remove your weakness, and you will be freed from lust."[60]

One day he talked about the efficacy of japam: "All power belongs to God. If anyone repeats the mantram, he will definitely get the result. For instance, when a farmer sows seeds, no matter whether they are placed in the ground straight or upside down, they shoot up all the same. He is everything — it is He who gives pain and again He who gives peace. One can overcome all obstacles by repeating the mantram."[61]

Subodhananda was a moderate eater. Once a devotee invited him to dine and he asked about the menu. The devotee humbly said: "What could we offer you, swami? We have arranged simple food — rice and lentils." Subodhananda went to the dining room and found that the devotee was actually serving various delicacies, but he ate only rice and lentils. In spite of the devotee's fervent request, he did not change his mind. The swami said to him, "The Master taught us that one should hold to the truth and keep his word."[62]

Days in Belur Math

In the early days of Belur Monastery, Subodhananda worked in the vegetable garden with Advaitananda. Brahmananda collected various kinds of fruit trees and flower plants from different parts of India and planted them in the monastery garden. Subodhananda used to make grafts of those trees and plants so that they could be preserved and planted in other places. Sometimes he would go with Akhandananda to collect *nageswar champa* (michelia champaka), which was a favourite flower of Sri Ramakrishna. He would also travel to raise funds for the Master's festival or to buy food for the monastery. He would nurse sick monks like a loving mother, cut vegetables, and manage the kitchen.

"One day," wrote a monk, "the bell was rung, but nobody came to cut the vegetables. Khoka Maharaj therefore cut five kinds of vegetables for the Master and asked the cook to offer those five items to him. He arranged to have rice, lentils, and boiled potatoes cooked for the monks. In the dining room, Swami Saradananda was pleased to have this simple menu. Then he asked, 'Have you not offered any vegetables to the Master?' Khoka Maharaj replied: 'Yes, five kinds of vegetables were offered to the Master; but since the monks did not come to cut the vegetables, I arranged this simple menu for them.' Immediately Swami Saradananda said in front of all the monks, 'Tomorrow I shall come to cut the vegetables.' This took care of the problem."[63]

Belur Math was Subodhananda's favourite place. In his later years he was reluctant to go anywhere else. Once when someone suggested that he go to a health resort to recuperate from his illness, he said, "It is better to live on rice and spinach at Belur Math than to have good food somewhere else." Every day, even when he was weak, Subodhananda would walk with a cane to Vivekananda's Temple at the southeast corner of the monastery. He told the monks: "The Master said that Swamiji was Lord Shiva Himself. To respect him is equivalent to worshipping Lord Shiva."[64] His room was adjacent to Swamiji's bedroom. Every morning he used to go to Swamiji's room and bow down to his portrait.

A monk recalled:

Khoka Maharaj was easy of access, and everybody felt very free with him. Many, on coming in contact with him, would feel his love so much that they would altogether forget the wide gulf of difference that marked their spiritual life and his. Yet he made no conscious attempt to hide the spiritual height to which he belonged. This great unostentatiousness was part and parcel of his very being. It was remarkable that he could mix so freely with one and all — with people of all ages and denominations — and make them his own. Many are the persons who, though not religiously minded, were drawn to him simply by his love and were afterwards spiritually benefitted.

The young brahmacharins and monks of the Order found in him a great sympathizer. He took the time to find out their difficulties and helped them with advice and guidance. He would be their mouthpiece before the elders, mediate for them, and shield them when they inadvertently did something wrong. One day a brahmacharin committed a great mistake, and was asked to live outside the monastery and to get his food by begging. The brahmacharin failed to get anything by begging except a quantity of fried gram and returned to the gate of the monastery in the evening. But he did not dare to enter the compound.

Khoka Maharaj came to know of his plight, interceded on his behalf, and the young member was excused. The novices at the monastery had different kinds of work allotted to them. Often they did not know how to do it. Khoka Maharaj on such occasions would come forward to help and guide them.

The swami was self-reliant and would not accept personal service from others, even if they were devotees or disciples. He always emphasized that one should help oneself as far as possible, and he himself rigidly adhered to this principle in his daily life. Even during times of illness he was reluctant to accept any service from others and avoided it until it became absolutely impossible for him to manage without it.

The swami's needs were few, and he was satisfied with anything that came unsought. His personal belongings were almost nil. He would not accept anything except what was absolutely necessary for him. In food as in other things he made no distinction and ate whatever came with equal relish. This great spirit of renunciation, always evidenced in his conduct, was the result of his complete dependence on God. In personal conduct as well as in conversation, he put much emphasis on self-surrender to God. He very often narrated to those who came to him for guidance the following story of Shridhara Swami, the great Vaishnava saint and a commentator on the Gita:

Spurred by a spirit of renunciation, Shridhara Swami was thinking of giving up the world when his wife died giving birth to a child. Shridhara felt worried about the baby and was seriously thinking about how to provide for the child before retiring from the world. One day as he was sitting deeply absorbed with these thoughts, the egg of a lizard dropped from the roof in front of him. The egg broke as a result of the fall and a young lizard came out. Just then a small fly came and stood near the young lizard, which it caught and swallowed in a moment. At this the thought flashed in the mind of Shridhara that there is a divine plan behind creation and that every creature is provided for beforehand by God. At once all his anxiety for his own child vanished, and he immediately renounced the world. Of course, the baby was taken care of by his relatives.

The swami's spiritual life was as marked by his directness as much as his external life was marked by its simplicity. He had no philosophical problems of his own to solve. The Ultimate Reality was a fact to him. Whenever he would speak of God, one felt that here was a man to whom God was a greater reality than one's own earthly relatives. He once said, "God can be realized much more tangibly than one feels the presence of a companion with whom one is walking." The form of his personal worship was singularly free from ritualistic observances. While entering the shrine, he was not obsessed by any awe or wonder, but would act as if he were going to a very near relation; and while performing worship he did not care to recite memorized texts. His relationship with God was just as free and natural as a human relationship. He realized the goodness of God, and so he was always optimistic in his views. For this reason his words brought cheer and strength to weary or despondent souls. Intellectual snobs or philosophical pedants were bewildered to see the conviction with which he spoke on problems that they had been unable to solve — their pride and arrogance notwithstanding.[65]

Subodhananda came from a well-to-do family. Once his relatives proposed sharing some of their family income with him, but he declined to accept it. He told them: "I am an all-renouncing monk; I don't need any money. Please serve the poor and the mendicants with that money."[66]

The disciples of Ramakrishna demonstrated that there is no high or low in work. Work is worship. Subodhananda would teach the new monks how to prepare betel-rolls and tobacco for offering to the Master in the shrine. With the help of the young boys he would uproot the thorny bushes from the courtyard. He was very methodical and punctual in his work. One day the lunch bell was late. He went to the person in charge of the kitchen and learned that there was a special food offering for the Master. The swami said to him: "The Master did not like to have his lunch after twelve noon. It is better to offer regular food to the Master at the right time and then arrange for special food later."[67] One day Subodhananda performed the worship in the shrine. While he was offering the fruits and sweets, the Master appeared before him and pointing to the sliced cucumber, said, "Please add a little salt to it."[68]

Subodhananda followed a daily routine: He got up at 3:30 a.m. He would smoke a hubble-bubble, then after washing, would go to the shrine at 4:00 a.m. and bow down to the Master. Then until 9:00 a.m. he would sit either on his bed or in a chair on the upper eastern veranda facing the Ganges: His calm appearance indicated that his mind was roaming in a mysterious realm. After tea he would take his bath, and then go to the shrine to bow down to the Master. Until lunch he would read some scriptures — especially the Puranas — sitting on an easy chair facing the Ganges. He loved the stories of the saints and divine incarnations of the Puranas. After lunch he would take a little rest. In the afternoon he would go for a walk, and in the evening he would sit quietly until supper. He did not like monks to misuse time in chatting and gossiping. It was not his nature to give unwanted advice to anybody; if anyone asked spiritual questions, he would answer in a simple way. One day he said to a devotee: "Do you expect anything when you present some gifts to your little brothers and sisters? One should love God like that. Say: 'Master, I offer my body and mind, my life, and everything to you. Give me shelter at your blessed feet. I don't want anything else.'"[69]

Towards the End

Towards the end, Swami Subodhananda suffered from various ailments including diabetes and blood dysentery. As a guru he travelled to many places in Bengal, Bihar, and Uttar Pradesh to spread the message of Sri Ramakrishna. He wrote in a letter: "The cause of my disease is excessive work. I didn't get the time to even walk. From morning to ten o'clock at night I talked to people and gave them spiritual instructions."[70] To recover his health he went to the Ramakrishna Ashrama in Jamtara, Bihar. One day when he was in critical condition, his attendant was fanning him. Suddenly he said to him: "Please move away from my bed. The Master, Holy Mother, and Swami Brahmananda have come. Can't you see them?"[71] Later Subodhananda said to his attendant that the Master had told him that he would be cured very soon.

In 1927 Subodhananda went to Varanasi, and in 1929 he went to Bhubaneswar for rest. Wherever he went, he initiated devotees and inspired them with the message of Sri Ramakrishna. In the beginning of 1931 he contracted tuberculosis, and in spite of all medical help, his body began to deteriorate. He wrote a letter from Belur Math: "Only the Master knows how long he will work through this body. I have no objection whether my body remains or dies."[72]

One day Shivananda asked the visiting doctor: "Have you seen that boy? How is he?" Neither the doctor nor the monks knew whom he was talking about. Then Shivananda said: "I mean that Khoka who lives in the room adjacent to mine. He is truly a child. He does not know how to take care of himself. Please check him carefully and arrange for proper medicine and diet."[73] Khoka Maharaj was then sixty-one.

A few days before his passing away, Subodhananda said to his attendant: "Mahapurush Maharaj [Swami Shivananda] was telling me, 'I pray to the Master that you get well and live many more years.' But I don't want to live anymore. I had a dream in the early morning the other day: I saw that I had left my body. I saw Swamis Brahmananda, Premananda, and Yogananda, but I didn't see Swamiji. I asked them, 'Please tell me, where is Swamiji?' They replied: 'He is not here. He is far above — absorbed in God.' 'It does not matter that he is far away, I am going to him.' Saying so, I left to find him. Then my sleep broke. I experienced tremendous joy there. They are living in a blissful city. It is hard to come back from there. All pain and suffering are here, in this world."[74]

In spite of all his suffering Subodhananda did not forget what the Master had told him: "Think of me twice a day." The terminal tuberculosis devoured all his energy, and he could not even change his position without help. Still, in the morning and before he went to sleep at night, he would lift his head with much effort and look at the picture of the Master behind his head and salute him with folded hands. What a touching scene! He didn't want the Master's words to be in vain. His love and devotion for his guru were outstanding.[75]

Subodhananda demonstrated in his life how to face inevitable death. When he was very sick, he could not read the scriptures, so his attendants would read to him *The Gospel of Sri Ramakrishna*, the Bhagavata, and the Upanishads. Sometimes in an inspired mood he would say: "The world with all its enjoyments seems like a heap of ashes. I don't feel any attraction for all these things." Again, he would say: "I don't depend on anybody in this world. If you say a few sweet words, people come to you; and, if not, they go away. Such is the nature of human beings! I only look at God.... I said to the Master: 'Enough of this world! Please take me with you.' 'Wait a few days more,' said the Master. Let it be. Let his will be done." If anybody asked about his pain, he replied, "When I think of the Master, I forget all physical suffering."[76]

Subodhananda was fully conscious and cheerful until the last. One morning when Swami Shuddhananda came to pay his respects to him, the swami asked, "Sudhir, how are you?" His body was so weak that it was difficult for him to keep his eyes open. When his attendants asked, "Swami, do you remember the Master, Holy Mother, and Swamiji?" Subodhananda replied, "Yes, I remember them all distinctly." An hour before his death, he looked intently at the picture of Sri Ramakrishna, and then suddenly his face glowed with a smile. A monk asked, "Swami, can you see the Master?" He nodded his head. Then his eyeballs turned from left to right, as if he was searching for someone. Again he smiled, and then passed away at 3:05 p.m. on Friday, 2 December 1932.[77] The monks chanted "*Jai Sri Ramakrishna*" and Vedic mantras, decorated his body with flowers and sandalpaste, and carried it to the burning ghat at Belur Math, near the Ganges, where it was cremated with sandalwood, ghee (clarified butter), and perfume.

The night before he passed away, Swami Subodhananda said, "My last prayer is that the blessings of the Master be always on the Order."[78]

Surrendering himself completely to Sri Ramakrishna, he conquered death. On his deathbed he would often say: "It does not matter if this body dies. I shall go to the Master joyfully."[79] And he did. Swami Subodhananda remained the same joyful little boy throughout his life — the ideal model of a divine child of Sri Ramakrishna.

15

ॐ

SWAMI AKHANDANANDA

Short-sighted people follow the path of the pleasant, which leads to bondage; the far-sighted tread the path of the Highest Good, which leads to liberation. As an ant sifts sugar from a mixture of sugar and sand, so a calm soul discriminates between these two paths and follows the latter. The path of the Highest Good is very rough and steep; that is why few succeed.

Those who possess a pure character relinquish worldly pleasures and seek spiritual bliss. It truly takes great effort to develop a noble character — but when it is formed, it is a source of tremendous energy and gigantic willpower. Only a person of noble character can be a true spiritual teacher and a great leader.

Swami Akhandananda spoke of how hard he worked to make his character strong and pure when he was a teenage boy: "I was extremely orthodox in those days and scrupulously observed all the brahminical customs in accordance with the scriptural injunctions. For example, I used to bathe four times a day in the Ganges without applying any oil to my body, and as a result my skin and hair became very dry. I was a vegetarian and cooked my own food. I was in the habit of chewing a myrobalan [a kind of bitter nut] after meals, so my lips became white.

"I used to practise *pranayama* [breathing exercises] along with my other morning and evening spiritual disciplines. I increased the volume of pranayama so much that my body began to perspire and shiver. I practised *kumbhaka* [breath retention] by diving into the Ganges and grabbing a stone. I was fascinated by this play with the prana."[1]

SWAMI AKHANDANANDA: SARGACHI, C.1934-35

Swami Akhandananda was born as Gangadhar Gangopadhyay on 30 September 1864, in the Ahiritola area of western Calcutta. His father, Srimanta Gangopadhyay, was a priest and Sanskrit teacher who also practised yoga and Tantra. Gangadhar's mother, Vamasundari, was a devout woman. After having three daughters, she prayed to God for a son, and thus Gangadhar was born.

Gangadhar was a vivacious, handsome boy. When he was eight years old, he had a large abscess between his eyebrows. He told the doctor to perform the surgery without anesthesia; the doctor was amazed at his stoicism. Gangadhar was extremely intelligent, and memorized the Gita and Upanishads. As a small child, he mastered the English alphabet in one day. Gangadhar was admitted to the Oriental Seminary, but he was not particularly interested in formal education. From his very childhood, Gangadhar was so compassionate that he once gave his own shirt to a poor classmate whose shirt was torn. Without telling his parents, he would secretly give food to beggars. He was a strong moralist and always helped his wayward friends.

Gangadhar was a close friend of Surendra Ghosh, a son of the famous dramatist and actor Girish Chandra Ghosh; together they formed an amateur theatrical party in North Calcutta. Gangadhar took roles in several dramas and earned some repute as an actor. But his theatrical ability could not hold in check his deep spiritual inclination.

Gangadhar was fascinated by the mendicants and by their stories about the holy places of India. He cherished a desire to see the Himalayas and the ashramas of the ancient sages. When Gangadhar was twelve, he was invested with the sacred thread; thereafter, he repeated the Gayatri mantram three times a day. Often he would make an image of Lord Shiva out of clay and worship Him with bel leaves and Ganges water.

In 1877 Gangadhar and his friend Harinath met Sri Ramakrishna at Dinanath Basu's house in Baghbazar. Seeing the Master in samadhi, Gangadhar's spiritual longing increased. Sometimes he would go to the cremation ground and imbibe the mood of renunciation by observing the impermanence of human life. Seeing Gangadhar's monastic tendencies, his mother was eager to arrange his marriage. Knowing her intention, Gangadhar said: "Mother, arrange my marriage quickly, and bring another 'mother' home. She will help you in cooking and other household work."[2] Gangadhar's mother understood the pure nature of her son, who considered all women to be his mother. After that she never again pestered him about getting married.

At twelve, Gangadhar met a monk at the Sarvamangala Temple in Cossipore, and left home with him without informing his parents. His parents wept for their only son, and searched for him in Varanasi, Vrindaban, Hardwar, and other holy places. As it turned out, however, Gangadhar had gone to Burdwan, sixty miles from Calcutta. The monk suggested that he return home, as he was too young for monastic life. When he did, his parents were overjoyed to have him home again.

In the Company of Sri Ramakrishna

In May 1883, when he was nineteen, Gangadhar visited Sri Ramakrishna at Dakshineswar. The Master received Gangadhar cordially, and made him sit on his small cot. He then asked, "Have you ever seen me before?" "Yes," Gangadhar replied. "I saw you once when I was very young at the house of Dinanath Basu in Calcutta." The elder Gopal was also present. Addressing him, the Master said with a smile: "O Gopal, listen to this! This boy says that he met me when he was very young. This little one had an early boyhood!"[3] Gangadhar looked exceptionally young for his age and moreover, he had a childlike demeanour.

Gangadhar later recalled his first meetings with the Master:

In the afternoon the Master asked me to go to the Panchavati after saluting the deities at the Kali and Vishnu temples. Later in the evening, as I returned to the Master's room, I heard music being played from the two *nahabats* [concert towers], and the temple garden was filled with the melodious sound of the vesper bells. The Master's room was dark, and there was a sweet smell of incense. The Master was seated on his cot, barely visible. He did not have any outer consciousness. As he had asked me to stay overnight at the temple garden, I did so. The next morning, when I was about to leave for Calcutta, he said to me with a smile, "Come again on Saturday."

After a few days I went to Sri Ramakrishna for the second time on a Saturday, and I was again made to stay overnight. In the evening, after the vesper service was over, the Master handed me a mat and asked me to spread it on the western veranda. He took his pillow and sat down on the mat. He then asked me to sit in a comfortable posture and to meditate. "It is not good to sit leaning forward or to hold the body too straight," he said.

That evening the Master initiated me by writing a mantram on my tongue. He then lay down putting his feet on my lap, and asked me to give them a little massage. I was quite strong, as I practised wrestling. No sooner had I begun to press his feet than he cried out: "What are you doing? The legs will be crushed! Press them gently." Immediately I realized how soft and tender the Master's body was, as if his bones were covered with butter. I was embarrassed, and I asked with some fear, "How then should I massage?" "Pass your hands over them gently," he replied. "Niranjan also did like you at first."[4]

On weekends many devotees would come to visit the Master. In order to avoid the crowd, Gangadhar would go on weekdays; sometimes he would stay overnight. This enabled Ramakrishna to imprint his way of life and teachings on the mind of his young disciple. Gangadhar reminisced:

One morning Sri Ramakrishna asked me to accompany him to the Panchavati, and there he told me to meditate facing the east. He left for a while, and when he came back he set my body straight. He remarked, "You become a bit bent during meditation." We then returned to his room. After that he asked me to carry a water pot and go with him to the chandni, the bathing ghat on the Ganges. He had his bath and returned to his room in his wet cloth. Before he put on his fresh cloth he asked me to sprinkle a little Ganges water on it. There was a picture of Mother Kali of Kalighat [Calcutta] in his room, which he saluted. Then he ate a little dry prasad of Lord Jagannath and gave some to me. Standing in front of the picture of Kali, he said several times, "Om Kali." He then put the palm of his right hand on his chest with the three middle fingertips touching the palm, and he stood there with half-closed eyes for some time. After that he took the offered fruits and sweets that had been sent to him from the Kali and Vishnu temples. He then drank a little bel sherbet and gave me the prasad, after which he sat on his small cot and smoked from a hubble-bubble.

When the food offering was over in the temples the Master took me to the eastern veranda of his room and said: "Go and take the prasad of Mother Kali. It is cooked in Ganges water and is very holy." I agreed. While walking through the courtyard I looked back and noticed that the Master was watching whether I was going to the kitchen of the Vishnu or Kali temple. I wondered why he had asked me to go to the nonvegetarian kitchen of Kali instead of the vegetarian kitchen of Vishnu. I did what the Master said, but I ate only the vegetarian dishes. I still remember the thick preparation of *chana dal* [lentils].

When I returned to the Master's room I found him waiting near the east door with a betel-roll in his hand. Giving it to me, he said: "Chew it. It is good to chew a couple of betel-rolls after meals. It removes bad breath."

Sometimes I would think: "The Master says that most of my habits, such as taking only self-cooked food, being a vegetarian, practising austerity, chewing myrobalan, and so on, are for old people. If they are not good, why shouldn't I give them up?"

One day I visited the Master and had prasad at the temple. A group of lay devotees came after his noon rest, and I spread a mat for them on the floor. One of them asked the Master, "Sir, is it good that these young boys come to you to embrace the monastic life, disregarding the householder's life?" The Master replied: "Look, you only see their present life, and not their previous lives in which they passed through these other stages. For instance, a man has four sons. One of them, having grown up, says: 'I shall not put oil on my body or eat fish. I shall eat only self-cooked vegetarian food.' The parents try to dissuade him from these habits and even threaten him, but the boy will not give up the path of renunciation. Yet the other three sons are set on enjoyment and swallow whatever they get. Look, it is because of the preponderance of sattva that this boy wants to renounce everything before he reaches manhood." Listening to this from the Master, my faith in keeping up my orthodox customs doubled.[5]

Sri Ramakrishna did not want his young disciples to be stuck in the obsolete customs of an older generation, yet at the same time he did not want to disturb their faith. He did not care for any kind of excessive behaviour in practising religion; he freed them from spiritual vanity. His way of teaching was simple and natural, and he knew how to make religion interesting. He taught individually according to the temperament of each disciple. The Master was never dry or boring: he would make jokes even while speaking on the most exalted topics. Once, during the Chariot Festival at Balaram Basu's Calcutta residence, the Master told Gangadhar and other young ones: "Well, my boys, sing and dance well. Then Balaram will give you *malpo* [a delicious sweet]." He was a loving father to his disciples as well as their friend.

Sri Ramakrishna taught from his own experience, not through knowledge acquired from books. Gangadhar later recalled:

Once I spent a night at Dakshineswar with several other disciples, and the Master had us all sit for meditation. While communing with our Chosen Deities, we often laughed and wept in ecstasy. The pure joy we experienced in those boyhood days cannot be expressed in words. Whenever I approached the Master he would invariably ask me, "Did you shed tears at the time of prayer or meditation?" And one day when I answered yes to this, how happy he was! "Tears of repentance or sorrow flow from the corners of the eyes nearest the nose," he said, "and those of joy from the outer corners of the eyes." Suddenly the Master asked me, "Do you know how to pray?" Saying this he flung his hands and feet about restlessly — like a little child impatient for its mother. Then he cried out: "Mother dear, grant me knowledge and devotion. I don't want anything else. I can't live without you." While thus teaching us how to pray, he looked just like a small boy. Profuse tears rolled down his chest, and he passed into deep samadhi. I was convinced that the Master did that for my sake.

One morning Sri Ramakrishna took me to the Kali Temple. Whenever I went there alone I stood outside the threshold, but on this occasion the Master took me into the sanctum sanctorum and showed me the face of Lord Shiva, who was of course lying on his back while Kali stood over Him. His face was not visible from outside the shrine, where one could only see the top of His head. The Master said, "Look, here is the living Shiva." I felt that Lord Shiva was conscious and breathing. I was astonished. How potent were the Master's words! Up to that time I had thought that this image was just like all the other Shiva images I had seen.

Sri Ramakrishna then gently pulled Mother Kali's cloth and placed Her ornaments properly. When we left the temple he was reeling like a drunkard. He was escorted to his room with difficulty and remained for some time in samadhi. I cannot describe the details of that day — the joy the Master poured into my heart cannot be communicated. After coming down from samadhi the Master sang many songs in an ecstatic mood.[6]

One day at Balaram's house Sri Ramakrishna told his would-be monastic disciples: "I spit upon lust and gold. Those who are attached to them will never have God-vision."[7] He repeated this several times to establish this idea in their minds. Another day in Dakshineswar, a beggar came to the Master's door and asked for some money. The Master called Gangadhar and, pointing to four pice, asked him to give them to the beggar. When Gangadhar had done this, the Master said, "Wash your hands with Ganges water."[8] This incident indelibly impressed on Gangadhar's mind the idea that money is rubbish, dirt. A true monk should be free from lust and gold. Later in life he wandered fourteen years all over India as a penniless monk, never touching money.

Once in Dakshineswar some nondualistic devotees came from Varanasi to visit the Master when Gangadhar was present. He later recorded their conversation in his memoirs:

One person asked, "Sir, how can He who is the Absolute Brahman, omnipresent and pervading the whole universe, incarnate Himself as man?"

"You see," the Master replied, "He who is the Absolute Brahman is the witness and is immanent everywhere. The divine incarnation is an embodiment of His power. The power is incarnate somewhere a quarter, somewhere else a half, and very rarely in full. He in whom the full power is manifest is adored as *Purna Brahman*, like Krishna. And three quarters of the Divine were manifested in Rama."

To this, one of the gentlemen said: "Sir, this body is the root of all evils. If it can be destroyed, all troubles will cease."

"The raw earthen pots when broken are made into pots again," the Master said, "but the burnt ones, once broken, can never be remade. So if you destroy the body before the attainment of Self-realization, you will have to be reborn and suffer similar consequences."

"But, sir," the gentleman objected, "why does one take so much care of his body?"

The Master answered: "Those who do the work of moulding, preserve the mould with care till the image is made. When the image is ready, it does not matter whether the mould is kept or rejected. So with this body. One has to realize the Supreme Self. One has to attain Self-knowledge. After that the body may remain or go. Till then the body has to be taken care of." The gentleman was silenced.

One of these visitors, Gadashankar, was a follower of Keshab Chandra Sen. The Master talked with him on the eastern veranda while I was there.

"Do you practise the brahminical rites daily?" the Master asked him.

"I do not like all these rituals," he said.

"You see," the Master went on, "do not give up anything by force. If the blossoms of gourds and pumpkins are plucked off, their fruits rot, but when the fruits are ripe the flowers fall off naturally. Do you believe in a God with form or in a formless God?"

"In the formless aspect," was the reply.

"But how can you grasp the formless aspect all at once?" the Master asked. "When the archers are learning to shoot, they first aim at the plantain tree, then at a thin tree, then at a fruit, then at the leaves, and finally at a flying bird. First meditate on the aspect with form. This will enable you to see the formless later."[9]

On another occasion, Gangadhar went to Dakshineswar and found that the Master was in samadhi. When he came down to normal consciousness, he spoke of God-vision and Self-realization, saying: "One's own Chosen Deity is one's own Self. The Chosen Deity and the Atman are identical. The vision of the Chosen Deity is equivalent to Self-knowledge."[10]

In the middle of 1885 Sri Ramakrishna developed throat cancer. He moved to Shyampukur in Calcutta for treatment, and then to Cossipore. Gangadhar began to serve the Master whenever he could, continuing all the while his spiritual disciplines and study. At night he used to meditate with Harinath on the bank of the Ganges. Gangadhar's father observed that his son was not interested in completing his education, so he found a job for Gangadhar in a merchant's office. Gangadhar worked there a few days and then gave it up. He then fully engaged himself in spiritual disciplines and service to the Master. He washed the dishes at the Cossipore garden house, and did all sorts of errands.

Even on his deathbed, Sri Ramakrishna took care of his disciples' needs like a loving mother, and chastised them for any mistakes. He told them not to misuse any articles or be extravagant, because the devotees supported him with their hard-earned money. One morning Gangadhar was in the Master's room. The doctor asked the Master not to talk because of his painful throat. However, out of motherly affection, the Master asked Gangadhar through a gesture, "Have you brushed your teeth?" Gangadhar nodded his head. On another occasion one of the attendants said, "I know." Immediately the Master raised his head from the pillow and remarked: "What do you say? You know? Never say that. Say, 'As long as I live so long do I learn.'"[11] Gangadhar learned a new lesson.

Sri Ramakrishna formed his monastic order at Cossipore and distributed ochre cloths to eleven of his would-be monastic disciples, saving one for Girish Chandra Ghosh. He gave ochre cloths to Gangadhar and Harinath on another day.[12]

Sri Ramakrishna passed away at 1:02 a.m. on 16 August 1886. Captain Vishwanath Upadhyay came, and after examining him, felt some heat in the body. He guessed that the Master was in samadhi. According to his instruction, Gangadhar rubbed *ghee* (clarified butter) on the Master's back the whole night. The Master's body was later cremated at the Cossipore cremation ground, and half of his relics were installed at Kankurgachi Yogodyana. Gangadhar was present on that occasion.

Wanderings in the Himalayas and Tibet

Some of the young disciples of Sri Ramakrishna resided at the Cossipore garden house for a couple of weeks and then moved to a dilapidated house at Baranagore, where they established the first Ramakrishna Monastery. Shashi began the worship service of the Master, while the others remained absorbed in meditation and study. On Christmas Eve of 1886, Gangadhar went with the other disciples to Antpur and took vows of renunciation. He returned home and told his father secretly that he would leave for the Himalayas very soon. His father gave his consent. In February 1887 Gangadhar took the ochre cloth that the Master had given to him and left the monastery without telling anyone. Only his noble father came to Howrah Station to see him off. He blessed his son: "Go, my son. Fulfill your mission in life. This world is unreal. I bless you: May you attain unflinching devotion to God."[13]

Gangadhar first visited Bodh Gaya, where Buddha attained nirvana. Near the Brahmayoni Hill of Gaya, he met the famous yogi Gambhiranath of the Natha sect, who affectionately told him: "My boy, stay with me. You will attain everything." Young Gangadhar replied: "My Master used to say that one cannot have a glimpse of the Infinite without seeing the Himalayas or the ocean. So I am eager to see the Himalayas." While at Gaya, he stayed at the house of Durgashankar, a devotee of Sri Ramakrishna. One day Durgashankar said to him: "I talked to you such a long time and I noticed your eyes never blinked. It is a sign of a divine nature. You are truly a disciple of Sri Ramakrishna."[14]

Pramadadas Mittra, a rich landlord as well as a great Sanskrit scholar, met Gangadhar at Durgashankar's house in Gaya. He had heard about Sri Ramakrishna from his friend Durgashankar, and now he was impressed upon seeing the young yogi Gangadhar. Pramadadas invited Gangadhar to his home in Varanasi. There he taught Gangadhar how to correctly chant the Upanishads and Sanskrit hymns in a melodious way. Gangadhar had a wonderful memory, and learned Vedic chanting after hearing it only once.

While in Varanasi, Gangadhar met the great saint Trailanga Swami, and received his blessing. He then went to see Swami Bhaskarananda with Pramadadas, who knew the great swami personally. Bhaskarananda was a great Sanskrit scholar, and he expressed his willingness to teach the Vedas to Gangadhar. The young man replied, "The power of sight which I would use for attaining knowledge by reading books, please turn it inward, so that I can experience the Atman." Bhaskarananda marvelled at him and remarked, "I see you are a yogi."[15]

One can learn more from a saint than from a library of a million books. Gangadhar absorbed the spiritual heritage of India from her holy places and saints. After staying a month in Varanasi, Gangadhar left for Ayodhya, the birthplace of Ramachandra. There he met Janakibarsharan, an all-renouncing mystic. He then went to Hardwar, in the foothills of the Himalayas, via Lucknow and Naimisharanya, an ancient Hindu cultural centre.

In March 1887 Gangadhar wrote to Pramadadas asking him to send a drum to Baranagore Monastery for the monks' vesper services. Thus he first introduced this great person to Swami Vivekananda and other disciples of the Master.

Early one morning in Hardwar, Gangadhar climbed up the Chandi Hill and there met Kamraj, a tantric saint. Kamraj was impressed with Gangadhar and asked him, "What do you want?" He replied, "I want that experience which is mentioned in the Gita — attaining *that* 'one grieves not and desires not'"(12.17). "Oh, you want Self-knowledge," said the saint. "You don't want my Divine Mother."[16] The saint's passionate love for Mother touched Gangadhar's heart.

Gangadhar then went to Rishikesh, a place for the hermits. There he saw mendicants practising their austerities, meditating, and discussing the Upanishads and the Gita. He found a thatched hut on the bank of the Ganges, where he practised meditation. Once a day, the manager of the *chatra* (a resting place for monks and pilgrims, where monks are given free meals) would ring a bell to call the mendicants there for food. Some days Gangadhar was so absorbed in meditation that he did not hear the bell. He would then beg food from villagers in the afternoon. At that time Rishikesh was dangerously infested with wild animals. Gangadhar heard from the mendicants that a few days earlier a tiger had grabbed a Vedanta monk and he had repeated loudly, "*Soham*" (I am He) until he died.

It is thrilling to read Gangadhar's entire travel account, which he recorded in his book *Smriti-Katha* (*From Holy Wanderings to The Service of God in Man*). He travelled hundreds of miles in the dangerous mountains of the Himalayas without carrying any money or any extra clothing, depending only on God. When a monk of the Mussoorie Hills heard that Gangadhar was going to Gangotri and Jamunotri (the sources of the Ganges and Jamuna, respectively) he offered some money and blankets to him, but he refused. Gangadhar accepted only a staff and proceeded on his journey.

Gangadhar walked sixty miles barefoot to reach Tihiri, where he rested awhile. He then continued his long walk over the high Himalayan range and visited Jamunotri and Gangotri, very important holy places, and most difficult to reach.

The spirit of service was ingrained in Gangadhar's nature. While on the way to Jamunotri, he came across a sick monk. With another person's help, he carried the monk to the nearest village, but could not save his life. Another time, in a cave at Gangotri he found a brahmin who had been starving for two days while fulfilling a vow to continually recite the Gayatri mantram. Gangadhar immediately begged food from some pilgrims and gave it to the brahmin.

Gangadhar stayed at Gangotri for a week, then decided to visit Kedarnath and Badrinath. He took the route via Chandravadani, a famous place sacred to the Divine Mother. While descending the steep Chandravadani Hill, Gangadhar lost his way. He closed his eyes and sat for meditation in that dense forest. He later wrote: "I got up and saying 'Victory to the Master,' I moved forward without caring for direction. It was almost impossible to stop my motion down the steep hill. I grabbed hold of shrubs and trees, my feet slipped, and at last I tumbled down into a corn-field. Two hill men were roasting sheaves of wheat for food. Seeing me, they were taken aback and said: 'How is it possible? Where did you come from? Who led you here? No human being has ever come down this way!' On hearing that I had come from the temple of goddess Chandravadani, they said, 'The Mother must have held you by the hand and brought you here.' I had actually felt that someone led me there by the hand. I had slipped down as much as two miles."[17]

Gangadhar wholeheartedly depended on Ramakrishna, and some-times he would follow a dangerous route in the Himalayas in order to test whether the Master was with him or not. One day, some woodcutters stopped him from continuing his journey because there was a bear on his path. "At one time," Gangadhar said, "in a Himalayan village I took shel-ter in a house and spent the first part of the night along with others and their cattle. But at midnight a tiger roared, and they were shivering out of fear. I silently got up and thought: 'What! I am a monk. Am I afraid of death?' I left the house and spent the rest of the night in meditation under a tree."[18]

Today it is relatively easy to travel to Kedarnath and Badrinath by car from Hardwar, but when Gangadhar was a young man it was extremely difficult and indeed dangerous to visit those inaccessible places. To the Hindus, the Himalayas are the abode of God and Vedanta mystics. Mystics love to stay away from people and remain in solitude absorbed in the con-templation of God. The vast mountain range of the Himalayas reminded Gangadhar of the Cosmic God Shiva and his wife Parvati, the daughter of the Himalayas.

Gangadhar later recalled: "When I first saw the entirely snow-clad, huge, and bright peak on which the temple of Kedarnath is situated, I was stupefied. . . . The temple of Kedarnath was on the lap of a huge peak and the entire peak was now revealing itself before me. It was as bright as the glowing morning sun. Thousands of soft rays were emerg-ing from the peak and they were all enveloping and overwhelming me. I thought to myself that I had come to this place of eternal light leav-ing the eternal darkness permanently behind. I could not look at the snow-white peak for long. My eyes became indrawn and the huge peak of the mountain appeared before me as an eternal, uncreated symbol of Shiva. This was not imagination. It was a divine experience. Nowhere else in the entire Himalayas can you see such a resplendent form of Shiva."[19]

From Kedarnath, Gangadhar went to Badrinath, a place sacred to Lord Vishnu, where Sage Vyasa compiled the Vedas and wrote the Puranas, and Shankara wrote his commentaries on the Upanishads, Brahma Sutras, and the Gita. It is a wonderful place to practise austerities. Gangadhar stayed in that spiritual place for some days and then decided to venture to Tibet via the Mana Pass. Shersingh, the head of the Mana village, warned him that the journey was dangerous: many people had died along the way. Before Gangadhar left, however, an official of the Thuling Buddhist Monastery of Tibet came to Mana to do some trading, and Gangadhar became acquainted with him.

Gangadhar started for Tibet with a trader, but partway into the journey, the trader pointed in the direction of the Thuling Monastery and went his own way. It was an arduous journey, and before he could reach the monastery Gangadhar fell unconscious on the ice. The next morning a monk happened to find him and carried him to the monastery. The lamas warmed him, thus saving his life. They discovered in Gangadhar the signs of a monk with unbroken chastity. When they saw the picture of Sri Ramakrishna that he carried with him, one lama asked: "Who is he? These eyes do not belong to an ordinary human being. This person must be a Buddha."[20]

Gangadhar learned the Tibetan language in fifteen days, and stayed there for three months. Observing the lamas' luxury, their love of money, food, and dress, he spoke to them on behalf of the poor. Because of this, the lamas kept him captive in the monastery and tortured him. One lama hit him on his shoulder with a sword in its scabbard. The poor people loved him, and once several of them told the lamas of his sympathy for them. Gangadhar was summoned again. This time the lamas said that they would cut open his jaw or keep him in lifelong imprisonment if he persisted in speaking out for the peasants. But with the help of some friendly traders, Gangadhar ran away. He returned to Badrinath via the Niti Pass.[21]

The next year Gangadhar again went to Tibet, this time to Daba. While going to Lhasa he was arrested. His trader friends had him released. Gangadhar then visited Mount Kailas and Manas Sarovar. The snow-clad Kailas is like a natural image of the Lord Shiva, and Manas Sarovar is a large lake with a fifty-mile circumference. There are eight Buddhist monasteries around the lake. A Buddhist monk taught Gangadhar a posture that helps to preserve body heat. When Gangadhar asked, "What am I supposed to do sitting in this way?" the monk replied, "Do nothing; just empty the mind."[22] On the way to Kailas, Gangadhar was attacked by robbers; he saved his life by giving them fried rice and molasses. On his way back he stopped at the Chekra village and became the guest of a rich gypsy. One day his host saw the picture of Ramakrishna next to Gangadhar's bed; as soon as he touched it, he lost outer consciousness. He asked Gangadhar: "Where did you get this picture? Please give it to me. I shall worship him every day. He is the veritable Buddha. Otherwise why did I become overwhelmed upon touching his picture. An ordinary human being cannot have such a facial expression."[23] Gangadhar again returned to Badrinath via the Niti Pass.

In July 1889 Gangadhar went to Tibet a third time. He planned to go to Lhasa but many of the Tibetans objected to his going, suspecting him of being a British spy. His former friends, too, felt differently, and advised him to leave Tibet as soon as possible. He made three determined efforts to reach Lhasa but failed. Gangadhar returned to Kashmir via Ladakh, where he was arrested by the British government. He was released when it was confirmed that he was a monk and had no political motive. As he was quite familiar with the Tibetan people, language, customs, and religious culture, the British government offered him a consul's post in Tibet, but he refused.[24]

With Swami Vivekananda

In June of 1890, after being away for three and a half years, Gangadhar returned to the Baranagore Monastery. Vivekananda and the other brother disciples were extremely happy to have him back and to hear of his adventurous travel. Swamiji affectionately called him "Ganges," as his name was Ganga-dhar, and sometimes "Ice Father," as his skin had been burned with cold. In the first week of July, Swamiji advised Gangadhar to take final monastic vows before Sri Ramakrishna's picture, in accordance with the Vedantic tradition. Gangadhar then became Swami Akhandananda (which means Undivided Bliss).

Swamiji now wanted to practise austerities in the Himalayas, so in mid-July he left the monastery, taking Akhandananda as his companion. Before their departure, they went to Holy Mother for her blessing. She blessed them, and told Akhandananda: "My son, you know the way of life in the mountains. Please take care of Naren, so that he may not suffer from lack of food."[25]

They first travelled to Bhagalpur, then to Baidyanath, Gazipur, and Varanasi, where they became guests of Pramadadas Mittra. Afterwards they visited Ayodhya and then proceeded to Nainital, in the Himalayas. One day Akhandananda bathed in the ice-cold water of a lake, and as a result he caught a severe cold accompanied by chest pain. From Nainital they went to Almora, where they joined Swami Saradananda and Vaikuntha Nath Sanyal. They planned to settle on the bank of the Ganges with the intention of practising sadhana. Unfortunately, however, Akhandananda was attacked by fever at Karnaprayag, and Swamiji became sick as well. At Srinagar, a doctor examined Akhandananda, diagnosed bronchitis, and advised him to go to the warm climate of the plains as early as possible. The party moved to Dehra Dun, and were joined there by Swami Turiyananda. After arranging for Akhandananda's medical treatment, Swamiji and the others left for Rishikesh to practise spiritual disciplines.

In late 1890, when Akhandananda had slightly improved, it was suggested that he go to Meerut for further treatment. Swamiji had also become very sick in Rishikesh; he and others joined Akhandananda in Meerut, where they became the guests of Dr. Trailokya Nath Ghosh. Swamis Brahmananda and Advaitananda also joined them, and Meerut thus became a second Baranagore Monastery. They lived there for nearly six weeks. While there, Akhandananda would bring books from the Meerut library for Swamiji, and he himself would also study. In the early part of 1891, Swamiji departed alone as an itinerant monk, and the other brothers went off in different directions.

In Northern and Western India

Akhandananda went to Delhi. While sitting on a park bench one day, he thought, "If I meet a devotee of the Master, I shall go to his house; otherwise I shall pass the night here." A Marwari gentleman was seated on the other side of the bench. Out of respect for a monk, he saluted Akhandananda and offered him some money, but Akhandananda would not touch it. Then the Marwari exclaimed, "I have seen only one great soul — Ramakrishna Paramahamsa of Dakshineswar — who completely renounced money." When Akhandananda inquired, he said that he was Lakshminarayan Marwari. He had once offered ten thousand rupees to Sri Ramakrishna, but the Master had refused to accept it. Akhandananda was very happy to meet another devotee of the Master, and introduced himself to him. Then Lakshminarayan joyfully took the swami to his house.[26]

Akhandananda stopped at Agra on his way to Vrindaban, the playground of Krishna. At Agra he met a Sufi who knew the Koran by heart. Akhandananda asked him, "What have you achieved from your lifelong sadhana?" The Sufi replied: "If you put a lemon in salt, it becomes saturated with salt; likewise I am saturated in God. This I have realized."[27]

In March 1891 Akhandananda arrived at Vrindaban and stayed for nearly four months. While at Vrindaban, he had a relapse of bronchitis. In May he moved to Etawah accompanied by Swami Nirmalananda. In Etawah, he studied Sanskrit grammar and Shridhara's commentary on the Gita. On the birthday of Krishna, Akhandananda had the vision of the Master standing near his head, saying, "Hello! Do the people know that I came?" This vision made his heart full of joy.[28] He then learned from a letter that Swamiji was in Jaipur, so he wanted to see him again.

Akhandananda went to Ajmere and there met Mr. Williams, a Christian devotee of the Master. Akhandananda wrote: "He considered Sri Ramakrishna an incarnation of Christ. He told me about his meeting with the Master: 'During my first visit with him, the Master spread a mat for me and another for himself. He said, "Look here, the two mats are an inch apart." "Two mats may be apart," I said, "but there is no distance between our hearts."'"[29] The Master instructed Mr. Williams at that time; he later went to the Himalayas to practise sadhana and there he passed away.

After visiting Abu, Ahmedabad, Baroda, Narmada, Junagad, Prabhas, Dwaraka, and Kachha-Mandavi, Akhandananda started on another journey. He walked eighty miles to see Narayan Sarovar, a holy lake in Gujarat. He was cautioned by the local people that the path was dangerous and haunted by robbers, but Akhandananda prepared himself to face them. He took a young boy as his guide and learned from him the words in Kutch dialect: "Take everything I have, but don't kill me." He had covered fifty miles when he met a pilgrim on the way, and then let the boy continue his own journey.

That part of the country was severely affected by famine and sparsely populated. In the afternoon Akhandananda noticed that four men wearing red turbans were following them diagonally. As the pilgrim was an elderly man, he remained a little behind the swami. When the men who had been following them approached Akhandananda, he asked, "How far is it to Narayan Sarovar?" "Six miles," one of them answered. Then all of a sudden, one of them grabbed his shoulder and thrust him onto the ground. Immediately, the swami said in their language, "Take everything I have, but don't kill me." Another robber then struck his back twice with a bamboo staff; luckily, his cotton shirt and backpack cushioned the blows. Two robbers with daggers in their hands ordered Akhandananda to remove his clothes. He kept on his *kaupin* (loin cloth) and handed everything else over to them. They searched his clothing and bundle, but found no money. They then realized that the swami was a genuine, penniless monk. In the meantime, the pilgrim arrived. Upon seeing the robbers, he fell to the ground, saying, "I am gone." Akhandananda asked the robbers not to hurt the old pilgrim. Knowing that they were poor, the swami offered his warm clothing to the robbers. The ringleader was very touched. He took the dust of the swami's feet and begged for his blessings. He then asked Akhandananda not to tell anyone about this episode, and then all of them disappeared swiftly.[30]

That evening Akhandananda reached Narayan Sarovar and became the guest at the local monastery. The swami had a high temperature, and his body ached terribly. As a result, he could not bathe in the sacred lake. The abbot gave Akhandananda a horse and a guide to accompany him on his journey, and at last he met Swamiji at Mandavi. Although Swamiji wanted to travel alone, they travelled together for a while in Bhuj and Porbandar. Then Swamiji left for Junagad, and Akhandananda moved towards Jamnagar via Kathiawar, Jitpur, Gondal, and Rajkot.

In June 1892 Akhandananda reached Jamnagar, where he lived for a year. There he started his mission — the service of God in man. He lived with a doctor, Kaviraj Manishankar, for four months and studied *Charak-Sushruta Samhita* (ayurvedic medical science). He also went to a Vedic school and learned to chant the four Vedas. He became acquainted with an old abbot of an affluent temple, who offered the swami his position as well as all of his wealth. Akhandananda declined, quoting a Hindi couplet: "The water is pure that flows, and the monk is pure who goes."[31]

Akhandananda then moved to the house of a banker by the name of Shankar Seth; he lived with him for four months. Shankar Seth was a devout and wealthy man, and had no children. Every day he performed worship, practised japam and meditation, and distributed food to the poor and mendicants. He became very fond of the swami and would give to charities according to his advice. When Akhandananda wanted to leave, Shankar asked him to stay and even offered to build a Ramakrishna temple on his land. This was unbearable for Shankar's nephews, who were supposed to inherit their uncle's property. They tried to kill Akhandananda by poisoning his coffee. As a result, the swami suffered from terrible diarrhoea and remained in bed for four days, gravely ill. Eventually, Kaviraj Jhandu Bhat, a local doctor, managed to save his life.

Akhandananda then went to Jhandu Bhat's house. Dr. Bhat was a remarkable physician and a highly spiritual person. He was seventy, yet extremely energetic for his age. He would give free medicine to the poor and would even visit them in their homes. He frequently recited the following two verses, which express his life's philosophy: "O Lord, I do not want any kingdom, nor heavenly pleasure, nor even escape from rebirth. But I do want the affliction of all beings tormented by the miseries of life to cease. O Lord, is there any way whereby I may enter into the hearts of all beings and always share the burden of their sufferings?"[32]

These verses touched Akhandananda's heart, and he came to realize that the highest ideal is to love and serve other human beings. Of course, Akhandananda had always been a loving and caring person, but in Jamnagar, Dr. Bhat roused his dormant inner feeling.

Akhandananda then went to Khetri in Rajasthan — via Baroda, Bhavnagar (where he learned of Swamiji's success in America), Bombay, and Abu, where he became the guest of Raja Ajit Singh, Vivekananda's disciple. Akhandananda lived in Rajasthan for nearly eight months. He observed the pitiful condition of the masses as well as the luxury of a handful of rulers and rich landlords. His heart melted for the downtrodden, and he drew his concerns to the local rulers' attention, asking them to ameliorate the poor condition of the masses. He wrote a letter to Swamiji in America, asking him for guidance.

Swamiji replied in early 1894: "Go from door to door amongst the poor and lower classes of the town of Khetri and teach them religion. Also, let them have oral lessons on geography and such other subjects. No good will come of sitting idle and having princely dishes, and saying 'Ramakrishna, O Lord!' unless you can do some good to the poor.... It is preferable to live on grass for the sake of doing good to others. The ochre robe is not for enjoyment. It is the banner of heroic work.... The poor, the illiterate, the ignorant, the afflicted — let these be your God. Know that service to these alone is the highest religion."[33]

Swamiji's encouragement pushed him further, and in 1894 Akhandananda began his campaign against poverty. He found that the root of all suffering was the appalling ignorance of the masses; hence, education became his prime objective. He moved from door to door impressing upon the residents of Khetri the need to educate their children. By his strenuous efforts he succeeded in raising the enrollment of the local high school from 80 to 257, as well as improving the teaching staff. He next visited the villages around Khetri and started five primary schools for the village boys. The maharaja of Khetri afterwards made an annual grant of 5,000 rupees for the promotion of education in his territory. At Akhandananda's request, the Sanskrit School at Khetri was converted into a Vedic School; he also raised money to buy books for the poor students. In addition he induced Maharaja Ajit Singh to allow his poorer subjects to see him on *durbar* (official reception) days, so that they could have direct access to their king.

People listen to the advice of the person who harbours no ill feelings and has no ulterior motives. Akhandananda was so bold that he did not hesitate to correct even the habits of kings. He later reminisced: "The maharaja of Khetri would rise late. One day I told him that those who eat too much and rise late can never attain prosperity. From then on the maharaja would rise early — even earlier than I. I would get up and find him standing and smiling at me. Some days he would be walking on the roof; and some days I would find him reading in the library with the help of a light."[34]

After his stay in Khetri, Akhandananda visited Jaipur, Chittor, Udaipur, and many other villages of Rajasthan. He asked the local rulers to start schools, distribute food among the poor, and support cottage industries. Some rich landlords would lend money to the farmers and then demand high interest. They did not like the swami's revolutionary ideas. Even the king of Udaipur became upset when Akhandananda refused to take food from the royal priest unless the poor people were fed first. Some of these enraged people threatened his life. Akhandananda was undaunted, however, and continued his mission. He succeeded in starting several schools and performing other philanthropic activities in Rajasthan. Akhandananda had wanted to lead an austere and contemplative life, but divine providence ordained that under his monastic garb, he would instead become a patriot, statesman, and philanthropist.

In September 1894 Swamiji wrote to his Madrasi disciples from America regarding the pioneering spirit of Sri Ramakrishna's disciples. He remarked, mentioning Akhandananda: "Look at the handful of young men called into existence by the divine touch of Sri Ramakrishna's feet. They have preached the message from Assam to Sindh, from the Himalayas to Cape Comorin. They have crossed the Himalayas at a height of twenty thousand feet, over snow and ice on foot, and penetrated into the mysteries of Tibet. They have begged their bread, covered themselves with rags; they have been persecuted, followed by the police, kept in prison, and at last set free when the Government was convinced of their innocence. They are now twenty. Make them two thousand tomorrow."[35]

Back to Alambazar Monastery

Towards the end of 1895 Akhandananda returned to the the Alambazar Monastery via Delhi, Etawah, Allahabad, and Varanasi. In 1892, the Ramakrishna Math had been moved from Baranagore to Alambazar, which is very close to Dakshineswar. It was a haunted house like Baranagore, therefore the rent was only ten rupees per month. The brother disciples were happy to have Akhandananda with them again after five years. The monastery was in poor financial condition. Akhandananda later recalled: "In the monastery we ate rice, lentils, and a hotchpotch vegetable curry. At night we ate *chapatis* [flattened bread] without butter."[36] But because their minds were filled with divine bliss, the hardship did not disturb them.

Monastic indolence is terrible; and Akhandananda was a man of action. He could not tolerate a monk who forgot his ideal, indulging in eating, sleeping, and gossiping. Akhandananda had so much energy and so much love for the Master that he travelled for nearly three weeks in remote villages to collect *nageswar champa*, a favourite flower of Sri Ramakrishna. During this trip he taught the villagers sanitation, health care, and so on. Akhandananda's gigantic heart cried for the poor, the destitute, and the sick. One day, when he was on his way to bathe in the Ganges, he found an old woman suffering from cholera. He cleaned her unconscious body, changed her clothing, and then sent her to the hospital.

In March 1896 the annual Ramakrishna festival was held at the Dakshineswar temple garden, and the devotees planned two kinds of prasad — one for the poor and another for themselves. Akhandananda had a democratic attitude and could not bear such an inequitable arrangement. He complained about this to Swami Brahmananda, who then ordered that one kind of prasad be prepared for everybody.

Akhandananda was a great organizer. While in Bengal, he met many pandits, educators, and political leaders, and consulted with them about starting a Vedic school. In 1897, when Swami Vivekananda returned from the West, Akhandananda worked hard to arrange a reception for him. He went to Satish Giri, the abbot of the Tarakeshwar Monastery and asked him to join Swamiji's reception, but he declined because Vivekananda was not a brahmin. When Akhandananda reminded him that Swamiji had been welcomed by the Shankaracharya of Sringeri Math and other religious orders of South India, Satish Giri apologized and explained to the swami that he had no time as he was occupied with other affairs.

In Alambazar, Akhandananda suffered from malaria. One day while he was sick, he had a spiritual experience. Before this, he had felt that the nondualistic experience "I am the Atman" is greater than the five kinds of dualistic relationships with God. While Akhandananda lay ill, however, he had the following vision: He saw the luminous form of baby Krishna in his room, and Krishna's mother, Yashoda, appeared from Akhandananda's own body. The baby was begging for food, so Yashoda began to sing and play with her little darling in order to pacify him. Sri Ramakrishna then appeared and said, "Look, what a wonderful scene!" Akhandananda joyfully exclaimed: "I don't care for nirvana, Master. This is wonderful! I don't care if I am born hundreds of times in my present state of mind."[37]

After that experience Akhandananda became imbued with the idea of being the mother, with all beings as his children. He recorded in his memoirs: "One sultry day some brothers were asleep in the front room of the monastery. I couldn't sleep because of the heat. Others were perspiring and their sheets were wet. I got up and began to fan them with great joy. Their perspiration dried; and they slept peacefully. But what a wonder! My body also became cooled within half an hour. I was thrilled to realize that I had developed the capacity to feel others' happiness and misery."[38]

In Murshidabad

In March 1897 Vivekananda went to Darjeeling for rest, and Akhandananda left for Navadwip — the birthplace of Chaitanya — and Murshidabad, an important historical site. He was thinking of returning to the Himalayas for the remainder of his days after seeing some of the notable places in Bengal. In Murshidabad district, however, the swami encountered a terrible famine. He saw death and dying everywhere. In the villages, he saw emaciated cattle and their herdsmen. At night he slept in a shop at Dadpur village, which belonged to the local ruler.

Akhandananda reminisced: "Early one morning I washed my hands and feet in the Ganges and was approaching the bazar when I discovered a Muslim girl of about fourteen, clad in dirty rags, weeping bitterly. She held at her waist an earthen pitcher, the bottom of which had given way." When the swami inquired the cause of her grief, she said: "Father, there is famine, and we have nothing at home to eat. At home we have only this pitcher for carrying water and two earthen cooking pots. There is no second vessel to carry water. My mother will beat me, so I am crying out of fear."[39]

Akhandananda happened to have four annas in his pocket. He took the girl to a shop and bought a pitcher for her as well as some puffed rice. Before he got his balance of three annas from the shopkeeper, he was encircled by a dozen children crying for food. He bought more puffed rice with the remaining coins and distributed it among the hungry children. At night he decided to leave that place as soon as possible, because he felt completely helpless and unable to relieve the poor. As he was leaving the village in the morning, a middle-aged woman approached him, saying: "Father, Gaya Vaishnavi, an old woman, is dying. Please do something for her." The swami expressed his inability to do anything, but later relented at her insistence. He went to see this old woman, who was suffering from diarrhoea and covered in filth. To save her life, the swami rushed to Jivan Krishna Das, the landlord of the village, and arranged daily food for her. He even begged a piece of cloth from a clerk for that woman. The old woman expressed her gratitude with tearful eyes, "Father, you must have been my son in my previous life."[40] Akhandananda replied: "Why your previous life? I am your son in this life."

Akhandananda then started towards Behrampur, the district town of Murshidabad. He stopped for one night at Bhabta village. In the morning, when he was about to leave, he heard a voice say: "Where will you go? You have many things to do here."[41] He heard the voice thrice, so did not proceed further. A teacher of the Bhabta school invited the swami to attend the Annapurna (the goddess of food) worship in Mahula, an adjacent village. While there, he fervently prayed to the Mother to save the lives of the poor people. Akhandananda was then offered a room in the temple complex, and thought deeply about his future plans. He began giving classes on the Gita to the villagers, and they fed him.

One day Akhandananda was invited by a brahmin for lunch; but in the morning when he learned that a farmer's family had been starving for two days, he began to cry to the Master, closing the door of his room. The host waited outside for a long time. At last the swami came out and said that he would accept his food provided he would send some food to this poor family. The host then agreed.

Akhandananda later wrote: "I carried a picture of Sri Ramakrishna with me. Every day after my bath in the Ganges, I would offer some flowers before it and pray to the Master with tears for the famine-stricken people. Thus I prayed every morning and evening. One day there was a response. I heard the Master's voice say: 'Wait and see what happens.'"[42]

On 15 May 1897 Akhandananda started famine relief work in Mahula and several other villages in the Murshidabad district. It was the first organized relief work of the Ramakrishna Mission which had been started by Swami Vivekananda on 1 May 1897 in Calcutta. Akhandananda wrote letters to his brother disciples in Calcutta and Madras requesting financial help. He wrote in detail about the tragic scenes of the dying people. The response was immediate: Swamiji sent two monks to help him. Seeing the appeal for relief in the newspapers, the Mahabodhi Society and some generous people of Madras and Calcutta sent money to him. Mr. E. V. Levinge, the district magistrate, and Mr. Panton, the district judge, also came forward to assist in Akhandananda's relief operation.

On 15 June 1897 Vivekananda wrote to him from Almora: "I am getting detailed reports of you and getting more and more delighted. It is that sort of work which can conquer the world.... Work, work, work, even unto death! Those that are weak must make themselves great workers, great heroes — never mind money, it will drop from the heavens.... It is the heart, the heart that conquers, not the brain. Books and learning, yoga and meditation and illumination — all are but dust compared with love. It is love that gives you the supernatural powers, love that gives you bhakti [devotion], love that gives illumination, and love, again, that leads to emancipation. This indeed is worship, worship of the Lord in the human tabernacle."[43]

Swamiji's letter increased Akhandananda's spirit of service a thousandfold. He later reminisced: "I read his letters over and over again and gained fresh strength within me. *Mantram va sadhayeyam shariram va patayeyam* — I shall either carry out my purpose or lay down my body — this mantram filled my heart. Oh, into what a current of activity did I then submerge myself!"[44]

Akhandananda's activities were so vast and far-ranging that it is almost impossible to record all of them. One day there was an earthquake, which was soon followed by an outbreak of cholera. The more Providence tested him, the more he continued his relief work. Akhandananda eventually opened an orphanage and started a school for the children. He nursed the sick, and taught the villagers the basics of hygiene. He also continued his preaching and distributed the *Teachings of Sri Ramakrishna* among the villagers.

At Shivnagar and Sargachi

When the relief operation in Mahula was over, Akhandananda decided to open a permanent orphanage. The Murshidabad district magistrate promised to give him financial help for this project. Madhusundari Barman, a rich landowner, was impressed with Akhandananda's work, so she donated one and a half acres of land to him for the ashrama, and offered him her office building in Shivnagar, near Sargachi, to use temporarily. Sargachi village is situated on Krishnanagar Road, six miles south of Behrampur.

In 1898 the Ramakrishna Monastery had been moved from Alambazar to Nilambar Babu's garden house at Belur. On Tuesday, 22 February 1898, Akhandananda arrived there to attend the festival of Sri Ramakrishna's birth anniversary. He carried from Behrampur two *pantuas* (a sweet made of cheese fried with butter and soaked in syrup) which weighed sixty-four pounds, and had been presented by a rich devotee. Swamiji saw those large sweets and asked him to offer them to the Master in the shrine.

Vivekananda then told a disciple: "Look, what a great hero he [Akhandananda] is in work! He is unaware of fear and death, and doggedly does his work 'for the good of many and the welfare of all.'" The disciple commented: "Sir, that power must have come to him as a result of great austerities." Swamiji replied: "It is true, power comes through practising austerities; again, working for others is also austerity. The karma yogis consider work itself as a part of austerity. As on the one hand, the practice of austerity intensifies altruistic feelings in an aspirant and actuates him to unselfish work, so also the pursuit of work for the sake of others purifies one's heart, and that leads him to the realization of the supreme Atman."[45]

It is worth mentioning how the disciples of the Master lived together in the monastery with much joy and amusement. Akhandananda later narrated this particular incident: "One day in Belur, Swamiji was telling the stories of his itinerant days and I was supplying the forgotten events to him. He scolded me: 'Don't talk too much. Keep quiet and meditate.' So I obeyed him. In the meantime, he talked about a fish in the Himalayas, and asked me, 'Hello, how big was that fish?' With my eyes closed, I raised my two hands and showed the size of that fish. All burst into laughter."[46]

Akhandananda also told another story that illustrates how strict Swamiji was about the monastery routine: "One night there was a discussion on various topics of Vedanta, such as reincarnation and whether a human soul is born in the subhuman plane or not. The brothers took sides in the debate and Swamiji became the umpire. He was smiling and listening, and sometimes he supplied points to the losing side. It continued till 2:00 a.m. Everybody went to sleep. But then at 4:00 a.m., Swamiji asked me to ring the bell so that the monks could go to the shrine for meditation. I said that they had gone to sleep only a couple of hours earlier, and that he should let them sleep a little more. Swamiji then firmly said: 'What! Because they have gone to sleep at two o'clock should they get up at six o'clock? Give me the bell. I will ring it. Did we start this monastery for sleeping?' When I rang the bell loudly, all got up yelling at me. But when they saw Swamiji smiling behind me, they silently followed the routine."[47]

After working hard for a year, Akhandananda fell sick at the Belur Monastery. On 30 March 1898, after he had recovered, he went with Swamiji to Darjeeling for a change. While they were gone, a plague broke out in Calcutta. In the first week of May, Swamiji and Akhandananda returned to Calcutta. There was terrible panic and chaos in Calcutta. In an attempt to comfort the people and plague victims, Swamiji wrote a pamphlet; Akhandananda distributed copies at the risk of his life. Sister Nivedita, Swamiji's Irish disciple, and Swami Sadananda also did extensive relief work in Calcutta. When the epidemic subsided, Swamiji left for Almora and Akhandananda returned to Sargachi.

The doers of good always encounter obstacles, but God gives them patience, perseverance, and strength. The more the current of a river is obstructed, the more vigorously it flows. Some selfish, rich people of Sargachi village could not bear Akhandananda's popularity. They put pressure on him to leave the place; they wrote adversely to Vivekananda about him; they even brought a legal suit against him. Swamiji said to him, "Don't be upset listening to public criticism."[48] It is said: "Criticisms are like ornaments to a pioneer."

Akhandananda faced terrible poverty in Sargachi. He wrote letters to some of his old acquaintances asking for financial help. Pramadadas Mittra of Varanasi wrote back to him mentioning that it is better for a monk to travel, study, and practise meditation and japam than to get involved in social service. On 19 October 1898 Akhandananda replied:

I am delighted that you have reminded me about my olden days. Those days are gone, and now a new era has sprung up. The Atman never changes, but life changes. Now I don't enjoy travelling anymore.

When I first went to the Himalayas, I was a different person. Now I wonder upon seeing myself. At that time I would avoid seeing human beings, and leaving the village, I loved to live in the secluded caves of the Himalayas surrounded by ferocious animals. In this way I lived for some years. Now I see God living in all human beings, and I have realized that service to man is service to God. God, as it were, is whispering in my ears, "Verily these human beings are the Vedic sages; they are divine incarnations like Rama and Krishna — they are everything."[49]

Where sincerity, unselfishness, and love exist, God sends help. A few largehearted local people — including some European officials, some silk merchants, and Maharaja Manindra Chandra Nandi of Kashimbazar — came forward to help Akhandananda build a permanent ashrama and orphanage. Akhandananda was a silent and unpretentious worker, so without caring for the city's fanfare, he continued to worship his living gods in the remote village. Putting aside the monastic ochre cloth, he put on knee-length pants, and tied his head with a handkerchief, and tilled the ground like other farmers. He lived on a farmer's diet — mixing lime and salt with rice soaked in water. He grew fruits, flowers, vegetables, and even cotton. Like Gandhi, he started to weave cloth on a spinning wheel. He arranged regular, practical schooling for his orphan boys, and at night he taught the illiterate adult villagers. He gave medicine to the sick people. When one of his orphans died, he cried like a loving mother who had lost her son.

The Passing Events

In October 1899 Akhandananda was invited by Raja Yogendranarayan, the ruler of Lalgola, to attend Durga Puja in his palace and also to distribute 15,000 pieces of cloth among the poor. On the second day of Mother's worship, Akhandananda learned of a devastating flood in the Bhagalpur district of Bihar. He immediately left for Bhagalpur, reaching it the next day. He was impressed by the relief work of Mr. Caming, the district magistrate of Bhagalpur. Mr. Caming asked Akhandananda to conduct relief work in the Ghogha area. The swami organized the local landlords, lawyers, teachers, and students to face the catastrophe. Swami Sadananda was sent from Belur Math, and the public generously helped the effort with money, food, and clothing. Akhandananda operated the relief work for two and a half months, serving fifty villages.

Akhandananda wrote to Swamiji, who was then in America, mentioning the relief work. On 21 February 1900 Swamiji replied from California: "I am very glad to receive your letter and go through the details of news. Learning and wisdom are superfluities, the surface glitter merely, but it is the heart that is the seat of all power. It is not in the brain but in the heart that the Atman, possessed of knowledge, power, and activity, has Its seat. 'The nerves of the heart are a hundred and one.' The chief nerve-centre near the heart, called the sympathetic ganglia, is where the Atman has Its citadel. The more heart you will be able to manifest, the greater will be the victory you achieve."[50]

Vivekananda returned to India in December 1900. He passed away a year and a half later, on 4 July 1902. When Akhandananda heard the news, he rushed to Belur Math. He cried for Swamiji and lived in the monastery with his brother disciples for a few days. He was depressed and felt emptiness all around. On the seventh day after Swamiji's passing, he went to Calcutta to meet Sharat Chandra Chakrabarty, a disciple of Swamiji. Later, Akhandananda told Miss Josephine MacLeod, an American devotee: "I have seen Swamiji after his passing away as clearly as I see you now, otherwise I could not live. Separation was so painful! I was going to commit suicide but was prevented by Swamiji. He caught my hand when I was about to jump under the running tram."[51] This vision filled his heart with joy and inspiration.

Akhandananda returned to his ashrama. He managed the orphanage and the ashrama activities from the Shivnagar office building for over twelve years. The land that had been donated was not sufficient for the ashrama, so in August 1912 he bought about thirteen acres of land in Sargachi village. According to the swami's plan, some rooms were constructed with thatched roofs in order to save money, and then in March 1913 the ashrama was permanently moved to the new location. Akhandananda planted flowering plants and fruit trees all around and made the ashrama like an ancient hermitage. Along with education, the swami concentrated on improving the agricultural and industrial activities amongst the villagers. The ashrama ran a full-fledged industrial school, teaching weaving, sewing, carpentry, and sericulture, which was the pride of the locality. One room of the ashrama was allotted for a library and charitable dispensary, and another room for the shrine. In the beginning he was not in favour of building a temple, as he was convinced that he was worshipping the living gods. Later, however, at his devotees' request he gave consent to build a temple for Sri Ramakrishna.

Akhandananda was a self-made man. He was a voracious reader, a linguist, a powerful speaker, a humourous conversationalist, and a good writer. His memoirs (*Smriti Katha*) and travel accounts (*Tibbater Pathe Himalaye*) were published serially in *Udbodhan* and *Basumati*, and later in book form. In 1906 when Abhedananda returned from America, he wanted Akhandananda to go with him to the West, but the latter declined. He preferred worshipping the poor living gods in the village rather than preaching Vedanta. He was respectful of the patriotism of Matsini and Garibaldi of Italy, and he was inspired by Florence Nightingale's and Booker T. Washington's spirit of service. He also had tremendous appreciation for the Indian national leaders, such as Mahatma Gandhi,

Balgangadhar Tilak, and Chittaranjan Das; he admired their self-sacrifice and service to the motherland.

Ramakrishna never cared for narrow, bigoted, closed-minded people, and his disciples resembled their Master in this respect. They continually learned wherever they found anything good, beneficial, and uplifting. Miss MacLeod once said to Akhandananda: "People say Swamiji was a great teacher, but I and many others knew him to be a great learner. He learnt from all, so he conquered all. He would always learn something, so he was always fresh, never monotonous — never repeating the same thing."[52]

Akhandananda also learned continually, and as a result he had encyclopedic knowledge. He encouraged the monks to keep diaries. He said: "If a monk travels in the Himalayas or any holy places, he should write in his diary vivid descriptions of those places, and also record the conversations of holy people. At the end of the year, all monks should deposit those diaries at the monastery, and some important things from their records could be published in the magazines of the Order. It would enhance the knowledge of the monks as well as the public."[53]

Swami Brahmananda passed away on 10 April 1922. On 2 May 1922 Swami Shivananda became the president, and Swami Akhandananda the vice-president, of the Ramakrishna Order. One day in Belur Math, Akhandananda noticed a monk reciting the Gita, the Chandi, and the Upanishads after his bath. A desire arose in his mind to follow the routine of the monastery. Suddenly he heard the Master telling him: "I have you and you have me. I pervade everything in this monastery. It is not necessary for you to chant in that manner. Eat, relax, move around, and have some fun. You will not have to supervise anything here." When Akhandananda narrated his experience to Shivananda, the latter remarked, "You are right."[54]

A monk once wrote about Akhandananda's childlike nature: "One day Gangadhar Maharaj came to the Udbodhan Office. Everyone began to pester him, 'Maharaj, you must feed us *rasagollas* [cheese balls soaked in syrup].' 'Where is my money?' he said. 'How can I feed you rasagollas?' But one of the young monks knew he had some money hidden in the cloth around his waist; so he put his hand there and touched his coins. At this Akhandananda dragged him to Saradananda in the adjacent room, and said: 'Look at this! What training have you given your boys? They want to extract a treat of rasagollas from me.' 'Very good!' answered Saradananda. 'Since they want it, why don't you feed them?' 'I see,' exclaimed Gangadhar Maharaj, 'you are also taking their side.' In fact he had brought that money to feed the monks with sweets. He was acting that way just to have some fun with us. He was also happy when we pestered him in that way."[55]

In April 1926 the first convention of the Ramakrishna Math and Mission was held in Belur Math. Some direct disciples of the Master along with other monks and devotees discussed the past, present, and future of the Order. Akhandananda gave a talk on 7 April during the final session of the convention:

The convention closes its sessions today. This is therefore the last occasion to speak to you in assembly. The wonderful life of the god-man Sri Ramakrishna, the magnetic spell of whose hallowed name and teachings has drawn you all together here, the undying stories of this unique manifestation, his unprecedented renunciation, his unfathomed love, sympathy and toleration, and above all his infinite moods of spirituality — these and such other aspects of the Master's life have been dwelt upon and interpreted by so many speakers in so many ways and will continue to be so done for how long who can say! But in thinking of him the idea that comes uppermost in my mind today is that the moment one saw him, one became transported to a spiritual elevation before which all distinctions and differences vanished; and even now if one could sincerely meditate upon the life or seriously think over and understand the true spirit of his harmony and toleration, one could no longer afford to cherish any bigoted or controversial ideas.

Sri Ramakrishna was never for a moment heard to denounce anyone because of his religious belief or profession if only he were sincere. He took man at his best and always gave him a lift from the plane where he stood. . . . If there was anything which he was never tired of denouncing most emphatically, it was hypocrisy. I remember one day a man denied the idea of the existence of God before him. And mark you what the Master, who was ever so deeply absorbed in ecstatic communion with the Divine Mother, said to him in reply: "Well, who told you that there is God? I would not ask you to believe in any such idea. But then, you cannot with reason deny that there is a Power working behind the universe. One may attribute any name to it, but it remains there all the same. Why not take it in that spirit and try to know more intimately what you believe in. Know this and be happy. To be sure, mere belief cannot give rest to your inner cravings. Knowledge — true knowledge of the mysteries of this phenomenal existence — alone can do that."

The same attitude of universal tolerance and sympathy for all irrespective of their religious beliefs and social or spiritual standing, we find manifested in Swami Vivekananda. And upon us also, the humble disciples of the Master, the full implications of this idea began gradually to dawn. The Master and Swamiji are really one; the one spirit as it were, manifested in twin personalities. What we find in the Master in the form of a seed, becomes fully developed in Swamiji. Swamiji is to Sri Ramakrishna what the commentary is to the *Vedanta Sutras*. The one is complementary to the other. They are in fact inseparable — the obverse and reverse of the same coin....

Sri Ramakrishna one day cried aloud from the housetop for those young spiritual seekers who were to come to him and pour forth their lives' offerings on the altar of his service, and they came. But that cry has not ended there; it is still ringing through the air and shall continue for aeons. Many have come after that, many are still coming, and many more will come in the future.[56]

Towards the End

In 1934, after the passing away of Shivananda, Akhandananda became the president of the Ramakrishna Order. From then on he lived in both Belur Math and Sargachi; but spent most of his time in Sargachi. In January 1934 there was a devastating earthquake in Bihar and many people were killed. In April Akhandananda went to inspect the Ramakrishna Mission's relief work there. His presence raised the morale of the people and he also inspired the monks to serve the afflicted as God. He returned to Belur Math on 10 May, and then went to Sargachi in the last week of May.

As president of the Ramakrishna Order, Akhandananda initiated a large number of people. On 4 November 1934 he went to Bombay and then Nagpur, where he inspired many seekers of God. Once somebody asked the swami: "On whom shall I meditate first — the form of the guru or the form of the *Ishta* [Chosen Deity]? Where shall I concentrate?" Akhandananda replied: "Sri Ramakrishna is the guru and he is the Ishta. There is no first or second about it. The heart is the best place for concentration. Think that you are seeing him face to face. He is seated in your heart. Those who are initiated can think of their own guru in the beginning if it helps them. There is no hard and fast rule. The only thing needful is constant recollectedness of the Lord."[57] Another time a devotee asked him if he had seen God. Akhandananda humbly replied, "Yes, while I was in the Himalayas, I saw God face to face."[58]

At the end of November Akhandananda returned to Calcutta, and then on 3 December 1934 he went to Sargachi. Sri Ramakrishna's centenary celebration was scheduled for February 1936. On 19 January 1936 Miss Josephine MacLeod went to the Sargachi Ashrama and said to the swami, "Give me your message for the coming centenary." Swami Akhandananda replied: "I have no message of my own. But I have received this message from the Lord: 'I am Infinite and Eternal. What is my centenary?'" Miss MacLeod said, "All right, I shall take this message with me."[59]

However, the Belur Math authorities repeatedly wrote to Akhandananda to send a message, as the celebration was only a few days off. They reminded him that the president's message was extremely important for Ramakrishna's centenary. Akhandananda later described how he wrote the centenary message: "That message was dictated by the Master. I was sleeping at night. The Master spoke from my heart: 'Since they are asking you so much, why don't you write this message: Truly, who can observe my centenary? I am Infinite and Eternal.' I couldn't wait for morning to write. I am an old man. Lest I forget, I picked up a pen and pad and wrote down the message."[60]

On 23 February 1936 Akhandananda arrived at Belur Math, and on 24 February he gave the inaugural message of the centenary. The following is the conclusion of the message, translated from Bengali:

The dawn of the New Age is breaking over the world — the blessed day that will illumine our hearts with the glory of its effulgence is at hand.

Knowingly or unknowingly the human race is moving forward along the path of liberation inspired by Sri Ramakrishna's message of the harmony of all religions and by his unique realization of the essential oneness of karma [action], jnana [knowledge], bhakti [devotion], and yoga [psychic control]. The day is not far off when the whole world will witness the establishment of a universal kingdom of peace, and when in loving response to the call of the Master, all people, forgetting their religious differences, will unite together and glorify the Master's message, "As many faiths, so many paths." Then only will the meridian light of the Master's advent illumine the hearts of humanity.

May the citizens of the world, on this blessed day, understand the meaning of the Master's coming and be hallowed. This and this alone is my fervent prayer. Peace, peace, and peace be unto all.[61]

Akhandananda stayed in Belur for a month. His body was feeble and it was difficult for him to even walk. A doctor examined him and found that he had diabetes. Nevertheless, he returned to Sargachi and continued his spiritual ministry. Akhandananda loved his village ashrama dearly and never liked to be away from it for long. However, he cherished a desire to give up his body in Belur Math, where Vivekananda had installed the relics of the Master. The swami's wish was providentially fulfilled.

On 5 February 1937, a cable was sent to Belur Math to inform the monks of Akhandananda's serious condition. Two monks arrived from Belur Math the next day, and, with the local doctor's approval, decided to take the swami to Calcutta for treatment. As Swami Akhandananda was carried on a stretcher to the railway station, some farmers on the street tearfully said to him, "Father, get well soon and come back." Akhandananda blessed them with a smile. The train left at 5:00 p.m.; he fell unconscious on the way. The train arrived at Calcutta at 11:00 p.m. He was first taken to Udbodhan by ambulance, and then to Belur Math at midnight via Dakshineswar. His bed was made ready next to Vivekananda's room. Several doctors tried their utmost to save this great soul. At last, at 3:07 p.m. on 7 February 1937, Swami Akhandananda passed away at the age of 72. His body was cremated on the bank of the Ganges, close to Swamiji's temple in Belur Math.

To see God in all beings is the culmination of the Vedantic experience. Swami Akhandananda had that experience, so he served all as God. A few years before his passing away, the swami told a monk his life's philosophy: "The Master has still kept me alive for his work. Distribute your Self among others and bring other souls within yourself. You will see how much joy you will get from it. On the other hand if you are always busy about yourself, you will be entangled within yourself, you will kill your Self, and you will die. [Not knowing the Self is akin to suicide or death.] The more you disseminate yourself among the people, the more you will attain bliss and that will lead you to Self-realization."[62]

16

ॐ

SWAMI VIJNANANANDA

S ri Ramakrishna was a spiritual phenomenon, and his spirituality
manifested in his spiritual longing and samadhi, in his singing
and dancing, in his conversations and stories, in his action and
behaviour, and even in his fun and frivolities. Many people consider
Ramakrishna to be an avatar or a great religious teacher; but it is also
interesting to observe his personal life behind the public gaze.

Needless to say, people would be surprised if they saw Ramakrishna
wrestling with a young man in his room at the Dakshineswar temple garden. But it was not unusual for the disciples of Ramakrishna to have an
ordinary situation turn into an extraordinary experience through the
influence of the Master. It is amazing to see how the Master transmitted
spiritual power to his disciples even in a playful way. Swami Vijnanananda
vividly narrated one of his dramatic and unconventional encounters with
Ramakrishna:

> I felt Sri Ramakrishna's room vibrating with a tangible atmosphere of
> peace, and the devotees present seemed to be listening in blissful
> absorption to the words that poured from the Master's lips. I don't
> recall what he said, but I experienced tremendous joy within. I sat
> there for a long time, my whole attention concentrated on Sri Rama-
> krishna. He did not say anything to me, nor did I ask him anything.
> Then one by one the devotees took their leave, and suddenly I found
> myself alone with him. The Master was looking at me intently. I
> thought it was time for me to depart, so I prostrated before him. As I
> stood up to go, he asked: "Can you wrestle? Come, let me see how well

SWAMI VIJNANANANDA, C.1925

you wrestle!" With these words he stood up, ready to grapple with me. I was surprised at this challenge. I thought to myself, "What kind of holy man is this?" But I replied, "Yes, of course I can wrestle."

Sri Ramakrishna came closer, smiling. He caught hold of my arms and began to shove me, but I was a strong, muscular young man and I pushed him back to the wall. He was still smiling and holding me with a strong grip. Gradually I felt a sort of electric current coming out of his hands and entering into me. That touch made me completely helpless. I lost all my physical strength. I went into ecstasy, and the hair of my body stood on end. Releasing me, the Master said with a smile, "Well, you are the winner." With those words, he sat down on his cot again. I was speechless. Wave after wave of bliss engulfed my whole being. I was pondering the fact that the Master had not won physically but his spiritual power had completely subdued me. Some time passed. Then the Master got up from his seat. Patting me gently on the back, he said: "Come here often. It is not enough to come once." Then he offered me some sweets as prasad, and I returned to Calcutta. For days the spell of that intoxicating joy lingered, and I realized that he had transmitted spiritual power to me."[1]

Ramakrishna later said of Swami Vijnanananda, "He wrestled with Krishna in his previous incarnation; he is not an ordinary person."[2]

Swami Vijnanananda's premonastic name was Hari Prasanna Chattopadhyay. He was born on Friday, 30 October 1868 in Etawah, Uttar Pradesh, where his father, Taraknath Chattopadhyay, worked in the commissariat of the British government. Hari Prasanna was the eldest of six children, two boys and four girls. As Taraknath's job transferred him to different places, the children lived with their mother, Nakuleswari Devi, at Varanasi, where Hari Prasanna began his primary education. In 1879 his mother moved with her children to their ancestral home at Belgharia, near Dakshineswar. Hari Prasanna entered the Hare School in Calcutta, and in 1882 he passed the Entrance examination.

From his childhood, Hari Prasanna had a religious temperament and a tremendous passion for truth. Once, when he was about fourteen, his mother falsely accused him of something and scolded him. He protested vehemently, and when he failed to convince his mother of his innocence he tore off his sacred thread and cried out, "If I tell a lie, I am not a brahmin." Nakuleswari Devi was taken aback, and became afraid that some misfortune might befall the family. Strangely enough, the very next day a cable from Quetta (Afghanistan) brought the news of his father's death. His mother, grief-stricken, said to Hari Prasanna, "See the result of your curse."[3]

Very little is known about his early life; however, Hari Prasanna once narrated the following incident from his boyhood: One day he heard a gun shot in the bamboo grove behind their house in Belgharia. He rushed to the grove and found a wounded monkey lying on the ground. He distinctly heard the monkey chant twice "Rama, Rama"; then, with folded hands it died. Hari Prasanna believed that monkeys are the devotees of Ramachandra and that they die chanting Lord Rama's name.[4]

Meetings with Sri Ramakrishna

Hari Prasanna was only seven years old when he first saw Sri Ramakrishna. He later recalled:

I first saw Sri Ramakrishna in 1875 at Belgharia in the garden house of Jaygopal Sen. The Master came to visit Keshab Sen in that retreat house. I was then a little boy. I was playing with my friends and then just by chance saw the Master there. At that time the paths of the garden house were covered with red brick dust. Many people came. The Master was seated in a room. After seeing him, I returned to my home nearby.[5]

The second time Hari Prasanna saw him, Sri Ramakrishna was immersed in samadhi at Dewan Govinda Mukhopadhyay's house in Belgharia. He later described the scene:

A young man [Narendra] was singing a devotional song, "*Jai, Jai Dayamaya, Jai Dayamaya*" [Victory to the compassionate Lord, Victory to the compassionate Lord]. Sri Ramakrishna was standing in the centre of the group, and another young man [Baburam] was holding him so that he would not fall. The Master was completely oblivious of his surroundings. He wore a white cloth. His face shone with a heavenly lustre and a smile played on his lips. His teeth were visible, and there was such a joyful expression on his face that it seemed as if it would crack — like a cracked melon! His eyes seemed to be gazing at something, and he appeared to be immersed in an ocean of bliss.[6]

Another thing that struck me has remained imprinted in my memory forever. From the base of the Master's spine right up to his head the whole column had become inflated like a thick rope. And the energy that rose upward towards the brain seemed to be spreading its hood and swaying its head like a snake dancing in joy.[7]

In 1883 Hari Prasanna entered Saint Xavier's College in Calcutta, and Sharat Chakrabarty (later, Swami Saradananda) and Ramananda

Chattopadhyay (later, the editor of *Pravasi*) were his classmates. On 26 November 1883 he and Sharat went by boat to see Sri Ramakrishna at Dakshineswar with another classmate, Barada Pal. Arriving in the afternoon, they saw the Master briefly as he was about to leave for Mani Mallik's house in Calcutta. However, the Master invited them to come to Mani Mallik's residence too, so they returned to Calcutta by boat. Hari Prasanna attended the festival at Mani Mallik's and returned home late that evening. He later described what happened: "My mother scolded me. When she heard that I had gone to see Sri Ramakrishna, she said: 'My goodness! You went to that crazy brahmin! He has deranged the brains of three hundred and fifty young men!' It was indeed mental derangement! Even now my brain is hot. I did not pay any attention to my mother's scolding."[8]

During his college days, Hari Prasanna visited Sri Ramakrishna several times at the Dakshineswar temple garden. He later related those wonderful reminiscences to some devotees. On Krishna's birthday, 18 August 1884, Hari Prasanna went to see the Master at Dakshineswar. That evening he decided to spend the night there. He recalled his experience:

Sometime later the Master gave me some *luchis* [fried bread] and sweets, which were the Divine Mother's prasad. Sri Ramakrishna made a bed for me and set up the mosquito curtain. I fell asleep as soon as I lay down. At midnight I woke up and found the Master walking around my bed, saying, "Mother, Mother." I was dumbfounded and could not understand what was going on. That night Sri Ramakrishna blessed me.[9]

The Master's disciples felt an irresistible attraction for their guru. They learned more by observing his exemplary life and listening to his talks than from books. Hari Prasanna described another night's stay with the Master:

One evening I went to Dakshineswar and expressed to the Master my desire to stay overnight. He gladly gave his consent. There was no suitable eating arrangement at night in Dakshineswar. Every night some prasad of the Divine Mother would be sent to the Master for his supper, and from that he would eat a little and distribute the remainder among those who stayed with him. The Master's night meal was very small — like a bird's food. He would eat a couple of luchis, a little farina pudding, and some sweets. When I saw the small quantity of prasad, I was upset. I realized that I would have to fast that night. I was then young with a well-built body and a large appetite. That little bit of prasad was not enough for me. Knowing what was in my mind, the

Master asked somebody to bring some *chapatis* [flattened bread] and vegetable curry for me from the nahabat. Even that amount of food was not sufficient for me, but I ate it and lay down on the floor in the Master's room.

At midnight I suddenly woke up and saw the Master pacing back and forth in his room. Sometimes he would go to the front veranda, muttering something, or he would chant the names of gods and goddesses while clapping his hands. During the day the Master talked and joked with the devotees; but now, at night, he was quite different. I was scared to death. I lay in bed, quietly observing the Master's madness. I could not get back to sleep. Sometimes the Master sang and danced, and sometimes he talked with someone. At last the night passed, and I was relieved. In the morning the Master was normal again.

When I returned home, my sister asked, "Where did you stay last night?" "At the temple garden of Dakshineswar," I replied. Immediately she exclaimed: "Did you stay with that mad brahmin of Dakshineswar? Don't go to that man again. He is really mad. I go there very often to bathe in the Ganges. I have seen him and I know about his madness." I listened to her words and smiled.[10]

Sri Ramakrishna was very concerned about his disciples' welfare. If any one of them did not visit him for a while, he would ask someone about that person. Once, when Hari Prasanna did not come to Dakshineswar for a long time, the Master sent for him. When he arrived, the Master asked why he had been absent for so long. Hari Prasanna replied truthfully: "Sir, I didn't feel like coming. Moreover, I try to meditate, but I find I cannot." "What do you mean you cannot meditate?" exclaimed the Master. After remaining silent for a few moments, he said, "Come near me." Hari Prasanna related what then transpired:

As I approached the Master, he asked me to stick out my tongue. When I did, he drew a figure on it with his finger. My whole body began to tremble, and I felt an unspeakable bliss within. Then the Master said, "Go to the Panchavati and meditate there." Following his instruction, I slowly moved towards the Panchavati. I walked with difficulty, intoxicated with joy from the Master's touch. Somehow I reached there and sat for meditation. Then I lost all outward consciousness. When I regained my ordinary state of mind, I saw the Master seated by me. He was rubbing my body with his hands. His face shone with a heavenly smile. I was still in an intoxicated mood. He asked me, "Well, how was your meditation?" "It was very good, sir," I replied. Then the Master said, "From now on you will always have deep meditation." He further asked, "Did you have a vision?"

I reported my experience to the Master as faithfully as I could. Then I followed him to his room. I was alone with him. That day he talked to me for a long time and gave me many spiritual instructions. I was overwhelmed by the Master's love and compassion for me. I had not realized before that he had so much feeling for me. Sri Ramakrishna's grace was boundless.

On that day the Master said to me: "Never get involved with women. Always be careful. Let there be no stain on your character. Never look at a woman, even if she is made out of gold. Do you know why I am saying all this to you? You belong to the Divine Mother, and you will have to do a lot of work for Her. A pecked fruit cannot be offered to the Mother. So I tell you, be careful."[11]

Hari Prasanna later recalled various episodes pertaining to his association with Sri Ramakrishna:

On one occasion I was massaging the Master's feet when a gentleman from Konnagar came to visit him. After he had left, the Master said, "You know, I can see the inside of a man's mind just as I can see the objects inside a glass case. I thought to myself: "Well, then he can also see everything in me. What a dangerous man he is!" But the Master would only speak of the goodness in others, not of their evil deeds or tendencies.[12]

Once during my college days when I went to visit the Master at Dakshineswar, I asked him, "Is God with form or without form?" The Master replied: "God is with form as well as without form, and again he is beyond both form and formlessness." Then I asked, "If God is all, is this cot also God?" He answered emphatically, "Yes, this cot is God, this glass, this utensil, this wall — everything is God." As he spoke, I experienced an inner transformation and was lifted beyond the realm of ordinary consciousness. My heart was illumined, and I saw the light of Brahman everywhere.[13]

During my youth I had read the philosophies of Kant, Hegel, and other great philosophers. One day I said to the Master: "Sir, what do you know about philosophy? Have you read the works of Kant and Hegel?" He replied: "What are you saying? Throw away all those books. Knowledge of God is not in any book. Those books are all products of ignorance." What a great statement the Master made! Later, finding no way out, I gave up arguing. In the beginning we need faith for God-realization.

Once at Dakshineswar the Master gave me an English book and asked me to read and explain it to him. It was stated in the book: "Speak the truth. Do not covet what belongs to another. Control your senses."

On hearing this, the Master felt elated like a boy and expressed his great delight. The Master's joy even now is deeply impressed in my mind. I think that his expression of great delight was due to the fact that if a person attains perfection in those three disciplines, he is sure to reach God. Whenever he heard any discussion about God, he would go into ecstasy.[14]

When the Master was blessed for the first time with the vision of the Divine Mother, he thought, "If this vision of mine is true, then let this big stone [which was in front of the nahabat] jump up thrice." Immediately, the stone did in fact jump thrice. Whatever he thought came to pass. Seeing this, the Master was fully convinced of the genuineness of his vision.[15]

Hari Prasanna was not able to spend a great deal of time with the Master, but the unbounded grace of his guru filled his heart. Towards the end of Sri Ramakrishna's life, pointing to his own picture, he told Hari Prasanna: "Look, I dwell in this picture. Meditate on me." "Yes, I will," replied Hari Prasanna.[16]

In 1885 Hari Prasanna passed the First Arts examination in the first division at Saint Xavier's College. He then moved to Bankipur in the state of Bihar, and entered Patna College to study for a B.A. degree. Hari Prasanna later recalled: "The day the Master passed away [16 August 1886] I saw him standing in front of me. I wondered: 'How did the Master come here? What is the cause of this vision?' The next day I read of the Master's passing away in the *Basumati* newspaper." Naturally Hari Prasanna grieved, but he remembered what the Master had once said to him: "Do you know why I love you? You boys are my very own. The Divine Mother has asked me to love you." Hari Prasanna later remarked: "I cannot express how much love the Master had for us. We don't have that capacity to love others. We became intoxicated seeing the Master, and now people are intoxicated just by hearing his name. How blessed they are!"[17]

As a Student and an Engineer

In 1887 Hari Prasanna graduated from Patna College and then went to the Poona College of Science to study civil engineering. He was a brilliant student and was greatly loved by his professors and classmates. In those days at the College of Science those who secured first and second places in their examinations would immediately get jobs either in the State Government of Bombay or in the Government of India. One of Hari

Prasanna's classmates, Radhika Prasad Roy, a poor and meritorious boy, needed a job badly. Hari Prasanna knew that he would secure one of the top positions, so a few days before the final examination he said to Radhika Prasad: "Brother, the financial condition of your family is not good. If you can get one of the two top positions in the examination, you will definitely get a government job. So I have decided not to appear for the examination this year."[18] He was true to his word. Although Radhika Prasad did not place first or second, he remembered Hari Prasanna's greatness all through his life.

Once in college Hari Prasanna protested the remark of a Christian missionary professor of geology who had sarcastically criticized the Hindu belief in reincarnation. As a result, the professor intentionally gave him a lower mark in geology than he really earned. Due to this mark, he placed second instead of first in his final examination. Despite this, after graduating in civil engineering in 1892, he was given the job of district engineer at Gazipur in Uttar Pradesh. While in this position, the Varanasi-Gazipur Road was built under his supervision. During this time he met Pavhari Baba, the great yogi of Gazipur, who was highly esteemed by Swami Vivekananda. As a government engineer, Hari Prasanna worked at Etawah, Bulandsahar, Meerut, and other places in Uttar Pradesh. During his years of government service he kept in close contact with his brother disciples and donated sixty rupees every month to the Ramakrishna Monastery. Sometimes the disciples visited him and stayed with him when they were sick, and he served them with loving care.

With Swami Vivekananda

Because his father died in his childhood, Hari Prasanna had to work until his family was financially secure. He provided for his mother and also for the education of his younger brother. As time went on, however, his uncle began to pressure him to get married. He became disgusted with these attempts to tie him to a worldly life and joined the Ramakrishna Monastery at Alambazar in 1896. He lived there humbly and spent most of his time in japam and meditation. He was a man of few words and did not care for chatting and joking as others did.

Swami Vivekananda returned to India from the West in 1897 and took Hari Prasanna with him on his travels in western and northern India. During this tour they visited the old Hindu temples of Rajputana. Vivekananda discussed the architecture of the future Ramakrishna Temple with him and expressed his own ideas as to how the temple should be built. On their return to the monastery, Hari Prasanna drew a sketch of the Ramakrishna Temple using Swamiji's ideas as his guide. He also consulted with Mr. Guithar, a noted architect. Swamiji was pleased when he saw the sketch and said, "This temple will certainly come up, but I may not live to see it.... I will see it from on high."[19]

On 13 February 1898 the Ramakrishna Monastery was moved from Alambazar to Nilambar Mukherjee's garden house at Belur. The site for Belur Math, the headquarters of the Ramakrishna Order, was purchased in March of 1898. Vivekananda entrusted Hari Prasanna with the task of remodeling the main building and constructing new buildings and the shrine for the monastery. Hari Prasanna drew up the site plan and building plans, prepared estimates, as well as supervised the construction. He did all of this single-handedly. When the construction was completed, Vivekananda consecrated the Ramakrishna Math on 9 December 1898. On 9 May 1899 Hari Prasanna formally took sannyasa, final monastic vows. Vivekananda told him: "Do as we have done. Take your sannyasa directly from the Master."[20] Accordingly, Hari Prasanna went to Sri Ramakrishna's shrine and took his monastic vows with the traditional *viraja homa* ceremony. He became known as Swami Vijnanananda.

One day Swamiji expressed a desire to build a ghat and an embankment on the bank of the Ganges for the Belur Monastery, so he asked Vijnanananda for an estimate. Fearing Swamiji might change his mind, Vijnanananda understated the cost and said it would be approximately three thousand rupees. This amount made Swamiji happy: He immediately consulted with Swami Brahmananda and ordered that the project be started. As the work proceeded, Vijnanananda realized that the cost would exceed his previous estimate. He humbly expressed his concern to Brahmananda who asked Vijnanananda to complete the project. Out of compassion for his younger brother, he accepted the responsibility of spending the extra money and risking a scolding from Swamiji.

Sometime later, Swamiji asked Brahmananda for the accounts. When he discovered that the expenses had already exceeded the original estimate, and the work was still unfinished, he became angry with Brahmananda and vehemently scolded him. The latter endured it calmly. When Swamiji returned to his room, Brahmananda went to his own room and closed the door and windows. After a while Swamiji regretted his bad temper. He then called Vijnanananda and said, "Could you check on what Raja [Brahmananda was called Raja or King] is doing?" Vijnanananda went to Brahmananda's room and found that the doors and windows were closed. He called for him but got no response.

When he reported this to Swamiji, he said: "You are a fool! I asked you to find out what Raja was doing; and you say, 'His door and windows are closed.' Go back again and tell me what he is doing." This time Vijnanananda pushed the door open and found Brahmananda on his bed, weeping. Vijnanananda said apologetically, "Maharaj, I am sorry; today you have suffered terribly for me." Brahmananda said: "Brother, can you tell me what wrong I have done that Swamiji could scold me so harshly? Sometimes it becomes so unbearable that I feel I should go away to some place in the mountains, leaving everything."

Returning to Swamiji, Vijnanananda reported that Brahmananda was crying. At this, Swamiji rushed to the room, embraced Brahmananda, and said tearfully: "Raja, brother, please forgive me. It is my fault that my temper is short and that I scolded you. Please pardon me." Meanwhile, Brahmananda had regained his composure. Seeing Swamiji weep, he was also moved. Then he said: "What does it matter? You have scolded me because you love me — that is all." But Swamiji continued: "Brother, please forgive me. I know how much the Master loved you and never uttered a harsh word to you. And I, on the other hand, for the sake of this petty work, have verbally abused you and given you pain. I am not fit to live with you. I shall go away to the Himalayas and live alone in solitude." "Don't say that, Swamiji," said Brahmananda. "Your scolding is a blessing. How can you leave us? You are our leader. How shall we function without you?" Gradually both of them became calm.

Vijnanananda later remarked: "I shall never forget that scene in my life. I never saw Swamiji weeping so bitterly. What a bond of love existed between them! Swamiji loved his brother disciples like a mother, and that is why he could not bear any shortcoming in them. He wanted them to be as great as himself; nay, even greater than himself. His love was incomparable."[21]

One hot summer day, while supervising the construction work of the embankment at Belur Math, Vijnanananda became thirsty. He noticed that Vivekananda was enjoying a cold drink on his upper veranda. Presently, one of Swamiji's attendants carried a glass to him and said, "Swamiji has sent this cold drink to you." Vijnanananda took the glass and found only a few drops at the bottom. He was disappointed and piqued by Swamiji's practical joke. However, he drank those few drops as prasad and, strangely enough, his thirst was instantly quenched. He was dumbfounded. In the evening Vijnanananda saw Swamiji, who asked with a smile, "Did you drink the cold juice?" "Yes, I did," replied

Vijnanananda. He then described his experience after drinking it, and Swamiji was pleased.[22]

Vijnanananda later reminisced about his Belur Math days with Swami Vivekananda:

> Swamiji used to call me "Peshan" [an abbreviation of Prasanna]. One day I was sitting on the upper veranda of Belur Math eating puffed rice. Swamiji was passing by. All of a sudden he grabbed a handful of puffed rice from my bowl and began to eat it like a boy. I remonstrated: "Swamiji, why don't you take another bowl of puffed rice? By eating the food that I have defiled you are making me feel guilty." Laughing, Swamiji left. [According to Hindu custom, a senior, or highly respected person, does not eat from the same plate with a junior person. A junior person would feel extremely ill at ease were this to happen.]
>
> I used to take snuff. Once Swamiji went to Calcutta and bought a pice worth of snuff in a packet. Handing it to me, he said, "Here is a wonderful present for you." I opened the packet and found the snuff. Seeing me happy, he was happy. But when he became grave, it was difficult to go near him. Then only Raja Maharaj could bring him back to the normal plane.[23]

At Belur Math Vijnanananda lived in a small room close to Swamiji's room. Once at two o'clock in the morning, Vijnanananda saw Swamiji pacing on the eastern veranda. Concerned, he got up and asked Swamiji why he could not sleep. Swamiji replied: "Peshan, I was sleeping nicely; but suddenly I felt a jolt, and my sleep broke. It seems to me that there must be a disaster somewhere and many people are suffering." That night Vijnanananda could not make sense of this statement. However, he later narrated: "The next morning I saw in the newspaper that at the same time Swamiji awakened, there had been a terrible volcanic eruption near the Fiji Islands, and many people were killed. I was surprised to read this news, and then I realized that Swamiji's nervous system was more responsive to human misery than a seismograph."[24]

Once in the dead of night at Belur Math, Vijnanananda heard a pathetic cry from Vivekananda's room. He thought that perhaps Swamiji cried out because he was sick. Vijnanananda silently entered Swamiji's room and asked, "Swamiji, are you not well?" Immediately Swamiji became quiet and replied, "Oh, Peshan, I thought you were sleeping." When asked the cause of his cry, Swamiji tearfully said: "Brother, thinking of the poverty and suffering of the people, I cannot sleep. My mind is restless with pain. So I am praying to the Master, 'Let good befall our people and let their suffering go away.'" Vijnanananda then consoled

Swamiji and asked him to sleep. That night Vijnanananda was deeply moved to see how intensely Swamiji felt for his countrymen.[25]

Vijnanananda had great love and respect for Holy Mother, but he seldom visited her in Calcutta. One day he went with Swamiji to Balaram's house in Calcutta while Holy Mother was staying there. Swamiji asked, "Peshan, did you salute Holy Mother?" "No, Swamiji, I did not." "What! Go right now and bow down to the Mother," said Swamiji. Accordingly, Vijnanananda went to Holy Mother and bowed down to her from a distance, bending his head to the floor. As soon as Vijnanananda got up, from behind he heard Swamiji say: "What is this, Peshan? Does anybody salute the Mother in this way? Bow down to her by prostrating yourself on the floor. Holy Mother is the Mother of the Universe." Swamiji then prostrated himself to the Mother, and Vijnanananda did likewise. Later Vijnanananda remarked, "I could not imagine that Swamiji would follow me to the Mother."[26]

Once while at Belur Math Vijnanananda was wondering about Swamiji's work in the West and his relationship with Western women. Seeing Swamiji alone in his room, Vijnanananda asked him frankly: "Swamiji, while you were in the West you associated with the women there; but didn't the Master teach the contrary in this respect? He used to say, 'A monk should not even look at the portrait of a woman.' He emphatically told me not to be close to women, however devoted they might be. So I am wondering why you did so."

Immediately Swamiji became very grave and his face and eyes turned crimson with anger. After a while he said: "Well, Peshan, do you think that what you have understood about the Master is all that he is? What do you know about the Master? Do you know that the Master eradicated the idea of the difference between male and female from my mind? Is there any distinction of sex in the Atman? Moreover, the Master came for the good of the entire world. Did he come to liberate only men? He will save all — both men and women. You people want to belittle the Master by measuring him with the yardstick of your own intellects. Whatever the Master told you is true; you follow that implicitly. But to me his instructions were different. He not only gave me instructions, he clearly showed me everything. He holds my hands — whatever he makes me do, I do."

Gradually Swamiji became calm. Noticing Vijnanananda's embarrassment, he said with a smile: "Can a nation rise or become great unless the primordial energy that lies dormant in women is awakened? I have travelled all over the world and found that women are neglected more or less everywhere, but this is particularly deplorable in India. That is why our nation has been degraded to such an extent. As soon as there is an awakening in women, you will see that the whole nation will rise up in its pristine glory. For that reason Holy Mother has come. With her advent there has been a stir among the women of all countries. This is just a beginning; you will see many more things later."[27]

A great soul sees greatness in others. In the last years of his life, Swamiji's mind was mostly absorbed in God-consciousness. One day Swamiji remarked: "I cannot say anything to Peshan because I see the Master in him." To this Vijnanananda responded: "The Master dwells in every being. It is no wonder that you see the Master in me through your divine sight." "No, Peshan," said Swamiji. "It is not like that. I see distinctly that the Master has made his habitat in you nicely." Vijnanananda humbly replied, "Swamiji, you see whatever you want to; but I don't understand it."[28]

Another time Vijnanananda asked Swamiji, "Well, does the Master accept the food which we offer in the shrine?" "Yes, he does," replied Swamiji. "A ray comes out from his third eye and touches the food. If you want, I can show it to you today in the shrine."[29] Vijnanananda fully believed what Swamiji had said, and proceeded no further. This mutual love and trust of Sri Ramakrishna's disciples made their lives joyful.

Vivekananda was a man of varying moods. Sometimes he was playful, and then everyone could approach him freely. But when he was serious, seldom would anyone dare to approach him. One day in a jovial mood, he said to Vijnanananda: "Peshan, it is time to write a new Smriti [scripture pertaining to social, moral, and ethical laws] according to the need of the present age. The old Smritis are now obsolete." Vijnanananda asked: "Swamiji, why will the people accept your Smriti?" Immediately Swamiji, like a querulous boy, complained to Brahmananda, "Rakhal, listen, Peshan says that the people won't accept my message." Brahmananda pacified him, saying: "What does Peshan know? He is a mere boy. The people will definitely accept your message someday or other." Like a reassured boy, Swamiji said joyfully: "Peshan, did you hear what Rakhal said? The people will positively accept my message."[30] Brahmananda's prophetic words came true!

At Allahabad (Prayag)

When the construction of the Belur Monastery was finished, Vivekananda advised Vijnanananda to start a centre at Allahabad (Prayag). This city is an important pilgrimage site because the confluence of three rivers

— the Ganges, the Jamuna, and the Saraswati — is located there. Accordingly, Vijnanananda left Belur Math in the early part of 1900, and after visiting a few holy places, reached Allahabad in the fall. He first stayed with his friend, Dr. Mahendra Nath Odedar, and then moved to the Brahmavadin Club. The club members practised meditation and prayer, held classes on the scriptures, sang devotional songs, and discussed spiritual topics. They were extremely happy to have Vijnanananda in their midst.

The club rented two rooms on the upper floor of a two-storey building — a small one (10 by 10 feet) for the shrine, and a larger one (18 by 10 feet) for a library and meeting room. In front of these rooms there was a long, roofless veranda. An open staircase by the side of the house extended from the ground to the veranda, then to the roof. On the roof there was a privy that was cleaned daily by a sweeper. There was no water or electricity in the house. Vijnanananda had to collect water from the street supply of the municipality, cook his own meals (rice and vegetable curry only) on two kerosene stoves, wash the pots and dishes, and do all the household work. In addition, he regularly did physical exercise and practised pranayama, breathing exercises. He spent mornings and afternoons in worship, japam, meditation, and study in the shrine room. In the evening, the club members would conduct a vesper service; he also gave classes on the Gita to club members in the library hall. He slept in this hall at night.

Vijnanananda loved to be alone and was a man of few words. If anybody asked for some advice, he would say: "Practise what you studied in the primary book in your childhood days: Always speak the truth and do not steal or covet others' things. Follow these two moral principles, and then everything else will take care of itself."[31]

During his early days in Allahabad, Vijnanananda would go for a daily bath before sunrise in the *Triveni* (literally, three braids), the confluence of three holy rivers. One day after his bath, while reciting a hymn to the Mother Ganges, Vijnanananda had a vision. The goddess Mother Triveni appeared as a beautiful young girl with three braids hanging down her back and then disappeared again into the water. He was overwhelmed by the vision. After chanting, when he began to walk towards the ashrama, he saw Mother Triveni walking in the same direction with her braids dangling. After a while she disappeared. When Brahmananda heard about this vision, he confirmed it as genuine. Vijnanananda himself said: "The test of a true vision is this: It leaves a lasting spiritual impression on the mind that generates awareness and bliss. I still get joy when I think of that virginal form of the Divine Mother."[32]

Swamiji had great affection for Vijnanananda, and called him the "Bishop of Allahabad." As a result of his intense, one-pointed spiritual disciplines, Vijnanananda had various kinds of visions and experiences. On the day Vivekananda passed away, Vijnanananda was meditating in the shrine of the Brahmavadin Club and he had a vision of Swamiji seated on the lap of Sri Ramakrishna. Vijnanananda became very anxious about Swamiji. He wondered, "Why have I seen Swamiji in this way?" The next day he received a cable from Belur Math with the sad news of Vivekananda's passing.[33]

In Allahabad, Vijnanananda did not make any effort to preach the teachings of Sri Ramakrishna. In fact, preaching was against his nature. He was satisfied leading his life according to the ideal of Sri Ramakrishna. He plunged into the inner realm, and seldom went outside the club. His simple, austere, God-centred life nevertheless attracted people, including Pandit Madan Mohan Malavya, a saintly and scholarly leader of India who founded the Varanasi Hindu University. The pandit was charmed to see in Swami Vijnanananda the living representation of Vedanta. The swami was completely indifferent to worldly comforts or any other external things. One day, seeing the swami's worn-out water jar, Madan Mohan remarked, "It needs replacing."[34]

A Vedanta scripture says: "If you want the knowledge of Brahman, shun crowds like a snake, good food like poison, and sex like the devil." Vijnanananda followed this advice to the letter. He was extremely punctual. During the daytime he would give interviews to earnest people, but if a person arrived even one minute late, he would not see him. At night he would not allow anybody to stay in the centre. His dress was quite unusual: a long loose shirt (either cotton or woolen) with many pockets, a piece of dhoti (cloth) reaching his knees, a couple of pairs of socks (even in the hot summer), worn-out shoes, and a cap that covered his ears. When he went somewhere by *ekka*, an open horse-carriage, people on the street would look at him with curiosity. Vijnanananda would make fun of them: "What are you looking at? A monkey? Yes, I am a monkey devotee of Lord Ramachandra."[35] This is the way mystics hide their true stature from the gaze of the public.

No one ever saw Vijnanananda wasting his time by indulging in chitchat or gossip, nor did he allow others to do so in the centre. When he was not practising his spiritual disciplines, he studied Vedanta literature thoroughly and regularly with Bhagavat Dat, an orthodox Vedic pandit of Allahabad. He also published a number of important books during his thirty-eight-year stay in Allahabad. In 1904 he translated *Sri*

Ramakrishna's Life and Teachings by Suresh Chandra Datta from Bengali into Hindi and published it as *Paramahamsa-Charitra*. His later publications were: *Jalsarvaraher Karkhana*, an engineering and waterworks manual in two volumes in Bengali; translations of Varahamihira's *Brihajjataka* and *Surya-siddhanta*, two ancient Sanskrit astrological and astronomical works, the first into English and the second into Bengali; and translations of Devi Bhagavata and Narada Pancharatra, two famous Hindu scriptures, from Sanskrit into English. Towards the end of his life, he was translating Valmiki's Ramayana from Sanskrit into English, but this was left unfinished. He later said of this experience: "When I sit down to translate the Ramayana, I forget the world. I see Rama, Lakshmana, Sita, and Mahavirji in front of me."[36]

During his early period of sadhana in Allahabad, Vijnanananda was very strict about women; he did not allow any women to visit the Brahmavadin Club, which was actually a men's club. One day the sweeper went somewhere to do errands, so he sent his young daughter to clean Vijnanananda's privy. She met the swami while walking down the steps, and greeted him with a smile. He did not want a woman to clean his privy, so he told her, "Starting tomorrow I don't need anybody to clean my privy." She reported this to her father. That evening the sweeper rushed to the swami and apologized. At first Vijnanananda said sternly to him: "I don't need anybody. I shall go to the public privy." Later, out of compassion, he told the poor sweeper, "If you want to serve me, please come; but don't send anyone else." Shivananda once remarked, "Even a she-fly has no entry in Hari Prasanna's ashrama."[37]

Let the reader not misunderstand: Vijnanananda did not hate women. But he was an ideal monk who followed his guru's advice without compromise. Later, when he moved to his own ashrama, his sister came to visit him. He arranged for her to stay in an inn. In 1918 his mother came to Prayag for a pilgrimage and holy bath during *Purna Kumbha* (an auspicious festival that falls once every twelve years). He arranged for her to stay in the ashrama guest house and served her wholeheartedly. He was a pure soul who had conquered lust — a great obstacle to spiritual life. Once he said to a monk in Allahabad: "I have never seen any woman even in my dreams [meaning, no lustful dreams]. . . . In my fifty-three years of life, the Divine Mother has never shown me Her bewitching form."[38] During a talk to the monks at Belur Math in 1937, Vijnanananda said: "Respect women as you respect Holy Mother in the temple. They are aspects of the Divine Mother. Bow down to them from a distance, because you are monks."[39] When Vijnanananda became president of the Ramakrishna Order, he initiated many women and was very kind and loving towards them. Once he said to a woman devotee: "Call on Holy Mother; you will achieve everything. The Master is very strict about bestowing his grace, but the Mother is very compassionate. I have achieved everything by her grace."[40]

Vijnanananda practised severe austerities fifteen hours a day for ten years while at the Brahmavadin Club. In 1910 he bought a house and a vacant plot across the road from it in the Muthiganj area of Allahabad. He turned the house into a Ramakrishna Monastery and built another house on the vacant plot for a charitable homeopathic dispensary. He took Brahmachari Panchanan from the Varanasi Home of Service as his assistant. Panchanan worked in the charitable homeopathic dispensary and he also served the swami from 1910 to 1924. He later left the Order. Vijnanananda continued to practise his sadhana in solitude as Sri Ramakrishna had directed: "Meditate in the mind, in the corner of the room, and in the forest." He was a yogi as described in the Gita: "He knows bliss in the Atman and wants nothing else. Cravings torment the heart: he renounces cravings. He is unperturbed by adversity, does not hanker after happiness, and is free from anger and fear. I call him a seer, and illumined" (2:55-56). However, the swami could not hide himself for long. Gradually people became aware of his spiritual greatness and began to come to him for guidance.

Allahabad has an extreme climate — very hot in the summer and severely cold in the winter. The ashrama had no electricity and moreover, it was very close to the main rail line in Muthiganj, which made it very noisy. It was unbearably hot in the summer, so Vijnanananda would meditate with a wet towel on his head. Despite these hardships, nothing could disturb the equanimity of Vijnanananda's mind. Sometime in 1916 or 1917 the swami suffered from acute blood dysentery for many days. He did not allow anyone to serve him; he only asked his assistant to keep a jar of cold water in his room. He endured the pain alone in his bed with his eyes closed, as if absorbed in deep meditation. If anyone offered to help, he would put his index finger over his lips to indicate "silence," and then would dismiss the person with a wave of his hand. Vijnanananda was an embodiment of forbearance, and finally was cured with homeopathic medicine.

In the beginning the financial condition of the Allahabad Ramakrishna Math was poor. There were only a few devotees and Vijnanananda had to take out a loan of 4,100 rupees in order to buy the house. A Muslim horse-carriage driver collected monthly subscriptions for the ashrama from some of those devotees. At that time the swami had not started to give initiation, so he had no disciples to assist him. He appointed Beni, a local boy, as his personal attendant.

In the early stages, there were no cooking facilities in the ashrama. Some devotees took turns cooking for Vijnanananda in their own homes and Beni would collect the food in a tiffin-carrier. The swami asked the devotees to cook simple meals for him, so they cooked only rice, lentils, and a vegetable. These devotees knew his temperament, so they never disobeyed him; they were happy to serve this great soul. Later, when the ashrama grew, Vijnanananda established cooking facilities and hired a cook. The swami was so fond of tea that he took it several times a day. He would buy the best tea available in the market and would invite everybody — visitors, servants, sweepers, and carriage-drivers — to his tea parties.

Vijnanananda believed wholeheartedly that all works of the ashrama belong to God, but the head of a centre is responsible if anything goes wrong. Once the doctor of the charitable homeopathic dispensary resigned. This created a great difficulty for the swami. He could not find a doctor immediately, and he was very concerned for the indigent patients. He pondered: "Well, it is the Master's work; I shall give medicine chanting his name." Vijnanananda had no knowledge of medicine, nevertheless he started to go to the dispensary every morning. He gave homeopathic medicine to the patients without asking about their diseases or physical problems. When the female patients tried to tell him their physical problems, the swami said: "Don't talk about your disease. Take the medicine and go home."

It was amazing: Every single drop of homeopathic medicine he gave cured each patient — not one had to return for a second dose. When this miraculous news spread, more patients began to appear every day. It became difficult to control the crowds. Then the swami brought in a doctor from Varanasi and was relieved of the responsibility. The doctor checked the stock of medicine and discovered that even the nitric acid bottles were empty. Frightened and amazed, he said to the swami, "Maharaj, you have cleared even the nitric acid!" Vijnanananda simply said: "I have given medicine in the name of the Master and the patients got well. There is no credit for me; I did as he asked me to do."[41]

In Varanasi

Sometime in the 1880s, probably while he was a government engineer, Vijnanananda met Trailanga Swami, a venerated saint of Varanasi. He later spoke about his visit: "I went to see him and found him lying naked in the hot summer sun. People said he had a dark complexion, but I found him as bright as molten gold. He seemed to me to be a great soul. He emanated a lustrous radiance, demonstrating the difference between ordinary mortals and spiritually powerful souls."[42]

Since Vijnanananda was an engineer, he was always consulted regarding the construction of the Ramakrishna Mission's hospitals or temples. In 1909 the swami went to Varanasi to supervise the construction of the Ramakrishna Mission Home of Service. While riding from the rail station to the centre, Vijnanananda's horse carriage suddenly overturned, and one of his legs was twisted inside a wheel. Although he was in severe pain, he was able to pull his leg out immediately. Vijnanananda reached the ashrama by another carriage, and the doctors took care of him quickly. That night he had a high temperature and a terrible headache. He thought to himself: "Lord Vishwanath, I have come to your city to work for the Master. This is an unselfish action! Why has this accident happened? The Master's work will suffer." Thinking thus, he fell asleep. Vijnanananda later narrated the following experience:

> It was 1:00 or 2:00 a.m. I saw Lord Shiva with matted hair and smiling face appear before me. I said: "Lord, have you come to take me? But I cannot go now; I have to complete the Master's work first." He didn't listen to me. Smiling, he came forward and then embraced me. Immediately my body became as cold as ice. I then said to him: "Good-bye now, Lord. I shall have to do the Master's work." Lord Shiva laughed and left. Strangely enough, in the morning I felt no fever and also my wounds were healed to some extent. Even now, sometimes I see that calm, smiling form of Lord Shiva.[43]

In 1918 while he was at Varanasi, Vijnanananda visited Sarnath, about six miles away. Sarnath is a historical site where Buddha gave his first sermon. Vijnanananda once mentioned to a professor from Sarnath that the images of Buddha and other deities looked beautiful and living when they were first excavated. But when they were later preserved in the Sarnath Museum, those images lost some of their solemnity and charm. Even so, these divine images are always inspiring. The swami described his visit to Sarnath and his experience:

> Once, during my morning walk, I decided to visit Sarnath. I had no previous plan to do so. After arriving there on foot, I looked around. While I was there, a guide informed me that there was a stone image containing carvings of Buddha's entire life story from his birth to mahaparinirvana [death]. The guide accompanied me there. While looking at the image I had a wonderful vision. I saw a formless ocean

of light, and the whole universe was gradually merging into it. Like a speck, I was watching that blissful glow with wonder, standing on the shore of the ocean of light. I was beside myself. Then in the twinkling of an eye the universe completely disappeared; and from the ocean of pure consciousness the compassionate, loving form of Buddha appeared. What a joy! Even now while describing it, I feel that joy. I was in that state for some time. Then I heard the guide's voice, "Let us go forward — let us go forward." Gradually I regained my normal consciousness. The guide thought that I had fallen asleep. I followed the guide, but I was extremely intoxicated. In the afternoon when I returned to the centre, the monks asked where I had been and said that lunch had been saved for me. I didn't tell them where I had been: I only said, "I don't feel like eating now." I quietly went to bed. That blissful intoxication continued for three days.[44]

Later, when I went to visit the temple of Vishwanath in Varanasi, I thought to myself: "Why have I come here? To look at a stone?" Then the same vision opened up. It was as if Vishwanath were telling me, "The light is the same here as there — Truth is one."[45]

On 5 February 1938 Vijnanananda again left Allahabad to visit the centre at Varanasi. After supper the monks and devotees assembled in his room and asked him to talk about Sri Ramakrishna. Instead of sharing his reminiscences, the swami asked, "Well, whom do you love — the Master or the Mother?" "We love both," came the answer. The swami said: "Then it is all right. The Master is Rama and Krishna, and the Mother is Sita and Yogamaya. As the king visits his subjects sometimes in royal dress and sometimes in disguise to evaluate their needs, so the Master came this time in disguise. . . . It is true: the Master will come back soon."[46]

The next day at 5:00 p.m. Vijnanananda went to visit the Durga Temple by car. He returned an hour and a half later and immediately went to bed. No one dared to ask him anything. He remained immersed in the thought of Mother Durga for quite some time. When his spiritual mood subsided, he sat in his chair and supper was served. Seeing the various dishes, he remarked: "Who can eat so many dishes? When I could eat, nobody gave me sufficient food. Now I cannot eat and people are serving me all kinds of food." After supper Vijnanananda told the monks: "The Americans respect Swamiji more than the Master. Swamiji had a wonderful, overwhelming personality. People felt inadequate in front of him. When we mentioned this to Swamiji, he said, 'It is the play of that mad brahmin [meaning the Master]; he is working through me.' Swamiji was very simple and a man of renunciation."[47]

Pilgrimage

In the latter part of his life, Vijnanananda visited various holy places. On 21 December 1931 the swami went to Ramakrishna Math in Madras. From there, he visited the temples of Lord Vishnu and Lord Shiva in Kanchipuram; then those of the Goddess Meenakshi and Lord Sundareshwara in Madurai. He proceeded to Trivandrum and from there travelled to Kanyakumari. He entered the temple and looked at the Mother Kumari, the Virgin Goddess, for an hour without blinking. From the seashore he saw Rock Island where Vivekananda had meditated and had a vision before he left for America. Vijnanananda then visited Rameswaram, Bangalore, Mysore, and Ootacamund, before returning to Madras. Vijnanananda told the devotees in Madras: "The goal of human life is to realize God because only that can give us real and permanent peace. Truly it is the ego, a product of ignorance, which has covered our God-vision. Once someone asked Sri Ramakrishna, 'Why can't we see God?' He immediately covered his face with a towel and asked: 'Can you see my face? No. Because this towel is the barrier; yet I am seated in front of you. Similarly, remove the veil of ignorance, which is between you and God and you will see Him everywhere.'"[48]

In 1932 he visited Chittrakut, where Lord Ramachandra stayed during his banishment; Dwaraka on the shore of the Arabian Sea, where Lord Krishna lived; Rajkot in Gujarat; and Bombay. In 1933 Vijnanananda went to Sri Lanka and visited three important Buddhist holy places: Kelani Temple, where it is said the Buddha visited three times; Kandy Tooth Temple of Buddha; and the Bo-tree of Anuradhapuram. In the same year Vijnanananda went to Delhi, Lahore, Peshwar, Landikotal, and Shillong.

In 1935 Vijnanananda went to see the famous Lingaraj Temple in Bhubaneswar. He then visited the Konarak Sun Temple. On another occasion he visited the Jagannath Temple of Puri. He later spoke of his experience there: "On entering the temple, I embraced Lord Jagannath. He seemed to be soft like a doll of butter."[49] He also visited Dinajpur, Tamluk, Kamarpukur (the birthplace of Sri Ramakrishna), and Jayrambati (the birthplace of Holy Mother). He then installed the foundation stone of the Ramakrishna Mission in Kanpur. At a later date he visited Dhaka and Barisal in Bangladesh.

When Sri Ramakrishna trained his disciples, he gave them the power necessary to transmit his spiritual heritage. Consequently, wherever his disciples went they would create such an uplifting atmosphere that everyone's mind would be filled with joy. Although reticent, when asked, Vijnanananda always talked about the Master and spiritual life. In Barisal he said to the devotees: "Only a few people can realize or understand God. This is not possible without purity of the heart. One should be extremely careful: Bad thoughts are like poison."[50] One day a judge's wife asked, "Maharaj, how can we control the restless mind?" "Punish the mind with a whip," replied the swami. The lady said: "The whip is in my hand, but the mind is far away. How can I thrash it?" Vijnanananda burst into laughter.[51] Another day he said to the devotees: "Chant the Lord's name; you will get peace." Then he mentioned the nature of the Soul, or the Atman: "The Soul is not matter. The Soul is beyond birth and death. The Soul is eternal. The individual soul is subservient to the Supreme Soul [Paramatman]."[52]

In December 1936 Vijnanananda went to Rangoon, the capital of Burma. The Burmese devotees were happy to meet a direct disciple of Sri Ramakrishna. On 11 December Vijnanananda went to see the famous reclining image of Buddha at Pegu, forty-five miles from Rangoon. He stood motionless in front of the image for a long time. His companions did not dare disturb him. After a while Vijnanananda regained a normal state of consciousness and they returned to the car. He remained silent and serious all the way back to Rangoon. Later, when repeatedly asked by the monks about his spiritual mood, the swami said: "Today Lord Buddha has graciously vouchsafed me his vision. I clearly saw that the reclining image of Buddha was living, as it were. How magnificent was the beauty of his luminous form!" After saying this, he again became silent.[53]

During his stay in Rangoon, Vijnanananda initiated some devotees. In the afternoons he answered the questions of spiritual aspirants. One afternoon a monk asked, "How can we still the mind?" Vijnanananda replied: "It is quite essential to practise japam and meditation regularly every day. Then gradually the mind will be calm and steady. Try to live alone. A real holy man lives in solitude." Later he added: "It is no use listening to too many spiritual instructions at one time. It is far better to hear and concentrate on a few instructions and practise them. Often some people take too many instructions but do not follow any at all — that does not bear any results. What good advice you have heard, try to translate into action."[54]

On 12 December 1936 Vijnanananda heard that Prince Edward VIII had renounced the throne of England in order to marry an American woman. The swami commented: "Look, the prince gave up such a vast empire, wealth, honour, and everything just for a woman! So a woman is greater than an empire, and again God is greater than a woman. Who renounces anything for God? God is the greatest of everything — upon gaining him one knows that there is no greater gain. But it is extremely difficult to attain him. The prince's renunciation of the empire is praiseworthy. Renunciation of any kind is good; it increases mental strength and dispassion. Today he has renounced the empire, perhaps in the future he may give up that woman."[55]

When his attendant came to bow down to him, the swami said: "Today you won't get food in the monastery. Edward VIII has given up such a vast empire; will you not be able to give up food for one day?" When the monk agreed to fast, Vijnanananda said: "Look, the king has renounced his kingdom for a woman! What a play of Mahamaya!"[56] The swami continued to praise renunciation, then finally said, "There is little hope of making any progress in spiritual life without renunciation."[57]

At Belur Math

On 9 December 1898 Vivekananda had consecrated Belur Math by worshipping the relics of Sri Ramakrishna. During this auspicious occasion, Swamiji had said to a disciple: "The Master once told me, 'I will go and live wherever it will be your pleasure to take me, carrying me on your shoulders — be it under a tree or in the humblest cottage.'"[58] Belur Math was very special to Vijnanananda, as it was to the other disciples and devotees of Sri Ramakrishna. Vijnanananda lived mostly in Allahabad, but from time to time Brahmananda asked him to oversee construction work for the Order. As described earlier, in 1909 he went to Varanasi and in 1910 to Kankhal (Hardwar) to supervise construction work. From 1919 to 1920 he supervised the construction of the Vivekananda Temple at Belur Math. After breakfast he would go to the construction site to guide the workers until 1:00 p.m. and return again in the afternoon. He always maintained his calmness during intense activity; he was truly a karma yogi. He reminded the labourers: "Look, work carefully. You are building the temple of Lord Shiva."[59]

One day Brahmananda asked Vijnanananda how the work was progressing. Vijnanananda reported that his work was suffering because there was a shortage of materials. Brahmananda said that the materials would arrive by boat before the next morning, but Vijnanananda doubted this. Thereupon a bet was laid and both retired for the night. Early in the morning Vijnanananda got up to see if the boat had come. It had not, so he returned to his bed, elated at the prospect of winning the bet. A little later, Brahmananda went out, saw the boat moored, and quietly retired. After daybreak Vijnanananda went to him and joyously demanded his winnings. "What for?" inquired Brahmananda. Then the disconcerting truth dawned upon Vijnanananda. Finding the tables turned on him, he said, "Well, I have no money; you must pay it for me." All laughed.[60] On another occasion, a similar result greeted Brahmananda's prediction about rain. Later, Vijnanananda narrated these incidents as a tribute to his illustrious brother monk.

The disciples of the Master had tremendous mutual love and respect for one another; this created solidarity within the Order. Once Brahmananda told some of his disciples: "Hari Prasanna Maharaj has come from Allahabad. Have you met him? Please go and pay your obeisance to him. He is a knower of Brahman; and having attained the supreme state of beatitude, he is calm and silent. It is difficult to recognize him; he generally eludes people."[61]

After Brahmananda passed away in 1922, Shivananda became president of the Ramakrishna Order. On 25 April 1933 Shivananda had a stroke. His right side was paralyzed and very soon his speech became impaired. A few months later Vijnanananda arrived at Belur Math to see him. When the monks asked Vijnanananda the reason for his surprise visit, he replied that a couple of days before he had been very disturbed about Shivananda's condition; then the Master appeared to him and said, "Don't worry; I am looking after him." "Immediately my anxiety ceased," said Vijnanananda. "Next it came to my mind that I must see this great soul who is protected by the Master. So I left for Calcutta yesterday."[62]

Although Shivananda could not talk, he was pleased to see his brother disciple and blessed him. Vijnanananda later described his experience: "That day Mahapurush [Swami Shivananda] laid his hand on my head; his touch changed my mental attitude. He passed on to me his great desire to help people spiritually and to assume responsibility for them. I now feel that as long as I live and have the least strength in my body I shall do the same and give the Master's name to all."[63] All these years Vijnanananda had lived a quiet and secluded life. He had avoided crowds, and spoke only occasionally to select individuals on spiritual matters. After this incident, however, he began to mingle more freely with people and to give initiation to seekers, refusing none.

In 1934, after Shivananda passed away, it was proposed that Swami Vijnanananda become a trustee and the vice-president of the Ramakrishna Math and Mission. Swami Akhandananda, the president, knew that his brother monk collected fountain pens as a hobby, so he wrote to him, "Brother, please give your consent and sign your name; and I shall present a fountain pen to you." Vijnanananda wrote back: "Brother, when you send me the pen, I shall sign my name with it." Akhandananda sent him a pen; the swami signed and became the vice-president of the Rama-krishna Order.[64] This incident shows the results of Sri Ramakrishna's training — his disciples had no desire for power or position. After becoming vice-president, Vijnanananda travelled widely and initiated many people. About initiation, he remarked: "When people come to me for a mantram, I take them to the Master's shrine and introduce them to him. Afterwards the Master will do what is necessary."[65]

On 20 December 1936 a devotee asked Vijnanananda at Belur Math: "One is supposed to repeat the mantram with joy, but quite often I feel depressed. What shall I do?" The swami replied: "Japam means repeating the Lord's name. It does not matter what mood you are in, you should continue your japam. Know for certain that you are separate from the mind. Don't pay any attention to whether you have joy or misery in your mind." Soon after, another devotee approached him for initiation. The swami at first declined, then said indignantly: "People take initiation and then write letter after letter. They do not practise spiritual disciplines according to the instructions. They only complain and disturb me." When the devotee finally persuaded Vijnanananda to accept him, the swami compassionately said: "All right. If you do not write me too many letters, come tomorrow morning for initiation."[66]

Once while at Belur Math Vijnanananda went to visit Kalighat in South Calcutta. There he had a mystical experience that he later narrated: "I was taken inside the temple. I saw and touched the Divine Mother's image; then while I was circumambulating the deity, the Mother, out of Her infinite mercy, revealed Herself unto me. She roused my *kundalini* [the serpent power that resides at the base of the spine] to the *sahasrara* [the thousand-petalled lotus on the crown of the head] and illumined it quickly."[67]

On another occasion he had a vision of Lord Shiva in the Art Studio of Calcutta. He described this experience: "I went alone to the studio and saw a beautiful picture of Lord Shiva. He was in a standing posture and had matted locks and a beard. A standing portrait of Shiva is rare. I gazed at it intently and was soon filled with ecstasy. The picture became living to me, and I felt that Lord Shiva would talk to me. I still vividly remember that sweet divine mood and I feel joy whenever I think of that picture."[68]

Sometimes after talking about his visions he would realize that some of his audience were sceptical. He would then change the topic and speak in a lighter vein: "You see, Rakhal Maharaj and I had all sorts of visions. Both of us had little sleep at night, so we used to see all those things. You are all young Bengalis; you do not have to believe in them."[69]

Vijnanananda considered Belur Math to be a genuinely holy place; it had been sanctified by the touch of Holy Mother and all sixteen of Sri Ramakrishna's direct disciples. Once the swami remarked: "Mother Annapurna [the goddess of food] is ever-present in Belur Math. It is a place of mendicants who have no money. But people bring food and all sorts of things. It is the grace of the Mother that the monastery store is always full.... Anybody who lives in Belur Math and practises japam and meditation intensely in solitude will attain spiritual experiences."[70] In 1937, after Akhandananda passed away, Vijnanananda became the president of the Ramakrishna Order.

"A Hidden Knower of Brahman"

Brahmananda once remarked, "Vijnanananda is a hidden knower of Brahman."[71] The Bhagavata gives a description of an illumined soul's way of life: "Though wise, he plays like a child unconcerned about status; though highly intelligent, he behaves like a fool without any plans; though learned, he speaks like one who is mad to avoid popularity; though established in the truth taught by the Vedas, he roams about like cattle with absolute unconcern for all established codes of conduct" (11.18.29). We must look at Vijnanananda's actions from this perspective in order to understand their true meaning; otherwise, he will be misunderstood.

Another important characteristic of Vijnanananda was his wonderful sense of humour. Although he seemed to be a serious person, he could make people laugh with his childlike simplicity, playful moods, jokes, and witty remarks. Humour has its place in religion: Although it is not accepted by many religions, it can actually be a mode of spiritual self-expression. Because a real Vedantin — a knower of Brahman — knows that the world is a dream, he can make fun of it.

One evening Vijnanananda pointed to the stars and said to his devotees: "They are my friends. How beautifully they are twinkling!" Soon after this a devotee asked the swami to tell a story. Immediately he said with a chuckle, "Am I your grandmother?" Then he continued: "Yes, everything is a fairy tale — really. If you can think of the world as unreal, how happy you will be! Trouble arises when you think of it as a reality."

In this connection he told the story of Diogenes, the famous Greek philosopher who considered the world to be a dream. One day some young students tied the philosopher's legs and pulled him over the street. His body was covered with cuts and bruises. Then the students asked, "Do you still think that the world is a dream?" Diogenes replied, "Yes, the world is a dream — but a painful dream."[72]

In 1933, on his way to Colombo, Sri Lanka, Vijnanananda stopped for a few days at the Madras Math. One day while he was removing his coat, sweater, shirt, and T-shirt, the young monks were watching him with great curiosity. One young monk commented: "Maharaj, Sri Ramakrishna compared the ego to an onion. If anyone removes the layers of an onion one after another, there will be nothing left. We see you are also removing your clothing like that." The swami said with a smile, "Five sheaths are within the body, and I put seven or eight more coverings over that, otherwise people will see my Atman."[73] All laughed.

Once Vijnanananda asked a disciple, "Have you ever seen a *bhut* [ghost]?" When the disciple replied, "No," the swami said: "There are five ghosts in your body. Do not fear. Chant the name of Rama; all the ghosts will run away. Where Rama's name is chanted, no ghosts can live."[74] *Bhut* means ghost and also element. The swami made a pun by saying *panchabhut*, i.e., five elements — space, air, fire, water, earth — that constitute the human body, as well as everything else in this universe.

In Allahabad Vijnanananda once told a young monk, "I shall make you hear Krishna's flute." At noon he took the curious monk outside and showed him a steamroller that was levelling the street. From time to time the driver pulled the whistle. As soon as he heard the sound, the swami said, "Listen, there is Krishna playing the flute!" The monk burst into laughter. Vijnanananda said with a jovial grin: "Why are you laughing? As Lord Krishna unselfishly does good to the world, so does that steamroller."[75]

As a knower of Brahman, Vijnanananda could read others' minds. The scripture says: "Tell the truth, but don't tell a harsh truth. However, if you love a person tell the harsh truth." Vijnanananda told people, when asked, what was good for them. Sometimes his words were pleasant and sometimes unpleasant. It was not posssible for him to flatter anyone or to utter an agreeable falsehood for the sake of courtesy. Once a fashionable modern girl came to the ashrama and sat abruptly in front of the swami. She then posed a question, "What is your advice to us?" His typical answer was, "Eat much, talk much, and quarrel much."[76] The girl was very embarrassed. Perhaps Vijnanananda sensed her quarrelsome nature, and intended for his sharp answer to remind her not to quarrel the rest of her life.

In January 1938 when Vijnanananda went to Belur Math for the dedication of Sri Ramakrishna's temple, he was almost constantly surrounded by people. He said: "Allahabad is a nice place. I have sufficient privacy there and not too many people come to me. But in Belur Math I am surrounded by a crowd almost continually — I can hardly breathe. Why do people come to see me? I am not a good-looking person, nor do I have any good qualities. Still people flock to me." His attendant replied: "Maharaj, you are a son and representative of Sri Ramakrishna; so seeing you they get peace." Later, on the Master's birthday, he greeted the devotees without taking any rest. He said to his attendant: "Today is an auspicious day, and the devotees are coming from a long distance just for a little peace. Let them come. It does not matter whether or not I get rest today."[77]

Sometimes Vijnanananda would enjoy light-hearted discussions. Once he was seated on the upper eastern veranda of Belur Math and two devotees were debating: Which is greater — self-effort or grace? They asked the swami, "Which one is greater?" Without answering their question, he asked a third devotee to say something. The high-spirited discussion continued and he listened. At last when all of them asked him for a solution, he said, "Whatever one thinks of as great, that is great to him."[78]

On another occasion he became the umpire of a debate between two devotees. One devotee said: "Maharaj, my friend says that knowledge is greater than devotion, but the Master said, 'Bhakti [devotion] has access to the inner court of a house and jnana [knowledge] can only go as far as the outer rooms.' He is not accepting the words of the Master." Vijnanananda signalled the other devotee to answer. That devotee said: "The Master declared: 'The sun of knowledge melts the ice of devotion.' So knowledge is greater than bhakti." When they could not reach any conclusion, the swami said: "Devotion is great to a bhakta and knowledge is great to a jnani. In the initial stage an aspirant experiences a difference; but after attaining perfection, he realizes that knowledge and devotion are the same."[79]

Sometimes the direct disciples of Sri Ramakrishna would tease each other or have fun with the young monks to ease the rigid routine of the monastery. Once a young monk expressed a desire to give a lecture. Brahmananda arranged a meeting on the veranda and asked all monks to be present. The speaker was formally dressed and had also put on a nice turban. Then Brahmananda announced, "I propose that Swami Vijnanananda take the chair and preside over the meeting." Immediately Vijnanananda got up and announced, "I now dissolve the meeting." All laughed and the meeting ended.[80]

The minds of knowers of Brahman always soar high. In order to help mankind, they cultivate some hobbies or desires to bring their minds down to the earthly plane. Vijnanananda had some interesting hobbies. He had a large collection of fountain pens, and most of them were very expensive. Sometimes he would go to Calcutta with his attendant to buy new pens. He once said about his method of writing, "I have several fountain pens which I fill with ink, and then I write."[81] Once when he was in Belur Math, Shivananda presented him with a good fountain pen and a flashlight. Another one of his hobbies was collecting tea sets. One day he went to the market and bought a German cup and saucer and showed them to Shivananda. While Vijnanananda was in Rangoon he bought a cup and saucer set made of ivory. Whenever he travelled he would carry a small suitcase that contained his tea sets and a flask of tea. He also had a wide selection of pocketknives and pocket watches. Some of these articles are still in the archives of the Ramakrishna Math in Allahabad.

Once Vijnanananda went to Belur Math and heard that Swami Shuddhananda had ridden in an airplane. He immediately asked to have a plane ride. An arrangement was made and he flew over the Belur Monastery.[82]

Allahabad is very hot in the summer. Because of that Vijnanananda had three beds — one in the courtyard, one on the veranda, and another in his room. He usually slept in the courtyard, but if it was raining he would sleep on the veranda, and if there was a severe rainstorm he would move to his room.[83] He allowed no one to clean his room except Beni, his faithful servant. The swami was very fond of Beni, a pure, guileless boy. Once Vijnanananda wrote a letter to Beni from Belur Math and asked a monk to write the address of the Allahabad Ashrama on the envelope. The letter was addressed to Dr. Beni Madhav, M.A.B.L., LL.D. The monk, out of curiosity, asked, "Maharaj, who is he?" The swami only smiled. Another monk indicated that it was Beni, the swami's servant. All laughed. Beni served Vijnanananda until the swami passed away. Vijnanananda left some money for Beni, which he donated to the centre, where he lived the remainder of his life.[84]

The Consecration of Ramakrishna Temple

Swami Vivekananda had expressed an earnest desire to have the relics of Sri Ramakrishna permanently housed in an enduring and imposing temple that would continue to inspire people for ages. Shivananda had laid the foundation stone for this temple on 13 March 1929. Afterwards, when the new temple site was selected in July of 1935, Vijnanananda had to re-lay the same stone one hundred feet south. It took nearly three years to construct the main part of the temple, then another year to complete it. In the early part of 1938, Dr. Carl G. Jung, the celebrated European psychologist, came to Belur Math. He asked Vijnanananda, "Did Swami Vivekananda give you the idea to build this Ramakrishna Temple?" "Yes, he did," replied the swami. "I made the first plan based on his ideas, but he did not like it. I revised the plan a couple of times and Swamiji approved the last one."[85]

The Ramakrishna Temple of Belur Math is a combination of Eastern and Western styles of architecture. The temple is 235 feet long, 140 feet wide, and the pinnacle of the dome is 108 feet high. On a marble pedestal in the shrine is an Italian marble statue of Sri Ramakrishna in the familiar samadhi (sitting) posture. The total cost of the construction was 800,000 rupees, of which 650,000 rupees was donated by Miss Helen Rubel and Mrs. Anna Worcester, two American devotees of Swami Akhilananda, the founder of the Ramakrishna Vedanta Society in Boston.

On 12 January 1938 Vijnanananda came to Belur Math from Allahabad for the consecration of the Ramakrishna Temple. On Friday, 14 January 1938, the swami got up early in the morning and put on a new ochre cloth. He sat quietly in his chair, waiting for the auspicious moment. He said to his attendant: "When I install the Master in the new temple, I shall say to Swamiji: 'Your consecrated deity has now been installed in the temple you planned. You said that you would watch from on high. Please see now that the Master is seated in the new temple.'"[86]

Vijnanananda's health was not good, so it was arranged for a car to take him from the Math building to the new temple. A monk brought the relics of the Master from the old shrine and handed them to Vijnanananda who waited in the car. Then the procession moved to the accompaniment of conches, bells, and the burning of incense. A group of singers led the procession, singing the famous Bengali song in praise of Sri Ramakrishna that begins with "*Eshechhe nutan manush dekhbi yadi ay chole*" (A new man has appeared; come, if you want to see him). The procession reached the new temple at 6:30 a.m. Vijnanananda entered the inner sanctum, placed the relics of Sri Ramakrishna on the altar, and offered the flowers. When the worship was over, he returned to his room.

After breakfast, his attendant asked him whether he had said anything to Swamiji. Vijnanananda replied: "Yes. I said to Swamiji, 'You told me that you would watch from on high. Please see now that the Master is seated in the new temple.' Then I vividly saw Swamiji, Rakhal Maharaj, Mahapurush Maharaj, Sharat Maharaj, Hari Maharaj, Gangadhar Maharaj, and others standing in the southwest corner watching the consecration ceremony."[87] After a while the swami said: "Now my work is over. Today I am relieved of the responsibility that Swamiji entrusted to me."[88]

His Passing Away

Some people in this world are selected by God to carry out His mission; it is God who decides what He will do through them and for how long. Sri Ramakrishna told Vijnanananda, "You belong to the Divine Mother and you will have to do a lot of work for Her." The swami obeyed his guru's order. He taught and inspired many people, less through lecturing than through his exemplary life, which was full of purity and renunciation. After the dedication of the temple, Vijnanananda began to prepare for his departure from this world.

He returned to Allahabad on 16 January 1938, then came back to Belur Math on 26 February for the birth anniversary of Sri Ramakrishna. He told the monks at Belur Math: "Please arrange to have someone else as your president. My failing health may not permit me to come here again."[89] His feet began to swell and a doctor diagnosed his condition as infectious dropsy. When his attendant insisted that he take medication, he said, "I have no faith in doctors." A monk suggested that the swami consult the famous physician who had treated Swami Shivananda. "Is there any doctor better than this one?" asked the swami. The monk replied, "Yes, there is one — Dr. Nilratan Sarkar." "Is there anybody greater than him?" "No, there is none. He is the best doctor here." Then Vijnanananda said: "Yes, there is one better still, and he is the Master himself. I am under his care."[90] This was his last visit to Belur Math.

On 8 March 1938 Vijnanananda returned to Allahabad; he continued his last task—translating the Ramayana from Sanskrit into English. Unfortunately, he could not complete it. One day he was joking with a devotee: "Do you know the meaning of the word *rum*? [In Bengali it sounds like Ram, i.e., Lord Ramachandra.] It is a kind of liquor. You cannot know it unless you drink it. Similarly, you cannot know the glory of God's name unless you chant it."[91] He decided to spend his last days chanting the name of the Lord. He refused medical treatment and gradually stopped eating. From time to time he drank some mineral water, tea, or lemonade.

A week before he passed away, a monk suggested that Vijnanananda consult an ayurvedic doctor. Vijnanananda gravely quoted a Sanskrit couplet, "Ganges water is the medicine and the Lord is the physician." He then waved the monk away. The swami calmly endured his pain; from time to time he murmured: "Mother, Mother," or "Master, let us go; let us go."[92] On 19 April a devotee came from Assam for initiation. Vijnanananda immediately initiated him while sitting in a chair. His voice and facial expression changed while initiating the devotee and no one could believe that he was on the verge of death. The swami once said, "As long as I have a little strength in my body, I shall distribute the Master's name."[93] He fulfilled his promise.

The news of Vijnanananda's serious condition spread. On Sunday, 24 April, some monks from Varanasi came with a doctor. No one dared to tell him to take allopathic medicine, so the doctor prescribed a homeopathic medicine and asked the attendant to give it to him mixed with water. The next day at 10:00 a.m. the doctor came again and asked Vijnanananda, "How are you?" "I am fine," replied the swami. His eyes were closed and his face was as serene as if he were immersed in meditation. When his attendants tried to change his position, he made a little noise "ah, ah," indicating that his end was imminent. A monk put a little Ganges water into his mouth and other monks began to chant, "*Om Namo Bhagavate Rama-krishnaya*" (Salutations to Bhagavan Ramakrishna). Vijnanananda's face beamed with joy and he passed away at 3:20 p.m. on Monday, 25 April 1938. The next day the monks and devotees carried his body to the confluence of the Ganges and Jamuna, placed it in a stone coffin, and then immersed it into that holy water where he had once had a vision of Mother Triveni.[94]

Swami Vijnanananda's life verified that God is not a myth, and that religion means the realization of God. His spiritual experiences silenced the speculation of those who only talked of religion, and removed the doubts of many agnostics and atheists. Once a prominent barrister of Calcutta said to the swami, "Maharaj, we don't understand God; we understand money, property, and the material world." Swami Vijnanananda listened to him with closed eyes. Then, placing his hand on his own chest, he said: "Whatever you say is true from your standpoint, but I have experienced the one pervading consciousness behind this manifested world. I have seen it with my own eyes." The barrister was speechless.[95]

Another time a monk asked the swami, "Do you see the Master even now?" Pointing to the picture of Sri Ramakrishna, Swami Vijnanananda replied: "The Master is there. He is always near me. Of course I see him, whenever it is necessary. He is guiding me."[96]

Sixteen Monastic Disciples of Sri Ramakrishna

left to right: Vijnananda, Akhandananda, Saradananda, Advaitananda,
Adbhutananda, Yogananda, Premananda, Brahmananda, Vivekananda, Turiyananda,
Shivananda, Ramakrishnananda, Subodhananda, Triguanatitananda,
Abhedananda, Niranjanananda

Painting by Swami Tadatmananda

Courtesy: Vedanta Society of Southern California

REFERENCES

Sri Ramakrishna (Introduction)

1. Christopher Isherwood, *Ramakrishna and His Disciples* (Methuen & Co.: London, 1965), 20.
2. *Life of Sri Ramakrishna* (Advaita Ashrama: Calcutta, 1943), 11.
3. Isherwood, 20.
4. Ibid., 21.
5. Ibid., 28-29.
6. *Life of Sri Ramakrishna*, 69.
7. Isherwood, 65.
8. Ibid., 85.
9. Ibid., 124.
10. Ibid., 148.
11. M., *Sri Sri Ramakrishna Kathamrita* (Kathamrita Bhavan: Calcutta, 1961), I:5.
12. M., *The Gospel of Sri Ramakrishna*, trans. by Swami Nikhilananda (Ramakrishna-Vivekananda Center: New York, 1969), 46.
13. *The Complete Works of Swami Vivekananda* (Advaita Ashrama: Calcutta, 1966), IV:185.
14. Ibid., 187.
15. His Eastern and Western Disciples, *The Life of Swami Vivekananda* (Advaita Ashrama: Calcutta, 1979), I:183.

Ch. 1 – Swami Vivekananda

1. Christopher Isherwood, *Ramakrishna and His Disciples* (Methuen & Co.: London, 1965), 188.
2. Romain Rolland, The *Life of Ramakrishna* (Advaita Ashrama: Calcutta, 1931), 250-51.
3. Swami Chetanananda, ed., *Meditation and its Methods* (Vedanta Press: Hollywood, 1976), 19.
4. His Eastern and Western Disciples, *The Life of Swami Vivekananda* (Advaita Ashrama: Calcutta, 1979), I:48.
5. Ibid., 107.
6. Romain Rolland, *The Life of Vivekananda* (Advaita Ashrama: Calcutta, 1931), 5.

7. Isherwood, 195.
8. *The Complete Works of Sister Nivedita* (Sister Nivedita Girls' School: Calcutta, 1967), I:22.
9. Swami Nikhilananda, *Vivekananda: The Yogas and Other Works* (Ramakrishna-Vivekananda Center: New York, 1953), 15.
10. Ibid., 15-16.
11. Isherwood, 203.
12. EW/*Life*, I.94.
13. Ibid., 96.
14. Ibid., 96-97.
15. Isherwood, 207-8.
16. Nikhilananda, 17.
17. Isherwood, 209.
18. EW/*Life*, I:124.
19. Isherwood, 210.
20. Ibid., 213.
21. EW/*Life*, I:128.
22. Shankari Prasad Basu, *Nivedita Lokamata* (Ananda Publishers: Calcutta, 1968), 320-21.
23. EW/*Life*, I:139-40.
24. M., *The Gospel of Sri Ramakrishna*, trans. by Swami Nikhilananda (Ramakrishna-Vivekananda Center: New York, 1969), 810-11.
25. *The Complete Works of Swami Vivekananda*, (Advaita Ashrama: Calcutta, 1966), IV:178,180.
26. Nikhilananda, 33-34.
27. *Complete Works* (1969), VII:206-7.
28. Nikhilananda, 35.
29. *Complete Works*, VII:248-49.
30. *Vedanta Darpan* (New York), May 1932:9.
31. RR/*Vivekananda*, 20.
32. Nikhilananda, 40.
33. Ibid., 45.
34. *Complete Works* (1970), V:137.
35. EW/*Life*, I:269.
36. Ibid., I:286.
37. RR/*Vivekananda*, 34.

38. Marie Louise Burke, *Swami Viveka-nanda in the West: New Discoveries* (Advaita Ashrama: Calcutta, 1983), I:66.
39. EW/*Life*, I:418.
40. *Complete Works*, V:314.
41. *Prabuddha Bharata*, 1945:44.
42. *Complete Works*, V:104-5.
43. EW/*Life*, I:448.
44. Ibid., I:452.
45. His Eastern and Western Admirers, *Reminiscences of Swami Vivekananda* (Advaita Ashrama: Calcutta, 1983), 258.
46. *Complete Works* (1968), VI:262.
47. Nivedita, I:17,30.
48. Nikhilananda, 110.
49. *Complete Works* (1970), III:110.
50. *Prabuddha Bharata*, 1978:125.
51. *Bharate Vivekananda* (Udbodhan Office: Calcutta, 1958), 478; *Udbodhan*, 25:731.
52. Nikhilananda, 137.
53. Ibid., 144; EW/*Life* (1981), II:383.
54. Nikhilananda, 146.
55. Ibid., 146.
56. Ibid., 149.
57. Nivedita, I:122.
58. Ibid., I:86.
59. *Reminiscences*, 265.
60. Ibid., 238.
61. Burke (1987), V:259-60.
62. Ibid., V:254.
63. Ibid., V:400.
64. *Reminiscences*, 384.
65. Ibid., 364.
66. *Complete Works* (1964), VIII:125-26.
67. EW/*Life*, II:518.
68. *Complete Works* (1970), I:461,474.
69. Nikhilananda, 155.
70. *Reminiscences*, 260-61.
71. Nikhilananda, 167.
72. EW/*Life*, II:590.
73. *Reminiscences*, 243.
74. *Udbodhan*, 38:59-60.
75. Nikhilananda, 174.
76. Swami Nirlepananda, *Swamijir Smriti Sanchayan* (Karuna Prakashani: Calcutta, 1967), 70-71.
77. Nikhilananda, 168.
78. Ibid., 172-73.
79. EW/*Life*, II:621.
80. Ibid., II:645.
81. *Reminiscences*, 242.
82. From Swami Siddheswarananda's Diary.
83. EW/*Life*, II:612-13.
84. Nikhilananda, 173.
85. EW/*Life*, II:632.
86. Nirlepananda, 18.
87. *Vedanta Darpan*, May 1932:10.
88. EW/*Life*, II:650-51.
89. Nikhilananda, 177.
90. EW/*Life*, II:653-54.
91. Ibid., II:654.
92. Nikhilananda, 178.
93. *Vedanta Darpan*, May 1932:10.
94. Nikhilananda, 179.

Ch. 2 – Swami Brahmananda

1. M., *The Gospel of Sri Ramakrishna*, trans. by Swami Nikhilananda (Ramakrishna-Vivekananda Center: New York, 1969), 669.
2. *The Gospel*, 332.
3. *Life of Sri Ramakrishna* (Advaita Ashrama: Calcutta, 1943), 323.
4. *The Gospel*, 534-35.
5. His Eastern and Western Disciples, *The Life of Swami Vivekananda* (Advaita Ashrama: Calcutta, 1979), I:94.
6. *Swami Brahmananda* (Udbodhan Office: Calcutta, 1941), 39.
7. *The Gospel*, 192.
8. Christopher Isherwood, *Ramakrishna and His Disciples* (Methuen & Co.: London, 1965), 180.
9. *The Gospel*, 194-95.
10. Isherwood, 180.
11. *Life of Sri Ramakrishna*, 324.
12. Isherwood, 180.
13. Swami Chetanananda, *They Lived with God* (Vedanta Society: St. Louis, 1989), 164.
14. *Brahmananda*, 44.
15. Brahmachari Akshay Chaitanya, *Brahmananda Lilakatha* (Nava Bharat Publisher: Calcutta, 1972), 9.
16. Swami Chetanananda, trans., *A Guide to Spiritual Life* (Vedanta Society: St. Louis, 1988), 60.
17. *The Gospel*, 270.
18. *A Guide*, 38.
19. Ibid., 49-50.
20. Ibid., 16.
21. Ibid., 152.
22. *Brahmananda*, 67.
23. Ibid., 57-58.
24. *A Guide*, 56-57.
25. *The Gospel*, 221.
26. *Brahmananda*, 68.

27. Swami Saradananda, *Sri Ramakrishna, The Great Master*, trans. by Swami Jagadananda (Ramakrishna Math: Madras, 1979), II:819.

28. Ibid., II:819.

29. *The Gospel*, 710.

30. Ibid., 715.

31. Ibid., 957.

32. Swami Prabhavananda, *The Eternal Companion* (Vedanta Press: Hollywood, 1960), 22.

33. *A Guide*, 52.

34. *The Gospel*, 833.

35. Ibid., 942-43.

36. Ibid., 994-95.

37. *Brahmananda*, 132.

38. *A Guide*, 18.

39. Ibid., 19.

40. *Prabuddha Bharata*, 1930:338.

41. Swami Gambhirananda, *Bhakta Malika* (Udbodhan Office: Calcutta, 1963), II:120.

42. *A Guide*, 20.

43. Ibid., 20-21.

44. Mahendra Nath Datta, *Ajatshatru Srimat Swami Brahmanander Anudhyan* (Mahendra Publishing Committee: Calcutta, 1975), 40-45.

45. Swami Purnatmananda, *Smritir Aloy Swamiji* (Udbodhan Office: Calcutta, 1990), 194.

46. *A Guide*, 37

47. *Brahmananda*, 180

48. Sharat Chandra Chakrabarty, *Swami Shishya Samvad* (Udbodhan Office: Calcutta, 1961), II:185.

49. EW/*Life* (1981), II:389.

50. *The Complete Works of Swami Vivekananda* (Advaita Ashrama: Calcutta, 1969), VII:252.

51. Swami Jagadiswarananda, *Swami Vijnanananda* (Ramakrishna Math: Allahabad, 1947), 243.

52. *Udbodhan*, Vivekananda Centenary Number, 262.

53. EW/*Life*, II:628.

54. Swami Gambhirananda, comp. & ed., *The Apostles of Sri Ramakrishna* (Advaita Ashrama: Calcutta, 1967), 96.

55. His Eastern and Western Admirers, *Reminiscences of Swami Vivekananda* (Advaita Ashrama: Calcutta, 1983), 329.

56. *Vedanta and the West* (Hollywood), 108:43.

57. *Udbodhan*, 56:43.

58. *The Eternal Companion*, 59.

59. Swami Ashokananda, *Swami Brahmananda* (Vedanta Society: San Francisco, 1970), 26.

60. Ibid., 26-27.

61. *The Apostles*, 98.

62. Swami Prabhananda, *Brahmananda Charit* (Udbodhan Office: Calcutta, 1982), 314-15.

63. *Lilakatha*, 169.

64. *Vedanta and the West*, 109:21.

65. Ibid., 109:21-22.

66. *Udbodhan*, 44:87.

67. Swami Nikhilananda, *Holy Mother* (Ramakrishna-Vivekananda Center: New York, 1962), 307.

68. Ibid., 307-8.

69. Ibid., 308-9.

70. Swami Kamaleswarananda, *Sri Ramakrishna Parikar Prasanga* (Calcutta, 1977), 32-33.

71. *Brahmananda*, 303-4.

72. Prabhananda, 255.

73. *A Guide*, 22.

74. Sister Devamata, *Days in an Indian Monastery* (Ananda Ashrama: La Crescenta, 1927), 146.

75. *The Story of a Dedicated Life* (Ramakrishna Math: Madras, 1959), 141.

76. *Prabuddha Bharata*, 1930:498.

77. *The Story*, 141.

78. *Days in Monastery*, 152,154.

79. Ibid., 160-61.

80. *Udbodhan*, 85:475.

81. Swami Narottamananda, *Raja Maharaj* (Udbodhan Office: Calcutta, 1954), 90.

82. Swami Mukteswarananda, *Smritikatha* (Calcutta, 1970), 93.

83. *Lilakatha*, 171.

84. *Smritikatha*, 156.

85. Ashokananda, 48-49.

86. *Smritikatha*, 164-66.

87. *Udbodhan*, 62:36.

88. *Vedanta and the West* (Memories of Maharaj), 59.

89. Swami Yatiswarananda, *Meditation and Spiritual Life* (Ramakrishna Ashrama: Bangalore, 1979), xix.

90. *Brahmananda*, 281.

91. From Gurudas Gupta's Diary.

92. *Lilakatha*, 81-82.

93. Ashokananda, 35.

94. *Prabuddha Bharata*, 1930:454.

95. *A Guide*, 150-51.
96. *Brahmananda*, 226.
97. *Smritikatha*, 81-83.
98. *Vedanta Kesari*, 1968:15.
99. *Udbodhan*, 48:11-12.
100. *Memories of Maharaj*, 39.
101. *Udbodhan*, 53:309-10.
102. *Udbodhan*, 48:13; *Ramakrishna Parikar*, 126.
103. *Lilakatha*, 236.
104. *Memories of Maharaj*, 28-29.
105. Ibid., 40-42.
106. *The Eternal Companion*, 162-63.
107. *A Guide*, 22-23.
108. *The Eternal Companion*, 155-58.
109. *Smritikatha*, 140-41.
110. *A Guide*, 95.
111. Ibid., 123-25.
112. Swami Chetanananda, *Swami Adbhutananada: Teachings and Reminiscences* (Vedanta Society: St. Louis, 1980), 100.
113. Swami Satprakashananda, *Sri Ramakrishna's Life and Message in the Present Age* (Vedanta Society: St. Louis, 1976), 129-30.
114. *The Eternal Companion*, 87.
115. Ibid., 78.
116. Ashokananda, 30-31.
117. Swami Aseshananda, *Glimpses of a Great Soul* (Vedanta Press: Hollywood, 1982), 72-73.
118. Satprakashananda, 183-84.
119. *Lilakatha*, 184.
120. Isherwood, 329-30.
121. Pravrajika Prabuddhaprana, *The Life of Josephine MacLeod* (Sarada Math: Calcutta, 1990), 157-58.
122. *The Gospel*, 493.
123. *Vedanta and the West*, 173:22-23.
124. *Sri Sri Ma O Sri Ramakrishna-Parsadganer Smritikatha* (Ramakrishna-Shivananda Ashrama: Barasat, 1965), 30-31.
125. *Memories of Maharaj*, 79.
126. *Udbodhan*, 85:472; *Smritikatha*, 99.
127. *Brahmananda*, 307-8.
128. Ibid., 308-9.
129. *Lilakatha*, 227.
130. *Udbodhan*, 70:672-73.
131. *Prabhananda*, 424.
132. *Udbodhan*, 24:249.
133. *Brahmananda*, 320.
134. *Memories of Maharaj*, 80.
135. *A Guide*, 78.

Ch. 3 – Swami Shivananda

1. From Swami Dhireshananda's diary (Told by Swami Ambikananda).
2. Swamis Vividishananda and Gambhirananda, tran., *For Seekers of God* (Advaita Ashrama: Calcutta, 1975), 34.
3. Swami Apurvananda, *Mahapurush Shivananada* (Udbodhan Office: Calcutta, 1949), 9.
4. Swami Vividishananda, *A Man of God* (Ramakrishna Math: Madras, 1957), 7.
5. *Mahapurush*, 16.
6. Ibid., 17-18.
7. Swami Chetanananda, ed. & trans., *Ramakrishna as We Saw Him* (Vedanta Society: St. Louis, 1990), 117.
8. Ibid., 117.
9. Christopher Isherwood, *Ramakrishna and His Disciples* (Methuen & Co.: London, 1965), 227.
10. *Mahapurush*, 27-28.
11. *A Man*, 262.
12. *For Seekers*, 28-29.
13. The First Disciples of Sri Ramakrishna, *Spiritual Talks* (Advaita Ashrama: Calcutta, 1968), 99-100.
14. *Ramakrishna as We*, 121-26.
15. *A Man*, 20-21.
16. *Mahapurush*, 51.
17. *A Man*, 21-22.
18. *Mahapurush*, 51-52.
19. M., *The Gospel of Sri Ramakrishna*, trans. by Swami Nikhilananda (Ramakrishna-Vivekananda Center: New York, 1969), 846.
20. *A Man*, 27-28.
21. *Ramakrishna as We*, 132.
22. *A Man*, 41-42.
23. Ibid., 55.
24. Ibid., 55.
25. Swami Apurvananda, comp., *Shivananda Vani* (Udbodhan Office: Calcutta, 1964), II:191.
26. *A Man*, 55-56.
27. *Mahapurush*, 117.
28. *A Man*, 63-64.
29. Ibid., 65.
30. Ibid., 66-70.
31. *Udbodhan*, Vivekananda Centenary Number, 262; *Shivananda Vani* (1955), I:163-64.
32. From Gurudas Gupta's Diary (Told by Swami Ambikananda).
33. *Mahapurush*, 359.

34. Ibid., 148.
35. Ibid., 142-43.
36. *A Man*, 78.
37. Ibid., 83-84.
38. Ibid., 84.
39. Ibid., 86.
40. *Mahupurushjir Patravali* (Udbodhan Office: Calcutta, 1953), 63.
41. Ibid., 74.
42. Ibid., 96.
43. *A Man*, 90.
44. Ibid., 92-93.
45. Ibid., 94-95.
46. Ibid., 99.
47. Ibid., 106.
48. Ibid., 109.
49. *Mahapurush*, 214-15.
50. *A Man*, 111.
51. Swami Apurvananda, comp. *Shivananda Smritisangraha* (Ramakrishna-Shivananda Ashrama: Barasat, 1968), II:145.
52. *A Man*, 114.
53. *Mahapurush*, 221.
54. From Gurudas Gupta's Diary (Told by Swami Jnanatmananda).
55. *Mahapurush*, 228-29.
56. Ibid., 231.
57. *A Man*, 127.
58. *Mahapurush*, 237.
59. *Patravali*, 289.
60. *A Man*, 146-47.
61. *Patravali*, 268.
62. *A Man*, 152-53.
63. Ibid., 156-57.
64. *The Ramakrishna Math & Mission Convention* (Belur Math, 1926), 22-38.
65. *A Man*, 153-54.
66. *For Seekers*, 186.
67. *Mahapurush*, 278-79.
68. *A Man*, 141-42.
69. *For Seekers*, 195.
70. *A Man*, 167-68.
71. *For Seekers*, 195.
72. From Gurudas Gupta's Diary (Told by Swami Nikhilananda).
73. *A Man*, 154.
74. *Sri Sri Mahapurush Maharajer Smritikatha* (Ramakrishna-Shivananda Ashrama: Barasat, 1960), 104.
75. *A Man*, 201.
76. Swami Kamaleswarananda, *Sri Ramakrishna Parikar Prasanga* (Calcutta, 1977), 128-29; *Shivananda Vani*, II:1.

77. Swami Satprakashananda, *Sri Ramakrishna's Life and Message in the Present Age* (Vedanta Society: St. Louis, 1976), 178-79.
78. His Devotees: Monastic and Lay, *Swami Shivananada: Reminiscences* (Bharatiya Vidya Bhavan: Bombay, 1971), 51-52.
79. *A Man*, 204-5.
80. *The Voice of India* (San Francisco), 1946:337-38.
81. *Smritisangraha*, I:261.
82. *Mahapurush*, 333; *Smritisangraha*, I:261-62.
83. *A Man*, 208-9.
84. *Smritisangraha*, II:43-44; Pravrajika Prabuddhaprana, *The Life of Josephine MacLeod* (Sarada Math: Calcutta, 1990), 172-73.
85. Swami Divyatmananda, *Divya Prasange* (Udbodhan Office: Calcutta, 1972), 71.
86. Ibid., 77-78.
87. *A Man*, 280.
88. *Smritisangraha*, III:454.
89. *For Seekers*, 238.
90. *Smritisangraha*, I:327-29.
91. Ibid., I:206.
92. Ibid., III:39-40.
93. Ibid., I:17.
94. Ibid., III:423.
95. Ibid., III:442-43.
96. *For Seekers*, 223.
97. *The Voice of India*, 1946:339.
98. *A Man*, 219.
99. From Gurudas Gupta's Diary.
100. *Mahapurush*, 350.
101. Ibid., 329.
102. *The Voice of India*, 1946:341.
103. *Mahapurush*, 367-68.
104. *The Voice of India*, 1946:341.
105. *A Man*, 351.
106. *Smritisangraha*, II:121.

Ch. 4 – Swami Premananda

1. M., *The Gospel of Sri Ramakrishna*, trans. by Swami Nikhilananda (Ramakrishna-Vivekananda Center: New York, 1969), 458.
2. Ibid., 487.
3. Swami Ashokananda, *Swami Premananda* (Vedanta Society: San Francisco, 1970), 8; Brahmachari Akshay Chaitanya, *Premananda Premakatha* (Navabharat Publishers: Calcutta, 1975), 29.
4. Ashokananda, 3.

5. The First Disciples of Sri Ramakrishna, *Spiritual Talks* (Advaita Ashrama: Calcutta, 1968), 80.

6. Swami Chetanananda, ed. & trans., *Ramakrishna as We Saw Him* (Vedanta Society: St. Louis, 1990), 99.

7. *Life of Sri Ramakrishna* (Advaita Ashrama: Calcutta, 1943), 377.

8. *Ramakrishna as We*, 101.

9. *Life of Sri Ramakrishna*, 379.

10. *Premakatha*, 14-15.

11. *Ramakrishna as We*, 102.

12. *The Gospel*, 458.

13. Ibid., 458.

14. Ibid., 488.

15. Ashokananda, 1.

16. *Ramakrishna as We*, 102-3.

17. Ibid., 103.

18. *The Gospel*, 716.

19. Ibid., 716-17.

20. *Ramakrishna as We*, 102-6.

21. Swami Chetanananda, *They Lived with God* (Vedanta Society: St. Louis, 1989), 182-83.

22. *Premakatha*, 25.

23. *Udbodhan*, 27:648.

24. Swami Prabhavananda, ed. & trans., *Swami Premananda: Teachings and Reminiscences* (Vedanta Press: Hollywood, 1968), 114.

25. *Ramakrishna as We*, 110-13.

26. Swami Abhedananda, *Epistles* (Ramakrishna Vedanta Math: Calcutta, 1970), 23-24.

27. Swami Tapasyananda and Swami Nikhilananda, *Sri Sarada Devi: The Holy Mother* (Ramakrishna Math: Madras, 1977), 253-54.

28. *Ramakrishna as We*, 110.

29. *Sri Sarada Devi*, 254.

30. *Ramakrishna as We*, 107.

31. Swami Nirlepananda, *Swamijir Smriti Sanchayan* (Karuna Prakashani: Calcutta, 1967), 12.

32. Swami Chetanananda, trans. & ed., *Spiritual Treasures: Letters of Swami Turiyananda*, (Vedanta Society: St. Louis, 1992), 126.

33. Swami Gambhirananda, *Bhakta Malika* (Udbodhan Office: Calcutta, 1963), I:200-1.

34. *Udbodhan*, 52:291-92.

35. *The Complete Works of Swami Vivekananda* (Advaita Ashrama: Calcutta, 1969), VII:143.

36. Ashokananda, 21; *Udbodhan*, 25:736-37.

37. His Eastern and Western Disciples, *The Life of Swami Vivekananda* (Advaita Ashrama: Calcutta, 1981), II:654.

38. Ashokananda, 32.

39. Ibid., 32.

40. *Premakatha*, 51-52.

41. Ibid., 63.

42. Ashokananda, 37.

43. *Premakatha*, 56.

44. *Udbodhan*, 48:420.

45. Ibid., 48:420.

46. *Premakatha*, 63.

47. *Swami Premananda* (Ramakrishna-Premananda Ashrama: Antpur, 1965), 142-43.

48. *Udbodhan*, 57:425.

49. Prabhavananda, 18-19.

50. *Swami Premananda* (Antpur), 152.

51. Prabhavananda, 115-16.

52. *Premakatha*, 97.

53. *Prabuddha Bharata*, 1941:564.

54. Ibid., 1941:564-65.

55. Ibid., 1933:596.

56. Prabhavananda, 14-15.

57. *Prabuddha Bharata*, 1933:596.

58. Prabhavananda, 16.

59. *Premakatha*, 78-79.

60. *Bhakta Malika*, I:204-5.

61. *Swami Premananda* (Antpur), 31.

62. *Premakatha*, 92.

63. Swami Gambhirananda, comp. & ed., *The Apostles of Sri Ramakrishna* (Advaita Ashrama: Calcutta, 1967), 140.

64. *Bhakta Malika*, I:215.

65. Sister Devamata, *Days in an Indian Monastery* (Ananda Ashrama: La Crescenta, 1927), 261.

66. Prabhavananda, 22-23.

67. Ibid., 23-24.

68. *Bhakta Malika*, I:209.

69. Swami Kamaleswarananda, *Sri Ramakrishna Parikar Prasanga* (Calcutta, 1977), 164-65.

70. Swami Nityatmananda, *Srima Darshan* (General Printers and Publishers: Calcutta, 1972), XII:105-6.

71. *Bhakta Malika*, I:215-16; *Premakatha*, 103-4; *Swami Premananda* (Antpur), 41.

72. Prabhavananda, 17; *Premakatha*, 199-200.

73. Swami Nikhilananda, *Holy Mother* (Ramakrishna-Vivekananda Center: New York, 1962), 261.
74. *The Complete Works of Swami Vivekananda* (Advaita Ashrama: Calcutta, 1968), II:14.
75. From Gurudas Gupta's Diary.
76. *Holy Mother*, 260.
77. *Swami Premananda* (Antpur), 80-81.
78. Ashokananda, 48.
79. *Swami Premananda* (Antpur), 105.
80. Ibid., 111.
81. Ibid., 29.
82. *Udbodhan*, 82:166.
83. *Swami Premananda* (Antpur), 40.
84. Ashokananda, 49.
85. Swami Omkareswarananda, *Premananda* (Ramakrishna Sadhan Mandir: Deoghar, 1946), II:145.
86. Prabhavananda, 92-94.
87. *Ramakrishna Parikar*, 172.
88. *Prabuddha Bharata*, 1930:533.
89. *Ramakrishna Parikar*, 173.
90. *Spiritual Talks*, 81-82.
91. Prabhavananda, 99.
92. Swami Omkareswarananda, *Premananda Jivan-Charit* (Ramakrishna Sadhan Mandir: Deoghar, 1952), 229-30.
93. *Swami Premananda* (Antpur), 127-28.
94. Ibid., 128-29.
95. Ibid., 132.
96. Ibid., 136-37.
97. Ashokananda, 52.
98. *Swami Premananda* (Antpur), 138-39.
99. Ashokananda, 52.
100. *Udbodhan*, 37:240.
101. Ibid., 33:572.
102. *Prabuddha Bharata*, 1918:215.

Ch. 5 – Swami Yogananda

1. Swami Siddhananda, comp., *Satkatha* (Udbodhan Office: Calcutta, 1964), 122-23.
2. Gurudas Barman, *Sri Ramakrishna Charit* (Calcutta, 1909), 202.
3. Swami Gambhirananda, *Bhakta Malika* (Udbodhan Office: Calcutta, 1963), I:151.
4. *Life of Sri Ramakrishna* (Advaita Ashrama: Calcutta, 1943), 394.
5. Ibid., 394.
6. Ibid., 393.
7. Swami Saradananda, *Sri Ramakrishna, The Great Master* (Ramakrishna Math: Madras, 1978), I:391-92.
8. *Life of Sri Ramakrishna*, 395.
9. Ibid., 395
10. *Udbodhan*, 43:529.
11. Ibid., 21:139-40.
12. *Sri Sri Mayer Katha* (Udbodhan Office: Calcutta, 1965), II:12.
13. *The Great Master* (1979), II:903.
14. Ibid., II:903-4.
15. *Udbodhan*, 43:531.
16. *Life of Sri Ramakrishna*, 398.
17. Ibid., 400.
18. *Vedanta and the West*, 187:58.
19. Chandra Sekhar Chattopadhyay, *Sri Sri Latu Maharajer Smritikatha* (Udbodhan Office: Calcutta, 1953), 175.
20. *The Great Master*, II:716.
21. Ibid., I:434.
22. *Life of Sri Ramakrishna*, 401.
23. Swami Chetanananda, ed. & trans., *Ramakrishna as We Saw Him* (Vedanta Society: St. Louis, 1990), 178.
24. Ibid., 178-79.
25. Ibid., 179.
26. *Bhakta Malika*, I:162-63.
27. Mahendra Nath Datta, *Srimat Vivekananda Swamijir Jivaner Ghatanavali* (Mahendra Publishing Committee: Calcutta, 1964), II:4-7.
28. *Latu Smriti*, 159.
29. *The Great Master*, II:760-61.
30. *Bhakta Malika*, I:167.
31. Swami Nikhilananda, *Holy Mother* (Ramakrishna-Vivekananda Center: New York, 1962), 99.
32. *Vedanta and the West*, 201:40-41.
33. Swami Gambhirananda, *Holy Mother Sri Sarada Devi* (Ramakrishna Math: Madras, 1955), 144-45.
34. *Udbodhan*, 38:753.
35. The Bible, Matthew 19:12.
36. *Vivekananda Ghatanavali*, I:35.
37. Ibid., II:116.
38. Ibid., I:33-34.
39. Ibid., I:32-33.
40. Ibid., I:233-34.
41. From Gurudas Gupta's Diary.
42. Swami Apurvananda, comp., *Shivananda Smritisangraha* (Ramakrishna Shivananda Ashrama: Barasat, 1970), III:216-17.
43. Swami Jagadiswarananda, *Navayuger Mahapurush* (Orient Book Company: Calcutta, 1949), 95.

44. Vaikuntha Nath Sanyal, *Sri Rama-krishna Lilamrita* (Calcutta, 1936), 311-12.
45. Her Devotee-Children, *The Gospel of the Holy Mother* (Ramakrishna Math: Madras, 1984), 78.
46. Swami Bhumananda, *Sri Sri Mayer Jivankatha* (Ramakrishna-Sarada Math: Calcutta, 1986), 148.
47. His Eastern and Western Disciples, *Life of Swami Vivekananda* (Advaita Ashrama: Calcutta, 1981), II:249-50.
48. *Bhakta Malika*, I:173.
49. *Holy Mother Sri Sarada Devi*, 187.
50. *Bhakta Malika*, I:180.
51. *Latu Smriti*, 339-40.
52. *Sri Sri Mahapurushjir Katha* (Udbodhan Office: Calcutta, 1934), 110-11.
53. Swami Apurvananda, comp., *Shivananda Vani* (Udbodhan Office: Calcutta, 1964), II:193.
54. *Navayuger Mahapurush*, 104.
55. *Mahapurushjir Katha*, 109.
56. *Kayastha Patrika*, Golden Jubilee Number (Calcutta, 1952), 9.
57. *Udbodhan*, 21:140-41.
58. Ibid., 21:141; The Gospel of Holy Mother, 111.
59. *Holy Mother Sri Sarada Devi*, 186.
60. Ibid., 185.
61. Swami Nirlepananda, *Swamijir Smriti Sanchayan* (Karuna Prakashani: Calcutta, 1967), 28.
62. *Mahapurushjir Katha*, 109.

Ch. 6 – Swami Niranjanananda

1. Chandra Sekhar Chattopodhyay, *Sri Sri Latu Maharajer Smritikatha* (Udbodhan Office: Calcutta, 1953), 400.
2. *Tattwamanjari* (Calcutta, 1905), 8:94.
3. Ibid., 8:94.
4. Swami Gambhirananda, comp. & ed., *The Apostles of Sri Ramakrishna* (Advaita Ashrama: Calcutta, 1967), 161.
5. Gurudas Barman, *Sri Ramakrishna Charit* (Calcutta, 1909), 216.
6. *Latu Smriti*, 400.
7. *Life of Sri Ramakrishna* (Advaita Ashrama: Calcutta, 1943), 382.
8. Swami Saradananda, *Sri Ramakrishna, The Great Master*, trans. by Swami Jagadananda (Ramakrishna Math: Madras, 1979), II:933.
9. Mahendra Nath Datta, *Ajatshatru Srimat Swami Brahmananda Maharajer Anudhyan* (Mahendra Publishing Committee: Calcuttà, 1975), 87.
10. Christopher Isherwood, *Ramakrishna and His Disciples* (Methuen & Co.: London, 1965), 221.
11. *Life of Sri Ramakrishna*, 383-84.
12. M., *The Gospel of Sri Ramakrishna*, trans. by Swami Nikhilananda (Ramakrishna-Vivekananda Center: New York, 1969), 448.
13. Ibid., 443.
14. Ibid., 810.
15. Ibid., 809.
16. *Tattwamanjari*, 8:95.
17. *The Great Master*, I:93-94.
18. Ibid., II:896.
19. *The Gospel*, 448.
20. Swami Chetanananda, *They Lived with God* (Vedanta Society: St. Louis, 1989), 298-99.
21. *The Gospel*, 932.
22. Ibid., 933.
23. Swami Gambhirananda, *Holy Mother Sri Sarada Devi* (Ramakrishna Math: Madras, 1955), 99.
24. Akshay Kumar Sen, `Sri Ramakrishna Punthi* (Udbodhan Office: Calcutta, 1949), 618.
25. Swami Gambhirananda, *Bhakta Malika* (Udbodhan Office: Calcutta, 1963), I:236-37.
26. *Latu Smriti*, 254.
27. *Punthi*, 611-12.
28. Vaikuntha Nath Sanyal, *Sri Ramakrishna Lilamrita* (Calcutta, 1936), 312-13.
29. Swami Jagadiswarananda, *Navajuger Mahapurush* (Ramakrishna Ashrama, Raghunathpur:1951), 2:289.
30. *Bhakta Malika*, I:238.
31. Mahendra Nath Datta, *Srimat Vivekananda Swamijir Jivaner Ghatanavali* (Mahendra Publishing Committee: Calcutta, 1974), II:8-9.
32. *Sri Sri Mayer Katha* (Udbodhan Office: Calcutta, 1969), I:100-1.
33. *The Complete Works of Swami Vivekananda* (Advaita Ashrama: Calcutta, 1968), VI:268.
34. Swami Abjajananda, *Swamijir Padaprante* (Ramakrishna Mission Saradapith: Belur Math, 1972), 308.
35. Ibid., 309.
36. Swami Chetanananda's Collection.
37. *Bhakta Malika*, I:245.

38. *The Apostles*, 167.
39. *Bhakta Malika*, I:248.
40. *The Gospel*, 813.

Ch. 7 – Swami Ramakrishnananda

1. Swami Chetanananda, ed. & trans., *Ramakrishna as We Saw Him* (Vedanta Society: St. Louis, 1990), 141.
2. Ibid., 152.
3. Sister Devamata, *Sri Ramakrishna and His Disciples* (Ananda Ashrama: La Crescenta, 1928), 78.
4. Sister Devamata, *Days in an Indian Monastery* (Ananda Ashrama: La Crescenta, 1927), 239.
5. *Life of Sri Ramakrishna* (Advaita Ashrama: Calcutta, 1943), 472.
6. Ibid., 472-73.
7. Swami Gambhirananda, *Bhakta Malika* (Udbodhan Office: Calcutta, 1963), I:349.
8. *The Story of a Dedicated Life* (Ramakrishna Math: Madras, 1959), 30.
9. Sister Daya, *The Guru and the Disciple* (Vedanta Center: Cohasset, 1976), 51.
10. M., *The Gospel of Sri Ramakrishna*, trans. by Swami Nikhilananda (Ramakrishna-Vivekananda Center: New York, 1969), 933-34.
11. *Bhakta Malika*, I:349.
12. Swami Saradananda, *Sri Ramakrishna, The Great Master*, trans. by Swami Jagadananda (Ramakrishna Math: Madras, 1979), II:881.
13. Swami Kamaleswarananda, *Sri Ramakrishna Parikar Prasanga* (Calcutta, 1977), 74.
14. Ibid., 92.
15. *Days in Monastery*, 31.
16. From Gurudas Gupta's Diary.
17. *Ramakrishna as We*, 150-53.
18. Ibid., 147.
19. Ibid., 148-49.
20. *Bhakta Malika*, I:351.
21. *Prabuddha Bharata*, 1911:189.
22. *Ramakrishna Parikar*, 64.
23. *The Story*, 32-33.
24. *Bhakta Malika*, I:351.
25. *The Gospel*, 952.
26. Ibid., 963-64.
27. *The Story*, 33.
28. *Bhakta Malika*, I:351-52.
29. *Ramakrishna as We*, 157-58.
30. Swami Chetanananda, *Swami Adbhutananda: Teachings and Reminiscences* (Vedanta Society: St. Louis, 1980), 54.
31. Ibid., 55.

32. *The Story*, 41.
33. His Eastern and Western Disciples, *The Life of Swami Vivekananda* (Advaita Ashrama: Calcutta, 1965), 166.
34. *Swami Adbhutananda*, 65-66.
35. Ibid., 66.
36. *Vedanta Kesari*, 1950:129.
37. *The Story*, 47.
38. *Days in Monastery*, 26.
39. *Ramakrishna Parikar*, 40-46.
40. *Life of Vivekananda*, 492.
41. *Udbodhan*, 64:635.
42. Swami Gambhirananda, comp. & ed., *The Apostles of Sri Ramakrishna* (Advaita Ashrama: Calcutta, 1967), 233.
43. *The Story*, 52.
44. *Bhakta Malika*, I:359.
45. *Vedanta Kesari*, 1951:92.
46. *The Story*, 55.
47. Swami Tapasyananda, *Swami Ramakrishnananda, the Apostle of Sri Ramakrishna to the South* (Ramakrishna Math: Madras, 1986), 140.
48. *Ramakrishna Parikar*, 47-48.
49. Tapasyananda, 130.
50. *Ramakrishna Parikar*, 48-49.
51. *Vedanta Kesari*, 1951:91-92.
52. Tapasyananda, 214-15.
53. Ibid., 132.
54. *The Story*, 68.
55. Tapasyananda, 144.
56. *Vedanta Kesari*, 1951:94.
57. *The Story*, 63.
58. Ibid., 64-65.
59. Tapasyananda, 142.
60. *Days in Monastery*, 22.
61. *Vedanta Kesari*, 1950:130.
62. Tapasyananda, 223.
63. Ibid., 226.
64. *Udbodhan*, 48:536.
65. *Vedanta Kesari*, 1951:90.
66. Tapasyananda, 135.
67. Ibid., 229-31.
68. *Ramakrishna Parikar*, 70.
69. *Vedanta Kesari*, 1951:91.
70. *The Story*, 130.
71. Tapasyananda, 135-36.
72. Ibid., 231-32.
73. *The Story*, 141.
74. *Swami Brahmananda* (Udbodhan Office: Calcutta, 1941), 233.
75. *The Story*, 141.
76. *Days in Monastery*, 33.
77. Tapasyananda, 126.

78. Ibid., 126-27.
79. Ibid., 132-34.
80. Told by Swami Prabhavananda.
81. *Vedanta Kesari*, 1951:95.
82. *The Story*, 143-44.
83. Tapasyananda, 216.
84. *Udbodhan*, 48:535.
85. Swami Tapasyananda, *Sri Sarada Devi: the Holy Mother* (Ramakrishna Math: Madras, 1958), 233.
86. Swami Nikhilananda, *Holy Mother* (Ramakrishna-Vivekananda Center: New York, 1962), 305.
87. *Udbodhan*, 28:749.
88. *Vedanta Kesari*, 1967:242.
89. *The Story*, 93.
90. Ibid., 97-106.
91. *Ramakrishna Parikar*, 54-55.
92. *The Gospel*, 443.
93. *Days in Monastery*, 32.
94. Tapasyananda, 175-76.
95. Ibid., 172.
96. Ibid., 181-82.
97. Ibid., 183.
98. Ibid., 183-84.
99. Ibid., 190-91.
100. *Days in Monastery*, 19-20.
101. Ibid., 27.
102. Ibid., 30.
103. Ibid., 30.
104. Ibid., 92-94.
105. *The Story*, 110.
106. Ibid., 110.
107. Ibid., 111.
108. Ibid., 111.
109. Brahmachari Akshay Chaitanya, *Premananda Premakatha* (Navabharat Publishers: Calcutta, 1975), 204-5.
110. Swami Jagadiswarananda, *Swami Ramakrishnananda* (Ramakrishna Mission: Midnapore, 1948), 179.
111. Ibid., 180.
112. Ibid., 180.
113. Ibid., 180-81.
114. *Vedanta Kesari*, 1949:220.
115. Tapasyananda, 168.

Ch. 8 – Swami Saradananda

1. M., *The Gospel of Sri Ramakrishna*, trans. by Swami Nikhilananda (Ramakrishna-Vivekananda Center: New York, 1969), 934.
2. Swami Gambhirananda, comp. & ed., *The Apostles of Sri Ramakrishna* (Advaita Ashrama: Calcutta, 1967), 169.
3. *Life of Sri Ramakrishna* (Advaita Ashrama, 1943), 472-73.
4. Swami Chetanananda, ed. & trans., *Ramakrishna as We Saw Him* (Vedanta Society: St. Louis, 1990), 163-64.
5. *Prabuddha Bharata*, 1927:438.
6. Brahmachari Prakash, *Swami Saradananda* (Basumati: Calcutta, 1936), 24.
7. Swami Saradananda, *Sri Ramakrishna, The Great Master*, trans. by Swami Jagadananda (Ramakrishna Math: Madras, 1979), II:862-63.
8. Ibid., II:881.
9. *The Apostles*, 175.
10. Swami Gambhirananda, *Bhakta Malika* (Udbodhan Office: Calcutta, 1963), I:307.
11. Swami Kamaleswarananda, *Sri Ramakrishna Parikar Prasanga* (Calcutta, 1977), 85; *Ramakrishna as We*, 204.
12. The First Disciples of Sri Ramakrishna, *Spiritual Talks* (Advaita Ashrama: Calcutta, 1968), 356; *The Gospel*, 207.
13. Brahmachari Akshay Chaitanya, *Swami Saradanander Jivani* (Model Publishing House: Calcutta, 1955), 30.
14. Swami Aseshananda, *Glimpses of a Great Soul* (Vedanta Press: Hollywood, 1982), xii.
15. *The Great Master*, II:950-51.
16. Akshay, 33.
17. Akshay, 37; *The Great Master*, II:991.
18. Prakash, 34-35.
19. Akshay, 44.
20. *Ramakrishna as We*, 175.
21. Akshay, 45.
22. Aseshananda, 13.
23. *Bhakta Malika*, I:311.
24. *The Gospel*, 985.
25. Prakash, 47.
26. Ibid., 53.
27. Akshay, 64.
28. *Bhakta Malika*, I:313-14.
29. Akshay, 70; Swami Bhumananda, *Jeman Dekhiachi* (Udbodhan Office: Calcutta, 1928), 78-79.
30. Akshay, 82.
31. Prakash, 92.
32. Aseshananda, 19.
33. Ibid., 19.
34. Ibid., 20.
35. Akshay, 89.
36. Aseshananda, 20-21.

37. A Western Disciple (Swami Atulananda), *With the Swamis in America* (Advaita Ashrama: Calcutta, 1946), 78-79.
38. Aseshananda, 23-24.
39. Ibid., 24.
40. Prakash, 110-12.
41. *Bhakta Malika*, I:321.
42. *Prabuddha Bharata*, 1927:444.
43. Prakash, 135.
44. *Udbodhan*, 29:664.
45. Ibid., 29:668-69.
46. Prakash, 136.
47. Swami Nikhilananda, *Holy Mother* (Ramakrishna-Vivekananda Center: New York, 1962), 270.
48. *The Apostles*, 184.
49. *Holy Mother*, 266.
50. Ibid., 267-69.
51. Ibid., 307.
52. From Gurudas Gupta's Diary.
53. *Jeman Dekhiachi*, 19.
54. Aseshananda, 79.
55. Christopher Isherwood, *Ramakrishna and His Disciples* (Methuen & Co.: London, 1965), 2.
56. Akshay, 150-51.
57. *Udbodhan*, 32:679-80.
58. *Bhakta Malika*, I:330-31.
59. Aseshananda, 248-49.
60. Akshay, 148.
61. Ibid., 191.
62. Aseshananda, 35-36.
63. Prakash, 298-99.
64. Akshay, 170-71.
65. *Prabuddha Bharata*, 1932:552-54.
66. Told by Swami Pavitrananda in Hollywood on 31 July 1973.
67. Aseshananda, 243.
68. *Prabuddha Bharata*, 1927:444-45.
69. *Bhakta Malika*, I:332.
70. Ibid., I:336.
71. *Bhakta Malika*, I:322; Akshay, 100-1.
72. Aseshananda, 52.
73. *Bhakta Malika*, I:342; Akshay, 225.
74. Akshay, 226; *Jeman Dekhiachi*, 314-15.
75. Aseshananda, 90.
76. *Jeman Dekhiachi*, 316.
77. *Prabuddha Bharata*, 1927:442-43.
78. *Udbodhan*, 37:84-85.
79. *Sri Sri Ma O Sri Ramakrishna Parshadganer Smritikatha* (Ramakrishna Shivananda Ashrama: Barasat, 1965), 74-75.
80. *Spiritual Talks*, 355.
81. Ibid., 358.
82. Ibid., 362-63.
83. Ibid., 367-70.
84. Ibid., 377-78.
85. Ibid., 383.
86. Aseshananda, 253-54.
87. *Prabuddha Bharata*, 1927:447.
88. *Udbodhan*, 32:638.
89. Aseshananda, 69.
90. Ibid., 69-70.
91. Ibid., 93.
92. Ibid., 88.
93. *Bhakta Malika*, I:343.
94. *The Ramakrishna Math & Mission Convention 1926* (Belur Math, 1926), 17-21. (Quoted from the edited version of *Glimpses of a Great Soul* by Swami Aseshananda, 192-96.)
95. *Parshadganer Smritikatha*, 76.
96. Aseshananda, 92.
97. Ibid., 92.
98. Akshay, 310.
99. Ibid., 310.
100. Ibid., 310.
101. Aseshananda, 96.
102. Akshay, 313.
103. Aseshananda, 250.
104. *Reminiscences of Pravrajika Bharatiprana* (Three typed pages from Swami Aseshananda's collection.)

Ch. 9 – Swami Turiyananda

1. Swami Ritajananda, *Swami Turiyananda* (Ramakrishna Math: Madras, 1973), 6.
2. Swami Jagadiswarananda, *Swami Turiyananda* (Udbodhan Office: Calcutta, 1964), 4-5.
3. Jagadiswarananda, 11.
4. Swami Chetanananda, trans. & ed., *Spiritual Treasures: Letters of Swami Turiyananda*, (Vedanta Society: St. Louis, 1992), 187-88.
5. Jagadiswarananda, 15; Swami Chetanananda, ed. & trans., *Ramakrishna as We Saw Him* (Vedanta Society: St. Louis, 1990), 194.
6. Ritajananda, 12.
7. *Life of Sri Ramakrishna* (Advaita Ashrama: Calcutta, 1943), 477-78.
8. Ritajananda, 12-13.
9. *Ramakrishna as We*, 190.
10. Ritajananda, 14; *Life of Sri Ramakrishna*, 478.

11. *Ramakrishna as We*, 189.
12. Ibid., 190.
13. Ibid., 190-91.
14. Ibid., 194.
15. Ibid., 191.
16. Ibid., 209.
17. Ritajananda, 19.
18. Ibid., 20.
19. *The Gospel*, 436.
20. Ibid., 801-2.
21. Ritajananda, 23.
22. Swami Atulananda, *Atman Alone Abides* (Ramakrishna Math: Madras, 1978), 163; A Western Devotee (Atulananda), *With the Swamis in America* (Advaita Ashrama, 1946), 59-60.
23. Ritajananda, 28.
24. Jagadiswarananda, 41-42.
25. *Atman Alone*, 163-64.
26. The First Disciples of Sri Ramakrishna, *Spiritual Talks* (Advaita Ashrama: Calcutta, 1968), 125.
27. Ibid., 126.
28. Ibid., 124, 127-28.
29. Jagadiswarananda, 55-56.
30. *Spiritual Talks*, 123-24.
31. Swami Niramayananda, *Swami Akhandanander Smriti-sanchaya* (Udbodhan Office: Calcutta, 1976), 51-52.
32. Ritajananda, 180.
33. Ibid., 43.
34. Ibid., 44.
35. Ibid., 49.
36. *With the Swamis*, 52-54.
37. Ibid., 70.
38. Ibid., 70-71.
39. Ibid., 52.
40. Ibid., 56.
41. Ibid., 71-72.
42. Ibid., 72.
43. Jagadiswarananda, 110.
44. *Prabuddha Bharata*, 1927:414.
45. His Eastern and Western Disciples, *Life of Swami Vivekananda* (Advaita Ashrama: Calcutta, 1981), II:534.
46. Ritajananda, 51.
47. Ibid., 54.
48. *Vedanta and the West*, 1952:135.
49. Ritajananda, 57.
50. *With the Swamis*, 97-98.
51. Ritajananda, 62.
52. *With the Swamis*, 96-97.
53. Ibid., 103.

54. Ibid., 104-5.
55. Ibid., 105.
56. *Vedanta and the West*, 1952:141.
57. Ritajananda, 72.
58. Ibid., 70.
59. *With the Swamis*, 111-12.
60. Ibid., 108-10.
61. Ibid., 98-100.
62. *Vedanta and the West*, 1952:141.
63. Ibid., 1952:141.
64. Ritajananda, 75.
65. Ibid., 74.
66. Ibid., 77.
67. *Prabuddha Bharata*, 1923:225.
68. Ibid., 1925:2.
69. Ibid., 1925:3-4.
70. *Spiritual Treasures*, 238-39.
71. Jagadiswarananda, 182-83.
72. Ritajananda, 89.
73. Ibid., 90.
74. Ibid., 91.
75. *Prabuddha Bharata*, 1925:53.
76. *Atman Alone*, 167-68.
77. Jagadiswarananda, 198.
78. Ibid., 198.
79. Ibid., 199-200.
80. *Spiritual Talks*, 327.
81. *Prabuddha Bharata*, 1925:101-2.
82. Ibid., 146-49.
83. Ritajananda, 114.
84. Ibid., 131-32.
85. *Spiritual Talks*, 192.
86. *Spiritual Treasures*, 156-57.
87. Ritajananda, 126.
88. Jagadiswarananda, 235.
89. Ibid., 239.
90. Ritajananda, 137.
91. Ibid., 139.
92. Ibid., 149-50.
93. Ibid., 155.
94. Ibid., 161.
95. Ibid., 175-76.
96. Ibid., 176-77.
97. Ibid., 186.
98. *Prabuddha Bharata*, 1922:331.
99. Swami Gambhirananda, comp. & ed., *The Apostles of Sri Ramakrishna* (Advaita Ashrama: Calcutta, 1967), 315-16.

Ch. 10 – Swami Adbhutananda

1. Swami Gambhirananda, comp. & ed., *The Apostles of Sri Ramakrishna* (Advaita Ashrama: Calcutta, 1967), 271.

2. Swami Chetanananda, *Swami Adbhutananda: Teachings and Reminiscences* (Vedanta Society: St. Louis, 1980), 12.
3. Chandra Sekhar Chattopadhyay, *Sri Sri Latu Maharajer Smritikatha* (Udbodhan Office: Calcutta, 1953), 491.
4. Ibid., 9.
5. Ibid., 8.
6. Ibid., 11.
7. Ibid., 17.
8. Ibid., 27.
9. Ibid., 31-32.
10. Ibid., 35-36.
11. Ibid., 36-38.
12. Ibid., 41-42.
13. Ibid., 53-57.
14. Ibid., 59.
15. Ibid., 173-74.
16. Ibid., 204-5.
17. Ibid., 65.
18. Ibid., 216-17.
19. Ibid., 93-94.
20. Ibid., 98.
21. Ibid., 179-80.
22. Ibid., 176.
23. The First Disciples of Sri Ramakrishna, *The Message of Our Master* (Advaita Ashrama: Calcutta, 1944), 43.
24. *Latu Smriti*, 181-82.
25. Ibid., 240.
26. Ibid., 103-4.
27. Ibid., 220.
28. Ibid., 221-22.
29. Ibid., 225.
30. Ibid., 225.
31. Ibid., 227-29.
32. Ibid., 222-23.
33. Ibid., 70-71.
34. Ibid., 75-76.
35. Ibid., 96.
36. M., *The Gospel of Sri Ramakrishna*, trans. by Swami Nikhilananda (Ramakrishna-Vivekananda Center: New York, 1969), 571.
37. *The Gospel*, 340; Swami Siddhananda, *Adbhutananda Prasanga* (Ramakrishna Mission: Lucknow, 1957), 120.
38. *Latu Smriti*, 211.
39. *The Gospel*, 504.
40. *Latu Smriti*, 143-44; *Swami Adbhutananda*, 41-42.
41. *The Gospel*, 884-85.
42. *Latu Smriti*, 241.
43. Ibid., 241.
44. Ibid., 251.
45. Ibid., 248.
46. Ibid., 248-49.
47. *Swami Adbhutananda*, 51-53.
48. *Latu Smriti*, 264.
49. Ibid., 267.
50. *Swami Adbhutananda*, 63-64.
51. *Latu Smriti*, 329.
52. Ibid., 329-30.
53. Ibid., 293-94.
54. Ibid., 334.
55. Ibid., 334-35.
56. Ibid., 308-9.
57. Ibid., 335.
58. Ibid., 335-36.
59. Ibid., 336-37.
60. Ibid., 305-6.
61. Ibid., 301-2.
62. Ibid., 309-11.
63. Ibid., 313.
64. Ibid., 314-15.
65. Ibid., 315-16.
66. Ibid., 317.
67. Ibid., 318.
68. *Adbhutananda Prasanga*, 98-99.
69. *Latu Smriti*, 318.
70. Ibid., 318-19.
71. Ibid., 319-20.
72. Ibid., 320-21.
73. Ibid., 342.
74. Ibid., 341-42.
75. Ibid., 343-44.
76. Ibid., 353-54.
77. Ibid., 346-47.
78. Ibid., 347-48.
79. Ibid., 352-53.
80. Ibid., 355-56.
81. Ibid., 357-58.
82. Ibid., 354.
83. Ibid., 361.
84. Ibid., 362-63.
85. *Prabuddha Bharata*, 1932:506-7.
86. *Latu Smriti*, 190.
87. Ibid., 419-20.
88. Ibid., 392-96.
89. Ibid., 433-34.
90. Ibid., 432.
91. Ibid., 423-24.
92. Ibid., 500.
93. Ibid., 439.
94. Ibid., 438-39.
95. Ibid., 450.
96. Ibid., 450-51.
97. *Swami Adbhutananda*, 93.

98. Swami Nikhilananda, *Holy Mother* (Ramakrishna-Vivekananda Center: New York, 1961), 263.
99. *Latu Smriti*, 382.
100. Ibid., 425-27.
101. Ibid., 435.
102. Ibid., 441.
103. Ibid., 446.
104. Ibid., 446-47.
105. Ibid., 474.
106. Ibid., 474-75.
107. Ibid., 190-92.
108. Ibid., 486.
109. Ibid., 482.
110. Ibid., 483.
111. Ibid., 484.
112. Ibid., 481.
113. Ibid., 484.
114. Ibid., 485.
115. Swami Chetanananda, trans. & ed., *Spiritual Treasures: Letters of Swami Turiyananda* (Vedanta Society: St. Louis, 1992), 275-76.
116. *Latu Smriti*, 80-81.

Ch. 11 – Swami Abhedananda

1. Swami Chetanananda, ed. & trans., *Ramakrishna as We Saw Him* (Vedanta Society: St. Louis, 1990), 223-24.
2. Swami Abhedananda, *Amar Jivankatha* (Ramakrishna Vedanta Math: Calcutta, 1964), 12-13.
3. *Ramakrishna as We*, 215-18.
4. *Amar Jivankatha*, 31.
5. Ibid., 42.
6. *Ramakrishna as We*, 219-20.
7. Ibid., 220.
8. Ibid., 221.
9. Ibid., 222.
10. Ibid., 223.
11. Ibid., 224.
12. *Amar Jivankatha*, 102-3.
13. Swami Saradananda, *Sri Ramakrishna, The Great Master*, trans. by Swami Jagadananda (Ramakrishna Math: Madras, 1979), II:1020-21.
14. *Amar Jivankatha*, 87-88.
15. Ibid., 91-92.
16. *The Great Master*, (1978), I:91-92.
17. His Eastern and Western Disciples, *The Life of Swami Vivekananda* (Advaita Ashrama: Calcutta, 1965), 135.
18. *Amar Jivankatha*, 92-93.
19. *Ramakrishna as We*, 224-25.
20. *Amar Jivankatha*, 108.
21. *Life of Vivekananda*, 141.
22. M., *The Gospel of Sri Ramakrishna*, trans. by Swami Nikhilananda (Ramakrishna-Vivekananda Center: New York, 1969), 961.
23. *Amar Jivankatha*, 111-15.
24. *Ramakrishna as We*, 225-26.
25. *Amar Jivankatha*, 117.
26. Ibid., 132.
27. Swami Gambhirananda, *Bhakta Malika* (Udbodhan Office: Calcutta, 1963), I:395.
28. Moni Bagchi, *Swami Abhedananda: A Spiritual Biography* (Ramakrishna Vedanta Math: Calcutta, 1968), 155-56.
29. Swami Chetanananda, *Swami Adbhutananda: Teachings and Reminiscences* (Vedanta Society: St. Louis, 1980), 64.
30. *Amar Jivankatha*, 210.
31. Ibid., 212.
32. *Swami Abhedananda*, 230.
33. *Life of Vivekananda*, 325.
34. *Swami Abhedananda*, 245.
35. Swami Gambhirananda, comp. & ed., *The Apostles of Sri Ramakrishna* (Advaita Ashrama: Calcutta, 1967), 259.
36. A Western Disciple (Swami Atulananda), *With the Swamis in America* (Advaita Ashrama: Calcutta, 1946), 11-13.
37. Swami Sambuddhananda, *Jeman Suniyachi* (Ramakrishna Ashrama: Howrah, 1970), I&II:162, 170.
38. Sister Shivani (Mary Le Page), *Swami Abhedananda in America* (Ramakrishna Vedanta Math: Calcutta, 1991), 96.
39. Ibid., 93-94.
40. Ibid., 97-98.
41. Swami Sankarananda, *Jivankatha* (Ramakrishna Vedanta Math: Calcutta, 1946), 179
42. Shivani, 105.
43. Marie Louise Burke, *Swami Vivekananda in the West: New Discoveries* (Advaita Ashrama: Calcutta, 1987), VI:266.
44. Shivani, 107-8.
45. Ibid., 109.
46. *Swami Abhedananda*, 308.
47. Shivani, 142-43.
48. *Swami Abhedananda*, 337.
49. Ibid., 346.

50. Shivani, 175.
51. Sankarananda, 416.
52. *Swami Abhedananda*, 373.
53. Swami Prajnanananda, *Man O Manush* (Ramakrishna Vedanta Math: Calcutta, 1959), 331.
54. *Swami Abhedananda*, 376.
55. Shivani, 197-98.
56. Ibid., 198.
57. Ibid., 200.
58. *Swami Abhedananda*, 413-14.
59. Ibid., 423.
60. Sankarananda, 504.
61. Ibid., 536.
62. *Swami Abhedananda*, 424.
63. *The Apostles*, 264-65.
64. Translated from an audio tape of a talk by Swami Abhedananda on All India Radio during Ramakrishna's Centenary celebration in 1936.
65. *Swami Abhedananda*, 435.
66. *Bhakta Malika*, I:418.
67. Rajendralal Acharya, *Swami Abhedananda* (Ramakrishna Vedanta Ashrama: Darjeeling, 1943), II:145.
68. *Jeman Suniyachi*, I&II:236, 183.

Ch. 12 – Swami Trigunatitananda

1. Swami Gambhirananda, *Bhakta Malika* (Udbodhan Office: Calcutta, 1964), II:2.
2. M., *The Gospel of Sri Ramakrishna*, trans. by Swami Nikhilananda (Ramakrishna-Vivekananda Center: New York, 1969), 685-87.
3. *Udbodhan*, 35:342.
4. Swami Gambhirananda, *Srima Sarada Devi* (Udbodhan Office: Calcutta, 1969), 161.
5. *The Message of Our Master* (Advaita Ashrama: Calcutta, 1944), 47.
6. Ibid., 55,43.
7. *The Gospel*, 803.
8. *Udbodhan*, 35:342-44.
9. *Bhakta Malika*, II:4.
10. *Udbodhan*, 35:344-45.
11. *Bhakta Malika*, II:9.
12. Ibid., II:9-10.
13. Ibid., II:10.
14. Mahendra Nath Datta, *Srimat Vivekananda Swamijir Jivaner Ghatanavali* (Mahendra Publishing Committee: Calcutta, 1964), II:124-25.
15. Ibid., II:125.
16. From Swami Dhireshananda's Diary (Told by Swami Nirvanananda).
17. Vaikuntha Nath Sanyal, *Sri Ramakrishna Lilamrita* (Calcutta, 1936), 314.
18. *Udbodhan*, 35:402.
19. Ibid., 35:402.
20. *Swamijir Jivaner Ghatanavali*, (1964), I:28.
21. Ibid., II:122-23.
22. *The Gospel*, 988-99.
23. *Prabuddha Bharata*, 1928:31.
24. Ibid., 1928:33
25. Ibid., 1928:31.
26. Ibid., 1928:31-32.
27. *Udbodhan*, 35:529.
28. Swami Omkareswarananda, *Premananda* (Ramakrishna Sadhan Mandir: Deoghar, 1939), I:142.
29. Ibid., I:144.
30. *Udbodhan*, 35:577, 42:492; *Bhakta Malika*, I:18-19.
31. *Talks with Swami Vivekananda* (Advaita Ashrama: Calcutta, 1990), 211-14.
32. Swami Nikhilananda, *Holy Mother* (Ramakrishna-Vivekananda Center: New York, 1962), 264.
33. *Udbodhan*, 35:530, 42:491.
34. Swami Gambhirananda, *Srima Sarada Devi* (Udbodhan Office: Calcutta, 1968), 247.
35. *Prabuddha Bharata*, 1928:131-32.
36. Ibid., 1928:132.
37. *Voice of Freedom* (San Francisco), May 1909:vi-viii.
38. *Prabuddha Bharata*, 1928:162.
39. *Udbodhan*, 37:303.
40. *Prabuddha Bharata*, 1928:163.
41. Swami Atulananda, *Atman Alone Abides* (Ramakrishna Math: Madras, 1978), 170-71.
42. *Prabuddha Bharata*, 1928:164-65.
43. Ibid., 1928:227.
44. *Atman Alone*, 171.
45. *Prabuddha Bharata*, 1928:230-32.
46. Ibid., 1928:465-67.
47. Ibid., 1928:524-25.
48. Ibid., 1928:355-56.
49. *Udbodhan*, 37:303.
50. *Prabuddha Bharata*, 1928:525.
51. Ibid., 1928:526.
52. Ibid., 1928:526.
53. Ibid., 1928:526-27.
54. Ibid., 1928:564-65.
55. Ibid., 1928:565-67.

Ch. 13 – Swami Advaitananda

1. *Udbodhan*, 49:144.
2. Ibid., 57:157.
3. M., *The Gospel of Sri Ramakrishna*, trans. by Swami Nikhilananda (Ramakrishna-Vivekananda Center: New York, 1969), 425-26.
4. From Gurudas Gupta's Diary (Mahendra Pal told this incident to Swami Arupananda).
5. *The Gospel*, 440
6. Chandra Sekhar Chattopadhyay, *Sri Sri Latu Maharajer Smritikatha* (Udbodhan: Calcutta, 1953), 165-66.
7. *The Gospel*, 932.
8. His Eastern and Western Disciples, *Life of Swami Vivekananda* (Advaita Ashrama: Calcutta, 1979), I:159.
9. *The Gospel*, 935.
10. *Latu Smriti*, 257.
11. Swami Gambhirananda, *Bhakta Malika* (Udbodhan Office: Calcutta, 1963), I:507.
12. *The Gospel*, 984.
13. Her Devotee-Children, *The Gospel of the Holy Mother* (Ramakrishna Math: Madras, 1984), 164.
14. From Gurudas Gupta's Diary.
15. Swami Abhedananda, *My Life Story* (Ramakrishna Vedanta Math: Calcutta, 1970), 90.
16. Christopher Isherwood, *Ramakrishna and His Disciples* (Methuen & Co.: London, 1965), 301.
17. Mahendra Nath Datta, *Srimat Vivekananda Swamijir Jivaner Ghatanavali* (Mahendra Publishing Committee: Calcutta, 1964), I:94-95.
18. *Udbodhan*, 49:206.
19. *Mahapurushjir Patravali* (Udbodhan Office: Calcutta, 1953), 46.
20. *The Complete Works of Swami Vivekananda* (Advaita Ashrama: Calcutta, 1969), VII:244.
21. *Latu Smriti*, 434.
22. Swami Apurvananda, comp., *Satprasange Swami Vijnanananda* (Ramakrishna Math: Allahabad, 1953), 71.
23. Ashutosh Mittra, *Sri Ma* (Calcutta, 1944), 206.
24. Swami Gambhirananda, comp. & ed. *The Apostles of Sri Ramakrishna* (Advaita Ashrama: Calcutta, 1967), 300.
25. *Vedanta and the West*, 131:22.
26. From Gurudas Gupta's Diary.
27. Swami Nirlepananda, *Swamijir Smriti Sanchayan* (Karuna Prakashani: Calcutta, 1967), 62; Vaikuntha Nath Sanyal, *Sri Ramakrishna Lilamrita* (Calcutta, 1936), 329.
28. *Complete Works* (1968), VI:442.
29. *Udbodhan*, 49:207.
30. *Bhakta Malika*, I:513-14.
31. *Udbodhan*, 57:158.
32. *Bhakta Malika*, I:516.

Ch. 14 – Swami Subodhananda

1. The Bible, Matthew 18:3.
2. *Swami Subodhanander Jivani O Patra* (Ramakrishna Math: Sonarga-Dhaka, 1935), 2.
3. Gurudas Barman, *Sri Ramakrishna Charit* (Calcutta, 1909), 337.
4. *Life of Sri Ramakrishna* (Advaita Ashrama: Calcutta, 1943), 489-90; *Swami Subodhananda*, 7.
5. *Ramakrishna Charit*, 333-36.
6. *Life of Sri Ramakrishna*, 490-92.
7. Ibid., 492.
8. Abani Gupta, comp., *Khoka Maharaj: Swami Subodhananda* (Calcutta), I:32.
9. M., *The Gospel of Sri Ramakrishna*, trans. by Swami Nikhilananda (Ramakrishna-Vivekananda Center: New York, 1969), 839-40.
10. *Ramakrishna Charit*, 342-43.
11. Christopher Isherwood, *Ramakrishna and His Disciples* (Methuen & Co.: London, 1965), 234.
12. *Swami Subodhananda*, 11.
13. Ibid., 11-12.
14. *Khoka Maharaj*, I:28.
15. Isherwood, 234.
16. *Udbodhan*, 88:624-25.
17. *Swami Subodhananda*, 79.
18. Swami Gambhirananda, comp. & ed., *The Apostles of Sri Ramakrishna* (Advaita Ashrama: Calcutta, 1967), 369.
19. Swami Gambhirananda, *Bhakta Malika* (Udbodhan Office: Calcutta, 1964), II:69.
20. *Ramakrishna Charit*, 346.
21. Chandra Sekhar Chattopadhyay, *Latu Maharajer Smritikatha* (Udbodhan Office: Calcutta, 1953), 217-18.
22. *Swami Subodhananda*, 102.
23. Ibid., 69.
24. *Udbodhan*, 88:624.
25. Ibid., 48:257.
26. Ibid., 88:624-25.

27. *Swami Subodhananda*, 61.
28. *Udbodhan*, 25:726-27.
29. Ibid., 88:624.
30. Swami Nityatmananda, *Srima Darshan* (General Printers and Publishers: Calcutta, 1969), II:292.
31. *Khoka Maharaj*, I:35.
32. *Ramakrishna Charit*, 344-45.
33. Ibid., 346.
34. *Udbodhan*, 88:625.
35. *Khoka Maharaj*, I:37.
36. *Swami Subodhananda*, 14.
37. Ibid., 115.
38. *Udbodhan*, 40:315.
39. *Khoka Maharaj*, I:55.
40. *Basumati*, Ramakrishna Centenary Number, 58.
41. *Khoka Maharaj*, I:73.
42. *Udbodhan*, 40:316-17.
43. Ibid., 35:48.
44. Ibid., 88:626.
45. *Khoka Maharaj*, I:49-50.
46. Ibid., I:60-61.
47. Isherwood, 235.
48. *Bhakta Malika*, II:83.
49. From Gurudas Gupta's Diary.
50. Isherwood, 235.
51. From Swami Dhireshananda's Diary.
52. *Khoka Maharaj*, 58.
53. Swami Gambhirananda, *Srima Sarada Devi* (Udbodhan Office: Calcutta, 1968), 325-26.
54. *Khoka Maharaj*, II:97.
55. Ibid., II:33.
56. *Bhakta Malika*, II:81-82.
57. Swami Jnanatmananda, *Punya Smriti* (Udbodhan Office: Calcutta, 1977), 101.
58. *Bhakta Malika*, II:82.
59. Ibid., II:82-83.
60. *Udbodhan*, 52:635.
61. Ibid., 88:626.
62. *Punya Smriti*, 104.
63. From Swami Dhireshananda's Diary.
64. *Udbodhan*, 35:64.
65. *The Apostles*, 374-77.
66. *Bhakta Malika*, II:85.
67. Ibid., II:83.
68. *Khoka Maharaj*, I:57-58.
69. *Udbodhan*, 40:315.
70. *Swami Subodhananda*, 93.
71. *Udbodhan*, 40:316.
72. *Swami Subodhananda*, 142.
73. *Bhakta Malika*, II:81.
74. *Swami Subodhananda*, 20-21.

75. *Udbodhan*, 35:63.
76. Ibid., 35:65.
77. Ibid., 34:656.
78. *Bhakta Malika*, II:89.
79. *Udbodhan*, 35:63.

Ch. 15 – Swami Akhandananda

1. Swami Chetanananda, ed. & comp., *Ramakrishna as We Saw Him* (Vedanta Society: St. Louis, 1990), 231.
2. Swami Annadananda, *Swami Akhandananda* (Udbodhan Office: Calcutta, 1960), 7.
3. Ibid., 10.
4. Swami Akhandananda, *Smriti Katha* (Udbodhan Office: Calcutta, 1937), 4-5.
5. *Ramakrishna as We*, 232-34.
6. Ibid., 234,238.
7. Ibid., 240.
8. Ibid., 236.
9. Ibid., 237-38.
10. Ibid., 241.
11. *Swami Akhandananda*, 20.
12. Ibid., 20.
13. Ibid., 26.
14. Ibid., 28.
15. Ibid., 29.
16. Ibid., 30.
17. *Smriti Katha*, 54.
18. Swami Niramayananda, *Swami Akhadanander Smriti-sanchaya* (Udbodhan Office: Calcutta, 1976), 61-62.
19. Swami Akhandananda, *In the Lap of the Himalayas* (Ramakrishna Math: Madras, 1980), 102.
20. *Swami Akhandananda*, 50.
21. Ibid., 51-52.
22. Ibid., 55.
23. Ibid., 55.
24. Ibid., 60.
25. Ibid., 65.
26. Ibid., 74.
27. Ibid., 74.
28. Ibid., 75.
29. *Smriti Katha*, 65-66.
30. Ibid., 73-76.
31. Ibid., 87.
32. Ibid., 98-105.
33. *The Complete Works of Swami Vivekananda* (Advaita Ashrama: Calcutta, 1968), VI:288.
34. Swami Niramayananda, *The Call of the Spirit* (Ramakrishna Math: Madras, 1984), 28.

35. *Complete Works* (1966), IV:352.
36. *Smriti Katha*, 133.
37. Ibid., 162-63.
38. Ibid., 163-64.
39. *Swami Akhandananda*, 122.
40. *Smriti Katha*, 225-26.
41. Ibid., 231.
42. Ibid., 239.
43. *Complete Works*, VI:400-1.
44. *Smriti Katha*, 241.
45. *Complete Works*, VII:110-11.
46. *Smriti-sanchaya*, 139-40.
47. Ibid., 50-51.
48. *Swami Akhandananda*, 165.
49. Ibid., 158-59.
50. *Complete Works*, VI:425.
51. *Smriti-sanchaya*, 17.
52. Ibid., 18.
53. *Udbodhan*, 53:610.
54. Ibid., 53:610.
55. *Prabuddha Bharata*, 1974:91.
56. *The Ramakrishna Math & Mission Convention* (Belur Math, 1926), 83-85.
57. *Smriti-sanchaya*, 64.
58. *Udbodhan*, 62:426.
59. *Smriti-sanchaya*, 18-19.
60. *Udbodhan*, 41:674.
61. Ibid., 38:124b; *Prabuddha Bharata*, 1936:281.
62. *Udbodhan*, 52:381.

Ch. 16 – Swami Vijnanananda

1. Swami Chetanananda, ed. & trans., *Ramakrishna as We Saw Him* (Vedanta Society: St. Louis, 1990), 246-47.
2. *Udbodhan*, 53:311.
3. Swami Jagadiswarananda, *Swami Vijnanananda* (Ramakrishna Math: Allahabad, 1947), 5-6.
4. Ibid., 6.
5. *Ramakrishna as We*, 243.
6. Ibid., 244-45.
7. Swami Vishwashrayananda, *Swami Vijnanananda: His Life and Sayings* (Ramakrishna Math: Madras, 1980), 8.
8. *Ramakrishna as We*, 245-46.
9. Ibid., 247.
10. Ibid., 247-48.
11. Ibid., 248-49.
12. Ibid., 249.
13. Ibid., 250.
14. Ibid., 250-1.
15. Ibid., 254.
16. Ibid., 254.
17. Ibid., 254-55.
18. *Swami Vijnanananda*, 9.
19. Swami Apurvananda, *Satprasange Swami Vijnanananda* (Ramakrishna Math: Allahabad, 1953), 11.
20. Vishwashrayananda, 17.
21. *Swami Vijnanananda*, 240-44.
22. *Satprasange*, 148-49.
23. *Udbodhan*, 41:301-2.
24. Suresh Chandra Das and Jyotirmay Basuroy, comp. & ed., *Pratyakshadarshir Smritipate Swami Vijnanananda* (General Printers and Publishers: Calcutta, 1977), 305-6.
25. Ibid., 314-15.
26. *Satprasange*, 187-88.
27. Ibid., 195-97.
28. Ibid., 126.
29. *Sri Sri Ma O Sri Ramakrishna Parshadganer Smritikatha* (Ramakrishna Shivananda Ashrama: Barasat, 1965), 89.
30. *Swami Vijnanananda*, 188.
31. *Udbodhan*, 42:662.
32. *Satprasange*, 14-15.
33. Ibid., 14.
34. *Udbodhan*, 42:663.
35. *Satprasange*, 16.
36. Vishwashrayananda, 32.
37. *Satprasange*, v-vi, 8.
38. Ibid., 8-9.
39. Ibid., 181-82.
40. Ibid., 180.
41. *Pratyakshadarshir Smriti*, 85-87.
42. *Satprasange*, 134-35.
43. Ibid., 123.
44. Ibid., 92-93.
45. *Prabuddha Bharata*, 1970:297.
46. *Udbodhan*, 45:223.
47. Ibid., 45:224.
48. *Udbodhan*, 43:285-86.
49. Vishwashrayananda, 32.
50. *Udbodhan*, 40:547.
51. Ibid., 40:602.
52. Ibid., 40:606.
53. *Satprasange*, 171.
54. Ibid., 177-79.
55. Ibid., 172-73.
56. Swami Divyatmananda, *Divyaprasange* (Udbodhan Office: Calcutta, 1972), 147.
57. *Satprasange*, 173.
58. His Eastern and Western Disciples, *The Life of Swami Vivekananda* (Advaita Ashrama: Calcutta, 1981), II:398.
59. *Parshadganer Smritikatha*, 88.

60. *Prabuddha Bharata*, 1938:295.
61. *Satprasange*, 20.
62. *Pratyakshadarshir Smriti*, 197.
63. Swami Vividishananda, *A Man of God* (Ramakrishna Math: Madras, 1957), 349-50.
64. *Divyaprasange*, 121-22.
65. *Satprasange*, 25.
66. *Swami Vijnanananda*, 43-44.
67. *Satprasange*, 22.
68. Ibid., 130-31.
69. *Udbodhan*, 71:310.
70. *Satprasange*, 139,112.
71. Swami Gambhirananda, *Bhakta Malika* (Udbodhan Office: Calcutta, 1964), II:116.
72. *Satprasange*, 72.
73. *Pratyakshadarshir Smriti*, 67.
74. *Swami Vijnanananda*, 107.
75. *Pratyakshadarshir Smriti*, 26-27.
76. Tarini Shankar Chakrabarty, *Swami Vijnanananda: The Beacon Light of Allahabad* (Allahabad, 1968), 3.
77. *Pratyakshadarshir Smriti*, 64-65.
78. Ibid., 9-10.
79. Ibid., 11.
80. From Dhireshananda's Diary (Told by Swami Siddheswarananda on 8 January 1947).
81. *Swami Vijnanananda*, 106.
82. *Divyaprasange*, 82.
83. *Pratyashadarshir Smriti*, 229-30.
84. Ibid., 66-69.
85. Ibid., 313-14.
86. *Satprasange*, 27.
87. *Divyaprasange*, 169.
88. *Bhakta Malika*, II:113.
89. *Satprasange*, 191.
90. *Vishwashrayananda*, 27.
91. *Satprasange*, 194.
92. *Swami Vijnanananda*, 212.
93. *Satprasange*, 31.
94. *Divyaprasange*, 189.
95. From Swami Shraddhananda's Diary.
96. *Pratyakshadarshir Smriti*, 106.

THE TEMPLE GARDEN OF DAKSHINESWAR, RAMAKRISHNA'S HOME FOR THIRTY YEARS
HE TRAINED HIS DISCIPLES HERE FROM 1880-1885

INDEX

Numbers in parenthesis indicate an entire chapter devoted to the individual. Numbers in bold indicate photographs. Abbreviations: RK=Sri Ramakrishna, HM=Holy Mother (Sarada Devi), SV=Swami Vivekananda, SB=Swami Brahmananda.

THEY LIVED WITH GOD
by Swami Chetanananda

This book is a sequel to author's present work entitled *God Lived with Them.* In twenty-eight short biographies, he brings alive Ramakrishna's principal lay disciples, and shows how they exemplified various facets of their Master's teachings. Moreover, this book presents a more complete picture of Ramakrishna himself, including many new stories about his life which have never been recorded in English.

Pp. xi+434   Rs. 100

RAMAKRISHNA
AS WE SAW HIM
by Swami Chetanananda

The author has helped to uncover the hidden personal life of Sri Ramakrishna by editing and translating the reminiscences of forty people who knew him. The selections represent a cross section of Ramakrishna's relatives, monastic disciples, householder disciples and devotees, and Brahmo devotees and admirers. Some of these people knew Ramakrishna well—they lived with him twenty-four hours a day. Others stayed with him only occasionally. Each chapter provides a vivid picture of Ramakrishna's life from a different, and intensely personal, perspective.

Pp. 496   Rs. 100

For a complete list of publications, please write to:
Advaita Ashrama
(Publication Department)
5 Dehi Entally Road, Calcutta 700 014
Email: advaita@vsnl.com • Website : www.advaitaonline.com